PASSENGERS
TO AMERICA

A Consolidation of Ship Passenger Lists from The New England Historical and Genealogical Register

Edited by Michael Tepper

GENEALOGICAL PUBLISHING CO., INC.
BALTIMORE 1977

Excerpted from
selected volumes of
The New England Historical
and Genealogical Register,
1847-1961

Reprinted with a New Introduction and Indexes
Genealogical Publishing Co., Inc.
Baltimore, 1977

Library of Congress Catalogue Card Number 77-72983
International Standard Book Number 0-8063-0767-6

Made in the United States of America

CONTENTS

Miscellaneous Lists

Appendix

INTRODUCTION

1

With the publication in 1975 of *Emigrants to Pennsylvania, 1641-1819*—a consolidation of ship passenger lists from *The Pennsylvania Magazine of History and Biography*—a pattern for further consolidations from periodical literature would appear to have been established. Using Harold Lancour's *Bibliography of Ship Passenger Lists, 1538-1825* as a guide to the literature, *Emigrants to Pennsylvania* consisted of twenty-six articles which originally appeared in *PMHB*, one of the oldest and most respected journals in the field of genealogy and local history. The consolidation of these articles satisfied several objectives: it united articles treating a common class of records; it provided access to material which had previously been difficult if not impossible to locate; and it otherwise reduced the labor of hunting about in a multi-volume periodical in pursuit of obscure and elusive data. Equally significant, perhaps, considering that few libraries lay claim to an unbroken run of *PMHB*, it secured the integrity of a homogeneous body of material.

In view of the achievement of the *PMHB* consolidation the undertaking, as it were, more than fulfilling its modest aims—there is little reason now to do anything less than plumb the richest mine of all and produce a similar consolidation of articles from the venerable *New England Historical and Genealogical Register*. Since 1847 this quarterly has been the very embodiment of authority, and it continues to this day to enjoy a reputation as the doyen of periodicals. Its continuity unparalleled, its range of contributions practically without equal, *NEHGR* offers almost limitless possibilities for genealogical study and invites consolidation along a great many lines. Indeed, a number of books before now have been comprised of articles excerpted from *NEHGR*, among them Henry F. Waters' *Genealogical Gleanings in England*, published in two volumes in 1901 and reprinted in 1969 by the Genealogical Publishing Company, with the inclusion of "New Series" (1907), and Albion M.

Dyer's *First Ownership of Ohio Lands,* published in 1911 and reprinted by the Genealogical Publishing Company also in 1969, to name but two. Nevertheless, a substantial body of material has eluded consolidation, particularly the embryonic group of articles on ship passenger lists.

While it is generally admitted that certain books on ship passenger lists derive from articles which had originally appeared in *NEHGR,* the complete body of literature on passenger lists as found in the multiple volumes of this periodical has never before been assembled, the task heretofore presenting some formidable obstacles. No doubt the accumulated bulk of this quarterly after 130 years of continuous publication has generally discouraged efforts at consolidation, for contributions in a wide range of categories have swollen to daunting proportions. Yet of the hundreds upon hundreds of articles published in *NEHGR,* there is hardly a group that claims a greater share of our attention than ship passenger lists, nor one that provides greater coherence and depth. However, even supposing a researcher could lay his hands on all the volumes of this periodical—an unlikely prospect at all but a handful of libraries—the task of singling out and examining contributions is prohibitive, for there are no less than thirty-five complete articles on ship passenger lists spread over approximately seventy-five quarterly numbers. Clearly, then, if any group of articles might profit from consolidation, ship passenger lists, in numbers alone, must be allowed pre-eminence.

The value of the Lancour *Bibliography* in reducing the literature on ship passenger lists to manageable proportions can hardly be overstated. Lancour provides us with a reliable key to a ponderous mass of material, the whole of which, representing even some of his more questionable entries and including some articles which already enjoy separate existence in book form, is herein excerpted in entirety from *NEHGR* and reproduced in a serviceable format, the 18,000 or so persons named in the lists conveniently cited in the index. Articles which originally appeared as continuations, some in as many as ten or fifteen issues, have been combined and appear here as single, cohesive units. Other groupings have been determined by logical relationships, an article consisting of *corrigenda,* for example, naturally following the article it corrects.

With the exception of four very brief articles—actually notes—assembled under the heading "Miscellaneous Lists" and eight articles which constitute the *Appendix,* the articles are arranged in chronological order by the date of embarkation or arrival. It might be noted that lists appearing in the *Appendix* cannot by any construction of the term be considered ship passenger lists; however, since they are cited in the Lancour *Bibliography* they are included here, if for no other reason but to reveal the full extent of Lancour's citations to *NEHGR* and to preserve bibliographical continuity. One such list, for example, is a list of persons who merely "wished" to emigrate to America, with no more manifest connection to a ship other than the fact that funds were apparently authorized to pay for the journey. Some of the other lists have even less foundation as passenger lists and one wonders why Lancour cited them in his *Bibliography*. Still, it may at least be said of this present compilation that it adheres strictly to the authorized canon.

2

Exceptions do not so awkwardly preponderate that we cannot here permit ourselves certain generalizations about the immigrants named in this collection of ship passenger lists. The majority of the immigrants, for example, were of British or Irish provenance; most sailed from the great ports of London, Liverpool, or Bristol and disembarked at New York or Boston. Most arrived during the 150-year period between the landing of the *Mayflower* and the start of the American Revolution, a great number settling in New England. And most were of yeoman or artisan stock or ranks beneath and were neither political refugees nor religious dissenters. Nor were many of them "adventurers" in any romantic sense of the term.

On the other hand some of the passengers identified in these lists were sturdy beggars and felons, and there are some here who were prisoners of war. There were a few gentlemen, in the landed sense of the term, and some speculators, and there were free-thinkers as well as separatists. And of course there were apprentices and a great many indentured servants. Quite a few sailed to ports other than New York or Boston. Indeed, in the largest cohesive group of passenger lists included in this collection, Gerald Fothergill's "Emigrants from England," the majority appear to have sailed to Maryland, presumably disembarking at the ports of Annapolis or Baltimore. And a far from insignificant number sailed to the West Indies, their ultimate destination, if other than the West Indies, unstated. In one group of passenger lists, however, Horatio G. Somerby's "Passengers for Virginia, 1635," many passengers designated as being bound for Virginia were in fact bound for New England, for as John G. Locke observes on page 108 ". . . at that early period, New England was oftentimes spoken of as 'North Virginia,' and was by some supposed to be within the bounds of Virginia proper, and perhaps being so considered, the prefix of 'North,' might be sometimes omitted."

Nevertheless, the various lists cannot be said to be over-ladened with data pertaining to the passengers. In all too many lists, in fact, information adheres too strictly to the limits of economy, at the very most consisting of an uneven mixture of references to age, family members, appearance, occupation, country of origin, place and date of departure or arrival, and reasons for emigration. But the genealogist is the undisputed master at shaping a pedigree from a laconic entry in a ship's manifest—a date, a reference to a place of origin, the given name of a child, or even the name of a servant—so there is doubtless enough here to repay his scrutiny.

3

Some 18,000 persons are named in this collection of ship passenger lists, all of whom arrived in America sometime between 1620 and 1836, though lists treating of seventeenth-century arrivals clearly predominate. Inevitably, therefore, some duplication of the passenger lists found in the celebrated *Hotten List,* i.e. John Camden Hotten's *Original Lists of Persons of Quality; Emigrants; Religious Exiles; Political Rebels . . . and Others Who Went From Great Britain to the American Plantations 1600-1700,* is bound to occur. Instances can be multiplied, but one example of over-lap and duplication of data embodied in the *Hotten List* is the list of passengers aboard the *Hercules* communicated by Mr. Eben Putnam, which commences on page 111. By a happy stroke both Putnam and Hotten worked from different copies of the same source material. Reproduction here of the Putnam article, therefore, broadens the basis upon which scholarly evaluations of the passenger list can be rendered and provides an additional check for accuracy. As it happens, the Putnam list is a much more comprehensive rendition of the list incorporated by Hotten. What is more, its appearance in *NEHGR* was the impetus for an article by Elizabeth French Bartlett —included here—containing some rather substantive revisions, so in the comparison of the two lists Hotten's is properly eclipsed. Similarly, data in Horatio G. Somerby's article, "Passengers for Virginia, 1635," can be found in whole or part in the *Hotten List,* but discrepancies in spelling and apparent errors in transcription and interpretation, necessitating careful comparison of the two lists, increases our enthusiasm for the Somerby list. On balance, however, this present collection of ship passenger lists is not intended to serve as a corrective to Hotten, nor even an adjunct, but is to be considered a companion volume, a distinct and, one hopes, equally useful contribution to the literature of genealogical reference.

Since the subject of duplication has been raised, it would be well at this point to observe that several articles incorporated in this collection have previously been constituted as books. Four such have been reprinted by the Genealogical Publishing Company, three of these reprints based on reprints originally undertaken by the New England Historic Genealogical Society itself; namely, "Two Early Passenger Lists, 1635-1637," by Eben Putnam (page 111*ff.*); "List of Emigrants to America from Liverpool, 1697-1707," by Elizabeth French (page 173*ff.*); and Gerald Fothergill's "Emigrants from England" (page 222*ff.*). GPC's reprint of the fourth article, Samuel Drake's "Founders of New England" (page 10*ff.*), is in fact reprinted from a much enlarged version of the article rather than the original article itself. Coincidentally, several of the unsigned pieces in this present collection of ship passenger lists can be found in the enlarged version of the Drake work, which is published under the title of *Result of Some Researches Among the British Archives for Information Relative to the Founders of New England.* The unsigned contributions referred to are "Emigrants in the Hercules of Sandwich" (page 123*ff.*); "Scotch Prisoners Sent to Massachusetts in 1652" (page 146*ff.*); "A Lyst of Pasingers Abord the Speedwell of London" (page 462); and "Passengers for New England" (page 463). An article by Henry Stevens, "Passengers for New England, 1638" (page 123*ff.*), was substantially revised by Drake and appears in his article "Founders of New England."

To be sure, other duplications occur, but there is as little reason to cavil over their inclusion here as with any of the forementioned articles. They are included because the scope of the work demands it. Either this consolidation is to embrace every article on ship passenger lists in *NEHGR* cited by Lancour, or it is to fail the most trifling expectations. It goes without saying, therefore, that every article cited by Lancour—every contribution no matter how ephemeral—has been incorporated in this collection. The reader may be satisfied that once he has perused this volume he will have no further recourse to *NEHGR* for ship passenger lists. The rationale of this type of consolidation, after all, is to cut secondary sources down to size by assembling all articles on a common subject, from a common source, in a single, convenient volume. One hopes the results are not disappointing.

ACKNOWLEDGEMENTS

The editor is indebted to the New England Historic Genealogical Society for permission to reproduce articles from the *Register* and to Mrs. Elizabeth Petty Bentley for providing the indispensable index of names. Mrs. Bentley's conscientious efforts have added immeasurably to the value of the work.

THE PASSENGERS OF THE MAY FLOWER IN 1620.

BY NATHANIEL BRADSTREET SHURTLEFF, M. D.

As EARLY as the year 1602, several religious people residing near the joining borders of Nottinghamshire, Lincolnshire, and Yorkshire, together with their pious ministers, being grievously oppressed by courts and canons, resolved to shake off the yoke of antichristian bondage, and, as the Lord's free people, to form themselves by covenant into a church-state, to walk in all his ways according to their best knowledge and endeavors, cost them whatever it might.

In the year 1606, by reason of the distance of their habitations, these people were obliged to assemble in two places and become two distinct churches; over one of which Mr. John Smith was established pastor, and among the others were Mr. Richard Clifton and Mr. John Robinson, two very excellent and worthy preachers.

In the fall of 1607, Mr. Clifton and many of his church, being extremely harassed, removed themselves and families to Holland, where, in the spring of 1608, they were followed by Mr. Robinson and the rest. They settled first at Amsterdam, where they remained a year; but finding that Mr. Smith's church, which was there before them, had fallen into contention with others, they, valuing peace and spiritual comfort above other riches, removed with Mr. Robinson, their pastor, to Leyden, Mr. Clifton remaining in Amsterdam, where he soon died.

Soon after their arrival in Leyden, they chose Mr. William Brewster to assist the pastor, as Elder of the Church. In their new place of abode they lived in love and harmony with each other, and on friendly terms of intercourse with their neighbors, till they removed to America.

By the year 1610, many had come over to them from various parts of England, and they had increased and become a great congregation.

In 1617, Mr. Robinson and his church began to think of emigrating to America, and, as a preparatory step, sent Mr Robert Cushman and Mr John Carver from Leyden over to England, to treat with the Virginia Company, and also to see if the King would grant them the liberty of conscience there, which was refused them in the land of their birth. Although the agents were not able to obtain from the King their suit for liberty in religion under the broad seal, as was desired, nevertheless, they prevailed so far as to gain the connivance of the King that he would not molest them, provided they carried themselves peaceably. In 1618, the agents returned to Leyden, to the great discouragement of the people who sent them; who, notwithstanding, resolved, in 1619, to send again two agents to agree with the Virginia Company; and at this time they sent Mr. Cushman a second time, and with him Mr. William Bradford, who, after long attendance, obtained the patent granted by the Company to Mr. John Wincob, which was never used.

Notwithstanding all these troubles, so strong was their resolution to quit Leyden and settle in America, that they entered into an arrangement with Mr. Thomas Weston, a merchant of London, for their transportation, and sent Mr. Carver and Mr. Cushman to England, to receive the money of Mr. Weston, to assist in their transportation, and to provide for the voyage. By direction, Mr. Cushman went to London and Mr. Carver to Southampton, where they finally joined with Mr. William Martin, who had been chosen to assist them.

A vessel of sixty tons, called the Speedwell, was bought and fitted in Holland, to be used in their transportation, and was designed to be kept for use in their new country. Mr. Cushman, in June, 1620, also hired at London the renowned May Flower, a vessel of ninescore tons, and also Mr. Clarke, the pilot.

Mr. Cushman, having procured the May Flower at London, and fitted it for the voyage, proceeded in it to Southampton, where he and Captain Jones, together with the other agents, remained seven days, until the arrival of the Pilgrims who left Leyden in July, embarking from Delft Haven.

On the 5th of August, both vessels, the May Flower, Capt. Jones, and the Speedwell, Capt. Reinolds, set sail from Southampton. The small vessel proving leaky, they both put in to Dartmouth about the 13th of August, where they remained till the 21st, when they set sail again. Both vessels were obliged to return a second time on account of the leakage of the Speedwell; and this time they put back to Plymouth, where they gave up the small vessel and dismissed those who were willing to return to London, Mr. Cushman and his family returning with them.

On the 6th of September, their number then consisting of one hundred persons, they made their final start, and arrived at Cape Cod on the eleventh day of November, when they signed the famous compact, and landed at Plymouth, in America, on the eleventh day of December, Old Style, or on the *twenty-first* of December, *New Style*, in the year 1620.

During their passage, one only died, William Butten, a young man, servant to Mr. Samuel Fuller, the physician of the new colony, who was included in Mr. Fuller's family, according to Governor Bradford, although dead at the time of the signing of the compact.

One person was born during the passage, Oceanus Hopkins, a son of Mr. Stephen Hopkins, who did not survive long after the landing.

At the commencement of the voyage, the number of passengers of the May Flower was one hundred, and at the time of the arrival at Cape Cod Harbor it was the same; one having died, and one having been born, thus preserving the integrity of the number. Both of these persons, however, are numbered among the passengers, and hence the number is generally stated as one hundred and one.

Peregrine White, son of Mr. William White, was born in Cape Cod Harbor, in November, after the signing of the compact and before the landing, and is not included with the voyagers. He enjoyed the distinction of being the first born white child in New England, of the Leyden Pilgrims.

The first child born after the landing on the twenty-second day of December, 1620, was a son of Mr. Isaac Allerton, but it did not survive its birth.

The May Flower has already been stated to have been a vessel of about ninescore tons, and was procured at London by Mr. Robert Cushman, who was debarred the privilege of coming over with the infant colonists, as it was necessary that he should remain in England, to keep together those who were left behind, and to provide for their future emigration, as he had done for that of those of the first passage. This he did by procuring the Fortune, and sailing from London in July, 1621, and arriving in New England on the 9th of November of the same year. It is also highly probable that he obtained the other early vessels, as he continued to be the agent of the Pilgrims till his death, which occurred in England, just as he was ready to come to spend the rest of his days in New England. In 1624, when the first division of land for continuance took place, Mr. Cushman, although in England, was placed at the head of the list of those who came in the May Flower; an act of justice alike creditable to our forefathers and honorable to him.

The May Flower not only brought over the first of the Leyden Pilgrims, but also, in the year 1629, with four other vessels, transported Mr. Higginson and his company to Salem; and in 1630, was one of the fleet which conveyed to New England Mr. Winthrop and the early settlers of the Massachusetts Colony.

A vessel bearing this name was owned in England about fifteen years or more before the voyage of our forefathers; but it would be impossible to prove or disprove its identity with the renowned May Flower, however great such a probability might be. It is known, nevertheless, that this identical famous vessel afterwards hailed from various English ports, such as London, Yarmouth, and Southampton, and that it was much used in transporting emigrants to this country. What eventually became of it, and what was the end of its career, are equally unknown to history.

The following list of passengers is made up from various sources. By referring to the list of those who signed the compact at Cape Cod, taken from Governor Bradford's folio manuscript, we know who signed the compact, and the number of persons in the family of each; who of the signers brought wives, and who died the first winter. By the pocket-book of Governor Bradford we know the names and dates of the deaths of sixteen who died the first season, and how many died before the arrival of the Fortune, on the 9th of November, 1621. By an examination of the Old Colony Records, we know to whom land was assigned in 1624, and what families were extinct at that time; and, as the families were arranged according to the vessel in which they came, and an acre was granted to each individual, we know how many were at that time in each family. Smith has also told us that none of the first planters died during the three years preceding the close of the year 1624. By the division of cattle, in the year 1627, a record of which was made at Plymouth, we know every individual who was living at that date, and the relative age of each person in every family. By wills, records, and gravestones, we know the ages of many of the Pilgrims and their children.

From such materials, and with such authorities, the following table has been constructed; and it is believed, that, although there is a possibility of the existence of small errors which can never be proved, the list is entirely or very nearly correct.

In order to save space and unnecessary printing, and to exhibit more readily for reference some of the most important facts, the following distinctive marks are made use of.

Those who signed the compact at Cape Cod, on the 11th of November, 1620, are in capitals.

The number in each family is indicated by the Arabic numeral.

Those who brought their wives have this mark, †.

Those who left them for a time in Holland or England are thus distinguished, ‡.

Those who died before the arrival of the Fortune on the 9th of November, 1621, have an asterisk, *.

Those who died before the division of cattle in 1627, are in italics.

The dates of those who died the first season are given as taken from Bradford's pocket-book.

JOHN CARVER, died in April, 1621. †*
Mrs. Carver, (his wife,) died in May, 1621. *
Elizabeth Carver, daughter of Mr. Carver and also wife of John Howland.
Jasper, (the boy of Mr. Carver,) died Dec. 6, 1620. *
John Howland.
Three others of this family died before 1627. * 8

WILLIAM BRADFORD. †
Mrs. Dorothy Bradford, (his wife,) drowned Dec. 7, 1620. * 2

EDWARD WINSLOW. †
Mrs. Elizabeth Winslow, (his wife,) died March 24, 1620–1. *
Edward Winslow, Jr., son of Edward.
John Winslow, son of Edward. 5

GEORGE SOULE. 1

WILLIAM BREWSTER. †
Mrs. Brewster, (his wife.)
Love Brewster, son of William.
Wrestling Brewster, son of William.
Mrs. Lucretia Brewster, wife of Jonathan, the oldest son of Elder Brewster.
William Brewster, son of Jonathan. 6

ISAAC ALLERTON. †
Mrs. Mary Allerton, (his wife,) died Feb. 25, 1620-1. *
Bartholomew Allerton, son of Isaac.
Remember Allerton, daughter of Isaac.
Mary Allerton, daughter of Isaac, and also wife of Elder Thomas Cushman.
Sarah Allerton, daughter of Isaac, and also wife of Moses Maverick. 6

MILES STANDISH. †
Mrs. Rose Standish, (his wife,) died Jan. 29, 1620-1. * 2

JOHN ALDEN. 1

SAMUEL FULLER. ‡
William Butten, (his servant,) died Nov. 6, 1620. * 2

CHRISTOPHER MARTIN, died Jan. 8, 1620-1. †*
Mrs. Martin, (his wife,) died the first winter. *
Solomon Martin, son of Christopher, died Dec. 24, 1620. *
One other of this family died the first winter. * 4

WILLIAM MULLINS, died Feb. 21, 1620-1. †*
Mrs. Mullins, (his wife,) died the first winter. *
Priscilla Mullins, daughter of William, and also wife of John Alden.
Two others of this family died the first winter. * 5

WILLIAM WHITE, died Feb. 21, 1620-1. †*
Mrs. Susanna White, (his wife,) afterwards wife of Governor Winslow.
Resolved White, son of William.
William White, Jr., son of William.
Edward Thompson, died Dec. 4, 1620. * 5

RICHARD WARREN. ‡ 1

STEPHEN HOPKINS. †
Mrs. Elizabeth Hopkins, (his wife.)
Constance Hopkins, daughter of Stephen and also wife of Nicholas Snow.
Giles Hopkins, son of Stephen.
Caleb Hopkins, son of Stephen.
Oceanus Hopkins, son of Stephen, born at sea. *

EDWARD DOTEY.

EDWARD LEISTER. 8

EDWARD TILLEY, died the first winter. †*
Mrs. Tilley, (his wife,) died the first winter. *
Two others of this family died the first winter. * 4

JOHN TILLEY, died the first winter. †*
Mrs. Tilley, (his wife,) died the first winter. *
One other of this family died the first winter. * 3

FRANCIS COOKE. ‡
John Cooke, (called the younger,) son of Francis. 2

THOMAS ROGERS, died the first winter. *
Joseph Rogers, son of Thomas. 2

THOMAS TINKER, died the first winter. †*
Mrs. Tinker, (his wife,) died the first winter. *
One more of this family died the first winter. * 3

JOHN RIDGDALE, died the first winter. †*
Mrs. Ridgdale, (his wife,) died the first winter. * 2

EDWARD FULLER, died the first winter. †*
Mrs. Fuller, (his wife,) died the first winter. *
Samuel Fuller, (called the younger,) son of Edward. 3

JOHN TURNER, died the first winter. *
Two others of this family died the first winter. * 3

FRANCIS EATON. †
Mrs. Eaton, (his wife,) died before 1627.
Samuel Eaton, son of Francis. 3

JAMES CHILTON, died Dec. 8, 1620. †*
Mrs. Chilton, (his wife,) died the first winter. *
Mary Chilton, daughter of James and also wife of John Winslow, the brother of Edward. 3

JOHN CRACKSTON, died the first winter. *
John Crackston, Jr., son of John. 2

JOHN BILLINGTON. †
Mrs. Helen Billington, (his wife.)
Francis Billington, son of John.
John Billington, Jr., son of John. 4

MOSES FLETCHER, died the first winter.	*	1
JOHN GOODMAN.		1
DEGORY PRIEST, died Jan. 1, 1620-1.	*	1
THOMAS WILLIAMS, died the first winter.	*	1
GILBERT WINSLOW, brother of Edward.		1
EDWARD MARGESON, died the first winter.	*	1
PETER BROWN.		1
RICHARD BRITTERIGE, died Dec. 21, 1620.	*	1
RICHARD CLARKE, died the first winter.	*	1
RICHARD GARDINER.		1
JOHN ALLERTON, (seaman,) died the first winter.	*	1
THOMAS ENGLISH, (seaman,) died the first winter.	*	1
Total,		101

The number of deaths of the first planters that occurred from the time the May Flower left England, to the year 1625, may be thus enumerated: —

In November, 1620,	1
In December, "	6
In January, 1620-1,	8
In February, "	17
In March, "	13
In April, 1621,	1
In May, "	1
From April 6 to November 9, 1621,	4
From November 9, 1621, to 1625,	0
Total,	51

Of these were, —		
Signers to the compact,		21
Wives of the signers,		13
Known members of families, viz: William Butten, Edward Thompson, Jasper, the boy, Solomon Martin, and Oceanus Hopkins,		5
Unknown members of the following families, viz:		
Of Carver's,	3	
Of Martin's,	1	
Of Mullins's,	2	
Of Edward Tilley's,	2	
Of John Tilley's,	1	
Of Tinker's,	1	
Of Turner's,	2	12
Total,		51

In the division of land in 1624, Henry Samson and Humilitie Cooper had land assigned them among those who came in the May Flower, and for this reason they have been generally believed to have been among the passengers of that vessel. If such is the case they can be placed in the family of Mr. Carver better than that of any other. But, as Mr. Cushman is also placed on that list, it may be reasonably inferred that others were put there for some other reasons, as perhaps Samson and Cooper, who are therefore excluded in this account.

John Goodman is marked in Bradford's manuscript as among those who died the first season. But as his name occurs among those who had garden lots in 1620, and also in the division of land in 1623, it must be inferred that he was marked by mistake, or else Mr. Prince committed an error in taking his copy for the Annals.

Three of the wives of the signers were left in Europe; namely, Bridgett, the wife of Dr. Samuel Fuller, Hester, the wife of Francis Cooke, and Elizabeth, the wife of Richard Warren. These afterwards came over in the Ann, in 1623.

Five lost their wives and married again; namely, William Bradford, who married widow Alice Southworth; Edward Winslow, who married widow Susanna White; Isaac Allerton, who married Fear Brewster, and afterwards, Joanna ———; Miles Standish, who married Barbara ———; and Francis Eaton, who married Christian Penn.

Others were married for the first time; namely, John Howland and Elizabeth Carver; George Soule and Mary; Love Brewster and Sarah Collier; John Alden and Priscilla Mullins; Resolved White and Judith Vassal; Giles Hopkins and Catherine Wheldon; Edward Dotey and Faith Clarke; John Cooke and Sarah Warren; Samuel Eaton and Martha Billington.

LEADERS IN THE WINTHROP FLEET, 1630

Communicated by J. GARDNER BARTLETT of Boston, Mass.

THE following list of some of the leading men who came to New England in the fleet with Winthrop in 1630 is preserved in the Colonial Office Papers, vol. 5, no. 78, in the Public Record Office, London.

A Note of the names of the principall undertakers for the plantation of the Mattachusetts bay in Newe England that are themselves gonne over with theire wives and children.

Mr Joh: Winthroppe Esqr: Governor, and three of his sonnes.
Sr Rich: Saltonstall Knight, three of his sonnes and 2 daughters.
Mr Isaake Johnson Esqr and the Lady Arbella his wife Sister to the Earle of Lincolne.
Mr Charles Fines the said Earles brother.
Mr Dudley, his wife, 2 sonnes and 4 daughters.
Mr Coddington and his wife.
Mr Pincheon and his wife and 3 daughters.
Mr Vassall and his wife.
Mr Revell.

[*Endorsed*]

The names of the New plantators In New England.
For the right honnorable the Lord Carleton.

This list raises a few interesting points. From various evidences it appears that the three sons brought by Governor Winthrop were Henry, Stephen, and Samuel. Sir Richard Saltonstall had four sons, Richard, Samuel, Robert, and Henry. Probably the youngest son, Henry, was the one left in England, and he came later to New England. The daughters were Rosamond and Grace. Charles Fiennes, born about 1607, was the fifth son of Thomas Fiennes, *alias* Clinton, third Earl of Lincoln, and a younger brother of Theophilus Fiennes, fourth Earl of Lincoln. He entered Christ's College, Cambridge, in Easter 1624, but did not proceed to a degree. He remained only a few weeks in New England, and then returned to England.* The four daughters brought over by Thomas Dudley were Ann, Patience, Sarah, and Mercy. His son Samuel Dudley, baptized 30 Nov. 1608, is known to have come with his parents; but who was the other son referred to in the list? The father married, 25 Apr. 1603, Dorothy Yorke, and when elected deputy governor, 17 May 1637, is called "senior," a term which implies a son Thomas then living in New England. The records of Emmanuel College, Cambridge, show that a Thomas Dudley, pensioner, matriculated in Easter 1624, and received his A.B. in Jan. 1626/7 and his A.M. in Apr. 1630. This may well have been the eldest son of Governor Dudley, born probably about 1606 and receiving his master's degree just before sailing in the Winthrop fleet, of which some of the vessels did not leave England until the end of April 1630. According to this list William

*Savage, in his Genealogical Dictionary, has erroneously confused this passenger with another person of the same name.

Pyncheon's only son John did not come with his parents, as has been commonly supposed. William Vassall and his wife soon returned to England, but came back in 1635, bringing then their children.

THE FOUNDERS OF NEW ENGLAND.

THIS designation is not intended to convey the idea that all the names of the founders of New England are contained in the following collection; while all such as emigrated with a view to a permanent residence during the first years of settlement, or previous to King Philip's war, well deserve to be numbered among the FOUNDERS OF NEW ENGLAND; and this, it is thought, sufficiently justifies the designation.

Nearly the whole of the following work was prepared during a residence in the British Metropolis, in the years 1858, 1859, and 1860. This statement is made that the reader may understand certain expressions; as, in speaking of New-England, *that* country is mentioned, and of England, as *this* country, &c. In all other respects it is presumed that the necessary explanations will be found in foot notes, or within brackets.

I had intended to accompany the work with some *indications* to antiquaries and genealogists, as to certain localities and means most likely to aid them in their investigations in England. But such a labor would require the compass of a work itself.

Such a work would not interfere at all with the valuable publication of Mr. Sims, of the British Museum, for what I had intended to do was to indicate the English localities of as many of our early New England emigrants as my collection of materials would enable me. So that, for example, a given name might be sought in a locality where it was known to have existed at the period of emigration. The importance of such a work will readily be perceived, but its accomplishment cannot be so readily performed. I shall therefore close these introductory observations with a few desultory remarks concerning researches, records, &c.

Whoever goes to England expecting to find the genealogy of any particular English family settled in New England at an early day, is pretty sure, in at least nine cases out of ten, to meet with disappointment. He will, if he looks for the names of Smith, Brown, Jones, &c., find enough of them; but, to connect an ancestor bearing one of these names, with the ancestor of a New England family of the same surname, is a desideratum of much uncertainty. The reason of this uncertainty is easily explained. In the first place, persons who emigrate are not often possessors of real estate, and hence deeds and wills seldom furnish indications referable to them. They leave no deeds or wills in the father land by which they can be traced. In the next place, very few emigrants from England were landholders, for the reason that for ages little or no land has been for sale in quantities within the reach of persons of moderate estates. William the Conqueror parcelled out all England to, comparatively, a few of his followers, and the dependents of those followers improved the vast domains by a sort of tenure, which in time grew into the leasing system, by which system, probably, above seven eighths of the present inhabitants of that country hold their places of residence and business.

As though the estates thus awarded were not sufficiently extensive, it not unfrequently happened that an estate, and sometimes several estates, reverted to the crown by confiscation; and such were conferred on some favorite already in possession of extensive domains; while the crown was careful to serve itself plentifully in the first place. The revenue to the sovereign from the crown lands, even to this day, are by no means inconsiderable.

It sometimes fell out that persons came into possession of lands by heirship, where the prospect originally appeared so small as to be scarcely worthy of attention. But such cases were always rare.

Hence, for the descendant of a New England emigrant to find his ancestor among the nobility or landed gentry of the period of the emigration, is about as certain as it would be to find him among those classes of the present day!

As the great body of emigrants to New England took no pains to transmit to their descendants any account of their ancestors, or even the places whence they came, it is pretty evident they had nothing to expect from the one, or any special regard for the other. Where parish registers have been preserved, some data are often found and made available in New England pedigrees. But they seldom indicate any connection with the so called higher classes.

Classes were and are very distinct in England. The class of servants, the class of tradespeople, the class of mechanics, &c., have continued for a long period of time. They mixed very little with those above them. Few of these ever became landholders, and few ever thought of a pedigree. Pedigrees may be said to have originated with the immediate descendants of the possessors of landed estates. They grew out of a necessity. Thus Genealogy became a *science*, and the learned pursued it as a useful and necessary branch of knowledge; and as such it is generally pursued in this country, especially in New England. There are those who pursue it with a notion that they are heirs to a great estate in England, left by some unknown ancestor. They may thus add something to the science of genealogy, and enlarge their own knowledge, while they will find no necessity to enlarge their pockets.

An exceedingly amusing article might be written upon the efforts of numerous families and individuals to obtain property left by their ancestors in England, at some remote period, as they imagine. And it may be pretty safely asserted, that the majority of such fortune hunters cannot trace their own line to their emigrant ancestor! Indeed, some have started for England to obtain, as descendants, the property of an individual who never had any descendants; and this knowledge was within the reach of everybody on this side of the Atlantic! But to take up space with these remarks may be considered unnecessary by the intelligent readers of the Register.

The sources of information in England have been greatly improved within the present century. Many restrictions upon the public records have been thrown off, and an immense amount of original papers, public and private, have found, and are daily finding, their way into that vast and well arranged and well conducted repository—the British Museum. And though it may be said that much remains to be done, in laying open, collecting, and arranging the records of England, at the same time it may be observed, that the extent and magnitude of what has already been done, could it be fully stated, would surpass belief.

It is high time the British government placed the ancient wills of the realm in a position to be consulted and used; especially those in the keeping of the Prerogative Court of Canterbury. This is the most extensive collection in the kingdom, and ought to be free for all genealogical and other literary uses. Yet the keepers of this repository are obliged to subject all applicants to heavy fees. In the beginning of 1859, an attempt was made to open Doctors' Commons to literary inquirers. A petition to Parliament was drawn up, ably setting forth the advantages which would accrue to the literary public by making that depository as free as the British Museum. This was headed by Lord Macaulay and other eminent gentlemen; but Parliament thought the time had not come for such liberality in Doctors' Commons, and thus the matter rests, and may possibly rest till another Sir Nicholas Harris Nicolas shall appear.

And here I may be pardoned for referring to that preëminent antiquary, who was cut off in the prime of life, while successfully advocating the cause of a free use of the public records, "whenever it could be done consistent with their safety." Few Americans who visit England to examine those records learn how much they are indebted to that gentleman; because he had by his perseverance rendered himself unpopular among some influential officials, who considered his course an infringement upon their interest. Sir Harris Nicolas, as he was familiarly called, possessed those rare qualities of mind which seemed to endow him with an intuitive knowledge, to that wonderful extent to which few eminent men have attained through a long life. This naturally subjected him to the envy of some and the jealousy of others. And hence his enlightened views, put forth with regard to the public records, were combated from different quarters, and with some success. And yet the entering wedge, which he so powerfully drove into the heavy doors of the public archives, not only retains its place, but is pretty sure eventually to accomplish the great and beneficent object of forcing them entirely open. That Sir Harris had co-workers is true, but they can take care of themselves. These remarks are made, because it is thought that not many Americans appreciate the labors of that gentleman, as, most likely, they are unacquainted with them. The majority of his publications are now obtainable; but it is highly probable that when antiquarian and historical societies are *advanced* enough to attempt to collect them, they will find them difficult to be had. The last place of residence of Sir Harris in London, was No. 55 Torrington Square, to which the devoted American antiquary will not fail to make a pilgrimage when he may visit the Metropolis of the British empire; or, rather, the Metropolis of the world.

It is not very surprising that the progress of collecting, arranging, and laying open to the public the muniments of the realm has been slow, if the magnitude of these muniments is but partially comprehended. Some idea may be formed on this head, by a comparison of our own records with those of England. This can be done only by a comparison of the length of time the two countries or governments have been in existence. A little reflection on this point may warrant the averment, that, if all the records of the United States were collected together, they would not occupy a space equal to that occupied by the British State Paper Office alone: to say nothing of the magnitude of those in the Tower of London, in the Rolls Chapel, the Chapter House, Remembrancer's Office, Treasuries of the King's Bench and Common Pleas Remembrance Office, Augmentation Office, British Museum, &c., &c. S. G. D.

FOUNDERS OF NEW ENGLAND.

In a large volume bound in vellum, now in the Rolls Office, Chancery Lane, London, are records of a few of the early emigrants to New England. On the cover of the volume containing the earliest of such records yet discovered, is this inscription:—

"A Booke of Entrie for Pafsengers by ye Comifsion, and Souldiers according to the Statuti^e^ pafsing beyond the Seas, begun at Chriftmas, 1631. and ending at Chriftmas, 1632."

In it were originally about two quires of paper, all of which is filled with the records indicated on the cover. The front of the book appears to have been intended for the entry of names of soldiers. The other end for emigrants, travellers, traders, &c. The part containing these entries is entire. The volume is not paged,* but the dates follow in order, which is ample for reference. The first entry of names of persons for New England which I can find is on leaf 6th, and is as follows:

vij Marcij 1631.—The names of such Men as are to be transported to New England to be resident there vppon a plantacon, have tendred and taken the oath of allegeance according to the statute, vizt.

Thomas Thomas	Walter Harris	Thomas Haeward
Thomas Woodford	Joseph Mannering	Edmond Wynsloe †
John Smallie	John Levins	John Hart
John Whetston	Thomas Olliver	Willm̄ Norton
Wm Hill	John Olliver	Robert Gamlin
Willm̄ Perkins		

xij° Aprilis, 1632.—The names of such Men women and children wch are to passe to New England to be resident there vppon a Plantacon, have tendred and taken the oath of allegeance according to ye Statute

John Barcrofte	John Greene	Abigall Greene
Jane Barcrofte	Perseverance Greene	Sara Johnes *mado oorvt.*
Hugh Moier	John Greene	Joseph Greene
Henrie Sherborn	Jacob Greene	

xxij° Junij 1632.—The names of such Men transported to New England to the Plantacon there p'r Cert. from Capten Mason have tendred and taken the oath of allegeance according to the Statute

William Wadsworth	Joseph Roberts	John Watson
John Tallcott	John Coxsall	Robert Shelley

---

* Nor are any of these volumes paged; hence referring to pages would be referring to what does not exist.

† June 5th, 1632, the ship William and Francis arrived at Boston. Among the passengers was Mr. Edward Winslow. Prince, in *Hist. and Antiqs. Boston*, 140.

Willm̄ Heath	Tobie Willet	John White
Richard Allis	William Curtis	James Olmstedd
Thomas Vffett	Nic° Clark	William Lewes
Isack Murrill	Daniell Brewer*	Zeth Graunt
John Witchfield	Jo: Beniamin	Nathaniell Richardes
Jonathan Wade	Richard Beniamin	Edward Ellmer
Robert Bartlett	William James	Edward Holmar
Jo: Browne	Thomas Carrington	Jo: Totman
John Churchman	William Goodwynn	Charles Glower

[I have looked through the volume and can find no others for New England.]

The next volume, containing records of persons emigrating to New England, is also in the Rolls Office. It was formerly among the records and documents at Carlton Ride.† I should not say it was *found* there, for I am not aware that it was ever *lost*, but, like thousands of other papers and books of records, it was deposited there for safe keeping. But, during the two hundred and twenty-four years which have elapsed since the volume was made, it has, during some part of that period, not been very *safely* kept, for near a third of it has been damaged by laying long in water or a damp place; yet this damage does not extend but two or three inches from the foot of the first pages, and nearly the whole of it can be read.

The volume contains about three quires of foolscap paper, and is bound in vellum. The first entry in it is "xxixth Decēbr: 1634," recording, that "*Wm Conasley*, aged 22 yeres," might "pass to Dort on his affairs."

The next entry (apparently made at the same time with the first) under the same date, is "*Samuell Sharpe* aged 55 years dwellen in London."

Several pages onward, date V° ffebr: [1634–5] is "*Samvel Sharp* 54 yeres old, dwelling in Layden."

About a third of the volume is taken up with recording the names of persons going to some part of the Low Countries,—Holland and Flanders,—some to reside and some to return. The last entry is of date 24th December, 1635.

The passengers for New England, Virginia, American islands, &c., are entered at the other end of the book. The first date there is "Vltiō Decembris, 1634," which is followed by a list of twenty-eight soldiers for "Guttorembeck." The list is prefaced thus: "Post festum Natalis Christi 1634. Vsqe ad festum Na: Christi 1635."

On the vellum wrapper or cover is this inscription:

"The Register of the names
of all ye Passinger[s] w^{ch}
Passed from ye Port of
London for an whole
yeare ending at
Xmas 1635."

[The various companies "desirous" of leaving England are entered in the order of their application, or nearly so, and hence those for different parts are so mixed up that a close inspection of the whole is indispensable, in making out a list for any one destination. My search was

---

* MS. perfectly plain.

† On the northerly side of St. James Park, now (1859) being demolished.

only for those who went for New England, and I feel quite confident none have escaped me. And the readers of the Register may rest assured, that, though critical antiquaries may not fully agree as to what every name in these lists is, the following is a *full* and perfect copy of all the lists yet discovered.

For the examining reader's benefit, I have underscored the occupations, and some other words or sentences, believing that by that method some relief would be afforded to the eye. I have intended to keep to the old orthography and use of capital letters, presuming that the descendants of those emigrants will ever desire to know how the exact record stands, as it is an indication of the state of literature, at least among educated clerks, of that age.

The notes being all my own, throughout, this announcement is to avoid signing each of them, or otherwise advertising the reader. Quotation marks, too, are generally omitted, as the beginning and ending of the record is sufficiently apparent without them. Clerical abbreviations are printed to accommodate modern type.]

xj° Marcij 1634. Theise vnder written names are to be transported to New England, having brought Certificate from the Justices of the peace and Minister of the p'ish, the p'tie hath taken the oathe of Allegeance and Supremacie *de p'ochia St. Egiddij Cripplegate.**

Peter Howson xxxi yeres† and *his wife* Ellin Howson 39 yeres old.

Turris London Theise vnder written names are to be transported to New England having brought attestacon and Certificate from the Justices of peace and Minister of the p'ish according to the LLs of the Councells ord^r^ the p'tie hath taken the oaths of Allegeance and Supremacie.

Thomas Stares 31 yeres
Suzan Johnson 12 "

---

16 Marcij 1634 Theis vnder written names are to be transported to New England imbarqued in ye Christian de Lo. Jo^h^ White M^r^ bound thither, the men have taken ye oath [of] Allegeance & Supremacie.
Mildred Bredstret.‡

ffrancis Stiles	35	Edward Preston	13
Tho: Bassett	37	Jo: Cribb	30
Tho: Stiles	20	George Chappell	20
Tho: Barber	21	Robert Robinson	41
Jo: Dyer	28	Edward Patteson	33
Jo: Harris	28	ffrancis Marshall	30
James Horwood	30	Ric^e^ Heylei ‖	22
Jo: Reeves	19	Tho: Halford	20
Tho ffoulfoot	22	Tho: Haukseworth	23
James Busket	28	Jo: Stiles	35
Tho Coop §	18	Henrie Stiles	40

* What I have underscored is in the margin, and *is* according to the MS.

† I have omitted to repeat the word "yeres" over the column of ages as entirely superfluous.

‡ In the margin of this list. St. Mildred's was destroyed in the great fire of 1666, and was rebuilt by Sr Chr. Wren.

§ Probably Cooper, but the MS. is as above, without abbreviation mark.

‖ The MS. appears to me plain.

Jane Morden	30	Jo: Stiles	9 mo.
Joan Stiles	35	Rachell Stiles	28
Henry Stiles	3		

22° Marcij 1634. Theis vnder written names are to be imbarqued in ye Planter Nic° Trarice Mr bound for New England p'r Certificat from Stepney p'ish,* and Attestacon from Sr Tho: Jay, Mr Simon Muskett Justices of the Peace. The men have taken the oathe of Supremacie and Allegeance.

Nicholas davies	40	James Lannin *A Glover*	26	
Sara davies	48	Robert Stevens *A Sawyer*	22	4 *Servants*
Joseph davies	13	John More *A labourer*	24	4 *Servants*
Wm Locke	6	James Haieward	22	4 *Servants*
Jo: Maddox *A Sawyer*	43	Judith Phippin	16	4 *Servants*

Primo Aprill 1635. In the Hopewell of London mr Wm Bundocke vrs† New England.

Joh Cooper 41 yeres
Edmond ffarrington 47
Wm Parryer§ 36
} of oney in Buckinghamsher theis have taken the othe of Alleg. and Supremacie

Geo: Griggs 42 of Landen‡
Phillip Kyrtland 21 of Sherington
nath: Kyrtland 19 of Sherington
} in Buckinghamsher.

Wibroe 42 yrs wife of Joh Cooper
Eliza: 49 yeis wife of Edmond ffarrington
Alyce 37 yeis wife of Wm Purryer

Tho: Griggs 15 yers
Wm: Griggs 14 "
Eliza: Griggs 10 "
Mary Griggs 6 "
James Griggs 2 "
} Children of Geo: Griggs aforsaid.

Alyce Griggs 32 wife of Geo: Griggs

Mary Cooper 13
Joh: Cooper 10
Tho Cooper 7
Martha Cooper 5
} Children of Joh: Cooper aforsaid

Phillip Phillip 15 yers sert to Joh: Cooper

Sarra ffarrington 14
Mathew§ ffarrington 12
Joh: ffarrington 11
Eliza ffarrington 8
} Children of Edw. ffarrington

Mary Purryer§ 7
Sarra Purryer 5
Katheren Purryer 18 mo
} Children of Wm Purryer

2° Aprilis, 1635.—Theis vnder written names are to be transported to New England imbarqued in the Planter Nic°: Trarice Mr bound thither the p'ties have brought Certificate from the Minister of St Albons‖ in

---

* Uniformly used for *parish.*

† Abbreviation of *versum* or *versus.* For, towards.

‡ I do not find *Landen* in most minutely written topographical works, but I find *Laundon* in Buckinghamshire.

§ I need not apprise the reader that I aim to preserve the exact spelling of names.

‖ Now St. Albans.

Hertfordshire, and Attestacõn from the Justices of peace according to the Lords Order.

Jo: Tuttell *A Mercer*	39	Mary Chittwood	24
Joan Tuttell	42	Tho: Olney *Shoemaker*	35
John Lawrence	17	Marie Olney	30
Wm Lawrence	12	Tho Olney	3
Marie Lawrence	9	Etenetus Olney	
Abigall Tuttell	6	Geo: Giddins *Husbandman*	25
Symon Tuttell	4	Jane Giddins	20
Sara Tuttell	2	Tho: Savage *Taylor*	27
Jo: Tuttell	1	Richard Harvie *A Taylor*	22
Joan Antrobuss	65	ffrances Pebody *Husbandman*	21
Marie Wrast	24	Wm Wilcockson *Lynen wever*	34
Tho: Greene	15	Margaret Wilcockson	24
Nathan Haford *seruant to* Jo: Tutell	16	Jo: Wilcockson	2
		Ann Harvie	22
Wm Beardsley *A Mason*	30	Willm̄ ffelloe *Shoemaker*	24
Marie Beadsley	26	ffrancis Baker *A Taylor*	24
Marie Beadsley	4	Tho: Carter	25 } *Servants* to Geo: Giddins *pred.*
John Beadsley	2	Michell Willmson	30 }
Joseph Beadsley	6 mo:	Elizabeth Morrison	12 }
Allen Perley *Husbandman*	27		

3 Aprill 1635.

James weauer *Statinor* 23
Edmond weauer *Husbandman* 28 dwelling in Anckstrey* in Herefordsher & his wife Margarett aged 30 yers

Theis vnder written names are to be transported to New England imbarqued in ye Hopewell Mr Wm Bundick. The p'ties have brought Certificates from the Minister & Justices of peace that they are no Subsedy† men they have taken the oath of alleg: and Supremacee.

Joh: Astwood *Husbandman*	26	Nazing in Essex.	
Jo: Ruggells	10	Jo: Ruggells *Shoemaker*	44
Martha Carter	27	Barbarie Ruggells *uxor*	30
Marie Elliott	13	Jo: Ruggells	2
		Elizabeth Elliot	8
p'r Cert: from Stanstede Abbey in com Hert.		Giles Payson	26
		Isack Morris	9
Laurence Whittimor *Husbandman*	63	Jo: Peat *Husbandman* of Duffill‡ p'ish in Derbieshere	38
Elizabeth Whittimor	57		
Elizabeth Turner	20	Edward keele	14
Sara Elliott	6	Jo: Goadby	16
Robert Day	30	Jo: Bill	13
Wm Peacock	12	Tho: Greene	15

* The only name in Herefordshire bearing any affinity to this is *Akenbury*, which is in Greytree Hundred.

† Always so written in the original. And so "Allegeance." The serious difficulties between Charles I. and his Parliament about raising money, gave rise to this matter of subsidy. The reader of English history does not require even this intimation, perhaps.

‡ Probably *Duffield*, in Appletree Hundred.

Isacke Desbrough *Husbandman*, of Ell-Tisley in com Cambridge	18
Eliz: Elliott	30
Lyddia Elliott	4
Phelip Elliot	2

Of St. Katherins

Robert Titus *Husbandman*	35
Hanna Titus *vxor*	21
Jo: Titus	8
Edmond Titus	5

Geo: Woodward *ffishmonger* 35 p'r Certi: from Sr Geo: Whitmor & Sr Nic° Raynton two Justices of ye Peace in London and from Jo: Thorp Minister of ye p'ish of St Buttolphs Billingsgate.

---

vjth Aprilis 1635.

Theis p'ties heerevnder mencioned are to be transported to New England: imbarqued in the Planter Nic° Trarice Mr bound thether: they have brought Certificates from the Justices of Peace and Ministers of ye p'ish that they are conformable to the orders of ye Church of England and are no Subsedy men: they haue taken the oath of Supremacie & Allegeance Die et An° pred.

Martin Saunders *A Currier*		40
Rachel Saunders *uxor*		40
Lea Saunders	3 *children*	10
Judith Saunders		8
Martin Saunders		4
Marie ffuller	3 *Servants*	17
Richard Smith		14
Rich Ridley		16

ffrancis Newcom *Husb:*		30
Rachell Newcom 20	*wife & 2 children*	
Rachell Newcom 2½		
Jo: Newcom 9 moneths		
Ant° Stannion *A Glover*		24
Daniell Hanbury		29
ffrancis Dexter		13
Willm̃ Dawes		15
Marie Saunders		15

Theis p'ties imbarqued in the Eliz: Mr Wm Stagg bound for New England p'r Cert from the Justices and Ministers of ye p'ish.

Clement Bates *A Taylor*		40
Ann Bates		40
James Bates	14	5 *children.*
Clement Bates	12	
Rachell Bates	8	
Joseph Bates	5	
Ben: Bates	2	

Jo: Wynchester	19
Jervice Gold *Servantes**	30

More for the Planter.

Richard Tuttell *Husbandman*	42
Ann Tuttell	41
Anna Tuttell	12
Jo: Tuttell	10
Rabecca Tuttell	6
Isbell Tuttell	70
Marie Wolhouston	30
Willm̃ Tuttell *Husbandman*	26
Elizabeth Tuttell	23
Jo: Tuttell	3½
Elizabeth Swayne	20
Margaret Leach	15
Ann Tuttell	2 *a qr.* [2¼]

Tho: Tuttell	3 *mo.*
Sycillie Clark	16
Marie Bill	11
Phillipp Atwood	12
Barthol: ffaldoe	16
ffrancis Bushnell *A Carpenter*	26
Marie Bushnell	26
Martha Bushnell	1
Willm Lea	16
Marie Smith	18
Hanna Smith	18
Ann Wells	15

---

* The scribe made a brace against *Jo: Wynchester*, and began to write *servant* against that name, but stopped when he had written *se* and wrote *servants* against *Jervice Gold.*

In the Hopewell Willm̄ Bundock Mr bound for New England, &c.

James Burgis	14	Marie Abbott	16
Alexander Thwaits	20	Marie Coke	14
Jo: Abbott	16	Marie Peake	15
Jo: Bellowes	12	Tho: Pell *A Taylor*	22
Jo: Johnes	18	Jo: Bushnell *A Glazier*	21

In the Rabecca of London Mr Hodges for New England.

Peter Vnderwood *A Husbandman*	22
Isabell Craddock	30

---

vijth Aprilis 1635. This p'tie vnder mencioned is to be imbarqued in the Planter bound for New England p'r Cert: from Alderman ffenn of his conformitie he hath taken the oath of Allegeance & Supremacie.

Richard ffenn 27

---

8 Aprilis, 1635. Theis p'ties herevnder mencioned are to be transported to New England: imbarqued in the Elizabeth of London Wm Stagg Mr bound thither: they haue taken the oath of Allegeance and Supremacie p'r Cert: from the p'ish of St. Alphage Cripple gate the Minister there.

Wm Holdred *Tanner*	25	Daniell Brodley	20
Roger Preston *Tanner*	21	Isack Studman	30

That theis 3 p'ties p'rd. are no Subsedie men: wee whose names herevnto are written belonging to Blackwell Hall, do averr they are none.

Robte ffarronds
Thomas Smith

Theis p'ties herevnder written are to be transported in the Planter: p'rd. p'r Cert: from the minister of Kingston vpon Thames in the County of Surrey of their conformitie and yt they are no Subsedy men.

Palmer Tingley* *A Miller*	21
Wm Butterick *An ostler*	20
Tho: Jernell *A Miller*	27

---

ixth Aprilis 1635. In the Elizabeth de London p'rd Mr Willm̄ Stagg bound for New England: Theis vnder written names have brought Cert: from ye Minister of Hauckust† in Kent: and Attestation from two Justices of Peace being conformable to the Church of England and that they are no Subsedy men:

James Hosmer *A Clothier*	28		John Ston	40
Ann Hosmer *vxor*	27		Edward Gold	28
Marie Hosmer	2	} *two*	Geo: Russell	19
Ann Hosmer	3 *mo.*	} *children*	Jo: Mussell	15
Marie Dounard	24	} *two*		
Marie Martin	19	} *servants*		

Nono die Aprilis 1635. In the Rabeca Mr Jo Hodges, bound for New England.

Jacob Welsh *husbandman*	32
Geo: Woodward	35

---

* I have no question as to this name, though the *T* is imperfectly made.
† *Hawkherst* then, now Hawkhurst.

Theis vnder written names are to be transported to New England imbarqued in the Rabecca p'rd.

Elizabeth Winchell	52	Wm Swayne	aged 16
Jo: Winchell	13	ffrancis Swayne	14

17th Aprill 1635. In the Eliza and Ane Mr Ro. Cowper* to New England.

Thomas Hedsall 47 yeres.

In the Encrease of London, Mr Robert Lea vrs New England.

Geo: Bacon†	43 yers		Eliza: Ward *a maid servant*	38	
Samuell	12	*children of the said* Mason [Bacon.]	Rebecca	18	*Children of the said* Tho: Jostlin
Joh:	8		Dorothy	11	
Susan	10		Nathaniell	8	
Tho: Jostlin‡ *Husbandman*	43		Eliza	6	
Rebecca *his wife*	43		Mary	1	

x° Aprilis, 1635. Theis vnder written names are to be transported in the Planter p'rd. Nic° Trarice Mr bound for New England p'r Cert. of the Minister of Sudburie in Suffolk and from the Maior of the Towne of his conformitie to the orders and discipline of the Church of England and that he is no Subsedy man; he hath taken the oath of Alleg: & Suprem:

Richard Haffell *Currier*	54		Alice Smith	40
Martha *vxor*	42		Elizabeth Coop	24
Marie Haffell	17	5 *daughters*	Jo: Smith	13
Sara Haffell	14		Job Hawkins	15
Martha Haffell	8			
Rachell Haffell	6			
Ruth Haffell	3			

In the Planter p'rd: Theis vnder names are to be transported to New England:

Eglin Hanford		46	Rodolphus Elmes§	15
Margaret Hanford	2 *daughters*	16	Tho: Stansley	16
Eliz: Hanford		14		

In the Elizabeth of London: Wm Stagg Mr bound for New England.

Willm̄ Wild 30 Peter Thorne 20 Alice Wild 40

xj° die Aprilis, 1635. In the Eliz: pred. wm Stagg Mr bound for New England: the p'ties vnder written have brought Certificate according to order.

Wm Whitteredd, *carpenter*	36	Jo: Wild	17
Elizabeth *vxor*	30	Samuel Haieward	22
Tho: whittredd *sonn*	10	Jo: Duke	20
Jo: Cluffe	22		

* *Cooper* elsewhere, but here it is *Cowper*.

† First written *Mason*, and afterwards erased and *Bacon* substituted; but the clerk omitted to do the same for the children.

‡ See pedigree of Joselyne, in Register, vol. xiv. pp. 15, 16.

§ Settled in Scituate. See Deane's *History of Scituate*. His wife was Catharine, dau. of John Whitcomb, whom he married in 1644. Their ninth child, Rodolphus, b. 1668, settled in Middleborough, had wife Bethiah ——, and son Elkanah. This son had nine children.

In the Planter p'rd: Theis vnder written names are to be transported to New England p'r Certificate according to order.

Sara Pittnei	22	Margaret Pitnei	22
Sara Pittnei 7 } 2 Childn		Rachell Deane	31
Samvell Pittney 1½ }			

---

xiij° Aprilis 1635. In the Elizabeth and Ann Mr Roger Coop bound for New England per Cert: from the Maior of Evesham in com̄ Worr and from the Minister of ye p'ish of their Conformitie

Margerie Washborn		49
Jo: Washborne	sons	14
Phillipp Washborne	sons	11

In the Elizabeth de Lo.* Wm Stagg M^r^ prd. theis vnder written names brought Cert: from the Minister of St. Saviors Southwark of their conformitie

Tho: Millet	30	Joshua Wheat	17
Maria Millet *vxor*	29	Jo: Smith	12
Versula Greenoway	32	Ralph Chapman	20
Henrie Bull	19	Tho Millet	2

The vnder written named is to be imbarqued in ye Increase Robert Lea M^r^ bound for New England p'r Cert: from Billercocay in Essex from the Minister of ye p'ish that he is no Subsedy man.

Wm Rusco *husbandman*	41	Sara Rusco	9 } *4 children*
et vxor Rebecca	40	Marie Rusco	7 }
		Samvel Rusco	5 }
		Wm Rusco	1 }

In the Increase, prd. Theis vnder written names are to be transported to New England: p'r Cert: from All Sts Staynings,† Mark Lane of their Conformitie to the Church of England

Tho: Page *A Taylor*	29	Edward Spurkes	22 } *2 servants*
Elizabeth Page *vxor*	28	Kat: Taylor	24 }
Tho: Page 2 } *2 children*			
Katherin Page 1 }			

The Elizabeth and Ann Roger Coop M^r^. Theis p'ties herevnder expressed are to be imbarqued for New England having taken the oaths of Allegeance and Supremacie and likewise brought Certificate both from the Ministers and Justices where their abidinges were latlie, of their conformitie to the discipline and orders of the Church of England and y^t^ they are no Subsedy Men.

Robert Hawkynns *husb.*	25	Richard Whitney	9
Jo: Whitney	35	Nathaniell Whitney	8
Jo: Palmerley	20	Tho: Whitney	6
Richard Martin	12	Jonathan Whitney	1
Jo: Whitney	11	Nic° Sension	13

---

* *de Lo.* of London. London is often abbreviated so, and sometimes *Lon: Lon̄.*, &c.

† *Allhallows* Stayning, probably. It escaped the great fire of 1666. In 1630 it was repaired and beautified, but not long after the fire, "it fell all down suddenly." *Strype's Stow's London.* It was anciently called the *stone* church; hence *stane* or *stayning. Ibid.*

Henry Jackson	29	Sara Cartrack	24
Wm Hubbard	35	Jane Dam̄and	9
Tho: Hubbard	10	Mary Eaton	4
Tho: Eaton	1	Marie Broomer	10
Marie Hawkynns	24	Mildred Cartrack	2
Ellen Whitney	30	Joseph Alsopp	14
Abigall Eaton	35		

In the Suzan and Ellin, Edward Payne Mr. for New England. Theis p'ties herevnder expressed have brought Certificate from the Minister and Justices of their Conformitie and that they are no Subsedy men.

John Procter *husb:*	40	Richard Saltonstall *husb:*	23
Martha Procter	28	Merriall Saltonstall	22
John Procter	3	Merriall Saltonstall	9 months
Marie Procter	1	Tho: Wells	30
Alice Street	28	Peter Coop	28
Walter Thornton *husb:*	36	Wm Lambart	26
Joanna Thornton	44	Sam̄vel Podd	25
John North	20	Jeremy Belcher	22
Mary Pynder	53	Marie Clifford	25
ffrancis Pynder	20	Jane Coe	30
Marie Pynder	17	Marie Riddlesden	17
Joanna Pinder	14	Jo: Pellam	20
Anna Pynder	12	Mathew Hitchcock	25
Katherin Pinder	10	Elizabeth Nicholls	25
Jo: Pynder	8	Tomazin Carpenter	35
Richard Skofield	22	Ann ffowle	25
Edward Weeden	22	Edmond Gorden	18
George Wilby	16	Tho: Sydlie	22
Richard Hawkins	15	Margaret Leach	22
Tho: Parker	30	Marie Smith	21
Symon Burd	20	Elizabeth Swayne	16
Jo: Mansfield	34	Grace Bewlie	30
Clement Cole	30	Ann Wells	20
Jo: Jones	20	Dyonis Tayler	48
Wm Burrow	19	Hanna Smith	30
Phillip Atwood	13	Jo: Buckley	15
Wm Snowe	18	Wm Buttrick	18
Edward Lum̄us	24		

---

15 May 1635. Penelopy Pellam 16 yers to passe to her brothers plantacō.

---

xiiij° Aprilis 1635. In the Increase of London Mr Robte Lea bouhde for New England. Theis haue taken the oathes of Allegeance and Supremacye, and haue brought Certificat of their conformity wch are this day filed.

Samuell Andrews	37	*Robert Cordell Gouldsmith in Limbert* street sent them a Way.*
Robte Naney	22	
Robte Sankey	30	
James Gibbins	21	

---

* So the MS.; no doubt *Lombard St.*, noted for jewellers.

Also Jane the wife of the bouesaid Saml Andrewes	30
Ellyn Lougie her Seruante aged	20
Jane Andrewes her daughter aged	3
Elizabeth Andrewes her daughter	2

All for new land in the Increase aforesaid.

---

xvth Aprill, 1635. In the Eliza. de Loñd. Wm Stagg vrs New England. Theis p'tis haue taken oathe of Allegeance and of Supremacy before Sr Wm Whitimor* Sr Nicho Ranton.

Rich. Walker	24	Tho Lettyne	23
Joh Beamond	23	Joh: Johnson	23
Wm Beamond	27	Willm̄ Walkor	15

---

15 Aprill, 1635. In the Eliza: and Anne de Lond. Roger Cooper vrs New England.

Percy Kinge, 24 yers, a maid seruant to Mr Ro: Crowley.

In the Eliza: de Lond. Wm Stagg vers New England James Walker 15 yers and Sarra Walkor 17 yers serute to Jno Browne *Baker* and to on Wm Bracey *linnen drap* in Cheapside Lond. p'r cert. of their Conformitie.

---

viijo Aprilis 1635. Theis vnder written names are to be transported to New England imbarqued in the Increase de Lo. Robert Lea Mr. The p'te pred having brought Certificates from the minister Justices of ye Peace of his conformitie to the Church of England.

Tho: Bloggett *Glover*	30	Daniell Blogget	4	*2 children.*
Suzun Bloggett *vxor*	37	Samvell Blogget	1½	

In the Increase p'rd. The p'tie vnder written hath brought Certificate from the Minister of Wapping and from two Justices of peace of his Conformitie to ye Church of England to passe in ye said ship for New England.

Tho: Chittingden *Lynnen wever*	51	Isack Chittingden	10	*2 Children*
Rabecca Chittingden *vxor*	40	Henr Chittingden	6	

Theis vnder written names are to be transported to New England imbarqued in the Suzan and Ellin Edward Payne Mr. The p'ties have brought Certificates from ye Ministers and Justices of the peace of they are no Subsedy men: and are conformable to ye orders and discipline of the Church of England.

Ralph Hudson *A drap.*		42	Den: Thwing	*Servants.*	16
Marie Hudson *vxor*		42	Ann Gilson†		34
Hanna Hudson	*3 Children.*	14	Judith Kirk		18
Eliz: Hudson		5	Jo: More		41
Jo: Hudson		12	Henry Knowles		25
Tho: Briggham		32	Geo: Richardson		30

---

* Easily taken for *Whitmore*, as the last *i* is not dotted; nor are half of that letter dotted in the whole MS.

† If this name is *Gilston* (and I know it is not) we should transcribe *Hudston, Atherston*, &c.

Ben: Thomlins	18
Edward Tomlins	30
Barbara Fford	16
Joan Broomer	13
Richard Brooke	24
Tho: Brooke	18
Symon Crosby *Husbandm:*	26
Ann Crosby *vxor*	25
Tho: Crosby *child*	8 weeks
Rich: Rowton *Husbandm:*	36
Ann Rowton *vxor*	36
Edmond Rowton *child*	6
Percivall Greene *Husbandm:*	32
Ellin Green *vxor*	32
Jo: Trane } 2 *Servants*	25
Margaret Dix } 2 *Servants*	18
Jo: Atherson	24
Ann Blason	27
Ben: Buckley	11
Daniell Buckley	9
Jo: Corrington	33
Mary Corrington	33

---

xv° Aprilis, 1635. Theis p'ties hereafter expiessed are to be transported to New England in ye Increase Robert Lea M^{r}: having taken the oathes of Allegeance and Supremacie: As also being conformable to the Government and discipline of the Church of England whereof they brought testimony p'r Cert. from ye Justices and ministers where there abodes have latlie been. (viz.)

Samvell Morse *Husbm:*	50
Elizabeth Morse *vxor*	48
Joseph Morse	20
Elizabeth Daniell	2
Philemon Dalton *A Lynnen weauer*	45
Hanna Dalton *vxor*	35
Samvel Dalton	5½
Wm White	14
Marthaw Marvyn *Husbandm:*	35
Elizabeth Marvynn *vxor*	31
Elizabeth Marvinn	31
Mathew Marvynn	8
Marie Marvynn	6
Sara Marvynn	3
Hanna Marvynn	½
Jo: Warner	20
Isack More	13
Samvell Ireland *Carpenter*	32
Marie Ireland *vxor*	30
Martha Ireland	1½
Wm̄ Buck *Plowrite*	50
Roger Buck	18
Jo: Davies *A Joyner*	29
Abram ffleming *Husband:*	40
Jo: ffokar *Husb:*	21
Tho: Parish *Clothier*	22
John Owdie	17
Wm Houghton *Butcher*	22
Willm Payne *Husb:*	37
Anna Payne	40
Wm Payne	10
Anna Payne	5
Jo: Payne	3
Daniell Payne	8 weeks
James Bitton	27
Wm Potter	25
Elizabeth Wood	38
Elizabeth Beardes	24
Suzan Payne	11
Aymes Gladwell	16
Phobe Perce	18
Henry Crosse *Carpenter*	20
Tho: Kilborne *Husb:*	55
ffrancis Kilborne *vxor*	50
Margaret Kilborne	23
Lyddia Kilborne	22
Marie Kilborne	16
ffrancis Kilborne	12
Jo: Kilborne	10
James Roger	20
Richard Nunn	19
Tho Barret	16
Jo: Hackwell	18
Symon Ayres *Chirurgion*	48
Dorothy Ayres	38
Marie Ayres	15
Tho: Ayres	13
Symon Ayres	11
Rabecca Ayres	9
Jane Rawlin	30
Symon Stone *Husbm:*	50
Joan Stone *vxor*	38
ffrancis Stone } *Children*	16
Ann Stone } *Children*	11
Symon Stone } *Children*	4
Marie Stone } *Children*	3
Jo: Stone } *Children*	5 *weeks*
Christian Ayres	7
Anna Ayres	5

Benjamin Ayres	3	Isack Worden (*Servants.*)	18
Sara Ayres	3 *months*	Nathaniell Wood (*Servants.*)	12
Steven Vpson *A Lawyer*	23	Elizabeth Streaton (*Servants.*)	19
Jo: Wyndell*	16	Marie Toller (*Servants.*)	16

17 Aprilis 1635. Theis p'ties herevnder expressed are to be transported to New England imbarqued in ye Elizabeth Wm Stagg M^{r}. Cert. from the Minister and Justices of the Peace of their Conformitie to the Church of England, they have taken the oaths of Allegeance and Supremacie.

James Bate *Husb:*	53	Mary Smith *filia*	15
Alice Bate	52	Peter Gardner	18
Lyddia Bate	20	Wm Hubbard	35
Marie Bate	17	Rachell Bigg	6
Margaret Bate	12	Patience ffoster	40
James Bate	9	Hopestill ffoster	14
Edward Bullock *Husb:*	32	ffrancis White	24
Elizabeth Stedman	26	Joan Sellin	50
Nathaniell Stedman	5	Ann Sellin	7
Isack Stedman	1	Edward Loomis	27
Robert Thornton	11	Jo: Hubbard	10
Margaret Davies	32	Jo: Davies	9
Elizabeth Davies	1	Marie Davies	4
Dorothy Smith	45	Jo: Browne	40

The p'tie herevnder named with his wife and children is to be transported to New England imbarqued in the Elizabeth and Ann, Willm Cooper M^{r}. bound thither the p'tie hath brought testimonie from the minister of his conformitie to the orders and discipline of the Church of England and from the two Justices of peace y^{t} he hath taken the oaths of Allegeance and Supremacie.

Alexander Baker	28	Christian Baker	1
Elizabeth Baker *vxor*	23	Clement Chaplin	48
Elizabeth Baker	3	Wm Swayne	50

27 Aprilis, 1635. Theis vnder written names are to be transported to New England Roger Cooper M^{r}. bound thither in the Elizabeth and Ann. The p'ties have brought Certificates from the Minister at Westminster and the Justices of the Peace, of his Conformitie; the p'tie hath taken the oaths of Allegeance and Supremacie.

Richard Brocke *A Carpenter*	31	Daniell Preston	13
Edward Sall	24		

29 Aprilis, 1635. These vnder written names are to be transported to New England imbarqued in the Elizabeth and Ann, Roger Coop^{r}, M^{r}. The p'ties have brought Certificate from the Minister of the p'ish and Justice of Peace of their conformitie to the orders and discipline of the Church of England and y^{t} they are no Subsedy men.

Rich^{h} Goard†	17	Tho: Lord *A Smith*	50

* Possibly *Wendell*, but the MS. is perfectly plain *Wyndell*.

† May as well be read Goare as Goard; for the terminal letter is *e* or *d*, and those letters are made exactly alike. The *d* is usually made a little taller than the *e*; but when used at the end of a word, and neither *d* nor *e* before occurring in the same word or name, it is not always possible to say which it is.

Dorothy Lord *vxor*	46	Aymie Lord	6
James Cobbett	23	Dorothy Lord	4
Thomas Lord	16	Wm Samond	19
Ann Lord	14	Josias Cobbett	21
Wm Lord	12	Jo: Holloway	21
John Lord	10	Jane Bennet	16
Joseph ffaber	26	Wm Reeve	22
Tho: Ponnd*	21	Christopher Stanley *Taylor*	32
Robert Lord	9	Suzanna Stanley *vxor*	31

4° Maij, 1635. Theis vnder written names are to be transported to New England imbarqued in the Eliz: and Ann p'rd. The p'ties have brought Certificate from the Minister and Justices of the Peace of their conformitie and that they are no Subsedy Men.

Hen: Wilkinson *A Tallow Chandler*	25
Robert Haus *A Soape boyler*	19

Theis vnder written names are to be transported to New England: imbarqued in the Abigall, Richard Hackwell Mr. The p'ties have brought Certificate from ye Minister and Justices of their conformitie to the orders and discipline of the Church of England.

Tho: Buttolph	32	Nathaniel Tylly	32
Ann Buttolph *vxor*	24	Peter Kettell	10
Wm ffuller	25	Tho: Steevens	12
Jo: ffuller	15	Eliz: Harding	12

6 Maij, 1635. Theis vnder written names are to be transported to New England, imbarqued in the Elizabeth and Ann, Roger Coop' Mr. The p'ties have brought Cert: from the Ministers where their abodes were and from the Justices of Peace of their conformitie to the orders and discipline of the Church of England and yt they are no Subsedy men: they have taken the oaths of Allegeance and Supremacie.

Samvell Hull†	25	Rich Goard	17
Wm Swynden	20	Wm Adams	15
†Jo: Halsey‡	24	†Henry Curtis‡	27
Vyncent Potter	21		

viij° Maij, 1635. In the Elizabeth and Ann p'rd. Roger Coop' Mr. Theis vnder written names are to be transported to New England imbarqued in the said shipp: They brought Cert: of their Conformitie to the Church of England and yt they are no Subsedy men.

John Wylie	25	George Orris	21
Jo: Thomson	22	Jo: Jackson	27
Edmond Weston	30	Elizabeth ffabin	16
Gamaliell Beomont	12	Grace Bulkley	33
Awdry Whitton	45		

Nono die Maij, 1635. Theis vnder written names are to be transported to New England, imbarqued in ye Suzan and Ellin, Edward Payne Mr.

* The MS. is undoubtedly *Ponnt;* that being the name understood by the clerk. It is nothing uncommon to find *d* and *t* thus confounded.

† Certainly *Hull* in the original ‡ So marked in the original MS.†

The p'ties haue brought Certificates from the minister of the p'ish of their conformitie to the Church of England, and that they are no Subsedy men: The p'ties haue taken the oaths of Allegeance and Supremacie.

Peter Bulkley	50	Richard Brooke	24
Tho: Brooke	20	Elizabeth Taylor	10
Precilla Jarman	10	Ann Lieford	13

In the Elizabeth and Ann p'rd. Roger Coop' M^r^. bound for New England.

Robert Jeofferies	30	Suzan Browne	21
Marie Jeofferies *vxor*	27	Robert Carr *a Tayler*	21
Tho: Jefferies } *Children.*	7	Calebb Carr	11
Elizabeth Jefferies } *Children.*	6	Rich. White } *Carpenters*	30
Mary Jefferies } *Children.*	3	Tho: Dane } *Carpenters*	32
Hanna Day	20	Wm Hilliard } *Carpenters*	21

---

xj° Maij, 1635. Theis vnder written names are to be transported to New England imbarqued in the Eliz. and Ann p'rd. The p'ties have brought Certificate from the Minister and Justices of Peace of their conformitie to ye orders and discipline of the Church of England, and y^t^ they are no Subsedy men.

Willm Courser *A Shoemaker*	26
Geo: Wylde *A Husbandman*	37
Geo: Parker *A Carpenter*	23

---

xij° Maij, 1635. In the Elizabeth and Ann, Roger Cooper, M^r^. bound to New England: Theis vnder written names are to be transported p'r Certificate from ye Minister of Bennandin* in Kent of their Conformitie to ye orders and discipline of ye Church of England.

John Borden	28	Jeremy Whitton	8
Joan Borden *vxor*	23	Mathew Borden	5
Nic^o^ Morecock	14	Eliz: Borden	3
Bennet Morecock	16	Thomas Whitton	36
Marie Morecock	10	Samvell Baker	30

---

14 Maij, 1635. Theis vnder written are to be transported to New England, imbarqued in the Elizabeth and Ann, Roger Cooper Mr. The p'ties haue brought Certificatt from the Minister of the p'ish of their Conformitie to the orders and discipline of the Church of England.

Richard Sampson *A Tayler*	28	John Oldham	12
Tho: Alsopp	20	Tho: Oldham	10
Robt. Standy	22		

---

xv° Junij, 1635. Theis vnder written names are to be transported to New England: imbarqued in the Abigall de Lo: Mr H. Hackwell: The p'tie having brought Certificate from the minister of Thisselworth† of his conformitie to the orders and discipline of the Church of England. He hath taken the oaths of Allegiance and Supremacie.

---

* Benenden, in the Lathe of Scray, Rolverden Hundred.

† *Thisselton* may be found mentioned in the Topographies of that time, but no *Thistleworth* or *Thesselworth*. *Thisselton* then, and *Thistleton* now, exist in Rutlandshire. But *Isleworth* in Middlesex was sometimes called *Thistleworth*.

Dennis Geere	30	Anne Pancrust	16
Elizabeth Geere *vxor*	22	Eliz: Tusolie	55
Elizabeth Geere } *Children*	3	Constant Wood	12
Sara Geere } *Children*	2		

19 Junij, 1635. Theis vnder written names are to be transported to New England imbarqued in ye Abigall: Hackwell Mr the p'ties having brought Certificate from the minister of the p'ish of the little Minories of his conformitie and opinion of the descepline of the Church of England.

Wm Tilly	28	Charles Jones	21
Robert Whiteman	20	Liddia Browne	16

Abord the James, Jo: May for N. England.

Tho: Ewer *Taylor*	40	Sara Beale	28
Sara Ewer	28	Elizabeth Newman	24
Elizabeth Ewer	4	Jo: Skudder	16
Tho: Ewer	$1\frac{1}{2}$		

xxth June, 1635. Theis vnder written names are to be imbarqued in the Abbigaill de Lo. Mr Hackwell, and boñd to New England, haue taken oathe of Allegance and Supremacie and Conformitie to ye Chh as p'adit from Two Justices of Peace and minister of St. Lawrence in Essex:

Henry Bullocke *husbandman*	40	Henry Bullocke } *Children*	8
Susan Bullocke *his wife*	42	Mary Bullocke } *Children*	6
		Tho: Bullocke } *Children*	2

More xxth 1635. In the Desire de Lond. Pearce, and boñd for New Eng. p'r Cert. frō ij Justices of Peace and minister of All Saintes* lionian in Northapton.

Wm Hoeman *husbm:*	40	Hanna Hoeman } 5 *Children*	8
Winifred Hoeman *his wife*	35	Jeremy Hoeman } 5 *Children*	6
Alce Ashbey *maid Servant*	20	Mary Hoeman } 5 *Children*	4
		Sarah Hoeman } 5 *Children*	2
		Abraham Hoeman } 5 *Children*	$\frac{1}{4}$

xxth June, 1635. In the Abbigall de Lond. Hackwell bñd for New England p'r Cert. frō of his Conformitie from Justices of Peace and minister Eaton Bray† in Com̄. Bedford.

Joh: Houghton 4 yers old

7 July, 1635. In the Defence de Loñd: Mr Edmond Bostocke vrs. New England p'r Cert. frō ij Justices of Peace and ministers frō Dunstable in Com̄ Bedfordshire:

Robert Longe *Inholder*	45	Anne } *Children*	10
Eliza: Longe *his wife*	30	Mary } *Children*	9
Luce Mercer *A seruant*	18	Rebecca } *Children*	8
Michell } *Children*	20	Joh: } *Children*	8
Sarra } *Children*	18	Zachary } *Children*	4
Robert } *Children*	16	Joshua } *Children*	$\frac{3}{4}$
Eliza } *Children*	12		

* There were numerous churches in Northamptonshire called All Saints, but none at any place bearing a name approaching to *Lionian;* and I am not able to make the record other than I have transcribed it.

† Near, and to the west of Dunstable.

xxth June, 1635. In the Defence de Lon̄d. Mr Pearce vers New England p'r Cert. frō two Justices of Peace and minister of Towcester in Com̄ Northampton:

Joh: Gould *husbandman*	25	Grace Gould *his wife*	25

xxij June, 1635. In the Abbigall de Lon̄d. Hackwell vers New England p'r Cert. frō minister of Craiebroke in Kent.

Edw: White *husbm:*	42	Jo^{h}: Allen *husbm:*	30
Martha White *his wife*	39	Anne Allen *his wife*	30
Martha White } *Children*	10	Cert. Herrnhill* in Kent.	
Mary White } *Children*	8		

In the Abigall, p'r Cert. from Justice peace and minister of Stepney:—

Geo: Hadborne *Glover*	43	Joseph Borebancke	24
Anne Hadborne *his wife*	46	Joane Jorden	16
Rebecca Hadborne } *Chil-dn:*	10	*Servants to Geo: Hadborne.*	
Anna Hadborno } *Chil-dn:*	4		

22th. In the Desire de Lond Edw: Boswell vrs New England p'r Cert. from Sr Henry Mildmaye and minister of Baddow in Essex:

Joh: Browne *Taylor*	27	Anne Leake	19
Tho: Hart } *his servants*	24		
Mary Denny } *his servants*	21		

26 Junij, 1635. In the Abigall, Robert Hackwell M^{r} to New England p'r Cert. from Northton Tho: Martin, maior, and 2 Justices.

Jo: Harbert *shoemaker*	23	4th July Henry Somner	15
Richard Adams	29	Eliza: Somner	18
Suzan Adams	26		

17 Junij, 1635 Theis vnder written names are to be transported to New England, imbarqued in the Abigall, Robert Hackwell M^{r} p'r Cert. from the minister and Justices of Peace of their Conformitie, being no Subsedy men. They haue taken the oaths of Alleg: and Supremacy being all Husbandmen:

Ralph Wallis	40	John Holliock	28
Ralph Roote	50	George Wallis	15
Jno ffreeman	35	Robecca Price	14
Walter Gutsall	34	Marie ffreeman	50
Richard Graves	23	Elizabeth Mere	30
Robert Mere	43	Jo: ffreeman	9
Samvell Mere	3	Sycllle ffreeman	1
Edmund Mañing	40	Jo: West	11
Tho: Jones	40	Mary Moninges	30
Geo: Drewrie	19	Mary Monninges	9
Wm Marshall	40	Anna Monnings	6
Thomas Knore	33	Michelaliell† Moñinges	3

* Am not quite sure I have spelled this name as the Clerk intended to spell it, but I am *quite* sure that he meant *Hearnehill,* as it should have been written in those days. But in these *degenerate* days it is written *Hernhill*—thus farther departing from what it took its name from originally.

† Notwithstanding the strangeness of this name the MS. is perfectly plain. See another version of it in *Reg.* i, 132. See also *Reg.* vii, 273; viii, 75; x, 176.

Elizabeth Ellis	16	Joan Wall	19
Ellin Jones	36	Wm Payne	15
Isacke Jones	8	Noel* Knore	29
Hester Jones	6	Sara Knore	7
Tho: Jones	3	Robt Driver	8
Sara Jones	3 *mo.*	John Mere	3 *mo.*
Cesara Covell	15		

In the Abigall p'red: p'r Cert: from the minister of their Conformitie and from the Justices that they are no Subsedy men:

Christopher ffoster	32	John Rookeman	45
ffrancis ffoster *vxor*	25	Elizabeth Rookman	31
Rebecca ffoster } *childn:*	5	Jo: Rookman	9
Nathaniell ffoster } *childn:*	2	Hugh Burt	35
Jo: ffoster } *childn:*	1	Ann Burt	32
Edward Ireson	32	Wm Bassett	9
Wm Almond	34	Edward Burt	8
Mary Jones	30	Tho: ffreeman	24
Awdry Almond	32	Wm Yates	14
Annis Almy	8	Elizabeth Ireson	27
Chri: Almie	3	Jo: ffox	35
John Strowde	15	Richard ffox	15
Edward Rainsford	26	Jo: Payne	14
Robt Sharp	20	Edmond ffreeman	45

Theis vnder written names are to be transported to New England imbarqued in the Blessing Jo: Lecester Mr. the p'ties having brought Cert. from the minister and Justices of their conformitie being no Subsedy men, tooke ye oaths of Alleg: and Supremacie:

Willm̄ Cope	26	Sara Robinson	1½
Richard Cope	24	Nico: Robertson	30
Thomas King	21	Jo: Mory	19
Jo: Stockbridge	27	Charles Stucbridge	1
Robert Saiewell	30	James Saiewell	1
Wm Brooke	20	Jo: Robinson	5
Gilbert Brooke	14	Ann Stockbridge	21
Nathaniell Byham	14	Suzan Saiewell	25
Jo: Wassell	10	Ann Vassall	42
W. Vassall	42	Suzan King	30
Rich: More	20	Judith Vassall	16
Robert Turner	24	Sara Tynkler	15
Eliza: Holly	30	ffra: Vassall	12
Ann Vassall	6	Thomazin Munson†	14
Margaret Vassall	2	Kat: Robinson	12
Mary Vassall	1	Mary Robinson	7
Elizabeth Robinson	32	Robt Onyon	26

29 Junij, 1635. Aboard the Abigall, Robt. Hackwell, Mr. for New England:

* This christian name I read *Noel;* but it is impossible to be certain what it is. It may be the nick-name for Oliver. If so it is the earliest occurrence of its use known to me. The last letter was reformed, which is the cause of the indistinctness.

† Plainly as I have transcribed it.

Joseph ffludd *A Baker*	45	Joseph ffludd	½
Jane ffludd *vxor*	35	Edward Martin	19
Elizabeth ffludd	9	Suzan Hathway	34
Obediah ffludd	4		

---

vltiº Junii, 1635. Abourd the Abigall, Robert Hackwell Mr p'r Cert from the minister of Stepney p'ish of their conformitie: and that they are no Subsedy men.

Henry Collins *starch maker*		29	Joshua Griffith	*Seruants*	25
Ann Collins *vxor*		30	Hugh Alley	*Seruants*	27
Henry Collins	*children*	5	Mary Roote	*Seruants*	15
Jo: Collins	*children*	3	Jo Coke	*Seruants*	27
Margery	*children*	2	Geo: Burdin	*Seruants*	24

In the Abigall p'rd p'r Cert from the minister and Justices according to order.

Edward ffountaine	28	Thankes Sheppard *vxor*	23
Ralph Sheppard	29	Sara Shepperd *daughter*	2

Primo die Julij, 1635. In the Abigall p'red.

Ann Gillam	28	John Cooke *servant*	17
Ben: Gillam *sonn*	1	Edward Belcher *servant*	8
Thomas Brane *husbandm:*	40	Ann Williams	10
Tho: Launder	22	Philip Drinker	39
William Potter *husb:*	27	Elizabeth Drinker *vxor*	32
ffrancis Potter *vxor*	26	Edward Drinker	13
Joseph Potter *weeks*	20	Jo: Drinker	8
Rich Carr	29	Margt: Tucker	23
Wm King	28	Ellner Hillman	33
George Rum*	25	Jo: Torry	32
Jo: Stantley	34	Jo: Emerson	20
James Dodd	16	Rich Woodman	9
Mathew Abdy	15	Elizab: ffreeman	12
Edward ffreeman *husb*	34	Alice ffreeman	17
Elizabeth ffreeman *vxor*	35	Hugh Burt	15
Edward ffreeman	15	Annis Alcoock	18
John ffreeman	8	Tho: Thomson	18
Jo: Jones	15		

Secundo die Julij. In the Abigall p'rd p'r Certificate from ye minister of Shoreditch p'ish and Stepney p'ish bound to New England.

John Deyking	28	Alice Steeuens	22
Jesper Arnold	40	Magaret Devocion	9
Alice Deyking	30	Ruth Bushell	23
Ann Arnold	39		

Theis vnder written names are to be transported to New England imbarqued in the Defence, Tho: Bostock Mr the p'tie hath brought testimony from the Justices of Peace and ministers in Cambridge of his conformitie to the orders and discipline of the Church of England: He hath taken ye oaths of Alleg: and Suprem̄:

---

* So the MS., and not *Ram*.

Adam Mott *A Taylor*	39	Jo: Mott	*children*	14
Sarah Mott *vxor*	31	Adam Mott		12
Henry Steevens *mason*	24	Jonathan Mott		9
John Sheppard *Husbm:*	36	Elizabeth Mott		6
Margaret Sheppard	31	Mary Mott		4
Tho: Sheppard	*mo* 3			

In the Defence p'rd Tho: Bostock Mr for New England p'r Cert: from the minister of ffenchurch of his conformitie, &c.

Tho: Boylson* 20

4th July, 1635. In the Abbigall de Lo: p'r Cert. from the minister and Justices of peace of St Ollives Southwark:

Ralph Mason *Joyner*	35	Richard Mason	*children*	5
Anne Mason *his wife*	35	Samuell Mason		3
		Susan Mason		1

In the Defence p'rd.

Elizabeth ffrench	30	ffrancis ffrench	10
Elizabeth ffrench	6	Jo: ffrench	*mo* 5
Marie ffrench	2½		

---

iiij July, 1635. In the Defence de Lond. Mr Thomas Bostocke, vrs New England p'r Cert: from the minister and Justices of peace of his Conformitie to ye Govmt. of Church of Engld and no Subsedy man.

Roger Harlakenden† 23 toke oathe of Allegance and Supremacie.

Eliza Harlakenden *his wife* 18 Mable Harlakenden *his sister* 21

Anne Wood	23	*Servants to ye aforesaid Roger Harlakenden.*	Wm ffrench	30
Samuell Shepherd	22		Eliza ffrench *his wife*	32
Joseph Cocke	27		Robert *a man servant*	
Geo: Cocke	25		Sarra Simes	30

6th July. In the Defence de Lond Mr Tho: Bostocke vrs. New England.

Joh: Jackson *wholesale man in Burchen Lane* 30

P'r Cert. from Sr Geo: Whitmore‡ and minister of ye p'ish.

---

* There will be found a pedigree of Boylston in the Hist. and Antiqs. of Boston, p. 726.

† In the *Visitation of Kent*, 1574, *Additional MSS. (B. M.) Vol.* 5532, *p.* 58 *b*, is the following pedigree:—

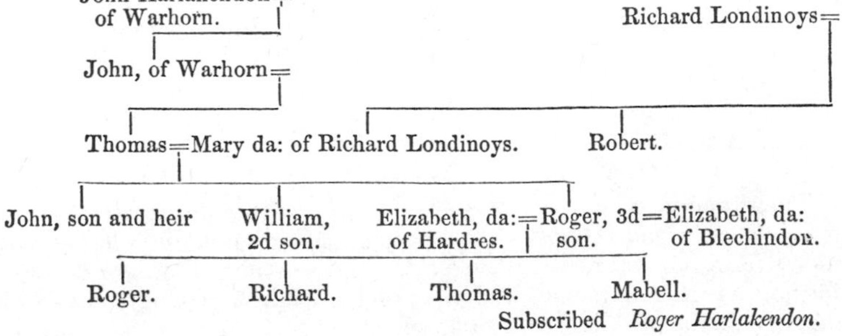

Subscribed *Roger Harlakendon.*

‡ The same spelt *Whittimor* in a previous page.

x° July, 1635. In the Abigall, Richard Hackwell Mr p'r Cert: from the minister and Justice of Peace of his conformitie to the Church of England and that he is no Subsedy man.

John Wynthropp	27	Tho: Goad	15
Elizabeth Winthropp	19	Elizabeth Epps	13
Deane Winthropp	11	Mary Lyne	6

In the Defence p'rd p'r Cert from the Justices and minister of his conformitie in the Church of England:

James ffitch *A Taylor*	30	Abigall ffitch *vxor*	24

---

xj° Die July, 1635. Theis vnder written names are to be transported to New England imbarqued in the Defence of London, Edward Bostock Mr p'r certificate of his conformitie in Religion and that he is no Subsedy man.

Richard Perk *a miller*	33	Isabell Perk	7
Margery Perk	40	Elizabeth Perk	4
Henry Duhurst	35		

---

14 July, 1635. In the Defence de Loñd. Mr Edmond Bostocke vrs New England p'r Cert. from the minister:

Robert Hill *servant to Mr Craddocke* 20

---

xviij° July, 1635. Theis vnderwritten names to be transported to New England in the Pide Cowe p'r Cert: from the minister of his conformitie and from Sr Edward Spencer resident neere Branford that he is no Subsedy man: hath taken the oathes of Alleg: and Suprem.

William Harrison	55	Wm Baldin	9
Joh Baldin	13		

Theis vnder written names are to be transported to N. England imbarqued in the defence p'red. p'r Cert: from the ministers and Justices of their conformitie and yt they are no Subsedy men:

Sara Jones	34	Dorothie Knight	30
Sara Jones	15	Nathaniell Hubbard	6
Jo: Jones	11	Richard Hubbard	4
Ruth Jones	7	Martha Hubbard	22
Theophilus Jones	3	Mary Hubbard	20
Rabecca Jones	2	Robert Colburne	28
Eliz: Jones	½	Edward Colborne	17
Tho: Donn	25	Dorothie Adams	24
Suzanna ffarebrother	25	ffrancis Nutbrowne	16
Eliza ffennick	25	Wm Williamson	25
Wm Sawkynn	25	Marie Willm̄son	23
W. Hubbard *Husb:*	40	Luce Mercer	19
Judith Hubbard	25	Jo: ffitch	14
John Hubbard	15	Penelope Darno	29
Wm Hubbard	13	Martha Banes	20
Wm Read	48	Jasper Gonn	29
Mabell Read	30	Ann Gonn	25
George Read	6	ffebe Maulder	7
Ralph Read	5	Sym: Roger	20
Justice Read	*mo.* 18	Jo: Jenkynn	26

Robert Keyne	40	Ben: Keyne	16
Eliz. Steere	18	Jo: Burtes	29
Sarah Knight	50	Mary Bentley	20
Ann Keyne	38		

---

13 July, 1635. Theis vnder written names are to be transported to N. England imbarqued in the James, Jn° May M^{r} for N: E: p'r Cert: from the minister of their conformity in Religion and that they are no Subsedy men.

Wm Ballard *husb:*	32	Nic° Buttry	33
Elizabeth Ballard	26	Martha Buttry	28
Hester Ballard	2	Grace Buttry	1
Jo: Ballard	1	Jo: Hart *shoemaker*	40
Alice Jones	26	Mary Hart	31
Eliza Goffe	26	Henry Tybbot *shoemaker*	39
Edmond Bridges*	23	Elizabeth Tybbott	39
Michell Milner	23	Jeremy Tybbott	4
Tho: Terry	28	Samvell Tybbot	2
Robert Terry	25	Remembrance Tybbott	28
Rich. Terry	17	Nic. Goodhue *clothworker*	60
Tho: Marshall	22	Jane Goodhue	58
Wm Hooper	18	John Johnson	26
Edmond Johnson	23	Suzan Johnson	24
Samvel Bennet	24	Eliza: Johnson	2
Rich Palmer	29	Tho: Johnson	*mo* 18
Anto Bessy	26	Ralph ffarman *Barber*	32
Edw: Gardner	25	Alice ffarman	28
Wm Colbron	16	Mary ffarman	7
Henry Bull	25	Tho ffarman	4
Salomon Martin	16	Ralph ffarman	2
Wm Hill *wheele write*	70		

Theis vnder written names are to be transported to N. England imbarqued in the Blessing, John Lester M^{r}. the p'ties have brought Cert: from the ministers and Justices of their conformitie in Religion and that they are no Subsedy men.

Jo: Jackson *Fisherman*	40	Richard Sexton	14
Margaret Jackson	36	Mary Hubbard	24
John Jackson	2	Mary Sprall	20
Jo: Manifold	17	Rich. Hallingworth	40
John Burules	26	Suzan Hallingworth	30
Jo: ffitch	14	Christian Hunter	20
Nic° Long	19	Eliz: Hunter	18
Christian Buck	26	Tho: Hunter	14
Barnabie Davies	36	Wm Hunter	11
Suzan Daues	16	Wm Hollingworth	7
Robert Lewes	28	Rich^{h} Hallingworth	4
Eliz: Lewes	22	Suzan Hallingworth	2
Edward Ingram	18	Eliz: Hallingworth	3
Henry Beck	18	Tho: Trentum	14
Jo: Hathoway	18	Tho: Bigges	13

---

* See Pedigree in New England Hist. and Gen. Register, viii, 252.

Jo: Brigges	20	Eliz: Lewes*	22
Robt. Lewes*	28		

Theis vnder written names are to be transported to New England imbarqued in the Love, Joseph Young M^{r}.

Willm̄ Cherrall *Baker*	26	Sara Harman	10
Vrsula Cherrall	40	Walter Parker	18
Jo: Harman	12	Willm̄ Browne *Fisherman*	26
ffrancis Harman	43	Mary Browne	26

---

23 July. Theis vnder written name is to be transportd to New England imbarqued in the Pide Cowe Mr Ashley the p'ty hath brought Certificate of his conformitie in Religion and Attestacon from the Justices that he is no Subsedy man:

Robert Bills *Husb:* 32

---

28 July, 1635. Theis p'sons herevnder expressed are to be transported to New England imbarqued in the Hopewell of London, Tho: Babb, M^{r} p'r Certificate from the minister of St Giles, Cripplegate, that they are conformable to the Church of England. The men have taken the oaths of Allegeance and Supremacie.

Thomas Tredwell *A Smith*	30	Tho: Blackly	20
Mary Tredwell	30	Tho: Tredwell	1

---

xjth Aug^{ti} 1635. In the Batcheler de Lo: Mr Tho: Webb vers New England:

Lyon Gardner	36	Eliza: Coles† *their maid sert.*	23
Mary Gardner *his wife*	34	Wm Jope	40

Who are to passe to new England, haue brought Cert: of their Conformitie.

---

21 Aug^{ti} 1635. In the Hopewell de Lo: Mr Babb vrs New England:

Henry Maudsley 24

Hath brought Cert. from the minister of his Conformitie hath taken the oathe of Allegeance.

---

xj^{o} Sept: 1635. Theis vnder written names are to be transported to New England imbarqued in the Hopewell p'r Cert: from the ministers and Justices of their conformitie in Religion to o^{r} Church of England: and y^{t} they are no Subsedy men. They have taken ye oaths of Alleg: and Suprem:

Wm Wood *Husb:*	27	Isack Robinson	15
Elizabeth Wood	24	Ann Williamson	18
Jo: Wood	46	Jo: Weekes *Tanner*	26
Robert Chambers	13	Marie Weekes	28
Tho Jnoson	25	Anna Weekes	1
Marie Hubbard	24	Suzan Withie	18
Jo: Kerbie	12	Robert Baylie	23
Jo: Thomas	14	Marie Withie	16

* It is not probable that there were two Lewises named *Robert*, and two named *Eliz:* of ages 28 and 22 respectively, but such is the Record.

† The MS. cannot be mistaken.

Samvel Younglove	30
Margaret Younglove	28
Samvel Younglove	1
Andrew Hulls	29
Anthony ffreeman	22
Twiford West	19
Roger Toothaker	23
Margaret Toothaker	28
Roger Toothaker	1
Robert Withie	20
Henrie Ticknall	15
Isack Heath *Harms* maker*	50
Elizabeth Heath	40
Elizabeth Heath	5
Martha Heath	30
Wm Lyon	14
Grace Stokes	20
Katherin Hull	23
Mary Clark	16
Jo: Marshall	14
Joan Grave	30
Mary Grave	26
Joan Clevin	18
Edmond Chippfield	20
Marg With	62
Tho: Bull	25
Joseph Miller	15
Jo: Prier	15
Richard Hutley	15
Daniell Pryer	13
Robert Edwardes	22
Robert Edye	25
Walter LLoyd	27
Ellin Leaves	17
Alice Alboñ	25
Barbary Rõfe	20
Jo: fforten	14
Gabriell Reldt†	18

xix Sept. 1635. Theis vnder written names are to be transported to New England imbarqued in the Truelove, Jo: Gibbs, M^r^ the mẹn have taken the oathes of Alleg: and Suprem:

Thomas Burcherd *laboring man*	40
Mary Burchard	38
Elizabeth Burchard	13
Marie Burchard	12
Sara Burchard	9
Suzan Burchard	8
Jo: Burchard	7
Ann Burchard	*mo* 18
Peter Place	20
Wm Beeresto	23
Geo: Beeresto	21
Edward Howe *husbandm:*	60
Elizabeth Howe	50
Jeremie Howe	21
Sara Howe	12
Ephraim Howe	9
Isacke Howe	7
Wm Howe	6
Jo: Sedgwick	24
Jeremy Blackwell	18
Lester Gunter	13
Zacharia Whitman	40
Sara Whitman	25
Zacha: Whitman	2½
Rabecca ffenner	25
Tho: Tibbaldes	20
Thomas Sterte	15
Jo: Streme	14
Ralph Tomkins *Husb:*	50
Kat: Tomkins *vxor*	58
Elizabeth Tomkins	18
Marie Tomkins	14
Samvel Tomkins	22
Richard Hawes	29
Ann Hawes	26
Anna Hawes	2½
Obediah Hawes	*mo* 6
Ralph Ellwood	28
Geo: Tayler	31
Elizabeth Jenkins	27
Wm Preston	44
Marie Preston	34
Wm Bentley	47
Alice Bentley	15
Margaret Killinghall	20
Jo: Bentley	17
Tho: Stockton	21
Geo: Morrey	23
Richard Swayne	34

* Probably *arms maker*. The MS. is clear as I have copied it. It was not uncommon in those days for English people to add the *h* to such words in writing, as many do yet in talking, as *hit* for *it*, &c.

† Possibly Rele. If so the final *e* is rather tall.

Sarah Haile	11	Edward Jeofferies	24
Samvel Grover	16	John Done	16
Eliz: Preston	11	Roger Broome	17
Sara Preston	8	Dorothie Lowe	13
Marie Preston	6	Jo: Simpson	30
Jo: Preston	3	Tho: Brighton	31
Wm Joes*	28	Tho: Rumball	22
Robert Browne	24	Edward Parrie	24
Tho: Blower	50	Jane Walston	19

A small parchment volume (also in the Rolls Office) labelled on the cover "T G 27.979 A A D 1637—13 Car. I" is occupied with a record of persons "desirous to pass beyond seas." Its upper right hand corner has been destroyed, by which much of the record is gone. It consists of but sixteen written leaves, and much the greatest portion of them is taken up with the names of persons going into Holland. It was originally a beautiful document, all in a splendid hand. What is not destroyed of the title of the volume is

"A Register of the - - - - - - - - - - - -
of such persons a - - - - - - - - - - - -
and vpwards and haue - - - - - - - - -
to passe into forraigne partes - - - - -
March 1637 to the 29th day of Septe -
by vertu of a commission granted to
Mr Thomas Mayhew gentleman."

The above extract will convey some notion of the extent of the injury which the book has received, from fire, acid or rats; probably acid.

The first entry is as follows:—

"March 28, 1637. The Examenation of Edmund Knappe: borne in great Killlngham and there dewling, gent. aged 25 yeares, is desirous to passe into holland to sarue the States."

I will note only a few others not going to New England.

WRIGHT.—Isacke, to go to layden in holland, there to inhabit. He was of Norwich in Norfolk, was born there, but his age the acid has destroyed. He was a single man.

PAGE.—Anne, wife of Robart Page to go to holland to see her friends and to return.

ROBENSON.—John, of Rye in Suffolk, aged 22, tayler, to pass to Rotterdam to seek of his trade and to retorne.

BROWNE.—John, borne in Norwich, gent. aged 55 trauiles into the Lowe Cuntres as Post for Letters and other wyes and retornes as his byssenes p'mts.

About four pages are filled with similar entries, and then comes the following:—

"These people went to New England with William Andrews of Ipswich, Mr of the John and Dorethay of Ipswich, and with William Andrewes his Sone Mr of the Rose of Yarmouth.

"Aprill 8th 1637. The examinaction of John Baker borne in Norwich in Norffolcke, Grocar aged 39 yeres, and Elizabeth his wife aged 31 yeares with 3 Children, Elizabeth, John and Thomas, and 4 Saruants, Marey Alxarson, aged 24 yeares, Anne Alxarson, aged 20 yeares, Bridgett

---

* *Ioes* or *Joes*. I cannot torture it into *Ives*.

Boulle aged 32 yeares and Samuell Arres aged 14 yeares ar all desiroues to goe for Charles Towne in New England ther to inhabitt and remaine.

"Aprill 8th 1637. The examinaction of Nicho: Busbie of Norwich in Norff. weauer, aged 50 yeares and Bridgett his wife aged 53 yeares with 4 children, Nicho: John: Abraham: and Sarath: are desirous to goe to boston in New England to inhabit.

"Aprill 8th 1637. The examinaction of Michill Metcalfe of Norwich, Dornix,* weauear, aged 45 yeares and Sarrath his wif, aged 39 yeares with 8 Children, Michill: Thomas: Marey: Sarrah: Elizabeth: Martha: Joane: and Rebeca: and his Saruant Thomas Comberbach, aged 16 yeares, are desirous to passe to boston in New England to inhabit.

"Aprill 8th 1637. The examinaction of John Pers of Norwich in Norff. weauear aged 49 yeares and Elizabeth his wife aged 36 yeares with 4 children, John: Barbre: Elizabeth and Judeth, and one seruant, John Gedney, aged 19 yeres, are desirous to passe to boston in New England to inhabit.

"April 8th 1637. The examinaction of William Ludken of Norwich in Norff. Locksmith, ther borne, aged 33 yeares, and Elizabeth his wife aged 34 yeares, with one child and one Seruant, Thomas Homes, are desirous to goe to Bostone in Newe England, there to inhabit and remaine."

The two next entries are partly gone.

" - - - - - of Norwich in Norff. cordwaynar, aged 28 years and
- - - - - - - with 4 children, Samuel, John, Elizabeth, and Debra,
- - - - - - - - aged 18 yeres, and Anne Williams, aged 15 yeres
- - - - - England to Inhabitt.

" - ncis Lawes, born in Norwich in Norff. and thar liuing, weauer, aged - - - idda his wife aged 49 yeares with one child Marey and 2 seruants, Samuell Lincorne aged 18 yeares and Anne Smith, aged 19 yeares ar desirous to passe for New England to inhabitt.

" - - - The examinaction of William Nickerson of Norwich in Norff. weauear aged 33 yeares and Anne his wife aged 28 yeares with 4 children, Nicho, Robartt, Elizabeth and Anne; ar desirous to goe to Bostone in New England ther to Inhabitt.

Aprill the 8th 1637. The examinaction of Samuell Dix of Norwich in Norff. Joynar aged 43 yeares and Ioane his wife aged 38 yeares with 2 children Presella and Abegell, and 2 Saruantes William Storey and Daniell Linsey, the one aged 23 the other 18 yeares; ar all desirous to pass to Boston in New England there to Inhabitt.

Aprill the 11th 1637. The examinaction of Henry Skerry of Great Yarmouth in the County of Norff. Cordwaynar, aged 31 yeares, and Elizabeth his wife aged 25 yeares, with one child Henry, and one Aprentice, Edmund Towne aged 18 yeares, ar desirous to passe for New England to inhabitt.

Aprill the 11th 1637. The examinaction of John Moulton of Ormsby† in Norf. husbandman, aged 38 yeares and Anne his wife, aged 38 yeares, with 5 children, Henry, Merey, Anne, Jane and Bridgett, and 2 Saruants, Adam Gooddens, aged 20 yeres, and Allis Eden aged 18 yers; ar all desirous to passe to New England, there to inhabitt, and abide.

---

* *Dornick*, a kind of stuff used for curtains, carpets and hangings, so called from *Doornick*, or *Tournay*, a city in Flanders, where it was first made.—PHILLIPS AND KERSEY.—*Dornix*.—BAILEY.—*Dornock*.—OGILVIE.

† In the vicinity of Norwich.

Aprill the 11th 1637. The examinacton of Marey Moulton of Ormsby in Norff. Wydow ageed 30 yeares and 2 Saruants; John Maston, aged 20 yeares and Merrean Moulton aged 23 yeares are desirous to go to New England to inhabitt and dwell.

Aprill the 11th 1637. The examinacton of Richard Caruear of Skratby* in the County of Norff. husbandman, ageed 60 yeares, and Grace his wife ageed 40 yeares, with 2 children, Elizabeth, ageed 18 yeares and Susanna aged 18 yeares, being twynes, mor 3 Saruants, Isacke Hartt, ageed 22 yeares, and Thomas Flege aged 21 yeares, and one Marable Vnderwood a mayd seruant, aged 20 yeares, goes all for New England to Inhabett and Remayne.

Aprill the 11th 1637. The examinaction of Ruth Moulton of Ormsby in Norff. Singlewoman aged 20 yeares, is desirous to passe for New England there to Inhabitt and dwell.

Aprill the 11th 1637. The examinaction of Robertt Page of Ormsby in Norff. husbandman, ageed 33 yeares and Lucea his wife aged 30 yeares, with 3 children, Frances, Margrett, and Susanna, and 2 Saruants, William Moulton and Anne Wadd; the one aged 20 yeares the other 15 yeares, and are all desirous to passe for New England to inhabitt and Remaine.

Aprill the 11th 1637. The examinaction of Henrey Dowe of Ormsby in Norff. husbandman ageed 29 yeares, and Joane his wife ageed 30 yeares, with 4 children and one Saruant Anne Maning, aged 17 yeares, are desirous to passe into New England to inhabitt.

Aprill the 11th 1637. The examinaction of Robertt - - - - - - Singleman, is desirous to passe - - - - - - - - - - - - - - -

Aprill the 11th 1637. The examinaction of Ellin Robenson of - - - desirous to passe into New England ther to - - - - - - - - - - -

Aprill the 11th 1637. The examinaction of William Williames of great Yarmouth - - - - - - - 40 yeares and Alles his wife aged 38 yeares with 2 children - - - - - - - - - ar desirous to goo for New England to inhabitt.

Aprill the 11th 1637: The examinaction of Elizabeth Williames of Yarmouth in Norff. Single woman aged 31 yeares, is desirous to passe into New England ther to inhabitt and Remaine.

Aprill the 12th 1637. The examinaction of Kathren Rabey of Yarmouth, a Wattermans wydow, ageed 68 yeares, is desirous to passe into New England there to remain with her Sone.

Aprill the 12th 1637. The examinaction of Richard Leeds of great Yarmouth, marrinar, ageed 32 yeares, and Joane his wife aged 23 yeares with one child are desirous to passe for New England and there to inhabitt and dwell.

Aprill the 12th 1637. The examinaction of Henry Smith of Newbucknam† husbandman, ageed 30 yeares, and Elizabeth his wife ageed 34 yeares with 2 children, John and Sethe ar desirous to passe into New England to inhabitt.

Aprill 13th 1637. The examinaction of John Ropear of New Bucknam, Carpentar ageed 26 yeares and Alles his wife ageed 23 yeares, with 2 children, Alles and Elizabeth, are desirous to goe for New England, there to Remaine.

[Then William Lambard and Samuell Clarke wanted to go to Holland, and so a large number of others; the record of which occupies some

---

* Probably *Scrattley*, now *Scratley*, a part of Ormsby.

† This name will be found in late Topographical works under *Buckingham New.*

eight pages. John Eyre of Norwich, grocar aged 40 wanted only to go and see the country and if he liked, to stay; otherwise he would come back in 3 months. Simond Sewell of Carlton Rod in Norf. aged 30, wanted to go to Holland only to see his friends, and to return in 3 months. Thomas Browne of Carlton in Suff. aged 18, to go to Layden to see an "onckell" and to return in three months. Robertt Chapman of Norwich "weauear" aged 37, to go to Holland to see the country, &c. &c.]

These people went to New England with William Goose, M[r] of the Marey Anne of Yarmouth.

[*Date gone.*] The examinaction of Thomas Paine* of Wrentom in Suffolcke weauear ageed 50 yeares, and Elizabeth his wife ageed 53 yeares with 6 children, Thomas, John, Marey, Elizabeth, Dorethey and Sarah are desirous to goe for Salem in New England to inhabitt.

May the 10th 1637. The examinaction of Margrett Neaue of great Yarmouth in Norff. wydow, aged 58 yeres, and Rachell Dixson—her grand child is desirous to passe into New England to inhabit.

May the 10th 1637. The examinaction of Beniemen Cooper of Bramton in Suffolck husbandman ageed 50 yeares, and Elizabeth his wife ageed 48 yeares with 5 children, Lawrence, Marey, Rebecca, Beniemen and Francies Fillingham his sone in Lawe ageed 32 yeares, allso his sister aged 48 yeares, and 2 seruants, John Kilin and ffeleaman Dickerson, are all desirous to goe for Salem in New England and there to inhabitt.

May the 10th 1637. The examinaction of Abraham Toppan of Yarmouth Cooper, ageed 31 yeares and Susanna his wife ageed 30 yeares with 2 children, Petter and Elizabeth, and one mayd saruant, Anne Goodin aged 18 yeares are desirous to passe to New England to inhabitt.

May the 10th 1637. The examinaction of William Thomas of Great Comberton in Worcestershire, husbandman, Singleman, aged 26 yeares is desirous to passe to Exerden in New England to inhabitt.

May the 10th 1637. The examinaction of John Thurston of Wrentom in Suff. Carpenter, ageed 30 yeares and Margrett his wife ageed 32 yeares, with 2 children, Thomas, and John, ar desirous to passe to New England to inhabett.

May the 10th 1637. The examinaction of Luce Poyett of Norwich, spinster, ageed 23 yeares is desirous to pass into new England and there to Remaine.

May the 10th 1637. The examinaction of John Borowe of Yarmouth, Cooper, ageed 28 yeares, and Anne his wife ageed 40 yeares is desirous to passe to Salam in new England, there to inhabitt.

May the 11th 1637. The examinaction of William Gault of Yarmouth, Cordwaynar, Singleman, ageed 29 yeares, is desirous to passe to new England and there to remayne.

May the 11th 1637. The examinaction of Joane Ames of Yarmouth, Wydow, ageed 50 years, with 3 children, Ruth, ageed 18 yeares, William and John; are desirous to passe for new England and there to inhabitt and Remaine.

May the 11th 1637. The examinaction of Augusten C - - - - - -
Alles his wife ageed 40 yeares - - - - - - - - - - - - - -
desirous to goe to Salam in New E - - - - - - - - - - - - - -

May the 11th 1637. The examinaction of John Darrell of - - - - -
passe into Salam in New England and there - - - - - - - - - -

* See N. Eng. Hist. and Gen. Reg., vol. v, p. 331.

May the 11th 1637. The examinaction of John Gedney of Norwich in Norff. - - - - - - - - - - - to passe for New England with his wife Sarah ageed 25 yeares - - - - - - - - Lediah, Hanah and John; mor 2 Seruants; William Walker ageed - - - - - - Burges ageed 26 yeares are desirous to passe for Salam.

May the 11th 1637. The examinaction of Samuell Aiers* of Norwch an apintes, ageed 15 yeares ar desirous to passe into New England to his Mr John Baker, as he had apointed him.

The examinaction of John Yonge of St Margretts, Suff. minister, aged 35 yeares and Joan his wife ageed 34 yeares with 6 children, John, Tho: Anne, Rachell, Marey, and Josueph, ar desirous to passe for Salam in New England to inhabitt.

[*Against the above entry, in the place of the date is written:*—] This man was forbyden passage by the Commisionrs and went not from Yarmouth.

May the 12th 1637. The examinaction of Samuell Grenfild of Norwich, weauear, ageed 27 yeares and Barbrey his wife ageed 35 yeares with two children; Marey, and Barbrey, and John Teed, his seruant, ageed 19 yeares, ar all desirous to passe into New England to inhabitt.

May the 12th 1637. The examinaction of Thomas Joanes of Elzing in Norff. Buchar, Singleman, ageed 25 yeres, is desirous to passe into New England and there to Remaine.

May the 13th 1637. The examinaction of Thomas Olliuer of Norwich Calinder, ageed 36 yeares and Marey his wife ageed 34 yeares, with 2 children, Tho: and John, and 2 seruants, Thomas Doged, aged 30 yeares, and Marey Sape, ageed 12 yeares, ar desirous to passe for New England to inhabett.

May the 15th 1637. The examinaction of William Cockram, of Southould in Suff. marinar, ageed 28 yeers, and Christen his wife, ageed 26 yeares, with 2 children and 2 Seruantes desirous to passe to new england to inhabitt.

[Then succeeds a list for Holland, &c. Thomas Welter of Norwich, Cordwaynar, aged 30, to go to Rotterdam to see some friends, to be gone 3 months. Anne Thompson and her dau. Bridgett, to go to Holland to see friends, for 2 months. Anne Thompson was the wife of John, and of the age of 60. They were of Yarmouth. Geo: Bartton of Wollerbe in Lincolnshire was allowed 2 months, to go to Holland "to parfett some acountes." His age 41. "Joseph Hayward of Norwich, dorinx weauear, aged 29," his wf. Sussanna, 26, and servant, Ester Brown, 21, to go to Rotterdam to inhabet. Elizabeth Fowlsom, wf. of Tho. Fowlsome, of Norwich, aged 27, to go to Newport in Flanders, and Bombake" to "seeck menes whych is left[?] her by a kinsman. Henry Ward of Worttwell in Norff. aged 19, to goe ouer Sarue the Stattes." Christopher Hatton of Norwich a pot sellers of earthen Vessells borne in Bradish in Norff. ageed about 36 yeares" to pass to Holland to buy commodities, and to return in a month. 17 May, 1623. John Checklie, aged xx yeeres, intending to passe over to Rotterdam to serve as a souldier hath tendred and taken the oath of allegeance, &c. &c. At the end of the entries is the Signature "Henry Hill Deputy for Mr Thomas Mayhew, Gentleman."]

---

* Nearly obliterated in the original, but I feel quite sure it is *Aiers*.

[The following Lists of New England Emigrants are from Her Majesty's State Paper Office. They cannot be referred to by volumes at present, as the papers, among which they are, are undergoing a re-arrangement; a condition which usually precludes examinations. But through the kindness of MR. SAINSBURY, under whose supervision they are being arranged and calendered, I have been indulged with the privilege of examinations, and allowed to make copies.]

IPSWICH.—A note of the names and ages of all the Passengers which tooke shipping in the Elizabeth of Ipswich Mr Williā Andrews bound for new Eng Land the last of Aprill, 1634.

John Sherman aged yeeres	20
Joseph Mosse	24
Richard Woodward	45
Rose [Woodward]* *his wife*	50
Edmond Lewis	33
Mary [Lewis] *his wife*	32
John Spring	45
Elinor [Spring] *his wife*	46
Thurston Raynor	40
Elizabeth [Raynor] *his wife*	36
Thomas Skott	40
Elizabeth [Skott] *his wife*	40
Henery Kemball	44
Susan [Kemball] *his wife*	35
Richard Kemball	39
Vrsula [Kemball] *his wife*	
Isaacke Mixer	31
Sarah [Mixer] *his wife*	33
Martha Scott	60
George Munninge	37
Elizabeth [Munninge] *his wife*	41
John Bernard	30
Phebe [Bernard] *his wife*	27
Thomas Kilborne	24
Elizabeth [Kilborne] *his wife*	20
John Crosse	50
Anne [Crosse] *his wife*	38
Robert Sherin	32
Humphry Bradstreet	40
Bridgett [Bradstreet] *his wife*	30
Henery Glouer	24
William Blomfield	30
Sarah [Blomfield] *his wife*	25
Robert Day	30
Mary [Day] *his wife*	28
Sarah Reynolds	20
Robert Goodall	30
Katherin [Goodall] *his wife*	28
Samuell Smithe	32
Elizabeth [Smithe] *his wife*	32
Thomas Hastings	29
Susan [Hastings] *his wife*	34
Susan Munson	25
Martin Vnderwood	38
Martha [Vnderwood] *his wife*	31
Henery Gouldson	43
Anne [Gouldson] *his wife*	45
Anne Gouldston	18
William Cutting	26
John Palmer	24
Danyell Pierce	23
John Clearke	22
John ffirmin	46
Rebecca Isaacke	36
Anne Dorifall	24

These p'sons aboue named tooke the Oath of Allegeance and Supremacy, at his Ma'ts Custome house in Ipswich before vs his Ma'ties Officers according to the order of the Lords and others of his Ma'ts most Honoble Priuy Councell: This xijth of Nouember 1634.

Ipswich Custome House
Phil. Browne
p'r Custor.

Tho Clere, Seċ
Edw: Man
Compt.

IPSWICH.—A Note of all the names and ages of all those which did not take the Oath of Allegiance or Supremacy being vnder age shipped in or Port. In the Elizabeth of Ipswich Mr Williā Andrewes bound for new England the last of Aprill 1634.

---

* For the sake of uniformity I have added the surnames of wives. I may have omitted the brackets in some cases. If so, it can lead to no error.

Ed: Lewis	John Lewis	aged 3 yeeres
	Thomas Lewis	3 quarters
Rich: Woodward	George Woodward	13
	John Woodward	13
John Spring	Mary Spring	11
	Henry Spring	6
	John Spring	4
	William Spring	3 quarters
Thurston Raynor	Thurston Rayner	13
	Joseph Raynor	11
	Elizabeth Raynor	9
	Sarah Raynor	7
	Lidia Raynor	1
	Edward Raynor	10
	Elizabeth Kemball	13
Tho: Scott	Elizabeth Scott	9
	Abigail Scott	7
	Thomas Scott	6
	Isaac Mixer	4
Hen: Kemball	Elizabeth Kemball	4
	Susan Kemball	1 and halfe
	Richard Cutting	11
Rich: Kemball	Henry Kemball	15
	Richard Kemball	11
	Mary Kemball	9
	Martha Kemball	5
	John Kemball	3
	Thomas Kemball	1
	John Lauericke	15
Geo: Munnings	Eliz: Munnings	12
	Abigail Munnings	7
Jno: Bernard	John Bernard	2
	Samuell Bernard	1
	Tho: King	15
Humph: Bradstreet	Anna Bradstreet	9
	John Bradstreet	3
	Martha Bradstreet	2
	Mary Bradstreet	1
Willi: Blomfield	Sarah Bloomfield	1
Sam: Smith	Samuell Smith	9
	Mary Smith	4
	Eliz: Smith	7
	Phillip Smith	1
Robt: Goodale	Mary Goodale	4
	Abraham Goodale	2
	Isaacke Goodale	half a yeere
Hen: Gouldson	Mary Gouldson	15

Ipswich Customehouse this xijth of Nouember 1634.

Phil: Browne p'r Custor.   Edw: Man Compt.   Tho: Clere, Sec.

IPSWICH.—A Note of the names and ages of all the Passengers which tooke shipping In the ffrancis of Ipswich, Mr John Cutting bound for new England the last of Aprill, 1634.

John Beetes aged yeeres	40	Robert Pease	27
William Haulton	23	Hugh Mason	28
Nicholas Jennings	22	Hester [Mason] *his wife*	22
William Westwoode	28	Rowland Stebing	40
Bridgett [Westwoode] *his wife*	32	Sarah [Stebing] *his wife*	43
Cleare Drap	30	Thomas Sherwood	48
Robert Rose	40	Alice [Sherwood] *his wife*	47
Margery [Rose] *his wife*	40	Thomas King	19
John Bernard	36	John Mapes	21
Mary [Bernard] *his wife*	38	Mary Blosse	40
William ffrebourne	40	Robert Cooe	38
Mary [ffrebourne] *his wife*	33	Anna [Cooe] *his wife*	43
Anthony White	27	Mary Onge	27
Edward Bugbye	40	Thomas Boyden	21
Rebecca [Bugbye] *his wife*	32	Richard Wattlin	28
Abraham Newell	50	John Lyuermore	28
ffrancis [Newell] *his wife*	40	Richard Pepy	27
Just Houlding	23	Mary [Pepy]	30
John Pease	27	Richard Houlding	25
Robert Winge	60	Judeth Garnett	26
Judith [Winge] *his wife*	43	Eliz: Hamond	47
John Greene	27	Thurston Clearke	44

These p'sons aboue named tooke the Oath of Allegance and Supremacy at his Ma'ties Custome house in Ipswch before vs his Ma'ties Officers according to the order of the Lords and others of his Ma'ties most honoble Priuy Councell the xijth of Nouember 1634.

Ipswich Custome house — Tho: Clere, Sec.

Phil: Browne p'r Custr. — Edw: Mann Compt.

IPSWICH.—A Note of all the names and ages of all those which Did not take the Oath of Allegiance or Supremacy being vnder age shipped in our Port In the ffrancis of Ipswich Mr John Cutting: bound for new England the last of Aprill, 1634.

Will: Westwood	John Lea	13
	Grace Newell	13
Robt: Rose	John Rose	15
	Robert Rose	15
	Eliz: Rose	13
	Mary Rose	11
	Samuell Rose	9
	Sarah Rose	7
	Danyell Rose	3
	Darcas Rose	2
Will: ffreebourn	Mary ffreebourne	7
	Sarah ffreebourne	2
	John Aldburgh	14
Jn°: Bernard	ffayth Newell	14
	Henry Haward	7

Abraha: Newell	Abraham Newell	8
	John Newell	5
	Isaacke Newell	2
Edward Bugby	Sarah Bugbye	4
John Pease	ffayth Clearke	15
	Robert Pease	3
	Darcas Greene	15
Rowland Stebing	Thomas Stebing	14
	Sarah Stebing	11
	Eliz: Stebing	6
	John Stebing	8
	Mary Winche	15
Mary Blosse	Richard Blosse	11
Tho: Sherwood	Anna Sherwood	14
	Rose Sherwood	11
	Thomas Sherwood	10
	Rebecca Sherwood	9
Robt: Cooe	John Cooe	8
	Robert Cooo	7
	Beniamin Cooe	5
Rich: Pepper	Mary Pepy	3 and half
	Stephen Beckett	11
Eliz: Hamond	Eliz: Hamond	15
	Sarah Hamond	10
	John Hamond	7

Ipswich Customehouse this xijth of Nouember 1634.

Phil: Browne p'r Custr. Edw Mann* Compt.

[The preceding lists are accompanied by a paper bearing the following record :—]

To the right houno^{ble} the Lords and others of his ma^{ties} moste honno^{ble} privie Councell.

The humble peticon and Certificates of John Cuttinge M^{r} of the shipp called the ffrancis, and William Andrewes Ma^{r} of the Elizabeth, both of Ipsw^{ch}.

Right houno^{ble} accordinge to yor Lo^{res} order wee heerewth presente vnto yor Lo^{pps} the names of all the Passengers that wente for newe England in the said shipps the Tenth daye of Aprill laste paste.

Humblie intreatinge yor Lo^{pps} (they havinge p'formed yor honno^{rs} order) that the bondes in that behalfe given may bee delivered back to yor peticon^{r}s.

And they as in dutie bound will daylie praye for yor houno^{r}s healthes and happynes.

SOUTH^{ON}.—A List of names of suche Passeng^{rs} as shipt themselues at the towne of Hampton, in the James of London of iij^{c} tonnes William Coop^{r} M^{r} v^{rs} New-England, in and aboute the v^{t} of Aprill, 1635.

Augustine Clem^{t}, sometime of Readinge† *Paynter*

---

* An evidence that the same *Mann* did not always spell his own name alike.

† In Berkshire.

Thomas Whealer *his servant*
Thomas Browne, of Malford,* *weav^{r}*
Hercules Woodman, of the same, *mercer*

John Euered } alias Webb†
Stephen Euered }
Gyles Butler
George Coussens
Thomas Colman
Thomas Goddard
John Pithouse
} of Marlborough‡ *laborers or husbandmen*

Anthony Morse }
William Morse } of Marlborough *shoomakers.*

John Hide, *Tayler,*
John Parker, *Carpenter*
Richard Walker, *shomaker*
Maudit Ingles,§ *ffuller*
Thomas Davyes, *Sawyer*
} late of Marlbrough

Thomas Carpenter, of Amsbury,|| *Carpenter*

William Paddey, *skinn^{r}* [*Cutler*
Edmund Hawes,
} late of London

Edmund Batter, *maulter*
John Smale, *his servant*
Michael Shafflin, *Tayler*
Josuah Verren, *Rep^{r}.*
Thomas Antram, *weav^{r}*
Thomas Browne, *his servant*
George Smythe, *Tayler*
Phillip Varren, *Roop^{r}*
John Greene, *surgeon*
} late of New-England.

Zacheus Courtis, of Downton,¶ *laborer*
Henry Rose, of Platford,** *laborer*
Nicholas Batt, of ye Devyes, *lennen weav^{r}*
Thomas Scoates, of Sarñ,†† *laborer*

John Pike,
John Musselwhite,
} of Langford,‡‡ *laborers*

Sampson Salter, of Caversham,§§ *fisherman*
Henry Kinge of Brencsley *laborer*
William Andrews of Hampsworth, *Carpenter*

John Knight }
Richard Knight } of Romsey, *taylers*

Thomas Smithe of the same, *weaver*
Nicholas Holte, thereof, *tanner*
Robert ffield of yealing, *laborer*
Anthony Thetcher of Sarm̄, *tayler* and
Peter Higdon *his servant*

James Browne
Lawrence Seag^{r}
} *youths* of Hampton of about 17 yeares old.

Henry Leũage }
William Parsons } of Sarñ *Taylers*

John Emery }
Anthony Emery } of Romsey, *Carpenters.*

William Kemp *servant*

The totall number of these men, youthes, and boyes are liij p'sons, besids the wives and Children of Dyvers of these.

Tho: Wurfris Coll^{r} ibm̄.   N. Dingley Compt^{r}
John Knapp Searcher

---

* Perhaps *Milford* in Hants.

† John Evered alias Webb settled at Chelmsford, Mass., and died 1668. J. W. D.

‡ In Wiltshire.

§ A name which has been subjected to much torture. Plain MAUDIT *Ingles* on this (original) record. On our (Boston) records, 2 April, 1638, *Maudit* Ings appears. No doubt the same. See *History and Antiquities of Boston*, 241, and elsewhere.

|| *Amesbury*, in Wilts.

¶ Several places bear this name, but *this* probably is in Wilts.

** Or *Plaitford*, in Wilts.

†† *Sarum*, Salisbury, in Wilts.

‡‡ Some twelve places bear this name in different counties. *Longford-steple* is in Wilts.

§§ Probably the same place called *Goñsham* in another list. In Oxfordshire.

[*On a separate sheet accompanying the above:—*]

Right ho^{rble}

After the p'formance of our most humble Duties, may it please y^{r} Lo^{ps} to receaue hereinclosed a list of the names of suche passeng^{rs} as tooke shippinge at this porte for New-England, and that onely in Aprill last in the good ship Called the James of London whereof William Coop^{r} went M^{r}. And thus in Due obedience and observance of yor hon^{rs} lre Dated the last of Decemb^{r} past. Thus wee humbly take leave. Southampton the xijth Day of June, 1635.

Yo^{r} Lo^{ps} most humble serv^{ts}
Tho: Wurfris, Coll^{r}
N. Dingley; Compt^{r}
John Knapp, Searcher

[*Direction.*] To the right ho^{rble} the lords of his ma^{ts} most honorable privie Counsell, this at Whitehall. London.

[The following list of Emigrants was printed in the New England Hist. and Gen. Register, vol. ii, 108, &c., but from a copy so erroneous, it was determined to reprint it in this place.]

The List of the Names of the Passeng^{rs} Intended for New England in the good shipp the Confidence of London of C C. tonnes, John Jobson, Mr And thus by vertue of the Lord Treas^{rs} warr^{t} of the xjth of Aprill, 1638.

Southampton, 24° Aprill, 1638.

	Ages.
Walter Hayne of Sutton Mandifeild* in the County of Wilts *Lennen weauer*	55
Eliz: Hayne *his wife*	
Thomas Hayne, John Hayne, Josias Hayne — *their sonnes vnder xvj yeares of age.*	
Suffrance Hayne, Mary Hayne — *their daughters*	
John Blanford — *their seruants*	27
John Riddet — *their seruants*	26
Rich Bidlcombe — *their seruants*	16
Peter Noyce of Ponton in the County of South^{n}† *yeoman*	47
Thomas Noyce *his sonne*	15
Eliz: Noyce *his daughter*	
Robert Dauis — *his seruantes*	30
John Rutter — *his seruantes*	22
Margarett Dauis — *his seruantes*	26
Nicholas Guy of Upton Gray, in the County of South^{n}, *Carpent'r*	50
Jane Guy *his wife*	30
Mary Guy *his daughter*	
Joseph Taynter — *seruants*	25
Robert Bayley — *seruants*	23
John Bent of Penton‡ in the County of South^{n} *Husbandman*	35
Martha Bent *his wife*	
Robert Bent, William Bent, Peter Bent, John Bent, Ann Bent — *their Children all vnder ye age of xij yeares*	
Roger Porter of Long Sutton in the County of South^{n} *Husbandm*	55
Joane Porter, Susan Porter, Mary Porter, Rose Porter — *his daughters*	
John Sanders of Lanford§ in the County of Wilts, *Husbandman*	25
Sara Sanders *his wife*	
John Cole	40

---

* *Sutton Manfield*, then; and I think, now, *Sutton Mandeville*.

† *Southampton.*

‡ There were then *Penton Grafton* and *Penton Mewsey*.

§ *Langford.*

Roger Easmen } *seruants* 25
Richard Blake 16
William Cottle 12
Robert King 24

John Roaff of Melchitt* Parke of Wilsheir *Husbandman* 50
Ann Roaff *his wife*
Hester Roaff *their daughter*
Thomas Whittle *their seruant* 18

John Goodenowe of Semley in Wilsheir *Husbandman* 42
Jane Goodenowe *his wife*
Lydia Goodenowe } *their daughters*
Jane Goodenowe

Edmvnd Goodenowe of Dunhead in Wilsheire *Husbandman* 27
Ann Goodenowe *his wife*
John Goodenowe } *their sonns 4 yeares and vnder*
Thomas Goodenowe
Richard Sangar *his seruant* 18

Thomas Goodenowe of Shasbury† 30
Jane Goodenowe *his wife*
Thomas Goodenowe *his sonne* 1
Vrsula Goodenowe *his sister*

Edmvnd Kerley } of Ashmore *Husbandmen* 22
William Kerley
Edmvnd Morres, of Keniton Magna in Dorsetsh^r *Carpenter*

Stephan Kent of England‡ 17
Margery Kent *his wife* 16
George Churche } *seruants* 16
Hugh Marche 20
Anthony Sadler 9

Nicholas Wallington, *a poore boy*
Rebecca Kent, *seruant* 16

John Stephens } of Goñsham§ in Oxon^r *husbandmen* 31
William Stephens 21
Eliza: Stephens *his wife*
Alice Stephens *his Mother*
John Lowgie } *seruants* 16
Grace Lowgie

Thomas Jones of Goñsham p^re *Tayler* 36
Ann Jones *his wife*
Four Children vnder x yeeres.
William Baunsh } *seruants* 24
Jude Donley

Martha Wild^r of Shiplocke|| in Oxfords^r *spinster*
Mary Wild^r *her Daughter*
Augustin Bearce 20
John Keene 17
Martha Keene 60
Eliza: Keene 13
Martha Keene
Josias Keene
Sara Keene

John Binson of Coñsham¶ in Ox: *husbandman* 30
Mary Binson *his wife*
John Binson } *their children vnder 4 yeares*
Mary Binson

William Ilsbey } *shoemakers* 26
John Ilsbey
Barbara Ilsbey *his wife* 20
Phillip Dauis *his seruant* 12

Joseph Parker of Newbury *Tanner* 24

---

* *Millchill Park.* Incidentally mentioned, and by only one Topographer that I have consulted.

† *Shaftesbury*, probably, in Dorsetshire.

‡ Rather an indefinite locality for so young a couple, but such is the record.

§ Perhaps *Godestow*. I find no *Goñsham*, early or late. There is also *Godington* or *Goddington*, a little to the N. E. of *Bicester*. *Godestow* is the site of an ancient Nunnery, and is now included in *Woolvercott*, a mile N. of Oxford.

|| *Shiplake*, by the Thames, two miles south of Henley.

¶ Doubtless the same place before named—*Goñsham*.

Sarah Osgood of Horrell,* *spinster*
Four children.
William Osgood } *children vnder xj years*
William Jones }
Margery Parke *seruant*

John Ludwell 50
Henry Hangert } *seruants* 40
David Whealer } 11

Richard Bidgood, of Romsey, *m^r^chant*

The number of the passengers aforementioned, greate and little, are Cx soules.

Tho: Wurfres Coll and Ser[r]
Hen: Champante Cust[r]
N. Dingley Compt[r]

[*Endorsement.*]—SO[u]THTON, 1638. The Cert. and List of the Passeng[rs] names gone for New-England in the Confidence of London in Aprill 1638.

SOUTHAMPTON.—The list of the names of Passeng[s] Intended to shipe themselues, In the Reuist of Hampton of CL. Tounes, Robert Batten M[r] for Newengland, And thus by vertue of the Lord Treasurers warrant of the second of May w[ch] was after the restraynt and they some Dayes gone to sea Before the Kinges Mat[ies] Proclumacon Came vnto South'ton.

No. of persons.		Ages.
5‡	John ffrey,§ of Basing,‖ *whelwrite ;* his wife and three children.	
4	Richard Austin, *tayler* (of Bishopstocke ;‖) his wife and two children	40
1	Robert Knight, his seruant, *Carpenter.*	
	Christopher Batt, of Sarum, *Tanner*	37
8	Anne [Batt] *his wife*	32
	Dorothie Batt, there sister, and fiue children vnder tenne yeares	20
	Thomas Good¶‖ } *serv^ts^*	24
3	Eliza: Blackston } *serv^ts^*	22
	Rebecca Pond } *serv^ts^*	10
	William Carpenter } of Horwell** *Carpent^rs^*	62
8	William Carpenter, Jun. } of Horwell** *Carpent^rs^*	33
	Abigael Carpenter and fower children 10 and vnder	32
	Tho: Banshott, *servt*	14
	Annis Littlefield and six children	38
9	John Knight, *Carpenter*	
	Heugh Durdal	
	Henery Byley of Sarū *tanner*	26
4	Mary Byley	22
	Tho: Reeues, *servt*	
	John Byley	20
42		

* There is a *Horil* in Hamshire, near Linington.

† There is an ancient Legend of "Sir Bevis of Southampton." A mount in the neighborhood still bears the name of Beavis' Mount.

‡ Against some of the families or parties no number is set in the original—omitted, doubtless, in the hurry of business. I have supplied them.

§ Settled at Andover, Mass. See Pedigree, Register, iii, 226. He and his sons spelled their names Frie. Their descendants changed it to Fry and Frye. J. W. D.

‖ In Hampshire.

¶ A little uncertain, as the two last letters are blotted.

** Probably *Horil.*

42

9	Richard Dum̄r of New england		40
	Alce Dum̄r		35
	Tho: Dum̄r		19
	Joane: Dum̄r		19
	Jane Dum̄r		10
	Steephen Dum̄r *husbandman*		
	Dorathie Dum̄r		6
	Richard Dum̄r		4
	Tho: Dum̄r		2
10	John Huchinson *Carpenter*	*Servants*	30
	ffrauncis Alcocke *vizg*		26
	Adam Moll, *tayler*		19
	Will. Wackefeild		22
	Nathaunel Parker of London *Backer*		20
	Samuel Poore		18
	Da'yell Poore		14
	Alce Poore		20
	Richard Bayley		15
	Anne Wackefield		20

61

The nombr of the passengrs aboue mentioned are Sixtie and one Soules.

Tho: Wurfres* Coll. and Searr

Hen: Champante Custr

D. Dingley Comptr

[*Endorsement.*]—Sōuthton, 1638. The Cert. and list of the Passengrs names gone for New England in the Bevis of Hampton, in May, 1638.

THE FOUNDERS OF NEW ENGLAND.

[Several Papers of the following description may serve to show that after **1638** a different system prevailed with relation to Emigrants leaving England for America.]

Whereas the Merchants Masters and Owners of the ship the Neptune haue by their Petition presented to the Board, being desirous to send the said shipp for New Englend, and from thence to Newfound land, and so to Spaine, for wines to bring for Bristoll and having fraighted her with Passengers and Prouisions as are here vnder written can not bee permitted by the officer of the Custome in that Port, to put to Sea wthout speciall order from the Bord. Did therefore this day Order that the Lo: high Treas. of England should bee hereby pleased and required forthth to giue direcōn to the officers of his Mates Customes there quietly to permit and suffer the said Marchants, master or owners to clere the said shipp the Neptune together with the number of passingers and the prouisions hereafter following, or so much thereof as his lp. in his judgment. shall find fitt; and that the Oaths of Allegiance, and Supremacy may be taken by all the passengers at Croconpill, by the officer appointed for that seruice as is vsual in like cases.

---

* I have disposed these names, in every instance, as they stand upon the original papers, and spelled them as they are spelt.

125 Passengers	2 Tonns of wine
150 barrells of beefe	100 gallons of Oyle
40 hogsheds of Mault	10,000 nayles
40 hogsheds of meale	one tonne and a half of strong water
150 dozen of stockens	10 dozen of hatts
150 dozen of shooes	4 barrells of powder
150 suits of Clothes	20 musketts
150 dozen of shirts	500 weight of small shott
150 dozen of drauers	15 hogsheads of oatemeale
20 dozin Monmouth Capps	10 hogsheads of pease
200 ells of cloth to make shirts	250 weight of pewter
20 pounds worth of iron tooles	500 weight of Sope
1000 weight of candles	2 Tonnes of vineger
20 dozen of Bootes	

[*Endorsement :—*] 17° Jan. 1639. Order for ye Neptune to goe wth passengers and Provisions to New England. Ent.

[I have met with but four papers of this description in my researches in the British Archives, and these are in Her Majesty's State Paper office. Thinking they might be interesting to the student in early New England history, I have transcribed them for this work. Besides showing what commodities were then in greatest demand in that country, it is also shown that not much more trouble was taken by the government about Emigrants than any other part of the cargo; as, for aught that can now be found, not even a list of the names of those were taken. Nor does it appear, that they were not sworn to *Allegiance* and *Supremacy* in *a lot.*

The form to each of these three lists or shipments of merchandize being the same, those forms to the other two lists are omitted. In the heading of the next form is, however, this addition: —"The Merchants, owners, &c. of the ship Fellowship of Bristol, sent the said ship the last year from that Port to New England laden with Passengers and Provisions, and from thence to New found land, and laded fish wch they carried to Malligo in Spaine, and there sould it, lading her from thence back to Bristoll wth wines, and paid his Matie great Sumes of money for the Customes thereof." Then the form proceeds as in the last.]

250 Passingers	10 tonne of wyne
300 Barrells of Beef	200 gallons of oyle
80 hogsheads of Mault	20,000 of nayles
80 hogsheads of meale	3 tonns of strong water
300 dozn. of stockings	20 dozn. of Hatts
300 dozen of shoes	8 barrells of powder
300 suits of clothes	40 Muskets
300 dozn. of shirts	1000 weight of small shott
300 dozen. of drauers	30 hogsheads of oatmeale
40 dozen. of Monmouth Capps	20 hogsheads of pease
400 ells of cloth to make shirts	500 weight of pewter
40 pounds worth of iron tooles	1000 weight of Sope
2000 weight of Candles	2 tonn's of viniger.

[*Endorsement :—*] 17 Jan. 1639. Order for 2 ships of Bristoll to goe to New England with passengers and provisions. Ent.

[The third of these documents is as follows :—]

17 Jan. 1639. Whereas George Foxcroft and other Merchants trading to New England, Spane, &c. and the owners of the shipp Desire of New-

england did by their Petn represent that haueing Estates lying in New-england aforesaid, in Clapboards pipe staues, hoopes, fish and other comodities, and intending to buy fish in the Newfound land to transtport into Spaine and other places ;—humbly besought the Boord that they might be permitted not only to proceed wth their said shipp in this voyage, but haue leaue to take in and carry such passengers and provisions for New England as shalbe offered, without wch helpe they can not proceed in their intencōns nor possesse themselues of their Estates in new England ; Wch their Wps taking into consideracoñ, did think fitt and this day Order &c· as before.]

50 passengers
15 firkins Butter
10 C waight Cheese
20 hoghd. Beefe
10 hoghd. Pork
30 quarters Wheat and wheat meale
20 quarters Rye and Rye meale
20 quarters Oats and Oat meale
150 quarters Mault and Barly
10 Barrills Powder
10 thousand Biskett
40 Barrills tallow and suet
200 dozn. shooes
10 dozn. Bootes
20 quarters Pease
50 hundred weight Candles.

The like Order for the ship called the William and George wth the Prouisions following, first

180 passengers.

[Then follows the invoice of merchandize, which being composed of the same items as those already copied, is omitted.]

[*Endorsement :*—] 17° Januarij, 1639. Order for 2 Ships to carry Passengers and Provisions to New England. Ent.

EMIGRANTS FOR ST. CHRISTOPHERS.

[Among a mass of MSS. exhibited to me in the Rolls Office, there was a very little book, with a vellum cover, about four by five inches, and containing but six leaves. The outside of the cover is thus inscribed :—]

" The Names of such as passed out of the poart of Plimworth Ano Dme 1634."

[What follows is an entire copy of the whole book.]

Plymouth ffebr: 1633. Passengers in the Robert Bonaventure for St Christophers

George fford of Exoñ,* aged 30 yeares.
Stephen Whittington, of Lincolne, 20 yeares.
John Thomas of St. Tiffey,† 26 yeres.
John Liddicott of St. Cullum,‡ 22.
Wm Clarke of Truro, 20.
Tho: ffrethy of Perintho,§ 24.
Michaell Bowden of Holston, 27.
John Badland of Northill, 22.
Richard Slavelie of Stoñehowse, 40
Richard Cocke of Wincklye, 33
Henry Rensby of St. Stephens, 28
Anthony Webb of Lanceston, 20

---

* Exeter.
† Perhaps St. Teath in Cornwall.
‡ Probably Columb in Cornwall.
‖ Perhaps Peramthon in Cornwall.

Gregory Sam of Chidleigh, 15
Christopher Carter of St. Gilt, 45
Martin Rooby of Guindiron, 23
Wm. Curke of Monteratt, 24
Henry Thomas of Luxulian, 15
Stephen Symon of Plimpton, 18
Mathew Arthur of Plimpton, 18
Jane Trewin of Plimpton, aged 26 yeares.
Wm Johnson of London, 32 "
Reignold ffrost of Tottnes, 15
John ffarren of Peter Tauey, 2
Wm Wndo of Bodmin, 33
Nichās Dabbin of St. Stephens, 40
Andrew Picke of Great Dalby, 34
John Penington of Symon Ward, 40
Tho Pollard of Paranenth, 23
Ellin Nauearro of Penryn, 20
Rawleigh Edye of Bodmyn, 15
Wm Dun of Truro, 16
Anth: Pearse of St. Breage, 16
Edward Trennueere of Helston, 18
Robt: Treneeghau, of Helston, 34
Tego Leaue of Corke in Ireland, 30
Rec. for these:
All husbandmen bound to serve here, some 3 and some 4 yeares.

1633. 1° mcij. In the Margarett for St. Christophers
Thomas Roseter of Washboro, 20 yeares.
Tho: Martin of Cardinham, 24
John Dustan, of St. Cullom, 26
Richard Williams of St. Cullom, 30
John Newdon of St. Tue, 20
Anth: Burrowes of Jacobstow, 20
Robert Oliver of Crediton, 20
Barth: Curnew. of Crediton, 18
Clement Barry of Exon, 22.
ffrancis Pedler of St. Breage, 28
Robt Pedler of St. Breage, 22
John Merry of Withiell, 28
Walter Burlace of Luggom, 22
Samuell fforgine of Wallen Lizard, 26
Richard Edward of St Virian, 28
Richard Symondes of Wantage, 28
Robt Paine of Marrozun, 29
Wm Badcocke of St. Hillary, 20
Simon Martin of St. Ives, 18
George Griffin of Marazion, 18
Tho: Sleman of St. Hillary, 18
John Sanders of Marozion, 18
Thomas Borinthon of Helston, 22
Wm Writt, of Marozion, 17
Nichas Warerman or [of] Marozion, 15

Samuell Purefoy of St. Ives, 13.
George Mathew of Ludswan, 23
Teage Williams, Irishman, 18
Rect. for them li s d 0 15 0

All husbandmen for the most pt as the former.

Joseph Boole
is Debuta ther.

[Here follows the whole of another book, similar in size and form to the last named :—]

A list of the names and surnames of those psons wch are bound for St Christophrs and haue taken the oath of Allegiance before me Mr William Gourney, Maior of Dartmouth, they being brought before me the twentyeth day of ffebruary in ye yeare of or Lord god 1634.

Imprimis William Haukins, of Exoñ, Glouer, aged 25 yeares or there abouts.

James Courtney, of Exoñ, A Blacksmith Aged 23 yeares or thereabouts.

Richard Skose of Newton Abbot, A Seafaringe Man; 37 yeares or thereabouts.

Francis Boyce of London, a Button hole maker, aged 25 yeares or thereabouts.

William Carkille, of Plimouth, a Saylemaker, aged 21 yeares or thereabouts.

William Gurge, of Exoñ, a shoemaker, aged 20 yeares or thereabouts.

Alce Whitmor, of Huniton in Devon, Spinster, aged 25 yeares or thereabouts.

Philipp Stephens of Ashbertan in Devon, Spinster, aged 28 yeares or thereabouts.

Sara Coose of Exoñ Spinster, aged 18 years or therabouts.

Judith Stevens of Exoñ, Spinster, aged 19 years or therabouts.

Margarett Harwood, of Stokegabriell in Devon, Spinster, aged 22 yeares or thereabouts.

Edward Morris, of Exoñ a Locker, aged 21 yeares or thereabouts.

Thomas Bryant of Bampton in Devonshire, a husbandman aged 23 years or therabouts.

Willyam May of Maymard in Somersett, a sea man aged 32 yeares or therabouts.

Hulinne Oneth, of St. Stevens in Cornwall, a husbandman, aged 34.

John Wille in Barnstable in Devon a ffeltmaker, Aged 35 years or therabouts.

Symon Weeks, of Exoñ, a Worsted weaver, aged 16 yeares or thereabouts.

Thomas Jermayne of Exoñ, an Ostler, aged 30 years.

John ffrench, of Washford in Ireland, a Seaman, 26 years.

Willen Bill of Great Torington in Devonshire, a husbandman, aged 28 yeares.

John Hocksley, of Stoke Cannon in Devon, a Taylor, aged 28 years.

James Ruosman, of London, a husbandman, aged 21 years.

Elizabeth Reed, of Exon, a spinster, aged 19 years or therabouts.

Mary Harte, of Lyme, a spinster, aged 18 years or therabouts.

Mary Hoppine, of Exmister, a spinster, aged 20 years.

Mary Harries of Stoke Pomneroy in Devon, aged 23 years or therabouts.

Elizabeth Quicke, of Barnstable in Devon, aged 18 years.

Elizabeth Hill of Brixam in Devon, aged 24 years.

Joane Shorte of Exon, Aged 20 years.

Joane Lauere, of Modbury in Devon, aged 19 years.

Jane Gouldinge of St. Thom: the Apostle in Devon, aged 16 years or therabouts.

James Worthy Deputy
for Mr Thoroughgood.

[The following list is from a paper without date. The Capt. *Hopson* mentioned in it is the Capt. *Hobson* of the New England Histories, probably.]

A List of Sea Men's Names wch Capt. John Hopson one of his Maties Councell in Virgenia desireth to be exempted from ye presse in Regarde of his Present intended Voyage of Virginia in ye good shipp called ye Vnity of ye Isle of Wyghte.

William Vpton, Mr:
Richard White, Mate
William Godfrie
William Minterne
William Poul
Thomas Wooden
Thomas Wise
Robert Carter
Nicholas Sallter
Nicholas Godfrie
John Persie
William Oden
John Orchard
John Smith
John Preston.

Her Maj. St. P. Office.

Omission in p. 306. After l. 6 should come in

Christian Luddington 18

[This work will now be found to contain complete lists of all the Emigrant Founders of New England, which have been brought to light, with the exception of two brief ones printed by Boys in his History of Sandwich. These are of easy access, as are those before printed in the Register: viz. in vol. i, pages 132, 377–9; vol. ii, page 407, and vol. ix, pages 265–8. Doubtless many of the Emigrants to Virginia, Barbadoes, and other Islands, found their way eventually to New England. All of these have been copied and the most of them printed in the Register. Those which have not been printed will soon be.

I have thought it proper to append to the preceding List of Early Founders of New England, the King's Commission to Archbishop Laud, for governing that country. And notwithstanding its great importance in New England History, I am not aware that a perfect copy of it has ever been published in that country. Mr. Hubbard has, in his valuable History of New England, given an abstract of it, and Governor Pownall has given it in Latin in an Appendix to the Fourth Edition of his "Administration of the Colonies."

For similar reasons I give also the Commission to Sir Ferdinando Gorges, which constituted him Governor of New England. Both of these papers are copied from the originals, with the best care I can take for their accuracy.]

COMMISSION TO ARCHBISHOP LAUD, AND OTHERS, TO GOVERN NEW ENGLAND.

A Commission for y[e]
makinge Lawes and Orders
for Government of English
Colonies planted in
Forraigne parts.
Dated xxviii° Aprilis
An° Caroli Regis x[mo]
Anōq Dm̄. 1634.

Charles by the grace of God King of England Scotland ffrañce and Ireland Defender of the Faith &c.

To the most reverend Father in God our welbeloved and most faithfull Councellor, William, by divine Providence, Archb[pp] of Canterburie, of all England primate, and Metropolitan, our welbeloved and most faithfull Councello[r] Thomas Lord Coventry, Lord Keeper of the greate Seale of England. The most reverend ffather in Christ, our welbeloved and faithfull Councello[r] Richard by Divine Providence Archb[pp] of Yorke Primate and Metropolitan, our welbeloved and most faithfull Cozens and Councellors, Richard Earle of Portland o[r] high Trēr of England, Henry, Earle of Manchester, Lord Keeper of our privie Seale, Thomas Earle of Arundell and Surrey Earle Marshall of England, Edward Earle of Dorsett, Chamberlaine to o[r] most deare Consort, the Queene And our welbeloved and faithfull Councello[r] Fraunces Lord Cottington, Chauncello[r] and Vnder Treasuro[r] of o[r] Exchequer, S[r] Thomas Edmonds, knight, Treasuror of o[r] Howshold, S[r] Henry Fane knight, Comptroller of the same Howshold, S[r] John Coke, knight, one of our prime Secretaries, and S[r] Fraunces Windebancke, knight, one of our prime Secretaries Greeting Whereas

Very manie of our subiects and of our late Fathers of blessed memorie our Soueraigne Lord James King of England, by meanes of Lycence Royall, not onlie with desire of enlarging y[e] Territories of o[r] Empire, but cheifely out of a pious and religious affection and desire of Propogatinge the Ghospell of our Lord and Saviour Jesus Christ, have Planted large Colonies of the English Nation in divers Partes of the world altogeather vnmanured and voyde of Inhabitants, or occupied of the barbaroas People that haue noe knowledge of Divine Wor[pp] Wee being willing graciouslie to provide a remedie for the tranquillitie and quietnes of those People, and being very Confident of your faith Wisdome, Justice and provident Circumspection, haue Constituted yo[u] the aforesaid Archb[pp] of Canterbury Lord Keeper of the greate Seale of England, The Archb[pp] of Yorke, The Lord Treasuro[r] of England, Lord Keeper of the privie Seale, The Earle Marshall of England, Edward Earle of Dorsett, ffra cis Lord Cottington, S[r] Thomas Edmonds knight; S[r] Henry Fane, knight, S[r] John Coke, knight, and S[r] Frauncis Windebancke, knight, or any five or more of yo[u] o[r] Commissioners. And to yo[u] five or more of yo[u] Wee doe giue and committ Power for the Gouernment and safetie of the said Colonies drawne, or w[ch] out of the English Nation into those partes shalbe drawne, to make Lawes Constitutions and Ordinances p'tayning either to the publique state of those Colonies or the private proffit of them, and concerning the lands, Goods, Debts and Succession in those partes, and how they shall demeane themselves towards forraigne Princes and their People, or how they shall beare themselues towards vs and our Subiectes as well in any forraigne Partes whatsoever, or on ye Seas in those partes or in their returne sayling home, or which may appertaine to ye maintenance of the Clergie Government, or to the cure of Soules amonge the People living and exercising Trade in those partes by designing out congruent portions arising in Tithes oblations and other thinges there accordinge to your sound descretions in politicall and Civill Causes, and by having the aduise of twoe or three Bpps for the setlinge, makeing and ordering of the busines for designing necessarie Ecclicall and Clergie Portions which yow shall cause to be called and taken to you, and to make Provision against the Violators of those Lawes Constitutions and Ordinances, by imposinge penalties and mulctes, imprisonmt (if there be cause, and that the qualitie of the offence doe require it by deprivation of member or life to be inflicted) with power also, (our assent being had,) to remove, displace ye Governor or Rulers of those Colonies for causes which to yow shall seeme lawfull, and others in their stead to Constitute, and to require an Accompt of their Rule and Government, And whome yow shall finde culpable, either by Deprivation from the Place or by Imposition of a mulct vpon the Goods of them in those Partes to be levied, or banishment from the Provinces in which they have been Governors, or otherwise to Chastice according to the qualitie of the fault And to Constitute Judges and Magistrates politicall and Civell for Civill Causes and vnder the power and forme which to you fiue or more of yow with the Bpps Vicegereull (provided by the Archbpp of Canterburie for the time being) shall seeme expedient And to ordayne Courtes Pretorian and Tribunall as well Ecclicall as Civell of Judgmente to determine of the forme and manner of proceeding in the same, And of appealing from them in matters and Causes as well Cryminall as Civill, Personall, reall and mixt, And to ye Seates of Justice what may be equally and well ordered and what crymes, faultes, or excesses of Contractes, or iniuries ought to belonge to ye Ecclicall Courte and Seate of Justice PROVIDED NEVERTHELESSE That the Lawes, Ordinances and Constitutions of this kind shall not be put in execution before or Assent be had therevnto in writing vnder or Signet, signed at least. And this Assent being had therevnto and the same publiquely proclaymed in ye Provinces in which they are to be executed. Wee will and Command that those Lawes, Ordinances, and Constitutions more fully to obtayne strength and be confirmed shalbe inviolablie observed of all men whom they shall concerne NOTWITHSTANDING it shalbe lawfull for yow five or more of yow as is aforesaid (although those Lawes Constitutions and ordinances shalbe proclaymed with our Royall Assent,) to change, revoke and abrogate them, and other new ones in forme aforesaid from time to time to frame and make as is aforesaid, and to new evills arisinge or daungers to applie new remedies as is fitting soe often as to you shall seeme expedient.

Furthermore you shall understand wee have Constituted you or every fiue of yow the aforesaid Archbpp of Canterbury, Thomas Lord Coventrie Lord Keeper of the Great Seale of England, Richard Archbpp of Yorke, Richard Earle of Portland, Henry Earle of Manchester, Thomas Earle of Arundell and Surrey, Lord Cottington, Sr Tho: Edmondes, Knight, Sr Henry Fane, Knight, Sr John Coke, Knight, and Sr Fraunces Windebancke, Knight, or Commissioners to heare and determine according to yor sound discretions, all manner of Complaintes, either against those Colonies or the Rulers and Gouernors at the instance of the parties greived, or at the Accusation brought from home or from thence, betweene them and their members to be moved, and to call ye Parties before you, and to the Parties and their Procurators from hence or from thence being heard, the full complement of Justice to be exhibited. GIVING vnto you, or any fiue or more of yow Power, that if you shall finde any of the Colonies aforesaid, or any of the Cheife Rulers vpon the Iurisdiction of others by vniust Possession or Vsurpation, or one against another makeing greivance, or in Rebellion against vs, or withdrawing from our Allegeance, or or Mandate not obeying (consultation first with vs in that case had,) to cause those Colonies or the Rulers of them for the Causes aforesaid, either to returne to England, or to Comañd them to other places Designed, euen as according to your sound discretions it shall seeme to stand with equitie, Iustice and necessitie.

MOREOVER WEE DOE GIUE vnto you or any fiue of you Power and speciall Comaund over all the Charters and Letters Patentes, and Rescriptes Royall of the Regions, Provinces, Islandes or Lands in other Partes graunted raising Colonies to cause them to be brought before yow and the same being reviewed, if any surreptiously, or vnduely hath bine obtayned; or that by ye same Privilege, Liberties or Prerogatives hurtfull to vs or or Croune or to forraigne Princes haue bine preiudicially suffered and graunted, the same being better made knowne vnto yow fiue, or more of yow, to command them according to the Lawes and Customes of England to bee revoked, and to doe such other thinges which to ye Government profitt and safeguard of the aforesaid Colonies and of or Subiectes resident in the same shalbe necessarie.

AND THERFORE wee doe Commaund yow that about the Premises, at Dayes and times which for thies thinges yow shall make provision, that you be diligent in attendance as it becometh yow Giuing in Precept also, and firmely enioyning, Wee doe giue Comañd to all and singular Cheife Rulers of Provinces into which the Colonies aforesaid have bine drawne or shalbe drawne and concerning ye Colonies themselves concerning others that haue any interest therein that they giue attendance vpon you and be observant and obedient to yor Warrantes in those Affaires as often as need shall require, and euen as in or name.

IN TESTIMONIE WHEREOF wee haue caused these or Lres to be made Patentes. Witnesse Or selfe at Westminster the 28th Day of Aprill in ye 10th yeare of or Raigne

By Writt from the Privy Seale

[*Endorsement.*] Willis

Commission for ye making Lawes and Orders for Government of English Colonies planted in foreign parts. Dated 28th April 1634.

State Paper Office.

COMMISSION TO SIR FERDINANDO GORGES AS GOVERNOR OF NEW ENGLAND: BY THE KING.

Manyfesting Our Royall pleasure for the establishing a generall Govern'mt in Our Territorye of New England for prevention of those evills that otherwise might Ensue for default thereof—

Forasmuch as Wee haue vnderstood and been credibly informed of the many inconueniences and mischiefs that haue growne and are like more and more to arise amongst Our Subjects allready planted in the parts of New England by reason of the severall opinions differing humors and many other differences springing up betweene them and daily like to encrease, and for that it rested not in the power of the Councill of New England (By our Gracious ffathers royall Charter established for those affaires) to redress the same, Without wee take the whole manageing thereof into Our owne hands, and apply therevnto Our immediate power and authority, Which being perceived by the principall undertakers of those businesses, They haue humbly resigned the said Charter unto us, that thereby there may bee a speedy order taken for reformation of the aforesaid Errors and mischeifs. And knowing it to bee a Duty proper to our Royall Justice not to suffer such Numbers of Our people to runne to ruine and so religious and good intents to languish for want of timely remedie and Soueraigne assistance Wee haue therefore graciously accepted of the said Resignation and doe approue of their good affections to a seruice soe acceptable to God and vs, And wee haue seriously aduised with Our Councill both of the way of Reformation and of a person meet and able for that imployment by whose grauity, moderation and experience Wee haue hopes to repair what is amiss and settlem^t of those affaires to the good of Our people and honour of Our Gouernm^t. And for that purpose Wee have resolued with Our selfe to imploye Our Servant fferdinando Gorges knight, as well for that Our Gracious ffather of blessed memory as Wee haue had for a long time good experience of his fidelity, circumspection and knowledge of his Gouernem^t in martiall and civill affaires, besides his understanding of the State of those Countreys wherein he hath been an immediate mover and a principall Actor, to the great prejudice of his estate, long troubles and the loss of many of his good ffreinds and servants in making the first discovery of those Coasts, and taking the first seizure thereof as of right belongs to vs Our Crowne and dignity, and is still resolued according to Our Gracious pleasure to prosecute the same in his owne person, Which resolution and most comendable affection of his to serve vs therin, as We highly approve, Soe Wee hold it a property of Our princely care to second him with Our Royall and ample authority Such as shalbee meet for an employment soe eminent and the performance of Our Service therin, wherof Wee haue thought itt fitt to make publick Declaration of Our said pleasure, That therby it may appear to our good Subjects the resolution Wee haue graciously to prouide for the peace and future good of those whose affection leads them to any such vndertaking, and withall to Signifye that Our further will and pleasure is, That none bee permitted to goe into any those parts to plant or inhabitt, But that they first acquaint Our said Gouerno^r therwith, or such other as shalbee deputed for that purpose during his aboad heer in England, And who are to receiue from him or them allowance to pass with his or their further directions where to sitt downe most for their perticuler commodityes and publick good of our Service (Sauing and reserving to all those that haue Joyned in the Surrender of the Great Charter of New England and haue Grants immediately to bee holden of us for their Severall plantations in the said Countrye, ffree liberty at all times hereafter to go themselues and also to send such Numbers of people to their plantacoñs as by themselues shall bee thought conuenient Heerby strictly charging and commanding all our Officers and others to whom it shall or may appertaine, to take notice of this our pleasure and to be careful the same bee firmely obserued as they or any of them shall answer the same at their vttermost perill. Giuen at the Court of Whitehall the 23. day of July 1637. and in the Thirteenth yeare of Our Raigne.

State Paper Office.

[The following Lists from the same volume as the preceding were copied and furnished to the Register by Mr. H. G. Somerby.]

Register of the names
of all ye Passinger w^ch^
Passed from ye Porte of
London for on whole
yeare Endinge at
Xp'^mas^ 1635

vi Januarii 1634

Theis under written names are to be transported to St. Christophers and the Barbadoes, James Romsey M^r^ bound thither have taken ye oath of Allegeance.

John Phillips	21	George Sutton	19	Tho: Carpenter	20
John Allin	23	Edward Jennor	24	Tho: Smith	17
Davie Johnes	24	Joseph Glade	20	John White	27
Wm White	30	Peter Monk	29	John Watkinson	22
Humfrey Davies	22	Richard Coke	38	Joseph Pardy	23
Wm Camion	21	Isack Peter	20	Robert Langredge	23
Edward Lampeugh	35	Phillipp Squier	20	Jn° Etherington	17
George Cliffe	26	Bartholomew Flade	24	George White	27
Abram Jn°son	27	Richard Lawrence	20	Tho: Cockey	25
Henrie Wells	23	Daniell Smith	20	Ant° Blackgrove	24
John Usher	26	John Symes	17	John Higgins	20
Edmond Knight	21	Robert Kett	22	Willm Hodgson	20
Tho: Rasbottom	23	Suzan Hudson	20	Tho: Jenkynns	23
Wm Griggson	14	Mary Sea	16	Jn° Greenewood	26
Richard Jones	23	John Shettleworth	28	John Place	22
Michell White	18	Richard Fryme	26	Wm Hayman	36
Richard Borne	24	Robt Holme	22	Edward Savage	20
Edward Fletcher	20	John More	28	Jo: Conniers	21
Francis Sowthe	19	Richard Pence	45	John Moore	30
John Conny	20	Edward Jones	21	Robt. Ground	22
Robert Skarvill	21	Mark Ellvyn	20	William Bruton	22
Edward Robinson	18	Henry Purslym	18	William Walton	22
John Holland	15	Richard Chitting	23	Willm Seward	26
Edward Ash	20	Tho: Marfutt	22	Henry Rymes	40
Tho. Sandby	17	Richard Edmonds	18	Henry Iles	17
Tho. Greene	24	Wm Prichard	25	Bryan Erle	21
Mark Theody	18	Tho: Arnold	18	John Fox	19
Willm Burt	22	Richard Chamblis	19	Robert Gilby	18
John Bowes	23	Edward Brunt	25	Robert Baker	50
Henry Cappledike	20	George Stokes	23	Tho: Peck	20
Robt. Stratford	16	Henry Fookes	21	Willm̄ Harris	35
Robert Holland	19	Robert Granger	21	John Towne	27
Tho: Borne	22	Wm Walter	26	Christian Mynnikyn	19
Edward Roberts	25	John Rods	20		
John Carter	26	Ezechell Clements	20		

17 Februarij 1634

Theis under written names are to be transported to the Barbadoes imbarqued in ye Hopewell Capten Tho: Wood M^r^ bound thither. The passengers have taken the oath of Allegeance and Supremacie.

Willm̄ Usher	22	Richard Clynton	23	Wm Owen	23
Rich. Hanby	23	Jn° Harrison	46	Jn° Free	25
Richard Jackson	17	James Read	19	Richard Gane	19
Joh. Hill	19	Dunston Rember	20	Thomas Richards	19

Name	Age
John Nicks	23
Martin Perkynn	20
Ant° Blades	24
Robert Dymond	29
Tho: Dayes	20
Wm Walker	21
Ralph Harwood	23
Phillipp Philpott	30
James Pallister	28
Richard Clark	21
Daniell Baker	20
John Tayler	23
Thomas Prosser	20
John Eaton	20
Tho: Smith	21
John Johnson	18
Richard Holmes	24
Ralph Terrett	24
Henry Tatnum	20
Alexander Smith	18
John Crapp	37
John Faux	36
Joseph Bryan	20
Nevill Hutchins	20
Wm Walters	22
Willm̄ Puttox	20
Archibald Weyer	18
Nathaniell Cobham	17
Jarvice Dodderidge	21
John Derborn	22
Willm Seriff	19
John Offword	24
Tho: Lee	20
Robert Richards	18
George Hiter	18
John Dreadd	17
Arthur Wynd	17
Richard Osborn	22
John Phillipps	37
John Steevens	13
John Reddhedd	28
Wm Gibson	18
Tho: Waterman	27
Tho: Jones	19
Jo: Nisom	23
Edward Layton	30
Wm Benson	28
John Whitehedd	23
Richard Barnard	23
Henry Long	21
John Wilks	22
Tho: Wellman	21
Tho: Gaton	25
Wm Allin	25
Tho: Letteny	20
Robert Porter	20
John Hughes	20
Henry Akyns	22
Robert Rember	21
Robert Mills	19
John Davies	25
Thomas Crowder	21
Richard Purnell	21
Robert Lynley	20
Henry Holmes	44
John Key	30
John Williams	21
John Fowler	24
John Owen	20
Owen Williams	21
Tho: Drow	26
Wm Bunystedd	21
Edward Jn°son	20
John Bownd	20
John Haies	30
John Lyon	18
Willm Corfer	24
Thomas Trigg	21
Robert Nisbett	19
Willm Caddy	21
John Cassedy	20
Alexander More	24
Richard Wellyn	25
Richard Griffs	24
Arthur Yeomans	24
Nicholas Hobson	23
Wm Marrow	25
Francis Dene	21
John Philpott	16
John Strattergood	18
Wm Cant	19
Henrie Speckman	27
John Yats	19
Wm Ranse	27
George Selman	16
Nicholas Blades	21
John Clark	24
Tho: Everie	19
Tho: Medwell	31
Jo: Basher	20
James Ellerton	18
Richard Hands	19
Medusala Watts	20
Tho: Hames	19
Phillipp Cartwrite	20
John Loftis	21
Michell Rocks	21
Jo: Ling	45
Tho: Sherman	26
Wm Jackson	30
James Goldingham	32
Rich. Rainolds	19
Jo: Nokes	20
Francs Symonds	21
Thomas Lurtray	21
James Anderson	19
Walter Jago	20
John Bead	22
John Young	19
Tho: Hubbard	20
Edward Browne	24
Wm Seere	22
Wm Levyns	22
Jo: Hamond	17
Edward Pullin	27
James Cullimor	22
Jo: Depark	28
Richard Walton	21
Robert Collie	20
Joseph Hepworth	33
Willm̄ Walters	32
Daniell Smith	33
Richard Trueman	24
Wm Masters	21
Jo: Clere	26
Randall Ogden	19
Tho: Browne	21

---

26 Martij 1635.

This under written name is to be imbarqued in the Peter Bonaventure Tho: Harman Mr bound for ye Barbadoes and St Christophers p' Certificate from St Andrewes p'rish Holborne: And attestacon from Justice Grimston, and Justice Sheppard hath taken the oaths of Allegeance & Supremacie.

William Banks 21 yeeres

To be Imbarqued In the Peter Bonavtr de Lond Capt. Harman Vss Barbades. Theis p'ties here under expressed have brought Certeficat from two Justices of peace that the toke the oathe of Allegn & S'ppremacie and Also cert frō ye ministr of the p'ishe the 3d Aprill 1635.

Tho: Hathorne aged	22 yers	Jane Maddockes	21	Margrett Ellgate	24
Wm Morrison	23	Alce Mare	22	Margrett Hartforde	22
Ralph Vaughan	22 & ½				

4th Aprill 1635

In the Peter Bonavtr de Lond Capt Harman for Barbades. Theis two p'ties brought Cert from two Justices of peace and the ministr of their Conformity accord' to order.

Wm Clerke	29 yers.	Tho: Sergeant	23 yers.

---

3 Aprilis 1635. At Gravesend.

Theis under written names are to be transported to St. Christophers imbarqued in the Paul of London, Jo. Acklin, Mr bound thither, there was Cert: brought from the Minister of St. Catherins of their conformitie of their discipline and orders to ye Church of England the men did take ye oath of Alleg. and Supremacie.

Ralph Reason	yeres 23	Wm Scarsbrick	23	Edward Gray	32
Edward Merrifield	19	Wm Church	21	Jo: Watts	21
Robert Wade	35	John Reinolds	23	Edward Fisher	27
Willm Haies	24	Henry Bagin	22	Rich Crowder	28
Geo: Rishford	24	Wm Lamyn	21	Rich Preston	21
Mathew Moyses	17	Hanna Roper	23	Rich Older	24
Robert Richardson	20	Henry Lee	30	Wm King	18
Jo: Mountain	20	Edward Smallman	21	Jo: Holmes	22
Jo: Willis	29	Robert Atkinson	23	Nico Sedden	20
Jo: French	18	Tho: Fearfax	22	Fra: Stott	32
Tho: Watson	29	Mathew Turner	46	Phillipp Jenings	25
David Evans	22	Edward Gass	20	Robert Spurr	24
Steeven Garret	19	Henry Sentence	20	Tho: Spendergrass	24
Wm Beddle	19	Edmond Davies	21	Nico Hollis	20
Richard Lock	20	Edward Barnes	16	Rich Danes	20
Abram Watson	19	Tho: Nott	18		
James Carter	25	Jo: Adams	16		

In the Peter Bonaventure, Tho: Harman Mr bound for the Barbadoes theis under written names p' order: they have taken ye oaths of Supremacie and Allegeance.

Tho: Berkynn	yeres 24	Wm Weston	16	James Robards	20
Jo: Westgarth	28	Wm Houseman	12	Rich Clark	19
Jo: Sweeting	26	Rich Chapman	40	Geo: Plankett	19
James Townson	29	Tho: Cutler	35	Wm Marrowdin	19
Rich Dawson	28	James Jackson	33	Jo: Alliday	20
Tho: Greenwood	15	Jo: Smitheman	23	Walter Gibson	25
Tho: Iveson	36	Robert Savage	21	Jo: Wynkles	20
Tho: Hywood	22	Geo: Penny	24	Jo: Vynn	17
Wm Banks	23	Jo: Pattman	23	Robert Roe	19
Jo: Greealy	20	Tho: Coke	30	Maurice Williams	18
Daniell Davies	26	Jo: Symonds	19	Dennis Mortagh	30
Robert Braban	29	Jo: Boone	12	Jo: Dukkarth	31
Jo: Thomas	25	Nico Evans	16	Rich Mansfield	22
Rich Leech	22	Jo: Mydhouse	15	Gregorie Ogell	15
Rich Abbott	20	Rich Hollinby	20	Wm Whitlock	31
Ambrose Huett	27	Wm Lodge	13	Jo: Long	20
Jo: White	25	Isack Pratt	22	Jo: Thompson	31
Jo: Weston	26	Jo: Evans	17	Tho: Farmer	22

Ric^{h} Brownley	19	Capten Jacob Lake	30	Tho: Lamberd	23
Mathew Westwood	18	Luke Stokes	35	Geo: Chapman	17
Jo: Mather	21	Richard Speed	35	Wm Aston	17
Robert Pendred	40	Phillipp Henson	21	Adrian Coke	27
David Robinson	20	Arthur Watkyns	25	Robert Philkyn	25
Willm Beckkitt	26	Jo: Joyner	25	Jno Sympson	29
Tho: Evans	20	Jo: Dent	30	Steeven Greenly	16
Jo: Hynd	24	Robert Jnoson	26	Mary Loveley	35
Wm Mecham	20	Jo: Sawcott	18	Ann Loveley	10
Roger Wills	20	Jo: Bunce	18	Margaret Lucocks	27
Tho: Tedder	19	Jo: Robinson	26	Annis Percy	24
Jo: Sessions	22	Ric^{h} Pell	22		
Daniell Dennis	22	Jo: Disherd	22		

---

xiiij° Aprilis 1635

Theis under written names are to be transported to the Barbadoes imbarqued in the Faulcon de London. Tho: Irish M^{r} p' Certificate from the Minister of the p'ish of their conformity to the orders of the church of England. The men have taken the oaths of Allegeance and Supremacie.

Gabriell Bolt	29	Jo: Belton	48	John Scott	16
Owon Bliss	30	Nicolas Flitcroft	16	Robert Jones	25
Geo: Say	26	Wm Bingham	18	Nathaniell Write	32
Bassell Terry	22	Humfrey Morris	18	John Jones	24
Marmaduke Turner	21	Jo: Dallinger	16	Tho: Wallis	27
Jo: Bassett	19	Jo: Rogers	34	Toby Hazell	20
Jo: Sheering	26	Jo: Spyer	32	Geo: Clark	15
Henrie Biddleston	17	Francis Smith	20	Tho: Roberts	18
Tho: Lett	22	Abraham Halloway	20	Marmaduke Crosby	28
Samvol Stor [or Ston, or Stow]	17	Joseph Drap'	21	Geo: Harris	17
		Tho: Bromby	50	Roger Sawter	17
James Burt	13	Jo: Bromby	27	Marie Perry	18
Charles Fall	19	Jesper Giggon	18	Elizabeth Elson	18
Wm Sonnott	20	John Brumwell	22	Bridget Gerden	19
Jo: Browne	20	Ric^{h} Dent	17	Kathorin Hill	20
Tho: Webb	18	Thomas Gualmay	22	Marie Newcom	17
Jo: Hopwood	20	Richard Snathe	19	Benedicte Sherhack	20
Nic^{o} Wade	19	Richard Cockman	20	Marie Crew	19
Robert Davers	14	Thomas Allin	22	Elizabeth Long	21
Henry Dye	20	Valentine Love	18	Winifred Hand	20
Edward Bull	22	Robert Hapley	21	Elizabeth Curtis	22
Farford Goldsmith	22	Tho: Metcalf	20	Wm Sturgis	18
Tho: Crispin	19	Wm Knight	30	Tho: Knowles	16
Francis Sheeres	26	Henrie Gilder	18	Peter Lostell	14
John Bathe	23	George Lee	16	Walter Holburd	24
Smith Baker	28	Ant^{o} Goldsworth	18		
James Hibbins	17	John Church	21		

---

16 Aprilis 1635.

Theis p'ties hereafter expressed are to be transported to the Island of Providence imbarqued in ye Expectacion Cornelius Billinge M^{r}, having taken the oaths of Allegeance and Supremacie: As likewise being conformable to the Church of England; whereof they brought testimonie from the Ministers and Justices of Peace, of their Abodes.

Francis Smith	36	Wm Lynlie	58	Jo: Baker	42
Tho: Palmer	18	Christian Whetston	19	Jo: Martin	30
Leonard Smith	22	Wm Cawdle	19	Wm Smith	20
Mathew Hamblen	38	Florence Dickenson	19	Ant^{o} Dowsell	20

Richard Slie 20
Francis Dales 20
Peter Ambrey 32
Tho: Feld 18
Edward Hassard 24
Richard Bull 17
Richard Reinolds 16
Wm Crakins 15
Jo: Totnell 16
Edward Horsham 14
Richard Trendall 16
Wm Read 16
Mathew Pippin 20
Mary Baker 42
Elisha Bridges 16
Willm̄ Thorp 30
Elizabeth Thorp 20
Elizabeth Thorp 2
Joan Felver 50
Margaret Rollright 45
Ellin Cooper 24
Elizabeth Coke 20
Marie Chaddock 20
Elizabeth Hamond 25
Alice Awbrey 29
Elizabeth Lawrence 26
Ann Noble 21
Marie Harrowigg 21
Millicent Leech 28
Marie Goodwyn 20
Katherin Webb 22
Elizabeth Scott 20
Marie Howes 18
Dorothy Lawrence 28
Elizab: Horsham 16
Alice Goldham 26
Richard Price 14
Richard Lane 38
Alice Lane 30
Samvell Lane 7
Jo: Lane 4
Oziell Lane 3
Jo: Atkinson 36
Love Atkinson 38
Elizabeth Owen 30
Marie Milward 21
Isack Barton 27
Abram Ray 20
Dorcas Horsham 40
Marie Griffin 17

24 Aprilis 1635.

Theis under written names are to be transported to the Island of Providence imbarqued in the Expectacion aforesaid, the p'ties have taken y oath of Allege :

Nicholas Riskym̄er 31
Wm Randall 26
Andrew Leay 24
Jo: Leay 25
Jo: Bloxsall 28
Sam: Goodenuff 22
Edward Hastings 23
Tho: Hobbs 18
Jo: Saracele 17
Tho: Wilson 18

Theis under written names are to be transported to the Barbadoes and St. Christophers, imbarqued in the Ann & Elizabeth Jo: Brookehaven, Capten and Mr having taken the oaths of Allegeance and Supremacie. As also being conformable to the orders and discipline of the Church of England and no Subsedy Men, whereof they brought test from the Minister of St. Katherins neere ye Tower of London

John Crofts 30
Jo: Mason 20
Jo: Oram 21
Christopher Fish 24
Owen Androwe 18
Robert Anderson 22
John Greene 25
Joseph Wallington 19
John Haieward 22
Thomas Martin 16
Edmond Holloway 17
Thomas Pierce 19
William Hayward 18
Edward Wilkinson 17
Richard Gale 16
Robert Tratt 21
Thomas Redman 16
Willm̄ Grubb 16
John Golding 21
Clement Hutchinson 20
Bartholomew Bennet 18
Thomas Tyler 21
John Prichard 20
Giles Barnes 19
Hugh Sadler 20
Harford Young 20
John Williams 16
Andrew Evans 16
John Barret 16
Joseph Walker 18
James Tate 17
John Smith 14
Nathaniel Bolton 19
Wm Laydon 17
Thomas Avery 18
Tho: Leake 18
Davie Williams 17
Willm̄ Harris 23
John Turpin 22
Francis Saidwell 18
Mathew Rogers 21
Bryan Bourk 19
Anto Taylor 26
Andrew Carr 23
Owen Garret 20
John Frazill 29
John Porter 24
Charles Pollington 26
Charles Jackson 18
Edward Bacon 25
Thomas Robinson 31
Patrick Conly 21
George Goddin 31
Arthur Roker 20
Tho: Dale 28
John Davies 19
Tho: Burton 19
Hugh Wynstonly 20
Bartholomew Draper 20
Robert Brook 25
Hugh Tawyer 18
Wm Greene 17
Patrick Connyer 20
Richard King 23
Willm̄ Barnes 17
Willm̄ Taylor 23
Robert Sennod 23
Thomas Perkynn 29
Willm̄ Longwith 26
Tho: Gullifer 28
John Davies 18
Richard Cawood 25

Richard Dynley	19	Alice Hilton	18	Michell Estplynn	18
Dennis Peke	20	Katherin Russell	20	James Bell	19
		Mary Powell	23	Frend Picto	20
WOMEN.		Debora Winke	21	John Whithedd	22
Katherin Lloyd	19	Rebeca Bedding	18	Jo: Mallion	21
Suzan Greene	20	Mathew Page	20	Tho: Bedlam	24
Margerie Barran	19	Ann Spicer	26	Tho: Lone	19
Elizabeth Benñing	18	Mary Jones	20	Thomas Wazell	21
Elizabeth Bruster	18	Margery Harding	20	Edward Garrard	26
Joan Smith	27	Marie Kinderslie	26	John Coke	22
Suzan More	21			Jeremy Hartley	30
Alice Dixon	21	Nicholas Greene	18	Gilbert Holdsworth	30
Jane Stafford	29	Robert Laycock	18		

2° Maij 1635.

Theis under written names are to be transported to ye Barbadoes imbarqued in the Alexander Capt. Burche and Gilbert Grimes Mr p' Certificate from the Minister where they late dwelt the men tooke the oaths of Alleg and Supremacie die et A° pred.

Willm Rapan yeres	29	Jo: Write	24	Jo: Cole	20
Leonard Staples	22	William Clarke	19	James Watts	35
Jo: Stanford	24	Edward Halingworth	46	Wm Crome	17
James Manzer	27	Richard Pomell	32	Phillipp Lovell	34
Jo: Watts	25	Henry Longsha	23	Uxor Elizabeth Lovell	33
Tho: Clark	26	Jo: Bush	22	Rowland Mathew	27
Michell King	27	Jonathan Franklin	17	Robert Sprite	30
Henry Broughton	20	Jo: Phillipps	20	Jo: Weston	41
Geo: Ventimer	20	Richard Cribb	19	James Smith	19
Robert Hardy	18	Tho: Browne	18	Jo: Smith	19
Tho: Dabb	25	Jo: Greenwich	21	Richard Lee	22
Geo: Norton	22	Jo: Nedson	19	Wm Seely	29
Wm Huckle	20	Edward Church	18	Edward Plunkett	20
Edward Kemp	29	Anto Threlcatt	19	Tho: Plunkett	28
Wm Powoll	19	Wm Willis	17	Rowland Plunkett	18
Ralph Promd	26	Clement Hawkins	16	Teaguo Nacton	28
Jo: Bullman	40	Lewes Hughes	19	Dormond O'Bryan	20
Jo: Watts	19	John Greene	22	Charles Galloway	19
Wm Dench	16	Richard Marshall	36	James Montgomery	19
Francis Peck	22	Mathew Calland	16	Jno McCoury	28
Jo: Benstedd	21	Lewes David	28	Samvell Priday	20
Symon Parler	24	Geo: White	18	Samvell Farron	30
Richard Howseman	19	Geo: Rudglie	17	Edmond Montgomery	26
Walter Jones	20	Dennis Mc Brian	18	Olliver Bassett	14
Phelix Lyne	25	Jo: Bussell	36	Parry Wy	15
Arthur Write	21	James Driver	27	Daniell Burche	14
Lewes Willms	21	Hugh Johnes	22	Richard Stone	13
Wm Pott	18	Tho: Gildingwater	30	Thomas Tayler	27
Thomas Gilson	21	John Ashurst	24	Edmond Nash	21
Nico Watson	26	James Parkinson	23	Jo: Herring	28
Olliver Hookham	32	Willm Young	21	Wm Beaton	24
Chri: Buckland	25	Wm Smith	18	Tho: Roe	22
Jo: Hill	23	Morgan Jones	31	Edward Banks	35
Anthony Skooler	20	Jo: Richard	30	Tho: Fludd	21
Jo: Anderson	21	Peter Flaming	16	David Collingworth	22
Wm Phillipps	17	Miles Farring	24	Wm Mathews	30
Jo: Befford	18	Robert Atkins	23	Tymothie Goodman	27
Henry Yatman	21	Beniamin Mason	23	Tho: Penson	20
Robert Duce	18	Tho: Rutter	22	Wm Anderson	36
Owen Williams	18	Jo: Howse	41	Geo. Merriman	41

Jo: Dellahay 27
Robert Lee 33
Jo: Jackson 24
Alexander de la Garde 27
Francis Marshall 26
Walter Lutterell 20
Jo: White 15
Jo: Burton 17
Symon Wood 14
Robert Mussell 14
Richard Fane 15
Robert Roberts 18
Wm Lake 14
Richard Iveson 16
Humfrey Kerby 18
Edward Cokes 17
Henry Morton 20
James Brett 17
Tho: Dennis 18
Tho: More 33
Jo: Lawrence 17
Wm Martin 13
Richard Phelpe 17

WOMEN.

Barbarie Reason 20
Jane Marshall 21
Diana Drake 19
Mary Inglish 17
Annis Barrat 20
Marie Lambeth 17
Ann Mann 17
Elizabeth Warren 17
Ann Skynggle 18
Alice Champ 20
Mathew May 21
Elizabeth Chambers 20
Elizabeth Farmer 20
Margaret Conway 20
Grace Walker 34
Edith Jones 21
Alice Guy 20
Mary Spendley 17
Ann Gardner 36

21° Maij 1635.

Theis under written names are to be transported to St Christophers, imbarqued in the Mathew of London, Richard Goodladd Mr p' warrant from ye Earle of Carlisle.

Thomas Knight yeres 21
Jo: Hill 18
Jo: Rawlins 18
Francis Penn 22
George Allerton 23
Rowland Millington 24
Rich Thomas 40
Roger Thomas 22
Richard Griggson 34
Jo: Bruñing 20
Robert Coke 32
Clinton Cutler 20
Tho: Turner 25
Jo: Wood 22
Wm Robinson 26
Edward Bicroft 22
Jo: Sturdy 26
Anto Netbie 20
Robert Wendever 25
Samvel Trese 20
Evan Jones 19
Gabriell Davies 38
Edward Eeles 20
Davie Thomas 40
Richard Honibym 31
Christopher Watson 21
James Hubbard 27
Wm Stoe 18
Mathew Tomlinson 31
Tho: Hall 25
Wm Marsh 26
Jo: Hatterton 38
Tho: Terrill 18
Robert Faucer 40
Miles Coventrie 18
Jo: Thomas 14
Tho: Reeve 24
Lewes Anbrey 13
James Walker 30
Tho: Vem 27
Geo. Ball 51
Tho: Gosling 22
Jo: Palmer 19
James Cotes 21
Wm Helaine 21
Mathew Hely 21
Originall Lowis 28
Jo: Thomson 34
Wm Brookes 25
Jo: Doe 22
Mathew Walker 19
Walter Collins 18
Jo: Clinton 19
Adam Chesterman 19
Hugh Hallowell 22
Wm Salmon 25
Jo: Lange 22
Richard Lane 28
Jo: Greene 29
Edward Warren 28
Jo: Paple 21
Robert Denten 26
Wm Elvyn 23
Geo: Tems 20
Geo: Swales 19
Marmaduke Read 25
Jo: Kibie 21
Tho: Garrett 20
Jo: Goslinn 20
Tho: Milward 18
Morgan Brint 19
Pierce Stapleton 22
Geo: Eaton 27
Leonard Hunt 38
Jo: Cave 34
Wm Barber 22
Jo: Hoddins 50
Alexander Tadde 38
Robt. Woodstock 40
John Offlent 20
Nico Watts 18
Richard Brookes 16
Tho: Hadbie 22
Tho: Reinolds 18
Darby Hurlie 18
Jo: Hilliard 35
Robert Lacie 21
Tho: Bell 14
Rowland Morton 17
James Hide 22
Richard Nelme 20
Tho. Hodges 20
Edward Thomson 18
Tho: Williams 18
Rich Lee 18
Walter Antony 23
Charles Caverlie 17
Tho: Coxson 21
Tho: Goodwin 30
Nico Wilcocks 21
Geo: Eeke 26
Rich Hubbard 18
Willm̄ Rush 20
Wm Dorn 22
Paul Bottell 32
Jo: Boswell 17
Jo: Woodgreene 16
Jo: Harlowe 16
Robert Warrington 20
Jo: Reinolds 20
Anto True 18
Wm Knight 13
Anto Williams 14
Jo: Barloe 22
Wm Parker 17
Jo: Wood 18
Jo: Payne 18

Daniell Lee 25
Tho: Powell 21
Jo: Smith 22
Geo: Dodd 17
Robt Sandley 20

Edward Mawfrey 15
Geo: Wade 16
Jo: Fulford 18
Geo: Smith 17
Thomas Powell 24

WOMEN.

Margaret Prichard 17
Jane Burrowe 17
Katherin Armstrong 20
Mary Barker 12
Elizabeth Speere 20

---

x Junij 1635.

Theis under written names are to be transported to the Bormoodes or Somer-Islands, imbarqued in the Truelove de London. Robert Dennis Mr being examined by the Minister of Gravesend concerning their conformitie to the orders and discipline of the Church of England as it now stands established: And took the oath of Allegeance.

Henry More 19
Wm Holt 19
Jo: Norman 19
Anto Gilliard 38
Robt. Stock 26
Tho: Foster 27
Robert Hart 30
Wm Pendleton 27
James Tayler 28
Chri. Hart 20
Richard Anderson 30
Tho: Richards 24
Jo: Norris 18
David Huswith 22
Henry Hill 24
Jo: Warren 19
Zeverin Viccars 18
Geo: Norman 25
Gabriell Stockwell 16
Tho: Torlie 27
Edward Goddin 16
Tho: Dorrell 22
Richard Cañon 24
Uxor, Elizabeth Cañon 23
Barnard Colman 26
Chri. Tuke 16
Wm Paul 20
Wm Bates 17
Samvell Short 24
Wm Hooper 18
Richard Hurt 17
Willm̄ Wells 17
Tho: Dene 17
Jo: A Negroe 18
Jo: Richards 21
Anto Bullock 19
Thomas Bassit 18
Edward Aldworth 13
Edward Vyncent 18
Jo: Truppatt 17
Anto Cooper 17
Jo: Lake 16
Rich Tayler 16

Tho: Mordin 18
Edward Sell 18
Roger Willm̄s 16
Jo: Baylie 18
Francis Woodcott 16
Jo: Bee 17
Rich Greene 17
Geo: Palmer 18
Tho: Smith 14
Nathaniel Willm̄son 17
Phillipp Wharton 14
Wm Henry 18
Geo: Saires 12
Nico Gaughton 14
Edward Hedley 13
Wm Sares 17
Robt Poole 20
Tho: Jones 17
Tho: Ervynn 16
Symon Barrott 16
Geo: Calverlie 14
Edward Parnell 16
Wm Lee 18
Wm Tayler 17
Edward Gibbs 17
James Reason 27
Jacob Wilson 18
Ben: Strange 18
Ralph Vennable 21
Tho: Bloes 10
Tho: Hedley 11
Tho: Thomson 17
Hen: Stonword 13
Sam̄vell Hubbard 16
Thomas Bull 13
Danioll Hammond 12
Geo: Morgan 12
Jo: Barnes 16
Abraham Claxson 17
James Aston 22
Rich Daughton 13
Mathew Steevens 12
Tho: Larkyn 15

David Jones 15
George Hanmer 24
Roger Hodges 17
Wm Powell 15
Sampson Meverill 20
Henry Carter 42
Jo: Yates 48
Jo: Browne 16
Francis Raynne 10
Francis Hedges 13
Davie Morris 18
Tho: West 17
Hugh Wentworth 44
Ann Taylor 24
Elizabeth Groves 35
Jo: Groves 1 qr.
Blanch Roberts 20

2 MINISTERS.

Jo: Oxenbridge 24
Henry Jennings 24

Benjamin Miller 30
Henry Fletcher 35
Edward Staughton 50
Josias Forster 43
Tho: Hall 24
Humfrey Smith 14
Francis Watson 16
Katherin White 18
Elizabeth Clark 18
Ellen Burrowes 30

Jo: Page 33
Tho: Jennison 21
Sara Page 31
Sara Page 3
Mary Page 3 mo.
Richard Harris 17
Jeffery Wright 18
Samvell Mayo 10
Marie Goffe 18
Jo: Brookes 12

Secundo die Septembris 1635.

Theis under written names are to be transported to St. Christophers: imbarqued in the William and John—Rowland Langram Mr have been examined by the Minister of Gravesend and tooke the oaths of Alleg. and Suprem̄: die et A° p'

James Lampley	19	Robert Richardson	33	Ezechell Rennam	15
Wm Greene	18	Robert Leake	38	Tho: Harden	15
Henry Daniell	20	Barnabie Brooke	20	Edward Brunt	26
Rowland Davies	20	Jo: Cock	18	Tho: Reinolds	16
Wm Reddish	20	Nic° Cobb	24	Wm Benn	24
Edward Brownish	20	Jo: Hinson	21	Phillip Skorier	26
Robert Fitt	18	Tho: Ekkersoe	24	Wm Worrall	23
Richard Lewes	26	Geo: Carter	28	Jo: Banson	27
Richard Corie	18	Rich Harris	26	Henry Bugland	21
Richard Christie	20	Henrie Nokes	27	Jo: Morton	24
Jo: Brant	24	Tho: Thompson	28	Jo: Ditchfield	22
Wm Williams	21	Samvell Knipe	23	Nathaniell Simpkins	26
Christopher Steevenson	19	Jo: Watton	25	Wm Procter	26
Tho: Barnes	20	Jo: Byrall	29	Edward Gressam	17
Robert Watler	20	Morris Parry	30	Wm Steevens	21
Andrew Young	40	Jo: Nayler	20	Tho: Whithedd	24
Francis Hudson	36	Edward Nayler	21	Tho: Clark	25
Jo: Parr	19	Geo: Noble	22	Wm Stiffiliynn	16
Wm Morley	24	Wm Cocks	20	Jo: Bonn	18
Rich Gavyn	21	Martin Sowth	19	Wm Dunbarr	15
Tho: Phillipps	35	Wm Greenelefe	26	Jo: Morrish	18
Jo: Willard	16	Jo: Sawnders	17	Alexander Glover	37
Tho: Hanmer	14	Tho: Hames	16	Edward King	25
Wm Burnham	21	John Pinkley	30	Jo: Kent	23
Walter Wall	16	Robert Thomson	22	Robert Lynt	21
Wm Bathoe	18	Wm Davies	30	Edward Bellis	21
Tho: Tupper	21	Richard Beare	28	Tho: Gill	30
Wm Baylie	23	Geo: Ford	19	Wm Grove	32
Tho: Brookes	21	Tho: Lowyun	20	Richard Mason	29
Nathanill Bernard	22	Jo: Drake	18	Manley Richardson	21
Tho: Price	20	Robert Outmore	38	Isack Beet	23
Geo: Frie	19	Hugh Hilton	23	John Pickering	25
Tho: Hart	25	Tho: King	27	Tho: Archbold	19
Mathew Addison	17	Lawrence Adderford	26	Mathew Wells	28
Theobald Wall	18	James Dockkie	17		

Tricessimo die Septembris 1635.

Aboard the Dorsst John Flower Mr bound for ye Bormodes.

John Redford	16	Jo: Mathews	16	Wm Thomas	17
Robert Ramsey	15	Robert Vardell	20	Rich Bunting	17
John Williams	16	Jo: Heth	21	Tho: Stokes	30
Willm Elliston	13	Nathaniell Bonnick	16	Wm Rosden	16
Lubas Wright	16	Jo: Denman	14	Nathaniell West	15
Humfrey Holt	18	Tho: More	18	Jo: Donn	14
Tho: Joyner	16	Wm Bruister	17	Edward Edwynn	15
Rich Tregagell	18	George Hubbard	16	Jo: Sell	15
Jo: Loe	18	Edw: Middleton	15	Tho: Ireland	10
Josua Woodcock	11	Francis Russell	23	Edward Davies	17
Robert Fisher	10	James Rising	18	Edward Simpson	13
Tho Sharp	17	Geo: Absolon	16	Edward Aldin	17
Jo: Rowland	21	Jo: Mosdell	24	Tho: Atkins	16
Wm Wheeler	22	Wm Stocker	19	Tho: Riley	16
Wm Pennington	18	Edward Morris	18	Wm Barnes	15

Jo: Day	16	Geo. Palmer	27	Sampson Lort	30
Wm Barrith	16	Wm Simpson	17	Jo: Miller	47
Jo: Tustin	16	Edward Simpson	13	John Johnson	23
Jo: Necklin	17	Edward Grubthorn	14	Richard Jennings	35
Jo: Harkwood	20	Jonas Goldenham	16	Uxor Sara Jennings	18
Humfrey Kemp	16	Judith Bagley	58	Richard Palmer	30
David Thomas	26	John Glassenden	14	Uxor Ellis Palmer	21
Willm Alburie	15	Wm Harding	30	Tho: Griffin	32
Arthur Thorne	33	Uxor Sarah Harding	30	Ann Griffin	35
Wm Cheeseman	20	Henry Rosse	31	Robert Ridley	23
John Mitchell	20	Tymothie Pynder	26	Elizabeth Ridley,	30
John Casson	18	Margaret Pynder	41	Edward Chaplin	20
Alexandor Brabant	30	Jane Dart	17	Wm Casse	19
Henry Fulcock	15	Geo: Tuck	40	Peternell Nowell	46
Jo: Mansfield	19	Ezia Vyncent	30	Christian Wellman	43
Willm Craft	15	Uxor Mathew	30	Eliz: Aldworth	15
Richard Haldin	14	Minister Daniell Wite	30		

2° die Octobris 1635.

Aboard the John of London James Waymoth M^r bound to St Christophers.

John Batcheller	26	Willm̄ Richardson	24	Jo: Sherlock	20
Samvell Parker	19	Edward Mekins	18	Tho: Frost	28
Tho: James	25	Jo: Clymer	30	Lewes Evans	25
Chri. Thomson	21	Richard Evans	21	Jo: Thomson	19
Alexandor Fleetwood	19	Henrie Feeld	25	Richard Townsend	19
Walter Lee	21	Henrie Radford	20	Mary Goodwin	18
Edward Dodson	21	Jo: Henman	19	Jane Goodwyn	20
Gilbert Clark	19	Tho: Walker	19	Martha Lilliot	20
Geo: Hoelis	19	Jo: Mulleneux	24	Elizabeth Murrin	21
Richard Elmes	21	Oswell Metcalf	22	Joan Hill	21
Richard Smith	22	Edward Cooke	22	Elizabeth Freeman	18

13° die Octobris 1635.

Aboard the Amitie George Downes M^r bound to St Christoph^rs.

Isack Drake	25	Tho: Pitts	24	Tho: Molton	20
Richard Ivoson	24	Jo: Thomson	25	David Owen	26
Robert Barne	33	Richard Webster	24	Henrie Rowles	22
Tho: Hernden	23	Lewes Jones	20	Nic° Alford	28
Edward Farr	28	John Coombes	26	Samvell Sakell	23
Wm Burrowe	19	George Coop'	20	Robert Jones	30
Tho: Brewyun	24	Mathew Preston	22	Jo: Browne	33
Marmaduke Borne	21	John Pynkston	27	Peter Salmon	20
Willm Creswell	22	Wm Geies	18	Jo: Saunderson	23
Henrie Hodgskynns	19	Willm̄ Vbank	20	Robert Rolfe	23
Robert Payne	21	Charles Parker	18	John Jack	27
George Hatrell	32	James Leachman	22	Tho: Yott	24
Jo: Hippsley	19	Wm Cartwrite	18	John Teirrer	24
Willm̄ Stanley	22	Richard West-Garrett	20	John Farmer	24
John Snape	22	Wm Harris	16	Wm Daughten	20
Isack Buck	33	Jer: Nicholls	16	Rich^h Skynner	20
Walter Ellitt	20	Tho: Rodes	20	Wm Egerton	20
Aymies Halfyard	19	Jo: Boughei	21	James Makyn	20
Oliver Johnes	25	Edward Grindall	21	Wm Harris	20
John Smith	23	Jo: Vaughan	23	Bastian Petite	23
Hamblet Sankey	22	Jo: Goddin	20	John Warren	20
Edward Porter	21	Richard Larkyn	32	Rich^h Phinnei	30
Tho. Galley	20	Richard Bodman	23	James Briggs	25

John Musick	19
Jo: Griddick	16
Wm Davies	40
Robt Heath	30
Tho: Baggelay	24
William Yateman	25
Richard Grind	11
Wm Galler	20
Robert Downe	35
John Hye	36
Edward Webb	17
James Johnson	28
John Avery	22
Daniell Cannelly	20
Rice Poke	30
Roger James	29
James Curtis	18
Clement Haines	22
John Fynn	22
Wm Goff	30
Andrew White	11
John Billinghurst	24
Morrice Davie	24
Wm Rule	20
Mary Wynd	18
Margaret Coles	21
Marie Merriton	21
Kat: Brewett	16
Ellen Channce	21
Ann Palmer	29
Alice Barker	3C
Patient White	44
Isack and Jacob } Twynns	2
Judith Lloyd	18
Marie Maxwell	21

---

20 Novembris 1635.

Theis under written names are to be transported to the Barbadoes, imbarqued in the Expedition, Peter Blackler Mr. The Men have taken the oaths of Allegeance and Supremacie. And have been examined by the minister of the Towne of Gravesend touching their Conformitie to the ordrs and discipline of the Church of England die et Ao prd.

Ministr Nicholas Bloxä als Jagles	yeres 31
Abram Holland	19
Thomas Hudson	16
Blackwell Lawrence	16
Leonard Briggins	17
Thomas Clark	27
Morgan Jenkins	32
Rich Pratt	18
Tho: Freeman	19
Willm Greefeson	26
Richard Wartumbee	21
Henry Bryan	21
Hugh Dawson	18
Mathew Beads	19
Charles Lambert	23
Jo: Lake	18
Jo: Smith	18
Anthony Hutchins	32
Willm Gibson	19
Jo: Williams	17
William Steward	21
John Pierce	18
Hugh Evans	18
Brian Aston	21
Nicholas Collon	19
Henry Field	24
Richard Smith	20
John Knowles	27
John Dickenson	24
John Mann	21
Tho: Peacock	17
Edward Steevens	53
Thomas Weekes	23
Hugh Cheswood	21
Jo: Coert	21
John Pike	30
George Blacklock	32
John Coleman	40
Wm Watts	28
John Bonner	18
Willm Snignell	18
Tho: Hobin	20
Francis Barnit	23
Willm̄ Buckley	26
John Clark	16
Phillipp Morlin	21
Henry Rawlins	25
Jo: Rudge	42
Edward Evans	22
John Hownsefield	20
Tho: Davie	20
Henry Gowde	19
Wm Mellison	25
John York	26
Wm Carpenter	19
John Wynter	23
Jo: Waller	17
John Sum̄es	20
John Heron	20
Willm Tayler	26
John Parlin	21
Wm Jackson	33
John Medgley	21
Wm Wreuch	21
Robert Hurt	19
James Farebank	26
Henrie Berrisford	32
James Nettleton	22
Thomas Armitage	24
Francis Mann	19
John Felkynn	20
John Jones	20
Richard Lightbound	22
Christopher Hartlie	19
Tho: Wood	23
Henrie Godfrie	36
Tho: Palmer	19
Jo: Humfrey	20
John Smith	22
Ambrose Greene	23
Jo: Hilliard	18
Jo: Browne	26
Willm Warr	19
Mathew Wilkinson	18
Mathew Gibbons	20
Wm Audley	18
James Kingston	22
Rich Smart	20
Wm Walters	26
Tho: Davies	23
Nathaniell Nordin	46
Wm Pitt	25
Jo: Chater	17
Jo: Chapman	24
Geo: Sterry	24
Abram Cheynei	22
Jo: Sturton	18
Jo: Edens	19
Lawrence Brock	18
Rich Best	18
Robert Hobbs	26
Peter Jones	30
Wm Topleife	18
Jo: Robinson	19
Morrice Jones	21
Henry Stint	18
Josias Weston	25
Francis Birkenhedd	24
Edward Jones	29
Ellis Williams	18
Wm Tayler	40
Tho: Burnham	18
Joseph Boyce	24

Jo: Rainescroft	23	Nic° Brogan	28	Launcelott Bromley	44
Henrie Bostock	19	Ant° Smith	18	Peter Spencer	15
Jefferie Shipp	24	John Spenceley	24	Thomas Phipps	15
Wm Brooke	26	Mathew Shore	46	Davie Thomas	20
Lanncelott Lacon	32	Thomas St Parlin	19	Willm̄ Greene	23
Wm Plomer	23	Dorothy Symonds	40	Jo: Watts	20
Wm Sheicrofte	17	Mary Lupton	30	Wm Lock	21
Wm Coke	18	Rich Horne	22	George Leas	20
Jo: Jennings	18	John Newton	29	John Spencer	19
Tho: Ossebrooke	27	Thomas Cowdell	17	Henry Antony	19
Jo: Davenport	30	Richard Gibson	25	James Fassitt	34
Geo: Burton	23	Nicholas Nevell	19	Henry Ellotts	23
Wm Morgan	20	George Tayler	20	Henry Coke	28
Davie Thomas	20	Wm Goad	21	Richard Dence	25
Rich Hannis	21	Wm Marritt	26	Wm Cosson	20
Peter Croningburk	20	Roger Eritage	22	Wm Thomson	20
Jo: Hall	29	Davie Dodderidge	20	Thomas Usherwood	28
Jo: Compton	26	George Fullwood	19	Wm Haning	30
Clement Backford	30	Rich Hamis	21	John Goad	22
Robert Browne	18	Ralph Webster	20	Richard Moncaster	32
John Key	32	Tho: Robinson	15	John Chesting	21
Howell Pryce	25	Joseph Thomlinson	26	Roger Sanford	35
Edward Aston	32	Baltazar Dederix	26	Wm Cornwell	20
Robt Edwards	38	James Smith	24	Wm Gosselin	21
Richard Ash	24	Nic° Flutter	27	Jo: Coop'	21
John Medley	26	Nic° Whithedd	24	Wm Price	22
Thomas King	24	Wm Hinkynn	26	Sam: Skynner	22
Richard Snowe	28	Thomas Gilbert	20	Robt. Dunstarr	34
Robert Filborne	18	Richard Seabright	21	Richard Buck	24
Pierce Morgan	23	Robert Greenewood	18	Nic° Lynton	22
Jo: Williams	17	Anthony Ashmore	33		

19 Dec: 1635.

Theis under-written names are to be transported to the Barbadoes imbarqued in the Falcon Tho: Irish Mr the Men have been examined by the Minister of the Towne of Grauesend touching their conformitie to the Church discipline of England: And also haue taken the Oaths of Alleg': and Suprem̄ die et A° prd

Arnold Ownstedd yeres	30	James Spencer	25	Jo: Burkett	21
Tho: Skyddell	28	Jo: Chubnell	21	Tho: Harrwell	29
Ant° Cadwold	23	Wm Gunter	22	Gregorie Booth	18
Phillipp Miller	21	Jo: Thurrogood	20	Edward Howe	19
Maximillian Prichard	20	Tho: Greene	16	Robt Clarke	18
Tho: Tisfin	28	Richard Richardson	36	Francis Martin	18
Jo: Butler	21	Robecca Burgis	17	Tho: Webb	22
Phines Trusedell	10	Richard Panke	19	Jo: Scott	42
Bryan Cowley	30	Leonard Robinson	20	Tho: Evans	20
Jo: Mason	19	Francis Buck	20	Wm Phillips	28
Robert Harris	42	John Hogg	21	James Cotesworth	21
Abram Shawe	20	Robert Symper	20	Ellinn Robb	27
Geo: Sabyn	21	Tho: Page	20	filia Elizabeth Robb	7
Wm Cartwrite	23	Dennis Britten	20	Tho: Clark	27
Nathan Murfitt	23	Jo: Rogers	18		
Jo: Barnett	20	James Wolton	22		

25 decembris 1635.

Theis under-written names passed in a Catch to the Downes ; and were put aboard the aforesaid shipp.

Tho: Davies	17	Griffinn Evans	40	Wm Coñisby	31
Henry Benson	19	James Terrill	20	Robert Tissall	30
Jo: Welsh	35	Elizabeth Cossen	25	Tristram Ford	21
Henry Southward	20	Jane Hickles	25	Elias Carpenter	20
Rich^{h} Newbolt	28	Henry Van Luccom	24	Richard Hames	18
Lawrence Keysie	28	Jo: King	30	Thomas Streter	21
James Robinson	15	Wm Flatter	18	James Lee	28
Ant^{o} Pope	28	Jo: Weston	27		
Jo: Lee	30	Tho: Clark	28		

---

29 August 1635.

William Norton xxv yeres old is to transport himself to New England and to imbarque himself in the Hopewell p' cert: from the Minister of his conformitie to the Church discipline of England: he hath taken the oaths of Allegeance and Suprem̄ die et An^{o} pr^{d}.

IIIIth Septr 1635.

Robert Edwards 27 yers who is to passe to Virginia hath taken the oath of Allegeance

Thomas Turner of age xlij yeres to passe to New England imbarqued in the hopewell hath brought Certificate of his Conformitie and tooke the oaths of Allegeance and Supremacie.

Viij^{o} die Sep.

A Turner Robert Pennaird of age 21 yeres and Tho. Pennaird x yeres old are to [be] imbarqued in Mr Babb bound to New England haue brought Certificates from Doctor Denison of his conformitie. he hath taken the oaths of Allege^{e} and Suprem

---

[On the fly leaf.]

Edward Towers 24 M^{r}chants Hope de Lo: Robt Page M^{r} for Virginia, to enter in the

---

21 July

Jane Gibbs of age 25 yeeres resident in Virginea to passe to Flushing about certen her affares

PASSENGERS OF THE MARY AND JOHN, 1634.

S. G. DRAKE, Esq. *Boston, May 31st,* 1855.

Dear Sir:—I communicate to you the following highly interesting documents for the Register, received through Mr. Cleveland of Salem. They will supply a gap, long bewailed, in the early history of Newbury, by giving us the name of the vessel, in which her first settlers came to this country, in 1634. The list of passengers by the "Mary and John," comprises many well-known names of residents of Newbury and its vicinity, and which also are well known to have been borne by the original planters of that ancient settlement. It will be seen by the Order in Council, that the emigrants were at first "made staye of, untill further order from their Lordshipps;" who eventually let them go, upon certain conditions, some of which seemed harder to them, perhaps, than they would be now considered. I understand the certificate of Mr. Whitehouse, at the end, to include the whole,—the Order in Council, the interesting abstract of the charter of Charles I, and the list of passengers.

The name of the master of the "Mary and John," is not very clear in my copy. It might be *Swyers* or *Savyres,*—and this latter might be a corrupt way of spelling the French name *Savory* or *Savary.* This is rendered less likely, however, by the fact, that this name is found in the list of passengers, spelled in a manner not departing very far from the modern mode. Although a matter of no consequence, the great point being the name of the vessel and her passenger-list, it has seemed to me most likely that *Sayres* was right, and misunderstood by some copyist, employed upon the documents. Especially, I am inclined to this opinion, since there occur evident mistakes in one or two other names; amongst these, *Hibbens* is converted into *Fribbens,* the first being the name of one of our "Assistants," and whose widow, as I regret to learn, by a note from one of our most eminent and excellent citizens and antiquarians, "was hanged for having more wit than benignity."

Respectfully, your obedient servant, G. L.

[The extracts from the Records of the Orders in Council which follow, are similar to a portion of the same, printed in the last volume (p. 135, &c.,) but as there are variations, it was thought proper to print them here, especially as they are necessary for the proper understanding of the circumstances of the emigrants.—EDITOR.]

New England—At Whitehall the last of February 1633. *Present.*

Lop. Arch Bp. of Cant—	Lo. Cottington
Lo. Keep^{r}	Mr V. Chamb^{r}line
Lo. Privie Seal	Mr Compt^{r}
Lo. high Chamb^{r}line	Mr Secretary Wyndibank
Earle of Kelly	

Whereas by a Warr^{t} bearing date 22nd of this Present the sev^{r}all ships following bound for New England & now lying in the River of Thames were made staye of untill further order from their L'opps Viz^{t}. the Clement & Job, The Reformation, The True Love, The Elizabeth Bonadventure, The Sea Flower, The Mary & John, The Planter, The Elizabeth & Dorcas, The Hercules & the Neptune.

For as much as the Masters of the said ships were this day called before the Board & several Particulars given them in charge to be performed in their said Voyage, amongst which the said Masters were to enter into several Bonds of One Hundred Pounds a piece to His Maj^{s}tys use before the Clarke of the Councell attendant to observe & cause to be observed & putt in Execuc'on these Articles following vizt.

1. That all & every Person aboard their Ships now bound for New England as aforesaid, that shall blaspheme or profane the Holy name of God be severely punish't.

2. That they cause the Prayers contained in the Book of Common Prayers establisht in the Church of England to be said daily at the usual hours for Morning & Evening Prayers & that they cause all Persons aboard their said Ships to be present at the same.

3. That they do not receive aboard or transport any Person that hath not Certificate from the Officers of the Port where he is to imbarke that he hath taken both the Oathes of Alleigeance & Supremacy.

4. That upon their return into this Kingdom they Certify to the Board the names of all such Persons as they shall transport together with their Proceedings in the Execuc'on of the aforesaid Articles—Whereunto the said M^rs^ have conformed themselves—It was therefore & for diverse other Reasons best known to their Lo^pp^s thought fitt that for this time they should be permitted to proceed on their Voyage, and it was thereupon Ordered that Gabriel Marsh Esqr. Marshalle of the Admiralty & all other His Maj'tys Officers to whom their said Warr^t^ was directed should be required upon Sight hereof to discharge all & every the said Ships & Suffer them to depart on their intended Voyage to New England.

Ex^t^. Jon Meantys.

An Abstract of His Maty's Charter for incorporating the Company of the Mattachusetts Bay in New England in America, Granted in the 4th yeare of His Highness' Reign of England, Scotland, France & Ireland, Anno. Domini, 1628—

And we do further of our especial Grace, certain Knowledge & mere mocion for us our Heirs & Successors—Give & Grant to the said Governour & Company & their Successors for ever by these presents, That it shall be lawfull & free for them & their Assigns at all & every Time & Times hereafter out of any of our Realms or Dominions whatsoev^r^, to take lade carry & transport for in & into their voyages, & for & towards the said Plantation in New England all such & so many of our Loving Subjects or any other strangers that will become our Loving Subjects & live under our Alleigeance as shall willingly accompany them in the said Voyages & Plantations, And also Shipping, Armour, Weapons, Ordnance, Powder, Shott, Corn, Victuals & all manner of Cloathing, Implements, Furniture, Beasts, Cattle, Horses, Mares, Merchandizes & all other things necessary for the said Plantation & for their use & Defence & for Trade with the People there & in passing & returning to & fro, any Law or Statute to the Contrary thereof in any wise notwithstanding—And without paying or yielding any Custom or Subsidy either Inwards or Outwards, to us our Heirs or Successors for the same, by the Space of Seaven years from the Day of the Date of these Presents—Provided that none of the said Persons be such as shall hereafter by Especial name be restrained by us our Heirs or Successors—

And for their further Incouragem^t^ of our Especial Grace & favor—We Do by these presents for us, our Heirs & Successors yield & grant to the said governour & Company & their Successors & every of them their Factors & Assignes that they & every of them shall be free & quit from all Taxes Subsidys & Customs in New England for the space of Seaven years, and from all Taxes & Impositions for the space of Twenty-one years upon all Goods & Merchandizes at any time or times hereafter Either upon Importation there, or Exportation thence, into our Realm of England or into any of our Dominions, by the said Governour or Company & their Successors, their Deputys, Factors & Assigns or any of them except only the Five Pounds p^r^ Centum due for Custom upon all such

Goods & Merchandizes as after the said seaven years shall be expired, shall be brought or imported into our Realm of England or any other of our Dominions according to the Ancient Trade of Merchants, which Five Pounds pr centum only being paid it shall be thenceforth lawfull & free for the sd Adventurers the same Goods & Merchandizes to export & carry out of our Dominions into Foreign Parts without any Custom, Tax or other Duty to be paid to us our Heirs or Successors or to any other Officer or Officers or Ministers of us, our Heirs or Successors,—

Provided that the said Goods & merchandize be shipp'd out within thirteen months after their first Landing within any part of the said Dominions—

This is a true Copy of His Maties Letters Patent aforesaid—Custom House London 30th Janury 1633

Anno. R. Caroli Nono—

John Wolstenholme
Collector.

The names of such Passengers as took the Oathes of Supremacy, & Alleigeance to pass for New England in tho Mary & John of London Robert Sayres master.

24th Mar 1633
William Trace
John Marshe
John Luff
Henry Traske
William Moudey
Robert Sever
Thomas Avery
Henry Travers
Thomas Sweete
John Woodbridge
Thomas West
Thomas Savery
Christopher Osgood
Phillip Fowler
Richard Jacob
Daniel Ladd
Robert Kingsman
John Bartlett
Robert Coker
William Savery
John Anthony, Left behind
Stephen Jurden
John Godfrey
George Browne
Nicholas Noyce
Richard Browne
Richard Reynolds
Richard Littlehall
William White
Matthew Hewlett *Her-*
John Whelyer [*cules*
William Clarke
Robert Neuman
Adrian Vincent

The 26th day of March.
Nicholas Easton
Richard Kent
Abraham Mussey
William Ballard
Matthew Gillett
William Franklin
John Mussey
Thomas Cole
Thomas Parker
James Noyce
John Spencer
William Spencer
Henry Shorte
William Hibbens
Richard Kent
Joseph Myles
John Newman
William Newbey
Henry Lunt
Joseph Pope
Thomas Newman
John Newman

For which we gave certificate, together, with five others whch are said to be left behind to oversee the Chattle to pass in the Hercules vizt.

The names of the Passengers in the Hercules of London, John Kiddey Mar: for New England—

These six Passengers took their Oathes of Supremacy & Alleigeance the 24th of March and were left behind the Mary & John as intended to pass in ye Hercules—Vizt.

John Anthoney
Robert Early
William Latcome
Thomas Foster
William Foster
Matthew Hewlett

} Cert. the six first to Mt'er Sayers as intended Secondh to Mr Kiddey to pass in the Hercules—

16th April 1634—Nathaniel Davyes
George Kinge
Thomas Rider
William Elliott
William Fifeilde
18 Henry Phelps—

These Proceedings were Copyed out of an Olde Book of Orders belonging to the Port of South'ton but now remaining at the Custom house in Portsmouth the 6th Day of December 1735—

pr Thomas Whitehouse.

MORE PASSENGERS FOR NEW-ENGLAND.

[Communicated by WILLIAM S. APPLETON, A.M., of Boston, Mass.]

The following has just been received from our associate member.

MY DEAR MR. APPLETON, *London, Sept.* 1870.

Amongst a bundle of miscellaneous manuscripts just turned up in the Public Record Office, I find, with other documents relating to New-England, the following list of passengers, which I have the pleasure of sending to you for publication in the Register. I remain, Yours very truly,

H. G. SOMERBY.

Bound for New England.

Waymouth
ye 20th of
March 1635.

1 Joseph Hall* of Somerss^t a Minist aged 40 yeare
2 Agnis hall his Wife aged 25 y^re
3 Joane Hall his daught^r aged 15 yeare
4 Joseph Hall his sonne aged 13 yeare
5 Tristram his son aged 11 yeare
6 Elizabeth Hall his daught^r aged 7 yeare
7 Temperance his daught^r aged 9 yeare
8 Grissell Hull his daught^r aged 5 yeare
9 Dorothy Hull his daught^r aged 3 yeare
10 Judeth French his srvaunt aged 20 yeare
11 John Wood his srvaunt aged 20 yeare
12 Robt Dabyn his srvaunt aged 28 yeare
13 Musachiell Bernard of batcombe Clothier in the County of Somersett 24 yeare
14 Mary Bernard his wife aged 28 yeare
15 John Bernard his sonne aged 3 yeare
16 Nathaniell his sonne aged 1 yeare
17 Rich: Persons salter & his srvant : 30 : yeare
18 Francis Baber Chandler aged 36 yeare
19 Jesope Joyner aged 22 yeare
20 Walter Jesop Weaver aged 21 yeare
21 Timothy Tabor in Som̄ss^t of Batcombe taylor aged 35 yeares
22 Jane Tabor his Wife aged 35 yeare
23 Jane Tabor his daugh^tr aged 10 yeare
24 Anne Tabor his daught^r aged 8 yeare
25 Sarah Tabor his daught^r aged 5 yeare
26 Willm̄ Fever his srvaunt aged 20 yeare
27 Jno. Whitmarsk aged 39 yeare
28 Alce Whitmarke his Wife aged 35 yeare
29 Jm^s. Whitmarcke his sonne aged 11 yeare
30 Jane his daught^r aged 7 yeare
31 Onseph Whitmarke his sonne aged 5 yeare
32 Rich: Whytemark his sonne aged 2 yeare

* The name should be Hull, as corrected in the case of the youngest two children. Rev. Joseph Hull was of Yarmouth, Mass., where his son Tristram left descendants.

33 Willm̄ Read of Batcombe Taylor in Som̄ss^{tt} aged 28 yeare
34
35 Susan Read his Wife aged 29 yeare
36 Hanna Read his daugh^{tr} aged 3 yeare
37 Susan Read his daught^{r} aged 1 yeare
38 Rich: Adams his srvante 29 yeare
39 Mary his Wife aged 26 yeare
40 Mary Cheame his daught^{r} aged 1 yeare
41 Zachary Bickewell aged 45 yeare
42 Agnis Bickwell his Wife aged 27 yeare
43 Jno Bickwell his sonne aged 11 yeare
44 Jno Kitchin his servaunt 23 yeare
46 George Allin aged 24 yeare
47 Katherin Allyn his Wife aged 30 yeare
48 George Allyn his sonne aged 16 yeare
49 Willm̄ Allyn his sonne aged 8 yeare
50 Mathew Allyn his sonne aged 6 yeare
51 Edward Poole his srvant aged 26 yeare
52 Henry Kingman aged 40 yeares
53 Joane his wife beinge aged 39
54 Edward Kingman his son aged 16 yeare
55 Joane his daught^{r} aged 11 yeare
56 Anne his daught^{r} aged 9 yeare
57 Thomas Kingman his sonne aged 7 yeare
58 John Kinghman his sonne aged 2 yeare
59 J^{n} Ford his servaunt aged 30 yeare
60 William Kinge aged 40 yeare
61 Dorothy his Wife aged 34 yeare
62 Mary Kinge his daught^{r} aged 12 yeare
63 Katheryn his daught^{r} aged 10 yeare
64 Willm̄ Kinge his sonne aged 8 yeare
65 Hanna Kinge his daught^{r} aged 6 yeare
66 Thomas Holbrooke of Broudway aged 34 yeare
67 Jane Holbrooke his wife aged 34 yeare
68 John Holbrooke his sonne aged 11 yeare
69 Thomas Holbrooke his sonne aged 10 yeare
70 Anne Holbrooke his daught^{r} aged 5 yeare
71 Elizabeth his daught^{r} aged 1 yeare
72 Thomas Dible husbandm̄ aged 22 yeare
73 Francis Dible Soror aged 24 yeare
74 Robert Lovell husbandman aged 40 yeare
75 Elizabeth Lovell his wife aged 35 year
76 Zacheus Lovell his sonne 15 yeares
78 Anne Lovell his daught^{r} aged 16 yeare
79 John Lovell his sonne aged 8 yeare
Ellyn his daught^{r} aged 1 yeare
80 James his sonne aged 1 yeare
81 Joseph Chickin his servant 16 yeare
82 Alice Kinham aged 22 yeare
83 Angell Hollard aged 21 yeare
84 Katheryn his Wife 22 yeare
85 George Land his servaunt 22 yeare
86 Sarah Land his Kinswoman 18 yeare

87 Richard Joanes of Dinder
88 Robt Martyn of Badcombe husbandm̄ 44
89 Humfrey Shepheard husbandm̄ 32
90 John Upham husbandman 35
91 Joane Martyn 44
92 Elizabeth Upham 32
93 John Upham Jun 07
94 William Grane 12
95 Sarah Upham 26
96 Nathaniell Upham 05
97 Elizabeth Upham 03
98 Dorss[t] Richard Wade of Simstuly Cop̄ aged 60
99 Elizabeth Wade his Wife 6
100 Dinah his daugh[r] 22
101 Henry Lush his srvant aged 17
102 Andrew Hallett his srvaunt 28
103 John hoble husbandm̄ 13
104 Robt Huste husbandm̄ 40
105 John Woodcooke 2
106 Rich: Porter husband 3

John Porter Deputy
Cleark to Edw:
Thoroughgood.

PASSENGERS FOR VIRGINIA, 1635.

Our valuable correspondent is at his post in London. The readers of the Register will remember that we gave notice on the cover of the last number, that H. G. Somerby, Esq., sailed for England on the 8th of October last, upon Genealogical and Antiquarian researches. We have received from him the extensive list of "Passengers for Virginia," which forms the substance of this article.

It was said of Dr. Johnson, by Boswell, that "he was born to grapple with whole libraries." By this, the extraordinary biographer undoubtedly meant no more than a library or two of *printed books.* Had he meant libraries of *manuscripts*, he would indeed have been thought extravagant, though speaking of an acknowledged Hercules in such matters. But our correspondent, though laying no claim to be a Hercules, yet, from the extract we here give from his letter, it will be seen, that he has already begun "to grapple" with *whole libraries of manuscripts.*

London, 18 Nov., 1847.

DEAR SIR, —

I arrived in London after a pleasant passage of twenty-four days, and immediately commenced with the manuscripts relating to pedigrees, &c., of which there are some two hundred folio volumes. After going through with these, I shall take up the county histories, &c., &c.

All the Heraldic Visitations I shall examine thoroughly. I have already been through with two counties, and made copious extracts. I have *passed* several American names, as I shall have sufficient to do for those who make it worth my while.

I send you an extract, which I have been permitted to copy from the original record in custody of the Master of the Rolls. This is the same record from which Mr. Savage made his valuable extracts of the New England Passengers. There are several other ship-loads for Virginia, Bermuda, St. Domingo, &c., some of which I shall extract and forward for the Register, as I find leisure.

On the cover of the Record is the following: "A register of the names of all ye passingers wch passed from ye porte of London for on whole yeare endinge at X^mas.^ 1635."

On the first page — "Post festum Natalis
Christi 1634 usque
ad festum Na: Christi
1635."

Then follows a list of those who went to St. Domingo, after which,

'These under written are to be transported to Virginca imbarqued in ye Merch^t^ bonaventure James Ricrofte M^r^ bound thither have taken ye oath of allegeance.'

You will perceive an apparent repetition of the name of Richard Champion. I can only say it is so in the original.

Although the passengers here given, went to Virginia, their names are not the less important to the student in New England History, for it is well known that great numbers came to New England from thence. And we feel assured, that by this and such lists, many points in family history will eventually be settled.

	Yeares.		Yeares.
Willm. Sayer,	58	Andrew Jefferies,	24
Bazill Brooke,	20	Wm. Munday,	22
Robert Perry,	40	Arthur Howell,	20
Charles Hilliard,	22	Jo: Abby,	22
Edward Clark,	30	James Moyser,	28
Jo: Ogell,	28	Mathew Marshall,	30
Richard Hargrave,	20	Wm. Smith,	20
Jo: Anderson,	20	Garrett Riley,	24
Francis Spence,	23	Miles Riley,	20
John Lewes,	23	Willm. Burch,	19
Richard Hughes,	19	Peter Dole,	20
John Clark,	19	James Metcalf,	22
Wm. Guy,	18	Jo: Underwood,	23
John Burd,	18	Robert Luck,	25
James Redding,	19	John Wood,	26
Richard Cooper,	18	Walter Morgan,	23

Henrie Irish,	16
George Greene,	20
Henry Quinton,	20
Jo: Bryan,	25
Robert Payton,	25
Tho: Symonds,	27
Michell Browne,	35
Jo: Hodges,	37
Jo: Edmonds,	16
Garrett Pownder,	19
Jo: Wise,	28
Henry Dunnell,	23
Symon Kenneday,	20
Tho: Hyet,	22
Tho: James,	20
Jo: Sotterfoyth,	24
Emanuell Bomer,	18
Leonard Wetherfield,	17
James Luckburrowe,	20
Tho: Singer,	18
Jesper Withy,	21
Robert Kersley,	22
Jo: Springall,	18
Tho: Jessupp,	18
James Perkyns,	42
Daniell Greene,	24
Wm. Hutton,	24
Jo: Wilkinson,	19
Hugh Garland,	20
Richard Spencer,	18
Humfrey Topsall,	24
Tho: Stanton,	20
Jo: Watson,	28
Tho: Murfie,	20
John Fountaine.	18
Henry Redding,	22
Loughton Bostock,	16
John Russell,	19
Tho: Ridgley,	23
Robert Harris,	19
Willm. Mason,	19
Victor Derrick,	23
John Bamford,	28
Geo: Session,	40
Jo: Cooke,	47
Tho: Townson,	26
Tho: Parson,	30
Tho: Goodman,	25
Phillip Conner,	21
Launcelot Pryce,	21
Uxor Thomazin,	18
Kat: Yates,	19
Alveryn Cowper,	20
Jo: Dunn,	26
Leonard Evans,	22
Tho: Anderson,	28
Edward Cranfield,	18
Jo: Baggley,	14
Tho: Smith,	14
Willm. Weston,	30
Tho: Townsend,	14
Edward Davies,	25
Mary Saunders,	26
Jane Chambers,	23
Margarett Maddocks,	21
Roger Sturdevant,	21
John Wigg,	24
John Greenwood,	16
Andrew Dunton,	38
John Wise,	30
Wm. Hudson,	32
Tho: Edenburrow,	37
John Hill,	50
Henry Rogers,	30
Robert Smithson,	23
Nics. Harvy,	30
James Grafton,	22
Daniell Daniell,	18
Reginell Hawes,	25
Geo: Burlington,	20
Jo: Hutchinson,	22
James Grane,	17
Richard Hurman,	20
Sam: Ashley,	19
Geo: Burlingham,	20
Elizabeth Jackson,	17
Sara Turner,	20
Mary Ashley,	24
Margerie Furbredd,	20
Margaret Huntley,	20
Richard Doll,	25
Tho: Perry,	34
Uxor Dorothy,	26
Ben: Perry,	4
Mary Carlton,	23
Abram Silvester,	40
Tho: Bolton,	18
Richard Champion,	19
Richard Champion,	19
Abram Silvester,	14
Elizabeth Nunisk,	20
Jo: Atkinson,	30
Rich: Hore,	24
Ralph Nicholson,	20
Robert More,	29
Joan Nubold,	20
Tho: Hebden,	20

PASSENGERS FOR VIRGINIA.

We are again enabled to lay before our readers a list of early emigrants to Virginia. It has just been received from our correspondent in London, H. G. Somerby, Esq., but of the precise locality of the original record, he does not advise us. It is probably from the same source as that we gave in the last No. of the Register; (pages 112 and 113,) namely, the records "in the custody of the Master of the Rolls."

These passengers, though they shipped to go to Virginia, it is quite probable that many intended to come to New England. It might have been difficult for some of them to have obtained permission to come here, while no objection might be made to their going to Virginia. Were we to enter into an examination of the list we doubt not we could show pretty conclusively that a large number of the persons named in it were not long after found in New England. At present we can only draw attention to the following names:—*Arthur Peach* was here in 1637, and in the war against the Pequots. And though he turned out to be a wretch, committed murder and was executed in 1638, Winthrop says he was "a *young* man of a good family." There was a *Thomas Arnold* at Watertown, 1640. *John Northy*, Marblehead, 1648; *Thomas Hall*, Cambridge, 1648. *Thomas Bulkely*, Concord, 1638; Rowley, 1643. This is a mere glance at a few of the names, and we do not pretend that they are the same individuals as those represented on our list. Some we think are, and others may prove to be so. — Ed.

15th May 1635. These under written names are to Virginea: imbarqued in the Plaine Joan, Richard Buckam Mr the pties having brought attestation of their conformitie to the orders & disipline of the church of England.

	Yeares.		Yeares.
Robert Briers,	21	Robert Hutt,	14
Jno. Johnson,	20	Jo: Raddish,	23
Robert Coke,	25	Tho: Bulkley,	32
Jo: Alsopp,	50	Robert Brooke,	33
Wm Piggott,	50	Richard Downes,	34
Wm Toplyf,	30	Arthur Peach,	20
Tho: Arnold,	30	Wm James,	26
Wm Paulson,	33	Tym Blackett,	40
Jo: Northin,	22	Roger Koorbe,	25
Tho: Turner,	21	Ann Perks,	27
Jo: Beddell,	22	Tho: Britton,	26
Jo: Barrowe,	26	Wm Collins,	34
Jo: Trent,	27	Jo: Resburne,	30
Jo: Coker,	21	Henry Jackson,	24
Henrie Donoldson,	25	Charles McCartie,	27
Wm Lavor,	22	Owen McCartie,	18
Chri: Davies,	22	Charles Flane,	18
Chri: Taylor,	25	Richard Lawrence,	20
Daniell Clark,	33	Tho: Godbitt,	20
Richard Day,	32	Nico Kent,	16
Robert Lewis,	23	Thomas Newman,	15
Luke Bland,	20	Peter Sudburrowe,	20
Jo: Warren,	27	Tho: Lloyd,	20
James Ward,	18	Wm Hitchcock,	27
Tho: Stamp,	32	Francis Barber,	18
Tobias Frier,	18	Edward Wheeler,	18
Willm: Steddall,	26	James Miller,	18
Chri: Thomas,	26	Jo: Shawe,	21
Richard Fleming,	24	Jo: Marshall,	21
Mathew Lem,	20	Jo: Aris,	19
Henry Perpoynt,	22	Robert Ward,	22
Tho: Hall,	21	Tho: Viper,	26
Edward Wilson,	22	Robt Shinglewood,	26
Jo: Palliday,	23	Geo. Smith,	34
Richard Wolley,	36	Jo: Hughes,	30
Willm Clark,	27	Geo. Talbott,	18
Wm Baldwinn,	24	Robert Gilbert,	18
Wm Collins,	20	Jo: Bennet,	18
Tho: Pitcher,	20	Jo: Rolles,	22
Joseph Nelson,	26	James Wynd,	23
Francis Gray,	15	Jno Marsh,	26
Samuell Young,	14	Ralph Wray,	64

PASSENGERS FOR VIRGINIA.

[Communicated by H. G. Somerby, Esq.]

28 May 1635. Theis under written names are to be transported to Virginea imbarqued in the Speedwell of London Jo: Chappell Mr being examined by the minister of Gravesend of their conformitie to the orders and discipline of the Church of England & have taken the oath of Allegiance.

	Years.		Years.
Henry Beere,	24	Jo: Deeby,	17
Jo: West,	30	Jo: Turner,	19
Richard Morris,	19	Samuell Holmes,	20
Nic° Tetloe,	35	Jo: Bever,	24
Wm Shipman,	22	Jo: Talbott,	27
Nathaniell Faierbother,	21	Edward Austin,	26
Richard Baylie,	22	Tho: Greene,	24
Wm Spencer,	17	Richard Browne,	19
James Lowder,	20	Wm Appleby,	32
Chrl: Metcalf,	19	Robert Parker,	21
Jeremy Burr,	20	Wm Cunningham,	21
Willm Basford,	19	Tho: Willis,	19
Jo: Watson,	22	Wm Straughan,	22
Jo: Gilgate,	22	Geo: Sympson,	19
Robt Spynk,	20	Richard Phillips,	20
Richard Rowland,	20	Arthur Saidwell,	25
Tho: Childs,	30	Melashus McKay,	22
Jo: Curden,	22	Richard Thomas,	20
Tho: Romney,	19	Katherin Richards,	19
Jo: Harris,	20	Marie Sedgwick,	20
Christopher Piddington,	18	Elizabeth Biggs,	10
Edmond Clark,	16	Dorothie Wyncott,	40
Jonas Smith,	22	Ann Wyncott,	16
Wm Hynton,	25	Phillipp Biggs,	6 mo.
Jo: Mowser,	22	Elizabeth Pew,	20
Samuell Tyres,	21	Francis Langworth,	25
Wm Steebens,	22	Chr: Reinolds,	24
Tho: Busby,	19	Abram Poore,	20
Richard Harvy,	32	Elizabeth Tuttell,	25
Tho: Robins,	17		

PASSENGERS FOR VIRGINIA.

[Communicated by Mr. Somerby.]

6 *January*, 1635.

Theis under-written names are to be transported to Virginia imbarqued in the Thomas & John Richard Lambard M^{r} being examined by the minister de Gravesend conserning their conformitie to the orders & disipline of the Church of England: And tooke the oath of Allegeance.

	yeares.		
Richard Pew,	23	Wm Aymie,	26
Richard Waynewrite,	24	Wm Hynton,	20
Chri: Houghton,	19	Jo: Edwardson,	22
Richard James,	24	Tho: Mann,	23
Francis Garret,	25	Robt. Aldred,	24
Richard Dally,	18	Zachary Taylor,	24
Edward Dix,	19	Humfrey Grudge,	21
Wm Chaplin,	18	Wm White,	22
Jo: Singleton,	18	Joseph Mennus,	21
Geo: Dickenson,	19	Wm Yard,	21
Geo: Hawkins,	19	Christopher Wheatley,	28
Henry Rastell,	30	Robert Heed,	27
Fra: Spight,	21	Edward Coles,	20

Morris Jones,	28	Jo: Moss,	21
Wardin Fossitt,	22	Jane Wilkinson,	20
Tho: Chamberlin,	20	Ann Brookes,	19
Jo: Shorter,	26	Katherin Wiseman,	19
Ant° Terry,	50	Jane Scott,	19
Robert Willms,	44	Jane Catesby,	20
Tho: Rosdell,	23	James Powell,	12
Thomas Terry,	25	Wm Mann,	25
Charles Wyngate,	22	Tho: Warner,	26
Jo: Hampton,	30	Tho: Ram,	19
Jo: Evans,	22	Griffin Jones,	21
Robert Sewar,	23	Tho: Tollie,	17
Richard Berry,	23	Wm Jones,	21
Owen Hughes,	27	Morris Parry,	30
Jo: Sutton,	24	Marmaduke Young,	24
Wm Stonhouse,	43	Willm White,	22
Wm Clark,	19	James Sherborne,	15
Jo: Dickenson,	22	Wm Gardener,	15
Tho: Bell,	17	Jo: Robinson,	19
Wm Bett,	20	Robert Turner,	16
James Cross,	21	Tho: Clark,	16
Sylas Foster,	22	Giles Terry,	33
Edward Mountfort,	20	Edward Cressitt,	20
Henry Newby,	24	Tho: Maggott,	17
Jo: Eeden,	19	Mary Ford,	22
Tho: Sherly,	23	Katherin Waterman,	20
Jo: Thompson,	24	Suzan Sherwood,	22
Henry Warren,	15	Grace Bycroft,	20
Jo: Wilkenson,	28	Francis Hunter,	19
Ralph Hudson,	17	Francis Ashborn,	20
Tho: Allin,	33	Wm Dixon,	18
Wm Jones,	17	Wm Smart,	20
Tho: Sharples,	20	Lawrence Preston,	21
Wm Crooke,	23	Wm Wheatlie,	17
Wm Bead,	15	Wm Lacy,	18
Lawrence Platt,	15	James Banks,	30
Robert Spenser,	21	Geo: Cobcratte,	22
Samuel Walden,	16	Geo: Kennyon,	25
Henry Morley,	25	Jo: Kennyon,	21
Ben: Easy,	13		

PASSENGERS FOR VIRGINIA.

[Communicated by H. G. Somerby, Esq., for the Antiquarian Journal.]

20th June 1635. Theis under written names are to be transported to Virginea imbarqued in the Phillip Richard Morgan Mr. the men have been examined by the minister of the towne of Gravesend of their conformitie to the orders & disipline of the Church of England: And tooke the oath of Alleg die et A° pred.

John Hart,	33	Tymothie Featlie,	23
John Coachman,	28	Wm Arundell,	32
John Reddam,	32	Alexander Leake,	22
John Shawe,	30	John Mason,	16
George Hill,	23	Willm Emson,	33
George Bonham,	31	James Habroll,	22
Wm Rogers,	35	Richard Jn°son,	19
Edward Halock,	22	John Lawters,	17
Ric: Dawson,	31	Thomas Edwards,	20
Peter Johnson,	36	Robert Davies,	28
Willm Bransby,	34	Richard Upcott,	26
Nicholas Rippen,	31	Thomas Peslett,	23
James Quarrier,	22		
Wm Taylor,	36	Women.	
James York,	21	Ellin Burgis,	45
Thomas Gorham,	19	Katherin Bowes,	20
Nathaniell Disnall,	23	Suzan Trask,	25
John Taylor,	16	Marcie Langford,	24
John Gorham,	18	Elizabeth Willerton,	18
Richard Wilson,	19	Sara Shawe,	18
Robert Morgan,	33	Marie Baker,	25
Samuel Milner,	18	Ann Barnie,	23

PASSENGERS FOR VIRGINIA.

[Communicated by MR. H. G. SOMERBY.]

23rd June 1635. Theis under-written names are to be transported to Virginea imbarqued in the America Willm Barker M^{r}; pr. cert: from the Minister of the Towne of Gravesend of their conformity to the orders & disipline of the Church of England.

Richard Sadd	23
Thomas Wakefield	17
Thomas Bennett	22
Steeven Read	24
Willm Stanbridge	27
Henry Barker	18
James Foster	21
Thomas Talbott	20
Richard Young	31
Robert Thomas	20
John Farepoynt	20
Robert Askyn	22
Samuel Awde	24
Miles Fletcher	27
William Evans	23
Lawrence Farebern	23
Mathew Robinson	24
Isack Bull	27
Phillipp Remington	29
Radulph Spragmy	37
George Chaundler	29
Richard Hersey	22
John Robinson	32
Edmond Chipps	19
Tho: Prichard	32
Jonathan Bronsford	21
Willm Cowley	20
John Shawe	16
Richard Gummy	21
Bartholomew Holton	25
John White	21
Thomas Chappell	33
Hugh Fox	24
David Morris	32
Rowland Cotton	22
William Thomas	22
John Yates	20
Richard Wood	36
James Somers	22
David Bromley	15
Walter Brookes	15
Symon Richardson	23
Thomas Jn°.son	19
Jo: Averie	20
John Croftes	20
Thomas Broughton	19
Benjamin Wragg	24
Henry Embrie	20
Robert Sabyn	40
George Brookes	35
Thomas Holland	34
Humfrey Belt	20
John Mace	20
Walter Jewell	19
Willm Bucland	19
Launcelot Jackson	18
John Williamson	12
Phillipp Parsons	10
Henry Parsons	14
Andrew Morgan	26
Willm Brookes	17
Richard Harrison	15
Thomas Pratt	17
John Ecles	16
Richard Miller	12
Robert Lamb	16
Thomas Boomer	13
George Dulmare	8
John Underwood	19
Willm Bernard	27
Charles Wallinger	24
Thomas Dymett	23
Ryce Hooe	36
John Carter	54

Women.

Elizabeth Remington	20
Katherin Hibbotts	20
Elizabeth Willis	18
Joan Jobe	18
Ann Nash	22
Elizabeth Phillips	22
Dorothy Standich	22
Susan Death	22
Elizabeth Death	3
Alice Remington	26
Dorothy Baker	18
Elizabeth Baker	18
Sara Colebank	20
Mary Thurrogood	19

4th July 1635. Theis under-written names are to be transported Virginea imbarqued in the Transport of London Edward Walker Mr p. Certificate from the Minister of Gravesend of their conformitie to the orders & disipline of the Church of England.

	yeres		
Olliver Van Heck	35	Henry Porter	30
uxor Katherin Van Heck	34	Patrick Woddall	20
Peter Van Heck	7	John Gee	18
Richard Maton	23	Richard Cooper	28
Wm Page	18	Richard Eggleston	24
Robert Kevyn	19	Wm Harbert	15
Peter Smith	25	John Wise	18
Brian McGawyn	3	Thomas Coles	32
Daniell Symson	17	Tho: Williams	18
Patrick Breddy	21	George Ashon	22
Henry Castell	22	Peter Sexton	20
Steeven Block	18	Tho: Johnson	23
Gowen Lancaster	28	Thomas Saunders	20
Robert Farrar	24	John Lee	16
Bryan Glynn	20	Robert Farest	20
Humfrey Hadnet	22	Richard Bick	18
Jo: Woddall	18	Willm Hardisse	22
Willm Wallington	32	Daniell Rose	25
Richard Sharp	15	Richard Anderson	17
Marmaduke Kidson	18	James Phillips	26
Jo: Godfrey	21	Robert Tynman	21
Richard Critch	27	Peter Waller	24
Ellis Baker	21	Richard Petley	22
Jonathan Neale	12	Roger Hollidge	19
Jo: Bush	17	Wm Reddman	18
Wm Nesse	23	Robert Greene	20
Jo: Spreate	20	Henry Meddowes	20
Tho: Steevens	25	George Johnson	19
Jo: Waters	29	John Voss	22
Robt. Fossett	26	Andrew Adams	18
Walter Downes	24	John Wilson	32
Symon Jones	40	Nathan Anley	28
Robert Jenkinson	18	Anthony Grimston	20
Francis Clark	28	Tho: Hatchet	19
Francis Bick	23	Robert Honniborn	21
Thomas Cranfield	14	Jo: Parson	18
Tho: Payne	23	Alexander Burlie	18
Phillip Jones	22	Wm Hart	26
John Goodson	21	Nathaniell Patient	16
Steeven Beane	20	Henry Armstrong	22
Geo: Barber	20		
Richard Wheatlie	32	Women.	
Richard Lloyd	28	Katherin Long	34
Henrie Barnes	22	Elizabeth Sames	19
Tho: Moore	21	Joan Hardiss	18
John Harrison	30	Elizabeth Riley	18
Wm Hudson	20	Ellin Rogerson	20
Wm Mason	30	Elizabeth Lincoln	23
Mark Briggoll	21	Elizabeth Corker	19

Ann Wandall	18	John Drue	26
Sibbell Lakeland	25	John Horne	21
Ellin White	26	Robert Medley	16
Wm White	7 weeks old	Richard Atkinson	21
Ellener Rogers	19	Jo: Pownd	20
Dorothie Charles	20	Edward Rede	17
Hester Brotherton	18	Francis Webster	27
Margaret Watson	18	Jo: Syard	38
Oliff Sprawe	21	Geo: Midland	19
Ann Bristo	22	Wm Watson	24
Ann Gudderidge	23	Harbert Judd	16
Rabecca Lane	22	John Fox	33
Elizabeth Yore	23	Henry Burkett	34
Ralph Golthorp	20	Bennet Freeman	20
Edward Thompson	24	Edward Salter	19
Wm White	37	Robert Covett	25
Robert Lewes	38	Tho: Moore	18
Barnabie Barnes	35	Jo: Russell	16
Edward Ison	20	Edward Hunt	19
John Somerton	24	Robert Beckwith	21
Jo: Russell	14	Jo: Witton	16
Robert Bateman	20	John Harris	28
Wm Cooke	20	Jo: Baylie	42
Henry Bannister	22	Jo: Hathorn	20
Tho: Richardson	26	Edward Drue	18
Jo: Waller	19	Jo: Arp	19
Richard Weaver	27	Edmond Pryme	16

PASSENGERS FOR VIRGINIA.

[Communicated for the Register, by H. G. Somerby, Esq.. ☞ The following list having been mislaid, appears here out of its order.]

6th July 1635. In the Paule of London Leonard Betts Mr bound to Virginia pr. certificate from the Minister of Gravesend of their Conformitie to the Church of England.

Adrian Ford	26
Wm East	23
Robert Caplin	22
Edward Wade	24
Tho: Greene	21
Jo: Jones	18
Tho: Barefoote	19
Robert Taylor	18
Jo: Richardson	22
Richard Hughes	20
Robert Markcom	22
Peter Price	23
John Davies	23
Nicholas Parker	23
John Gill	19
Jo: Aynis	21
Aron Everett	20
Launcelott Limrick	20
Wm Strange	25
Wm Palmer	18
Phillip Bagley	19
Cyprian Warner	21
Henry Dudman	18
Tho: Hitchcock	22
Giles Collins	20
Jo: Machem	18
Robert Wile	28
John Thompkins	25
Silvester Thatcher	21
Anto Potts	27
Mark White	25
Wm Hickey	22
Francis Searle	28
Willm Riddell	16
Jo Potter	26
William Capell	25
Jo: Myntee	16
Wm Harefinch	30
Symon Simes	15
Anthony Day	22
Richard Eggleston	16
Jo: Courtney	32
Robert Underwood	30
Wm Quynie	40

Nicholas Clarke	31
Samuell Symonds	30
Jo: Gill	34
Matthew Bennet	18
Willm Hind	35
Margaret Hinde	30
Augustin Harwood	25
Katherin Wilson	28
2 Childr. { Robert Wilson	6
Richard Wilson	5
Leonard Wood	22
Wm Postell	22
Charles Ford	33
John Scott	26
Thomas Flesney	23
John Heron	18
Tho: Baker	16
Willm Hughes	20
Jo: Coxshedd	14
Peter Pryer	26
Benjamin Hooke	20
Jo: Gibbs	35
Geo: Dawe	25
Hugh Beacon	25
Jo: Bishopp	23
Samuell Davies	24
Women.	
Grace Alderman	22
Mary Husband	20
Alice Fuller	22
Elizabeth Raynton	16
Elizabeth Collins	20
Dorothie Bradlie	18
Grace Jones	24
Sybill Courtney	33
Joan Bowden	24
Annis Sceden	22
Joan Colchester	23
Elizabeth Stacie	20
Dorothy Day	17
Ann Emmerton	20
Martha Holland	24

PASSENGERS FOR VIRGINIA.

[Communicated by H. G. SOMERBY.]

27th July 1635. Theis under written names are to be transported to Virginea imbarqued in the Primrose Captan Douglass Mr. p Certificate under ye Ministers hand of Gravesend, being examined by him touching their Conformitie to the church discipline of England The Men have taken the oathe of Allegeance & Supremacie.

	William Spranson	28	Jo: Beetell	20
fetch off by Mr. Secretary Windebanks Warrant	Jo: Symonds	18	Francis Ratford	20
	Richard Webb	36	Jo: Morfin	20
	Luke Snoden	21	Jo: Lee	25
	W^m. Starling	18	Jo: Balme	34
	Lawrence Whitehorse	17	Jo: Stronde	17
	Robert Nutall	18	W^m. Fox	21
	Robert Williams	21	Tho: Pynch	32
	Wm Thorncome	19	Rich: Gill	26
	Tho: Wiggin	21	Henry Dikes	33
	Chr: Legg	19	W^m. Shawe	25
	Henrie Robinson	26	Henry Smith	22
	Jo: Sherrick	19	Ralph Hunt	22
	Jo: Palmer	18	Jo: Lupton	25
	W^m. Alderton	35	James Rydie	45
	Tho: Clifton	25	Garret Cooke	20
	W^m. Browne	19	Jo: Merie	17
	Alexander Masie	21	Olliver Clifford	18
	Geo: Lee	16	Willm White	23
	Tho: Beane	21	Tho: Mortimer	20
	Jo: Pen	16	Jo: Ridge	16
	George Cottingham	20	Tho: Vinson	18
	Jo: Swifte	23	Francis Dellicat	20
	Geo: Fowler	22	Tho: Ridge	23
	Tho: Farraby	26	Richard Cary	17
	Robert Sharpe	21	Tho: Mannings	16
	W^m. Evans	25	Walter Marshall	17
	W^m. Harris	50	Jo: Shipley	21
	Thomas Coke	24	Tho: Smith	18
	Abram Swifte	23	Jo: Johnson	21
	Olivor Fayrie	25	Jo: Wicks	26
	Oliver Symon	30	Ric^d. West	21
	Henry Maggit	29	Francis Marsh	28
	Tho: Bales	18	Tho: Adams	21
	W^m. Allinson	25	Philip Davies	25
	Jo: Hull	24	Edward Dannell	18
	Mathew Burr	27	Henry Chapman	19
	Tho: Daggett	21	Jo: North	22
	Jo: Baldwin	27	Charles White	18
	Tho: Braxton	20	John Parry	27
	Henry Banbridge	18	Godfrey Hundley	24
	Nic^o: Petting	24	Richard Watts	24
	Geo: Wade	19	Clement Doun	22
	W^m. Perce	19	Rich: Staniford	25

Ben: Gregorie	24	Tho: Mason	19
Edward Mills	30	Tho: Saker	16
Robert Eclie	14	Jo: Marsh	33
Rich: Kellum	16	Jo: Weeks	18
Robert Page	17	Edmond Ardington	20
Jo: Baldwyn	21	Christo: Banbridge	19
Ellis Harman	18	Eliz: Maynard	22
Jo: Bottomly	19	Ann Jackson	23
Wm. More	16	Jo: Molin	30
Samvel Boswell	23	Margaret Clark	21
Wm. Swifte	21	Wm Clark	1
Wm. Griffin	21	Ellin Haly	55
Jo: Norman	20	Sicillia Weston	37
Richard Wards	13	Jane Prym	18
Francis Jarvice	14	Ann Visher	20
Tho: Thomas	20	Kat: York	19
Luke Richardson	17	Dorothy Jakes	29
Jo: Fletcher	18	Aymie Humfrie	23
Robt. Harris	20	Margaret Jn°son	20
Robert Feats	25	Marie Saker	24
Jo: Saker	30	Ellin Sutton	20
Wm. Johnson	26	Jo: Saker	1
Wm. Parry	16	Tho: Poole	43
James Hall	18	Jo: Whetson	20
Robert Benton	18	Thomazin Mills	38

Theis under written names are to be transported to Virginea imbarqued in ye Merchants Hope Hugh Weston Mr. p examinacon by the Minister of Gravesend touching their conformitie to the Church discipline of England & have taken the oaths of Allege. & Suprem:

Edward Towers	26	Rich; Jones	26
Henry Woodman	22	Tho: Wynes	30
Richard Seems	26	Humfrey Willms	22
Allin King	19	Richard Williams	18
Rowland Sadler	19	Jo. Ballance	19
Jo: Phillips	28	Wm. Baldin	21
Vyncent Wharter	17	Wm. Pen	26
James Whithedd	14	Jo: Geerie	24
Jonas Watts	21	Henrie Baylie	18
Peter Loe	22	Rich: Anderson	50
Geo: Brooker	17	Robert Kelum	51
Henry Eeles	26	Richard Fanshaw	22
Jo: Dennis	22	Tho: Bradford	40
Tho: Swayne	23	Wm. Spencer	16
Charles Rinsden	27	Marmaduke Ella	22
Jo: Exston	17	Edward Roberts	20
Wm Luck	14	Martin Atkinson	32
Jo: Thomas	19	Edward Atkinson	28
Jo: Archer	21	Wm Edwards	30
Richard Williams	25	Nathan Braddock	31
Francis Hutton	20	Jeffery Gurrish	23
Savill Gascoyne	29	Henry Carrell	16
Rich: Bulfell	29	Tho: Ryle	24

Gamaliel White	24	Jo: Saunders	22
Richard Marks	19	Tho: Bartcherd	16
Tho: Clever	16	Tho: Dodderidge	19
Jo: Kitchin	16	*Women*	
Edmond Edwards	20	Ann Swayne	22
Lewes Miles	19	Eliz: Cote	22
Jo: Kennedy	20	Ann Rice	23
Sam Jackson	24	Kat: Wilson	23
Daniell Endick	16	Maudlin Lloyd	24
Jo: Chalk	25	Mabell Busher	14
Jo: Vynall	20	Annis Hopkins	24
Edward Smith	20	Ann Mason	24
Jo: Rowlidge	19	Bridget Crompe	18
Wm. Westlie	40	Mary Hawkes	19
Jo: Smith	18	Ellin Hawkes	18

Primo die Augusti 1635

Theis under written names are to be transported to Virginea imbarqued in the Elizabeth de Lo Christopher Browne M^r^. examined by the Minister of Gravesend touching their conformitie to the order and discipline of the Church of England the men have taken the oaths of Alleg^e^ & Supremacie.

Jo: Benford	20	Samvel Growce	38
Lodowick Fletcher	20	W^m^. Glasbrooke	26
Jo: Bagbie	17	Edward Dicks	30
Robt. Salter	14	Jo: Bennett	18
Edward White	18	Michell Saundby	25
Steeven Pierce	30	W^m^. Thurrowgood	13
Rich. Beauford	18	Samvell Mathew	14
Ric^h^. Chapman	18	Tho: Frith	17
Andrew Parkins	18	*Women*	
Jo: Baker	16	Katherine Jones	28
Jo: Walkero	16	Eliz: Sankster	24
Jo: Vaughan	17	Ellin Shore	20
Jo: Austin	24	Alice Pindon	19
Paul Fearne	24	Sara Everedge	22
Thomas Royston	25	Margaret Smith	28
Jo: Taylor	18	Elizab: Hodman	20
Yeoman Gibson	16	Moules Naxton	19
Tho: Leed	16	Marie Burback	17
Geo: Trevas	18	Eliz: Rudston	40
W^m^. Shilbom	38	Eliz: Rudston	5

PASSENGERS FOR VIRGINIA.

[Communicated by H. G. Somerby.]

vij° Augusti 1635

Theis under written names are to be transported to Virginea imbarqued in the Globe of London Jeremy Blackman M^{r}. have been examined by the Minister of Gravesend of their Conformitie & have taken the oaths of Alleg^{e} & Supremacie.

Minister John Goodbarne	30	W^{m}. Savory	25
Edward Lewes	21	Edward King	21
Jo: Whitwham	26	Nathaniel Rogers	17
Jo: Babington	20	Michell Victor	18
W^{m}. Satchill	22	Wm Sharp	21
Tho: Gowen	18	W^{m}. Smotherly	14
Symon Moody	20	Robert Arnold	30
Thomas Tucker	21	Jo: Thatcher	22
Jo: Walton	20	W^{m}. Nash	22
Jo: Ramsey	30	Peter Payton	22
Richard Bates	16	Robert Baldry	18
Willm. Bowler	14	Edward Langstell	18
Henry Hopes	23	James Scott	21
Wm Barnes	22	W^{m}. Andrews	18
George Nettelford	19	Jo: Bland	26
Thomas Parker	22	Philip Westlake	20
Philip Meredith	12	Jo: Marwood	17
Robert Coppyn	11	Jo: Griffith	20
Wm. Browne	20	Jo: Howgate	17
Robert Yates	25	Luke Hanes	27
Wm. Griffith	18	Jo: Stibbs	19
Clough Berne	19	Jeffery Wynch	20
James Copley	22	Richard Abbott	25
Tho: Blithe	20	Rich. Steevenson	19
W^{m}. Howard	16	Tho: Smith	30
Jo: Hale	14	Ant^{o} Carter	22
Nicholas Tayler	17	Geo: More	25
Benedict Rolls	16	Robert Gannock	20
Martin Perkins	18	W^{m}. Burton	20
Wm Emns	22	Mathew Bateman	20
Davie Vaughan	18	Jo: Bynstedd	20
Jo: Seaton	19	Michell Hayms	21
Tho: Bowyer	19	Tho. In^{o}son	21
Abram Bentley	20	John Whitfield	20
Rich. Adams	22	Henry Morton	23
John Russell	15	Allin Hamock	32
Henry Smithick	26	George Forth	27
Tho: Grigg	16	Charles Smith	22
Christopher Legg	18	Mathew Morton	19
Randall Burne	20	W^{m}. Lewes	25
Humfrey Buckley	18	Richard Wells	26
Henry Ston	27	Richard Guy	23
Phillipp Shenningham	17	Jo: Swann	18
Tho: Sharp	17	Edward Lene	32

Tho: Sawell	29
Tho: Whaplett	21
Mabell Eaton	27
Sara Cleyton	27
Ann Levynns	31
Mary Willis	22
Ann Creede	22
Julien Merideth	38
Lucie Bucklie	18
Joan Jernew	30
Eliz: Jernew	25
Robert Scriven	18
Robert Isham	14
Jo: Armsby	30
Wm. Lemon	19
Michell Whitley	23
Jo: Mannings	20
Wm. Barloe	19
Edward Hollingbrigg	27
Wm. Manifold	20
Gregorie Allin	17
Wm. Talbott	14
Geo: Hawley	17
Edward Hodgokynns	21
Mark Gill	22
Tho: Harrwood	26
Abram Watson	17
Allin Rippin	28
John Hobson	25
Tho: Chapman	26
Rich. Cooke	46
Richard Townsend	28
Nicholas Jernew	28
Tho: Wallis	32
Willm. Scarfield	22
Samvell Stringer	17
Nic°. Reinolds	38
John Peter	20
Richard Wollman	22
Edward Clerborn	20
Nicholas Bate	24
Wm. Bate	35
Robert Vass	19
Richard Ward	23
Geo: Aldin	20
Wm. Warner	25
Geo: Grace	25
Christopher Hamond	32
Jacob Averie	33
Geo: Averie	28
Francis Bullock	26
Richard Upgate	21
Ann Willett	23
Joyce Robinson	20
Margaret Baylie	20
Mary Brackley	20
Francis Townsend	21
Francis Townsend	2
Tho: Needham	13
Tho: Axstell	35
Jo: Reddman	46
Robert Mastrie	32
Robert Crouch	15
Tho: Owen	23
Tho: Knibb	23
Robert Wattum	26
Debora Barrie	23
Jo: Tyler	16
Tho: Gregorie	15
Tho: Tate	22
Tho: Hancock	15
Fra: Pepper	16
Wm. Saunder	19

P°. Aug:ti 1635.

Theis under written names are to be transported to Virginea, imbarqued in the Safety. John Grant Mr.

	yeres
John Hardon	27
Richard Haieward	33
Barthol: Hoskyns	34
Ant°. Hries	24
Jo: Catts	23
Jo: Wazen	19
Henry Gadling	16
Richard Hopkins	25
Robert Sutton	17
Robert Pitway	27
Mary Pitway	4
Jo: Jones	29
Mathew Gouch	22
Robert Boddy	19
Jo: Carter	22
Thomas Heath	23
Jo: Hornwood	21
Francis Barker	21
Wm. Tighton	24
Christopher Wynn	20
Jo: Heming	25
Ralph Sympkynn	28
James Barnes	25
Chri: Stope	24

Robert Lendall	20
David Kisfin	24
Wm Symonds	32
Tymothy Trallopp	21
Henry Dugdell	20
John Lownd	16
Tho: Jennions	24
Robert Perkins	25
Jo: Martin	23
Edmond Farsell	20
W^{m}. Hassell	24
Edward Gifford	30
Roger Gilbert	16
Richard Allin	22
Jo: Wilkinson	14
Francis Vycas	25
Willm Davies	27
James Atkinson	16
Nic^{o}. Watson	16
Jo: Taylor	18
Arthur Raymond	20
Edward Spicer	21
Robert Harwood	17
Richard Foster	16
Jo: Bell	30
Gabriell Fisher	36
Tho: Browne	18
Cornelius Maies	12
Stephen Gorton	35
Jo: Gloster	23
Jo: Pigeon	15
Thomas Thorne	13
Jo: Write	15
Richard Preston	17
Andrew Stretcher	14
Alexander Harvie	15
Edmond Jenkins	15
Nic^{o}. Watson	17
Jo: Bag	16
James Pattison	21
W^{m}. Lowther	24
Edward Saunders	40
James Bethell	27
Jo: Browne	25
Jo: Gibson	30
Tho: Belk	37
Geo: Tucker	22
Jo: Curtis	20
Robert Glencster	25
Henry Buckle	30
Jo: Newman	20
Thomas Gardiner	22
Jo: Newman	24
Robert Frister	20
Richard Field	20
Geo: Habbittell	26
Willm Kareswell	20
Wm Grayson	20
Richard Alderley	26
Henry Dalleper	18
Rich. Hudson	30
Jo: Hill	22
Edmond Mullendux	20
Humfrey Blackman	16
Richard Cotton	20
James Allin	19
Martin Church	16
Henry Gilbert	34
W^{m}. Gay	20
Brian Kelley	20
Lewes Smith	22
Tho: Doe	33
Thomas Saunders	13
Edward Saunders	9
Thomas Carter	25
Thomas ap Thomas	30
Richard Caunt	36
Richard Moss	20
John Perryn	21
Hugh Le Roy	19
Thomas Reynolds	15
Joan Allin	20
Marie Booth	19
Jane Cutting	17
W^{m}. Hindsley	23
Katherin Smith	18
Thomazin Broad	24
Ann Waterman	18
Joan Turner	21
Jane Foxsley,	25
Richard Wright	23
Jo: Butler	21
Jo: Hendry	24
Richard Brookes	20
Jo: Martin	17
Geo: Castell	21
Jo: Billings	26
Tho: Wrenn	20
Robert Pister	44
Marie Lerrigo	19
Margaret Homes	23
Alice Ashton	20
Hanna Waddington	16
Elizabeth Holloway	26
Eliz: Gold	17
Elizabeth Frisky	24

Eliz: Smith	50	Rose Hills	22
Margaret Gard	24	Ann Crofts	16
Margerie Smith	22	Grace Tubley	20
Elizab: Pister	16	Margaret Snales	22
Elizabeth Ward	25	Ann Holland	19
Joan Griffige	35	Ann Fossitt	34
Eliz: Turner	44	Dorothy Moyle	24

PASSENGERS FOR VIRGINIA, JULY, 1635.

[Communicated by H. G. Somerby, Esq.]

Theis under-written names are to be transported to Virginea imbarqued in the Alice, Richard Orchard, M^r^. the Men have taken the oath of Allegeance & Suprem.

Edward Hughes	21	Robt. Baxter	21	Rowland Sadgerner	21
James Morfy	21	Jo: Bently	34	Wm. Massingburd	23
Robert Haggar	30	Jo: Holdsmorth	20	Jo: Hutton	17
Tho: Askew	21	Jo. Wright	21	Elizabeth Dew	32
Ric^d^ Cooke	21	Charles Peacock	28	Ann Dew	9 mo.
Miles Atkinson	22	Chri: Hudson	30	Rachell Adams	16
Rowland Vaughan	19	Jo: Smith	20	Avis Deacon	19
Richard Natt	18	Jo: Cooper	20	Hanna Glifford	20
Fra: Jenkinson	28	Edward Waggett	20	Eliza: Blanch	20
Willm Kendridd	20	Jo: Viccars	35	Sophia Rottrio	16
Jo: Wilson	29	Tho: Atkinson	27		

Theis under written names are to be transported to Virginea imbarqued in the Assurance de Lo: Isack Bromwell & Geo: Pewsie M^r^. examined by the Minister of the Towne of Gravesend of their conformitie in o^r^. Religion. the men have taken the oath of Allegeance & Supremacie.

	yeres		yeres		yeres
Robert Brian	27	Tho: Pagett	41	Sara Rayne	18
Maudlin Jones	60	Mathew Holmes	21	Andrew Underwood	22
Ann Shawe	32	Elias Harrington	22	Philip Johns	22
Jo: Duncombe	46	Richard Smith	35	Henrie Marshall	35
Sith Haieward	30	Tho: Robinson	24	Henry Heiden	30
Richard Hamey	38	Evan ap Evan	19	Elizabeth Sherlocke	29
Wm. Holland	35	Jo: Browne	21	Tho: Hurlock	40
Henry Snow	26	Robert Frithe	23	Samuel Handy	25
Marie Southwood	22	Tho: Wilkinson	23	Jo: Gater	36
Francis Roweson	29	James Southern	19	Joan Gater	23
Richard Glover	24	Margerie Baker	39	Wm. Lee	36

Josua Titloe	19
Jo: Middleton	23
Robert Haiward	22
Samuel Powell	19
Wm. Robbell	19
Robert Wyon	22
Mathew Dixon	18
John Wheeler	23
Jo: North	24
Mountford Newman	27
Robert Steere	17
Wm. Lake	35
Humfrey Wilkins	19
Ant^{o} Stilgo	21
Tho: Deacon	19
Robt. Rigglie	19
Beniamin Pillard	18
Robert Davies	28
Jo: Smith	20
Walter Meridith	33
Tho: Phillips	24
James Kingsmill	18
Jo: Bowton	20
Walter Chapman	44
James Arnold	37
Richard Leake	18
Tho: Edwinn	13
Hundgate Baker	22
Jo: Abrock	20
Tho: Hall	15
James Edwin	18
Edward Comins	28
Dennis Hoggin	24
Jo: Friccar	25
Richard Ridges	19
Edward Davies	27
Theodorics Bakewell	21
Jo: Dermot	21
Jo: Morgan	27
Tho: Baycock	46
Ric^{d} Rogers	48
Ric^{d} Lockley	51
Jo: Jakes	20
Tho: More	19
Jo: Baker	22
Nehemiah Caston	21
Robert Mayes	28
Richard Barnes	38
Jo: Buttler	50
Warram Tuck	20
Jo: Jones	30
Wm. Colture	19
Robert Silby	19
Ric^{d} Bruster	26
Jo: Swanley	21
Wm. Charles	21
Anthony Lee	21
Willm Williams	28
Henry George	19
Jo: Billings	21
Wm. White	18
Robert Lovett	20
Job Jefferie	19
Henrie Haler	22
Richard Symons	30
James Sparks	57
Richard Kirbie	32
James Hingle	40
Tho: Saunderson	24
Wm. Spicer	20
Willm Thomas	19
Henry Madin	30
Edward Ednall	21
Tho: Jefferies	22
Nic^{o} Jackson	22
Tho· Spratt	23
Tho: Leonard	18
Jo: Gater	15
Nic^{o} Gibson	22
Jo: Roberts	46
Geo. Mosely	20
James Ravesh	20
Jo: Hales	21
Robert Handley	19
Jo: Aymies	18
Jo: Tayler	21
Wm. Roffin	18
Ric^{d} Halsey	13
Ant^{o} Otland	18
Robert Oldrick	18
Wm. Hall	21
Jo: Copeland	19
John Goad	18
Jo: Pooly	17
Francis Geyer	18
Tho: Craven	17
Ric^{d} Lucas	16
Geo. Cullidge	18
Lawrence Barker	26
Jo: Bowes	20
Jo: Woodbridge	32
Jo: Johnson	20
Jo: Chappell	38
Geo. Whittaker	32
Richard Liversidge	24
Henrie Wood	20
Robert Max	21
Jo Warren	18
Tho: Turner	18
Jo: Garland	19
Jo: Humfrey	23
Isack Ambrose	18
Wm. Huncote	35
Tho: Williams	19
Tho: Foxcrofte	19
Tho: Hobbs	22
Charles Collohon	19
Marie Averie	22
Sara Alport	25
Maria Lee	22
Elizabeth Bateman	23
Thomazin Markcom	26
Tho: Beson	24
Chri: Dixon	24
Isack Kemp	23
Jeremie Slie	19
Jo: O'Mullin	18
Ant^{o} Proctor	16
Henry Doun	23
Roger Quintin	21
Wm. Small	18
Wm. Coleman	16
Ant^{o} Andrewe	21
Jo: Richardson	18
Wm. Claddin	17
Tho: Gudderedge	17
Rodger Burley	17
Tho: Burd	16
Henry Butler	14
Jo: Budd	15
Jno Marshall	35
Wm. Read	30
Edward Mitchell	18
Robert Drewrie	16
Ric^{d} Welle	17
Jo: Cotes	17
Jo: Stubber	17
Henry Lee	18
Ric^{d} Ball	17
Jo: Cooke	17
Tho: Syer	14
Jo: Patridge	18
Jo: Johnson	24
WOMEN	
Isbell Davis	22
Isabell Hakesby	23
Joan Vallins	17
Marie Chambney	28
Elizabeth Allcott	20
Frances Bakewell	30
Elizabeth Payne	21
Elizabeth Hughson	22
Elizabeth Raynard	20
Marie Olliver	21
Alice Riall	18
Rebecca Parmeter	19
Marie Middleton	17
Ann Goldwell	17
Ann Griffin	26
James Brooks	28
uxor Alice Brookes	18
Dorcas Mercer	30
Ellin Davies	23
Alice Harris	21
Eedie Holloway	22
Sara Coggin	20
Elizabeth Baker	20
Dorothie Davies	17
Kat: Fulder	17
Eliz: Dicks	18
Sara Greene	20
Margaret Ricord	20
Winnifred Congrave	22
Mathew Plant	23
Jo: More	28
Elizabeth Powell	17
Marie Shorter	26
Marie Lee	14 weeks
Mathew Clatworthy	25

PASSENGERS FOR VIRGINIA. 1635.

Communicated by H. G. SOMERBY, Esq.

Theis under-writtten names are to be transported to Virginea imbarqued in the Transport of London Edward Walker Mr p. Certificate from the Minister of Gravesend of their conformitie to the orders & discipline of the Church of England.

	yeres.
Olliver Van Heck	35
uxor Katherin Van Heck	34
Peter Van Heck	7
Richard Maton	23
Wm. Page	18
Robert Kevyn	19
Peter Smith	25
Brian Mc Gawyn	8
Daniell Symson	17
Patrick Breddy	21
Henry Castel	22
Steeven Block	18
Gowen Lancaster	28
Robert Farrar	24
Bryan Glynn	20
Humfrey Hadnet	22
Jo: Woddall	18
Willm Wallington	32
Richard Sharp	15
Marmaduke Kidson	18
Jo: Godfrey	21
Richard Critch	27
Ellis Baker	21
Jonathan Neale	12
Jo: Bush	17
Wm Nesse	23
Jo: Spreate	20
Tho: Steevens	25
Jo: Waters	29
Robt. Fossett	26
Walter Downes	24
Symon Jones	40
Robert Jenkinson	18
Francis Clark	28
Francis Bick	23
Thomas Cranfield	14
Tho: Payne	23
Phillip Jones	22
John Goodson	21
Steeven Beane	20
Geo: Barber	20
Richard Wheatlie	32
Richard Lloyd	28
Henrie Barnes	22
Tho: Moore	21
John Harrison	30
Wm Hudson	20
Wm Mason	30
Mark Briggoll	21
Henry Porter	30
Patrick Woddall	20
John Gee	18
Richard Cooper	28
Richard Eggleston	24
Wm Harbert	15
John Wise	18
Thomas Coles	32
Tho: Williams	18
George Ashon	22
Peter Sexston	20
Tho: Johnson	23
Thomas Saunders	20

	yeres.
John Lee	16
Robert Farest	20
Richard Bick	18
Willm Hardisse	22
Daniell Rose	25
Richard Anderson	17
James Phillips	26
Robert Tynman	21
Peter Waller	24
Richard Petley	22
Roger Hollidge	19
Wm Reddman	18
Robert Greene	20
Henry Meddowes	20
George Johnson	19
John Voss	22
Andrew Adams	18
John Wilson	32
Nathan Anley	28
Anthony Grimston	20
Tho: Hatchet	19
Robert Honnibom	21
Jo: Parson	18
Alexander Burlie	18
Wm Hart	26
Nathaniell Patient	16
Henry Armstrong	22

WOMEN.

Katherin Long	34
Elizabeth Sames	19
Joan Hardiss	18
Elizabeth Riley	18
Ellin Rogerson	20
Elizabeth Lincoln	23
Elizabeth Corker	19
Ann Wandall	18
Sibbell Lakeland	25
Ellin White	26
Wm White	7 weeks old
Ellener Rogers	19
Dorothie Charles	20
Hester Brotherton	18
Margaret Watson	18
Oliff Sprawe	21

	yeres.
Ann Bristo	22
Ann Gudderidge	23
Rabecca Lane	22
Elizabeth Yore	23
Ralph Golthorp	20
Edward Thompson	24
Wm White	37
Robert Lewes	38
Barnabie Barnes	35
Edward Ison	20
John Somerton	24
Jo: Russell	14
Robert Bateman	20
Wm Cooke	20
Henry Bannister	22
Tho: Richardson	26
Jo. Waller	19
Richard Weaver	27
John Drue	26
John Horne	21
Robert Medley	16
Richard Atkinson	21
Jo: Pownd	20
Edward Rede	17
Francis Webster	27
Jo: Syard	38
Geo: Midland	19
Wm Watson	24
Harbert Judd	16
John Fox	33
Henry Burkett	34
Bennett Freeman	20
Edward Salter	19
Robert Covelt	25
Tho: Moore	18
Jo: Russell	16
Edward Hunt	19
Robert Beckwith	21
Jo: Wilton	16
John Harris	28
Jo: Baylie	42
Jo: Hathorn	20
Edward Drue	18
Jo: Arp	19
Edmond Pryme	16

PASSENGERS TO VIRGINIA.

[The following lists of passengers to Virginia were furnished to the Register hy Mr. Somerby, some years since, together with those at that time published; but by some accident were lost or mislaid, and never printed. Mr. Somerby has obligingly sent us another copy, which we now present to our readers.]

Ultimo July 1635.

Theis under written names are to be transported to Virginea imbarqued in ye Merchants Hope Hugh Weston Mr p' examinacōn by the Minister of Gravesend touching their conformitie to the Church discipline of England, and have taken the oaths of Allege and Suprem:

Edward Towers	26	Edward Roberts	20	Richard Williams	18
Henry Woodman	22	Martin Atkinson	32	Jo: Ballance	19
Richard Seems	26	Edward Atkinson	28	Wm Baldin	21
Allin King	19	Wm Edwards	30	Wm Pen	26
Rowland Sadler	19	Nathan Braddock	31	Jo: Gerie	24
Jo: Phillips	28	Jeffery Gurrish	23	Henrie Baylie	18
Vyncent Whatter	17	Henry Carrell	16	Rich: Anderson	50
James Whithedd	14	Tho: Ryle	24	Robert Kelum	51
Jonas Watts	21	Gamaliel White	24	Richard Fanshaw	22
Peter Loe	22	Richard Marks	19	Tho: Bradford	40
Geo: Brooker	17	Tho: Clever	16	Wm Spencer	16
Henry Eeles	26	Jo: Kitchin	16	Marmaduke Ellu	22
Jo: Dennis	22	Edmond Edwards	20		
Tho: Swayne	23	Lewes Miles	19	WOMEN.	
Charles Rinsden	27	Jo: Kennedy	20	Ann Swayne	22
Jo: Exston	17	Sam Jackson	24	Eliz: Cote	22
Wm Luck	14	Daniell Endick	16	Ann Rice	23
Jo: Thomas	19	Jo: Chalk	25	Kat. Wilson	23
Jo: Archer	21	Jo: Vynall	20	Maudlin Lloyd	24
Richard Williams	25	Edward Smith	20	Mabell Busher	14
Francis Hutton	20	Jo: Rowlidge	19	Annis Hopkins	24
Savill Gascoyne	29	Wm Wostlie	40	Ann Mason	24
Rich: Bulfell	29	Jo: Smith	18	Bridget Crompe	18
Rich: Jones	26	Jo: Saunders	22	Mary Hawkes	19
Tho: Wynes	30	Tho: Bartcherd	16	Ellin Hawkes	18
Humfrey Willm̄s	22	Tho: Dodderidge	19		

Primo die Augusti 1635.

Theis under written names are to be transported to Virginea imbarqued in the Elizabeth de Lo Christopher Browne Mr examined by the Minister of Gravesend touching their conformitie to the order and discipline of the Church of England the men have taken the oaths of Allege and Supremacie.

Jo: Benford	20	Jo: Vaughan	17	Sam̄vell Mathew	14
Lodowick Fletcher	20	Yeoman Gibson	16	Tho: Frith	17
Jo: Bagbie	17	Tho: Leed	16	Jo: Austin	24
Robt: Salter	14	Geo: Trevas	18	Paul Fearne	24
Edward White	18	Wm Shelborn	20	Thomas Royston	25
Stephen Pierce	30	Sam̄vel Growce	38	Jo: Tayler	18
Rich: Beanford	18	Wm Glasbrooke	21		
Rich: Chapman	18	Edward Dicks	30	WOMEN.	
Andrew Parkins	18	Jo: Bennett	18	Katherine Jones	28
Jo: Baker	16	Michaell Saundby	25	Eliz: Sankster	24
Jo: Walker	16	Wm Thurrowgood	13	Ellin Shore	20

Alice Pindon	19	Elizab: Hodman	20	Eliz: Rudston	40
Sara Everedge	22	Moules Naxton	19	Eliz: Rudston	5
Margaret Smith	28	Marie Burback	17		

P° Aug^{ti} 1635.

Theis under written names are to be transported to Virginea imbarqued in the Safety, John Grant M^{r}.

John Hardon yeres	27	Alexander Harvie	15	Robert Glenester	25
Richard Haieward	33	Edmond Jenkins	15	Henry Buckle	30
Barthol: Hoskyns	34	Nic° Morton	17	Jo: Newman	20
Ant° Haies	24	Jo: Bag	16	Robert Trister	20
Jo: Catts	23	James Pattison	21	Richard Field	20
Jo: Wazen	19	Wm Lowther	24	Geo: Habbittoll	26
Henry Gadling	16	Edward Saunders	40	Willm Kareswell	20
Richard Hopkins	25	James Bethell	27	Wm Grayson	20
Robert Sutton	17	Jo: Browne	25	Richard Wright	28
Robert Pitway	27	Jo: Gibson	30	Jo: Butler	21
Mary Pitway	4	Tho: Belk	37	Jo: Hendry	24
Jo: Jones	29	Geo: Tucker	22	Richard Brookes	20
Mathew Gouch	22	Tho: Jennions	24	Jo: Martin	17
Robert Boddy	19	Robert Perkins	25	Geo: Castell	21
Jo: Carter	22	Jo: Martin	23	Jo: Billings	26
Thomas Heath	23	Edmond Farrell	20	Tho. Wrenn	20
Jo: Hornwood	21	Wm Hassell	24	Robert Pister	44
Francis Barker	21	Edward Gifford	30	Marie Lerrigo	19
Wm Tighton	24	Roger Gilbert	16	Margaret Homes	23
Christopher Wynn	20	Richard Allin	22	Alice Ashton	20
Jo: Heming	25	Jo: Wilkinson	14	Hanna Waddington	16
Ralph Sympkynn	28	Francis Vycas	25	Elizabeth Holloway	26
James Barnes	25	Willm Davies	27	Eliz: Gold	17
Chri: Stope	24	Richard Alderly	26	Elizabeth Frisby	24
Robert Lendall	20	Henry Dalleper	18	Eliz: Smith	50
David Kisfin	24	Rich: Hudson	30	Margaret Gard	24
Wm Symonds	32	Jo: Hill	22	Margerie Smith	22
Tymothy Trallopp	21	Edmond Mullendux	20	Elizab: Pister	16
Henry Dugdell	20	Humfrey Blackman	16	Elizabeth Ward	25
John Lownd	16	Richard Cotton	20	Joan Griffige	35
James Atkinson	16	James Allin	19	Eliz: Turner	44
Nic° Watson	16	Martin Church	16	Joan Allin	20
Jo: Taylor	18	Henry Gilbert	34	Marie Booth	19
Arthur Raymond	20	Wm Gay	20	Jane Cutting	17
Edward Spicer	21	Brian Kelley	20	Wm Hindsley	23
Robert Harwood	17	Lewes Smith	22	Katherin Smith	18
Richard Foster	16	Tho: Doe	33	Thomazin Broad	24
Jo: Bell	30	Thomas Saunders	13	Ann Waterman	18
Gabriell Fisher	36	Edward Saunders	9	Joan Turner	21
Tho: Browne	18	Thomas Carter	25	Jane Foxsley	25
Cornelius Maies	12	Thomas Ap Thomas	30	Rose Hills	22
Steven Gorton	35	Richard Caunt	36	Ann Crofts	16
Jo: Gloster	23	Richard Moss	20	Grace Tubley	20
Jo: Pigeon	15	John Perryn	21	Margaret Snales	22
Thomas Thorne	13	Hugh le Roy	19	Ann Holland	19
Jo: Write	15	Thomas Reynolds	15	Ann Fossitt	34
Richard Preston	17	Jo: Curtis	20	Dorothy Moyle	24
Andrew Stretcher	14				

21st August 1635.

Theis under written names are to be transported to Virginea imbarqued in the George Jo: Severne Mr bound thither pr. examination of the Minister of Gravesend etc.

Michaell Masters yeres	21
Tho: Morecock	26
Jo: Gillam	21
Tho: Gillam	18
Humfrey Higginson	28
Mathew Silsby	31
Tho: Bullard	32
Tho: Rogers	15
Nowell Lloyd	16
Ann Higginson	25
Francis Foster	18
Robert Scotchmore	39
Jo: Evans	19
Rabeca Palmer	19
Arthur Bodilies	19
Peter Maning	25
Daniell Bowyer	30
Michell Williams	18
Chri: Kirk	23
Richard Genney	20
Christopher Thomas	21
Walter Walker	23
Jo: Pope	28
Anto Hodgskins	22
John Bell	21
Ann Layfield	30
Jo: Hutchinson	47
Alice Levett	16
Mary Burtwezill	18
Alice Watson	30
Joan Ludcole	18
Nathan: Wilson	23
Theodor Rogerson	20
Wm Thompson	22
Jo: Jones	17
Michel Hedly	24
Edward Abbs	07
Wm Golder	22
Tho: Hand	20
George Fox	14
Jo: Dagnie	20
Wm Hawkes	22
Ralph Cleyton	20
Tho: Best	33
Jo: Hunt	23
Jo: Feld	20
Eliz: Bristowe	17
Mary Robinson	18
Elizabeth Woodbridge	22
Bryan Hare	27
Roger Cutts	20
Wm Dickenson	21
Wm Mitchell	15
Marie Neele	13
Ann Cooper	20
Geo: Taylor	20
Henry Kilby	27
Jo: Fynch	27
Geo: Quither	25
Tho: Mothropp	21
James Homer	24
Jo: Ray	21
Rich Dixon	20
Tho: Peacock	19
Jo: Rogers	18
Griffith Hughes	24
Ann White	19
Jo: Quyle	15
Tho: Allin	17
Jo: Butler	13
Tho: Purnell	16
Valentine Bishopp	11
Wm Clowdeslie	26
Richard Verdin	24
Jo: Baddam	40
Elias Wiggmore	24
Suzan Hare	24
Richard Hide	24
Robert Dunham	30
Jo: Goodridge	19
Jo: Tiffiny	19
Henry Cutling	40
Leonard Richardson	43
Jesper Hodgskyns	24
Jo: Wynn	25
Tho: Howell	20
Lawrance Barwick	20
Jo: Musgrave	07
Edward Lillie	19
Jo: Goodson	25
Michell Prymm	25
Alexander Greene	40
James Bankes	35
Oliff Gibbins	18
Constance Foster	23
Wm Scott	24
Ralph Browne	23
Robt. Morrison	21
Edward Greene	6
Tho: Banks	4
Eliz: Banks	9 mo.
Jo: Allin	21
Lewes James	30
Tho: Wiggins	20
Sara Merriman	20
Arthur Figiss	40
Wm Hinshawe	20
Roger Nevett	20
Mathew Price	20
Rich James	33
Wm Neesun	21
Tho: Buck	17
Geo: Smith	20
Joseph Mills	20
Tho: Rogers	16
Jo: Richards	17
Wm Saic	17
Geo: Cranwell	23
Jo: Weston	20
Francis Blake	18
Tho: Maynard	22
Jo: Price	34
Peter Starkie	22
James Hamkins	17
Joseph Warrwell	17
Francis Young	21
Tho: Connier	23
Tho: Perry	18
Jo: Staunton	27
Tho: White	16
Rich: Phillyps	14
Jane Swifte	23
Margery Carter	23
Gressam Parkins	19
Wm Block	23
Tho: Gadsby	19
Minister Richard James	33
Ursula James	19
Arthur Figiss	33
Francis Havercamp	17
Edward Jones	22
Henry Hawley	34
Robert Burr	19
Wm Miller	29
Wm Curtis	19
Tho: Beomont	29
Jo: Covell	18
Joan Vizard	18
Wm Steevens	22
Tho: Horrocks	22
Mary Soanes	26

Theis under-written names are to be transported to Virginea imbarqued in the Thomas Henry Taverner Mr have been examined by the Minister of Gravesend touching their conformitie in or Religion etc.

Jo: Lewes	16
Wm Greene	18
Walter Smith	20
Wm Burton	24
Jo: Hill	15
Joseph Browning	20

Tho: Fouch	16	Jo: Collopp	22	Joan Looker	20
Edward Sawnders	20	Peter Ricard	19	Suzan Jennoway	26
Wm James	18	Henry Gew	20	Edward Robins	33
Jo: Tullie	20	Wm Adams	24	Geo: Dawe	23
Jane Gibbs	27	Robt James	18	Joseph Preston	20
Mary Chadd	17	Jo: Bromton	20	Ananiah Dyer	24
Jane Colerack	22	Rich: Wheeler	24	Roger Wilkyns	33
Alice Wright	21	Robert Wells	30	Jo: Boothe	19
Edward Erle	45	Jo: Gressam	22	Peter Harbynn	21
Richard Crane	32	Teague Quillin	20	Tho: Maltman	17
Adam Crowe	19	Wm Peas	19	Nic° Folly	16
Jacob Denton	20	Bartholm: Furbank	20	Hugh Fouche	17
Hugh Stanley	16	Robert Johnson	27	Michell Hutchinson	16
Beniamin Symes	42	Mary Johnson	23	Wm Pallmer	17
Mary Jolly	21	Alice Jn°son	22	Wm Chamberlin	16
Eliz: Ayres	26	Eliz: Johnson	18	Nathan Tooly	19
Humfrey Awdry	21	Mary Lucie	20	Henry Wilson	12
Edward Johnson	28				

Theis under written names are to be transported to Virginea, imbarqued in the David Jo: Hogg Mr have been examined by the Minister of Graves-end etc.

Edward Browne	25	Henry Melton	23	Jo: Lamb	22
Samuel Troope	17	David Lloyd	30	Tho: Nunn	22
Wm Hatton	23	Donough Gorhue	27	Jo: Steevens	19
Daniel Bacon	30	Geo: Butler	27	Edward Crabtree	20
Robert Alsopp	18	Addam Nunnick	25	Wm Barber	17
Teddar Jones	30	Jo: Stann	27	Ann Beeford	25
Tho: Siggins	18	Edward Spicer	18	Martha Potter	20
Abell Dexter	25	Jo: Feelding	19	Gurtred Lovett	18
Rich. Caton	26	Jo: Morris	26	Jane Jennings	25
Henry Spicer	28	Richard Brookes	30	Margaret Bole	30
Tho: Granger	19	Robert Barron	18	Mary Rogers	20
Jo: Bonfilly	21	Jonathan Barnes	22	Margaret Walker	20
Roger Mannington	14	Henry Kendall	17	Freese Brooman	20
Josua Chambers	17	Tho: Poulter	31	Eliz: Jones	20

24° Octobris 1635.

Aboard the Constance Clement Campion Mr bound to Virginea.

John Wade yeres	21	Rich: Steere	24	Elizabeth Brewer	17
Garret Nicholson	23	Tho: Leer	18	Isack Bever	24
John Burrowes	18	Wm Prichard	34	Alice Brass	15
Wm Belt	21	James Cotes	22	Tho: Moore	26
Thomas Simpson	24	James Revell	20	Wm King	21
Tho: Patrick	22	Wm Andrewes	20	Jo: Mitchell	22
John Till	20	Lymon Jarr	14	Tho: Hall	21
Joseph Prichard	17	Wm Hunt	21	Robert Ellis	22
Wm Bennerman	18	Tho: Jackson	23	James Haies	28
Rich. Tayler	18	Miles Coke	23	John Hancock	17
John Griffin	26	Chri: Chambers	24	Rich Gray	21
Sam̃uel Jackson	21	Davie Williams	24	Wm Tyse	20
Geo: Atkinson	16	Nic° Huggins	24	Tho: Watkin	35
Robt Sexton	24	Jo: Davies	20	Charles Hughes	50
Tho: Pursell	26	Willm Jones	25	James Symons	20
David Lupton	23	Henrie Richardson	21	Jo: Clark	38
Henrie More	20	Roger Williams	19	Geo: Dycs	38
Michell Suckliff	18	Jo: Wythins	24	Jo: Palmer	12
George Atterborne	20	Tho: Jay	25	Griffin Maymor	21

Frances Marsten	19	Sampson Alkynn	24	Mary Parker	15
Steephen Pack	22	Jo: Coke	24	Wm Hulett	19
Geo: David	22	John de Cane	20	Walter Jenkyns	30
Henrie Johnson	27	Jo: Elliott	36	Edmond Porter	35
Jo: Ashcrofte	33	Wm Gillam	27	Edward Herrott	35
Mathew Gowghe	28	Tho: Smith	24	Hugh Douglass	22
Tho: Digglin	22	Ant° Miles	11	Walter Colly	19
Robert Baskerville	22	Chri: Boyce	38	Joan Carraway	22
Nathaniell Young	20	Tho: Saddock	17	Tho: Hart	18
Tho: Hodson	20				

Aboard the Abraham of London John Barker Mr bound to Virginea.

Tobie Sylbie	20	Francis Tippsley	17	Jo: Bullar	32
Robert Harrison	32	Emanuell Davies	19	Jo: Clanton	26
Willm Lawrence	22	Wm Williams	25	Alexander Symes	19
John Johnson	35	Roger Mathews	28	Ant° Parkhurst	42
Wm Fisher	25	Jo: Masters	23	Jo: Hill	36
Steeven Tayler	17	Willm Mathews	18	Alexander Gregorie	24
Tho: Penford	30	Jo: Britten	18	Martin Westerlink	20
Wm Smith	25	George Preston	20	Patrick Wood	24
Tho: Archdin	18	Robert Toulban	23	Tho: Kodby	25
Rich Morrice	17	Henry Dobell	20	Roger Greene	24
Walter Piggott	19	George Brewett	18	Willm Downes	24
Richard Watkyns	20	Francis Stanley	23	Jo: Burnett	24
Jo: Braunch	13	Willm Freeman	46	Tho: Allin	31
Jo: Clark	20	Edward Griffith	33	Simon Farrell	19
Gabriell Thomas	30	Willm Manton	30	Tho: Clements	30
David Jones	21	Owen Williams	40	Wm Hunt	20
Alexander Maddox	22	Tho: Flower	32	Katherin Aldwell	33

EMIGRANTS IN VESSELS, "BOUND TO VIRGINIA,"

AND MEMORIAL OF WILLIAM CLARKE, OF WATERTOWN AND WOBORN.

[Communicated by John G. Locke, Esq., of Boston, member of the N. E. H. G. Soc.]

In Volume II. p. 211, of the Register, there are introductory remarks, prefacing a list of "Passengers for Virginia," in which it is intimated that some of the emigrants to America, who took passage in vessels "bound to Virginia," found their way to New England, at an early period, and instances of names being found in or near Boston, identical with names found in the lists of passengers, are cited. The reason assigned that "It might have been difficult for some of them to have obtained permission to have come here, while no objection might be made to their going to Virginia" may perhaps be a good reason, and applicable to some cases, but there is another fact which to me has much weight, and that is, that some of the said vessels which are noted as "bound to Virginia," were in fact bound to New England, for at that early period, New England was oftentimes spoken of as "North Virginia," and was by some supposed to be within the bounds of Virginia proper, and perhaps being so considered, the prefix of "North," might be sometimes omitted.

But my intention is not now to establish this point, but to state some facts which conclusively show that some of the passengers in the vessels "bound to Virginia," *did* in fact, settle in Massachusetts.

Thomas Arnald, who came over in the "Plaine Joan," whose name is registered May 15, 1635, then aged 30, and William Clarke, in the same vessel, aged 27, — and Thomas Smith, who came in the "Primrose," and whose name is registered July 15, 1635, and Margaret Clark, who came in the same vessel, then aged 21, (she had a son William, aged 1 year,) are all found at Watertown, as will appear by a deed of a lot of land in Watertown, from said William Clarke, to Timothy Hawkins, bearing date 1651. The land is described as follows: "A parcel of Upland commonly called by the name of great divident, in the town aforesaid, (Watertown) being the first lot in the third division, containing thirty five acres. Bounded upon the South side with the land of John Page, (and) the common, on the West with the land of *Thomas Smith*, upon the North, with the land of Richard Sautle and Samuel Thatcher, upon the East, with the common, which land was granted by the townsmen of Watertown, to *Thomas Arnald*, and by him conveyed to the said William Clarke."

The deed is signed by William Clarke, and
1 (2) mo 1651. Margary Clarke.

Here we find the *four* names which I have before enumerated, in one document. At what period these persons came to Watertown, I am not able to say. Thomas Arnald was there in 1640, and William Clarke was made a freeman, May 16, 1629, and had a daughter born at Watertown, in 1640.

The facts I have stated, prove conclusively, that the Virginia bound emigrants did settle at a very early period in Massachusetts.

The name of William Clarke, was common in that day. A William Clarke aged 19, came over in 1635, in the "Thomas and John;" and one of that name, whose wife's name was Sarah, sold land in Dorchester, to Robert Stiles, in 1659. He was not the William of Watertown, as the wife Margery, of the latter, was living in 1681, at the death of her husband. William of Watertown, bought sixty acres of land in Watertown, of Thomas Boyden, in 1650. Within a few years, he moved to Woborn;

for on the 17 (1) mo. 1663–4, I find his name to a document relating to the sale of some lands in Woburn, which land, he with William Simonds certifies, was sold about two years previous to the date noted.

The numerous families of Clarke of the present day, cannot claim him for an ancestor, for I think he left no sons. He had a son William in 1635, then one year old, born in England — who probably died, as he does not mention him in his Will, and no other sons are therein named. The children of whom I have found any account were,

MARY, born at Watertown, 10 (10) mo. 1640, married William Locke, Dec. 27, 1655, who emigrated in the "Planter," in 1634, and who is the earliest emigrant of that name, and the ancestor of all the Lockes who can trace their origin to Massachusetts. He lived in Woburn, and d. in 1720.

ELIZABETH, was born at Watertown, 26 (9) mo. 1642, and m. George Brush, of Woburn, in 1659.

HANNAH, b. ——— m. William Frissell, of Concord, in 1667. He d. at Concord, in 1684.

LIDEA, b. ——— m. ——— ———, and was a widow with two children, (daughters) when her father died in 1681. I have been unable to find her husband's name.

By the Will of the father, "all his houseing and lands in the bounds of Woburn — and all his other estate of household and Cattell" are bequeathed to his grand son, John Locke, who he says, "has been a liver with me for many years;" making a condition that his grandson, John, shall pay to his daughters, Elizabeth and Hannah, and to the two daughters of his daughter Lidea, certain sums, and grants the use of his houseing and lands, during her life, to his wife Margaret.

TWO EARLY PASSENGER LISTS, 1635–1637

Communicated by EBEN PUTNAM of Wellesley Farms, Mass.

THE two passenger lists given in this article were copied from the records of Sandwich, co. Kent, England, Yearbooks C and D, 1608–1642, by J. A. Jacobs, Esq., of Sandwich, alderman of that town, honorary curator of its archives, and well known as a local antiquary, and through his courtesy the contributor of this article is enabled to present them to the readers of the REGISTER.

Notwithstanding the fact that the existence of these lists has long been known, although for a time their exact location in the records was forgotten, this is the first time they have been printed in complete form.

Partial copies, omitting the names of the children and also of the individuals grouped under the heading "Servants," but giving the numbers of such persons accompanying the various heads of families, were first printed by William Boys in his "History of Sandwich," published at Canterbury, England, 1786–1792, pages 750 and 752. In 1843, in *Collections of the Massachusetts Historical Society*, Series 3, vol. 8, pages 274–276, the late James Savage, as a part of his article entitled "Gleanings for New England History," reprinted these lists from the "History of Sandwich," and suggested that the name of each child and servant, perhaps the age also, might be found in the original record. The lists were reprinted again, in a more concise form, in the REGISTER, vol. 15, pages 28–29 (January 1861), and also, from the REGISTER type, in Samuel G. Drake's "Founders of New England," Boston, 1860, pages 82–85. The late Horatio G. Somerby also copied these lists from the "History of Sandwich," and his copy, preserved in the Somerby Manuscripts, vol. 3, pages 58–61, differs from Savage's printed copy only in punctuation and occasionally in capitalization. The lists do not appear in Hotten's "Original Lists," New York, 1874.

A comparison of the text given in this article with the text printed by Savage shows, apart from punctuation and spelling, some different readings in the column in the first list headed "Certificates" and here and there some differences in names. According to Savage, seven children accompanied Robert Brooke; but the complete list gives the names of only six, of whom four bore the surname Brooke and two the surname Gallant. In other cases, also, it sometimes happens that not all of the children accompanying the head of a family are his own.

Aside from the corrections made by Mr. Jacobs to the printed lists of signers of certificates and heads of families, the names of seventy-seven children and kinsfolk of the heads of families emigrating and the names of forty-three servants, many of whom founded families in New England, have been brought to light in this copy. Under the heading "Servants" are included apprentices; and in many cases the persons so listed were relatives of the head of the family, and in some instances married children of their master, this fact showing that the social position of such masters and servants was the same.

The value of these lists will be readily recognized by all interested in New England history and genealogy. That Savage's suggestion, that, if the original lists could be inspected, undoubtedly the additional names would be recovered, has not resulted hitherto in the publication of the complete lists is a matter of some surprise.

Where necessary, explanations of readings in the text are given in footnotes, and notes on some of the passengers, arranged alphabetically by surnames, follow the two lists.

A list of all such persons as imbarqued themselves in the good shipp called the Hercules of Sandwich of the burthen of 200 tonnes or thereabouts whereof next under God John Witherley was master and therein transported from this town & port of Sandwich to the plantac̄on called New England in America together with a breif note of the certificates from the ministers where they have dwelt of their conversac̄on and Conformity to the orders and discipline of the Church, and that they had taken the oath of Allegeance and Supremacy according to an order of the Lds of his Mat^s Most Noble privie counsell of the last of December 1634 Videlt

Certificates	M^rs of families	Children	Servants
ffrom Mr Gee Vicar of Tenterden and from Jno Austen Mayor of Tenterden & ffregift Stace Jurat there dated 4 Mch 1634	Nathanel Tilden of Tenterden in Kent yeoman & Lidia his Wief	Joseph Thomas Stephen Marie Sara Judeth Lidia	Thos Lapham Geo Sutton Edwd fford Edwd Jeakins Sara Couchman Marie Perien James Bennet
ffrom the Same 2 Mch 1634 4 Mch 1634	Jonas Austen of Tenterden & Constance his Wief	Jonas Austen Lidia Robinson-Austen a litle childe	
ffrom Saml Marshall Mayor of Maidstone Thos Swinnok Jurat Edwd Duke & Robt Barrell Ministers there 14 Mch 1634	Robt Brooke of Maidstone in Kent Mercer & Anne his Wief	Thos Brooke Saml Brooke Elys Brook Dorothie Brooke	

		Abra: Gallant James Gallant	
ffrom Wm Culpeper Caleb Banckes, Edwd Duke & Hen Crispe ffrancis ffroiden cler. 14 Mch 1634	Thos Hayward of Aylesford in Kent Taylor & Susanna his Wief	Thomas John Elizabeth Susan Martha	
Mayor Maidstone &c as above 14 Mch 1634	Wm Witherell of Maidstone School Master & Mary his Wief	Saml Daniel Thomas	Anne Richards
ffrom Edw Chute Edmd Hayes Vicar of Ashford Elias Wood pson of Hinxhill 4 Mch 1634	ffannet not Wise Ashford Hemp-dresser*		
ffrom Mr Thos Warren Rector of St Peters Sandwich 14 Mch 1634	Thos Boney & Edwd Ewell† Shoemakers of Sandwich		
ffrom Mr Thos Gardener Vicar of St Maries in Sandwich 17 Mch 1634	Wm Hatch of Sandwich Merchant & Jane his Wief	Walter John Willm Anne Jane	Wm Holmes Joseph Ketchrell Simon Ketcrell Robt Jenings Symon Sutton Lidia Wells
ffrom Mr John Gee &c of Tenterden as above 15 Mch 1634	Saml Hinckley of Tenterden & Sara his Wief	Susan Sara Mary children and Elzab a kinswoman	
ffrom Thos Warren of Sandwich	Isaac Cole of Sandwich Carpenter	Isaac &	

*In this list as printed by Savage and others this entry reads: "Fannett . . . . of Ashford, hemp dresser." This passenger is undoubtedly identical with Faintnot Wines, flax-dresser, who was an inhabitant and proprietor of Charlestown, Mass., in 1635, was admitted to the church there 4 Nov. 1643, was freeman 29 May 1644, and died 25 Feb. 1664/5. In his will, dated 1 Sept. 1663, he mentions wife Bridget and various relatives, but no children of his own. Cf. Savage's Genealogical Dictionary and Pope's Pioneers of Massachusetts.

†"Hen. Ewell" in list as previously printed.

14 Mch 1634	& Joane his Wief	Jane	
Edwd [*sic*, ? Edm^d] Hayes Vicar of Ashford 12 Mch 1634			Rose Tritton of Ashford
The Same "	Thos Champion of Ashford		
Thos Warren of Sandwich & Thomas Harmon Vicar of Headcorn Mch 1634	Thos Besbeech of Ashford*	Mary Alice Elzab Egelden Jane Egelden Sara Egelden John Egelden	Thos Neuley Joseph Pacheury Agnes Love
Jno Gee &c of Tenterden as above 28 Feb / 1 Mch 1634	John Lewis of Tenterden & Sarah his Wief	Sarah Lewes	
Jos Leech Vicar of Bow in London 19 Mch 1634	Parnell Harris of the parish of Bow in London		
Edwd Nicholls Vicar of Northbourn 2 Feb 1634	Ja^s Sayers of Northbourne Kent Taylor		
Edm Hayes Vicar of Ashford in Kent 21 Mch Jno Honnywood / Thos Godfrey } Justices	Comfort Starre of Ashford in Kent Chirurgeon	Thomas Comfort Mary	Saml Dunkin, John Turkey, Truth shall prevail Starre
Robt Gorham Jurat of Great Chart in Kent 20 Mch 1634	Joseph Rootes of Great Chart		
Wm Sandford Rector of Eastwell in Kent 16 Mch 1634	Emme Mason of the parsh of Eastwell widow [?]		

*"Sandwich" in list as previously printed.

Thos Gardner of Sandwich as above 26 Mch 1634	Margaret Wief of Wm Johnes late of Sandwich now of New England painter	
Thos Jackson of St George Canterbury Feb 1634	John Best of the same Parish Taylor	
John Phillips minister of Faversham 5 Mch John Knowler Mayor Wm Thurston Jurat	Thos Brigden of the same town husbandman & . . . his Wief	twoe children

M^d^ That all those that have noe Certifictats affixed that they had taken the oath of Supremacy & Allegeance tooke the said oathes before the Mayor of Sandwich

The Mayor & Jurats of Sandwich

A true Roll or list of the names sirnames and qualities of all such persons which have taken passage from the Town & Port of Sandwich in the County of Kent for the American plantacons since the last cerificate of such passengers returned into the office of Dovor Castle from the said town of Sandwich
11 May 1637

	Children	Servants
1 Thos Starr of Canterbury yeoman & Susan his Wief	Constant Starr	
2 Edwd Johnson of Canterbury Joyner & Susan his Wief	Edward George William Mathew John Susan Martha	John ffarle John Ingland Ann Norcott
3 Nicholas Butler of Eastwell yeoman & Joice his Wief	John Henry Lidia	John Pope John Gill Richd Jenkin Marg^t^ Angells Christian Spice

4 Samuell Hall of Canterbury Yeoman & Joane his Wief		Edwd Page John Granger Grace Granger
5 Henry Bachelor of Dovor Brewer & Martha his Wief		John Bucke Susan Bucke Saml Taylor Margerie Walker
6 Joseph Bachelor of Canterbury Taylor & Elzabeth his Wife	Marke Bachelor	Thos Granger Edwd Harnet Mary Call
7 Henry Richardson of Canterbury Carpenter & Mary his Wief	John Henry Elisabeth Mary Rachell	
8 Jarvese Boykett of Thanington* Carpenter		Steven Granger
9 John Bachelor of Canterbury Taylor		
10 Nathaniel Ovell of Dovor Cordwinder		Thos Granger
11 Thos Calle of Feversham husbandman & Bennet his Wieff	Thomas John Margaret	
12 Wm Eaton of Staple husbandman & Martha his Wief	John Martha Albe	Jonas Eaton
13 Joseph Coleman of Sandwich Shoe maker & Sara his Wief	Joseph Zacharie Sara Mary	

*"Charington" in the list as previously printed; but there is no English parish of that name, while there is a parish of Thanington in Kent.

14 Mathew Smith of Sandwich Cordwinder & Sara* his Wief — Mathew, John, Hanna, Elisabeth

15 Marmaduke Peerce of Sandwich Taylor & Mary his Wief — John Hooke his apprentice

In Witness whereof wee the Maior & Jurats of the towne & porte of Sandwich aforesaid have hereunto caused the seale of the Office of Maioraltie to be put & sett dated the nynth day of June in the twelveth yeare of the reigne of our sovrayne lord King Charles by the grace of God of England 1637

NOTES

Austen, Jonas, of Staplehurst and Tenterden, co. Kent, and of Cambridge, Hingham, and Taunton, Mass., passenger in the *Hercules*. For his family and ancestry cf. REGISTER, vol 67, pp. 161–166. His wife Constance was the widow of William Robinson of Tenterden, and Lydia Robinson, who appears among the children accompanying Jonas Austen to New England, was the daughter of Constance Austen by her former husband.

Bachelor, Henry, of Dover (formerly of Canterbury), co. Kent, and of Ipswich, Mass., brewer, whose name appears on the second passenger list, was of the parish of St. George, Canterbury, and was a bachelor, aged about 35, on 15 Apr. 1637, when a licence was granted for his marriage with Martha Wilson, of the same parish, virgin, aged about 32. In this licence he is called Henry Bacheller. The marriage was to be solemnized at Thanington, and Joseph Bachelor of Canterbury, tailor [probably a brother of Henry Bachelor], was bondsman. (Cowper's Canterbury Marriage Licences, Second Series, column 74.) He settled at Ipswich, Mass., and died 2 Feb. 1678/9. His widow died 4 Apr. 1686. (Cf. Savage's Genealogical Dictionary and Pope's Pioneers of Massachusetts.)

Bachelor, John, of Canterbury, co. Kent, and of Salem, Mass., tailor, whose name appears on the second passenger list given above, was probably a younger brother of Henry and Joseph Bachelor of the same list. He settled in Salem, deposed in 1658, aged about 47 years, and died 13, 9 mo. 1675. For his family cf. Savage's "Genealogical Dictionary" and Pope's "Pioneers of Massachusetts."

Bachelor, Joseph, of Canterbury, co. Kent, and of Salem and Wenham, Mass., tailor, whose name appears on the second passenger list given above, was of the parish of St. George, Canterbury, and was a bachelor, aged about 24 and upwards, on 22 Dec. 1628, when a licence was granted for his marriage with Elizabeth Dickinson, of the same parish, virgin, aged about 15, daughter of Susan Dickenson, of the same parish, widow. In this licence he is called Joseph Batcheler. The marriage was to be solemnized at Thanington. (Cowper's Canterbury Marriage Licences, Second Series, column 74.) The printed "Register Booke of the Parish of St: George," Canterbury, p. 24, contains the record of the baptism of Elizabeth Dickenson, daughter of

*"Jane" in the list as previously printed.

Robert Dickinson, 10 Apr. 1614. The same parish register also shows that John, son of Joseph Bacheler, was buried 1 May 1631 (p. 184), that Mary and Martha, daughters of Joseph Bachelor and Elizabeth Diconson his wife, were baptized 20 June 1634 (p. 32) and were buried the same day (p. 185), and that Mark, son of Joseph Bacheler and Elizabeth Dickinson his wife, was baptized 4 Oct. 1635 (p. 32). Joseph Bachelor settled at Salem, whence he removed to Wenham. He died in 1 mo. 1647/8. (Cf. Pope, Pioneers of Massachusetts, p. 26.) He was probably a brother of Henry and John Bachelor, whose names appear on the same passenger list.

Besbeech, Thomas, of Biddenden, Frittenden, Headcorn, and Sandwich, co. Kent, of Scituate in the Plymouth Colony, and of Sudbury, Mass., passenger in the *Hercules*, was a widower when he emigrated to New England, his wife, Anne Baseden, whom he married at Biddenden, 14 Jan. 1618/19, having been buried at Frittenden 21 Apr. 1634. The Frittenden registers contain the record of the baptisms of two daughters of Thomas Besbeech, viz., Sara, 6 Jan. 1621/2, and Alice, 29 June 1624. For his parentage, family, and connection with the Fosters cf. REGISTER, vol. 67, pp. 33–36. The parentage of the four Egelden children who accompanied him in the *Hercules* has not been discovered, although many records and a pedigree of the Iggledens of co. Kent are printed in REGISTER, vol. 65, pp. 174–187.

Brooke, Robert, of Maidstone, co. Kent, and Anne, his wife, passengers in the *Hercules.* A licence for the marriage of Robert Brooke, of Maidstone, silk-weaver, and Sarah Pierse, of the same parish, virgin, daughter of Samuel Pierse, of the same parish, yeoman, was granted 3 June 1618, and the marriage was solemnized 4 June 1618, the contracting parties being recorded as Robert Brook and Sara Peirse (Canterbury Marriage Licences, First Series, column 66, and Marriage Registers of All Saints, Maidstone, p. 39). A licence for the marriage of Robert Brooke, of Maidstone, tailor, bachelor, aged about 25, and Ann Dirrick, of the same parish, widow, aged about 25, relict of William Dirricke, late of the same parish, tailor, deceased, the marriage to take place at Harrietsham, was granted 20 Apr. 1621 (Canterbury Marriage Licences, Second Series, column 144). Robert Brooke and Elizabeth Peckham were married at Maidstone, 19 Jan. 1628/9 (Marriage Registers of All Saints, Maidstone, p. 46). Robert Brook, tailor, and Ann Lawrence, widow, were married at Maidstone, 11 Sept. 1634 (*ib.*, p. 49). A licence for the marriage of Robert Brooke, of Maidstone, tailor, widower, and Mary Garnet, of the same parish, virgin, aged about 28, whose parents were dead, was granted 10 Aug. 1637, and the marriage of Robert Brooke and Mary Garlett was solemnized at Maidstone, 5 Sept. 1637 (Canterbury Marriage Licences, Second Series, column 144, and Marriage Registers of All Saints, Maidstone, p. 51). In the REGISTER, vol. 61, p. 385, in a communication from the Committee on English Research of the New England Historic Genealogical Society, Mr. Joseph Gardner Bartlett states that the Robert Brooke of the marriage licence of 1621 was the man who came to New England in the *Hercules*; but the Robert Brook who married Ann Lawrence, widow, 11 Sept. 1634, may have been the passenger in the *Hercules*, and in that case probably all of the four Brooke children were children by a former wife, who was, perhaps, the bride in one of the earlier marriages (including that of 1621) given in this note. Savage (Genealogical Dictionary) states that a Robert Brookes of New London, 1650, was perhaps the passenger in the *Hercules*. Pope (Pioneers of Massachusetts) says that the Robert Brooke of the *Hercules* resided at Marblehead. There seems to be no proof that he remained in New England. If he returned to England, he may be the man whose marriage at Maidstone, in 1637, is given above in this note. The surname Callant, of which Gallant is probably another form, was a common one in Maidstone at that period, and perhaps Abraham and James Gallant, who are listed among the children accompanying Robert Brooke to New England, were his stepsons.

Bucke, John and **Susan,** whose names appear on the second passenger list given above as servants of Henry Bachelor, are found in the printed "Records and Files of the Quarterly Courts of Essex County, Massachusetts." Susan Bucke was charged with slandering Henry Bachelour, 4 Nov. 1645, but the verdict was for the defendant (p. 87); and she brought action against Henry Bachelour, 29 Sept. 1646, for detaining goods (p. 109). At the court held at Ipswich

26 Mar. 1650 John Buck was fined for stealing ½ bushel of wheat, and was ordered to pay his dame 7s. 6d. (p. 188).

Calle, Thomas, of Faversham, co. Kent, husbandman, whose name appears on the second passenger list given above, settled at Charlestown, Mass. Cf. Savage's "Genealogical Dictionary" and Pope's "Pioneers of Massachusetts." Thomas Green of Malden, Mass., had a wife Margaret, who according to Savage, "Genealogical Dictionary," vol. 2, p. 306, was "perhaps" a daughter of the first Thomas Call, Thomas Green's "brother Thomas Call" being one of the executors of his will. This passenger list, which shows that Thomas Calle had a daughter Margaret, confirms Savage's conjecture.

Hatch, William, of Ashford, Wye, and Sandwich, co. Kent, and of Scituate in the Plymouth Colony, passenger in the *Hercules*. For his family and ancestry cf. REGISTER, vol. 70, pp. 245–260. His wife was Jane Young of Thanington, co. Kent. His son Walter was probably his child by a former wife. Two of his children by his wife Jane were buried at Wye.

Hinckley, Samuel, of Tenterden, co. Kent, and of Scituate and Barnstable in the Plymouth Colony, passenger in the *Hercules*. For his family and ancestry cf. REGISTER, vol. 65, pp. 287–290, 314–319, and vol. 68, pp. 186, 188–189. His wife, whom he married at Hawkhurst, co. Kent, 7 May 1617, was Sarah Soole, baptized at Hawkhurst 8 June 1600, daughter of Thomas and Mary (Iddenden) Soole of Hawkhurst. Their oldest child, Thomas Hinckley, the well-known Governor of the Plymouth Colony, was baptized at Hawkhurst 19 Mar. 1619/20. A son and a daughter of Samuel and Sarah (Soole) Hinckley were buried at Tenterden, and another son and daughter who were baptized at Tenterden probably died young in England. It is to be noticed that their son Thomas was not among the children who accompanied them in the *Hercules*, as Savage (Genealogical Dictionary) conjectures and Pope (Pioneers of Massachusetts) states, but that the four children of the passenger list were their three daughters, Susan, Sarah, and Mary, and a kinswoman, Elzab, i.e., Elizabeth.

Hooke, John, see Peerce, Marmaduke.

Johnson, Edward, of Canterbury, co. Kent, and Woburn, Mass., whose name appears on the second passenger list given above, was the well-known author of the "Wonderworking Providence of Sion's Savior in New England." For his family and ancestry cf. REGISTER, vol. 67, pp. 169–180, and the "Johnson Genealogy," by Alfred Johnson, Boston, 1914, pp. 137–142. His wife was Susan Munnter. They had eight children, of whom one, William, was buried at Canterbury and seven were brought by them to New England.

Pacheury, Joseph, who appears on the passenger list of the *Hercules* as servant of Thomas Besbeech, is probably identical with the Joseph Patching or Patchen who married at Roxbury, 10 Apr. 1642, Elizabeth Ingulden or Iggleden, widow of Stephen Iggleden. Cf. REGISTER, vol. 65, p. 187, Savage's "Genealogical Dictionary," and Pope's "Pioneers of Massachusetts."

Peerce, Marmaduke, of Sandwich, co. Kent, tailor, whose name appears on the second passenger list given above, is evidently the Marmaduke Percy of Salem, Mass., who was tried in 1639 for the murder of his apprentice (probably the John Hooke of the same list) and was finally acquitted. Cf. Winthrop's "History of New England," vol. 1, p. 384 (Savage's second edition).

Pope, John, who appears on the second passenger list as a servant of Nicholas Butler, settled in Dorchester, Mass., where his master, Nicholas Butler, settled. The latter removed to Martha's Vineyard about 1651, but John Pope continued to live in Dorchester, had a wife Alice, and died 18 Oct. 1686, leaving a widow, Margaret, and children. In his "History of the Dorchester Pope Family," Boston, 1888, the late Rev. Charles Henry Pope maintained that this John Pope was the son of the John Pope, who, with wife Jane, was in Dorchester as early as 3 Sept. 1634 and is called "John Pope senior" in an entry in the town records dated 27, 11 mo. 1645 [1645/6.] Mr. Pope held to this theory in spite of the fact that the will of the elder John Pope, proved 5, 4 mo. 1649 (the testator died 12, 2 mo. 1646), and that of his widow, Jane Pope, dated 18 Apr. 1662, mention no children except a daughter. They had had a son John, born 30, 4 mo. 1635, who undoubtedly died before his father, and a son Nathan, who was born and died in 5 mo. 1641, but their daughter, Patience Blake, must have been their only surviving child. The presence in Dorchester of the John Pope who, according to Rev. Charles Henry Pope, was the son of "John Pope senior" is explained by the fact that his master, Nicholas Butler, with whom he came to New England, settled in Dorchester, and no relationship between this servant of Nicholas Butler and "John Pope senior" has been proved. The immigrant ancestor of the Dorchester Pope family was, therefore, the John Pope who came from Kent as one of the servants of Nicholas Butler.

Spice, Christian, whose name appears in the second passenger list given above as servant of Nicholas Butler, is probably identical with the "Christian Spisor a maide servant" who is found in Rev. John Eliot's record of members of the Roxbury church.

Starr, Thomas, of Canterbury, co. Kent, and of Boston, Mass., whose name appears on the second passenger list given above, was, according to Savage (Genealogical Dictionary), a younger brother of Comfort Starr, who was a passenger in the *Hercules*, but this relationship seems doubtful. Cf. Burgis Pratt Starr's "Starr Family," p. ii.

Starre [Starr], **Comfort,** of Ashford, co. Kent, and of Cambridge, Mass., Duxbury in the Plymouth Colony, and Boston, Mass., passenger in the *Hercules*. For him and his family cf. REGISTER, vol. 64, pp. 73–74, and the "Starr Family," by Burgis Pratt Starr, Hartford, Conn., 1879.

Tilden, Nathaniel, of Tenterden, co. Kent, and of Scituate in the Plymouth Colony, passenger in the *Hercules*. For his family and ancestry cf. REGISTER, vol. 65, pp. 322–333. His wife was Lydia Huckstep, baptized at Tenterden 11 Feb. 1587/8, daughter of Steven and Winifred (Hatch) (Wills) (cf. REGISTER, vol. 67, pp. 47, 48). Nathaniel and Lydia (Huckstep) Tilden had twelve children baptized at Tenterden. Five of these children were buried at Tenterden, and seven accompanied their parents to New England. Their daughter Mary married 13 Mar. 1636/7 Thomas Lapham, and their daughter Sarah married on the same day George Sutton, both of these men appearing in the passenger list as servants of Nathaniel Tilden.

TWO EARLY PASSENGER LISTS: ADDITIONS AND CORRECTIONS. — In July 1921 Mr. Eben Putnam of Wellesley Farms, Mass., communicated to the REGISTER (vol. 75, pp. 217–226) a very important article containing a complete copy of two lists of passengers sailing from the port of Sandwich, co. Kent,

England, for New England, the first list giving the names of the passengers in the *Hercules*, in the spring of 1634/5, and the second list the names of other passengers migrating to New England up to the late spring of 1637. These lists are preserved in the borough records of Sandwich; and partial copies, giving the names of the heads of families and their wives, with the numbers only, but not the names, of the children and servants in the various families, were published before the end of the eighteenth century by William Boys in his "History of Sandwich" and have been reprinted in divers American publications from 1843 on. Mr. Putnam's article, in addition to making a few changes in the previously printed lists of signers of certificates and heads of families, revealed the names of seventy-seven children and kinsfolk of the heads of the emigrating families and also the names of forty-three servants, many of whom founded families in New England. As I copied these lists, *verbatim et literatim*, in 1911 from the Sandwich records, I submit in this note a few corrections and one addition to the lists as given in Mr. Putnam's copy, which was made for him by J. A. Jacobs, Esq., of Sandwich, an alderman of that borough and honorary curator of its archives. The references are to the pages of volume 75 of the REGISTER.

Page 218, column 3. Delete the hyphen after "Lydia Robinson." The third child accompanying Jonas Austen, described as "[*blank*] Austen a litle childe," was Mary Austen, baptized at Tenterden, co. Kent, 5 Aug. 1632. (Cf. REGISTER, vol. 67, pp. 162, 166.)

Page 218, column 3. The original list gives the names of *five* (not four) children of Robert Brooke, as follows: Thomas Brooke, Sam: Brooke, John Brooke, Eliz: Brooke, Dorothie Brooke.

Page 219, column 2. The name given as "ffannet not Wise" should be "Fannetnot Wines" or "Faunetnot Wines." In the Ashford parish register the Christian name appears as "Faint not."

Page 219, column 2. For "Thos Boney & Edwd Ewell Shoemakers of Sandwich" read "Thomas Bony & Henry Ewell of Sandwch shoemakers."

Page 219, column 4. For "Joseph Ketchrell" and "Simon Ketcrell," among the servants of William Hatch, read "Joseph Ketchell" and "Simon Ketchell."

Page 219, column 3. The original list gives the surname of Samuel Hinckley's children as "Hinckley," the spelling which he always used; but for "Elzab a kinswoman" the reading should be "Eliz: Hincle a kinswo," the surname of this girl, who was a niece of Samuel Hinckley, being spelled as her father, Stephen Hincle or Hinckle of Milton by Sittingbourne, co. Kent, spelled it, omitting the *y* and reverting to the earlier form of the name. (Cf. REGISTER, vol. 65, pp. 288, 315, 317, 318.)

Page 219, column 1. For "Thos Warren of Sandwich" read "Mr Tho: Warren rector of St Pr p'ish in Sandwich."

Page 220, column 3. The name of the daughter of Isaac Cole should be "Anne," instead of "Jane."

Page 220, column 1. For "Edwd" as the Christian name of the vicar of Ashford read "Edm:." Other entries also show that his name was Edmund.

Page 220, column 2. For "Thos Besbeech of Ashford" read "Tho: Besbeech of Sandwch in Kent."

Page 220, column 4. For "Joseph Pacheury," as the second servant of Thomas Besbeech, read "Joseph Pacheing."

Page 220, column 1. The name of the vicar of Bow should be "Jo: [i.e., John] Leech."

Page 220, column 4. The surname of the second servant of Comfort Starre should be "Turvey" or "Turbey."

Page 220, column 1. For "Robt Gorham Jurat of Great Chart" read "Robt Gorham curat of great Chart."

Page 220, column 2, last line. Delete the interrogation mark in brackets after the word "widow," the original entry reading "Emme Mason of the p'ish of Eastwell wid."

Page 221, column 1. For "Thos Gardner of Sandwich" read "Mr Tho: Gardiner vicar of St Maries in the p'ish of Sandwch."

Page 222, column 2. The name of the last child of William Eaton is written "Albe," the line over it indicating the omission of one or more letters.

Page 223, column 1. For "Sara," as the Christian name of the wife of Mathew Smith, read "Jane."

It may be added that the statement in Register, vol. 75, p. 217, that these lists do not appear in Hotten's "Original Lists," is incorrect, since they are printed on pp. xix–xxi of that work.

Boston, Mass. Elizabeth French Bartlett.

EMIGRANTS* IN THE HERCULES OF SANDWICH,

Of 200 tons, John Witherley, master, bound for "the plantation called New England in America, with certificates from the ministers where they last dwelt, of their conversation, and conformity to the orders and discipline of the church, and that they had taken the oath of allegiance and supremacy."

Nathaniel Tilden of Tenterden, yeoman, wife Lydia, seven children, and seven servants. Certificates from Mr. Jno. Gee, Vicar of Tenterden, 26 Feb. 1634, Jno. Austin, Mayor of Tenterden, and Fregift Stace, jurat, 4 Mar. 1634.†

Jonas Austen, of Tenterden, Constance, his wife, and four children. Certificates from Mr. Jno. Gee, 1st Mar. 1634, Jno. Austin, Mayor, and Fregit Stace, jurat, 4 Mar. 1634.

Rob. Brook, of Maidstone, mercer, Ann, his wife, and seven children. Certificates from Samuel Marshall, mayor of Maidstone, Tho. Swinnok, jurat, Edw. Duke and Rob. Barrel, ministers, 14 Mar. 1634.

Tho. Heyward, of Aylesford, taylor, Susannah, his wife, and five children. Certificates from William Colepeper, Caleb Bancks, Edw. Duke, Han. Crispe, Franc. Froiden, cler. 14 Mar. 1634.

Will. Witherell, of Maidstone, schoolmaster, Mary, his wife, three children, and one servant. Certificates from Sam. Marshal, mayor of Maidstone, Tho. Swinnuck, Edw. Duke and Rob. Barrel, cl. 14 Mar. 1634.

Fannett . . . . of Ashford,‡ hemp dresser. Certificates from Edw. Chute, Edm. Hayes, vicar of Ashford, Elias Wood, parson of Hinxhill,§ 4 Mar. 1634.

Tho. Boney and Han. Ewell, of Sandwich, shoemakers. Certificate from Mr. Tho. Warren, rector of St. Peters, in Sandwich, 14 Mar. 1634.

Will. Hatch, of Sandwich, merchant, Jane, his wife, five children and six servants. Certificate from Mr. Tho. Gardener, vicar of St. Mary's, Sandwich, 17 Mar. 1634.

Sam. Hinkley, of Tenterden, Sarah his wife, and four children. Certificates, Mr. Jno. Gee, vicar of Tenterden, Jn. Austin, mayor, Fregift Stace, jurat, 15 Mar. 1634.

Isaac Cole, of Sandwich, carpenter, Joan his wife, and two children. Certificate from Mr. Tho. Warren, rector of St. Peter, Sandwich, 14 Mar. 1634.

A servant. A certificate from Edm. Hayes, vicar of Ashford, 21 Mar. 1634.

Tho. Champion, of Ashford. Certificate from Edm. Hayes, vicar, 12 Mar. 1634.

Tho. Besbeech, of Sandwich, six children and three servants. Certificates from Tho. Warren, rector of St. Peter's, Sandwich, 13 Mar. 1634. Tho. Harman, vicar of Hedcorn, 6 Mar. 1634.

Jno. Lewis, of Tenterden, Sarah his wife and one child. Certificates from Jno. Gee, vicar of Tenterden, 20 Feb. 1634. Jno. Austin, mayor, and Fregift Stace, jurat, 1st Mar. 1634.

---

* From the History of Sandwich, by William Boys, 4to, Canterbury, 1786–92.
† The year in this list must be understood 1634–5.
‡ In Kent, doubtless; though there were at that day no less than eight Ashfords.
§ Hinksell, Hinxell. The same, in Kent.

Parnel Harris, of Bow, London. Certificate from Jos. Leeth, vicar of Bow, London. 19 Mar. 1634.

James Sayers, of Northburn,* taylor. Certificate from Edw. Nicholls, vicar of Northburn, 2 Feb. 1634.

Comfort Starre, of Ashford, chirurgion. Three children and three servants. Certificates from Edm. Hayes, vicar of Ashford, 21 Mar. 1634. Jno. Honnywood, Tho. Godfrey, justices.

Jos. Rootes, of Great Chart. Cert. from Rob. Gorsham, curate of great Chart, 20 Mar. 1634.

Em. Mason, of Eastwell, wid. Certificate from Will. Sandford, rector of Eastwell, 16 Mar. 1634.

Margt. wife of Will Jones, late of Sandwich, now of New England, painter. Certificate from Tho. Gardiner, vicar of St. Mary's, Sandwich, 26 Mar. 1634.

Jno. Best, of St. George's, Canterbury, taylor. Certificate from Tho. Jackson, minister of St. Georges, Canterbury, ult. Feb. 1634.

Tho. Bridgen, of Faversham, husbandman, his . . . . . wife and two children. Certificates from Jno. Phillips, minister of Faversham, 5 March, 1634, Jno. Knowler, mayor, and Will. Thurston, jurat.

[In another part of the same work the following list is found, " of persons who have taken passage from the town and port of Sandwich for the American Plantations since the last certificate of such passengers returned into the office of Dover Castle." Whether their destination was for New England is left to conjecture. However, it is pretty certain that some of them found their way there eventually. The list is " certified under the seal of office of mayoralty, 9 June, 1637."]

Thomas Starr, of Canterbury, yeoman, Susan, his wife, and one child.

Edward Johnson, of Canterbury, joiner, Susan, his wife, seven children and three servants.

Nicholas Butler, of Eastwell, yeoman, Joice, his wife, three children and five servants.

Samuel Hall, of Canterbury, yeoman, Joan, his wife, and three servants.

Henry Bachelor, of Dovor, brewer, Martha, his wife, and four servants.

Joseph Bachelor, of Canterbury, taylor, Elizabeth, his wife, one child and three servants.

Henry Richardson, of Canterbury, carpenter, Mary, his wife, and five children.

Jarvis Boykett, of Charington, carpenter, and one servant.

John Bachelor, of Canterbury, taylor.

Nathaniel Ovell, of Dovor, cordwinder, and one servant.

Thomas Calle, of Faversham, husbandman, Bennett, his wife, and three children.

William Eaton, of Staple, husbandman, Martha, his wife, three children, and one servant.

Joseph Coleman, of Sandwich, shoemaker, Sara, his wife, and four children.

Matthew Smith, of Sandwich, cordwinder, Jane, his wife, and four children.

Marmaduke Peerce, of Sandwich, taylor, Mary, his wife, and one servant.

* In Kent, Northborne in some early topographies.

PASSENGERS FOR NEW ENGLAND, 1638.

[The following list of early emigrants or passengers was obtained for the New England Historic Genealogical Society, by Henry Stevens, Esq., one of its members, lately resident in London.]

Southampton, 24° Aprill, 1638.

The List of the names of the Passengers intended for New-England, in the good shipp, the Confidence of London, of 200 tonnes, John Jobson $M^{r.}$—— and thus by vertue of Lord Treasurers warrant of the 11th of Aprill, 1638.

Names.	Residence.	Occupation.	Ages.
Walter Hayne,	Sutton, Mandifield, Co. of Wilts.,	Lennen Weaver,	55
Eliza, his wife,			
Thomas Hayne,			
John Hayne,	their sonnes, under 16 years of age.		
Josias Hayne,			
Saffranc,	their daughters.		
Mary,			
John Blanford,			27
John Riddet,	their servants,		26
Rich: Bildcombe,			16
Peter Noyce,	Penton, Co. of $South^{n.}$	Yeoman,	47
Thomas Noyce, his sonne,			15
Elizabeth Noyce, his daughter.			
Robert Davis,			30
John Rutter,	his servants,		22
Margaret Davis,			26
Nicholas Guy,	Upton Gray, Co. of Southampton,	Carpenter,	50
Jane, his wife,			30
Mary Guy, his daughter,			
Joseph Taynter,	servants,		25
Robert Bayley,			23
John Bent,	Penton, Co. of Southampton,	Husbandman,	35
Martha, his wife,			
Robert Bent,			
William Bent,			
Peter Bent,	his children, under 12 yeares of age.		
John Bent,			
Ann,			
Roger Porter,	Long Sutton, Co. Southampton,	Husbandman,	55
Joane Porter,			
Susan Porter,	his daughters,		
Mary Porter,			
Rose Porter,			
John Sanders,	Lanford, Co. Wilts.,	$Husbd^{m.}$	25
Sara, his wife,			
John Cole,			40

Names.	Residence.	Occupation.	Ages.
Roger Casman, } servants,			15
Richard Blake, } servants,			16
William Cottle, } servants,			12
Robert King, } servants,			24
John Roaff,	Melchitt Parke, Wilsheir,	Husbd$^{m.}$	50
Ann, his wife,			
John Roaff, } their sons, 4 years & under,			
Thomas Roaff, } their sons, 4 years & under,			
Richard Sangar, his servant,			18
Thomas Goodenowe,	Shasbury,		30
Jane, his wife,			
Thomas Goodenowe, his sonne,			1
Ursula, his sister,			
Edmund Kerley,	Ashmore,	Husband$^{n.}$	22
William Kerley,	Ashmore,	"	
Edmund Morres,	Reniton Magna, Co. Dorset,	Carpenter,	
Stephan Kent,	England,		17
Margery, his wife,			16
George Churche, } servants,			16
Hugh Marche, } servants,			20
Anthony Sadler, } servants,			9
Nicholas Wallington, a poore Boy,			
Rebecca Kent, servant,			16
John Stephens,	Gowsham, Co. Oxoñ,	Husband$^{n.}$	31
William Stephens,	"	"	21
Eliza, his wife,			
Alice, his mother,			
John Lowgie, } servants,			16
Grace Lowgie, } servants,			
Thomas Jones,	Gowsham,	Tayler,	36
Ann, his wife, &			
Four children under 10 years,			
William Baunche, } servants,			24
Jude Denley, } servants,			
Martha Wilder,	Shiplocke, Oxfordshire,	Spinster,	
Mary Wilder, her daughter,			
Augustin Bearce,			20
John Keene,			17
Marthe Keene,			60
Eliza Keene,			
Martha Keene,			
Josias Keene,			
Sarah Keene,			
John Binson,	Gowsham, Oxfordshire,	Husbandmn,	30
Mary, his wife,			
John Binson, } their children, under 4 years,			
Mary Binson, } their children, under 4 years,			
William Ilsbey,		Shoemaker,	26
John Ilsbey,		"	

Names.	Residence.	Occupation.	Ages.
Barbara, his wife,			20
Philip Davies, his servant,			12
Joseph Parker,	Newbary,	Tanner,	24
Sarah Osgood & 4 children,	Horrell,	Spinster,	
William Osgood, William Jones, } children under 11 years, &			
Margery Parke, servant,			
John Ludwell,			50
Henry Haugert, } servants,			40
David Whealer, } servants,			11
Richard Bidgood,	Romsey,	Merchant.	

Signed THO: WULRRIES, Col: & Suff.
HEN: CHAMPANTE, Cust:
N. DINGLEY, Comp^tr.

The number of the passengers afore mentioned, greate & little, are 110 soules.

(S. P. O. Am: & West Indies. v. 375.)
(New England.)

CORRECTIONS OF NAMES, PLACES, &c.

RELATING TO NEW ENGLAND EMIGRANTS, WRONGLY GIVEN IN THE MASS. HIST. COLL. AND IN THE N. E. H. G. REG.

[Communicated by H. G. SOMERBY, Esq.]

N. E. Hist. Reg. Vol. 2, page 108.

For Walter Hayne, Eliza, his wife, Sutton, Mandifield, *r.* Eliz: his wife, Sutton-Mansfield.—Saffranc, *r.* Suffrance.—Nicholas Guy, Upton Gray, *r.* Upton.—Mary Guy his daughter, *r.* Mary his daughter.—Robert Bent, William Bent, Peter Bent, John Bent, Ann, his children, under 12 yeares of age, *r.* Robert, William, Peter, John and Ann their children: all under ye age of XII yeares.—Joane Porter, Susan Porter, Mary Porter, Rose Porter, *r.* Joane, Susan, Mary, & Rose.—Roger Casman 15, *r.* Robert Easman, 25.—John Roaf, Ann his wife, John Roaf, Thomas Roaf, their sons, 4 years & under, *r.* John Roaf, Ann his wife, and Hester their Daughter. Richard Sangar, his servant, *r.* Thomas Whittle, their servant.—Omitted in the Reg. John Goodnowe, 42, of Semly in Wilsheir Husbandman Jane his wife, Lydie & Jane their daughters. Edmund Goodnowe of Dunhead in Wilsheire Husbandman, 27 Ann his wife, John and Thomas their sonns, 4 years & under. Richard Sangar his servant. 18.—For Edmond Morres, Reniton, *r.* Keniton.—George Churche, r. George Marche.—John Stephens, of Gowsham, *r.* Caversham.—Thomas Jones, Gowsham, *r.* Caversham p^va.—John Binson, Gowsham, *r.* Caversham.—Philip Davies, *r.* Phillip Davis.—Sarah Osgood, Horrell, *r.* Sarah Osgood of Herrell.

PASSENGERS TO AMERICA.

UNDER this head we propose to print lists of passengers and memoranda of the arrival of vessels in America. Contributions to this series of articles are solicited from our friends.

No. I.

ARRIVALS IN BOSTON, MASS., MAY TO JUNE, 1712.

From Manuscripts belonging to the New-England Historic, Genealogical Society.

Massachusets Impost Office, Boston.

Vessells Entered in ye Month of March, 1711–12

8th John Row ye Sloop Dorcas & Mary from Fyall
No Passengers
10th John Mathews ye Sloop Content from South Carolina
No Passengers
Ebenezr Swan ye Brigtt Fraternity from Turtuda
No Passengers
24th Allexeandr Duncan ye Swallow from Mary Land
No Passengers
John Gardner ye Sloop Seartryall from Virginia
No Passengers
John Mitchell ye Sloop Hanah & Mary from N Carolina
No Passengers
Henry Cally ye Bark Seaflower from Fyall
No Passengers
Thomas Bell ye Sloop Mary from Pocomoke Verginia
No Passengers
Nathanll Harris ye Sloop Vergin from Maryland
No Passengers
Moses Abbott ye Sloop Swallow from N Carolina
No Passengers

Dated Boston, March 31st 1712.

p' DAN: RUSSELL, Comer

Massachusets Impost Office Boston.

Vessells Entred in ye Month April 1712

ye 4th John Dimon ye Sloop Aduenture from Stt Christophr
No Passengers
Arthur Rexford ye Sloope Rose from Antigua
No Passengers
Michall Gill ye Ship John Gally from Turtuda
No Passengers but Marreners
5th James Killying ye Sloop Mary from North Carolina
No Passengers
Thomas Ienkins ye Sloop Vnion from Virgina
No Passengers

John Venteman ye Ship Han^a^ & Eliz^a^ from Turtuda
No Passengers
Wm Marsh ye Sloop W^m^ & Sarah from New York
Joseph Thorn } Planters
John Wright }
Dan^ll^ Lawrance }
7th Joseph White ye Ship Sheppard from Turtuda
No Passengers
John Breet ye Brig^tt^ Katherine from Holland
No Passengers
8th Peter Papillon ye Ship Sarah from London
Twenty Nine Marriners
James Gouge Gentleman
William Carkett ye Sloop Endeavor from Virgina
No Passengers
John Tuffton ye Sloop Tryall from Surenam
No Passengers
Benj^a^ Juery ye Sloop Endeavor from S^tt^ Christophers
No Passengers
9th John Petty ye Sloop Dubertus from North Carolina
No Passengers
William Cook ye Sloop Dimond from Mounseratt
No Passengers
John Royall ye Sloop Speadwell from North Carolina
No Passengers
10th Joseph Jenkins ye Sloop Vnity from North Carolina
No Passengers
12th Andr^r^ Gibson ye Brig^tt^ Succes from Glasgow
John Alron } Traders
Patrick Cheap }
Robert Clarke }
George Seiruin A Youth for Education
Peacock A Cordwainer
14th Amos Story ye Sloop Friends Aduenture from Turtuda
No Passengers
Thomas Dalling ye Sloop Dragon from Fyall
No Passengers
Richard Fifield ye Ship Eliz^a^ from Turtuda
No Passengers
Francis Norris ye Brig^tt^ Martha & Hanah from Mounseratt
Allexcander Baker Marin^r^ & his Seruant
Haynes } belonging to New York
Scott }
Thomas Lathrop ye Sloop Johan^a^ & Thankfull from N. york
No Passengers
Robert Sanders ye Sloop Daniel from Virginia
No Passengers
15th John Cooper ye Sloop Black Cock from Virginia
No Passengers
Andrew Meade ye Sloop Macy from Virginia
No Passengers
19th William Thomas ye Ship Succes from Surenam
Johanes Vanharbergreen Merch^tt^

26th Phillip Callender ye Sloop Ann from New York
No Passengers
Francis Biluton ye Sloop Fisher from Philedelpha
No Passengers
28th Nathll Mason ye Sloop Eliza from Stt Georges
No Passengers but Marreners
Thomas Vernam ye Barque Vnion from Barnstable
No Passengers
Thomas Landell ye Sloop Betty from Antigua
No Passengers
George Huntington ye Brigtt Macy from London
No Passengers but Marriners
Edward Tyng ye Brigtt Hope from Fyall
William Wilson Merchtt
and Six Marreners
29th Lewis Hunt ye Barque Hopewell from Surenam
John Seylor A Saylor

Dated Boston April 30th

p' DAN: RUSSELL Comer

Massachusets — Impost Office Boston

Vessells Entered in ye Month of May 1712

1st John Foster ye Sloop Maulborough from Antigua
No Passengers
3d William Alden ye Brigtt Stt John Battis from Anopolis
No Passengers
5th Thomas Miors ye Ship Friendship from South Carolina
John Jorden, A Merchtt
John Wakefield ye Brigtt. Lisbon Merchtt. from Lisbon
No Passengers but Marriners
Daniel Marshall ye Brigtt. Lepard from Nevis
No Passengers
12th Joseph Penwell ye Sloop Orringtree from Newfd Land
No Passengers
13th John Jenkens ye Brigtt Jera & Thoms from Madera
No Passengers
Jona Bull ye Sloop Two Brothers from Anopolis
No Passengers
15th John Secomb ye Sloop Swallow from Madera
No Passengers
17th John Hayes ye Ship Marcy & Sarah from Barbados
Sarah Blanchard A Marryed Woman
Aibel Macumber ye Sloop Speadwell from Jamaica
Brattle Oliver Merchtt
John Rogers Phissihon
David Jones Seruent
Thomas Simpson ye Sloop Succes from Barbados
No Passengers
19th Peter King ye Ship John & Mary from Barbados
No Passengers
William Euerton, ye Brigtt Releaf from Madera
No Passengers

20th Newcomb Blaque ye Ship Neptune from Barbados

Benja Wright Josiah Jackson Samll Hill Samll Rooke Thomas Jones Smith	Merchtts

21st George Phillips ye Brigtt Aduenture from Surenam
No Passengers
23d Charles Howell ye Sloop Dubertus from New London
Zacharia Rogers Cordwainer
Two Marriners
29th John Pumroy ye Sloop Sarah & Mary from N:Fd Land
No Passengers
Joseph Atkins ye Pink Sarah from Newfound Land
No Passengers
William Euerton ye Sloop Anna from Bristoll & Fyall
Eleazer Armitage
William Hutton ye Ship Jamaica Gally from Jamaica
Lenord Vassell Esqr & his Sone & Dafter
David Preshaw ye Ship Expedition from North Brittan
John Nicolls Chrgeon
James Nerne Gentleman
Robert Cuningham & Two Marrenirs
31st Thos Wenmouth ye Ship Eueling from Biddyford
Wm Dumer & Two Seruents, Indimion Walker & 4 Seruents
Francis Wainwright & one Seruent
Jeffry Farmer Merchtt John Irwin Curgeon
Dated Boston May 31st 1712

p' Danl Russell, Comr

Massachusets Impost Office Boston

Vessells Entred in ye Month of June 1712

17th Richard Loue ye Ship Peter & Phillip from London

John Channing	Peter Whalton
Mary Anthram	Christian Snowman
Ann Anthram	Isac Varenne
Mrs Selby and her Child	Capt John Woodward
Abram De Senne	Edward Mobeley
Henry Whitton	Mr Payne
Mr Bayley his Wife & Two Childn	John Coats & his Sone
Madam Proctor	Mrs Shad
Lydia	John Brewstow the Negro

p' Danl Russell, Comr

No. II.

Arrival about 1685.

Communicated by Arthur M. Alger, of Boston.

In the Colonial Records in the State House, Boston, vol. 61, p. 288, is a petition to the Hon. Simon Bradstreet, signed by Thomas Banister, Thomas Cobb, James Thornbeck, George Clarke, Ralph Killcup, bearing date Aug.

12, 1685. We gather from it that they with their families were passengers in a ship which had lately arrived from England, and, on account of a false report that they had brought the small-pox with them, were confined on an island in the harbor, where they had no shelter and were without fresh water. The petition set forth that they had all had the distemper in Old England many years ago, with the exception of four persons who had it on board ship, but had been well six weeks and upwards. They therefore prayed to be admitted within bounds, that they might provide for themselves and families.

Leave was given them to come ashore on the following day.

Two of the petitioners, Thomas Banister and George Clarke, settled in Boston; the latter afterward removing to Roxbury.

PASSENGERS AND VESSELS THAT ARRIVED IN AMERICA.

UNDER this head we propose to print lists of passengers and memoranda of the arrival of vessels in America. Contributions to this series of articles are solicited from our friends.

No. III.

THE SUSAN AND ELLEN, 1638.

From the GENEALOGY OF THE LOOMIS FAMILY.

[The Loomis Genealogy, noticed in the REGISTER for April last (*ante*, p. 272), contains the following document, copied from the original in the possession of the Hon. J. Hammond Trumbull, LL.D., president of the Connecticut Historical Society. It is a draft (unsigned) of the deposition of Joseph Hills, afterwards of Malden, taken 30th July, 1639.—ED.]

Joseph Hills of Charlestowne, in New England, Woollen Draper, aged about 36 yeares sworne, saith upon his oath that he came to New England undertaker in the ship called the Susan & Ellen of London whereof was master Mr. Edward Payne, in the yeare of our Lord one thousand six hundred thirty and eight, the 14th yeare of the raigne of our Sou^r^aigne Lord the King that now is, and this d^pt^ knowes that divers goods and chattells, victualls & commodities of Joseph Loomis late of Brayntree in the County of Essex, Woolen-draper, wch were put up in three butts, two hogsheds, one halfe hogshed, one barrell, one tubb & three firkins, transported from Malden in the County of Essex to London in an Ipsw^ch^ Hye, were shipped in the said ship upon the eleventh day of Aprill in the yeare abovesayd, and this deponent cleared the said goods wth divers other goods of the said Joseph Loomis and other mens, in the Custome-house at London, as may appeare by the Customers bookes, and this dep^t^ saith that the said goods were transported into New England in the said ship where she arrived on the seaventeenth day of July in the yeare aforesayd.

No. IV.

MORE EARLY PASSENGERS TO NEW-ENGLAND.

Communicated by HENRY F. WATERS, Esq., of Salem.

These p^r^sents are to certifie unto whome it may concerne that wee Thomas Cromwell[1] & John Cromwell whoe have beene long inhabitants here in ye towne of Salem, in the county of Essex in new England, doe testifie that wee haue known Hugh Joanes[2] as one coming from England in the same ship with us in to the contry aboue thirty yeares agoe (& as wee un-

[1] Thomas Cromwell is supposed to have been a son of Giles Cromwell, of Newbury, and John to have been a grandson of the same, being son of Philip and nephew of Thomas. H. F. W.

[2] Hugh Joanes m. 1st, Hannah Tomkins, June 26, 1660; she died May 10, 1672; he m. 2d, Mary Foster, 31st 10 mo. 1672. I suspect that these two wives were cousins, one a dau. of John, son of Ralph Tompkins, and the other a gr. dau. of the same Ralph by a dau. who m. John Foster. H. F. W.

derstood abord Mr Strattons ship*) that he came from uincanton† and was servant to Mr Robert Gutch) & his sister & Elizabeth Due & Margarett White & James Abbot & John Vinning as wee understood came from the same plaice, & the same Hugh Joanes that came along with us into the country is now liuing.

Taken upon the corporall oathes of the s^d Thomas and John Cromwell in Court at Salem the 27: June 1682 & alsoe the said Hugh Joanes then p̃sonally appeered in court being in health.

Attestes HILLIARD VEREN Cler:

[Essex Co: Deeds, B. 6, p. 168.]

No. V.

CAPT. DOBLE'S PASSENGERS, 1763.

Communicated by JOHN S. H. FOGG, M.D., of South Boston.

List of Capt. Doble's Passengers, who arrived [at Boston] from Newfound Land December, 1763.

Matthew Brimigum
Lawrance Glinden
William Murry
Morris Jack
William Ryan
James Cowen
Jonas Jackson
James Gorman
Richard Sprusin
John Welch
Edmund Hearn—Hospital
John Burk Ditto
Martin Grady
John Crole
Patrick Ashing Ditto
Edmund Butler
Daniel Flerta
Patrick Day
Dennis Dennavan
John Woodlock
Patrick Welch
William Lee
Simon Mulley—died at sea
Valentine Connel
Patrick Murphy
John Mejory
Robert Page
Gilbert Steel
Nicholas Flernin
Thomas Dunn
John Murray
William Brown
George Barstow

PASSENGERS AND VESSELS THAT HAVE ARRIVED IN AMERICA.

UNDER this head we propose to print lists of passengers and memoranda of the arrival of vessels in America. Contributions to this series of articles are solicited from our friends.

No. VI.

A List of Ships which arrived in New England in 1630.

From Prince's New England Chronology, Appendix to 1630.

No.	Names.	Whence set sail.	When set sail.	When arrived.	Where arrived.
		England.	1630	1630	*New-England.*
1	Lion	Bristol	Feb. *dd*	May e.	Salem
2	Mary-John	Plymouth	March 20	May 30	Nantasket
3	Arbella	Yarmouth	April 8	June 12	Salem
4	Jewel	at the	ditto	June 13	
5	Ambrose	Isle of	ditto	June 18	
6	Talbot	Wight	ditto	July 2	
7	May-Flower	S. Hampton	May	July 1	Charlestown
8	Whale	ditto	ditto		
9	Hopewell	ditto	ditto	July 3	(Salem)
10	Wm. & Fran.	ditto	ditto		
11	Tryal	ditto	ditto	July 5	Charlestown
12	Charles	ditto	ditto		Salem
13	Success	ditto	ditto	July 6	(Salem)
14	Gift		May e	August 20	Charlestown
15	Another *dd*		June *dd*		
16	Handmaid		August 6	October 20	Plymouth
17	Another set out by a private merchant. *dd*				

These seventeen ships arrived all safe in New England, for the increase of the population here, this year, 1630. *dd*

[Note.—The letters *dd* in italics, denote that the authority for the statements is Gov. Dudley's letter to the Countess of Lincoln, which is printed in the *New Hampshire Historical Collections*, vol. iv. pp. 224–49; *Force's Tracts*, vol. ii. Tract 4; Young's *Chronicles of Massachusetts*, pp. 301–41; *Massachusetts Historical Collections*, 1st series, vol. viii. pp. 36–47. The other facts seem to be derived from Winthrop's *History of New England*.—Ed.]

No. VII.

Capt. Jenner's Ship, 1677 or 1678.

Copied by Henry F. Waters, A.B., from the Essex County Court Files.

Thomas Clark of Chelmsford Clerk Testifieth and saith that about seuenteen years since he came ouer from England wth Capt Thomas Jenner late of Charlestowne Decēd and with him came m[r] ffrances Willoughby the Reputed son of y[e] Honourable ffrances Willoughby Esq[r] of s[d] Charlestowne decēd, passenger, which said ffrances Willoughby died on board said ship of ye distempr of ye Small Pox,* and was then in his sight and view solemnly thrown ouerboard into ye Deep, and further testifieth that he was very well acquainted wth the said ffrances Willoughby junr in England before he took ship, and yt he spake to him about an hour before his death.

THOMAS CLARK.

Charlestowne March 8th 94–5

The reverend mr Thomas Clark made oath to the truth of the above written before me THOMAS HINCHMAN, Justice *peace.*

No. VIII.

ARRIVALS IN BOSTON, MASS., JUNE, 1712.

From Manuscripts belonging to the N. E. HISTORIC, GENEALOGICAL SOCIETY.

Massachusetts Impost Office Boston

Vessells Entered in the Month of June 1712

ye 2d - Samll Hatch ye Brigtt John & George from Madara & Fyall
No passengers
John Ellery ye Brigtt Mayflower from Fayall
No passengers
Thomas Dimond ye ship Vpton from Fyall
No passengers
3d Wm Partridge ye Sloop Hana & Eliza from Fyall
No passengers but Marreners
Philip Jenkens ye Ship Marlborough from Bristoll
Thomas Moffatt Merchtt Edward Fisher Merchtt
John Goodson Ditto Samel Storke Ditto
Samll Carter Puterer
Wm Atwood, John, John Jones } Marreners
5th Joshua Furbur ye Sloop Betty from Fyall
No passengers but Marreners
6th Jethro Furbur ye Sloop Tryall from Fyall
George Alvis & 3 Seruents
Willis Finderson Merchtt
James Huistin Corurgon
John Filmore ye Ship Mary from Topsham
Joshua Norman
Caleb Norman
Thoms Langaford
Edward Pentrall
Eliza Bartlet & her Son
Richard Short, John Youlden, Mary Souton, Eliza Dande, Eliza Teague } Seruants
Thomas Neck ye Barqe Prosperity from Topsham
William Edwards A Gentleman
ye 9th Joseph Arnold ye Sloop fortune from Proudendce
No passengers
10th Henry Davis ye Sloop Speadwell from Fyall
No passengers

* Savage states that Francis Willoughby, Jr., died of the small-pox, June 15, 1678; but he is mentioned in his brother William's will, Sept. 1, 1677, as then deceased. See REGISTER, XXX. 77.—ED.

11th Thomas Couerly ye Sloop Hanah & Mary, Surrenam
No passengers
Wm Glouer ye Sloop Mary from St Thomases
No passengers but Marreners
12th Timothy Williamson ye Sloop Seatryall from Virgina
No passengers
Thomas Hunt ye Ship Prouidence from Georges
No passengers
13th Thomas Clarke ye Sloop Mounseratt from Faro
No passengers
Joseph Berry ye Sloop Wm from Madera
No passengers
Jona Bassett ye Sloop Mary & Abigall from New London
Mary Jess
Pripila a free Negro
ye 16th Theopolis Grigory ye Ship Oley Frigett from London
Thomas Staples A Bricklayer
John Lewis A Joyner
Samll Tibbs A Masson
& Three Marriners
Richard Loue ye Ship Peter & Phillip from London
forty five Seruants Male & Female
James Atchison ye Ship Sarah Gally from London
Richard Harris } Marriners
Paul Gerrish }
Roger Foot }
Hercnls Braillsford }
Samll Whittwall } all Timbermen
Thomas Wharton } Robert forrister Ditto
James Goodwin }
17th John Allexandor ye Ship Queen Ann from London
Capt Bedgood, Capt Whale } Marenrs
Capt Winter & Mr John Rogers }
Mr Henry Marsh A Gentleman
Mrs Francis Tarrant with a Maid & Man Seruant
Mrs Dilly & Children
Fourteen Traids Men
Thirteen Marriners
David Jones A Taylor
Obadiah Wakefield ye Brigtt Prince Eugene from London
William Cooper A Ropemaker
Samll Still a Ditto
Arno A Glouer
Raulins A Joyner
18th Robert Luist ye Brigtt Dolphin from Neuis
John Swiniton A Cooper
19th Samll Northy ye Sloop Elizabeth from North Carolina
No passengers
23d Benja Goold ye Sloop Mary from Fyall
No passengers but Marriners
27th Nathll Mason ye Sloop Elizabeth from N Foundland
Anthony Poer A Nantuckett man
28th John Welch ye Sloop Eliza from Barbados
No passengers

30th Thomas Burnton ye Ship Margrett from barbados
No passengers
Francis Plaisted ye Ship John & Dorothy from Barbados
John Hooper Gentleman
Dated Boston June 30th 1712
p̃ DAN: RUSSELL Comr

PASSENGERS AND VESSELS THAT HAVE ARRIVED IN AMERICA.

UNDER this head we propose to print lists of passengers and memoranda of the arrival of vessels in America. Contributions to this series of articles are solicited from our friends.

No. IX.

THE VOYAGE OF THE JONATHAN TO NEW ENGLAND, 1639.

Communicated by HENRY F. WATERS, A.B., of Salem, Mass.

At a County Court held at Cambridge the 6th of the 2d mo: 1652:

Richard Barnes Plive agst Tho: Blanchard Deft for with holding a debt of Twenty poundes given him by his mother whiles shee was a widow. The jury found for the plive, damages twenty pounds and costs of court thirty shillings.

Tho Blancher testifieth that Agnes Bent made her will and gave her estate to Richard Barnes and Eliza: Plimpton and to pay five pounds to Eliza. Plimpton and twenty pounds to Richard Barnes and gave tenn pounds to John Bent and five pounds to Tho Plimpton. the Rest to be divided betweene Richard Barnes and Eliz: Plimpton. Deposed before me,

INCREASE NOWELL.

I, John Rutter beinge of age 37 yeares or there about doe testifye to this honored Courte that goodman Blanchard told me that hee had twenty pounds of Richard Barns in his hande the wch twenty pound his wife did desire him to pay to her sonne Richard Barnes when he should be of age. Sworne in Court 5 (8) 1652.

William Marble and Elizabeth his wyfe aged 40 yeares a peece or there abouts do joyntly and sevrally depose and say—That aboute a yeare since the said Will'm askeing what estate Richard Barnes had in his father Thomas Blanchards hands the said Barnes answered he had none at all, but the estate that his mother and his grandmother gave him was in his unkle's hands at Sudberry.

Thomas Eames of Medford aged 34 yeares or there abouts deposeth and sayth That about the latter end of the month of October (51) as nere as this depo^{nt} remembreth This Depo^{nt} and Richard Barnes were discourseing about some wood, and fell into some speeches about Thirty pounds wch the said Barnes sayed he had of his unckle Bent or might have it when he would, but hee sayd he made account to haue Twenty pounds more the next Court, and this Depo^{nt} asked of whom he should haue it, and Barnes answered that he should haue it of his unkle Bent, and this Depo^{nt} asked him how he would come to haue it, for this Depo^{nt} thought that that Thirty pounds was all that had belonged to him. And the sayd Barnes answered againe and sayd That it was twenty pounds that his mother gaue him, and this Depo^{nt} asked him how he could proue it and what evedence he had for it. And the sayd Barnes answered againe That his father in law Thomas Blanchard had the bonds for it and would help him to gett it.

[Extracts from] "Reasons of Thomas Blanchard for the Review of this action."

Upon marriag of Thomas Blanchard wth Agnes the mother of Richard Barnes the said Agnes haueing 30^{lb} estate gaue 20^{lb} thereof to the said Richard her sonn and tenn pounds to the said Thomas her husband.

This 20^{lb} was giuen to Richard Barnes by his mother before her marriage, and was put into the hands of John Bent her brother. John Bent upon his comeing to New England put it into the hand of Mr. Peter Noyse. Mr Peter Noyse being asked why he would take Richard Barnes his 20^{lb} wth him to New England and leaue the said Barnes in old England, Mr. Noyse said he would cleare his hand of it and came the Tewsday following to John Bents house, where also his mother dwelt, and layed downe the money on the table in the p^{r}sence of widdow Bent her sonn John Bent and his wyfe and Thomas Blanchard: and then the said Widdow Bent sayd that shee would receiue it, so Mr Noyes and Thom Blanchard went away for that tyme.

A little after Mr Noyse receuied of Widdow Bent 80^{lb} for land or [ ] out of land 20^{lb} of wch 80^{lb} was Richard Barnes and so came for New England. About a yeare after Mr Noyse returned to England and enjoyed his land againe and beccame debtor to widdow Bent for the 80^{lb}. A little after Mr Noyse widdow Bent and others came for New England and Mr Noyse had the moneys vizt 80^{lb} still in his hand and since hath given account of it and hath payd it. It seems Mr Noyse payd this money to widdow Bent her executors vizt to John Bent for Richard Barnes and to Elizabeth Plympton executors. * * * * * * * * *

When Agnes was nere death in the ship she desired her husband Thom Blanchard that when he came to New England, that he would endeavour that her children might have their owne or their due, shee knoweing that it was in M[r] Noyse his hands for her sonn Barnes; her young child dyed shortly after in the ship. And her husband Thom Blanchard promised that he would, and hath since endeavoured it for her son Rich[d] Barnes as appears, &c.

I Peter Noyes doe testify that I payd fiue pound out of the estate of Agnis Bent by her order for the passage of Thomas Blanchard wife and alsoe I lent Thomas Blandchard twenty shillings after I arriued at Boston by the apoyntment of Elizabeth Plympton the now wife of John Rutter.

The testymony of John Bent is that he placed his mother and hir 2 granchildren befor he came out of England; that she had suficient in hir owne hand to discharg for hir expences and that she came over to new England w[th]in less then one yeare after I cam over.

Samuell Hides aged 42 yeares or there abouts deposeth and sayth

That about thirteene yeares since this Depo[nt] came ouer into New England in a shipp w[th] Thomas Blanchard and sayth that there was an old woeman lay in a cabbine in the shipp w[ch] this depo[nt] doth not remember that shee came forth all the tyme that shee was at sea untill she was brought forth to be buried, and sayth there was a bigg gerle there but this depo[nt] did not see her to doe anything about the old woeman or if she did it was very little. But this depo[nt] doth well remember that he saw the sayd Thomas Blanchard doe much about her and had light about her very much on nights untill shee dyed.

Thomas Gould aged 45 yeares or there abouts deposeth and sayth. That about thirteene yeares since this Depo[nt] comeing ouer in a shipp w[th] Thomas Blanchard here into New England this depo[nt] saw none nor knew none that had care of an old weoman w[ch] this depo[nt] app[r]hended to be the s[d] Blanchards mother in law, but the said Blanchard; there was a mayde of some stature but this depo[nt] perceiued that she did little or nothing in cookeing to the sayd old weoman yet this depo[nts] cabbine was ouer against them, neither did this depon[t] see her up on nights about her but this depont well remembers that he saw the said Thomas Blanchard take much paynes about the old weoman as of his owne famyly.

ffrances the wyfe of goodman Cooke of Charlestowne aged 44 yeares or there abouts deposeth and sayth.

That shee this depo[nt] come into New England in the same shipp wth Thomas Blanchard in the yeare 1639 and lying in the next cabbine to him and his wiues mother sayth that the said Thomas Blanchard did wholly take care and paynes wth his wiues mother all the way ouer (except some little help some tyme of a weake gerle who was a kinsweoman of hers) and the old weoman what wth her age and what wth her sicknes, for she was sick all the way his trouble and paynes wth her was such that it was unseemely for a man to doe, but there was no other saue that little helplesse gerle his kinsweoman, and continued his care and paynes wth her all the way from London to Nantaskith and endured very much wth her untill the shipp came to Nantaskith and ancored there and this depo[nt] came away before shee was dead.

At a County Court held at Charlestowne 21 (4) 1653 Blanchard vs Barnes in an action of Review—

The 5th of October 1652.

I John Bent doe testify that when my brother in law Barns was dead my father aduised my sister to sell her right in some lands that came by her husband barns w[ch] she sold and it came to fowerteene or fifteene pound and thereupon my father made it up twenty pounds upon this condition that she should reserue it for a portion for the boy and she consented thereunto. And further before Thomas Blanchard maryed my sister she told him of the twenty pound which shee had reserued for the boy and told him that shee would not marry wth him unles he would consent unto it and promise that the boy should haue it when hee came of age, to which Thomas Blanchard consented and promised that the boy should haue the twenty pounds when he came of age.

I John Groute do further testifie to this Honored Court that I did heare Thomas Blanchert affirme in the Court at Boston y^{t} ye 20^{lb} giuen to Richard Barnes by his mother was in his handes and that did deliv^{r} it Mr Peeter Noice on such a table in his house at Penton. This also I John Rutter do testifie, further at another time he did say to me and to John Rutter y^{t} he had a writeing under Mr Noice his hands to show for it, and that he would go to Brantre and fetch it for me, but the next day when he came to us he tould us y^{t} he did loose it by the way.

I William Marble Aged about 36 yrs testify that at the Court att Cambridge I heard Thomas Blanchard say Brother Bent did not these eys of myne and those eys of yours se Mr Noice bring in Richard Barnes 20^{lb} his mother gaue him and lay it downe uppon a table in yor house; at which John Bent stood sylent a little while and then Replyed Bro^{r} you^{r} are decieued and After another little pause sayd it was in my mothers house.

Mr Noyes i	05	00	0	Peter Noyes	02	10	0
John Waterman	05	00	0	anie bent	05	00	0
Nicholas Noyes	05	00	0	Elezabeth plemten	05	00	0
Dorevti Noyes	05	00	0	Richard barnes	02	10	0
Abigale Noyes	05	00	0	agnis Blanchet	05	00	0
William Stret	05	00	0				
					50	00	0

Rec^{d} in pt ffor the fraught of goods for John Waterman } £ 2 s 10 0

4 hds fraught	03	0	0	mele	10	19	0
4 fferkines	00	10	0	Butter	04	19	0
4 kelderkines	01	00	0	Licores	02	00	0
1 barrill	00	10	0				
3 packes 3 barilles	01	10	0		17	18	0
2 chests	02	00	0		50	00	0
					08	10	0
	08	10	0				
				10 passengers	76	08	0

	£	s	d
Rec^{d} this 12th of Aprill 1639 of Mr Peter Noyes the sum of ffifty pounde ffor his one and ffameleyes pasage to New England	50	00	0
Rec^{d} more ffor ffraught of goods	08	10	0
Rec^{d} more ffor mele and 4 ferkines of Buter and 2 cases of Licores	17	18	0
	76	08	0

ꝑ mee FFRA: NORTON.

[*From the Middlesex County Court Files.*]

The testimonie of us Inhabitants now of Newburie whose names are here under written, who about thirteen yeares past came ouer in a ship called the Jonathan of london with Thomas Blanchard now of Charlstowne, at what time his wife dyed in the ship hee was conceiued to be very poore and in greate necessity by reason of his wiues and his childrens sicknesse, that the passengers made a gathering for him in the shippe to helpe to put his child to nurse his wives mother also being sicke all the while wee were at sea and wee knew no other man that looked to her but Thomas Blanchard, but there was a maide which was her neece tended her —— —— ffurther I Anthony Som̄erby testifyes that about the time the ship came to Anchor in Boston Harbor the woman his mother in law dyed, And Thomas Blanchard procured to carry her to shore to be buried, I knew no other man that was about it but hee.

ffurther Nicholas Noyes testifyes that old Goody Bent came up from Andeuor to London in a waggon with the carryers, And Thomas Blanchard tooke care of her and her goods from Andeuor to the ship and she was with Thomas Blanchards family about a month at London, and that there was a gathering among christians in england to help him ouer.

taken upon oath in the court held at Ipswich ths 28th of (7) 1652.

NICHOLAS NOYES
ANTHONY SOMERBY.

[*From the Essex County Court Files.*]

PASSENGERS AND VESSELS THAT HAVE ARRIVED IN AMERICA.

UNDER this head we propose to print lists of passengers and memoranda of the arrival of vessels in America. Contributions to this series of articles are solicited from our friends.

No. X.

VOYAGE OF THE SHIP UNITY, 1680.

Communicated by HENRY F. WATERS, A.B., of Salem, Mass.

Warrant to attach "the body of George Penny Command^r of the ship Unity of London and take bond of him to ye value of one hundred pounds, with sufficient suretye or suretyes, for his appearance at ye next County Court to be holden at Salem, then and there to answer the complaint of Henry Lillye Glover or his lawfull atturney, and is in an action of the case for that ye said Penney did after an unhumane and unchristian manner abuse the Plaintiffe and his wife, by forcing them (contrary to agreement with him made in London) to ye piching of Ocum, without which doing they should have nither victualls nor drinke allowed them for their support, also debarring them of their dyett notwithstanding they were kept dayly at worke, and by turning them out of thir Cabbin, that they were forced to lye upon the hard boards, they being passengers in the said ship, By which abuses the plaintiffe and his said wife their lives were endangered and their healths very much impaired; which is very much to ye plaintiffes damage," &c. Dated in Boston this 27th of Octob^r 1680

NAT BARNES p Curiam
for the towne of Boston.

Humphrey Davie signs as surety for Capt. Penny on his bond to abide the order of the Court, 27 Oct. 1680.

Bond of "Henry Lilly and Ann Lilly his wife both of the Old Street nere the Citty of London"—"in the sume of Twenty ffoure pound of good and Lawfull money of New England to be paid"—"unto George Penny of Wapping near the Citty of London marriner"—"Dated the third day of June 1680."—the condition being that Lilly and his wife shall pay Capt. Penny twelve pounds of lawfull money of N. E. "wth in six Dayes after the arrivall of the ship Unity at Boston," &c.

"Sealed and delivered in ye p'sence of
Soloman Hobartt Nath: Brigge."

"The deposition of Richard Secombe aged 35 years Lancelott Lake aged 31 years" (made 30 9mo 1680) "Witnesseth:—That George Penny Comand^r of ye ship Unity of London did within few days sayle from ye Lands end of England command Henry Lilly and his wife passengers in ye said ship to ye picking of Ocum; without performing of wch they should nither have victualls nor drinke for their support and nourishment, constituting and appointing Richd Kennett his Chyrurgeon to be their superviseer y^t they did dayly performe the same, ye said superviseer of ye Ocumites telling them often no worke no victualls. They were likewise both at ye same time put to very short allowance both in victualls and drinke in so much that there was not according as we did conjecture above one pound of beef for six passengers and y^t but thrice a week to; the drink for ye most part either very salt, or else as thicke as puddle, and of y^t to such as it was not a pint a day a passenger. But notwithstanding this dayly worke y^t was thus imposed upon them and they within few days sayle from ye Lands end of Engld they were forced to such miserable short allowance, yet for no reason at all him thereunto moving they were both turned out of their cabbins and forced to lye upon the hard boards, and in that state continued untill they were almost destroyed through this their hard usage; and after all this before ye ship came to an anchor before Boston they were clapt as close prizoners into ye Gunroom there closely to be secured not having ye liberty to go a shore."

"The deposition of Mary Newby aged 34, Johanna Secombe aged 30, Peter Hicks aged 18." (taken 1st Nov. 1680) "witnesseth—That notwithstanding this worke imposed upon them they were both brought to very short allowance both of victualls and drinke, not having a pound of beef as we sopose for six passengers, and of that to but thrice a weeke, ye fish likewise rotten, and the beer as thicke as puddle water, or else salt and of that to not a pint a day a passenger. That some few days sayle from ye lands end of Engld Georg Penny command^{r} of ye ship unity of London, commands Henry Lillye and his wife to ye picking of ocum without which they should have nither victualls nor drinke for their support, wch worke they were forced to undergo or else perish ; and Richd Kennett was sett over them as superviseer that they did dayly performe the same he carrying about him a Rope of a considerable bignesse for to chastise them if they were negligent of this their dayly servitude ; teling of them no worke no victualls. That upon the fourteenth of August they were both turned out of our cabbin and forced for to lye upon the boards untill they were almost killed through sicknesse and want of provisions, and before they came to an anchor before Boston they were cast as prizeners into ye gunroom, and their cloathes into ye hole, and not suffered to go a shore for to relieve their necessityes."

"The Deposition of William Newsham aged about 22 years sworn" (11 Nov. 1680) "saith that hee being one of the passengers belonging to the Ship Unity George Penny com̄ander in her late voyage from London to New England hath severall times in the voyage observed m^{r} Lancelott Lake a passenger in s^{d} ship to bee very much discontented by reason of contrary windes, and also heard him say if wee did not meete wth a fair winde within two or three dayes or some such little time wee should never arrive at Boston, and persisted in such kinde of murmuring most part of the voyage, and also incensing the seamen and passengers betwixt decks against the master, that at last it was grown to that height of insolency with them that I did not apprehend myself to bee in safety ; whereupon I desired the master to spare me some powder which I obtained of him to load my pistols ; three or four dayes after perceiving no alteration the s^{d} seamen and passengers, wee that lay in the great Cabbin consulting with the master for the safety of our selves ship and goods thought it the securest way to possess our selves of the small armes belonging to the gunroome wch wee did by takeing some into the great cabbin and some into the Round house and afterwards wee found an alteration in the seamen and passengers who from that time were peaceable and quiet. And whereas it is reported that the master should say hee was God and Lord of that wooden world I never heard any such expressions from him, nor can I imagine hee would so say ; but the cooke of s^{d} Ship who is said to bee the Author of s^{d} report is a person of very little credit and be haved himselfe so rudely and prophanely in swearing singing base songs and drunkenness that daily complaints were brought of him to the master wch occasioned difference between the master and him so that I feare hee may speake out of prejudice."

"The Deposition of George Hilliard Gunner of the Ship Unity of London George Penny ma^{r}. Nicholas Matthews Cooper of the s^{d} ship and Richard Kennett Chyrurgion of s^{d} Ship.

That whereas there is a complaint made by some passengers y^{t} came over in s^{d} ship for want of provision, wee do hereby testify that the least of the allowance ordered by the master was no less for ffive men or women or children then one peice of beife a day mess peice cut at London and two pound and a halfe of fflower with pease eleven pints a day for the Ships company and passengers ffour pound of bread a peice every weeke, and as for ffish wee heard no complaint of any want, every mess had a pound and a halfe of butter every weeke and as for beare and water ye least allowance was three pints of water and beare a day for a man women and children except about one weeke at ye end each person was put to a quart a day wch was the least allowance during the whole voyage."

The case was committed to the Jury, who found for the plaintiff "six pound damag in money and costs of court 41^s 10^d."

In addition to the above there is a memorandum showing that one James Rose must have complained "for that the said peny did after ae cruell and barborus manor beat and abuse the plaintive being ae passinger in his ship from London hether to boston by tying hime to the capstall and beat him with ae great tard rope of above thre inchis round which was all most as hard as Iron and thrue the plaintive ovar ae grinston and he the said peny with five of the seamen which he the said peny did reqiar to asist hime most horabilly abucs the said rose all most unto death and allso denyed the plaintive of all manor of relefe with sevarell other great and horabill abusis whearby the said James rose is greatly damnefied."

[*From Essex County Court Papers.*

PASSENGERS AND VESSELS THAT HAVE ARRIVED IN AMERICA.

UNDER this head we propose to print lists of passengers and documents and memoranda concerning the arrival of vessels in America, and the passengers in them. Contributions to this series of articles are solicited from our friends.

No. XI.

A Ship which Arrived at Boston, Dec. 1, 1673.

Communicated by Henry F. Waters, A.B., of Salem.

The Testimoney of George Booth aged about 35 yeares.
Saith that he came from England in a ship with Henry Dispaw Senr: and Henry Dispaw Junr: & knew them both to be servants to m^r John Gifford, and that they did ariue at Bostone the first daye of December in the yeare 1673: Herlackendine Simonds* testifieth to what is aboue and beneath

* Mr. Symonds was then returning from England after a visit of more than fifteen months, the most of which time he claimed that he had passed in waiting for a power of attorney from Henry Bennet, of Ipswich, to secure a legacy of one hundred pounds, bequeathed to him by his brother, William Bennet, of London, vintner, whose son-in-law, Henry Jennings, also a vintner, lived at the White Hart, without Bishopsgate. Those interested in the Symonds family may like to learn that there is a deposition on file, in this case, signed 19 Aug. 1673, by John Symonds, Esq., of Yeldham, which, he says, is about forty miles distant from his, Jennings's, abode.

written, being a passenger coming ouer sea with them, to be truth to my best knowledg: Taken upon oath: 1: 10mo: 75: by all ꝑties:

W^{m}: HATHORNE Assistant.

Likewise Alce the wife of George Booth abouesaid aged about 35 yeares: testifieth to the very same that is aboue written.

" ARTICLES of Agreement indented and made this eleventh day of the month of August Ann^{o} Dn^{i}: 1673. & in the five & twentieth yeare of the Reign of our Sovereign Lord King Charles the Second &^{c} Between John Wright of Writsbridge Esqr. John Giffard of New-England merchant & Ezekiel Fogg citizen & Skinner of London of th' one part, And Henry Dispaw Senr. & Henry Dispaw jun^{r} of Horsemenden in the County of Kent Potters of the other part," &c.

Essex County Court Papers, B. xxiv. L. 24 and 27.

No. XII.

SHIP NATHANIEL OF DARTMOUTH, WHICH ARRIVED ABOUT 1662.

The deposition of Nicholas Bartlett and Damaris Phippeny, Sept. 2, 1706, about this voyage, is printed in the REGISTER, vol. xxviii. 378.

SCOTCH PRISONERS SENT TO MASSACHUSETTS IN 1652, BY ORDER OF THE ENGLISH GOVERNMENT.

London, this 11: of Nouembe^{r} 1651:

M$^{R.}$ THO: KEMBLE

Wee whose names are vnder written, freighte^{rs} of the sh[ipp] John & Sara whereof is Cōmande^{r} John Greene Doe Consigne the said shipp & servants to be disposed of by yow for ou^{r} best Advantage & account & the whole proceed of the Servants & vojage Retourne in a jojnct stocke without any Division in such goods as you conceive will turne best to acco^{nt} in the Barbadoes & consign[e] them to M$^{r.}$ Charles Rich for the aforesajd acco^{tt} & w^{t} other pay yo^{w} meete with fit for this place send hither & take the Advise & Asistance of Capt Jno Greene in disposall of the Servants Dispatch of the shipp or w^{t} else may any wajes concerne the vojage thus wishing the shipp a safe vojage & God's blessing on the same not doubting of you^{r} best care & dilligence, Remajne:

Signatum et Recognitum in p^ncja — you^{r} loving freinds Jo: Beex
Jo: Nottock notarius publ: — Robt Rich
Willjam Greene

Entred & Recorded at the Instant Request of the said Mr Tho: Kemble.
ꝑ Edw: Rawson Recorder 13th May 1652.

London this 11th : of Nouember^{r} , 1651 :

CAPT. JN^{o}: GREENE

Wee whose names are vnder written freighte^{r}s of you^{r} shipe the John & Sara doe Order yow forthwith as winde & weather shall permitt to sett sajle for Boston in New England & there deliver our Orders and Servants to Tho: Kemble of charles Toune to be disposed of by him according to orde^{r}s wee have sent him in that behalfe & wee desire yow to Advise with the sajd Kemble about all that may concerne that whole Jntended vojage vsing you^{r} Jndeavo^{r}s with the sajd Kemble for the speediest lading you^{r} shipp from New Eng: to the barbadoes with provisions & such other things as are in N. E. fit for the West Jndjes where yow are to deliuer them to M$^{r.}$ Charles Rich to be disposed of by him for the Joinct acco^{nt} of the freighte^{r}s & so to be Retou^{r}ned home in a stocke vndevided thus desiring your Care & Industrje in Dispatch and speed of the vojage wishing you a happy & safe Retourne wee remajne you^{r} loving freinds

Signatnm et Recognitum — John Beex
in pncia: Jo: Nottock: notar Publ: — Rob$^{t.}$ Rich
13 May 1652. — Will. Greene

Entred & Recorded ℱ Edward Rawson Recorde$^{r.}$

A list of the passengers aboard the John and Sarah of London John Greene m^{r} bound for New Englan[d]

Donald Roye
James Moore
Walter Jackson
Michaell ffossem
Daniell Simson
John Rosse
Sander Milleson
Daniell Monlow
Henry Brounell
James farfason
Alester lowe
Daniell Hogg
Hugh Mackey
Daniell Mackannell
John Croome
John Macklude
Dan: Mackwell
**** Mackunnell
John Hudson
John Mackholme
John Deme
**** More
John Crag
Robe^{r}t Monrow
Hill Mackie
John Mackdonell
Allester Macknester
John Edminsteire
Wm Banes
Patrick Jones
Andrew Wilson
Daniell Monwilliam
John Mackenthow
John Jamnell
David Mackhome
Murtle Mackjlude
Salamon Sinclare
John Gurden
Wm Macken
John Cragon
John Graunt
Alestre Mackrore
Daniell Mackendocke
Gellust Mackwilliam

James Milward
Wm Dell
James Micknab
Glester Macktomas
Almister Mackalinsten
John Coehon
Robe^{r}t Jenler
Edward Dulen
John Hogg
James Mickell
John Mackalester
Daniell Macknell
Patrick Jimson
John Hanoman
Andrew Jerris
James Jackson
Patricke Tower
Wm Mackannell
Dani** Mackajne
Senly Mackonne
James English
Dan** Mackennell
John Mackey
Danniell Gunn
James Ross
John Wilson
David Jeller
George Quenne
John Jenler
John Woodell
George Perry
John Monrow
Wm Clewston
Daniell Mackhan
Alester Mackhene
Alester Simson
Richard Jackson
James Camell
Dan: Martjn
John Hogg
John Robinson
John Rosse
John Rosse
Hugh Monrow

Thomas Bereere
Sjmon Russell
John Morre
Edward Punn
Sannde^{r} Morrot
W^{m} ffressell
John Boyc
John Buckanen
Patricke Morton
Dan[i]ell Makalester
James Michell
Sander Mackdo[n]ell
James Gurner
Wm Teller
Origlais Mackfarson
Nicholas Wallis
John Murrow
Robe^{r}t Higben
John Muckhellin
Allester *****
Dan: Mackhellin
***** *****
Charles Lesten
Wm Stewart
John Morro
Edward ffressell
David Hinne ?
Daniell blacke
Daniell Sessor
Patricke Mackhatherne
Alexande^{r} Tompson
Danell Kemper
Daniell How
John Brow
***** *****
Henry Mack***
John Robinson
Daniell *****
Patricke *****
Patricke *****
P**** *****
***** *****
***** [Mac]kfarson
***** Macklyne

***** Monrow
***ster Macknell
Daniell Robinson
[J]ames Shone
John Anderson
James Graunt
Patricke Crosshone
John Grant
John Scott
Dan: Gordon
Dan: Ross
John Hogg
Patrick Mann
Ansell Sherron
James Ross
David Hamilton
Patricke Mackneile
David Rosse
Amos Querne
Alestre Hume
Neile Johnson
Alester Rallendra
Rory Hamilton
James Robinson
David Bukanon
David Sterling
Daniell Macknith
Robt Mackfarson
Wm Munckrell
Neile Camell
Semell Mackneth
John Mackane
Dan Shuron
Rory Machy
Patrick Graunt
Patricke Harron
James Rowe
Sander Simson
James Gorden
Charles Robinson
Alester Robinson
Patricke Robertson
Alester graunt
Neile Macketh
Patricke Macknith
Daniell Macknith
James hedericke
James Mackhell
John Curmickhell
David Hume
Patrick Macktreth
David Anderson
Wm Beames
David Monwilljam
John Sterling
John Mann
Wm Dengell
Daniell Mann
Sander Mackcunnell
Cana Mackcurnall
Patricke Mackane
Ansel Sotherland
Sander Miller
James Pattison
Alexander Graunt
Thomas Graunt
Neile Carter
Dan: Mackneile
John Shenne
Robt Mackajne
Dan: Hudson
Neile Murrow
John Cannell
Evan Tiler
Jonas Murrow
Alester Mackhele
Edward Dengle
James Kallender
Jonas Ross
Neile Mackhone
James Graunt
David Tenler
James Mackally
Wm Mackajne
Alester Tooth
Austin Stewart
Laughlell Montrosse
Wm Mackontoss
Neile Mackajne
James Mackreith
John Mackforsen
James Hamilton
John Graunt
James Murrow
Wm Carmackhell
James Mackneile
Samuell Mackajne
Dan: Graunt
Cha: Stewart
Neile Stewart
David Macketh
David Jameson
Dan Simson
George Hame
James Crockford
David Kallender
David Patterson
Alester Anderson
Patricke Smison
Robt Boy
John Wilson
Patricke Jacson
Wm Mackajne
Dan: Mackhoe
Dan: Mackajne
Alester Ross
Neile Murkstore
Wm Mackandra
John Boye
Wm Graunt
James Graunt
Henry Smith
Wm Hidrecke
Cana Macktentha
Niele Hogg
Robt Mackhane
Robt Stewart
David Simson
Laughleth Gordon
Neile Jameson
Patrick English
James Benne
David Milward
Wm Anderson
Sander Mackey
Patrick Sotherland
Daniel Oneale
John Woodall
Christopher Wilson
John Murrow

The persons afore named passed from hence in the ship afore mentioned and are according to order Registed heare,

Dat. Search office, Grauesend 8th. Nouember, 1651.

GILES BARROW }
EDW: PELLING } Searchers.
JOHN MORRIS }

Jn the Jno & Sara of London John Greene mr for New England: | Robt Rich mrt Jronworke household stuffe & other provisions for Planters and scotch prisoners free by ordnance of Parliament dat 20th of October 1651.

S
G R No 1 two trusses of goods for planters shipt the viiith of Nouember 1651 mrkt & nombred as in the magent.

JOHN BRADLEY Sr wth ye Armes of ye Comonwealth.

Entred & Recorded at the Request of mr Thomas kemble. 14 May 1652

℈ EDWARD RAWSON Recorder.

The following is from Governor Hutchinson's Collection of Original Papers and may furnish some light in respect to the above mentioned prisoners sent to this country and sold for slaves, no doubt, by order of the English Government, as a sort of banishment for their rebellion. It is probable that some of them were sent to Barbadoes, as all their names do not seem to appear in any other way in this country, except on this list.

Extract from a Letter written by Rev. John Cotton to the Lord General Cromwell, dated at "Boston in N. E. 28. of 5th 1651," respecting some prisoners of the same class of persons included in the above list sent over before these arrived. They all probably were taken at the battle of Dunbar, Sept. 3, 1650, when Cromwell was victorious and four thousand were slain and ten thousand made prisoners.

"The Scots, whom God delivered into your hands at Dunbarre, and whereof sundry were sent hither, we have been desirous (as we could) to make their yoke easy. Such as were sick of the scurvy or other diseases have not wanted physick and chyrurgery. They have not been sold for slaves to perpetual servitude, but for 6 or 7 or 8 yeares, as we do our owne; and he that bought the most of them (I heare) buildeth houses for them, for every four an house, layeth some acres of ground thereto, which he giveth them as their owne, requiring 3 dayes in the weeke to worke for him (by turnes) and 4 dayes for them themselves, and promiseth, as soone as they can repay him the money he layed out for them, he will set them at liberty."

SERVANTS TO FOREIGN PLANTATIONS FROM BRISTOL, ENGLAND, TO NEW ENGLAND, 1657–1686

Contributed by GORDON IRELAND, J.S.D., of Cambridge, Mass.

It may be recalled that England's efforts to suppress the kidnapping and transportation of children and the indigent and friendless made somewhat better progress under the Commonwealth than throughout the rest of the Seventeenth Century. The Interregnum Parliament passed on May 9, 1645 an Ordinance prescribing penalties for the stealing away of children, and in particular charging marshals of ports with the duty of diligently searching outgoing ships and vessels to discover children stolen for overseas. Various port cities, in which of course the evils culminated, slowly took steps of their own to better conditions and enforce the law. The Council of the City of Bristol, which had then a monopoly of the Virginia trade, after some earlier half-hearted efforts, finally passed on Sept. 29, 1654 an Ordinance which provided that before embarkation persons bound as servants for overseas were to be articled and enrolled as were the city apprentices. Enrollment books were opened the next day, and listing began with an attempt to record not only the servants' and bond-masters' names and the destination, but the servant's place of origin, at first a brief summary of the terms of the articles of bondage, and later the name of the vessel and her master. Gradually, with the increase of routine in the business, the details were cut down, so that the bulk of the entries show only the servant, bond-master, destination, and date of entry. As this type of emigration waned, in some thirty years, the books were allowed to lapse.

The servants' embarkation record for the City of Bristol was contained in two volumes (I, 1654–1663, 545 pages; II, 1663–1679, 318 pages) which were discovered in forgotten recesses of the City Hall when an Archives Department was established by the City in 1924.

The servants' names, destinations, and pages of record have been published under the title "Bristol and America" (London, 1929). There are some 10,000 entries, from Sept. 30, 1654 to the last regular entry in August, 1679, with 500 or more scattered in the last pages from March 27, 1680 to June 12, 1686; and the places of origin, where given, range all over the British Isles, with, of course, the counties of Gloucester and Somerset predominating. Destined for the most part to Virginia, Maryland and the Bermudas, it was found that 163 servants were entered as for New England; and after obtaining from the Bristol Archives Department all further available information from the original record books, including especially the date of entry in each case, the complete record as to those persons bound for New England is here presented. To make the material as useful as possible, there have been listed alphabetically the names of the emigrants themselves (Table I), thus indicating incidentally possible family groups; the bond-masters (Table II), showing dates and servants under one man; and the vessels (Table III), showing servants on the same voyage, where known.

TABLE I

No.	*Name of Servant*	*To Whom Bound*	*Date of Entry*	*Record Book*	*Record Page*
1	Adams, Thomas	Samuel Nichols	Jan. 28, 1662	I	537
2	Addams, William yeoman	George Garner	May 12, 1657	I	79
3	Alston, Rooo	Thomas Dennis	Feb. 24, 1661	I	472
4	Axall, Humfrey	Francis Raynes	Aug. 12, 1678	II	308
	On the *Releife* of Boston, William Marshall, Master				
5	Aylesworth, John	George Warren	Apr. 27, 1674	II	248
6	Backster, Thomas	Samuel Nicholas	Mar. 17, 1662	I	544
7	Baker, Thomas	Hugh Tucker	May 25, 1674	II	250
8	Ball, Mary	Philipp Cooke	July 18, 1678	II	307
	On the *Relorne* of Boston, Thomas Edwards, Master				
9	Barber, Armfry	Thomas Donning	Jan. 23, 1661	I	466
	At the end of 4 years to have £10.				
10	Barnes, Hugh	Thomas Elbridge	Mar. 5, 1663	II	26
11	Bartlett, Henry	John Franck	May 15, 1667	II	101
12	Bates, Anne	Edward Horte	Feb. 27, 1662	I	542
13	Bayly, Richard	Robert Ellott	Mar. 16, 1667	II	128
14	Baywell, George	Samuel Nickolls	Feb. 20, 1661	I	471
15	Beale, Samuell	Christopher Holder	May 5, 1670	II	182
16	Bennet, John	Phillipp Mathews	Feb. 4, 1662	I	538
17	Beverlin, Lenox	William Roberts	May 11, 1674	II	249
18	Binner, Elizabeth	Thomas Jones	Feb. 20, 1661	I	471
19	Bowen, John	John Nicholas	Mar. 9, 1662	I	543
20	Brayne, Robert	John Pitman	Feb. 23, 1668	II	160

No.	Name of Servant	To Whom Bound	Date of Entry	Record Book	Page
21	Brimsly, Simon	Richard Pugsly	Feb. 26, 1661	I	473
22	Britten, William	Thomas Burroughs	March, 1679	II	316
	On the *Supply*				
23	Brookes, Thomas	Samuel Nickolls	Feb. 20, 1661	I	471
24	Browne, Richard	Thomas Moore	Mar. 31, 1679	II	316
	On the *Saphire* Ketch				
25	Bull, John	Thomas Bedford	Mar. 6, 1667	II	127
26	But, Richard	Edward Thomas	Feb. 13, 1662	I	540
27	Cary, Richard	Thomas Harris	Mar. 6, 1662	I	542
28	Cawley, Robert	Thomas Elbridge	July 15, 1662	I	500
29	Challoner, Arthur	William Roberts	May 11, 1674	II	249
30	Chamblis, Morris	Thomas Elbridge	Mar. 5, 1663	II	26
31	Chresseham, Daniell	Thomas Harris	Mar. 6, 1662	I	542
32	Churchell, Robert	John Coock	Mar. 28, 1671	II	202
	On the *Society*				
33	Clarke, Jeremy	John Alden	Feb. 23, 1670	II	201
	On the French ship of Boston				
34	Clarke, Thomas	John Turner	Feb. 17, 1661	I	470
35	Clhoone, John	Thomas Oldfeild	June 13, 1669	II	163
36	Clothier, Jeremiah	John Vineing	Mar. 6, 1662	I	542
37	Colston, Joseph	John Griffen	May 11, 1670	II	183
38	Comes, Henry	Christopher Smith	Jan. 26, 1668	II	159
39	Conaway, Mary	Thomas Bedford	Mar. 6, 1667	II	127
40	Corneborough, Nathaniel	John Morgan	Feb. 8, 1663	II	25
41	Daves, William	William Titherly	Apr. 16, 1669	II	162
42	Davis, Evan	Samuel Tipton	May 14, 1675	II	267
43	Davis, Silvanus	William Hayman	Feb. 6, 1662	I	539
44	Davis, Thomas	John Smith	May 16, 1671	II	204
	On the *Laurell* for Nevis, Jamaica or New England, John West, Master				
45	Davy, Thomas	David Foy	Mar. 2, 1667	II	127
46	Dickeson, John	John Sunderland	June 15, 1669	II	163
47	Dodge, John	Josias Kootes	June 30, 1674	II	250
48	Dymock, Allice	Samuel Nichols	Feb. 17, 1662	I	541
49	Edward, William	John Stokes	June 7, 1670	II	183
50	Edwards, Roger	Samuel Nickolls	Feb. 10, 1661	I	469
51	Everet, John	William Hayman	Jan. 27, 1662	I	537
52	Eyre, Thomas	Giles Merwick	June 6, 1684		(p. 173)
	of East Farendon; on the *Rainbow*, William Stermy, Master				
53	Fisher, William	Thomas Hobson	Feb. 10, 1674	II	265
54	Foskew, Richard	Thomas Oldfeild	Aug. 19, 1670	II	188
	On the *Content*				
55	Found, Moses	Philipp Cooke	July 12, 1678	II	307
	On the *Retorne* of Boston				
56	Freeman, John	Nicholas Smale	Feb. 6, 1662	I	539
57	Freind, John	Samuel Nicholls	Jan. 19, 1662	I	535
58	Froame, Thomas	Grace Smith	Feb. 23, 1669	II	180
59	Frost, Nicholas	Thomas Orchard	Mar. 24, 1662	I	545
60	Fry, Thomas	Thomas Bedford	Mar. 9, 1667	II	128
61	Fryer, John	Thomas Oldfield	May 6, 1669	II	162
62	Gatlock, Joane	Thomas Jones	Feb. 20, 1661	I	471

No.	*Name of Servant*	*To Whom Bound*	*Date of Entry*	*Record Book*	*Record Page*
63	Gatly, John	Thomas Jones	Feb. 20, 1661	I	471
64	Gausset, William	Samuel Nicholas	Feb. 9, 1662	I	539
65	Geare, John	Josias Kootes	June 30, 1674	II	250
66	Genings, Francis	Richard Shipway	Aug. 10, 1662	I	509
67	Giles, Marke	Thomas Elbridge	Mar. 5, 1663	II	26
68	Glenton, Thomas	John Shipway	Aug. 7, 1662	I	508
69	Goddard, Henry	Peter Ware, planter	Mar. 30, 1686		(p. 182)
	of Whatden, sergeweaver; on the *Bossterne Merchant*, William Curtis, Master				
70	Gough, John	Thomas Donning	Feb. 14, 1661	I	469
	To have £10				
71	Greene, Roger	John Legg	Feb. 24, 1661	I	472
72	Griffen, Rice	Thomas Hollard	Feb. 16, 1674	II	265
73	Harris, George	Oliver Stratton	Feb. 23, 1670	II	201
	On the *Robert and Hester*				
74	Harris, John	John Dale	Mar. 8, 1670	II	201
75	Hedon, Richard	John Codnell	Feb. 20, 1684/5		(p. 176)
	of Landbathurne; on the *Laurell*				
76	Holborne, Thomas	Christopher Holder	Mar. 25, 1669	II	181
77	Huffe, Mary	Mathew Lambes	Feb. 14, 1662	I	540
78	Hughes, Thomas	Daniel Sam	Apr. 22, 1669	II	162
79	Iles, Timothy	Thomas Donning	Jan. 23, 1661	I	466
	At the end of 7 years to have £10				
80	Jarvis, Joane	John Cary	May 7, 1674	II	248
81	Jenkins, William	Anthony Ailiffe	Feb. 27, 1657	I	122
	of Ragland				
82	Jinkins, Evan	Samuel Nickolls	Feb. 20, 1661	I	471
83	Jones, Hugh	Mary Norman	Mar. 4, 1669	II	180
84	Jones, Katharine	Philipp Cooke	Aug. 7, 1678	II	308
	On the *Rotorne*, Thomas Edwards, Master				
85	Jones, Thomas	Richard Martin	June 27, 1666	II	72
86	Jones, Thomas	Matthew Stephens	May 1, 1674	II	248
87	Jones, William	William Lewis	Feb. 4, 1662	I	538
88	Lacy, Elianor	John Morgan	Feb. 8, 1663	II	25
89	Lane, Charles	Henry Baker	Mar. 21, 1676	II	298
	On the (*Speedwell?*), Daniel Legg, Master				
90	Langford, Thomas	George Gallop	Feb. 27, 1657	I	122
	of Netherbury				
91	Leech, Edward	Edward Thomas	Feb. 13, 1662	I	540
92	Lonnon, John	William Tytherly	Feb. 26, 1667	II	127
93	Lugg, Andrew	Samuel Tipton	May 14, 1675	II	267
94	Martin, Joane	Christopher Christopher (?)	Apr. 8, 1671	II	203
95	Martin, John	John Devill	Feb. 27, 1657	I	123
	of Tedbury				
96	Medcalfe, Paule	Edward Feilding	Feb. 27, 1657	I	122
	of St. Dunstone, London				
97	Meredith, Elizabeth	Thomas Dennis	Feb. 24, 1661	I	472
98	Miles, John	William Curtis	Mar. 30, 1686		(p. 182)
	of Whatden, sergeweaver; on the *Bostern Merchant*, William Curtis, Master				
99	Miles, Susanna	William Curtis	Mar. 30, 1686		(p. 182)
	of Whatden, wife of John; on the *Bostern Merchant*, William Curtis, Master				

No.	*Name of Servant*	*To Whom Bound*	*Date of Entry*	*Record Book*	*Page*
100	Millard, Robert	Ann Runnings	Apr. 7, 1671	II	202
101	Minny, Thomas	Thomas Martin	Apr. 8, 1671	II	203
	On the *New found Land Merchant*				
102	Moreton, John	John Morgan	Feb. 8, 1663	II	25
103	Morris, William	Henry Baker	May 14, 1675	II	267
104	Moxham, Joseph	Isaac Sheere	Sept. 28, 1675	II	277
105	Norton, Edward	Charles Answeare	Apr. 2, 1663	II	1
106	Olliver, Francis	Edward Thomas	Feb. 4, 1662	I	539
107	Paviott, John	Edward Watkins	Feb. 19, 1668	II	160
108	Pen, William	John Vance	May 28, 1675	II	267
109	Pitman, John	Jonathan Pitman	Mar. 12, 1663	II	26
110	Powell, Nicholas	John Beed	Feb. 27, 1657	I	123
	of St. Peters, co. Hereford				
111	Powell, William	Henry Baker	May 14, 1675	II	267
112	Price, William	Richard Folluit	May 2, 1679	II	316
113	Pritchard, Thomas	Richard Foluit	May 2, 1679	II	316
114	Provender, John	Isaac Ealton	Feb. 8, 1663	II	24
115	Randell, Marke	Thomas Archer	May 7, 1662	I	485
	On the *Huntsman*				
116	Reece, Ann	Samuel Nicholas	Feb. 12, 1662	I	540
117	Reece, Richard	Aldworth Elbridge	May 20, 1668	II	130
118	Richards, Oliver	John Berry	Feb. 20, 1663	II	25
119	Roach, John	John Nicholls	May 23, 1665	II	44
120	Robert, John	Henry Baker	May 14, 1675	II	267
121	Roberts, John	Hugh Tucker	May 13, 1674	II	249
122	Robins, William	Thomas Hollard	Feb. 25, 1674	II	266
123	Rogers, William	Thomas Donning	Feb. 24, 1661	I	472
124	Round, Martha	William White	May 25, 1674	II	250
125	Sall, Lawrence	Samuel Nickolls	Mar. 5, 1661	I	474
126	Saunders, Thomas	Joseph Bowry	Apr. 4, 1679	II	316
	On the *Saphire Ketch*				
127	Say, Thomas	Mathew Buck	Jan. 7, 1663	II	22
128	Sclanders, John	William White	May 25, 1674	II	250
129	Sherman, William	Thomas Moore	May 19, 1668	II	130
130	Sherwood, John	Samuel Nichols	Jan. 21, 1662	I	536
131	Sloper, Anthony	John Alden	Mar. 6, 1670	II	201
	On the French ship of Boston				
132	Sparks, Henery	Edward Tocknell	Aug. 28, 1666	II	73
133	Stone, Richard	John Moore	Feb. 26, 1674	II	266
134	Strowd, Thomas	William Allen	July 16, 1668	II	132
135	Sturmy, Charles	Samuel Nichols	Jan. 28, 1662	I	537
136	Sturmy, Thomas	Samuel Nichols	Feb. 28, 1662	I	537
137	Swayne, Henery	Edward Tocknell	Aug. 31, 1666	II	73
138	Symkins, Michaell	Thomas Elbridge	Feb. 8, 1663	II	24
139	Talbot, Christopher	Richard Folluit	May 2, 1679	II	316
	On the *Benjamin* of Boston				
140	Tayler, Matthew	Matthew Stephens	May 1, 1674	II	248
141	Thomas, Sarah	Thomas Savadge	Mar. 15, 1669	II	181
142	Thomas, William	Thomas Elbridge	Aug. 13, 1662	I	510
143	Thorne, Thomas	Samuel Nickolls	Feb. 20, 1661	I	471
144	Thornes, Nathaniel	Dennis Moone	Apr. 10, 1679	II	316
	On the *Supply*, David Sannd, Master				
145	Tidcombe, Ann	Philipp Cooke	July 18, 1678	II	307
	On the *Retorne* of Boston, Thomas Edwards, Master				

No.	*Name of Servant*	*To Whom Bound*	*Date of Entry*	*Record Book*	*Record Page*
146	Towne, Daniell	William Hiscox	Mar. 5, 1661	I	474
147	Trowbridge, John	Richard Martin	May 13, 1669	II	162
148	Tucker, Edward	John Sunderland	May 28, 1669	II	162
149	Vowles, Allexander	John Nicholas	Mar. 5, 1662	I	542
150	Wall, Humphry	Hugh Tucker	May 25, 1674	II	250
151	Warin, John	Phillip Mathews	Mar. 9, 1662	I	543
152	Warner, Anne	George Lane	Feb. 8, 1661	I	469
153	Wattkins, Priscilla	Philipp Cooke	Aug. 7, 1678	II	308
	On the *Retorne*, Thomas Edwards, Master				
154	Waynehouse, Thomas	Samuel Tipton	May 14, 1675	II	267
155	Webster, Henry	Henry Cott	Apr. 1, 1663	II	1
156	Wharton, Ann	Philipp Cooke	July 18, 1678	II	307
	On the *Retorne* of Boston, Thomas Edwards, Master				
157	White, Martha	John (Devill?)	Feb. 27, 1657	I	122
	of Michaell Deane				
158	Whittle, Thomas	Daniel Legg	Mar. 16, 1676	II	298
	On the *Speedwell*				
159	Williams, John	Thomas Elbridge	Apr. 30, 1662	I	483
	On the *Huntsman*				
160	Williams, John	John Griffen	May 5, 1670	II	182
161	Wolfe, Henry	John Davis	May 13, 1662	I	486
162	Wood, John	Thomas Oldfield	May 21, 1669	II	162
163	Wrentmore, John	Joseph Bowry	Apr. 4, 1679	II	316

Table II

Bond-Master	*Dates of Entries*	*Servants Numbers*
Ailiffe, Anthony	Feb. 27, 1657	81
Alden, John	Feb. 23–Mar. 6, 1670	33, 131
Allen, William	July 16, 1668	134
Answeare, Charles	Apr. 2, 1663	105
Archer, Thomas	May 7, 1662	115
Baker, Henry	May 14, 1675 (3), Mar. 21, 1676 (1)	89, 103, 111, 120
Bedford, Thomas	Mar. 6–9, 1667	35, 39, 60
Beed, John	Feb. 27, 1657	110
Berry, John	Feb. 20, 1663	118
Bowry, Joseph	Apr. 4, 1679	126, 163
Buck, Mathew	Jan. 7, 1663	127
Burroughs, Thomas	March, 1679	22
Cary, John	May 7, 1674	80
Christopher, Christopher	Apr. 8, 1671	94
Codnell, John	Feb. 20, 1684/5	75
Coock, John	Mar. 28, 1671	32
Cooke, Philipp	July 12–Aug. 7, 1678	8, 55, 84, 145, 153, 156
Cott, Henry	Apr. 1, 1663	155
Curtis, William	Mar. 30, 1686	98, 99
Dale, John	Mar. 8, 1670	74
Davis, John	May 13, 1662	161
Dennis, Thomas	Feb. 24, 1661	3, 97
Devill, John	Feb. 27, 1657	95 (157?)
Donning, Thomas	Jan. 23–Feb. 24, 1661	9, 70, 79, 123
Ealton, Isaac	Feb. 8, 1663	114

Bond-Master	*Dates of Entries*	*Servants Numbers*
Elbridge, Aldworth	May 20, 1668	117
Elbridge, Thomas	Apr. 30, 1662 (1)	10, 28, 30, 67, 138,
	July 15–Aug. 13, 1662 (2)	142, 159
	Feb. 8–Mar. 5, 1663 (4)	
Ellott, Robert	Mar. 16, 1667	13
Feilding, Edward	Feb. 27, 1657	96
Folluit (Foluit), Richard		
	May 2, 1679	112, 113, 139
Foy, David	Mar. 2, 1667	45
Franck, John	May 15, 1667	11
Gallop, George	Feb. 27, 1657	90
Garner, George	May 12, 1657	2
Griffen, John	May 5–11, 1670	37, 160
Harris, Thomas	Mar. 6, 1662	27, 31
Hayman, William	Jan. 27–Feb. 6, 1662	43, 51
Hiscox, William	Mar. 5, 1661	146
Hobson, Thomas	Feb. 10, 1674	53
Holder, Christopher	Mar. 25, 1669–May 5, 1670	15, 76
Hollard, Thomas	Feb. 16–25, 1674	72, 122
Horte, Edward	Feb. 27, 1662	12
Jones, Thomas	Feb. 20, 1661	18, 62, 63
Kootes, Josias	June 30, 1674	47, 65
Lambes, Mathew	Feb. 14, 1662	77
Lane, George	Feb. 8, 1661	152
Legg, Daniel	Mar. 16, 1676	158
Legg, John	Feb. 24, 1661	71
Lewis, William	Feb. 4, 1662	87
Martin, Richard	June 27, 1666, May 13, 1669	85, 147
Martin, Thomas	Apr. 8, 1671	101
Mathews, Phillip	Feb. 4–Mar. 9, 1662	16, 151
Merwick, Giles	June 6, 1684	52
Moone, Dennis	Apr. 10, 1679	144
Moore, John	Feb. 26, 1674	133
Moore, Thomas	May 19, 1668, Mar. 31, 1679	24, 129
Morgan, John	Feb. 8, 1663	40, 88, 102
Nicholas, John	Mar. 5–9, 1662	19, 149
Nicholas, Samuel	Feb. 9–Mar. 17, 1662	6, 64, 116
Nicholls, John	May 23, 1665	119
Nicholls (Nichols), Samuel		
	Jan. 21–Feb. 28, 1662	1, 48, 57, 130, 135, 136
Nickolls, Samuel	Feb. 10–Mar. 5, 1661	14, 23, 50, 82, 125, 143
Norman, Mary	Mar. 4, 1669	83
Oldfield (Oldfeild), Thomas		
	May 6–June 13, 1669 (3),	35, 54, 61, 162
	Aug. 19, 1670 (1)	
Orchard, Thomas	Mar. 24, 1662	59
Pitman, John	Feb. 23, 1668	20
Pitman, Jonathan	Mar. 12, 1663	109
Pugsly, Richard	Feb. 26, 1661	21
Raynes, Francis	Aug. 12, 1678	4
Roberts, William	May 11, 1674	17, 29
Runnings, Ann	Apr. 7, 1671	100
Sam, Daniel	Apr. 22, 1669	78
Savadge, Thomas	Mar. 15, 1669	141

Bond-Master	*Dates of Entries*	*Servants Numbers*
Sheere, Isaac	Sept. 28, 1675	104
Shipway, John	Aug. 7, 1662	68
Shipway, Richard	Aug. 10, 1662	66
Smale, Nicholas	Feb. 6, 1662	56
Smith, Christopher	Jan. 26, 1668	38
Smith, Grace	Feb. 23, 1669	58
Smith, John	May 16, 1671	44
Stephens, Matthew	May 1, 1674	86, 140
Stokes, John	June 7, 1670	49
Stratton, Oliver	Feb. 23, 1670	73
Sunderland, John	May 28–June 15, 1669	46, 148
Thomas, Edward	Feb. 4–13, 1662	26, 91, 106
Tipton, Samuel	May 14, 1675	42, 93, 154
Titherly (Tytherly), William	Feb. 26, 1667, Apr. 16, 1669	41, 92
Tocknell, Edward	Aug. 28–31, 1666	132, 137
Tucker, Hugh	May 13–25, 1674	7, 121, 150
Turner, John	Feb. 17, 1661	34
Vance, John	May 28, 1675	108
Vineing, John	Mar. 6, 1662	36
Ware, Peter, planter	Mar. 30, 1686	69
Warren, George	Apr. 27, 1674	5
Watkins, Edward	Feb. 19, 1668	107
White, William	May 25, 1674	124, 128

TABLE III

Ship	*Ship's Master*	*Dates of Entries*	*Servants Numbers*
Benjamin		May 2, 1679	139
Bostern (Bossterne) Merchant	William Curtis	Mar. 30, 1686	69, 98, 99
Content		Aug. 19, 1670	54
French ship of Boston		Feb. 23–Mar. 6, 1670	33, 131
Huntsman		Apr. 30–May 13, 1662	115, 159, 161
Laurell	John West	May 16, 1671	44
Laurell		Feb. 20, 1684/5	75
New found Land Merchant		Apr. 8, 1671	101
Rainbow	William Stermy	June 6, 1684	52
Releife of Boston	William Marshall	Aug. 12, 1678	4
Retorne of Boston	Thomas Edwards	July 12–Aug. 7, 1678	8, 55, 84, 145, 153, 156
Robert and Hester		Feb. 23, 1670	73
Saphire Ketch		Mar. 31–Apr. 4, 1679	24, 126
Society		Mar. 28, 1671	32
Speedwell	Daniel Legg (?)	Mar. 16–21, 1676	89 (?), 158
Supply	David Sannd	March–Apr. 10, 1679	22, 144

GENEALOGICAL GLEANINGS AMONG THE ENGLISH ARCHIVES.

Communicated by J. Henry Lea, Esq.

Bristol Apprentice Books.

These invaluable records preserved at the Council House at Bristol are rightly guarded with jealous care by the custodians, and it was only with considerable difficulty that I obtained access to them, thanks to the influence of His Excellency our Ambassador in England, the late Lord Bishop of London,* Senator Hoar, Alderman Hall of Bristol, and others, whose kind endorsements proved an "Open Sesame!" to the Treasure House, and to whom I am under deep obligation for the great privilege of being admitted to what is probably the first thorough examination of these priceless records. To Mr. Lane, the courteous Treasurer of the City, and his assistants I am also under deep obligation for unfailing courtesy and patience during the weeks spent in their examination.

The series, as preserved, dates from 1532; but the earlier pages of the first volume are so mutilated that it is impossible to fix the exact date of the earliest entry. They continue in almost unbroken series down to our own time, and the pages teem with information regarding every part of the kingdom, the Bristol of that day ranking little if at all below the City of London in trade and commerce, and youths of all grades of society, (younger sons of gentry as well as yeomen,) were sent to the busy city of the West to learn a trade and develop later into members of the great body of merchants who had made, and were making, Bristol rich and famous.

Hundreds of pages of my note books are filled with extracts which as yet I have been unable to classify or index, and many of which I may have the pleasure in future of laying before the readers of the Register; but the direct references to America are few until we reach the sixth volume, in which, for the first time, we find a number of entries of apprentices bound to go abroad. Unfortunately this volume, to us the most full of interest of the series, is the most defective of all. The first 41 pages have perished, the first entry being 21 June, 1660, and leaving a gap from Vol. iv,† which ends in December, 1658, of about eighteen months. Pages 42 to 53, inclusive, cover the period from 21 June to 25 November, 1660; then another gap to page 246, which begins 6 April, 1668, and runs to page 324 where the book ends at 23 March, 1669. Volume vii. is not paged, but begins 16 May, 1670, (showing a loss of two months in one or both books,)

* I cannot print these lines without more than a passing word of gratitude to the Right Reverend Mandell Creighton, first of English historical scholars and most courteous of English gentlemen, to whose ready and helpful kindness I owe so much of what success has attended my labors abroad during the past fifteen years. From the freedom of the Bodleian Library, which was the first, to the help accorded me at Bristol, which was the last, I was under constant obligation for favors received which I have a melancholy pleasure in acknowledging in this brief but sincere tribute to his memory.

† Vol. v. has utterly disappeared.

and runs on without a break to the end of Vol. viii. in January, 1671; this is interrupted by Vol. ix., 1670–1684, (the latter having no apprentices bound beyond sea,) but the latter again interrupted by Vol. x., 1676–1677, and Vol. xi., 1677–1684. There is a break of three years to the next Vol. (xii.), and from this time the foreign entries are discontinued.

The entries which follow are taken from Vols. vi. to xi. inclusive, and I think comprise *every reference to New England* contained in them. There are very many, I think hundreds, of references to Virginia, Bermuda and the different West India Islands, with which Bristol was in closer touch than with our colony; but lack of time, already far overrun in my stay in Bristol, made it impossible for me to take them all, and I was forced to content myself with those mentioned and a few whose names had a special interest and meaning to me. I have strongly urged upon the gentlemen of the Council and the Lord Mayor of the City, (to whom my discoveries in their records came somewhat in the light of a revelation,) the advisability of printing them verbatim, and, as my suggestion seemed to be favorably received, it may be that they will some day be made accessible to all in this way, and preserved in enduring type for the use of future generations of genealogists.

1670. viij Julij. Barthol: Penn bound to Jonas Moxley 4 y^s^ Virg^a^ *

xxv Augusti Jane ffisher bound to Henry Aley for 8 yr^s^ Virg^a^; Rathornis (*sic, perhaps name of ship?*)

2 7^ber^ Andrew Lloyd bound (*to*) Tho: Cary 4 yr^s^ Virginia. †

14 September. Thomas Clement bound to William Rodney for 4 years in the ship Rich'd., Mr. Hramel (?) M^r^. Barba^d^. ‡

do. John Batchello^r^, John Bowen, John Owen, bound to John Norman for 4 years in Virginia in the ffrancis and Mary, John England, M^r^.§

30 September. Richard Andrew to Basswell Newton 4 years in the John. ‖ (*Virg. was first written, and Bar^d^. over it.*)

3 October. Elizabeth Cople bound to John fferne for 4 yr^s^ Virg^a^ in the Vnichorne Mr. Coop, M^r^. ¶

23 ffebruary. Jeremy Clarke bound to John Alden for 6 years in New England in the ship called the ffrench ship of Boston.**

* I have already printed this entry and the admon. of the emigrant to his father, John Penn, 1677, in the Penn notes in Register for July, 1900, p. 327.

† See notes under Cary, 1679, page 334, *post*.

‡ See notes under Cæsar Rodney, 1657, page 335, *post*.

§ Can this John Batchellor have been the freeman of 1670, mentioned by Savage, who died at Reading in 1705? John Norman cannot be either the John of Salem, 1631, and Marblehead 1648, who died at Salem 1673, or the later John of same place, son of Richard, who died 1713, aged 67. Of John Bowen or John Owen (*quere, if not the same man?*) I find no trace in New England, and it seems probable that these were really Virginia emigrants.

‖ Newton is a notable Virginia name, and it may well be that this Basswell Newton should give us a clue to the parentage, hitherto vainly sought, of George Newton who appears at Norfolk in 1670 (Lower Norf. Court Rec., vii., 58) and who is believed to have come from Barbadoes. See also under apprenticeship of William, son of Brian Newton, in 1593.

¶ See the will of John Ferne of St. Vedast, Foster Lane, London, 1620 (P. C. C. Soame 8) printed by me in Register for April 1900, page 192. The John Ferne of the Apprentice Books is most probably the son John of this will. His Admon. is probably either 5 July or 23 Mar. 1680, *ibid* page 193.

** This and the following entry certainly relate to the John Alden of the Mayflower, and may prove of great value in locating his place of origin in England. That he was *not* of Southampton, where he embarked, is about all that is known with certainty re-

6 March.	Anthony Sloper is bound to John Alden for 6 years in New England in the ship called y[e] ffrench ship.
viij March.	Jo[n] Harris bound to Jo[n] Dale 4 years (*in*) New England ship (*blank*) Thomas Savidge M[r]. *
1671. 16 May.	Thomas David bound to John Smith for 4 years in Nevis, Jamaica or New England, in the ship Lawrell, John West, M[r].
3 June.	William Davis bound to Tho: Norman for 4 years in Virginia in the Catherine, Robert Dapwell, M[r].
8 June.	Edward Davis bound to William Merrick for 4 years in Barbadoes, in the Planter, Bartholimy Jeffares M[r].
v. July.	Mary Jones bound to John Mason for 4 years in Virginia, in ship Triall, William Smith M[r].†
11 July.	William Davis bound to John Mason for 4 years in Virginia, in the ship Triall, William Smith M[r].
19 August.	Hester Garberry bound to Thomas Hungerford 4 years in Virginia (*in ship*) Steven, M[r] Scott M[r].‡
24 August.	Susannah Davis bound to Thomas Daniell 4 years (*in*) Maryland.
1676. 23 August.	James Penn bound to Ralph Smith 4 yeeres in Virg[a] Shipp St. John, Peter Wraxall Master.§
1677. 1 May.	Richard Davis bound to Thomas Pearce 4 yeares in Newfoundland (*in ship*) Hopewell - - - Holbruke (*Master*)‖

garding him; and this connection with Bristol furnishes a clue which may be well worth following up, and I shall perhaps have more to say of the Aldens hereafter. Jeremy Clark is certainly not identical with the Jeremiah Clark who was of Newport in 1640, nor does it seem possible that this could have been the latter's son of the same name, returning to New England. Neither can I identify Anthony Sloper; Richard Sloper of Dover 1657, who died 1716, being the only one of the name mentioned by Savage.

* This is probably John Dale who was of Salem in 1682, and died 9 Feb., 1700. John Harris of Boston, who married 20 Mar., 1675, Susanna Breck of Dorchester, is probably identical with this apprentice, as he would then have been just released.

† A John Mason was of Norfolk, Virginia, in January, 1640. See Lower Norfolk Court Records, Vol. I., fo. 54[b].

‡ Thomas Hungerford may perhaps be the Thomas Hungerford of Hartford and Haddam, Conn., son of Thomas of the same who died in 1663. Thomas the son was born about 1648, and so would have been 23 years of age in 1671. The name is so unusual that this might well be the same, although called of Virginia. I am engaged in an exhaustive study of the Hungerfords, and may be able later to clearly identify this man. There was a Thomas Hungerford, son of Henry and Eleanor (Stevens) Hungerford, baptized at St. James, Bristol, 14 Dec. 1616; he was apprenticed 28 Nov. 1631, to John Roome, Jr., carpenter, and married 20 April 1640, to Mary White at St. James; he had children—Elizabeth, bapt. 10 Feb. 1640-1, Ann, 7 Aug. 1642, and William, 24 Mar. 1643, all at same Church, and after that date his name disappears from the Registers; but he can hardly be identical with the first Thomas of Hartford, unless Savage is in error in locating him there so early as 1639. Perhaps, however, the Thomas of New London, 1650, was another man and, if so, very probably identical with the Bristol Thomas. His age, if it could be ascertained, would greatly assist identification.

§ This entry I have already printed in the REGISTER for July, 1900, p. 327.

‖ The following will, showing a Davis connection with Newfonndland many years earlier, may be noted in this connection:

Will of Thomas Davis of Cittie of Bristoll, merchant, in good health ("*of St. Leonards*" *on dorso.*) Dated xx October 1630, 6 Charles. To wyfe Mary my dwelling in Corne Street, purchased of S[r] George Snigg for three lives, with remainder to my daughters. To sonn Richard my 1-12 adventure in Bristolls Hope at newfoundland, said sonn under 25 years of age. My daughters Susanne & Marie Res. Legatees. To my wyfe aforsaid the house at Stony Hill in w[ch] Richard Boswell apothecary late dwelled, with rem. to sonn Richard, and said wyfe Extrx. Witn:—Walter Stephens & Elizabeth Pringe. Pro. 9 March 1637 in P. C. C. & reissued at Bristol 17 October 1637, by oath of Extrx. (*Sic. but pro. 16 Oct. 1637 in P. C. C. Reg.*)

Cons. Bristol Files &
P. C. C. Reg. Goare 129.

1678. 12 July. Moses ffound bound to Phillip Cooke 9 yeeres in New England (*in*) the ship Retorn of Boston. *

7 August. Katherine Jones bound to Phil: Cooke 4 years in New-england, Shipp Return, Thomas Edwards M[r].

25 January. Samuel Peckford bound to Christopher Pitt 4 years in Barbadoes and Nevis. †

1678–9. March (n. d.) William Britten bound to Thomas Burroughs 7 yeeres in New England shipp Supply, David Sanders Master.

1679. xxxj March. Richard Browne bound to Thomas Moore 4 yeeres (*in*) New England, Saphire Ketch (*blank*) Boury (*Master.*) ‡

iiij April. Thomas Sanders bound to Joseph Bowry M[r] of the Sapha Ketch 4 yee[rs] in New England.

April 10 Nathaniel Thomes bound to Dennis Moone Jun[r] 4 yeeres in New England shipp Supply Ketch, David Sand[r]s (*Master.*)

11 Maij. Christopher Talbott bound to Richard ffollint 4 yee[rs] in New England shipp Benjamin of Boston, Arth: Tanner (*Master.*) §

Thomas Pritchard bound to same 4 yeers same place.

1679. 16 October. George Hopton bound to ffrancis Cattkins (*or Caltkins*) 6 yeares (*in*) Maryland, shipp Richard and James, Thomas Opie, M[r].‖

7 November. David Jones bound to George Cary 5 yeares in Virg[a] (*in*) shipp ffrancis and Mary.¶

1680. 22 July. Andrew Wanklyn (*or Wauklyn?*) bound to George Cary 4 yeeres in Virg[a] shipp Samuel, William Sanky, M[r].¶

24 September. Edward Davis bound to Thomas Cary for 4 yeares in Virginia in shipp ffactor, Robert Drew, M[r].¶

do. Ann Douding bound to Marmaduke Williams 4 yeares in Maryland, ship Richard and James, Tho: Opie, M[r].**

* This cannot be either the Phillip Cooke of Cambridge, 1647, who died 1667, or his son of same name, bapt. there 5 May, 1661; as the latter would have been but 17 years of age in 1678.

† The Pickfords are a well known family of Cheshire and Derby. They came to America late in the 18th century, and settled in Maine. See under Jeddiah Pickford, 1669, for notes concerning them. The West Indian connection here shown is interesting, as Thomas Pickford, half-brother of John, the Maine emigrant, was a planter in Trinidad, and died there in 1805.

‡ This is probably the Thomas Moore of Boston, mariner, who died in 1690, as noted by Savage.

§ Christopher Talbott was of Boston, tanner, in 1686.

‖ I am making an exhaustive study of the interesting family of Hopton, but am unable, as yet, to place this George Hopton. The name is very unusual in the family. I should be glad to know if he has left descendants in Maryland.

¶ The Carys of Virginia are a very well known family, founded in this country by Miles Cary of Bristol, son of John and Alice (Hobson) Cary, who was in Virginia as early as 1640. Thomas Cary is probably the second son of Miles, who died in 1708, aged 60 years. I fail to place George Cary in the pedigree—perhaps Virginia Records may help in this. I am inclined to believe that John Care of Barbadoes, distiller, deceased in 1683, was identical with John Cary of Bristol (brother of Miles) who disappears from the Bristol records after 1660. I have a singularly perfect pedigree of this old Bristolian stock from William Cary, Sheriff of Bristol, 1532, and Mayor 1546. Of this family was also James Cary, merchant, of Charlestown, 1647, according to Stow MS., 670, fo. 229–30. He was son of William and Alice (Goodal) Cary, and was bapt. at St. Nicholas, Bristol, 14 April, 1600; he married Eleanor Hawkins, and had one son, Robert, bapt. 9 March, 1625, and buried 5 March, 1626, at St. Stephen's, Bristol; his other children being probably born here. He died 2 Nov. 1681, aged 81, which fact, as well as the name of his wife, accords with Stow MS.

** The Parish Registers of St. Werburgh, Bristol, give the following:

1652. George, sonn of Marmaduke Williams, of St. Steevens parish buried February 21.

1659. Elizabeth, daughter of Marmaduke Williams and Wealthian his wife of St. Stephen's buried April 25.

do. Thomas Williams bound to the same 4 yeeres in Maryland in same shipp.

1683. ffebruary 11. Nicholas son of John Care late of the Island of Barbadoes, Distiller, apprenticed to Hugh Rainstorp, mariner, (*naute*) and Martha his wife. [See note, page 334.]

The foregoing concludes the direct American references contained in the Apprentice Books, so far as covered by my notes, but the following entries, selected at random from my still unindexed note books, will give an idea of the scope and great value of these records.

1657. 15 August. Cezar Rodney son of William Rodney, of Catcott, co. Somerset, Gent., apprenticed to William Tippet of Bristol, Haberdasher, and (*blank*) his wife.

This William Rodney was the fourth and youngest surviving son of Sir John Rodney, Knt., of Rodney Stoke, Somst., by his wife Jane, daughter of Sir Henry Seymour, Knt., (brother of Edward, Duke of Somerset, and of Queen Jane Seymour.)* He was born about 1610, and having married Alice, daughter of Sir Thomas Cæsar, Knt., Baron of the Exchequer, had by her Anthony, Cæsar, William, and probably other children. Anthony was a colonel in the army, and was grandfather of George-Brydges Rodney, the famous English admiral; Cæsar seems to have remained in Bristol; and William, who was born about 1652, became a convert to Quakerism, and came to America with William Penn in 1682, settled in Kent County, Delaware, and, through his son Cæsar, was grandfather of Cæsar Rodney, born 7 October, 1728, delegate to the Continental Congress and signer of the Declaration of Independence, for the State of Delaware. I shall have more to say of this interesting family when my collection of their wills is completed. The William Rodney already cited† may be confidently identified with the father of our American emigrant, and the Barbadoes connection there shown may give a clue to further and valuable information concerning the family when the island records are examined.

The Registers of Christ Church, Bristol, show the following entries:

1660. March 14. William sonn of William Rodney and Rachel his wife bapt.‡

1666. April 8. Alice daughter of Cesar Rodney by his wife Sarah bapt.§

1688. June viij. Anthony Thatcher, son of Peter Thatcher, late of Rangeworthy co. Glouc., Tanner, apprenticed to John Poyte of Bristol, Pipemaker, and Barbara his wife.

The above entry struck me at once as of great possible value in giving a clue to the hitherto vexed question of the paternity of Rev. Peter Thacher of Sarum, and his brother Anthony, which has been so long and vainly sought for in Wilts. and Somerset, as we have here a most significant com-

* A very interesting 17th century Genealogy of this family, written by Sir Edward Rodney, Knt., elder brother of William, has just been printed in the *Genealogist*, n. s., Vol. xvi., 207, Vol. xvii., 6 and 100.

† See apprenticeship of Thomas Clement in 1670, page 332, *ante*.

‡ I do not with certainty identify this William, who can hardly be the father of our emigrant, married to a second wife; as at this period the custom of giving two or more sons the same Christian name had fortunately fallen into disuse.

§ This is clearly the Cæsar of the apprenticeship of 1657, married and settled in Bristol.

bination of the two characteristic family names in Gloucestershire, a county which has never, I believe, been examined for the name. The date is of course late, and could represent only collateral members of the family, but may well serve to guide us to their place of origin. The following extracts show other occurrences of the name in the Bristol Books:

1601. xj March. Arthur Thatcher* son of John Thatcher of Burington,† co. Somst., Husbandman, apprenticed to Edmund Hedges and Alice his wife.

1613. 2 March. John Thatcher son of William Thatcher late of Pyrton, co. Wilts., Husbandman, dec'd., apprenticed to Richard Stockman, Sherman, and Johanna his wife.‡

1671. 30 June. William Thatcher, son of John Thatcher of Wrinton (*i.e. Wrington*), co. Somst., Coordwinder, apprenticed to John Comberbach, Sen:, Horner, and Elizabeth his wife for 7 yeares.§
(*This is twice entered, in Vols. viii. and ix.*)

1707. August xi. Nathan Thatcher, son of Peter Thatcher of Thornbury, co. Glouc., Tanner, apprenticed to John Trickey, Weaver, and Sarah his wife.

* Simon and then Joseph were first written and crossed out, and Arthur written over the last.

† Will of John Thatcher of Berington, co. Somst., husbandman, sicke in bodye. Dated xv maye, 1603. To be buried in churchyard of Berrington. To dau. Jsable Thatcher iij[li] of money & the pane at Rickeford. To dau. Elizabeth iii[li] & her owne mother's apparell. To son James Thatcher the best pane & greate crocke. To (*son*) Arthur Thatcher all the money that is to be received of Edmund Hedges of Bristowe. I forgive Symon Thatcher all he oweth me, if so be that he shall paye vnto Jsable Thatcher xxx[s] that I owe vnto her or ells not. My wyfe Margaret Thatcher, Res. Leg. & Extrx. Overseers—John Tristram & James Thetcher. Witn:—John Tristram, Clerk, & James Thetcher. Pro. at Wells, 28 July, 1606, by Extrx.

Cons. Wells file no. 79.

John Thatcher, senior, was buried at Berrington, 3 August, 1605. (Bish. Trans.)

‡ Will of Edward Thatcher of Pirton, co. Wilts., husbandman, sicke in bodye. Dated 10 Maye 1595, 37 Elizabeth. To be buried in churchyard of Pirton. To O[r] Ladye Church of Sarum 4[d]. To Parish Church of Pirton 5[s]. To poor of parish 20[s]. To John Thatcher, the sonn of William Thatcher, my lease at Longcutt with remainder to his brother Bennett Thatcher. To sonne Thomas Thatcher, my dwelling at woulson, my Lease w[ch] he now occupyeth there, he to paye £16. of my debts— i. e. £11 to William Rippington & £5 to Richard Russley, both of Moulsonne. To John, sonn of William Thatcher, one fallowe Cowe & best bed & one greate Candlesticke. To Benedict, sonn of William Thatcher, one browne Cowe shorte horned, Coverlett & paire of sheetes next best. To Edward, sonn of Thomas Thatcher, one fallowe heifer, Bed with payer of sheetes of the third sorte & one Candlesticke. To Thomas Thatcher, sonn of Thomas Thatcher, a tagged blacke Cowe somethinge crooked horned & payer of sheetes. To Arnold Thatcher, sonn of said Thomas, two weaneling Calves. To daughter in lawe Ellynor Marshe a white Couerlett, payer blanketts, platter, pottinger, Sawcer, little Cawdron, her mother's weddinge Ringe & her best partlett, she to take her legacy quietly without troubling my Exor. & her stocke—1 Cowe 13[s] 4[d], 1 quarter of Barley price 10[s], 3 sheepe, 3 lbs. of wooll prise 3[s]. To children of John Sparkman, late of Buskett, Dec'd., (*i.e. Burscott in Berks*) £4 which I received of him for his childrens vse. My sonne william Thatcher, Res. Leg. & Exor. Overseers—my welbeloued in xpiste John Shurmer & John weaving & to them 5[s]. Due to me by Humfry Edwards of Maggett mill 46[s]. 8[d]. by Richard wicksey 53[s]. 4[d]. Witn:—Thomas Elbrough, Richard Adams & Robert Prue, Vicar of Pirton. Pro. at London 4 Oct., 1595, by Thomas Lovell, Not. Pub., Atty. for Exor. named.

P. C. C. Scott 62.

§ The Wrington Parish Registers show only the following entries:
1647.—October vij—Sarah daughter of Richard Thetcher & Sarah his wiffe baptized.
1655.—Intentions of Marriage of John Thatcher of this parish, Cordwinder, and Mary Dotin of St. James in Taunton, singlewoman, were published 17, 24 June and 1 July 1655.

Baptisms and Burials searched to 1650 only, Marriages to 1675. Wrington is near Berrington in the same Hundred—*i. e.* Brent with Wrington.

1714. January xviij. William Thatcher, son of Peter Thatcher of Bristoll, Tanner, apprenticed to Jona: Mason, Hallier, and Marie his wife. 2 January 1715, was turned over to William Roach, Hallier, and Dinah his wife for rest of terme.

1629. 8 March. Robert Beaton, son of Robert Beaton of Mudford, co. Somst., yeoman, dec'd., apprenticed to Thomas Whittinghame, Joyner, and Marie his wife.

1688. May 10. Georg Beaton, son of Jonathan Beaton late of vpgher Compton, (*i. e. Upper Compton,*) co. Dorset, yeoman, dec'd., apprenticed to William Barnsdale, Grocer, and Jane his wife for 7 years. His mother to find his apparell.

These Beatons were of a family long seated at Upper and Nether Compton in Dorset, and descendants of theirs became Quakers and came to Pennsylvania in the 18th century. The name is frequent in Bristol records. John Beaton, grandfather of this Jonathan Beaton, married Mary daughter of Thomas Napper of Tintenhull, co. Somst.*

1677. vj November. Vzziel Chancy, son of Jsaac Chancy of Andover,† co. Hants., merchant, apprenticed to Richard King, Junr., merchant, and (*blank*) his wife, for 7 years.

1689. 1 May. Charles Chauncy, son of Jchabod Chauncy,‡ Doctor in Medicine of the City of Bristoll, apprenticed to vzziel Chauncy,§ mercer, and (*blank*) his wife for 7 years. The father to find his apparell.‖

1705. November 9. Nathaniel Sheppard, son of William Sheppard late of Bristoll, Merchant, apprenticed to Charles Chancy, Mercer, and (*blank*) his wife.

1705. June 5. Stanton Chancy, Merchant, is admitted into the Libts. of the Cittie for this he was Apprentice of Mikaell Pope and paid 4^s 6^d. Burgess Books, iv., fo. 339.

The family of the distinguished President of Harvard College needs no introduction to New England readers, as the history is well known. I shall have some further notes to submit regarding them from testamentary sources, but the wills of four of the name have already been printed in the Register** by Mr. H. F. Waters.

1669. 3 December. Jedida Pickford, son of James†† Pickford of Macklecfeild, co. Cest., gent., dec'd., apprenticed to John Dymer, Grocer, and Elizabeth, his wife.

* See Pedigree of Napper, in Visitation of Somst., 1623, from Harl. MS. 1141.

† See his will, 1711 (P. C. C. Barnes 46), Register, 39, page 167.

‡ In the registers of St. Michael's, Bristol, I find this entry:
1669.—m^r^. Eichabod Chuncy and mrs. Mary King married August 12.
His will pro. 10 Dec. and 17 Feb. 1691 at London, his son Stanton then a minor (P. C. C. Fane 138 & Vere 233).

§ Uzzaliel Chauncey committed suicide—the long and interesting testimony at his inquest, held 1 September 1696, may be found in Brit. Mus., Add. MS. 5540, fo. 29.

‖ Charles Chauncy was not admitted to the freedom of the city until 1703, as we learn from the following entry in the Burgess Books:
1703—October 15—Charles Chauncey, Mercer, is admitted into the Libts: of the Cittie, for that he was Apprentice to Vzzell Chancey and paid 4^s 6^d.

** See Register, Vol. 39, page 166, and references there given.

†† "Jacobi" in the entry in the Apprentice Book, but the wills show that this is merely the latinized form of James.

Referring to my comment on this family, under Samuel Peckford apprenticed in 1678,* who was a putative member only of the Cheshire stock, we are now dealing with a certainty in this Jedidiah Pickford, who became a prosperous merchant of Bristol, and whose position in the pedigree is well assured by his own and his brother's wills which follow:

Will of Jonathan Pickford of Macclesfield in co. Cest., gentleman. Dated 25 February 1689. A very long and intricate will, mentions: Grandfather James Pickford, dec'd., wife Alice, son John and younger son James, brother Jeddediah Pickford, father James Pickford, dec'd., mother-in-law Alice Williamson, daughters Priscilla, Alice and Grace Pickford, sister Ellen, wife of William Fletcher; Exors. Robert Sandiford of Knotlands in co. of Lanc., Gen:, John Corker of Hurdsfield, co. Cest., gent., and William Fletcher of Derby, in co. Derby, gent., and Alice his wife. Fine pendant Seal of letters J. P. and a Palm Tree. Witn: Alls williamson, James Andrews and John Andrew. Pro. 23 May, 1690, by Exors.

Inventory as of Jonathan Pickford, late of Althill in parish of Ashton-under-line, co. Lanc., Gent., taken 6 May 1690, by Ralph Sandiforth of Deanshutts, Robert Hopkin of Netherlees, Samuel Andrew of Alt and John Andrew his son. Sum Totall 378 - 6 - 0. Cons. Ct. Cest. Files.

Will of Jedidiah Pickford of St. Nicholas parish in the City of Bristoll, merchant. Dated 3 March 1693 (4). Names sister Hellen, wife of William Fletcher of Derby, Malster; Sister Alice, widow of brother Jonathan Pickford, dec'd., and her son James, eldest son John and daughter Priscilla; Nephew James Fletcher, son of sister Hellen; Nephew James Pickford aforesaid to be Exor. (*He was then a minor but attained his majority in March 1697.*) Overseers—William Opie, Esq., Jacob Beale, Mercht, and Henry Bradley, Ironmonger. Witn:—John Watkins, John Plaister and Edmund Brand. Pro. at London 24 March 1693 (4). P. C. C. Box 62.

The following, tho only other entry of the name found in these books, seems to be of an altogether different family:

1548. xxix September. Thomas Pytchforde, son of Thomas Pytchforde of Preston, co. Salop, husbandman, apprenticed to Roger Bailie and Helen his wife (*no trade named*).

1593. 8 November—William Newton, son of Brian Newton of lancaster in co. Lancaster, apprenticed to John Griffith of the city of Bristoll, grocer, and (*blank*) his wife, for 9 years.

As has been mentioned under Basswell Newton, in 1670,† there was a George Newton who appeared at Norfolk, Va., in 1670, and believed to have come to America via Barbadoes. He was a young man on his arrival, and then unmarried, but before 1678 he had married Frances, daughter of Lemuel Mason, a leading citizen, and died in 1694. His eldest son George was sent to school at Lancaster in England, as we learn from a deposition of his in 1738,‡ and the inference is a natural one that his father came from that neighborhood.

Brian Newton, the father, was son of Edmund Newton of Lancaster, Mercer, by Isabell his wife, daughter of William Curwen, Mayor of Lancaster, and was bapt. there 1 March, 1 and 2 Phillip and Mary. From the will

* See page 334, *ante*.
† See page 332, *ante*.
‡ Lower Norfolk Court Records, Vol. 14 (No. 12), fo. 202.

and admon. which follow, we learn that William Newton did not remain in Bristol but returned to Lancashire, and died there, evidently unmarried, in 1636. His burial is found in the Tunstall, Lanc., Register as 25 January, 1636.

Will of Brian Newton of Canffield in parish of Tunstill, sick and weak. Dated — March 1622. To be buried in the churchyard of Tunstall. My wife Jennet to mayntayne Jeny newton, my son James his daughter. To son James £3 - 9 - 0 w[ch] my son Thomas oweth me. To son William closes bought of Edmund Batty of overtowne, lying in Tunstall. Daughter Elizabeth Newton. John Smith, J[r], a debtor. My wife Jennet and dau. Elizabeth Exors. Witn:—William Thornton, Roger Canfild and John Williamson, clerk. Bond of William Newton of Cantfield, yeoman, and Francis Batty of Tunstall, in £90. Inventory dated 29 April 1623, by William Thornton, William Gybson, Bryan Robinson and Francis Carington.

Arch. Richmond Files.

Admon. of William Newton of Canfield in Tunstall, granted 18 May 1637, to James Newton of Canfield, linen webster (*no relationship given, but probably brother*). Sureties – John Canfield and Robert Canfield of Thornton in Lonsdale, co. Lanc., husbandman, in £100. Inventory 28 March 1637, by John Hodgshon, William Gibson, Thomas Smith and Robert Towne.

Arch. Richmond Files.

These will conclude, for the present, my extracts from the Bristol City books. As my note books are indexed and put in order, I shall have more to say regarding certain families named in them.

MORE PASSENGERS TO NEW-ENGLAND, 1679.

Communicated by HENRY F. WATERS, Esq., of Salem.

THE following extracts were taken from papers now contained in Vol. xxxii., leaves 19 to 22 inclusive, of "Essex County Court Papers," having been used as evidence in the case of Mr. John Barton, "cherurgeon," vs. Capt. Nicholas Manning, "for non-payment according to agreement at two shillings & six pence per head for all the passengers that came over in the Ship Hannah & Elizabeth, from England, * * * * to the number of about forty seven passengers."

Many of the names contained in this list of passengers I do not find in Savage. Mrs. Anstiss Manning, who heads the list, was the widow of Mr. Richard Manning, of St. Patrick's parish, Dartmouth, Eng., and the five following names are those of her children. I have been told by a lineal descendant that her maiden name was Calley. Her dau. Sarah (third on the list) married John Williams, of Salem (son of John and Elizabeth (Skerry) Williams, and grandson of George and Marie Williams), and had, among other children, Sarah who married Gamaliel Hodges, Anstiss who married John Crowninshield, and Mary who married Joseph Lambert, thus being the common ancestress of three of the most prominent and influential families in the east parish of Salem. The name of Anstiss has been brought down to this day among her descendants in the Crowninshield, Pickman, Derby, Stone, and Dunlap families.

Margaret Willing may have been she who married John Richardson, of Woburn, in 1689. The name of Bouey (Bovey) is found in Salem now. Cane, it will be noticed, is spelled "Cann" on the doctor's list of patients. Towsey suggests the family name of the late Secretary Toucey, of Conn. Dearield may be meant for Darrell, and Goarding (or Gourding) for Gordon. Mr. John Calley may be he who was afterward one of the most influential citizens of Marblehead, and widely known as "Capt. John Calley, esq." The deposition of "m^r John Calley" shows him to have been 49 yrs. of age.

These extracts have been made with careful attention to the spelling in the original MSS.

The names of all ye passengers that came in ye shipe Hannah & Elizabeth m^r Lott Goarding com̄ander Capt Nicholas Manning undertaker of ye said shipe.—

m^{rs} Anstist Manning Senr
Anstist Manning Junr
Margrett Manning
Sarah Manning
Jacob Manning
Thomas Manning
Elizabeth Walsh
Joane Brownestis
Margrett Willing
Annis ffoord
Anne Killigroue
Margrett Bouey
Grace Stiuer
Mary peirce
Stephen Bickford
Robert Cane
Joseph Manning
Richard oliver
Richard Thomas
Wm Hutchings
& his wife
George Martine
& his wife
Thō Knollman
John Norway
James Tomling
m^r Thomas Towsly
& his wife
& his child
& his seruant boy
Moses Dearild
James Mudd
Richard Goarding
m^r Aron Smith
m^r John Cally Senr
John Cally Junr
Thomas Baker

m^r John Jackson
& his wife
Clement Jackson
Sarah Jackson
Agnes Jackson
m^{rs} Joan Deareing
Sarah Dearing
Joseph Dearing

All these Eight was agreed upon between Captain Manning, & John Jackson for thirty pounds for theire passages from Dartmouth to New England, m^r John Jackson doeing his labour in ye said shipe

The depositions of m^r Lott Gourding comand^r of ye shipe Hannah & Elizabeth & Benj^m Rawlings Seaman of ye said shipe testifyeth & saith that all those names aboue written were passengers in ye aboue named shipe Capt Nicholas Manning sole Undertaker of all passengers & concerns, & farther saith nott Both Sworne in Boston this 4th day of November 1679

Before me JOHN RICHARDS. Com̄isn^r.

The deposition of m^r Lott Gourdinge Comander of ye pinke Hannah & Elizabeth aged 32 years or thereabouts, testifyeth & saith, that Capt. Nicholas Manninge sole undertaker of ye said pinke did shipe John Barton chyrurgeon; as chyrurgeon of ye said shipe, which place he did act & officiate in as a chyrurgeon & did administer to seuerall, especially to ye said Mannings servants, & was as chyrurgeon of ye said shipe from ye day that he was shiped by the said Manning—itt being ye twenty third of may, untill ye fourtenth of September following & as to ye contract made between them, ye halfe Crowne a head was to be paid at ye place where the passengers come on boord, & as tis alsoe coustomary throughout England and further saith nott Sworne in Boston Novem. 14. 1679

Before me JOHN RICHARDS: Comsnr.

The deposition of Jacob Manning aged Eighteen yeares and Anstice Manning: testifieth & saith. that D[r] Barton lay on bord the Shipp Hannah & Elizabeth of Boston. Lott Gorden Commander about five or six weekes in Dartmouth & had his victualls abord upon Nicholus Mannings Accompt all that time & so came from thence a passenger to New England: also, a great Chest of his brought in the hold of the s[d]. shipp.

Owned by y[e] defend[t] that D[r] Barton was soe longe abord after he was shiped & came ouer in y[e] ship & his chest in Court at Salem 27 : 9 : 79 :
HILLIARD VEREN Clc:

Medicines Expended upon A Voyage from Dartmouth to New England in y[e] Shipe: Hannah & Elizabeth Lott Gourding Coand[r], but Capt Nich[ll] Manning Undertaker wth theire Names Maladies & Medicines

1679	NAMES.	MALADIES.	MEDICINES.	£	s	d
May 27	Hen Dawson	An Itching Humor	letting a s blood	0	1	0
	Nath Stanbury	paine in his head & teeth	6 purging pills wth Rosin of Jallap	0	2	0
			oile of Cloues & origanû for his teeth	0	1	0
June 28	Rich Goarding	Bite wth a Dogg on ye wrist	Oyntments Emplaisters Balsam for seauen dayes	0	5	0
July 4	Robt Cann	A Bruise vpon his fingers, wth a chest in ye Hold	Oyntments & Emplaisters for seuerall dayes . .	0	2	0
10	Jos Manning	A Broken shinn	Seuerall Emplaisters . .	0	1	0
	Annis ffoord	An Extream Cold	A Diaphoritick Bolus . .	0	1	0
12	Goodwif Martin	Naturall Obstructions & very faint	Syrup of Saffron ʒ iiij Gascons[1] powder ʒ s .	0	3	6
	Annis Jackson	Stomachacall paines	Syrup of Saffron ℥ s . .	0	1	0
	Rich Goarding	A great Cold, swelling of y[e] Amigdalls[2] & a feauer	An Oyntment for his throat	0	0	6
			A sweating Bolus . . .	0	1	0
			A potion of physicke . .	0	1	6
13	— — —	— — —	A Refrigerating powder 3 ƒ	0	1	0
			A somniferous Bolus . .	0	1	0
			More oyntment	0	0	6
			A pectoral syrup ℥ iiij .	0	1	4
			A liquorish sticke . . .	0	0	2
			A pectorall Refregerating Decoction	0	2	0
14	Marg[rtt] Manning	paine in her head	Emplaisters for her temples	0	1	0
15	Thō Knollman	Blistred his hand & fingers	Emplaisters & oyntment .	0	1	0

[1] Undoubtedly meant for Gascoign's Powder, and apparently identical with the "Compound Powder of Crabs-Claws," for which an old Dispensatory in my possession furnishes the following recipe:—"Take of prepared Pearls, of Crabs Eyes, red Coral, the whitest Amber, Calcined Hartshorn, and Oriental Bezoar, ana ℥ i., of the Powder from the black Claws of a Crab, the Weight of all the other, and make them into a fine Powder, which is to be formed into Balls with a Solution of Gum Arabic." * * * * * * "It was in the former Dispensatory ordered to be formed into Balls, with a Jelly made of Vipers Skins, but that difference is of no great moment."

[2] The tonsils, sometimes called the almonds of the throat.

	Annis Jackson	Costiue body	A suppository	0	0	6
16	Anne Killigroue	Costiue body	A suppository	0	0	6
			purging pills 6	0	1	6
17	Annis Jackson		purging pills 6	0	2	0
20	Mary peirce	Cutt ffinger	Emplaisters	0	0	6
	Nath. Stanbury	Bruised ffinger	Emplaisters Unguents	0	1	0
21	Ben : Threenedles	A Roosty naile in his hand	Emplaisters	0	1	0
	mr Tom Towsey	paine in his head & Swelling of ye Amigdalls	A suppository	0	0	6
			A sweating Bolus	0	1	0
22	— — —	— — —	An Oyntment for his throat	0	0	6
			A suppository	0	0	6
			6 purging pills	0	1	6
July 22	Goodwife Hutchins	Tooth ach	Oile of Cloues	0	0	6
			Blistering Emplaisters	0	1	6
23	— — —	— — —	Oile of Cloues	0	0	6
			Emplaisters for her temples	0	0	6
	Goodman Hutchins	Much troubled wth flemye	A pectoral Syrup	0	1	0
29	Stephen Bickfoord,	Wormes	purging pills wth Mercurius dulcis	0	1	0
			flower of Brimston	0	1	0
31	mr Goarding	Broken hands & fingers	Emplaisters	0	1	0
	margrett Bouy	Cutt & Bruise in her nose & eybrow	Emplaisters & Balsams for 6 dayes	0	6	0
Aug 4	An Killigroue	Histericall vapors	Suppository	0	0	6
			A compound Clyster wth Histericall Carmanitiue seeds	0	2	6
			An Histericall bolus	0	1	6
			A stomachicall Emplaister	0	1	0
8	Joane Brownstist	Hystericall ffitts	Spiritt of Castor & oile of Amber seuerall times	0	3	0
9	Thō Knollman	A Cold & feauer	A Diaphoretic bolus	0	1	6
			A somniferous Julap	0	1	0
10	— — —	— — —	both ye same againe	0	2	6
				3	5	0

That I John Barton chyrurgeon doe owne this to be ye whole truth as witnesse my hand

J. Barton

Passengers in the ship Nathaniel of Dartmouth.—The following is from the Book of Notarial Records, clerk's office, county of Essex, Massachusetts.

"The affidavitts of Nicholas Bartlet and Damaris Phippeny the former aged about 86 yeares the latter about fifty nine Testifie and say yt they came from England forty four yeares agone in the Ship Nathaniel of Dartmouth John Adams of said Dartmouth Commander, and that there came with them Christopher Babbidge of Tatness in the County of Devonshire, son of Roger and Hester Babbidge of Tatness aforesaid;" that the said Xtopher is now living in Salem, that he had three brothers named Richard, Roger, and John, and one sister called Jone; that he served his time with one George Markes of Tatness aforesaid, Taylor; that these deponents were next neibours to them in Tatness; and that he married one Agnes Triggs of the same place, and is now present at the giving of this deposition. Sept. 2nd, 1706."

Chicago, Ill.

E. S. Waters.

Newcomb.—Griffith Owen of Phila, Physitian also testifies that Richard Newcomb of Salem is the only son of Richard & Mary of Burlington N. J. who came over from Leicestershire about 1704. Salem in N. E., May 9, 1717.

E. S. Waters.

DEPORTATIONS FROM SCOTLAND, 1685

Deportations from Scotland in 1685.—The following is transcribed from a photostat supplied by the Scottish Record Office, H. M. Register House, Edinburgh: Forasmuch as there being ane address made to the Lords of his Majesties privy Councill, by William Arbuckles merchant in Glasgow Desyreing that In regaird he hath a ship now lying in the road of Leith bounding for his Majesties plantations in New England He might be allowed to have some of those prisoners who wer lately taken as being engadged with the late Earl of Argyle upon caution to transport them in maner underwritten The Lords of Councill upon consideration of the forsaid address Doe hereby give and grant the persons underwritten being in number fiftein to the said William Arbuckles supplicant viz: Duncan Mcviccar John Thomsone Murdoch Mcisack Donald Thomson John Clerk & John Clerk Archbald McUrich Daniel Ker Neil Mchatton Donald Mcviccar Angus Mciver Angus McKellor Duncan Mccallum Archbald Mcadam and John Mcmillan all prisoners under the laigh parliament hall. In regaird the said William Arbuckles hath found sufficient caution, acted in the books of privy Councill. to transport the forsaids persones and each of them to his Majesties plantations in new England and report a certificat of there landing under the hand of the governor of the place where they shall land there to his Majesties privy Councill And that under the penalty of One thousand Merks Scots money in caice the said certificat be not reported betwixt and [*sic*] the ninth day of July next to come in the year of God 1686 Or in caice of his not trasporting them as said is (sea hazard, Mortality fforce and pyratts being alwise excepted) (Privy Council Register, *Acta*. Feb.-Dec. 1685. No. 81).

The unsuccessful rising of Archibald, ninth Earl of Argyll, against James II and VII took place in the spring of 1685; the Earl, after being captured, was beheaded on 30 June. The above order, with many others relating to the transportation to North America of those condemned for participation in the rebellion, is printed in "The Register of the Privy Council of Scotland", 3rd series, vol XI.

Lord Neil Campbell (died in 1692), brother of the Earl, came to Perth Amboy in the same year with a number of followers (see William A. Whitehead, "Contributions to the Early History of Perth Amboy", New York, 1856); for other information see "The Lord Neil Campbell Myth", by Meredith B. Colket, Jr. (*The American Genealogist* vol. XIV, 1938, no. 3; *The New York Genealogical and Biographical Record,* vol. XVI (1885), p. 6; also "A Scots Earl in Covenanting Times: The Life of the 9th Earl of Argyll", by J. Willcock, 1907; "The Commons of Argyll" (Oban, 1935); "Inveraray Papers" (Oban, 1939), both by Duncan C. MacTavish, the former of which gives a "List of Rebells in Argyll Shyr and Tarbert Shyr" made up after the rising; and "Kintyre in the Seventeenth Century", by Andrew McKerral, C.I.E. (Edinburgh, 1948) which has a chapter on the episode and appendixes concerning Highland and Lowland families in the district, where Argyll landed in May 1685 to gather recruits.

Several of the surnames in the above order—McCallum (Malcolm), McIsaac, McKellar, McMillan, McVicar, McIver—are Argyllshire names, but without territorial descriptions it is not possible to identify the persons. Mr. McKerral mentions (pp. 129, 170) among persons from Kintyre examined by the Privy Council after the rebellion, and whose fate is not known, Murdoch McIsaac in Machrimore, captured at Dunbarton; Duncan McVicar, aged about sixteen, son of Andrew McVicar in Balnaglek, bailie of Campbeltown; John Clark in Lochkilkerran (*i.e.* Campbeltown), schoolboy; and Donald Thomson in Jarbert, aged fifteen. The first two stated that they had been pressed. Some information about the McIsaacs or McKesaigs, later known as Malcolms, is given in *Publications of the Scottish History Society,* 3rd series, vol. IX (1926).

Among other persons who emigrated was the Reverend David Simson or Simpson, minister of Southend, Kintyre, who went to New Jersey where he died by 1695 (McKerral, pp. 105, 121). Part of the deposition made concerning the rising by his son, David, who succeeded him at Southend, is printed in "Inveraray Papers". Lieutenants Archibald Campbell of Askomill and Hugh Campbell, of the 71st (Fraser's) Highlanders, prisoners of war in Massachusetts in 1776-1777 (The Register, vol. CXIII, Jan. 1959, p. 12), were grandsons of the Reverend David Simson, Jr.

The Scottish merk was worth thirteen shillings and fourpence Scots money, which in the seventeenth century was the equivalent of one shilling one penny and a third sterling (McKerral, pp. 180-181). Arbuckles' bond was thus for £666.13.4 Scots, or £55.11.1⅓ in English money.

New York, N. Y. Colin Campbell.

LIST OF EMIGRANTS TO AMERICA FROM LIVERPOOL 1697–1707 [1]

Transcribed by Miss ELIZABETH FRENCH, and communicated by the Committee on English Research

If I find Jno Lealand bound to Virg or Maryland I must write to his father a Tapeweaver in Salford.

Richard Hilton Apprentice to m^{r} Bryan Blundell for 11 Yeares to Comen[ce] from his first Arrivall in Virginea Or Maryland, Indenture dated 28 of October 1697.

Martin Heyes, Apprentice to Thomas Johnson j^{r} Esqr (or Assignes) for 4 Yeares to Comence from his first arrivall in Virginea Or Maryland Indent[ure] dated ye 27 day of October 1697.

William Mosson Apprentice to Lewis Jenkins for 5 Yeares to Comence from his first Arrivall in Virginea Or Maryland Indenture dated the 29 day of October 1697

Isabell Conley Apprentice to Lewis Jenkins for 7 Years to Comence from hir first Arrivall at Virginea Or Maryland Indenture dated y^{e}: 23 day of Octobr 1697

Margery Blundell to Henry Farar for 4 Years to Virginea [or] Maryland Indenture dated ye 11 : day of Novb^{r} 1697.

Law: GillGrist to Henry Farrar for 7 Years to Virginea [or] Maryland Indenture dated ye 11 day of Novr 1697

Tho: Silvester to Henry Farrar for 7 Years to Virginea Or Maryland Indenture dated ye 11 day of Novr 1697

Isabel Conley to Lewis Jenkins for 7 Years to Virginea Or Maryland Indenture dated ye 23 day of Novr 1697.

J^{no} Leek to m^{r} Lewis Jenkins for 5 Years to Virginea Or Maryland Indenture dated ye first day of December 1697

Wm Ludloe [?] of Bradfrd in Yorkeshire App^{r} to m^{r} Wm Chantrell for 5 years to Virgin^{a} or Maryland

Wm Gibson to Randle Galloway for 4 Years to Virginea or Maryland Indenture dated ye first day of December 1697—

J^{no} Webster to Randle Galloway for 8 Years to Virginea or Maryland

[ ] Green (p^{r} m^{r} Parrs order) to Wm Chantrele for 4 yeares.

[ ] Haddam (p^{r} ditt order [ ] same.

[ ] 97 Paul Leighmans Indnt to Randle Galloway for 9 yea[rs].

J^{no} Moores Indnt to Randle Gallowa[y] 9 yeares

Jan 3 }
[]b 7 } Georg. Worrs of ye County of Lancast App. to Ra[n]dle Galloway for Eight Yeares to Virginea or Maryland [] now

[1] This list, comprising over 1500 names, is to be found in the back of vols. 5 and 7 of the Records of the Corporation of Liverpool, deposited in the Town Clerk's Office, Leasing Department, Liverpool. The entries were originally arranged chronologically, but vol. 5 has been rebound and the pages have been misplaced. The entries are apparently not official, and most of the writing can only be described as scribbling. The writer or writers—the entries seemingly being made by three different scribes—were evidently employed to draw up the indentures. The words "pd." and "delivered" in the margin appear to refer to the indentures, and there is one entry stating that twenty shillings was paid for four indentures.—E. F.

The use of apostrophes at the end of words has been rendered necessary to represent the signs of abbreviation in the original manuscript.

drawn pr Capt Claytns man.

ditto die } Richd Jones of Carnarvon Apprentice to Randle Galloway for Eight Yeares to Virginia or Maryland this Indent. was drawn p Capt Claytn man.

Janu' : 5 97 } Maudlin Dauis of Ruthin of Wales App' to m^{r} Wm Webster to Virgin or Maryland for 5 yeares delivred

Katherine Perry of Ruthin to him for ye same time. deliverd.

Joan Rowland of Bangor in Wales to him for ye same time deliv

Richard Jones of Denbyshire for ye same time delid

Edward Jones of Willison in Cheshire for ye same time deli'd

Thomas Cook of Frodsham for ye same time delid

Willm Smith of Dover for 4 yeares delid

Jan' 8. 97. John White of Cicester in Glocester shire 4 years [delid]

Jno Tonnard for Barbadoes

Not p' 8. 97 Hugh Gryffeth of Denby to Randle Gallowai 4 yeares

Not p' Wm Gryffeth to ye same for ye same time

10 Hugh Partington to Randle Galloway 4 yeares

11 James Walker to ditt 4 yeares

10 J^{no} Thomas of St Asaph to Randl Gall 4 years

20 Hugh Roberts of Anglesay in wales to Jonath Livesey 4 years

20 J^{n} Gryffin of Carnarv 4 years

Ann Jones of Anglesey to ditt 6 yeares.

To J^{no}. Marshall Mast of Y^{e} Ann And Sarah

Henry Ripley of York	4 years.
Daniel Showland of Cork	4 years
J^{no} Wilson [?] of Nycrofte in Lecestershire	4 years
James Eccles of Loughlavin in Ireland	4 years

J^{no} Steward of London 4 years

April 19–98 Thomas Evans of Denbyshire Carpent. App^{r} 4 years for Pensylvania to Richd Adams & Wm Lewis

---

For Barbadoes or some of ye Barbba' Islands

May ye 5–1698

Joseph Stile of Talkell Hill[2] Staffordshi' bond' 4 years 6 m^{o} James Gordon

ditto die Wm English of Fur in Scotland 4 yeares

ditto die Samul Wallington of Presbury 4 yeares

ditto die Roger Sharples of Lealan' 4 yeares

ditto die Richd Hughes of Mould 4 yeares

May 11–'98 Thom' : Prichard of Beaumaris 7 yeares

ditto die Peter Jones of Flintshire 4 yeares

May 16 J^{no} Prior of Pisor in Flintshire 4 yeares

June 7–98 Wm Russel of Kinsale 4 yeares

July 5. 98 Joseph Stile of Staffordshire ap^{r} m' Gordon 4 4 yeares[3]

Wm English of Scotland 5 4 yeares[3]

[2] Talk o' th' Hill.

[3] This entry crossed out.

June 21–98 Jane Horton [or Foster] of Windle Apr. to m' Edw. Tarleton 4 yeares
June 21–98 Richd Cowlund [?] of Thornton Leicastia app^{r} to m^{r} Gordon 7 yeares—16
William Wilson of Langton in s^{d} County to ditto 8 yeares 15
June 27 Jonathan Davis to ditto 4 yeares 4 yeares 19
— 27 Augustine Ca [rr?] 4 yeares 4 yeares 17
— 27 Richd Werton to ditt 4 yeares 4 years 18

July 2^{d} 98 J^{no} Mason son of J^{no} Mason of ye Citty of London Marrin^{r} deceas^{d} App^{r} to m J^{no} Thomas to Virginca or Maryla fr 7 years · Seaven Yeares } 7 yeares
Wm Mason Apr to ye same fr. 7 yeares 7 yeares

July 7 '98 William Holt of Preston o th Hill in Cheshire Apr' to m
p' Edward Tarleton to Virgin or Maryland for 4 yeares } 4
p' Georg Oldham to ditto 4 yeares 4

July 8 to m' James Gordon for Barbadoes Humphry Roberts 7 yeares 11 Carnarvanshire
Wm Gryffith Cardiganshire 4 yeares 12
Peter Prier Denbyshire 7 yeares 13
J^{no} Browne of Lincolnshire Stationer 4 yeares 6
Maurice Roberts of Denbyshire 7 yeares 10
Richd Merton of Denbyshire 7 yeares 9
J^{no} Hughes of Merionithshire Sawyer 4 yeares 8
Peter Matthew Denbyshire 4 yeares 7

July 8. 98. Henry Dauis son of Charles Dauis of Denby Apr to m^{r} Peter Atherton for 4 yeares } 4 yeares
Jno Roberts Son of Edwd Roberts of Queckleys. Flintshire } 4 yeares
J^{no} son of J^{n} Lloyd of Abergelly Denbyshire 9 yeares
July 19. 98 Laurence Dounes of Maxfield[4] to m^{r} Ja: Gordon 4 yeares

---

July 13. 98 Hugh Powell of Dublin; blacksmith to m^{r} Gordon 4 years 14
July 19. 98 Ann Green of Bretherton to m^{r} Tarleton for 4 year
Mary Smith of Grosli Parish Flintshire to ditto 4 yea'

July 22 Richd Evans of Carnarvan to m^{r} Gordn 4 years 1
Elkana Telson 7 years 2
Wm Roberts of Denbyshire 4 years 3
July 27. 98 Thomas Lloyd of Cardiganshire to m' Thomas 4 years
27. 98 Watkin Prier of Cardigan to m' Thomas 4 years
July 27. 98. J^{no} Harrison of Babington to m' J^{no} Thomas to Virginia 8 yeares
Wm Chanceller of Harbro in Yorkshire to ditto 7 yeares
Rowland Jones of Ruthen to ditto 5 yeares
Elin Cook of London Spinster 5 yeares
Margarett Daughter of J^{no} Blake of London to ditt 4 yeares.

Macclesfield.

	Jno Bird of Preston in Oxfordshire [*sic*] 4 yeares	
July 29. 98	Gaynold Thomas of Carnarvon to m' Tarletn 4 yeares	
July 29. 98	Thomas Row of Flintshire Taylor apr to mr Gordon 4 yeares	
Aug 13 1698	Joseph Troughweare of Crosbie in Cumberland Taylor Apr. to m' Henry Brown for Virginia or Maryland for	4 yeares
	Wm Kitchin of Erton in Cumberland Taylor to ditto for 4 yeares	
Augt 17	John Stedman of Padnam[5] Lancast to m' Edwd Tarlton to Virg for 4 yeares.	
Augt 23	Jno Prescott to mr Jno Thomas for	4 yeares
Augt 24	Jno Pritchett of Wrexam to m' Jno Thomas	7 yeares
	Tho: Powell of Wrexam to ditto	7 yeares
	Hugh Jones of Wrexam to ditto	7 yeares
	Hugh Lealand of Westhoughton to ditto	7 yeares
	Ann Blyth of York Citty Spinst. to ditto	4 yeares
2d Sept	Thomas Ellis of Dalirauen in Wales to Do	7 yeares

Augst 27	Joseph Reyburne of Waser in Staffordshire shoomaker Appr. to mr Bryan Blundell for Virginea.	5 yeares
29	Thomas Dunbalin son of Wm Dunbalin to m' Tarleton	6 yeares
29	John Foster of Bethopricke to ditto for	4 yeares
29	John Kirk App to ditto	4 years
29	Jno Jones of Wrexam Hannah his Wife and a Child	4 yeares
30:	Gryffith Thomas Labourer	4 yeares
30:	Eliz: Markley of Latham	5 years.

Augst 31	Jonas Dauis of Corke to mr Jno Thomas	4 year
31	Richd Owen of Flintshire to ditt	4 year
31	Henry Bond son of James Bond near Garstan to ditt	7 year
Sept 2d	Thomas Ellis of Dalmen in Wales to ditt for	4 year
Sept 5	Eliz: King daughter of Abra' King of Dublin to mr Porter	4 year
	Charity Barlor of Kilkenny to ditto for	5 years
Septr 7th	John Thelfell of Preston Gardiner to m': H: Browne	4 years
7.	Jno Dobson of Bolton in Lancashir to ditt	4 year
7:	Ralph Kettle of Warmingham in Cheshire to ditt	4 year
7.	Henry Bell of Carlisle to ditt	4 years
7.	James Boudler of Ossesstry[6] in Shropshir ditt	4 year
Septr 10	John Owen to John Thomas	4 Years
10	Edwd Jones to Do	4 Years
13	Robert Tongue to m' Henry Browne for	4 Years.
14	Eliz: Wilson of Kirkham in ye fild to mr Edwd Tarleton	4 yeares
14	Edwd Steele of Westtirlie to mr Thomas	4 Yeares
14	Jno Ducker of Tarvin Taylo. to m' Thomas	4 yeares

[5] Padiham.
[6] Oswestry.

14 Richd Darrel of Chester to m' Thomas 4 years
14 Eliz Barlow of Knutsfrd to m' Thomas 4 years
14 Hannah Vaughan of Chester to m' Thomas 4 yeares

---

febru' 17 97 William Ertome of ye Citty of London Apprentice to Wm Webster to Virginea or Maryland for 4 year
Jan 28 Jane Evans Denbyshire to m' Webst 5 years delivd
Jan 28 Henry Evans Denbyshire 4 yeares delivd
Jan 28 Mary Gryffith of Merionthshire 4 years delivd
28 Ame Watkins Denbyshire 4 year delivd
28 Robert Matthew Denby 9 years delivd
28 Robert Jones of Denbyshire 4 years delivered

Febr 24th Elizabeth Jones near Ruthen to m' Webt 5 years delivd
Ann Jones of Rixam 7 delivrd
Robt Williams near Ruthen 7 delivrd.
Tho: Davies of Denby 7 delivd
Mary Tue of Houghtonton [*sic*] in Cheshire 5 delivd
Tho: Babington of Aperton[7] in Cheshire 9
Joan Williams of Ruthen 5. delivd
Ellen Hughes of Ruthen 5 delivd
Thomas Owen of Denby 7 delivd
Katherine Hughes of Ruthen 5 delivd

Feb 28 Richd Edward 4 year of Denby deliverd
delivd 2 March 4.97 Wm Bennet of Ashburne Darbyshire delivd

March 10. 97 Thomas Steward of Widdenbury[8] Chester 7 yeares delivd
10. 97 Thomas Whitaker of Eastquein Cheshire 8 yeares delivd
10. 97 Jno Bright Uxbridge Middlesex 4 year delivd
10. 97 Jno Dauis of Wopping Middlesex 4 year delivd
10. 97 Georg Baddon of Clee Shropshire 4 years delivd
10. 97 Edwd Buckley of Bugleton[9] Cheshire 4 year delivd
11. 97 William Dickinson Farn[10] Chesher 4 year delivd
12. 97 Joseph Jinkins of Warton in Chesher 4 year delivd

March 16. 97 Samuel Low of Nutsford Chesher 4 yeares delivd
16. 97 Thomas Farrel of Dublin 4 yeares delivd

March 21. John Baggeley Apr to Wm Webstr his selfe 4 year delivd
21. Joseph Brosier of London [ ] 5 years delivd
21. John Stol of Sunhen 9 year delivd
21. Margery Hunt of Knutsford Cheshir 5 year delivd
March 23 97/8
Henry Prescott of Wigan to m' Wm Webster 4 years delivrd

[7] Appleton.
[8] Wybunbury.
[9] Buglawton.
[10] Farndon, probably.

delvd 3d March 24
Ann Coulburne of Preston 8 years
delvd 4. Peter Fothn' of Tatnal[11] in Cheshir 4 years
March 24 97 fit Hugh Jones of Wrixan to m' Wm Webster 9 years delivd
fit Jno LLoyd of Denbyshire 8 yeares delivd
fit Charles Webster of Denby 8 yeares delivd
fit William Hughes of Denbyshire 8 delivd
fit Edwd Hughes of Flintshire 9 delivd
delivd Edwd Howel of St Asaph Flintshire 9 delivd
fit Jno Morgan of Denbyshire 8 delivd
Edwd Roberts of Denbyshire 6 delivd
fit Gabriel Roberts of Flintshire 4 delivd
fit Thomas Hughes of Ruthen 5 delivd
fit Robt Hughes of Denbyshire 4 delivd
fit Thomas Roberts of Denbyshire 5 delivd
fit Thomas Perrey of Denby 4 delivd
Owen Hughes of Ruthen in Wales 8 delivred

April 1 fit 98 Eliz. Roberts of Denbyshire m' Wm Webstr 7
fit Margtte Wms of Anglesey 5
fit Dorathy Edwards Denbyshire 7
fit James Yates near Blackburn 4

April 13 Charles Shehy [?] of Dublin 4 yeares delivd all
Thomas Moor of Dublin 4 yeares delid all
Jno Edmunds of Merionthshire 4 yeares deld all

April 13. 98 Robert Warner of Glocestershire 4 yeares delivd
Thomas Morris of Shropshire 4 years delivd
Richd Worden of Essex 4 yeares delivd

Jan 21 Robt Hughes of St Asaph to mr Webster delivd
Jan 21 Wm Ellis of Clantastelh in Wales 7 years delivd
Jan 21 John Alvin of Shaftsbery in Dorsetshire delivd
Jan 21 John Hughes 7 years delivd
Jan 21 William Dauis of Caires in Wales 7 years delivd
Feb 18 Thomas Humphrey 9 year Mr Webster delivd
Feb 18 Edwd Jones Merionithshire 4 year
Feb 18 Eliz Gryffeth five yeares delivred
Jan 28 97 Richd Jones of Carnarvan to Wm Webster for 4 yeares delivd
28 97 Ann Watkins 4 years
Feb 28 Jno Thomas 9 year Denby
Jn 28 Finlh Morris 9 year Denby delivd
feb 28 Wm Hughes 9 year Denby delivd
Feb 28 Tho Roberts 9 year Denby delivd
Feb 28 Jno owens Carnarvanshire 6 year delivd
Feb 28 Owen Jones of Anglesey 4 year delivd
28 Christian Ireland of Chester 4 years delivd
28 John Jones of Anglesey 4 years delid
28 Henry Perry Montgomerishire 4 year delivd

[11] Tattenhall.

Feb 3. 97 Jacob Boulton of Ashton Canes[12] in Wilshire Seu' to m' Jonatha' Lievsley for three yeares
William Darter Apprentice to ye same for 3 yeares & borne in ye same Parish
William Prior of Flintshir Apprentice to ye same for 4 year yeares.

Feb. 16. Henry Brobbin of Warrington 5 yeares to Wm Webster deliv^d
Feb. 16. J^no Brobbin ye same tearme deliv^d
Feb 16 Eliz. Brobbin ye same tearme delivrd
Feb 16 Mary Cloud of ye same same tearme deliv^d
Jan. 28 Mary Norman of of Egermun'[13] same tearme deliv^d
Jan. 28 Isabel Troughton of Caton same tearme deliv^d
Feb 16 Mary steel Harperthe in Cheshire same time deliv^d
Jan. 28 Wm Moor of Antrim in Ireland 4 years deliv^d
Feb. 16 Katherine Williams 4 year of Carnarvanshire deliv^d
Jan 28 Mary Williams Flintshire Five yeares delivred

Feb : 18 Robert Clark 4 yeares to m^r Wm Webs^t deliv^d

July 30 98 Mary Jones daughter of J^no Jones of Wrixam in Denbyshire Appr to m' J^no Thomas for 4 yeares
August 4. 98 Robt Jones of Denbyshire 4 year
Edwd Jones of Wrixam 7 year
Thomas Duckes of Tarvin in Cheshire 7 year
Mary Cowly hir marke 4 year
9 Robt Faux of Denbyshire 4 year

Aug^st 10. 98 Henry Jones of Flintshire to m^r J^no Thomas for –years
Alice Harlow of Widmore[14] in Herefordshire 4 yeares
Richd Edwards of Cardiganshire 9 years
J^no Williams of Cardiganshire 7 years
J^no Staton of Congleton Cheshire 0 years
J^no Harris of Cardiganshire 7 years.

Aug^st 16 : 98 Eliz. Jones of Denbyshire to m^r J^no Thomas for 5 yeares
17 Rowland Thomas of Anglesey Taylor 5 years
Robt Hughes of Conaway Taylor 4 years
Richd Woods of Adlington Lancashire 7 years
Wm Lawson of Lievsay Lanc. 7 years

Mr. Lewis Jinkin' Servants

Richd Alcock of Bolton Taylor App^r 5 yeares
J^no Houseman of Bolton Taylor Apr 5 yeares
Rob : Chalis Castleton in Derbyshire 4 yea
Jo : Bramwale of Preston 4 years
Wm Rycroft of Preston 4 years

[12] Ashton Keynes.
[13] Egremont.
[14] Wigmore.

7br 17	Edward Hardman Apprentice to John Neild of Pensilvanie to go to Pensilvane for five Yeares		5 Yeares
7br 20	Richd Newell to Do for Pensilvane		5 Yeares

7br 19	Tho: Marland to mr Browne	Virginea	7 Yeares
7br 19	John Carneagee of Aberdeene in Scotland to mr Browe	Virginea	4 Yeares
7br 20	John Harrison of Ashton under Line to mr Browne	Virginea	7 Yeares
7b 15. 98	Charles Ellis of Macclesfield to mr Brown	Virginea	5 Yeares
	Edwd Thorncroft of Sutton in Cheshir to mr Brown	virginea	5 yeares
7b 16	John Davies of Denbygshire Grocer to Do	Virginea	4 Yeares
7. 16	Humphrey Howell of Merionethshire to Do	Virginea	4 Yeares
7br 17	John Wynn of Denbyshire to Henry Browne		5 Yeares
7br 20	John Walker of Ashton under Line to mr Browne		5 Yeares
7br 20	John Beecham of Chester to Do		4 Yeares
7b 20	Thomas Walker of Ashton under Line		7 Yeares
7b 15	Robt Rallestr of Leeds to Richd Bridg for mr Thomas	Virginea	4 yeares
7br 15	James Jameson of New Castle to mr Edwd Tarleton	Virginea	4 Yeares
7br 17	Robert Pollet son of Robert Pollett late of Bolton to mr Tarleton	Virginea	9 Yeares
20	John Nichols to mr Edward Tarleton		4 Yeares
7br 20	Samuell Hemming to DO.		4 Yeares
7br 20	John Price of Merionethshire Chirurgeon to mr Thomas		4 Yeares
7br: 22	Thomas Wilding of Litchfield to William Bushell to Virginia		5 Yeares
7b 27	Richd Owen of Carnarvanshire to mr Thomas		4 Years
7br 27	John Lamb of Levpoole to Ezekiell Parr		4 Yeares
7b' 27	John Ricketts of Lavanshie in Wales to Do		4 Yeares
do die	Jonathan Clarke of Little Mesle in Lan' to m' H. Browne		7 Yeares
27 7b'	Mary Terpin of Lithan in fild to mr Wm Porter		5 Yeares
28 7br	Mary Floyd of Shroesbery in Shropshire to mr Ezekiell Parr		5 Yeares
28 7br	Jane Hide of Manchest' Spinst' to m' Nicholes Smith		5 Yeares
7b. 30. 98	Matthew Moretown of Presberry in Cheshir to mr Henry Brown for 4 years		4 years

---

8b. 5. Robt Voughan son of Thomas Voughan neer Salp. to mr And. Leed 5 years

---

To mr Nicholas Smith to Virginea Or Maryland

Wm Hudson 5 Yeares October ye: 13th: 1698
Miles Grimshaw 5 Yeares ditto die.
Mary Boardman 5 Yeares ditto die

8b 17. 98 Tho: Higham of Warrington Toban [?] to m' Scarburrough 4 year.

The Names of ye: Servants that Goes to Virginea in ye Loyalty Capt Henry Browne Commander Octobr 19th 1698

Ralph Kettle of Warmingham in Cheshire	4 Yeares
Robt: Tongue of Farnoth[15] neare Manchester	4 Yeares
John Threlfell of Preston Gardiner	4 Yeares
Charles Ellis[16] of Macclesfield	5 Yeares
Alexdr Sinkler of Glascow	4 Yeares
John Wright of Middlesex	4 Yeares
Wm Tayler of Scarbrick	8 Yeares
James Streete	Tenn Yeares
Thomas Walker of Ashton vnder Line	7 Yeares
David Tayler of Mottrom in Cheshir	8 Yeares
John Beecham of Cheshir	4 Yeares
John Walker of Ashton vnder Line	5 Yeares
Georg Low of Gawsworth Cheshir	Tenn Yeares
George Brasfelld	Eleaven Yeares
John Carneagee of Aberdeene in Scotland	4 Yeares
Charles Tayler of Mottrom in Cheshire	7 Yeares
John Harrison of Ashton vnder Line	7 Yeares
Robert Bower[17] of Macclesfeild in Cheshire	7 Yeares
James Bouldler of Augettree[18] in Shropshire	4 Yeares
John Dobson of Bolton Lanc'	4 Yeares
Edwd ThorniCroft of Sutton in Cheshire	5 Yeares
Tho: Marland of Ashton vnder Line	7 Yeares
Humphrey Howell of Merionethshire	4 Yeares
John Davies of Denbigshire Grocer	4 Yeares
Edwd Perry of Denbigshire	4 Yeares
Tho: Vpton of Presberry in Cheshire	Tenn Yeares
John Wynn of Ruthin in Denbigshire	5 Yeares
Jonathan Clark of Little Messin Lanc	7 Yeares
Nathaniel Tayler of Mottrom in Cheshre	9 Yeares
Tho: Tayler of Mottrom in Cheshre	Eleaven Yeares
Mathew Moreton of Presberry Cheshire	4 Yeares
Joseph Troughweare of Crosby in Cumberland Tayler	4 Yeares
Wm Kitchen of Erton[19] in Cumberland Tayler	4 Yeares
Joyce Cooper of Carnarvanshire 4 yeares	4 Yeares
Henry Bell of Carlisle 4	4 Yeares
Tho: Wilding of Litchfield App. (to Wm. Bushell Meate of ye Loyalty) to serve in Virginea for ye Tearme of	5 Yeares
Ja: Barton Apprentice to Janes [*sic*] Hawkshaw to Monserratt	4 Yeares

15 Farnworth.
16 A Charles Ellis, son of William Ellis of Macclesfield, was baptized there Aug. 2, 1678.
17 A Robert Bower, son of Francis Bower of Poynton, was baptized at Prestbury (the mother church of over thirty surrounding townships and chapelries, including Poynton and Macclesfield) 18 Aug. 1678.
18 Clearly as printed. May stand for Oswestry.
19 There is a Hutton in Cumberland, for which this may stand.

LIST OF EMIGRANTS TO AMERICA FROM LIVERPOOL 1697–1707

Transcribed by Miss Elizabeth French, and communicated by the Committee on English Research

The Names of all the Servants that Goes to Virginea in the Ship Concord J^{no} Walls Commander October ye 25th 1698 Bound to Ezekiel Parr.

h Jane Johnson of Wigan Spinster 4 Yeares
h Isaac Carpenter 4 Yeares
h John Prescot[20] of Wigan Tayler 4 Yeares
h Roger Tayler of Abram in ye County of Lanc husband 4 Yeares
h Oliver Whalley als Wood 7 Yeares
h Alice Catterall of Wigan 4 Yeares
h Elizabeth Ashton of Wigan Spinster 4 Yeares
h Sarah Heyes 4 Yeares

[20] John, s. of Thomas Presscot of Daltone, b. 16 Nov., bapt. 22 Nov., 1633 at Upholland, parish of Wigan.

h	William Scott of Wigan 7 Yeares	
h	Francis Cattarall of Wigan 4 Yeares	
h	John Gasway 4 Yeares	
h	William Fox 4 Yeares	
h	James Exx 4 Yeares	
h	James Butterworth[21] Weaver	4 Yeares
h	John Leyland of Abram Weaver	4 Yeares
h	Mary Moss	4 Yeares
h	Joshua Spencer of vpHolland[22]	7 Yeares
h	Mary Gibbs of Wigan	4 Yeares
h	Jno Wood	4 Yeares
h	Alice Heaton	4 Yeares
h	Richd Heaton	4 Yeares
h	Edward Heaton	4 Yeares
h	Margaret Kearfoote of Wigan Spinster	4 Yeares
h	Eliz: Heaton	4 Yeares
	all bound at Wigan ye Countnsts [*sic*] writt here	
h	Charles Wilkinson of Burnley in Lancashire	7 Yeares
h	Eliz: Rollins of Raiby[23] in Cheshire	4 Yeares
h	Edward Wilson[24] of Tarleton in Lanc	5 Yeares
h	Joseph Stanthrop of Yorkshire Tanner	4 Yeares
h	Ann Eccles of Preston	4 Yeares
h	Charles Coup[25] of Bolton Tayler	4 Yeares
h	James Gambell of Nantwich	4 Yeares
h	Thomas Clayton of Preston	7 Yeares
h	Martha Lloyd of Shroesberry in Shropshire	5 Yeares
h	James Boardman[26] of Bolton Butcher	4 Yeares
h	Thomas Turner of Warrington	4 Yeares
h	Hester Ford of Wigan Spinstr	4 Yeares
h	Daniel Lyon of Rainford Blacksmith	4 Yeares
h	Thursden Mather of Hinly in Lancashire	4 Yeares
h	James Dangerfeild of Rapahannock River in Virginea	4 Yeares
h	Ellen Peatiason of Fild Lanc'	4 Yeares
h	John Lamb of Leverpoole	4 Yeares
h	John Ricketts Joyner	4 Yeares
h	Eliz: Crompton[27] of Berry in Lanc'	5 Yeares
h	William Thomas of Carnarvanshire	4 Yeares
h	John Johnson of Ipston in Staffordshr Shoomaker	4 Yeares
h	Edward Houghton of Macclesfield	4 Yeares

---

servants to Mr Jn Marsden Merc' who went wth ye Submission

2 9b 98 Paul Riglie of Hey in Lancashire 7 Yeares

[21] James, s. of Adam Butterworth, bapt. 22 Aug. 1680 at Upholland. Adam Butterworth bur. 25 June 1690 at Upholland.

[22] In the parish of Wigan.

[23] Ribby (?)

[24] Edward, s. of John Wilson of Bretherton, bapt. 10 Apr. 1675 at Croston, of which parish Tarleton was a part.

[25] Charles Coope, s. of Laurence and Elizabeth of Bolton, bapt. 25 Dec. 1674 at Bolton.

[26] James Boardman, s. of Andrew and Deborah of Little Bolton, bapt. 14 May 1676 at Bolton.

[27] Elizabeth, dau. of William Crompton, b. 15 Apr., bapt. 23 Apr. 1680 at Bury. William, s. of William Crompton, b. 3 Mar., bapt. 12 Mar. 1656-7.

2 9^{b}	Jeremiah Jones[28] of Berry	7 Years
7	David Bevis of Burstan in Staffordshire	7 Years
7	J^{n} Newton of Bolton	7 Years
7	Wm Fartley of Orrel near Wigan Husband'	4 Years
7	J^{n} Winstantly[29] of ye sam husband'	4 Years
7 9^{b}	Isaac Firth of Bradford in Yorkshire	5 Years
7	Joseph Parr of Little Hilton[30] Lancashire	5 Years

Decem 8 1698 Nath: Fogg bound to Mr Abram Dyson for 4 Years

---

An Acc^{t} of ye Servants to Virgin' that went ꝑ ye Ann & Sarah m' J^{no} Marshall M^{r} for Virginea & bound to himself[31]

Novemb. 4. 98 J^{no} Bruin of Chester Shumaker 4 years

Novemb^{r} 11. 1698.

	Tho: Hawkshaw son of George Hawkshaw of Dennam,[32] Cheshire	5 years
	Herbert Son of Tho: Patterson late of Chester Chapman	7 yeares
	Walter Cramp Son of Wm Cramp of Willington in Shropshire	7 yeares
	J^{no} Son of J^{n} W^{ms} of Widdenbury[33] in Cheshire	5 yeares
	Thomas son of Thom^{s} Jennison late of Lunt in Lancashire	7 yeares
	J^{no} son of J^{no} Shaw of Congleton in Cheshire	7 years

An Acc^{t} of Servants that went to Virginea in ye Ship Lamb of Dublin. m' Wm Burnsides Mast^{r}

9b. 15. 1698	Judith Butterworth of Middleton in Lancas'	5 yeares
	Sarah Celliam of Manchester	5 yeares
	Ann Sickley of Chadle in Cheshire	5 yeares
	Martha Peak of Broden in Lancash'	7 yeares
	Ann King of Cletherou	5 yeares
	Matthew Newall of Mincheld[34] in Cheshire	7 yeares
	Wm Sheapheard of Manchest	7 yeares
	Jonath' Preestley of Sneland in the County of York	7 yeares
	Wm Guy of Duckenfield in Cheshire	5 yeares
	Jno Penberry of Manches^{r}	7 yeares
	Rob Leafield of Lancast'	5 yeares
9b ^{r} 17	Abigail Burnett of Manches^{r}	5 yeares

An Acc^{t} of Servants That went to Virginnia in the Shipp Society of Leverpoole Mr Jonath Lievsley Master

Octob^{r} 23^{d}. 98	And: Martin of Huttale in Lanc	9 Yeares
	John Ramsbotten in County Lanc.	5 Yeares

28 Jeremiah Jones, s. of Richard Jones of the Lees, b. 4 June, bapt. 13 June, 1675 at Bury.

29 John, s. of Henry Winstanley of Billing, bapt. 11 Apr. 1680 at Upholland, parish of Wigan.

30 Little Hulton.

31 This heading and the seven entries under it are crossed out in the original. *Vide infra*, where the list is repeated in somewhat changed form.

32 Dunham.

33 Wybunbury.

34 Minshull.

Novem^r ye 1st	John Brown of Cledle[35] Parish Nea Stockport	5 Yeares
2^d	Isaac Taylor of Newton in the County of Lanca'	5 Yeares
	Eliz^a: Williams of Clutton in ye County of Chester	8 Yeares
	Geo: Wisson of Inglewhite in ye County of Lancaster	5 Yeares
4th	Mary Clowd of Brewerton[36] in County of Chester	6 Yeares
	Jane Banks of Chorley in Lancasher	6 Yeares
11th	John Tayler of Coulden in County of Lancashire	5 Yeares
	Robt Noblett of Aston Bank in Lancashire	6 Yeares
30th	Ayley Blackwell of Brewerton in Cheshire	6 Yeares
Decr 13th	Jno Briggs of Waddington in Yorkshire	5 Yeares

Acc^t of Serv^{ts}: y^t Went to Virginnia in ye Globe Mr Simpson Master

Decr ye 2^d	John Strachine of Scotland	4 Years
3	Alexander Marsh of Aughton Lancashire	8 Yeares
Pd for {	Homer Rodan of Scotland to Mr Neilson	4 Yeares
	James Douglass of Scotland D^o	4 Yeares
5	Peter Holland of Middle Witch	6 Yeares
15	James Corry of Scotland	4 Years

1698 An Acc^t of Servants Thatt went to Virginnia in the good Shipp Called the St John Baptest: Mr Nicholas Franch.

October 24th	John Thompson of Cumberland	7 Yeares
	John Rudd of Liverpoole Webster	4 Yeares
	Peter Winstanley[37] of Oriell	4 Yeares
	Abram̄ Rudd of Rachdale Clothier	4 Yeares
	John Gilburt of Holtbridge in Essex	4 Yeares
	John Morgan of Apsom[38]	4 Yeares
	John Fisher of Holmes Chappell	4 Yeares
	Samuell Williams of Wrixham	10 Yeares
	William Collins of Bristoll	4 Yeares
	Thomas Williams of Wrixham	10 Yeares
	Robert Lewis of Denbyshire	4 Yeares
	John Redding of Canterbury	4 Yeares
	Daniell Child of Whitechappele	4 Yeares
	Richard Lewis of Branford	4 Yeares
	Robert Finch of Wrixham	10 Yeares
	Elizabeth Holding of Lanc Spinster	4 Yeares
26th	Caelia Woods of Berry in Lanc	6 Yeares
	Elizabeth Hunt of Wrixham	4 Yeares
	Ruth Davies of Wrixham Spinster	4 Yeares
	Henry Woods of Derry	4 Yeares
28	Alexander Challinor of Macclesfield	4 Yeares
	Ann Evans of Wrixham	4 Yeares
Novem̄ ye 18	Edward Clark of Uttertter[39] in Stafford	4 Yeares
	Edward Williams of Rixam	4 Yeares
	John Taylor of Wellington in Shropshire	4 Yeares

[35] Cheadle(?)
[36] Brereton(?)
[37] Peter Winstonle, s. of John of Orrel, bapt. 26 Dec. 1669 at Upholland. John, s. of Thomas Winstanley of Billing, bapt. 13 Sept. 1646 at Upholland.
[38] Epsom, Surrey(?)
[39] Uttoxeter(?)

28	John Cheetum of Oldham in the County of Lancaster	4 Yeares
	Jam̄ Pye of Lyddgate in the County of Lancaster	4 Yeares
29th	Marg[t] Renndle of Pilling, Indent[d] to John Fox, Mate of the s[d] shipp,	7 Yeares
Dec[r] 5	Newman Steward of the County of Norfolk	4 Yeares
31	William Hodgkins to m' Conly of Blackly in Worcetsh'	4 Yeares

---

An Acc[t] of Serv[ts] That Went to Virginnia in the Ann and Sarah M[r] John Marshall Master
Novem : 4th : 98

	John Bruin of Chester	4 Yeares
7	Mich[l] Godwin of Winchester	4 Yeares
11	Jn[o] Shaw of Congleton in Chesshire	7 Yeares
	Tho : Jennyon of Lunt in Lancashire	7 Yeares
	Jn[o] Williams of Chesshire	5 Yeares
	Walter Crampton [40] of Willington in Shropshire	7 Yeares
	Herbert Patterson of Chester Chapman	7 Yeares
	Thos : Hawkshaw of Dannam [41] in Cheshire	5 Yeares
16th	Jn[o] Hoague of Cload in Cheshire	9 Years
19th	Wharton Fallowfield of Pennyroth[42] in Cumberland	4 Years
24	William Wood of Tarvin in Cheshire	5 Yeares
26	Jn[o] Lloyd of Weppen in Flintshire	8 Years
Dec[r] 2	Jn[o] Lyon of Huntspear in Somersetshire	4 Yeares
5	Jn[o] Baker of Astberry in Cheshire	5 Yeares
7	Jn[o] Shaw of Millhouse in Lancashire	4 Yeares
9	W[m] Heaton of Heaton in Lancashire	4 Yeares
10	Job : Howard of Sawford by Manchester	5 Yeares
	Ann Dumbile of Middle Witch in Cheshire	4 Yeares
	Sarah Pinkston of D[o]	4 Yeares
16	Jn[o] Rothell of Toddington[43] in Lancas' :	5 Yeares
16th	Sam[ll] Mccreky of Carlisle in Cumberland	5 Yeares
	Elis[a] : Valentine of Leverpoole	6 Yeares
20th	Dan :[ll] Walker of Stand of Polkington in Lancashire	4 Yeares
22d	Joseph : Brosents of Burnby in Lancashire	4 Yeares
	Adam Mottershed[44] of Macclesfield in Cheshire	4 Yeares
23	John Milener of Holebrook in Yorkshire	5 Yeares

An Acc[t] : of Servants That went to Virginnia in the Ship Called the Eleanor of Liverpoole Nicholas Reynolds Master
Septem[r] : 5 : 1698

	Charles Barber of Kilkenny	5 Yeares

[40] The ton of Crampton has been added and crowded in. *Vide ante* for the original form of the list.
[41] Dunham.
[42] Penrith.
[43] Tottington.
[44] Adam, s. of Roger Mottersheade of Mottram, bapt. 7 Aug. 1677 at Prestbury, of which parish Macclesfield was also a part.

	Elizabeth King of Dublin	4 Yeares
	Martha Jackson bound but remaned	4 Yeares
24th	John Pennant of flintshire	7 Yeares
27	Mary Terpin of Lathom in field	5 Yeares
October 18	John Posthous of Harding in Wales	5 Yeares
19	Ralph Haliwale of Bolton falsified his name it was Thoms	4 Yeares
22	Diana Johnson[45] of Presberry in Chesshire	4 Yeares
	Marg^{t} Bantum of Coppl in Lancashire	4 Yeares
	Mary Smallwood of Bartumlee in Cheshire	4 Yeares
Novem^{r} 2^{d}	Peter Shellom of Presberry in Cheshire	7 Yeares
	Thomas Upton of Presberry d^{o}	4 Yeares
Gone [*crossed out*]		
	Martha Jackson[46] of Presberry d^{o}	5 Yeares
	John Upton[47] of D^{o}	5 Yeares
	Elizabeth Upton of D^{o}	4 Yeares
4th	Susanna Pound of Devon Widdowe	4 Yeares
7th	John Haggarty Ireland	4 Yeares
19th	William Beck of Underbarraugh in Westmoreland	4 Yeares
	Robt Lawson of Burnick in Lanceshire	4 Yeares
	Richd Holmes of Preston in Lanca :	4 Yeares
	Peter Jones of Anglesey	4 Yeares
	Hugh Owen of Anglesay	4 Yeares
	William Owen of Anglesay	4 Yeares
22^{d}	James Morden of Bristoll	7 Yeares
28	Elizabeth Wilson of Carleton in County of Lancas :	4 Yeares
29	John Hartopp of Coventry	4 Yeares
30	John Porter of Wimsley[48] Parish in Chesshire	4 Yeares
Novem^{r}: 17th :	James Barbur bound to John Tyrer	7 Yeares
Dec^{t} 2^{d}	Katherine Ritchley of Ayre in Scotland	
3 :	Wm Blundell of Cheedley Holme[49] in Cheshire	5 Yeares
9th	Rp^{h}. Relshaw of Lendy in Yorkshire	7 Yeares

An Acc^{t} of Servants that went to Virginea in the Ship Barbadoes Merc^{t} and were bound to m^{r} Cuthbert Sharples

23–9b 98	Josiah Mayeres of Macklesfield in Cheshire	4 Yeares
23	Jane Swindle of Maxfield Mem^{d} She was bound to Aldem^{n} Houghton	5 Yeares
25	Thomas Yates of Whiston	5 yeares
25	Aaron Summers of Kellen in Lancash^{r}	5 yeares
25	Wm Davies of Mosteyn in Flintshire	5 yeares
1 xb	J^{no} France of Huddersfield in Yorkshire	4 yeares
1 :	Elizabeth Dickin of Denby in Wales	4 yeares
1 :	Mary Holme[50] of Bolton	4 yeares
2. 9b.	Joyce Cooper of Carnarvanshire	4 yeares

[45] Dyana, dau. of John Johnson of Falibroome, bapt. 4 Feb. 1678-9 at Prestbury.
[46] Martha, dau. of Peter Jackson, bapt. 1 Feb. 1681 at Prestbury.
[47] John, s. of James Upton of Newton, bapt. 28 Jan. 1679-80 at Prestbury.
[48] Wimbersley.
[49] Cheadle Hulme.
[50] Mary Holme, dau. of Timothy of Little Bolton, bapt. 25 Apr. 1680, Marah Holme, dau. of Jas. and Margaret of Bolton, b. 29 Nov., bapt. 2 Dec., 1677 at Bolton.

1. xb	Mary Case[51] of Bolton	4 yeares
1	Sarah Gibbons of Maclesfield	4 yeares
2	Benjamin Roy^{l} [52] of Macklesfield	7 yeares
28.8b	Samuel Dagnell of St Hellen in Lancash^{r}	5 yeares
xb. 5	Wm Cragge of Dent in Yorkshire	5 yeares
12	Robt Ward of Bolton in Lancashire	6 Yeares

An Acc^{t} of Serv:^{ts} That Went to Virginnia in the Shipp Called the Submission of Leverpoole Thomas Seacome Master

Octob^{r}: 7 : 1698	William Relict of Gatlemellit in Flintshire	Bound	4 Yeares
	John Young of Wandsor in Surrey	To Mr John	4 Yeares
	William Bradshaw of Long Green in Chesshire	Hughes	4 Yeares
12th	John Adams of Shotten in Flintshire		4 Yeares
14th	John Thompson of Coalrain in Ireland	Bound to	4 Yeares
	Henry Woods of Chester	Mr Jno Hughes	4 Yeares
24th	Mary Standish of Stafford, Spinster		4 Yeares
	Mary Faulkner of Manchester, Spinster		4 Yeares
	Martha Newton of Macclesfield		4 Yeares
25th	Joan Witter of Tapperly in Chesshire		4 Yeares
28th	Philip Finn of Harding Parish in Wales		4 Yeares
	John Finn of D^{o}		6 Yeares
Novem^{r}: 2^{d}	Robert Middleton of Oacks Parish in Derby Shire		4 Yeares
	Ellin Barlow of Macclesfeild in Cheshire		4 Yeares
	Tho: Williams of Carnarvan in Wales		5 Yeares
	Fran: Glanford of Buckinhamshire		4 Yeares
	And: Hamilton of Edenborough		4 Yeares
16th	Richd Fin near harding in Flintshire		4 Yeares
23	William Pelkington[53] of Brindle		5 Yeares

Acc^{t} of Servants that Went to the West Indies in the Ann and Mary, John Dann Master, and bound to him, 169$^{8}/_{9}$

March the 28: 169$^{8}/_{9}$	Thomas Roper of Wrightingham in Lancashire Aged (19) Yeares bound for	4 Yeares
Aprill the 4th:	Henry Halewood of Ormskirk in Lancashire Aged (25) Yeares bound for	4 Yeares

---

Mem^{d} if Peter Atherton of Cuerdly aged about Ten Yeares Comes to Offer himself he is apprentice to Tho: Richardson of the same place. A Gray Wastecoat, & Gray Stockings a Jockey Capp: Flaxen hair'd

---

51 Mary Care, dau. of Samuel and Martha of Bolton, b. 29 Nov., bapt. 2 Dec., 1677 at Bolton.

52 Benjamin Royle, s. of Henry Royle, bapt. 30 Sept. 1673 at Macclesfield.

53 William Pilkington, s. of John, bapt. 17 Feb. 1680–1 at Brindle. John Pilkington and Agnes Waring m. 24 July 1676 at Brindle. John Pilkington churchwarden of Brindle in 1679.

Acc^{t} of Servants bound to Mr Wm Middleton Master of the Irish Lawrell of Leverpoole bound for Newfoundland as Viz^{t}:

		[Age]	[Term]
Feb: 21 $\frac{1699}{1700}$			
	Henry Powell of Wells in Sommersetshire	21 –	4
	James Tucker of Wells	20 –	4
	Thomas Jones of Carnervan	20 –	4
Runn	Thomas Jackson of Blakeley in Lanc'	19 –	4
Feb: 27	Wm Williams of Narbot in Pembrookshire	21 –	4

Acc^{t} of Servants bound to Capt Edwd Tarleton and Went to Newfoundland in the (Yorkshire) Lawrell of Leverpoole as Viz^{t}:

Feb^{ry}: 27 : $^{1}\frac{699}{700}$			
	Evan Owen of Ossesstry[54] in Shropshire	20 –	4
	Thomas Williams of Carnarvan in Wales	12 –	9
28th	Hugh Reddish of Kearsly Near Bolton in Lanc'	19 –	4
	John Stock of Rachdale in Lanc'	23 –	4
	John Barnes of Hazledine[55] in Lanc'	15 –	7
	John Wood of D^{o}	13 –	8
	John Bretherton of Nantwich in Cheshire	20 –	4

Acc^{t} of Serv^{ts} that Went to New England in the Virginnia Merch^{t} Edmund Ball Master 1699

Imp^{rs}: Mar: 3^{d} 99		years of Age	Years to serve
	Jane Radcliff of Rachdale in Lancashire Spinster	20	7
	Mary Gleddale of Hepworth in Yorkshire	20	7
	Danill Clows of Osterfield in Staffordshire	23	6
	John Holgrave of Hazledine[56] in Lancashire	28	7
	James Nuttes of Blakebourne d^{o}	18	7
	Paul Widdop of Hallifax in Yorkshire	26	7
	John Walker of Tithrton[57] in Cheshire	19	7
	Christophr Patrick of Great Musgrove in Westmoreland	20	7
	Mathew Mooreton[58] of Presbury in Cheshire	20	7
	John Jones of Clanderry Denbyshire Wales	17	7
	James Thompson of the Kingdom of Scotland	19	7
	Josiah Maires of Macclesfield in Cheshire	19	7
	Mary Dawson of Leades in Yorkshire	22	7
	Margaret Jones of Ritchin in Denbyshire	32	7
	James Chaddock of Rotchdale in Lancashire	22	7
	Jane Swindle of Macclesfield in Cheshire	23	7
	Edward Cook of Hope Parish in Derbyshire	19	7
	Richard Thomas of Dublin in Ireland	18	7
	Nicholas Hurd of Possenby[59] in Cumberland	19	7

[54] Oswestry.
[55] Haslingden.
[56] Haslingden.
[57] Titherington.
[58] Matthew, s. of Matthew Moreton, bapt. 22 Nov. 1676 at Prestbury.
[59] Ponsonby.

	Thomas Stringer of Buckton in Yorkshire	22	7
	John Beaver of Hepworthe in Yorkshire	22	7
	Jonath: Hartly of Martown in Yorkshire	18	7
	Edward Glover of Manchester in Lancashire	20	7
	Hugh Hughles [*sic*] of Anglesey in Wales	19	7
	Peter Bole of Paynton in Cheshire	20	7
	Margarett Todd of Ingleton in Yorkshire	19	7
	Mary Tayler of Ratchdale in Lancashire	22	7
	James Clarke of Newtown heath in Cheshire	17	7
	Edward Faux of Flint in Wales	19	7
	Math: Williams of Blew Morrice in Wales	26	7
	Humph Salsbury[59a] of Glandiray in Denbyshire	19	7
	Marg^{t} Bishop of Loughbourough in Lecestershire	25	7
	Peirce Tickle[60a] of Limb in Cheshire	17	10
	John Smith of Craven in Yorkshire	17	7
Turnd off	John Williams of Woolwich in Kent	29	7
4th	John Roadly of the City of Norwich	17	7
6	Dan^{ll} Clew of Manchester in Lancashire	21	7
	John Rothett of Blackbourn in Lancashire	19	7
	Maudlin Lewis of Carmarthen Town in Wales	15	7
Turnd off	John Mills of Oldham in Lancashire	12	10
Run	{ Joseph Bell of New Castle upon Tine	23	7
Run	{ Lawrence Scotland of Scotland	21	7
	Ann Singleton of Firwood[60] in Lancashire bound to Mr John Moody	23	7

An Acc^{t}: of Servants that went to Pensilvania, Virginnea or Marly in the good Ship the Experiment of Leverpoole Cavaleiro Christian Master; all bound to Mr John Hughes of the s^{d} Ship Aug^{s}: 16. 1699

June 20th: 1699		Yeares of Age	Yeares to serve
	Mary Lee of Peake in Derbyshire Spinster	19	6
	Richard Worrall of Bridget Parish in the City of Chester Tayler	21	5
July 4th	Stephen Fletcher of the City of London Taylor	21	6
	William Windsor of Potters Marson in Leicestershire Blacksmith	18	6
July 11	James Johnson of Sawford in Lancashire Weaver	23	5
	Ellin Acres of Sephton in Lancashire Spinster	22	6
	Ellin Rushton of Whaley Parish in Lancashire	18	6
July 20th	George Griffith of Colin[61] in Flintshire	23	6
22^{d}	Marg^{t} Plaise of Stairbourne in Yorkshire	20	6
	John Rhodes of Hallifax Parish in Yorkshire Weaver	21	5

[59a] Humphry Salsbury and Mary Milborn m. at Boston, Mass., 11 July 1707.
[60a] Peirce Tickle and Jane Ratleife m. at Boston, Mass., 26 May 1707.
[60] Firgrove (?)
[61] Colwyn (?)

Aug^s: 4th	Marg^t Ellis of Merryonithshire in Wales	28	5
	Wm Ellis of the same	26	5
	Elizabeth Wharton of Frodsham Parish in Cheshire	22	6
	Jane Lackey of Carrickfargus in Ireland	18	5
Aug^s: 9th	John Jones of Northey in Flintshire	28	5
15th	John Richard of Clanarman Parish in Denbyshire	16	7

M^{dm} Richard Berlow Apprentice to Wm Hoome of Manchester Dyer Ou [*sic*] Runn his Master Aug 22: 1699. to Send a note to his s^d Master to Enquire whether he is Consenting to his Goeing to Sea or not.

Servants Bound to Mr Richard Murfey Master of the Lamb of Doblin Bound to Verginnia

Septemb^r 4° 1699:		Age
	Phebe Leed of Oldham in Lancashire	19–05
do	Robert Owen of Seale in Cheshire Taylor	18–05
do	Mary Speakman of Clifton in Lancashire	20–05
do	Thomas Lindsay of Pendleton in Lancashire	16–09
do	Ellen Holt of Rachdale in Lancashire	27–05
6°	John Andrew of Oldham in Lancashire	22–04

Septr 19° 1699	Mary Atkinson of Nottingley in Yorkshire Bound to Mr Henry Smith of Liverpoole Merch^t	21–5
9 br 20°: 99	Joseph Elwood of Garston Taylor To Henry Smith	19–4

October 7°: 1699	John Nuttong of Burnley in Lancashire to Mr Robert Fleetwood	12–10

To Mr Lewis Jenkins

9 ber 9° 1699	Richard Edwards of Denbyshire		14–7
	John Edward	d°	18–5
	Robt Powell	d°	20–6
	Robt Davies		21–6

		Age	Yeares
Septr 12th	John Nicholson of Lancaster bound to Mr Thomas Tyler to go to new England for Seaven Yeares	20	7
14°	John Thomas of Clandethlow in Carmarthenshire bound to Capt Clayton for ye West Indies	18	7

Servants bound to Thomas Bowling of Exton in Lancashire husbandm': Octobe 14°: And Went in the Elizabeth for Viginniae or Maryland: Gilbert Leivsay Master

		age	
Octob^r: 14°	James Hall of Exton in Lancashire	11	12
1699	Joshua Holden of Heath Charnock in Lancashire	16	08
p^d	Thomas Colson of Chorley	18	08
	William Dickinson of Flucton in Yorkshire	14	08
	William Conly of Ouse Walton in Lancashire	09	13

Servts: Bound to Mr Bryan Blundele Mastr of the Mulberry October the 24o: 1699

8ber 24o: 99	Isaac Scofield of Chatherton[62] near Manchester	13:11
	James Scofield his brother	11:11
	Edward Lunt of Maile[63] in Lanc'	13:11

8ber 26: 99	William Scott of Portsmo to Mr John Parker	14:07

9ber. 10	Jacob Rylance of Morley in Cheshire to Richard Singleton	24:5

Servants Bound to Mr Henry Brown Master of the Loyalty bound for Virginnia or Maryland

		Age
8ber 24o: 99	Francis Boardman of Gorton near Manchester	21–4
	Ann Williams of Denbyshire	22–7
	Jam: Kershaw of Blakely in Lanc'	18–7
	Wm Kinder of disley in Cheshire	16–7
	Math Stabbs Sen of Rushton in Staffordshire	44–6
	Math Stabbs jun' of Ditto	15–9
	Edward Stabbs of Ditto	16–8
	Ewen Lommas[64] of Bury in Lancr	21–5

An Acct of Servants bound to Mr Wm Porter of Leverpoole Merchant and went in the Shipp Eleanor for Virginnia or Maryland Mr Nicholas Reynolds Master 1699

Janry 2th 1699	Constant Jeoffrys of St Asaphs in Wales	16–5
3d	Elizabeth Edwards of Yarmouth	18–5
10	Charles Quarryer of Sandbich in Cheshire	25:4
	Mary Steele of Beeston Castle in Cheshire	25:4
	Jane Wright of Skipton in Yorkshire	15:7
	Mary Anderton of Leverpoole in Lancashire	20:4
19th	John Travers of Denbyshire	14:7
	Mary Jones of Carnarvan in Wales	18:5
20th	Samwell Smallwood of London & his Wife Martha	35:27: Each 4
	Wm Huntington of Middlewich in Cheshire	28:4
	Ellen Masterman of Ornskirk	20:5
	Eliza. Galliburn of Blackbourn	18:5

[62] Chadderton (?)

[63] Mill or Meols (?)

[64] The following items refer to Bury: Owen, s. of John Lommas, b. 19 Apr., bapt. 27 Apr., 1679. John, s. of Richard Lomax, Taylor, b. 24 Mar., bapt. 28 Mar., 1650. John, s. of Richard Lomax, Elton, b. 28 July, bapt. 6 Aug. 1648. John, s. of Richard Lomax, Goosford, b. 4 Sept., bapt. 12 Sept., 1647. Wife of Richard Lomax, Taylor, d. 2 Oct., bur. 3 Oct., 1652. Richard Lomax, Taylor, d. 12 May, bur. 13 May, 1651. Anne, w. of Richard Lomax, Cooper, d. 28 June, bur. 30 June, 1651-2. Wife of Richard Lomax, Carpenter, bur. 27 Apr. 1661. Richard Lomax, Shipobotham, d. 15 Mar., bur. 18 Mar., 1671-2. Izabell, wife of Richard Lomax, d. 5 July, bur. 7 July, 1673. John Lomax and Esther Howorth, both of Bury, m. 13 Feb. 1671-2. John Lomax and Elizabeth Greenhalgh, m. 12 Aug. 1672. John Lomax and An Low of Bury m. 7 Jan. 1672-3. Jon Lomax Curate of Bury in 1694. John Lomax Churchwarden in 1685. Richard Lomax of Redwells Churchwarden in 1651. Esther, dau. of James Howorth of Elton, b. 7 Mar., bapt. 13 Mar. 1650. Elizabeth, dau. of John Greenhalgh, Catholic, b. 19 Nov., bapt. 24 Nov., 1653.

	Tho: Hodgkinson of Preston	19:4
	Math. Thorp of the City of York	24:4
	John Thorp of Mossen near Manchester	13:8
	Steph Thomas of Twissock in Denbyshire	15:7
	Edward Jones near Wrexham in Wales	20:7
Feb: 9:	Richard Dalton of Carlisle in the County of Cumberland	26:4
19	David Curran of the City of Dublin	30:4

1699/1700

Servts: bound to Mr John Rimmer Master of the Good Ship Planter bound for Newfoundland Mar: 18°: 1699

March ye 18th	James Day of Doublin in Ireland	22–5
	James Garnette of Rainhill in Lanc'	22–5

LIST OF EMIGRANTS TO AMERICA FROM LIVERPOOL 1697–1707

Transcribed by Miss Elizabeth French, and communicated by the Committee on English Research

Servts: Bound to Wm Benn Master of the Elizabeth and Ann bound for Montserratte in the West Indies

March ye 19° 99/700	Lawrence French of Galloway in the Kingdome of Ireland	26:4
	William Spence of Cambridg	20:5
	John Lindsey of Ballenmenough in the County of Antram Ireland	18:9
	Robert Joyce of Tane in the County of Galloway in the Kingdom of Ireland	25:4
March 26. 1700		
	Wm Thompson of London Marr'	31:4
	Thomt: Pickering of Great Budworth in Cheshire	29:4
	William Davies of Belfast	24.4
	Richard Messenger of Creeklard[65] in Wiltshire	31:4

To Mr Gravill Parifie

Aprle: 20°: 1700	Richard Jones[66] Bury in Lanc'	15:9

[65] Cricklade.
[66] Richard, s. of Richard Jones de Leeys, b. 25 Mar., bapt. 1 Apr., 1687 at Bury.

An Acc[t] of Servants Bound to M[r] Peter Atherton and M[r] Richard Bridg for Acc' of s[d] M[r] Peter Atherton to go in y[e] good Ship Lamb to Virginea or Maryland: and Shipt on board hir this the 8th day Septem[r] 1699.

July 14. 99	W[m] Evans of Denbyshire aged 23 yeares	23– 5 yeares
	Andrew Pritchett of Carnarvanshire aged	23– 5 yeares
	Thomas Berkett of Kendall	17– 7
	W[m] Hubbart of Hilmartin Parish, Wiltshire	21– 4
	Thomas Barlow of Manchester	19– 5
	J[no] Jones of Northrop Flintshire	19– 5
	Tho: Hughes of Denbyshire	14– 9
	Hugh Robert of Denby Town	13–10
	W[m] Gryffith of Rathbone near Wrexham	13–10
	Peter Evans neer Denby	14–10
	Hugh Morris of Little Church in Denby	14–10
	Robert Price of Denby Town	13–11
	Peter Dauis of Denby	13–11
	Henry Parrey of Olky in Flintshire	20– 1
	J[no] Dauis of Denby Town	13–11
	W[m] Roberts of Grandyel in Denbyshire	14– 9
	W[m] Williams of Denby Green in Wales	14–10
	Tho: Owen of Abergelly[67] in Denbyshire	25– 5
	J[no] Dauis of Denby Town aged	28– 5
	Lewis Jones of Beaumauris	30– 5
	Jane French of Holme near Lancas'	21– 4
	Edw[d] Guy of Aughton in Lancashire	34– 5
	Margarette Lloyd of Denby Town	20– 4
	Evans Hughes of Anglesey	13– 8
	Edw[d] Bumber of Denbyshire	14–10
	J[no] Williams of Denbyshire	12–10
	Robert Edwards of Merionithshire	22– 5
	J[no] Morrice of Denbyshire	16– 9
	Rich[d] Williams of Denbyshire	12–11
	Hugh Pierce of Denbyshire	35– 6
	Martha Hughes of Denbyshire	17– 5
	Ann Sammell of Meryonithshire	15– 7
	Rich[d] Jones of Denbyshire Taylor	19– 7
	David William of Denbyshire	21– 5
	Joseph Hart of Warwychshire	16–10
	Benjamin Bagshaw	12– 9
	Maurice Jones of Denbyshire	17– 7
	Richard Edwards of Denbyshire	19– 6
	J[no] Gryffith of Denbyshire	17– 7
Aug' 5	Rich[d] Stannor of Northwich Cheshire	17– 8
11	Peirce Hughes of Molleyn	15– 9
	Margarette Jones of Carnarvanshire	17– 5
Aug[st] 19	Rich[d] Tomlinson of Waddington in Yorkshire	31– 5
	Mary Taylor of Brurton[68] wood	34– 4
	Thomas Howarth of Limb in Suffolk Taylor	21– 4
21	J[no] Dene of y[e] City of London	14– 7

[67] Abergele.
[68] Brereton (?)

	Richd Faulkner of Ludlow in Shropshire	15– 7
	Mary Whitaker of Manchester	21– 4
	Alice Diggles of Eccles Parish	27– 4
	Joseph Crosbie of Nassburrough in Yorkshire	24– 5
24	Wm Barton of Scazebrick	28– 5
	Richd Hughes of Denbyshire	14– 8
	Jno Thomas of Merionithshire	10–12
	Gryffith Arthur of Denbyshire	21– 5
	Wm Edmunds of Denbyshire	12–12
	Tho: Francis of Carnarvanshire	24– 5
	Jno Morris of Carnarvanshire	20– 6
	Thomas Lloyd of Flintshire	13– 8
	Margarette Evans of Carnarvanshire	18– 5
	Nathaniel Waring of Floor in Northamptonsh	37– 5
7b. 4	Evan Roberts of Denbyshire	15–10
	Henry Owen of Abergelley parish in Denby	38– 5
	Elizabeth Thomas of Anglesey	26– 4
	Ann Owen of Abergelly	38– 5
	Rowland Thomas of Anglesey	34– 4
	William Dauis of Cothelwell in Meryonthshire	19– 5
	Edwd Furrington of Chester Watchmaker	20– 5
	Jno Fuller of Market Drayton in Shropshire blacksmith and Mary his Wife	26– 4
	Jacob Sherwood of Okingham in Cheshire	13– 8
	Henry Proctor of Walton	16– 7
	Richard Barlow of Manchester ran away	20– 6
	Jno Cartwright of Manchester ran away	19– 6

Acct of Servts: bound to Mr John Walls Mastr: of the Concord bound for Virginnia or Maryland December the 7o: 1699.

8ber: 25o: 99	Joseph Monk of Clayton i'th Moores in Lanc: Carpent'	22 : 4
	Jennet Monk his Wife	26 : 4
	Eleazer Fletcher of Leadon in Yorkshire	25 : 4
	Robert Twiddale of Fixby in do	23 : 4
	Ann Harrison of Scazbrick	19 : 5
	Margt Corrwinn of London	20 : 4
	Ann Richardson of Wallesley	20 : 4
	Elizabeth Cave of Warten Moore near Manchester	27 : 4
	Eliza Hunter of St. Albans Denbyshire	12 : 9
	Wm Hall of Burnley in Lanc'	21 : 4
	Jno Walker of Henley	19 : 4
	Wm Preston of Wittenborow[69] in Chester	22 : 4
	Eleanor Drury of Shrewsberry	23 : 4
	Richard Shaw of Ratchdale	21 : 4
	Thom' Connily of London	26 : 4
	Jane Bennet of Sutton in Cheshire	23 : 6
	John Jones of Llandurneugh in Denbyshire	13 : 9
Runn	Patk Dunkin of Sneeton in Yorkshire husbandm'	35 : 4
	Margt Lamb of Dalton in Lancashire	21 : 6
	John Leasiter of Hotsfield[70] in Cheshire	22 : 4

[69] Wybunbury (?)
[70] Hoofield (?)

	Wm Snalshaw [*sic*][71] of upholland in the County of Lanc'	22 : 4
16 : xb. 99	Richd Haddock of Lealand aged 14 yeares	14 : 11
xber 28	Edwd Warrington of Macclesfeild	27 : 5
	Wm Thomas of Carnarvanshire	35 : 5
	John Harrisson of Denbyshire in Wales	21 : 5
Jan. 3	Tho Hughes of Holliwell	25 : 5

December the first James Ridgway of Prestbury in Cheshire to Capt Wm Clayton for the Island of St Kitts Aged 22: 3 bound

Decr : 16th : 99 { John Woods (a Poor Child) of Aughton in Lancashire by Consent of the Overseers of Aughton aforesd. To Capt Clayton for Seaven Yeares at St Kitts in the West Indies
Joshua Taylor do of Do by Do to Do for Tenn Years at St Kitts Richard Latham and Thomas Harker Overseers

---

Maurice Griffith enquired for ye 26 2b 99
James Holme of Ormeskirke Taylor

Bound to Mr Jonath Leivsay

		Age	Yeares
Septembr : 25o 1699	Charles Mills[72] of Bury in Lancashire	16	8
October 11	Margarett Hughes of Anglesay in Wales	22	5
do	Katherine Maddock of the City of Chester	16	8
Novemr 25o	George Holt of Hallifax in Yorkshire	17	7
do	Robert Reynolds of Clanledon in Denbyshire	19	6
do	George Reynolds of do	17	6
do	Evan Edwards of Ebellah in Merryonithshire	26	5
do	Wm Humphrey of Beltworth in do	16	8

Bound to Mr William Fletcher

1699 xber 20	James Seacome of Preston Patrick in Westmoreland	20 : 8
Janry : 27	Peter Holland of Conway in Denbyshire	26 : 4
Feb : 2	Thomas Phithian of Mossen in Cheshire	28 : 4
Feb : 6	Jno Lethberrie of Hilton in Darbyshire Carpenter	22 : 4
ead die	Tho : Lethberrie of ye same husbandm'	25 : 4

Bound to Mr Lawrence Thompson p Acct of Mr Houghton

Aprill 10th 1700

Antho Stuart of Scotland	34 : 5
Jonath Crimes of Sandyway in Cheshire	21 : 5

Bound to M' Samuel Waring

Nicholas Brooke of Stradford in Lanc	12 : 9
Joseph Munck of Hazleinden[73] Husbm	22 : 4

[71] Probably Smalshaw, a name frequently found in the Registers of Upholland.
[72] The following items refer to Bury: Charles, s. of John Mills, b. 12 May, bapt. 21 May, 1682. John, s. of John Mills, b. 19 Jan., bapt. 4 Feb., 1657-8. John Mills of Walmersley in the parish of Bury and Sarah Greggory in the parish of Ratlife m. at Newhall 19 May, 1656.
[73] Haslingden.

Acc^t. of Servants That went to Virginia With Mr Gilbert Leivsay [ ] the [ ] 1699 in the Elizabeth of Leverpoole

	Age	Servd years
Elizabeth Addison of Kirby Staven[74] in Westmoreland	24 –	05
Mary King of Leverpoole	24 –	05
James Syddale of Ellingborough in Lancashire	18 –	06
Sarah Allison of Cuerdly d^o	24 –	04
Adam Simner[75] of Lealand	19 –	04
William Water of Walton le dale in d^o	17 –	05
Marg^t Lavinsley of Wrighton	19 –	07
John Brascoup of Burnley	18 –	05
Abram̄ Scowfield of Manchester	23 –	05
Ann Kirkome of Gorome Hills	23 –	04
Jane Willington of Barton	21 –	04
Adam Leasiter of Kersley	15 –	07
John Liphot of Bolton	21 –	04
George Seddon[76] of d^o	16 –	07
John Smethurst[77] of d^o	18 –	07
John Houseman[78] of d^o	20 –	04
Marg^t Sharpless of Heaton	23 –	05
Sarah Sherwood of Congerton	17 –	05
Elizabeth Nichols of Wiggan	30 –	05
Alex^r Jones of Denbyshire	12 –	10
Marg^t Waring of Queens County in Ireland	22 –	04
Elizabeth Ward of Eaton [?] in Lancashire	40 –	04
William Ward of d^o	13 –	10
Henry Butterfeild of Hallifax	16 –	08
Rober Maurice of Denbyshire	20 –	04
Richard Harris of Denby shire	26 –	04
Tho: Radcliff of Radcliff in Lanc	21 –	05
Mary Midclare of Macclesfield	21	05
Henry Ascroft of Aughton	20	04
James Birchenough of Wildbore Clough in Cheshire	25 –	04
John Johnson of Gorsworth in d^o	40 –	04
Mary Clayton of Adlington in d^o	24 –	04
Sarah Hilton of Hazlinton in d^o	25 –	04
William Pickering of Macclesfield	14 –	07
Henry Turner of Macclesfield	19 –	04
James Pickering[79] of Macclesfield	20 –	04
Ann Vavasor of Sporington in Yorkshire	23 –	05

[74] Kirkby Stephen.

[75] The following items refer to Leyland: Adam, s. of Thomas Somner, taylor, of Leyland, bapt. 12 Oct. 1680. Thomas Sumner and Ellin Whittle of Leyland m. 6 Dec. 1674. Thomas Sumner and Elizabeth Rochett, both of Leyland, m. 23 July 1677. Thomas Somner and Ellin his wife of Leyland Mosside bur. 10 Dec. 1680.

[76] George Seddon, s. of Thomas and Jennet of Bolton, b. 17 Jan., bapt. 23 Jan., 1680-1 at Bolton.

[77] John Smethurst, s. of James and Alice of Bolton, b. 1 Mar., bapt. 6 Mar., 1686-7.

[78] John Houseman s. of James and Mary, bapt. 15 Feb. 1679-80.

[79] The following items refer to Macclesfield: James, son of James Pickering of Macclesfield, bapt. 27 Sept. 1675. James, s. of James Pickering of Macclesfield, bapt. 1 June 1676. James Pickering and Frances Ouldfield, both of Macclesfield, m. 22 June 1673.

Ralph Smith of Bolton in Lanc'	15 – 07
Ralph Kershaw of Longworth	23 – 04
Charles Physick of Latham	8 – 14
James Gill of Latham	17 – 05
Wm Physick of Latham	17 – 05
Tho: Physick of d^o	11 – 10
Ellen Physick of d^o	37 – 04
James Barnes of Hazledine Parish in d^o	28 – 04
Will Ollerhead of Tervin in Cheshire	21 – 05
Mary Goare of ormskirk in Lanc	22 – 06
Margery Fairclough of Chorly in d^o	14 – 07
$Marg^t$ Fairclough of d^o	16 – 06
Ann Fairlclough [*sic*] of d^o	37 – 04
Wm Fortclough [*sic*] of d^o	12 – 10
Ann Ashley of Boaden in Cheshire	20 – 05
Tho: Robertshaw of Downham in Lancashire	21 – 04
Wm Coverly of Downham in d^o	25 – 04
Robert Emett of d^o	18 – 05
Tho: Bulcock of d^o	22 – 04
Christopher Smith of d^o	20 – 04
Will Bulcock of d^o	17 – 05
Will Shenock of Downham	16 – 06
Joseph Monk of Clayton in Lanc	20 – 04
Will Hertland of Clerk Hill near Burnley	11 – 11
John Horne of $Bishop^k$ of Durham	20 – 04
John Williams of Cryddun in Carnarvanshire	12 – 10
William Pollard of Burnley in Lanc'	21 – 04
$Marg^t$ Coales of y^e Isle of Man	16 – 05
Frances Jackson of City of Chester	17 – 05
Ellen Smith of Sommerset in Lanc'	20 – 06
Ann Waller of Winton in Westmoreland	19 – 04
Joseph Wennington [of] Wheales in Cumberland	20 – 04
Jane Whitehead of Tarleton in Lanc'	17 – 04
John Terroy of London	23 – 04
John Walmsley of Ackrington in Lanc'	20 – 04
Nicholas Whittle [80] of Lealand	22 – 04
Kath Robinson of Hootown in Cheshire	20 – 04
Rober Turner of Tarleton and his daughter	28 : 4 – 05 : 17
Isabel of d^o and Son Thomas	20 : $\frac{3}{4}$ – 05 : $20\frac{1}{4}$
$Rich^d$ Snailum [81] of Bretherton	26 – 04
Robert Woods of Bretherton	14 – 06

Account of $Serv^{ts}$ bound to M' Samuell Smith Since 10th of $Octo^r$ 1700

	Yers – Age
William Muddiford of Yorkshire	5 – 27

$Serv^{ts}$ to M' Thomas Presson 23^d $Octo^r$ 1700

Thomas Hamson of Kilton in Lanc	5 – 22

---

[80] Nicholas, s. of Nicholas Whittle and Alice Parker, a bastard, bapt. 19 Apr. 1676, at Leyland.

[81] Richard Snailem and Anne Porter, both of Bretherton, m. 3 Feb. 1696-7 at Croston.

An Acct of Servants bound to m' Ralph Wmson 9b. 23. 1699

Eliz.–Ellis of Leedes	aged 20 yeares –	6
Amie Pritchard of Hallywell	aged 23 –	6
James Stewart of Northumberlan'	12 –	10
Mary Howard of Rightington Lanc'	25 –	6
Agnes Sherman of Malstonn [82] Westmorland	17 –	6
Jerom' Taylor of Doncasd' Yorksh'	26 –	5
Jno Lipscom of Sudbery near Bristol	27 –	5
Wm Hussy of Wellington Somersetsh'	20 –	5
Tho: Williams of Monmouth in Wales	30 –	4
Ann Ellis[83] of Leeds Yorkshire	23 –	6
Elizabeth Waters of Westhoughton Lanc'	22 –	6
Jno Glave of Hope parish in Flintshire	19 –	5
Tho: Ascome of Padyam [84] in Lancash'	12 –	12
Arthur Dewhurst of Whiston in Lanc'	10 –	12
Tho: Walker of Barnacre in Lanc'	27 –	4
Mary Walker of Barnacre	22 –	4
Tho: Widop of Wadsworth in Yorksh'	17 –	7
Jno Williams of Mosteyn Flintsh'	14 –	8
Hugh Kenardy of Scotland	35 –	5
Wm Woolfet [85] of Bolton Lanc	15 –	7
Jno Johnson of London	22 –	5
Tho: Robinson of Richwood Oxfordshr	25 –	4
Ann Hughes of Denbyshire	28 –	6
Daniel Kennion of Berry Lanc	18 –	5
Jno Murrough of Northumberl'	14 –	10
Josh.' Tunstall of Billing	18 –	6
Ann Penry of Rochdall	18 –	6
Adam Auger of Northumberl'	12 –	11
Charles Mendam of Norridg Citty	19 –	5
Jno mtt Donell [*sic*] of Scotl'	19 –	6
Jno Alicer of Taunton Somersetsh'	21 –	5
Jno Pennington of Little Emsell in Yorsh'	25	5
Tho: Hudson of Maun in Yorksh'	19 –	5
Robt Southworth of Kinsley Staffordsh'	16	7
Jno Low of Ashton in Lanc	30 –	4
Mary Statham of Lichfield	20 –	6
Daniel Burridg of Shrewsberry	26 –	5
Alexand Blandford of Plimouth Devonsh'	22 –	6
Ellis Scowfield of Rochdall	25 –	5
Jno Ashworth of Rochdall	30 –	5
Xpr. Tyrer of West-Derby	18 –	6
James Thelwell of Cuerdley Shoomak'	22 –	5
Ann Walker of Manchest'	19 –	6
Grace Edmund [of] Carnarvansh'	20 yeares –	6
Thomas Ewes of Colehill Warwicksh'	20 –	4

82 Mallerstang.

83 At St. Peter's Church, Leeds: Ann, child of Samuel Ellis of ye Nether Headrow, b. 5 June, bapt. 18 June, 1673. Samuel Ellis and Elizabeth Threlford of Lower Headdrow m. 6 Apr. 1669.

84 Padiham.

85 William Woolfet, s. of Edward and Elizabeth of Little Bolton, b. 27 Dec., bapt. 30 Dec., 1683 at Bolton.

Margtte Brown of Witham Cumberl'	18 –	5
Edw' Gryffin of Carmarthen	25 –	5
James Toppin of Garston	22 –	4
Mary Jones of London	20 –	5
James Wilson of Cardigan	24 –	4
Wm Plumb of Hollinfare	16 –	9
Wm Sedden of Hinley	20 –	5
Eliz: Cotton near Blackburne	18 –	7
J^{no} Wainwright of Halewood	11 –	11
Sarah Eaton of Budworth	20 –	4
Eliz: Marsh of Budworth	16 –	6
Tho: Mosse of Budworth	16 –	6
Joseph Elwood	19 –	4
J^{no} Beckett Bricklayer of the City of York	30 –	4
Joseph Briggs of Ratchdale	18 –	7
Isaac Harrisson of of [*sic*] Ditton	13 –	7
Thomas Daw of Birtinwood Lancashire	25 –	5
Jeremiah Cronage of Leeds: Yorkshire	17 –	4

9b. 24	Samuel Sadler of Wittnough Cheshir' Milwright	To m' Lund m' Houghtons friend	23 yeares bound for 5 yeares

---

Febre: 22° 1699

Thom' Parke of Much Hool in the County of Lanc. aged 21 Appr to m' Tho: Hayes for Acc^{t}. of Thom. Johnson j^{r} Ery [*sic*] 4 yeares

J^{no} Sutherland Son of James Sutherland of Elgin in Scotlan' aged ab. 15 to ye same fr 7 yeares

---

Febru: 27. 1699

	Evan Owen of or near Ossestry in Shropshr' ag^{d}	20 yeares –	4
27; 1699	Tho: Williams of Carnarvan in Wales	12 yeares –	9

To m' Wm Benn.

March 21. 1699

Robt Jayes of Tuam County of Galloway in Ireland 4

To Capt Clayton

March 26–1700

Wm Thompson of London Mason ag^{d} 31 – 4
who went also in ye ship wth m' Wm Benn

Bryan Blundell Servants to Henry Williams of Cornarvanshire 9 – 16

John Thomas [of] Cornarvanshire 6 – 19

November 7th 1700 Serv^{ts} to Mr John Henry of Maryland

John Key of Yorkeshire 4 – 25

William Jackson of Lancashire 4½ – 27

Samuel Simpcock to John Cocke		6 - 24

8b. y^e^: 15. 1700

	Ann Buckley of Salford to m' Robt Moon	6 yeares aged	22
16	Henry Williams of Flintshire	9 yeares ag^d^	15
8^br^ 21°	Benedictus Chestain of Mancheste	6	18
	Jane Buckley of Salford	6	19
	Thomas Bradbury Weston	5	24
	Mary Pye Knowsley	5	30

Serv^ts^ with John Charters Octo^r^ 16 - 1700

francis Fanco' [of] Norrmondy	4	25
John Wilson [of] Denbishire	4	21
John Rowlands [of] Denbishire	4	24
Henry Griffin [of] Denbishire	4	20

---

17 October 1700 Serv^ts^ to Mr Basnett

John Nutter of Yorkshire	8 - 14

Servants bound to Mr Augustine Woodward to Virginia the 12^d^ day of Octo^r^ 1700 in the Virginia Merch^t^.

	Y^s^ old	Yeares
Elizabeth Leafield of Lancashire	20 -	7
Mary Masson of Cheshire	20 -	5
Margarett Vpton of Cheshire	18 -	4
Anne Wharton of Cheshire	17 -	5
John Coloct of Nottinghamshire	11 -	11
Martha Kilshaw of Cheshire	18 -	4
Elizabeth Naylor of the City of Chester	18 -	5
Jeremiah Doucker of the Citty of London	20 -	4
Thomas Pope of the Citty of London	20 -	4
Elizabeth Hughes of Flintshire in Wales	20 -	7
John Griffith of Denbishire in Wales	12 -	9
Richd Owens of Cardiganshire in Wales	18 -	7
Mary Williams of Anglesie in Wales	11 -	11
Henry Roberts of Flintshire	21 -	7
John Thomas of Flintshire	11 -	11
John Robert of Flintshire	12 -	10
Thomas Roberts of Flintshire	14 -	8
Evan Owens of Carnarvanshire aged	11 -	11
William Robinson of Northumberland	16 -	7
William Stafford of Cheshire	17 -	6
John Spooner of Derbyshire	32 -	4
John Balie of Lancashire	20 -	4
Kath: Thomas of Wales	22 -	5
Evan Evans of Wales	25 -	4

Servants bound to Mr William Part to Virginia the Nineteenth day of November in the Elizabeth & Judeth

John Mathews of Whitehaven	17 - 5
John Medley of Yorkshire	19 - 7

Nicholas Butterworth of Yorkshr^{e} 19 - 7
Henry Walbanck of d^{o} 24 - 5
Robt Ratt[ ] D^{o} 22 - 5
William Boy D^{o} 22 - 5
Rab^{m}. [*sic*] Shaftin 21 - 5

Servants bound on board Mr Jonathan Leivsay
Edm^{d} Knowles of Boulton aged 15 - 7

---

xb 16 1700 Servants bound to Mr Henry Browne
John Oglebie [of] Edenboraugh, Aged 19 Yeares, According to the Custome
John Horsbell of the Same Aged 16 Yeares D^{o}
William Maddock of Chester 21 - 5
Charles Edw^{ds} of Wales 12 - 12
John Loyd of d^{o} 11 - 13
Wm Edwards d^{o} 10 - 14
Tho : Mathews d^{o} 9 - 15
Michal Hughes d^{o} 15 - 7
Tho Owens d^{o} 17 - 7
Edwd Jones d^{o} 15 - 9
Sam. W^{m}so' d^{o} 14 - 10
Jo^{se}h Griffith d^{o} 17 - 7

Servants bound To m' Daniell Murphy To Virginia in the Shill [*sic*] John Baptist the Twelfth of December 1700
Elizabeth Thompson of Chester 28 - 5
Isabella Sellors of Liverpoole 24 - 7
John Mills of Lansh 12 - 9
John Barroms of Kent 16 - 5
Thomas Duglas of Northumberland 29 - 4
James Johnson of Lanc' 21 - 4
Wm Hicks of Elesmore 22 - 4
Richard Style of Cheshire 19 - 4
Timothy Hicks of Elesmore 16 - 4
Samuell Breerely of Lanc 15 - 7
Edward evans of denbishire 12 - 7
Jonie Fletcher of Staffordshire 22 - 4
Ellen Foster of Namtwich Aged 27 - 4
John Morgan of Wales 13 - 7
Margrett Hebbett of Cheshire 21 - 4
Sarah Clough of Holywell 17 - 6
Elizabeth Rogers of Cheshire Aged 18 - 6
Hester Jones of Cheshire 18 - 6
Howell Jones of Cheshire 23 - 4

An Account of Servants bound to Mr Thomas Leskonby for Virginia on board the Shipp Globe the Twenty Third day of January 1700
Alexander Harginson of Newcastle aged 5 - 8
John Gage of the City of London 22 - 4
Daniell Steward of the City of London 15 - 8

	Mary Booth of Lancashire	22 –	4
	Anne Birch of Lancashire	20 –	4
	Richard Rowlands of Westmoreland	24 –	4
	Elizabeth Pamwitt of Cumberland	22 –	5
	Henry Justice of Chester	21 –	5
	Samuell Gurdain of Lanc	28 –	4
	Thomas Fenne of Lancashire	24 –	4
	Anne Humphrys of Herefordshire	22 –	5
	Robert Whitacre of Lancashire	19 –	4
	Robert Siddall of Whithington neare Manchester	23 –	4
R : :	Edwd Fitchgerrard of London aged 30 Yeares		4

LIST OF EMIGRANTS TO AMERICA FROM LIVERPOOL 1697–1707

Transcribed by Miss Elizabeth French, and communicated by the Committee on English Research

Servants bound to Mr Henry Smith for Virginia on board the Anne & Sarah the Twenty Third day of January 1700.

William Morris of Lancashire	36 –	4
Mary Morris of the same vx^r	30 –	4
Richard Simons of Liverpoole	21 –	4
Mary Boucker of Lancashire	22 –	4
Elizabeth Lunt of Lancashire	23 –	4
Richard Abraham of Lanc'	20 –	5
James Hall of Northumberland	26 –	5
James Wilson of Northamptonshire	20 –	5
John Bowker of Lancashire	21 –	4
Abraham Bowker D^o	18 –	4
William Briggs of Lanc'	22 –	4

Servants bound to Virginia on board of the Robert and Elizabeth to Mr Ralph Williamson 27th January 1700

Elizabeth Naylor of Exiter	26 –	4
Henry Scoffield of Lanc^r	40 –	4
Andrew Bird of Shropshire	18 –	4
John Whitacre of Lanc^r	30 –	4
Nathaniell Lidnescey of Hampshire	26 –	4
Peter Gowen of Yorkshire	20 –	4

	Mary Mills of Lancashire	23	5
	Thomas Thornley of Cheshire	16	7
	Owen Jones of Anglisie	20	4
	Barbury Lensey of Yorkshire	20	4
	John Frankland of Middlesex	21	5
	Elizabeth Briggs of Hull	19	4
	Richard Radley of Manchester	37	4
	Thomas Most of Lanc'	19	4
	James Maddock of Lanc'	30	4
	Christopher Marsden of Lanc'	20	5
	Samuell Browne of Whiston in Lanc'	16	7
	Susan Lea of Cheshire	29	4
	Anne Edward of Wales	25	5
	Elizabeth Camell of Lanc^{r}	16	8
	Elizabeth Davies of Shrowsbury	24	5
Run away	Diana Molyneux of Chester	20	5
	Sarah Bridg of Cheshire	25	5
	James Cartwright of Shropshire Bridgnorth	30	5
Run away {	Thomas Pearson of Newcastle	21	4
	Daniell Williams of Herefordshire	24	4
	Robt Goodwin of Lanc^{r}	22	4
	John Harrison of Liverpoole	21	4
	Thomas Hardman of Lanc^{r}	30	4
	Evan Evans of Mountgomeryshire	40	5
	Margarett Evans of d^{o}	30	5
	William Wright of Rudlandshire	30	4
	Elizabeth Wright D^{o}	30	5
	Rachell Pattison [of] Cheshire	19	5
	Martha Marchie	19	5
	Jonathan Plowman of Yorkshire	12	10
	Peter Harrison of Lanc'	24	4
	paid by Mr Marsden		
	Wm Pers of Lancashire	21	4
	Richd Rustin of Chalk in Weltshire Tayl'	21	4
	J^{n} Heal of Cirencest' in Glowstershir Tay^{l}	21	4
	J^{no} Gath of Carlisle 5 year	20	5

Servants bound to M' William Everard the Eleaventh day of February 1700: on board of the Shipp the Lambe of Liverpoole

Richard Lewis of Mereonithshire	11	7
William Davies of Dorsetshire aged	24	4
Thomas Jones of Denbishire	29	4
William Davies of Denbishire	21	4
Joseph Gibson of Travellin in Wales	16	7
Thomas Worrall of Nantwich	20	4
Thomas Davis of Denbishire	21	5
Robert Morris of Shropshire	22	4
Robert Hughes of Carnarvanshire	15	9
John Hodgkinson of Liverpoole aged	9	11
Randle Carters of Cheshire	20	6
James Towning of Lodg.[86]	17	5

[86] Lodge, Yorks, or The Lodge, Shropshire (?)

	Christopher Parkinson [87] of Chipping	17 –	5
	John Peares of Flintshire	18 –	7
	Randle Fidians of Cheshire	22 –	4
	John Dod of Denbyshire	30 –	4
	David Jones of Denbishire	19 –	7
	Griffith Hughes of Wales	18 –	5
	Thomas Briscoe of Chester	22 –	4
Run	David Williams of Mountgomeryshire	35 –	4

rememb. Hugh Topping of Waringh'

Servants bound to to [*sic*] M' John Hughes the Tenth day of February 1700

	Mary Owery of Denbishire aged	15 –	8
	Margarett Nicholls of Flintshire	26 –	5

Serv^{ts} to M' John Charters on board the Lambe of Liverpoole 11th Feb^{r}y 1700

	Robert Oglebie of Lanc'	17 –	4
	John Brittin of Lancashire	22 –	4

Serv^{ts} bound to M' Tho: Heyes To Antego this 8 day of March 1700

Paid } 1° Apr 1701 }	John Low of Lanc' Aged	16 –	6
	William Lealand of Boulton in Lanc	13 –	7

Nov 1° 1701	Serv^{ts} to Mr Tho: Williamson		
	Joshua Rycroft of Cheshire Aged	12 –	8
Nov: 1° 1701	Servants bound to M' William Part		
	Ralph Cockett of Dunyan [88] Aged	15 –	7
	Elizabeth Stansel [A]ged 21 Yeares	21 –	4
	Robert Jackson of Lanc' A[ged]	15 –	7
	Ellen Roson of Lanc' Aged	20 –	4
	Mary Harefoote of Ormshire	19 –	4
November 8th	1701		
	Serv^{ts} bound to Mr John Gore		
	Elizabeth Wright of Cheshire Aged ab^{t} [89]	21 –	5
Ship7Serving	Joseph Tagg of d°	20 –	5
men p^{d}	Michaell Aldridg of Yorkeshire	40 –	4
per J^{n}:	Richard Pearson of Northampton	26 –	5
Cockshutt	Easter Miers of Lanc^{r}	20 –	5
	Mary Oragehead of Cheshire	20 –	5
	Abigall Bradshaw of d°	27 –	5
No: Eighth:	Servants bound to Mr Samuell Medgley		
	Eliz Oakes [of] Cheshire	18 –	4
p'	Alice Slator d°	20 –	4

[87] The following items refer to Chipping: Christopher, s. of Robert Parkinson of Chepin, bapt. 5 Mar. 1681-2. Robert, s. of John Perkinson of Cock hill, bapt. 12 May 1661. Robert, s. of Richard Perkinson of Chippin, bapt. 26 Sept. 1655.

[88] Dunham (?)

[89] This and the six items following it are crossed out in the original.

Jane Robinson [of] Lancaster 20 - 4

25 Octo^br 1701 Tho Buttler Son of Wm Buttler to Ganther Carefoote for 7 Yeares

---

Serv^ts to M' Edwd Tarleton 21 of November 1701

Walter Richards of Herefordshire 33 - 4

Serv^ts to Mr Basnett

Eliz Voughan of the City of London 20 - 7

4° Decem^r 1701. Serv^ts to Mr John Greene

William Peares of Carnarvanshire 12 - 9

---

4 Decem^r 1701 Servants bound to William Gurdon

		aged
	James Smallwood [of] Cheshire Aged	27 - 4
	Ann Goodwin d°	22 - 4
9	Richd Dinsdall of Wenswide in Yorkshire	32 - 4

Serv^ts to M' Nehemiah Jones 4 december 1701

Joseph Gregg Apprentice of Ashton 22 - 5

Servants bound to m' Michael Wentworth 28th 9b 1701

Thomas Greene of Yorkshire aged between 27 yrs for 6 yeares

Joshua Thompson of Yorkshire aged about 20 yeares for 6 yeares

---

Jan 3 1701 John Medecine App to m' Andrew Clark for 9 yeares, ye s^d John Medecine aged about 13 yeares

---

Janu' 5 1701 Serv^ts to m' Henry Brown

John Patience of Wiltshire husband' aged about 34 yeares

James Hamer of Acper in Lancashire near Wigan is suspected to go abroad & I am Oblig^d to Stop him.

Serv^ts bound to John Ball

	Y
John Whitehead of Wrixen in Lanc^r Aged	15 - 9

Servants bound to Thurstan Brachall

Mary Allam of Warrington 20 - 5

12th February 1701

Serv^ts bound to Mr Augustine Woodward

	Age	time
Wm Beniford of Cheshire	15 -	9
John Askie of Cheshire	14 -	9
Sarah Heanes of London Spinst'	21 -	5

21 Feb	Melicent Astly aged 12 years	12 -	7
	Mary Taylor of Staffordshire	18 -	5
	Eliz: Thomas of Wrexam	30 -	5
	Eliz: Morris of Leverp[l] Spinstr	25 -	4
24 Jan'	Mary Jones of Brecknockllin	17 -	5
	James Feshel of Cheshire	30 -	4
	Margtte Hughes of Whitby in Cheshire	13 -	9
	Ann Hardgrace of Lancashir	22 -	4
	W[m] Brindley of London Shoomakr	25 -	4
	Hannah Yales of Chester Spins'	20 -	5
March 5 1701	Margarette Welsly of Speak	19 -	6

To m' Edw' Smalley

Feb 26	Ann Pugh of Much Woolton	20 -	4
Feb 4	Tho: Chorter of Manchest to Adam Oldfiel 2: [*sic*]	-	5

Servants to m' W[m] Benn M[r] of y[e] Eliz & Ann to Virgin'

Feb[r] 19	J[no] Howard of Witherilach Lancashir	28 -	5
Feb 24	William Gedlin of Lancashir	18 -	5

June 29 1702	Servants to m' Thomas Jameson of Maryland		
	Edw[d] Jaspers of Namptwich in Cheshire Tayl[r]	21 -	4
July 1	Alexand[r] Tyror to m' Thos Jameson	19 -	9
July 1	William Hoyl of Hallifax in Yorkshire	12 -	11
July 3	Richard Anderton of Knowesley	13 -	9

July 6	W[m] Edge of Manchest[r] Serv[t] to W[m] Evrard	17 -	7
14	Jane Chadwick of Clievland near Yorkshire	24 -	5

To m' Smalwood & m' Everard

Aprel 19th 1702

		Yeares	
	Abraham Su[ ] of Leeds Yorkshire to m' Smalwood aged	15	9
June 19 1702	Moses Rithwell of Chester	16 -	7
June 27	Jno Marshall [of] Southampton	15 -	8
July 6	Ann Heward[90] of Berry Lancashire	20 -	7
6	Jane Knight of Congleton	30 -	7
6	Anna Crosfield of Cartmell Lancar	18 -	7

Aug. 14 1702	Luke Perrey to m' [*blank*]		
	to m' Stephen H [*blotted*]		
8b. 6 1702	John Earthead of Brinly in Lancashire	18 -	7
8b y[e] 10 1702	James Burl of Westmoreland Ag'	27 -	4

		ag'	time
8b. 15 1702	Henry Wilson Servant to m' W[m] Peters	14 -	7

[90] At Bury: "An," dau. of Roger Hewood, b. 20 Nov., bapt. 10 Dec., 1682. Roger Hayward of Moorside d. 22 Mar., bur. 23 Mar., 1698.

Servants to m' Nehem. Jones

Janu' first	Thom' Hart of Ashton	17 –	7
	Mary Morris of Ashto	18 –	6
	Jno Tyrr of Liverpoole	18 –	6

9b 17th 1702 Richard Peling Son of Georg Peling late of ye Citty of Chester Shoomaker aged about 16 Yeares hath bound himselfe a Serv to Barbadoes or any other of ye Charyb-bee Island for 7 yeares, after his Arrival at Barbadoes or one of ye sd Islands

---

		age	yrs
xb. 7. 1702	Mary Fish of Whittle in ye Woods Lancas Appr to m' Gilb: Eden Or his Assigns to Virg. or Maryland [91]	29 –	5

---

xb. 8. 1702 Jane Morgan servt: to m' Jno Lancast 14 –

		Age	year
xb. 16. 1702	Richard Hatton of Tarbook to sd Andr' Clarke of Belfast	29	4
xbr 21	Wm Philips of Cork in Ireland to m': Jno Lancst	48	4
xb. 26 1702	Jno Fooles of Cabin in Lancast husbndm'	25	4

Jan: 8. 1702	Roger Preswicke of Manchr Taylor to Randle Platt	20	4
Jan: 9: 1702	Ralph Bate of Croft hus to Capt. Henry Brown	22 :	5
Jan 13 1702	Timothy Dickinson of Stockport Chap'	35 :	4
Jan. 16 1702	Alice Steel of Knutsford in Cheshire	21 :	4
Jan. 20: 1702	Robt Buckley of Cronton	15 :	9
20:	Ann Steed of Sephton	25 :	5
20:	Mary Woods [92] of Bolton	23 :	5

To Tho Wmson

March 5th 1702			
	Richard Forber of Whiston	17 :	6

To m' Ralph Wmson

March 17 1702			
	Kather' Williams of Abborguelley [93] in Wales	18 :	6
17	Wm Parrey of Ridgland [94] in Wales	18 :	6

To m Wm Robinson

March 17: 1702			
	Jno Mercer Son of Jno Merce' of Eurton Shoo-make'	15 :	6

---

[91] This entry crossed out in the original record. *Vide infra* for duplicate entry.
[92] Mary Wood, dau. of Samuel and Dorothy of Breightmet, b. 27 Jan., bapt. 29 Jan., 1682–3, at Bolton.
[93] Abergele.
[94] Raglan (?)

An Acc^{t}: of Serv^{ts}: in ye Tabitha and Priscill Capt Wm Tarleton Comand^{r}

		Age	Year
28 : Ja' 1702	Jno Harrison of Liverpoole Assign^{d} to m' James Tildesley	24	4
Feb 3	Jno Humphrey of Denbyshire to m' Geo': Tyrer & Assign^{d} to m' Tildesly	12 :	9
7 xb.	Mary Fish of Whittle in ye Woods in Lancaste' Spins^{t} to m'. Eden Ap. to m'. Tildesley	29 –	5
18 xb.	Richd Webb son of Edw'. Webb of London In-keep, to m' Geo : Tyrer assign^{d} to m' Tildesly	16 :	7
9 Ja'	Jane Granth' of Olringham in Cheshire	23 :	4
1 Jan'	Ann Tool of Fingall in Ireland Spinst^{r} to m' Wm Tarleton & by him assign^{d} to m' James Tildesley	21 :	4
6 : Feb	James Hatton of Boughton in Cheshir	14 :	7
29. Jan'	Eliz : Valentine of Liverpoole	21 :	5

March 20 : 1702

	Ellen Hughes of Denbishire to Daniel Faurell Carpen^{t} of ye Brittania	21 :	5

An Acc^{t} of Serv' Bound to m' : J^{no} Charters Anno 1702

		Age	Yeares
January 20.	James Low of Prescott	15 :	4
28.	Mary Robinson of Thornton of Dalamores[95] in Cheshire Spinst	20 :	4
Feb 20 :	Eliz : Wright of Liverpoole Spinst^{r}	15 :	4
17 :	Jinnet Roy^{l} of Preston in Lancash' Spins^{t}	19 :	4
Jan 18 :	Eliz : Dixon of ye Town of Lancs^{r} Spins^{t}	20 :	4
18 :	Mary Fletcher[96] of Macclesfield in Cheshire Spinst	16 :	4
29 :	James Brown of Carleton in Cumberland	21 :	4
March 10	James Aldorson of Helig in sneidale in ye County of York	22 :	4
10	J^{n} Hunter of Askrigg in Yorkshire	18 :	4
Apr^{l} 9. 1703	Eliz : Hughes of Wrexam	21 :	5
9 :	Marg^{tt} Gaylen of Ruthin	36 :	5

To m' : Samuel Sanford

Feb. 15. 1702	Peter Wilson of Carlisle	12 :	9
25	Thom' Rawson of Wrexam in Wales	14 :	6
March 27	Wm Heyes	16 :	7

To m' Joseph Briggs

Janu' 19. 1702

	Thom' : Elleson of Preston on ye Hill in Cheshire	12 :	9
20 :	Eliz : Johnson of Macklesfield in Cheshire	25 :	4
12 :	Ezekiel Holms of Frodsham	15 :	7
6 :	Wm Hamlet of Wavetree	10 :	11

---

95 Thornton-le-More or, as it was probably called at that time, Thornton de la More.

96 Mary, dau. of Alexander Fletcher of Macclesfield, bapt. 1 May 1687 at Macclesfield.

To m' : J^{no} Gore

Ap' 2. 1703	J^{no} Ashton of Whiston	20 : 5
	Anne Steed of Jure Lan	21 : 5
	Richd Jakeman of Skipton brawn Yorksh	22 : 4
	Mary Woods of Bolton	22 : 5
	Robt Buckley near Preston	13 : 9
March 17	Richd Ronell of Livrpoole	20 : 4
3	[*blank*] Penkell	20 : 5
Feb. 27	Peter Penkell Pieer [*last two words crossed out*]	12 : 11

To m'. Richard Lathom

		age : year
April 6. 1703	Richd Ingam[97] of Wood Plumpton in Lanc	30 : 4
Ap'. 10. 1703	John Jackson son of Rich^{d} of Preston Inkeep^{r}	— 4

To m' Thos Leavins

April 7	Wm Isherwood of Bolton Lancast	16 : 7

April 12. 1703	to m' J^{no} Gore John Pelton of [*blank*] in Lancashire	13 : 9
15. 1703	Easter Deakin of Toxteth Park in Lancashire	22 : 5
21: 1703	James Johnson	18 : 7
26: 1703	Ann Linacre of Livrpoole	38 : 4

Servants bound to m' Thomas Hughes

xb. 17. 1702	Edwd Tatlocke of Childwall in Lancashire	22 : 5
March 23. 1702/3	Kath' Prier of Carmarthenshire	21 : 5
Ap'. 1. 1703	Pemberton Proudlow of Sandwich in Cheshire	15 : 9
	Steph' Christian	30 : 4
Ap'. 20: 1703	J^{no} Evans of Anglesy in Roskallin[98] Parish	12 : 9

To m' Henry Brown

April 26. 1703	J^{no} Poston Off Shrewsberrey	17 : 5

April 26. 1703	Ruth Lingard to m' Joseph Briggs	18 : 4

April 26. 1703	Evan Jones of Carnarvansh to m' J^{n} Charters	30 4

April 29. 1703	Thom' Wharton of Eurton to m' Richd Wright in ye Brittan to Virgin'	19 : 5

[97] Richard Ingham and Ellin Porter, both of Wood Plumpton, m. 18 Sept. 1692.
[98] Rhoscolyn.

LIST OF EMIGRANTS TO AMERICA FROM LIVERPOOL 1697–1707

Transcribed by Miss ELIZABETH FRENCH, and communicated by the Committee on English Research

Servants bound to M' Nathn^{l} Hughes 2 Augt 1702

	Dorathy Tipping of Garston Lancasr	21 :	4
16. April 93 [*sic*]	Mary Adrick of Barton Lanc	21 :	4
17. Feb. 1702	Mary Moor of Aughton Lan'	25 :	4
28. 8b. 1702	Eliz : Sharp of Pelton Lanc	18 :	4
23. 8b. 1702	Margar^{tt} Taylor of Ratclffe Lancast	18 :	5
16 Feb. 1702	Ellen Owen of Farnith Lanc'	20 :	4
7 March 1702	Georg Burgesse of Preston	22 :	4
20 Janu' 1702	Henry Lea of Pickdell	14 :	6
	mem there is one & half more Owing for.		

---

		yeares
Octob 9 1703	Wm Watson[99] Son of Saml Watson late of Macclesf^{d} in Cheshire gent Servt to m' Bryan Brundell	4

An Acc^{t} of Servants bound to m J^{no} Smalwood to go in ye Lamb

			age	years
Augst	13 1703	Philip Stockton of Clayton Parish Lanc	14 :	7
	14	James Dawson of Lealand	14 :	8
7b	17	Sarah Johnson [of] Pontefract in Yorksh'	22 :	5
	20	Tho : Slater of Manches^{t}	20 :	5
	30	Alice Chadwyck of Brindle Lancasr'	20 :	5
	13	Ellen Hodgson of Thornton	:	5
	9	Henry Lloy^{d} of Conway in Wales	15 :	8
8b	1	Jno Living of Manchest'		
	4	Mary Platt of Preston on ye Hill Chesh	23 :	4
	8	Eliz Lewis of Foodild Parish Cheshir	23 :	5
		Mary Stewart of London	25 :	7
		[ ] of Cheshire		

To m' Jno Birch

9b. 1 1703	Thom Prestidg of Vardy Green, near Manches'	15 :	7

To m Peter Man

Janu : 25th1703	Mary Fletcher of Whiston Spinst aged	21 :	5

To m' J^{no} Laurill

Janr 12 1703	Kath' Hughes of Arlslie in the County of Salip Spinst	22 :	4

[99] "Gulielmus Watson filius Samuelis Watson generosi et Sarae vxoris Eius natus fuit Primo Die Martij Baptizatusq in Capella Parochiali de Macclesfeild Decimo Tertio die Die Ejusdem mensis Annoque domi 1672–3." From the Church Registers of Macclesfield. This Latin entry, which is in a large and elaborate hand, covering half a page, in contrast to the carelessly written and abbreviated form used in other entries, shows the social importance of the family.

ead die Margtte Dickinson of Wavertree Spinst 22 : 4
Feb 7 1703 Alice Bertinsh' of Manch' Spinst 21 : 4
Fbr ead die Hannah Hairclipe of Hallifax in y[e] County of York Widow 27 : 4
Feb. 4. 1703 William Yates of Prescott husbandm' 18 : 4
2. 1703 Ellen Whitlisse of Hinley Spinst. to m Rich[d] Gildart but Assign' to Cap[t] Lancst' 15 : 7
Febr. 9 1703 Sam[l] Hartless of Sanbych in Cheshire to m' : Thom' Williamson but assigned to m' J[n] Lancast'

To m' Peter Hall

March 31. 1704 William Strickland Appr. to m' Peter Hall 14 : 10

To m' : Nathaniel Hughes to go in y[e] : great Eliz :

April 5	Eliz : Cooper of Hanforth Spinst : in Cheshire	24 :	4
5	Ann Lingard of M[cc]lesfield in Cheshire	24 :	4
5	Mary Williams of Holywell Spinst	16 :	5
5	Mary Lawrence of Liverpoole Spr	24 :	4
5	Ann Bowland of Chester Spr	20 :	4
22	Hanna Croswell of Livrp Spr	22 :	4
M' 5	Thomas Hughes of Walton [ ]withems	15 :	5

To m' William Par[t]

		age	years
July 15. 1704	Marth' Wilson of Macclesfield in Cheshire Spinst	21 :	5
Aug[t] 1. 1704	Jane Richson of Workington in Cumberland Spinst	25 :	5
Aug[t] 10: 1704	Jane Miller of Macclesfield in Chestr Spinst	22 :	5
10 : 1704	Ralph Langley of Tamouth[100] in Warwyckshire	16 :	4
10 : 1704	Elizabeth Meakin of Dublin Spins[t]	16 :	5
19 : 1704	Jane Clements of Dublin Spinst	21 :	4
7b 11 : 1704	Elizabeth Butler daughter to Eliz : Watkinson of York Widow ℘ her Mother Consent	8 :	12
11. 1704	Eliz : Watkinson herself	27 :	4

7b. 13 : 1704 To [ ] Blundell Esq ; & sent to his Broth.' m.' Rich[d] Blundell in Virgin.' and hee went in y[e] Ship wth W[m] Part. J[no] Blundell of Crosbie Parva 20 : 7

8b. 17 : 1704 Jonath' Tapley of Norley in Cheshire Taylor to m' Low 22 : 5
To m : Joseph Parr.

9b. 16. Eliz : Actin of Tunbridg Spinstr (in Kent 18 : 4

To m' : J[no] Lancst'

16 : 9b. 1704 Richard Berrey of Dalton in Lancashire 16 : 7

---

[100] Tanworth.

20: 9b. 1704 To m' : Thom' : Leekenber
Thom : Dickinson of or near Leeds in Yorkshire 15 : 6

---

to m' Jno Bamster
age year
Decemb. 18. 1704 Ann Wainwright of Farnworth 20 : 5

To m' : Ezekiel Parr
Decembr 20. 1704 Mary Woolley of Bishops Castle in Shropshire 26 : 4
ead die Kath' Woodier of Rigat in Surrey 24 : 4

To m' Wm Williamson for acct of m'. Johnson
xb. 27. 1704 Mary Mills of Leeke[101] in Shropshire 16 : 4
ead Die Grace Robinson of Heptonstall in Yorkshire 21 : 4

To Aldm : John Cockshutte
xb. 28. 1704 Hannah Bridg of Manchester Spinster 20 : 4
30 : Kath Arch-Deacon of Bramhall town in ye County of Kilkenny In Ireland Sp. 19 : 4

To Aldm : Richd Houghton
xb. 30. 1704 Jno Bonns of Oustan in ye County of Lincoln Taylor

---

To m' : Thomas Williamson age
Janu : 5. 1704 Roger Finch of Standish House[102] Carpenter 45 : 4
ead die Wm Finch of ye same and son to Roger Finch 16 : 7

To mr : Randle Platt.
Thomas Taylor of Liverpoole 14 : 7

To m' Jno Wright
April 27. 1705 Jno Aspinwall son of Henry Aspinwall of Ashton in ye County of Lancast to S : xprnos[103] or any other of ye Char'ybbee Islands age 17 time 4

To m' : Edward Rochdale
Ap. 27. 1705 Eliz : Parker Daughter of Thomas Parker late Bolton in Yorkshire 20 – 5
May 1. 1705 Hannah Hewitte of Heplinsdale in Yorkshire spinster 21 – 4
ead die Ann Booth[104] of Bradford in Yorkshire spinster 16 – 4
ead die Mary Heywood of Great Newton in Staffordshire 18 – 5

[101] Lake.
[102] Is this Standish Hall in the parish of Standish?
[103] St. Christopher.
[104] At Bradford: Ann, dau. of James Booth of Heaton, bapt. 29 Dec. 1689. Ann, dau. of James Booth of Shipley, bapt. 30 Dec. 1689. James Booth and Ann Pollard m. 7 Feb. 1688-9.

May 22. 1705	Ellen Holme[105] of Manchester in ye County of Lanc Spinst	19 – 4
June 1 : 1705	Mary Cooper of Prescott in ye County of Lanc Spinst	17 – 6
5 :	Jane Stewart of ye City of London Spins^t	14 : 6
14	Ellen Croston of Westhoughton in ye County of Lanc Spins^t	17 – 5
18 :	Isabel Jones of Rigland[106] in Wales Spinst^r	25 : 4
20 :	Roger Son of Roger Prestidge of Manchs^t in ye County of Lanc	15 : 7
21 :	Thomas Hough of Middle Hilton[107] in ye County of Lanc	14 – 7
27 :	Kath' : Langdon of Whittle in ye County of Lanc	21 – 5
July 3 :	Ann Brown of Leland in Lancashire	21 – 5
3 :	Mary Heap of Blackbourne in Lancashire	21 – 5

To m' : Joseph Preem

7b. 11	Mary Thornton of ye Parish of Stoke in Cheshire Spins'	17 – 6
7b. 11	James Brown of Sheilds in Northumberland	17 – 6
7b. 8	Joannah Meredith of Much-wenlock in Shropshire Spn	21 – 5
7b. 8	J^{no} Hughes of Langadwin in Montgomeryshire in Wales	14 – 7

To m' : Henry Smith to ye Charybbee Islands Virgin' or Maryland.

9b. 3. 1705	Thomas Mere of Hulton in ye County of Lancas^r husbandm'	5 –16

To m' : Edward Tarleton j^r

9b. 27. 1705	Wm Smethurst al Hilton[108] of Middleton in ye County of Lancas^t & Son of Andrew Hilton Husbandm	14– 7
9b. 29. 1705	Jane ye Daughter of Henry Ellison of West Derby husban'	17– 5
xb. 8. 1705	To M' : J^{no} Marsden Edwd Ashton of Winwyck Parish	21– 4
xb. 10. 1705	To M' Wm Tarleton Thomas Whalley of Middleton	15– 7

To Thomas Fawsette

xb. 6. 1705	Lawrence Cockshutte of Ecclesell in Lancashire Fustian Weaver	20– 5

[105] Ellen, dau. of John Hulme, Shrewfold, bapt. 26 Dec. 1684 at Didsbury, in the parish of Manchester.

[106] Raglan.

[107] Middle Hulton.

[108] Andrew Hilton of Middleton had eleven children b. betw. 1668 and 1689, when there is a break in the records until 1695. He was bur. 25 Feb. 1696-7. This emigrant was b. abt. 1691. He may have been a son, legitimate or illegitimate, of the above. Andrew, son of William Hilton, bapt. 6 Aug. 1643 at Middleton.

	To m' Henry Schofield in Potomock in Maryland	Age	Years
9b. 21. 1705	Jno Lucas of Eccles in Lancash' Webster	17 :	5
28	Thom' : Hayes of Huddersfield in Yorkshire Chandlr	30 :	4

To m' Jno Smalwood

9b. 9. 1705	Jn Millard in Wedgberry[109] in Staffordshr Nailr	14 :	7
8 :	George Lord of Tatnell[110] in Cheshire White Cooper	30 :	4
6 :	Jno Bradburd of Bradley near Frodsh' in Chesh'	22 :	5
7b. 3	Jno Walmesley of Lievsay in Lancast' husband'	13 :	7
was returnd' 3	Sam̄l Berrey of Aston in Cheshire Husband	13 :	7
18	Francis Vandery of Colchestr' in Essex husb'	18 :	6
18	Jno Bricknell of Colches' hus'	20 :	6
18	Jno Bow of Colchest husb'	19 :	6
3	Thom' : Chaddock of Pendleton Pole husband	12 :	7
Janr 4	To m'. Jno Marsden, but m' : Smalwood pays for them. Jonathan Heendrey of Eccls Parish	14 –	9

1705 Memo. That when Mr Thomas Preeson went in ye ship called ye Augustine but now called ye Thomas and Elizabeth, hee owd me for drawing the 4 Lad Indentures ; and three shillings six pence besides.

To m'. Jno Wright

Jan'. 4. 1705	Wm Roberts of Beau mauris Shoomaker pd	21 –	4

To m'. Matthias Gibson

Jan'. 4. 1705	Jno Taylor of Bedford in ye County of Lancst Agd. pd	16 –	5

To m'. Jn Crane 22d 9b 1705

	James Woods of Derby in Derbyshire aged — to be allowed on Acct	12 –	9

To m'. Ralph Wmson Jan 4. 1705

	Ellen Roberts near Holywell Spinst	19 –	4
	Ann Whitacre near Clitherou	21 –	4
	Eliz : Dene [of] Great Sankey	27 –	4

Janr 19. 1705	John Hougland of Kelson[111] in Cheshire to mr Jno Periesel for Virgin or ye Charybben	16 :	5

	To m'. Hugh Patten	Age	Years
Janu' 22d 1705	Jacob Jackim of Haughton in ye County of Chester	15 –	8
Jan'. 22. 1706	Adam Mosley of Mackelesfield Forrist in Cheshire	15 –	8

109 Wednesbury(?).
110 Tattenhall.
111 Kelsall(?).

To Mr John Percivall Febr 2 : 1705

Febuy ye 21^{t} Robt Harrison[112] of Bretherton in Lanc aged about Fifteene yeares to serve in y^{e}: Plantations for Seaven Yeares

---

Feb : 2 : 1705

To Mr Thomas Amery Ellen Low of Hay near Wigan aged about sixteene yeares to serve in Virginea or Maryland seaven Yeares p^{d}

March 6 1705/6 Margtt Cholmondeley of Coat Cales in Lansh' p^{d} ag^{d} 20 7 yeares

---

Feb : ye 5 : 1705

To Mr William Oliver, Elizabeth Brookes of Bridgwater in Somersetshire aged about Thirty Yeares to serve in Virginea or Maryland for Fowr Yeares p^{d}

Ditto Die

To Wm Oliver Sarah Needham of Buxton in Darbishire aged about 19 Yeares to Serve in Virginea or Maryland for 4 Yeares.

To Mr Lancaster

		Age	Time of Service Yeares
Feb.	Elizab Stanley of Leverpoole Spinst aged	26	– 7
1705	Mary Winstanley[113] of Upholland in y^{e} : Co : Lanc'	17	– 5
	Elizabeth Yeoman of Anglesey in Wales	20	– 5
	Alice Crompton of Freckeleton in Lanc'	25	– 5
	Elizabeth Fauster of Samsberry[114] in Lanc'	21	– 5
	Mary Greenhalgh of Chorley in Lanc'	15	– 5
	Ann Greenhalgh of Chorley in Lanc'	20	– 5
	Ellen Bradshaw[115] of upholland in Lanc'	14	– 7
	Annas Liniare of Leverpoole in Lanc'	30	– 4
	Ellen Leed of Sawick[116] in Lancashire	26	– 5
	Jane Vexon of Houghton in Lanc	16	– 5
	Sarah Reed of Wrixham in Wales	20	– 5
	John M^{ck}Gee of Scotland	15	– 5

Margaret Griffith aged about Eleven years of Carnarvanshire to serve 7 Yeares to Mr Lancaster or Assignes

---

To Mr Ralph Williamson

Age	yeares of Service

[112] Robert Harrison, "son of a Beggar Woman," bapt. 17 Apr. 1692 at Croston, part of which parish was Bretherton.

[113] At Upholland, parish of Wigan: Mary, dau. of James Winstanley of Winstanley, bapt. 23 Dec. 1684. Mary, dau. of John Winstanley of Orrall, bapt. 11 Jan. 1690. John, s. of John Winstanly of Orrell, bapt. 1 May 1664.

[114] Samlesbury.

[115] Eline, dau. of John Bradshaw of Upholland, Senior, bapt. 16 July 1692 at Upholland.

[116] Salwick.

February 1705	Ann Cuquith of prescot in Lancashire	22	4
	Dorithy Davies of Denby in Wales	20	4
	To Mr Edward Tarleton		
February 1705	Ralph Banckes of Bold in Lancashire	14	7
	Robert Evans and Ann his wife of Dodleston Cheshire		4
March 6 1705/6	Georg Robinson of Astick in Yorkshire	13	6
6	Thom' Hill of Hollingworth in Lancash	16	7
21	Wm Fallar of or near Chedel in Cheshir	17	5
23	Ralph Collier of Rochdale Cloathworker	25	4
	To m' Tho: Dutton Narrgat'		
March 23. 1705/6	Jane Platt of Sropenhall[117] in ye: County of Chestr Singlewoman	18	7
ead die	Martha Platt of ye: same place Single'	14	8
ead die	James Platt of ye: same	12	9
April 6. 1706	Eleoncr Holford of Croton in Cheshire	15	6
February 1705	To mr Parr and Worthington		
	Ellen Sedden		
	Robert Benson		
	Michl Hogg		
	Alex Orrell		
	Alice Steele		
	Alice Monding		
	Ann Chandler		
	Ellen Pierson mem'd Sarah Mere		
	Mary Worrall		
	To Mr Jno Lancaster Ann Cooke of Wales aged about 18 yeares to serve 5 years.		
February 1705	To Mr Ezekiel Parr	age	Time of Service years
	Margaret Tongue of Manchester Spinster	19	5
	Ellen Taylor of Mchester	19	5
	Margtte Roberts of Merionetshire in Wales		5
	Mary Thornton of Stanney in Cheshire	18	5
	Prudence Smalwood of Malpus in Cheshire	20	5
	To m' Tho: Williamson Mercht		
March 26. 1706	Roger ye son of James Rigby of Heay in ye County of Lan'	11	8
March 26. 1706	To mr: Jno Smalwood w': goes in ye: Jno & Thomas) Wm Sharples[118] of Lealand in ye: County of Lancst Taylor	25	4

[117] Plainly so in the original, but probably meant for Gropenhall.

[118] At Leyland: William, s. of Roger Sharples of Leyland, bapt. 30 Nov. 1679. Roger Sharples and Anne Fareclough, both of Leyland, m. 18 Dec. 1677.

March 28. 1706 to m' Thom' Williamson
Jonath' Delnow of Trafford in ye County of Chester pd 11 - 9

To m' Wm Everard
April 1t 1706 Tho: Edge Son of Thom': Edge of Milton Green in Cheshire pd 16 - 7

To m' Georg Battersly
April 12. 1706 Thom': Brown of Mansfield in Nottinghamshire pd 15 - 7

To Capt Tarlet
April 15. 1706 Wm Lucas of Worseley in Eccls Parish in Cheshire pd 19: 4

To m' Jno Tunstall
April 18. 1706 Elizabeth Brining of Samsbery[119] in Lancashir 17: 7
Ann Harrison of Frodsham in Cheshire 18: 7
Wm Robinson of Wimerley[120] near Garston in Lacast 17: 7
Apr'. 22. 1706 Richd Glouer 22: 7
April 27. 1706 Mary Greaues of Halton in Cheshr Singlewoman 27: 7
Ann Whalley of Broughton in Lanc. 23: 7
Ann Kerchin of Scazbricke 26: 7
29. 1706 Ellen Fisher of Wrightlington 18: 7

To Thomas Johnson Esqr: for ye use of ye Ownrs
June 21. 1706 of Richard Rogerson of Bunbery in Cheshire pd age 18 Time 07

To m' Thom' Woodward
July 20th 1706 Ambrose Wynne of Mould in Flintshire 20: 06

To m': Gilbert Lievsay, p Capt Edward Rochdale
July 16 Thomas Jackson of Millam in ye: County of Cumberland Taylo' 18: 04
Augt 3 Jane Lievsay of Samsbury[121] in ye: County of Lancst Spinst 20: 05
6. Mary Taylor of Burnley in ye: County of Lancsr Spinstr 17: 05
8. Jane Williams of Denbigh in Wales 29: 04
7b. 9. Elizabeth Willson of Ellell in ye County of Lancastr Spinstr 19: 05
16. Rowland Evans of Lang Gelly[122] in Wales Age 12: 07
8b. 3. Ellis Davies of Reabban[123] near Wrexham in Wales 20: 04

[119] Samlesbury.
[120] Wimbersley.
[121] Samlesbury.
[122] Llangwyllog.
[123] Ruabon.

8. Eliz: Eccleston of Polton in Lancashire Spinst[r] 20: 05
14: Joannah Meredith of Much Wootton in Shropshire Singlewom' 22: 05
15. J[no] Jordan of Sheffield in Yorkshire pd 15: 08

To Capt[t] J[no] Wright for Virgin', Maryland, or any of y[e] Charybbee Islands — age yeares

December 9 1706 Tho: English of Cresleton[124] in Cheshire 14 7

To m': Andrew Moore or Manchs[t] Jan'. 25. 1706 — Age Yeares

William Dale son of James Dale Late of Manches[t] Taylor 15 5

Tho: Morley Son of W[m] Morley late of Walden in Kent Brickmk[r] 16 – 5

John Heyes Son of George Heyes of Manchester Schoole Mast[r] January y[e] 28th 1706 p[d] 15 – 5

To M[r] Thomas Hughs of Liverpoole Jan[r] 28 1706

Roger Ellors of Rochdale a father and Motherless Child 14 – 7

John Walker of Cockerham, a Fatherless Childe 12 – 9

John Grene of [ ] 14 – 7

Margaret Jones of Holiwell in Flintshire 16 – 7

These 4 Serv[t] were bound p Ad[m] J[no] Clievelands order to m': Thomas Hughes and the charg[e]. (being Twenty shillings) place[d] to s[d] Ald[m]. Clievelands Acc[t]:

---

21. xb: Margtte Smith of Lowton 16 – 5
21 ib: Mary Brown of Langton 19 – 5

To m': Thomas Williamson Merch[t] Febr: 4: 1706

Rebeccah Shaw[125] of Macclesfield in y[e] County of Chest[r] 20 5

Aarron Thornley[126] of Macclesfield p' 15 – 6

To m' Georg Tyrer Janu'. 4. 1706. Rob[t] Dixon of Ulfall[127] in Cumberland 16 – 7

Feb. 12. 1706 Thomas Wild of Polton Taylor 20 – 5

12: 1706 Gilbert Periew[l] Son of James Periew[l] of Lymme Cheshire 15 – 7

To m': J[no] Molyneux Merch[t] Edmund Atherton of Bolton Smith 20: 4

---

[124] Christleton.

[125] At Macclesfield: Rebecca, dau. of Edward Shaw of Crooked yard, bapt. 11 Mar. 1671–2. Rebecca, dau. of Samuel Shaw of Macclesfield Forest, bapt. 7 May 1672.

[126] Aaron, son of John Thornley of Macclesfield, bapt. 6 May 1691.

[127] Ulpha.

Feb. 21st 1706 Mr Andrew More of Manchester
Mary Williamson Daughter of Samll Williamson late of Manceser 15 – 6

Feb. 27. 1706
To m' Thomas Preem Kather' Robinson of Wrexham Denbyshire 20 – 5
Martha Lloyd of Wrexham pd 20 – 5
March 17. 1706/7 To m': Anthy Booth Jno Davies of Wrexham in Denbyshire but to serve in a sloop or to ye: Charybbees 17 – 5
Wm Robinson Son of Tho: Robinson late of Dunfreeze in Scotl' 18 – 5
Henry Wainwright Taylor Son of Jno Wainwright late of Rainhill pd 18 – 4

March 21. 1706/7 to m Georg Duddell, Wm Leatherland of Sutton Weaver 20 – 7

Alice Leech[128]

EMIGRANTS FROM ENGLAND.

Transcribed by GERALD FOTHERGILL, Esq., of New Wandsworth, London, England, and communicated by the Committee on English Research.

THE following lists of emigrants were discovered by Gerald Fothergill, Esq., of London, England, among Treasury Records in the Public Record Office, Chancery Lane, London, and were secured for REGISTER publication by the Society's Committee on English Research. The lists comprise about six thousand names.

PORT OF LONDON, 11 TO 18 DEC. 1773.

Name	*Age*	*Occupation*	*From*	*Ship*	*To*	*As a*
Thos Ramsey	17	Gentleman	Edingboro	Eagle	Jamiaca	Planter
John Harlow	30	"	London	Aiadne	Dominica	"
Willm Thomas Esqr	—	refused to give any answer				
W. H. Ricketts	19	Gentleman	Southampton	Esther	Jamiaca	Planter
H. Ferguson	20	"	Aberdeen	"	"	"
Will Clark	22	Baker	Surrey	"	"	for Employment
Will Shillingford	18	Gentleman	Hertfordshire	"	"	going to his Father
M. A. Warwall	32	Bookkeeper	London	La Soy Plant	Dominica	for Employment
John Hill	24	Baker	"	Elizabeth	Virginia	Indented Ser^{vt} for four years
Willm Smith	42	Taylor	Surry	"	"	" " " " "
Willm Morgan	31	Husbandman	Dublin	"	"	" " " " "
Thos Weatherley	21	Edge tool Maker	Kent	"	"	" " " " "
S. Wetherell	31	Bricklayer	Lincolnshire	"	"	" " " " "
Thos Hanham	21	Plaisterer	London	"	"	" " " " "
John Turner	25	Cordwainer	"	"	"	" " " " "
Edwd Deneau	45	Schoolmaster	Eaton	"	"	" " " " "
John Howard	25	Smith	Surry	"	"	" " " " "
Aaron Palpernan	29	Bookkeeper	Bucks	"	"	" " " " "
John Carry	24	Stone Mason	Fifeshire	"	"	" " " " "
Willm Emmins	27	Husbandman	Lincoln	"	"	" " " " "
Thos Sewell	22	Bookkeeper	Westminster	"	"	" " " " "
Tho's Draper	22	Silk Dyer	London	"	"	" " " " "

Sam[l] Young	21	Cordwainer	Westminster		Virginia	Indented Ser[vt] for four years
Will[m] Wingfield	30	Husbandman	Berks	“	“	“ “ “ “ “
Will[m] Howard	26	Schoolmaster	Worcester	“	“	“ “ “ “ “
Rob[t] Hoggart	21	———	———	“	“	“ “ “ “ “
Rob[t] Dellemore	22	Brazier	London	“	“	“ “ “ “ “
Chas Taylor	41	Bricklayer	‘	“	“	“ “ “ “ “
Thos German	26	Schoolmaster	Ireland	“	“	“ “ “ “ “
Lewis Bryant	22	Plaisterer	Bath	“	“	“ “ “ “ “
Rob[t] Bagwell	23	Schoolmaster	Westminster	“	“	“ “ “ “ “
Will[m] Rice	26	Husbandman	Essex	“	“	“ “ “ “ “
John Saunders	42	Perukemaker	London	“	“	“ “ “ “ “
James Demsay	21	Husbandman	London	“	Virginia	“ “ “ “ “
John Low	23	Blacksmith	Herts	“	“	“ “ “ “ “
Tho's Williams	30	Labourer	London	“	“	“ “ “ “ “
Geo Clark	18	Stocking Weaver	Gloucestershire	“	“	“ “ “ “ “
Edw[d] Pemberton	30	Blacksmith	Stafford	“	“	“ “ “ “ “
Pat[k] Reiley	25	Husbandman	Ireland	“	“	“ “ “ “ “
James Major	27	Butcher	“	“	“	“ “ “ “ “
Tho's Stape	21	Woolcomber	Somerset	“	“	“ “ “ “ “
Isaac How	24	Husbandman	Suffolk	“	“	“ “ “ “ “
Jn[o] Sangster	21	Carpenter	Reading	“	“	“ “ “ “ “
Jn[o] Patterson	22	Gardener	Aberdeen	“	“	“ “ “ “ “
Jas Lambert	21	Gardener	Middlesex	“	“	“ “ “ “ “
John Asher	28	“	Edingboro	“	“	“ “ “ “ “
Jas Whitehead	27	Cordwainer	“	“	“	“ “ “ “ “
Thos McKoin	28	Schoolmaster	London	“	“	“ “ “ “ “
Will[m] Merssey	23	Husbandman	Bucks	“	“	“ “ “ “ “
Will[m] Gunn	32	Husbandman	Sunderland	“	“	“ “ “ “ “
Bar[w] Walker	28	Sawyer	Bucks	“	“	“ “ “ “ “
Geo Lambert	25	Cordwainer	Westminster	“	“	“ “ “ “ “
Benj[m] Richards	35	Mast Maker	Deptford	“	“	“ “ “ “ “
John Orpwood	25	Joyner	Oxford	“	“	“ “ “ “ “
Rich[d] Miller	21	Necklace Maker	London	“	“	“ “ “ “ “
Thos Thairjames	21	Bookkeeper	“	“	“	“ “ “ “ “
Peter Westphal	24	Husbandman	“	“	“	“ “ “ “ “
Terence McDonald	30	Painter	“	“	“	“ “ “ “ “
John Thornber	35	Peruke Maker	“	“	“	“ “ “ “ “
Cha's Watson	23	Baker	Surry	“	“	“ “ “ “ “

Name	*Ag*	*Occupation*	*From*	*Ship*	*To*	*As a*
Bem^{n} Edwards	22	Bro^{d} Cloth Weaver	Somersetshire	Elizabeth	Virginia	Indented Ser^{vt} for four years
Thos Borden	21	Husbandman	Nottingham	"	"	" " " " "
Willm Allison	18	Labourer	London	"	"	" " " " "
Tho's Turtle	21	Husbandman	Cambridge	"	"	" " " " "
Willm Boyle	26	Husbandman	Ireland	Virginia	"	" " " " "
Jno McCloud	28	Labourer	London	"	"	" " " " "
Alex^{d} Nuir	21	Weaver	Scotland	"	"	" " " " "
Robt Ogelvie	19	Husbandman	London	"	"	" " " " "
Robt Tuder	18	Leather dresser	"	"	"	" " " " "
John Oakeley	19	Peruke Maker	"	"	"	" " " " "
Jno Weatherfield	20	Blacksmith	"	"	"	" " " " "
Jno Leek	17	Whitesmith	Worcester	"	"	" " " " "
Jno Onwin	17	Baker	Greenwich	"	"	" " " " "
Thos Pemberton	20	Bricklayer	Chester	"	"	" " " " "
John Welch	31	Malster	Surry	"	"	" " " " "
Thos Wood	23	Schoolmaster	"	"	"	" " " " "
Jos^{h} Stevenson	25	Carpenter & Joyner	Westminster	"	"	" " " " "
Benj^{m} Smith	24	Bricklayer	"	"	"	" " " " "
John Yeates	24	Weaver	"	"	"	" " " " "
Arch^{d} Obrian	24	Butcher	Dublin	"	"	" " " " "
Benjn Parrott	32	Carpenter	London	"	"	" " " " "
John Garth	39	Sawyer	"	"	"	" " " " "
Willm Parker	22	Edge tool Maker	Deptford	"	"	" " " " "
Richd Thomas	36	Haberdasher	London	"	"	" " " " "
John Dawson	22	Ostler	Surry	"	"	" " " " "
Thos Howard	28	Surgeon	London	"	"	" " " " "
Elizabeth his Wife	23		"	"	"	" " " " "
Willm Fogg	23	Blacksmith	Warwickshire	"	"	" " " " "
Willm Kilman	23	Blacksmith	Scotland	"	"	" " " " "
Richd Harris	35	Gardener	London	"	"	" " " " "
Jno Ockershanson	25	Baker	"	"	"	" " " " "
Ja's Jameson	21	Husbandman	"	"	"	" " " " "
Jno Carl Ketler	21	Taylor	"	"	"	" " " " "
Peter Cagaux	26	Cooper	"	"	"	" " " " "
Alex Chesailler	21	Hatter & Painter	"	"	"	" " " " "

John Young	21	Blacksmith	"	"	"	" " " " "
George Dane	33	Cabinet Maker	"	"	"	" " " " "
Jos Cheauvant	20	Gilder	"	"	"	" " " " "
Peter Auber	26	Dyer	"	"	"	" " " " "
Peter Challe	23	Blacksmith	"	"	"	" " " " "
Chas Disbonne	30	Taylor	"	"	"	" " " " "
Peter Macquet	34	Locksmith	"	"	"	" " " " "
Beate Lowis Pack	28	Farmer	"	"	"	" " " " "
Willm Ashburne	28	Cutler	"	"	"	" " " " "
Thos Hill	35	Schoolmaster	Essex	"	"	" " " " "
Anto Chevaillier	21	Brickmaker	Westminster	"	"	" " " " "
Willm Burgess	34	Weaver	London	"	"	" " " " "
Sarah Harris	21	Sempstress	"	"	"	" " " " "
Henry Brandes	33	Cordwainer	"	"	"	" " " " "
Jos Isaac	19	Perukmaker	"	"	"	" " " " "
Antho Lawrence	36	Cabinet Maker	"	"	"	" " " " "
Jas Flemming	26	Husbandman	Cornwall	"	"	" " " " "
Jas Campbell	26	Attorney	London	Westerhall	Grenades	Lawyer

Port of Liverpool, 11 to 18 Dec. 1773.

James Chaffers	33	Gentleman, Merchant	Wales	St. Peter	Jamaica	To Trade
John Smith	20	Gentleman Merchant	London	" "	"	" "
Elizabeth White	28	Lady	Jamaica	" "	"	going to her husband
Two black Girls	25	Slaves	"	" "	"	Servt to Mrs White

Pill a Creek to the Port of Bristol, 11 to 18 Dec. 1773.

Willm Jones	50	Merchant	Bristol	Indian King	Tobago	to Merchandise

Port of London, 18 to 25 Dec. 1773.

Frederick Faber	23	Merchant	London	Simond	Grenades	to settle at the Grenades
James Dowling	43	Sadler	Jamaica	Mary	Jamaica	going back to his home
George Johnson	15	Gentleman	Edinbourg	Augustus	Jamaica	to settle in Kingston
John Fairar	16	Clerk	London	London Merchant	Nevis	going as a Clerk
Sarah Crooke	25	Lady	"	Dorsetshire	St. Kitts	going to her husband
Samuel Hunter	20	Merchant	"	"	" "	to settle as a planter

Name	*Age*	*Occupation*	*From*	*Ship*	*To*	*As a*
Edm[d] Elsegood	24	Merchant	London,	Dorsetshire	St. Kitts	to settle as a planter
George Ewang	19	Carpenter	Edingbourg	Greyhound	Dominica	to get employment
Rob[t] Young	32	Carpenter	"	"	"	" " "
Peter Donaldson	33	Mason	"	"	"	" " "
Thos Mitchell	23	Blacksmith	"	"	"	" " "
Thos Gordon	17	Bookkeeper	Aberdeen	Charming Nelly	Jamaica	to a planter
Peter Spath	29	Sugar Baker	London	London	"	for employment
Thos Leming	27	Gardner	Yorkshire	Britannia	"	" "
Philpot Frusilla	26	Bricklayer	London	"	"	" "
James Bell	24	Stone Cutter	Scotland	"	"	" "
Willoughby Smith	19	Carpenter	Norfolk	Carolina	Virginia	Indentured Servant
William Durred	15	Husbandman	Isle Ely	"	"	" "
Jos[a] Fish	19	Bricklayer	Bristol	"	"	" "
John Cole	21	Carpenter	London	"	"	" "
John Webb	21	Husbandman	Gloucestershire	"	"	" "
James Smith	23	Bookerkeeper	London	"	"	" "
John Holmes	32	Carpenter	"	"	"	" "
German Campion	29	Sawyer	Derby	"	"	" "
William Fulcher	21	Carpenter	Norwich	"	"	" "
John Goodley	23	Perukemaker	Surrey	"	"	" "
George Craig	27	Gardener	Middlesex	"	"	" "
Henry Coats	37	Taylor	Yorkshire	"	"	" "
Daniel Wellett	27	Schoolmaster	London	"	"	" "
Thomas Barget	26	Taylor	"	"	"	" "
Arthur Raynells	23	Husbandman	Dublin	"	"	" "
John Wright	23	"	London	"	"	" "
William Cartis	25	Carpenter	"	"	"	" "
Henry Spence	25	Tallow Chandler	"	"	"	" "
John Fry	18	Husbandman	Hants	"	"	" "
Edward Price	33	Husbandman	Warwickshire	Susanna	"	" "
William Bowen	20	Bricklayer	Surry	"	"	" "
William Baldwin	22	Carpenter & C[a]	London	"	"	" "
Richard Dennis	24	Husbandman	Worcester	"	"	" "
William Parker	25	Butcher	Surry	"	"	" "
John Grimes	25	Bricklayer	London	"	"	" "

Robert Alfred	22	Husbandman	Devonshire	"	"	" "
John Wigham	23	Gardner	Lancashire	"	"	" "
John Wastenays	20	Bricklayer	London	"	"	" "
Robt Mayo	23	Carver	"	"	"	" "
Page Marsh	28	Weaver	"	"	"	" "
John Palrim	21	Cabinet Maker	"	"	"	" "

PORT OF PLYMOUTH, 18 TO 25 DEC. 1773.

Richd Hobbs	33	———	Plymouth	———	St. Christophers	to reside as a planter
Ann Hobbs his sister		———	"	———	" "	to reside there

PORT OF LONDON, 25 DEC. 1773, TO 2 JANUARY 1774.

James Irwin	22	Physician	London	Nancy	Antigua	to Practise abroad
Charles Hamilton	16	Servant to Mr Irwin	"	"	"	going with his master
William Lewis	27	Attorney at Law	"	West Indian	Jamaica	for pleasure
John Gray	25	Gentleman	"	" "	"	on Business
Sarah Gray	25	His Wife	"	" "	"	" "
Elizabeth Soley	14	———	"	" "	"	to see her friends
Richard Battey	25	Gentleman	"	" "	"	on Business
John Tomlinson	16	No trade	"	Gibbons	Barbadoes	to see his father
Diana Sinclair	21	———	"	Fanny	Jamaica	for Health
Elizabeth Achenhed	13	———	"	"	"	her native Country
Ann Perry	19	———	Wolverhampton	"	"	to see her Relations
Alexand^{r} English	20	No trade	London	"	"	
Robert Jas Cleaton	20	" "	"	"	"	to reside there
Ann Duff	10	a Negro Child	"	"	"	" " "
Samuel Charmichael	10	" " "	"	"	"	" " "
Charles Aberdeen	20	Clerk	"	Reward	Fortold	to a Merchant
Alexander Forfor	20	"	"	"	"	as a planter
John Giles	32	"	"	"	"	" " "
Florence Frett	21	———	"	"	"	" " "
John Cooper	16	———	"	"	"	" " "
Jane Moir	15	Lady	"	"	"	to see her friends
Phœbe Bentley	51	"	"	"	"	" " " "
Ann Frett	22	"	"	"	"	going with her husband
Plunkett	18	Clerk	"	"	"	to a planter

Name	Age	Occupation	From	Ship	To	As a
Robt Gibbs	19	Clerk	London	Reward	Fortold	to a planter
Jno Rennie	25	Clergyman	Middlesex	Unanimity	Georgia	to settle there
John Lane	28	Councellor	Middlesex	Harrott	Barbadoes	to settle there
Thos Barwick	26	Clerk	"	Dominica	Dominica	" " "
J Greme	30	Gentleman	Surry	Fortune	Boston	to see his friends
D Greme	26	Servant	Middlesex	"	"	" " " "
Peter Eglington	24	Mathematical Inst Maker	London	Etty	Maryland	Intented servt for four years
Jas Roddick	26	Groom	Oxford	"	"	" " " " "
Patrick Redmond	21	Labourer	Ireland	"	"	" " " " "
James Benning	25	Baker	London	"	"	" " " " "
John Morien	23	Plasterer	"	"	"	" " " " "
Mathw Holfredshaw	22	Sadler	"	"	"	" " " " "
Edwd Coursey	28	Husbandman	Essex	"	"	" " " " "
Willm Mitchell	28	"	Scotland	"	"	" " " " "
Patrick Allen	25	Bricklayer	London	"	"	" " " " "
George Craggs	25	Husbandman	"	"	"	" " " " "
William Roy	39	White smith	Gloucester	"	"	" " " " "
Edward Wilkins	39	Stone mason	Warwick	"	"	" " " " "
John Ware	23	Labourer	Ireland	"	"	" " " " "
James Sims	35	Bookkeeper	London	"	"	" " " " "
Willm George Stevens	37	Plumber	London	"	"	Indentered servt for for years
Wm Armatage	30	Plasterer	Surry	"	"	" " " " "
Willm Shepherd	21	Husbandman	Wilts	"	"	" " " " "
Walter Simpson	21	Cooper	London	"	"	" " " " "
Geo Lorrimore	21	"	"	"	"	" " " " "
Andrew Malm	23	Labourer	"	"	"	" " " " "
James Stokes	14	"	"	"	"	" " " " "
William Webster	23	Hatter	"	"	"	" " " " "
Tho's Rule	27	Gardener	"	"	"	" " " " "
James Brookes	27	Painter	Somerset	"	"	" " " " "
Willm Jenkins	39	Carpenter	Surry	"	"	" " " " "
Richd Bolton	36	Cordwainer	London	"	"	" " " " "
James Stuard	22	"	Cumberland	"	"	" " " " "
Alexr Stevenson	28	Weaver	London	"	"	" " " " "
Thos Smith	22	Ostler	Middlesex	"	"	" " " " "
John Beardmore	23	Painter	London	"	"	" " " " "

Thomas Harrison	21	Hair Dresser	Licestershire	“	“	“ “ “ “ “
Richard Gervan	18	Labourer	London	“	“	“ “ “ “ “
Thomas Heates	16	Picture frame Maker	“	“	“	“ “ “ “ “
Elizabeth Mosley	20	———	Shewsbury	“	“	“ “ “ “ “
William Luscombe	16	Labourer	Somerset	“	“	“ “ “ “ “
Thomas Clarke	18	Husbandman	Essex	“	“	“ “ “ “ “
Charles Hill	16	Baker	London	“	“	“ “ “ “ “
Thomas Uzzell	17	Gardener	Kent	“	“	“ “ “ “ “
Benjamin Beale	21	Groom	London	“	“	“ “ “ “ “
Lucy Lloyd	20	———	“	“	“	“ “ “ “ “
Susanna Clark	17	———	“	“	“	“ “ “ “ “
Mary Wilkinson	19	———	Southwark	“	“	“ “ “ “ “
Thomas Williams	22	Blacksmith	Monmouth	“	“	“ “ “ “ “
David Raid	19	Weaver	Scotland	“	“	“ “ “ “ “
Robert Hewes	31	Painter	London	“	“	“ “ “ “ “
William Chadwick	24	Labourer	“	“	“	“ “ “ “ “
Edwd Kirkham	22	Gardener	Somerset	“	“	“ “ “ “ “
John Fox	26	Turner	Surrey	“	“	Indentured Servt for four years
Lawrance Bergh	21	Sailmaker	London	“	“	“ “ “ “ “
Joseph Jennings	24	Groom	London	“	“	“ “ “ “ “
John Farrell	25	“	Worcester	“	“	“ “ “ “ “
Evan Guynne	22	Clerk	London	“	“	“ “ “ “ “
Grace Fox	23		Surry	“	“	“ “ “ “ “
Sarah Baldock	23		London	“	“	“ “ “ “ “
Geo Preston	21	Weaver	“	“	“	“ “ “ “ “
John Collins	39	Taylor	Ireland	“	“	“ “ “ “ “
Tho's Kenneday	23	Husbandman	Essex	“	“	“ “ “ “ “
Henry Clayton	36	Schoolmaster	London	“	“	“ “ “ “ “
Geo Young	25	Husbandman	Kent	“	“	“ “ “ “ “
Joseph Powell	25	“	London	“	“	“ “ “ “ “
Thoms Carrol	10	Shoemaker	Ireland	“	“	“ “ “ “ “

PORT OF PLYMOUTH, 25 DEC. 1773 TO 2nd JAN. 1774.

Capt Geo Bruce	35	Engineer I H M Servce	London	Greyhound	Dominica	
Mrs Bruce	30	———	“	“	“	
George ———	15	Mulatto	“	“	“	
Ann Took	21	Servant	“	“	“	

Port of Portsmouth, 25 Dec. 1773 to 2nd Jan. 1774.

Name	*Age*	*Occupation*	*From*	*Ship*	*To*	*As a*
Chas Sharpe Esq	36	Gentleman	St Kitts	Charles Shayse	St Kitts	to superentend his plantations
Mr Horne	26	Surgeon	London	" "	" "	to practise his profession
Mr Frayer	20	Gentleman	Scotland	" "	" "	to Visit his brother at StVincent

Port of Newcastle, 25 Dec. 1773 to 2nd Jan. 1774.

Robt Brown	32	Watchmaker	London	Squirrell	Grenades	In expectation of better business
John Dutton	15	No Employment	Berkshire	Nancy	"	to live with a relation as Clerk

Port of Whitehaven, 25 Dec. 1773 to 2nd Jan. 1774.

Thos Campble	26	Stationer	Penrith	Prince George	Jamaica	to sell Books

Port of London, 2nd to 9th Jan. 1774.

Geo Webb	—	Planter	Nevis	Clytus	Nervis	to settle there
Mrs Webb	—	his Wife	"	"	"	" " "
John Bevell	45	Merchant	Barbadoes	Richmond	Barbadoes	going home
William Bennett	20	Farmer	Worcester	Britannia	St Vincent	to settle there
Joseph Israel	20	Planter	Jamaica	Parnasus	Jamaica	to his plantation
Peter Israel	18	"	"	"	"	" " "
William Israel	17	"	"	"	"	" " "
John Mackay	15	Husbandman	Inveness	Amelia	Philadelphia	Indented Servant
Thos Cannum	17	Weaver	Norfolk	"	"	" "
John Bird	16	Sawyer	London	"	"	" "
Willm Collup	15	Labourer	"	"	"	" "
John Garrett	15	"	"	"	"	" "
Joseph Clark	18	Baker	Yorkshire	"	"	" "
Nathl Banister	15	Bargeman	Westminster	"	"	" "
John Price	18	Weaver	London	"	"	" "
Richd Ham	16	Husbandman	Cornwall	"	"	" "
Richd Kenny	16	"	Kent	"	"	" "
John Cook	15	Labourer	Southwark	"	"	" "

William Cole	16	"	Ipswich	"	"	"	"
Danl Donovan	16	Husbandman	Ireland	"	"	"	"
John King	17	Weaver	London	"	"	"	"
Joseph Harvey	18	"	"	"	"	"	"
Willm Bonner	15	Labourer	"	"	"	"	"
James King	21	Husbandman	Greenwich	"	"	"	"
Edwd Dawkins	29	Printer	London	"	"	"	"
Henry Webber	25	Cordwainer	"	"	"	"	"
John Chapple	16	Brickmaker	"	"	"	"	"
Saml Robinson	16	"	"	"	"	"	"
Willm Page	15	Labourer	Middlesex	"	"	"	"
Richd Griffin	15	Nailer	Worcestershire	"	"	"	"
Tho's Hazlewood	16	Labourer	Norwich	"	"	"	"
Willm Foster	17	"	"	"	"	"	"
John Finch	15	"	"	"	"	"	"
John Jenkins	17	Gardner	"	"	"	"	"
Peter Dominica	17	Joyner	London	"	"	"	"
Joseph Webster	19	Labourer	Norwich	"	"	"	"
James Donovan	27	Husbandman	Ireland	"	"	"	"
Tho's O'Brian	27	"	"	"	"	"	"
John Hayes	26	"	"	"	"	"	"
Patrick O'Brian	25	"	"	"	"	"	"
Willm Skirrey	27	Bricklayer	Middlesex	"	"	"	"
John Berner	24	Taylor	"	"	"	"	"
Willm Spencer	15	Labourer	"	"	"	"	"
Thos Lusby	16	"	Lincoln	"	"	"	"
Tho's Aldin	21	Weaver	Norfolk	"	"	"	"
Willm Gyles	22	Cooper	Southwark	"	"	"	"
John Dradge	24	Weaver	London	"	"	"	"
Henry Soley	27	Heelmaker	"	"	"	"	"
Willm Sworder	26	Husbandman	"	"	"	"	"
Joseph Roe	15	Labourer	"	"	"	"	"
Thos Fred Norton	27	Watchmaker	"	"	"	"	"
Chas Cox	26	Husbandman	Lamberth	Chance	Maryland	"	"
James Norton	25	Labourer	Middlesex	"	"	"	"
Willm Clark	30	Sailmaker	Rotherhith	"	"	"	"
John Fox	21	File Maker	London	"	"	"	"
Willm Barker	22	Bricklayer	Portsmouth	"	"	"	"
Willm Lyons	22	Husbandman	London	"	"	"	"

Name	*Age*	*Occupation*	*From*	*Ship*	*To*	*As a*
Rich[d] Jones	17	Sawyer	Sussex	Chance	Maryland	Indented Servant
James Dixon	25	Stone Mason	Lambeth	"	"	" "
Samuel Johnson	21	Tavern Waiter	London	"	"	" "
Rob[t] Gunnick	21	Labourer	Bristol	"	"	" "
Philip M[c]Donald	31	Perukemaker	London	"	"	" "
Tho's Foster	29	Bricklayer	Epsom	"	"	" "
Edw[d] Stone	20	Plaisterer	Surry	"	"	" "
Thos Clark	33	Stone Mason	London	"	"	" "
Margaret Moore	21	Spinster	Somerset	"	"	" "
Sarah Cripps	25	"	London	"	"	" "
Mary Vidler	23	"	"	"	"	" "
Thos M[c]Kenzie	19	Perukemaker	Edingbourg	"	"	" "
Joseph Jones	35	Printer	London	"	"	" "
Charles Gray	25	Working Goldsmith	"	"	"	" "
Jeremiah Bryant	32	Husbandman	Dublin	"	"	" "
Will[m] Hopkins	33	White Smith	London	"	"	" "
Ann His Wife	33	———	"	"	"	" "
Peter Mair	35	Gardener	Essex	"	"	" "
Edw[d] Broffee	23	Husbandman	London	"	"	" "
James Fenning	21	Brick & Tile maker	Kent	"	"	" "
Tho's Tucker	26	"	Islington	"	"	" "
Thos King	28	Bricklayer	London	"	"	" "
Will[m] French	46	Sailmaker	Cornwall	"	"	" "
John Wright	22	Silk Weaver	London	"	"	" "
Jas Ansley	21	Gardner	"	"	"	" "
Henry Dodson	23	Paper stainer	"	"	"	" "
Edw[d] Kelly	36	Husbandman	Devon	"	"	" "
John Brown	20	Servant	London	"	"	" "
Betty Hughes	21	Spinster	"	"	"	" "
Patrick Manyor	27	Gardner	Essex	"	"	" "
Ann Wilmott	27	Cookmaid	Middlesex	"	"	" "
Michael Burn	17	Husbandman	Essex	"	"	" "
Luke Burn	40	"	"	"	"	" "
Will[m] Johnson	40	Cornwainer	London	"	"	" "
Alex[r] Daniel	15	Husbandman	"	"	"	" "

James Skroger	16	"	"	"	"	"	"
Robt Bennett	24	Harness Maker	"	"	"	"	"
Adam Richardson	21	Skinner	Gloucester	"	"	"	"
Geo Todd	16	Labourer	Rotherhithe	"	"	"	"
James Taylor	32	Husbandman	London	"	"	"	"
John Robinson	30	Perukemaker	"	"	"	"	"
Richa Broadfield	34	Husbandman	Surry	"	"	"	"
Francis Francis	27	Felmonger	Oxford	"	"	"	"
John Lowell	24	Butcher	Bath	"	"	"	"
John Haner	24	"	Buckingham	"	"	"	"
Francis Sim	33	Husbandman	Pool	"	"	"	"
Lewis Vesar	23	Hairdresser	St James's	"	"	"	"
Joseph Reeves	17	Labourer	London	"	"	"	"
Willm Green	15	"	"	"	"	"	"
Hugh Jones	25	Nailer	Ireland	"	"	"	"
James Townsend	24	Copper plate printer	London	"	"	"	"
Giles Hodges	28	Glover	"	"	"	"	"
Caleb Hayes	25	Sawyer	Wiltshire	"	"	"	"
Thomas Stephenson	22	"	Newcastle	"	"	"	"
Richd Hancock	21	Biscuit Baker	Surry	"	"	"	"
James Coward	21	Gardener	Dorsetshire	"	"	"	"
Fergus Newton	24	Fish Hook Maker	London	"	"	"	"
Mary McCullock	17	Spinster	"	"	"	"	"
Dennis Burn	17	Labourer	Ireland	"	"	"	"
John White	35	Cooper	Surry	"	"	"	"
Willm Lovell	34	Coachman	London	"	"	"	"
Geo Holton	21	Weaver	"	"	"	"	"
James Bell	24	Stone Mason	Southwark	"	"	"	"
Mathias Keys	23	Plaisterer	London	"	"	"	"
Jemima Keys	22	Nett hook Maker	"	"	"	"	"
Mary Pether	21	Dairy Maid	Somerset	"	"	"	"
James Lytham	19	Weaver	Middlesex	"	"	"	"

EMIGRANTS FROM ENGLAND.

Transcribed by GERALD FOTHERGILL, Esq., of New Wandsworth, London, England, and communicated by the Committee on English Research.

Name	Age	Occupation	From	Ship	To	As a
PORT OF PLYMOUTH, 2nd TO 9th JANUARY 1774.						
Fredk Corsar Esqe	35	Planter	London	Westerhall	Grenades	to reside there
Mrs Corsar	30	———	"	"	"	" " "
A Child	2	———	"	"	"	" " "
Mary Latham	20	Servant	"	"	"	" " "
Charles OConnor	28	Planter	"	Le Soy planter	Dominica	" " "
Moses Rogers	28	Merchant	"	Lawrent	"	" " "
Alexr Cockburn	30	Planter	"	"	Grenades	" " "
Mrs Cockburn	26	———	"	"	"	" " "
PORT OF PORTSMOUTH, 2nd TO 9 JANUARY 1774.						
Major Russell	35	Gentleman	London	Willm & Elizabeth	Antigua	to settle on his Estate at Virginia
Bertie Antwizle	40	"	Antigua	" " "	"	to supd his plantation
Robert Jefferson	20	"	"	" " "	"	" " "
Mr Kensley	35	"	"	" " "	"	" " "
Mrs Scott	28	———	"	" " "	"	" " "
Mr Hotson	25	Gentleman	London	" " "	"	to survey his Estate
Mr Wilson	24	"	"	" " "	"	to settle his account
PILL A PORT OF BRISTOL, 2nd TO 9 JANUARY 1774.						
Alex Lunningham	41	Factor	Bristol	Dominica a Packet	Dominica	on Business
PORT OF LONDON, 9th TO 16 JANUARY 1774.						
John Bevell	45	Merchant	Barbadoes	Richmond	Barbadoes	going home
William Bennett	20	Farmer	Worcester	Britannia	St Vincent	to settle
Joseph Israel	20	Planter	Jamaica	Parnassus	Jamaica	going to his plantation
Peter Isreal	18	"	"	"	"	These three were inserted in a
William Isreal	17	"	"	"	"	former weeks account

Geo Perry	23	Blacksmith	Staffordshire	Nancy	Musquette shore	to settle
John Smith	17	A Clerk	London	"	" "	as a clerk
William Marshall	50	Mariner Wife & 10 Children	"	"	Maryland	Refused further account
Rev Dan Betvel	40	Clergyman	Essex	"	"	" " "
Rachael his Wife	30	& three Children	"	"	"	" " "
Elizabeth Shenirn	50	Mother to Rachl Betvell	"	"	"	" " "
Joseph Hubbart	40	Merchant	London	"	"	" " "
No. dropped						
Robt Norton	23	Labourer	Shopshire	Trecothick	Grenades	for employment
Willm Hart	22	"	London	William & Mary	Jamaica	" "
John Valantine	23	Watchmaker	Derby	" "	"	" "
George Mayo	35	Merchant	Birmingham	Emerald	Teneriffe	on Business
Richd Powell	21	Carpenter	London	Nancy	Maryland	Indented Servant
Willm Westley	22	"	Surry	"	"	" "
John Knight	26	Blacksmith	Oxfordshire	"	"	" "
Geo Gingley	28	Biscuit Baker	Surry	"	"	" "
Thos McCarty	22	Schoolmaster	Southwark	"	"	" "
James Bailey	31	Bricklayer	"	"	"	" "
William Vaughan	32	Woolcomber	Barnstable	"	"	" "
James Southward	24	Ship Carpenter	Rotherhithe	"	"	" "
Simon Nicholson	41	Husbandman	Middlesex	"	"	" "
Thos Clark	40	"	NewingtonSurry	"	"	" "
Peter Amsley	36	"	Westminster	"	"	" "
John Reed	32	Schoolmaster	Middlesex	"	"	" "
Nathaniel Welch	32	Gardner	Lincolnshire	Friendship	Virginia	" "
Benjm Chapman	21	Labourer	Middlesex	"	"	" "
Isaac Reed	30	Husbandman	Essex	"	"	" "
Fredk Hilliar	27	Carpenter	Brentford	"	"	" "

PORT OF LONDON, 15th TO 23 JANUARY 1774.

James Lawrence Esqre	35	Gentleman	London	Henry	Jamaica	on Pleasure
H.Y.ScrymgerimEsqre	18	"	Scotland	"	"	to Merchandize
David Sirright	20	"	"	"	"	on Business
John Chambers	22	"	London	"	"	" "
Saml Lightfoot	25	Surgeon	"	"	"	" "
Nathl Lambden	21	Bricklayer	Berkshire	"	"	" "
Nathl Webster	20	Gentleman	London	"	"	" "

Name	*Age*	*Occupation*	*From*	*Ship*	*To*	*As a*
Daniel Elder	21	Bookkeeper	Scotland	Assistance	Barbadoes	to see his friends
Alex^{r} Miller	19	“	“	“	“	“ “ “ “
Willm Elder	21	“	“	“	“	“ “ “ “
Willm Wilson	38	Planter	London	Carolina	Carolina	as a planter
Benj^{m} Blackburn	28	Clergyman	“	“	“	to settle there
Robt Rose	20	Planter	“	“	“	as a planter
George Ogier	15	“	“	“	“	“ “ “
Robt Knight	26	“	“	“	“	“ “ “
Henry Chapman	30	Jeweller	“	“	“	to work at his business
Henry Maskal	19	Clerk	“	“	“	as a Clerk
John Williams	30	Cabinet	“	“	“	for Employment
Thos Vernan	22	Silk Throwster	“	“	“	“ “
Peter Milne	28	Talyor	“	Charming Sally	Jamaica	to follow his business
Alex^{r} Perry	25	“	“	“ “	“	“ “ “ “
Charles Smith	27	Gardner	“	“ “	“	“ “ “ “
Nathanel Price	22	Woolen Weaver	Norwich	Peggy	Maryland	Indented Servant
Abraham Angel	27	“ “	“	“	“	“ “
John Stevens	26	Husbandman	Kent	“	“	“ “
Jane Griffiths	23	Housemaid	Middlesex	“	“	“ “
Richd Amott	26	Carpenter	“	“	“	“ “
James Rassey	24	“	“	“	“	“ “
John Lavender	27	Blacksmith	Essex	“	“	“ “
John Bay	24	Silk Weaver	Middlesex	“	“	“ “
Charles Bay	26	“ “	“	“	“	“ “
Edward Hatfield	31	Labourer	Kent	“	“	“ “
Henry Harrod	30	Husbandman	London	“	“	“ “
Joseph Nuttall	36	Silversmith	“	“	“	“ “
James Banning	21	Labourer	“	“	“	‘ “
Lawrence Thompson	25	Weaver	Norfolk	“	“	“ “
Abraham Blouse	20	Husbandman	Essex	“	“	“ “
Stephen Hughes	33	Labourer	London	“	“	“ “
William Harrison	18	Husbandman	Lincolnshire	“	“	“ “
Benj^{m} Taylor	21	Painter	Cambridge	“	“	“ “
Barnaby Scully	22	Weaver	London	“	“	“ “
Richd Humphry	40	Husbandman	Kent	“	“	“ “

Charles White	21	Gardner	London	"	"	"	"
Martha White	21	His Wife	"	"	"	"	"
Thos Wilson	18	Labourer	"	"	"	"	"
John Hudson	20	"	"	"	"	"	"
Daniel Smith	30	"	"	"	"	"	"
James Best	22	"	Berkshire	"	"	"	"
Stephen Cooper	31	Bricklayer	London	"	"	"	"
William Head	23	Cardmaker	"	"	"	"	"
Thomas Hudson	22	Baker	Sunderland	"	"	"	"
Thomas Halyer	36	Paper Maker	Kingston on Thames	"	"	"	"
John Harding	23	Stone Mason	London	"	"	"	"
Thos Hare	21	Weaver	"	"	"	"	"
Thos Hoskins	25	Husbandman	"	"	"	"	"
Saml Stanton	33	Cabinet Maker	"	"	"	"	"
Edwd Smith	34	Labourer	Waterford	"	"	"	"
John Streat	23	Breeches maker	Nottingham	"	"	"	"
Willm Evans	35	Perukemaker	Southwark	"	"	"	"
Robt Whittle	38	"	London	"	"	"	"
James Silver	32	Baker	"	"	"	"	"
John Wall	35	Labourer	"	"	"	"	"
Willm Taylor	21	Groom	Hampshire	"	"	"	"
Saml Batt	22	Labourer	Southwark	"	"	"	"
Peter Notley	27	Tavern Waiter	Dorchester	"	"	"	"
John Norton	30	Malster	Bristol	"	"	"	"
James Harman	20	Taylor	Cambridge	"	"	"	"
John Gaeling	33	Rope Maker	Devonshire	"	"	"	"
George Baker	29	Carpenter	Cheshire	"	"	"	"
John Nichols	23	Shoemaker	London	"	"	"	"
Robt Jones	22	Tobacconist	"	"	"	"	"
Richd Thompson	22	Sawyer	"	"	"	"	"
David Helley	21	Labourer	Ireland	"	"	"	"
Thomas Holmes	29	Servant	London	"	"	"	"
Philip Nevil	24	Husbandman	"	"	"	"	"
Thos Onsman	19	Butcher	Yorkshire	"	"	"	"
John Williamson	18	Labourer	London	"	"	"	"
Maurice Higgins	22	Dyer	"	"	"	"	"
Willm Price	19	Carver & Gilder	"	"	"	"	"

Name	Age	Occupation	From	Ship	To	As a
Alex^{r} Bain	27	Sawyer	Scotland	Peggy	Maryland	Indented Servant
James Baker	27	Tallow Chandler	Yorkshire	"	"	" "
Willm Steward	24	Flax dresser	London	"	"	" "
Francis Musgrave	27	Linen Weaver	"	"	"	" "
Lancelot Taylor	26	Carpenter	Norwich	"	"	" "
George Colton	30	Butcher	Kent	"	"	" "
John Smith	21	Groom	London	"	"	" "
John Summers	24	Blacksmith	"	"	"	" "
Willm Falkner	21	"	Lambeth	"	"	" "
Joshua Andrews	23	Cabinet Founder	London	"	"	" "
Geo Jennings	33	Groom	"	"	"	" "
John Mathews	25	Perukemaker	"	"	"	" "
Elizabeth Smith	25	Servant	"	"	"	" "
John Edwards	16	Cordwainer	Plymouth	"	"	" "
John Parkhurst	26	Weaver	London	"	"	" "
Benj^{m} Spencer	21	Labourer	Surry	"	"	" "
Henry Bateson	23	Carpenter	"	"	"	" "
Lawrence Gaskell	24	Stone mason	Yorkshire	"	"	" "
Joseph Scott	18	Plaisterer	London	"	"	" "

Port of Plymouth, 15 to 23 January 1774.

Sarah Williams S^{r}	42	———	London	Rachael	Grenade	to reside at Grenade
Sarah Williams J^{r}	18	———	"	"	"	" " " "

Pill Port of Bristol, 15 to 23^{d} January 1774.

John Bird	29	Merchant	Bristol	Neptune	Grenade	on Business
John Wllliams	22	Clerk	"	"	"	" "

Port of Falmouth, 15 to 23^{d} January 1774.

				Packet Boats		
Colin Cambell	36	———	———	Le De Spencer	Carolina	No further Account
Fra^{s} J. Pickard	30	———	London	Grenville	Antigua	" " "
Anthony Calvert	50	———	———	"	"	" " "

PORT OF LONDON, 24 TO 30th JANUARY 1774.

Thos Stephenson	30	Merchant	London	Susanna	Jamaica	on Business
Peter McKenzie	20	Planter	“	“	“	to his plantation
Sarah Blyth	30	Spinster	“	“	“	to see her friends
Thos Mills	28	Carpenter	“	Northside Planter	“	to settle there
Catharine Wilson	23	Spinster	“	Hope	“	going to her Mother
Richd Grievely	47	Planter	Sussex	“	“	to his Plantation
Charles Holdsworth	31	“	Jamaica	St. James	“	“ “ “
Willm Weston	21	Gentleman	London	Ashley	“	For pleasure
Henry Cook	17	“	“	“	“	“ “
Adam Obryne	25	“	“	“	“	“ “
Saml Mabletuft	21	Farmer	Durinton Lincoln	Jenny & Polly	Maryland	Indented Servant
George Wild	24	Shoemaker	London	“ “	“	“ “
Thos Harpman	21	Whitesmith	Warwickshire	“ “	“	“ “
Geo Blackham	21	Husbandman	“	“ “	“	“ “
Thos Bowen	23	Brass Founder	London	“ “	“	“ “
John Dogharty	21	Surgeon	Ireland	“ “	“	“ “
Morgan Sweeny	30	Husbandman	London	“ “	“	“ “
Barnaby Baxter	30	“	“	“ “	“	“ “
John Wilherson	39	Sawyer	“	“ “	“	“ “
Richd Aston	21	Footman	“	“ “	“	“ “
James Owen	21	Butcher	“	“ “	“	“ “
William Stroud	21	Cooper	Berks	“ “	“	“ “
John Vowells	22	Schoolmaster	London	“ “	“	“ “
Adam Argent	22	Cordwainer	Essex	“ “	“	“ “
John Hewlett	21	“	London	“ “	“	“ “
Willm Smith	34	Clerk	Salisbury	“ “	“	“ “
Peter Chapman	35	Husbandman	Lincoln	“ “	“	“ “
Willm Savage	18	Footman	Northampton	“ “	“	“ “
Moses Jones	18	Post Chais Driver	Essex	“ “	“	“ “
Thos Payne	28	Husbandman	Herts	“ “	“	“ “
John Burton	21	Gardner	Bedford	“ “	“	“ “
Thos Jones	22	Groom	Salap	“ “	“	“ “
Willm Emerton	28	“	London	“ “	“	“ “
John Lee	35	Cordwainer	“	“ “	“	“ “
James Place	22	Bookkeeper	“	“ “	“	“ “

Name	*Age*	*Occupation*	*From*	*Ship*	*To*	*As a*
John Wier	22	Brass Founder	London	Jenny & Polly	Maryland	Indented Servant
Willm Rolph	22	Cordwainer	Hertfordshire	" "	"	" "
Abraham Berthand	21	Schoolmaster	London	" "	"	" "
John Blackmore	27	Carpenter	Stepney	" "	"	" "
Willm Ayres	25	"	London	" "	"	" "
Geo Ferrer	19	Coopersmith	Deptford	" "	"	" "
Thos Bishop	21	Poulterer	London	" "	"	" "
James Canan	20	Braizier	Lincoln	" "	"	" "
Willm Parker	19	Cordwainer	"	" "	"	" "
James Collins	19	Footman	London	" "	"	" "
John Blaney	29	Cordwainer	Oxford	" "	"	" "
David Cuthbert	19	Brazier	Scotland	" "	"	" "
John Ellison	19	Hatter	Liecester	" "	"	" "
Willm Kumber	18	Painter	Middlesex	" "	"	" "
John Bradford	18	Labourer	London	" "	"	" "
Edmund Carthew	18	Husbandman	Cornwall	" "	"	" "
Geo Hewitt	22	Weaver	London	" "	"	" "
Saml Meakins	29	Cabinet Maker	"	" "	"	" "
John Evans	24	" "	"	" "	"	" "
Thos Smith	29	Husbandman	Stafford	" "	"	" "
Henry Simmonds	22	Weaver	London	" "	"	" "
Geo Field	23	Perukemaker	"	" "	"	" "
Anthony Tapp	27	Smith	Southwark	" "	"	" "
Benj^{m} Paris	37	Weaver	London	" "	"	" "
Joseph Howard	21	Boxmaker	"	" "	"	" "
Willm Arnold	21	Groom	York	" "	"	" "
Richard Payne	27	Footman	Kent	" "	"	" "
Richd Dixon	24	Husbandman	London	" "	"	" "
James Farrell	21	"	"	" "	"	" "
Daniel Goodshalk	22	Ropemaker	"	" "	"	" "
Jeremiah Hooper	39	Husbandman	Gloucester	" "	"	" "
James Robertson	21	Wheeler	Hoxton	" "	"	" "
John Smith	42	Skinner	Surry	" "	"	" "
John Thomas	28	Coachman	London	" "	"	" "
Patrick Coffee	30	Husbandman	Meath	" "	"	" "

Joseph Botheley	22	Taylor	Durham	" "	"	Indented Servant
Willm Deacon	22	Husbandman	London	" "	"	" "
James Belliason	25	Taylor	Middlesex	" "	"	" "
Richd Green	35	Wool comber	Coventry	" "	"	" "
John Hall	22	Taylor	Enfield	Minerva	Philadelphia	" "
Andrew Smith	24	Baker	Stepney	"	"	" "
Robert Stevens	26	"	Kent	"	"	" "
Thomas Brown	22	Weaver	London	"	"	" "
John Sinsgreen	35	Brass founder	"	"	"	" "
John Moody	18	Husbandman	"	"	"	" "
Henry Ray	16	Labourer	"	"	"	" "
John Hall	15	"	Kent	"	"	" "
Edwd Griffis	25	Husbandman	Southwark	"	"	" "
Peter Tiebant	30	Turner	London	"	"	" "
John Freeman	21	Weaver	"	"	"	" "
Ann Tiebant	21	Wife of Peter Tiebant	"	"	"	" "
Margaret Smith	22	Housemaid	Essex	"	"	" "
Dropped						
Christopher Xelander	22	Farmer	London	"	"	" "
Ann Maria Xelander	28	His Wife	"	"	"	" "
Sarah Yoxall	21	Servant	Middlesex	"	"	" "
Elizabeth Addis	24	"	London	"	"	" "
Samuel Hix	16	Cabinet Maker	"	"	"	" "
John Pinsent	16	Cooper	"	"	"	" "
Thos Camp	17	Perukemaker	Surry	"	"	" "
Richd Walton	19	Chimney Sweep	Oxford	"	"	" "
Willm Wade	19	Sawyer	London	"	"	" "
Charles Smith	15	Labourer	"	"	"	" "
John Cannon	18	Tallow Chandler	"	"	"	" "
Thos Harris	19	Labourer	Southwark	"	"	" "
Elizabeth Burdett	18	Servant	London	"	"	" "
Elizabeth Hopkins	18	"	"	"	"	" "
Catharine Reynolds	21	"	"	"	"	" "
Elizabeth Rawlins	19	"	"	"	"	" "
Lionel White	22	Taylor	Suffolk	"	"	" "
Jacob Carter	27	Sawyer	London	"	"	" "
John Heny Hartwig	22	Baker	"	"	"	" "
John Galloway	22	Cooper	"	"	"	" "

Name	*Age*	*Occupation*	*From*	*Ship*	*To*	*As a*
Gallia Galloway	21	His Wife	London	Minerva	Philadelphia	Indented Servant
Mary Lyons	16	Spinster	“	“	“	“ “
Daniel Vautier	22	Silk Throwster	“	“	“	“ “
Patience York	18	Spinster	“	“	“	“ “
Jane Vaughan	19	“	“	“	“	“ “
Catherine Hart	21	“	“	“	“	“ “
Thomas Cook	23	Shoemaker	“	“	“	“ “
Thomas Beard	28	Carpenter	Worcester	“	“	“ “
Alice Beard	27	Wife of the above	“	“	“	“ “
Willm Powell	15	Labourer	Westminster	“	“	“ “
Willm Jefferys	15	“	Southwark	“	“	“ “
Geo Pringle	28	Copper Smith	London	“	“	“ “
Pat^{k} Reilly	22	Husbandman	“	“	“	“ “
Thos Neale	18	Labourer	“	“	“	“ “
Stephen Sanger	40	Gent^{s} Steward	Wiltshire	“	“	“ “
Lydia Powell	21	Housemaid	London	“	“	“ “
John Short	33	Painter	“	“	“	“ “
Richard Willoughby	24	Gent^{n} Servant	Kent	“	“	“ “
Elizabeth Jones	23	Servant	London	“	“	“ “
John Brown	23	Labourer	Ireland	“	“	“ “
John Shepherd	22	“	London	“	“	“ “
Letitia Waters	23	Servant	Coventry	“	“	“ “
Thos Bussey	22	Labourer	London	“	“	“ “
Thos Gray	23	Painter	“	“	“	“ “
Ann Young	24	Servant	Westminster	“	“	“ “
John Hind	40	Cooper	“	“	“	“ “
Richd Whaling	20	Husbandman	Essex	“	“	“ “
James Fellgate	24	Groom	Suffolk	“	“	“ “
Richd Lewis	15	Labourer	Kent	“	“	“ “
Geo Sammony	16	“	Herford	“	“	“ “
James Croix	15	Servant	Essex	“	“	“ “
John Naile	16	Labourer	London	“	“	“ “
Charles Hazletine	16	Labourer	Norwich	“	“	“ “
Joseph Screech	15	“	Devonshire	“	“	“ “
Archilas Parker	15	Silk Weaver	York	“	“	“ “

Catherine Vesal	19	Spinster	London	Minerva	Philadelphia	Indented Servant
Elizabeth Bond	20	“	Southwark	“	“	“ “
Chloe Levingstone	27	“	London	“	“	“ “
James Gillie	21	Joyner	“	“	“	“ “
Thos Hardie	21	Harpsichord Maker	“	“	“	“ “
Lewis Martin	34	Clerk & Bookeeper	“	“	“	“ “
Thos Stewart	18	Wire Drawer	“	“	“	“ “
Thos Hudd	22	Smith	Bristol	“	“	“ “
Joseph Hieatt	18	Baker	Oxford	“	“	“ “
John Thoresby	26	“	Middlesex	“	“	“ “
Willm Evans	40	Carpenter	“	“	“	“ “
James Bailey	22	Gardner	“	“	“	“ “
Robert Taylor	26	Butcher	Portsmouth	“	“	“ “
Willm Rodd	20	Cooper	London	“	“	“ “
Charles Lozum	15	Labourer	Essex	“	“	“ “
James Harper	15	“	London	“	“	“ “
Thos Morpeth	15	Husbandman	Worcester	“	“	“ “
James Bryant	16	Labourer	London	“	“	“ “
John Fitzpatrick	24	Husbandman	Southwark	“	“	“ “
Abraham Andrade	24	Clerk & Bookkeeper	London	“	“	“ “
Robert Davidson	21	Anchor Smith	“	“	“	“ “
George Fisher	36	Cock	“	“	“	“ “
John Raguet	22	Distiller	“	“	“	“ “
Thos Wade	16	Tallow Chandler	Westminster	“	“	“ “
Powell Charbonmir	32	Skinner	London	“	“	“ “
Ann Edwards	18	Servant	“	“	“	“ “
Willm Barrett	16	Labourer	“	“	“	“ “
Tobias Danss	40	Furrier	“	“	“	“ “
John Wiederkum	23	Taylor	“	“	“	“ “
Henry Bennett	23	Gunsmith	Birmingham	“	“	“ “
Willm Pollard	28	Skinner	Southwark	“	“	“ “
Michael McKnally	18	Stone Sawyer	“	“	“	“ “
Willm Reilly	35	Upholsterer	London	“	“	“ “
Lawrance Gorman	23	Cordwainer	“	“	“	“ “
John Moor	21	Frame Sawyer	Worcester	“	“	“ “
Joseph Griffiths	30	Footman	Kent	“	“	“ “
Thos Caraghen	19	Cordwainer	London	“	“	“ “
John George	16	Labourer	Southwark	“	“	“ “

Name	*Age*	*Occupation*	*From*	*Ship*	*To*	*As a*
Alex^{r} Drisdale	19	Smith & Farrier	London	Minerva	Philadelphia	Indented Servant
Willm Bateman	23	Seal Engraver	Westminster	"	"	" "
Mary Parsons	23	Ladys Maid	"	"	"	" "
John Ryland	16	Labourer	Middlesex	"	"	" "
John Penny	28	Clerk & Bookkeeper	Plymouth	"	"	" "
Henry Jones	21	Labourer	Westminster	"	"	" "
Ann Turner	21	Servant	"	"	"	" "
Thos Curtis	24	Silk Dyer	London	"	"	" "
Willm Haslop	22	Painter	London	"	"	" "

PORT OF HULL, 24 TO 30 JANUARY 1774.

Mark Cooke	18	Clerk	Hull	Jamaica Packet	Kingston	Merchants Clerk

PORT OF LONDON, 30 JANUARY TO 7th FEB. 1774.

John Robertson	24	Gardner	Scotland	Jenny	Maryland	Indented Servant
Willm Little	20	Servant	Surry	Pemberton	St. Kitts	to Service
Hugh Duncason	18	Carpenter	Scotland	Friendship	St. Vincents	to settle there
P. W. Birleck	18	Gentleman	London	Pemberton	St. Kitts	" " "
P Folkard	28	Ironmonger	"	"	" "	" " "
J. Padmore	15	Gentleman	"	"	" "	" " "
John P. Schott	30	Gentleman	"	"	" "	" " "
Charles Monro	18	Bookkeeper	"	Capel	Jamaica	for Employment
George McKenzie	17	Bookkeeper	"	"	"	" "
Robt Ware	15	Bookkeeper	"	"	"	to his Uncle
Richard Miller	21	Cooper	"	"	"	to follow his trade

PORT OF PLYMOUTH, 30 JAN. TO 7 OF FEB. 1774.

Sir Fra^{s} Laurent Knt.	40	———	London	Mary	Grenada	to reside at Grenada
Mr Foukett	30	Planter	"	"	"	" " " "
Thos Frith	20	Gentleman	"	"	"	" " " "
And^{n} Whitmore	15	Clerk	"	"	"	" " " "
—— Lambert	30	Servant	"	"	"	" " " "
—— Vanderdy	28	"	"	"	"	" " " "

Pill a Creek Port of Bristol, 30 Jan. to 7th Feb. 1774

John Smith	29	Clerk	Gloucestershire	——	Pensacola	Secretary to Chief Justice at Pensacola
John Williams	27	Seaman	Bristol	——	Jamaica	
Oliver Besley	26	Merchant	Barnstaple	——	"	on Business
Joseph Besley	23	"	"	——	"	" "
George Blackmore	35	"	"	——	"	" "
Thos Colston	29	Blacksmith	Shipton Mallett	——	Philadelphia	for want of Employmt
Lewis Wilson	23	Gentleman	——	——	"	to return home
Thos Stephens	26	Clerk	Willington	——	"	for want of Employmt
John Stephens	24	Sadler	"	——	"	" " " "
John Hew	24	Clothier	"	——	"	" " " "
Twenty three Convicts	—	——	No Particulars Place of Residence	——	Maryland	
Js Webb	24	Mason	Willington	——	"	Indented Servant
Wm Sully	21	Labourer	"	——	"	" "
Jas Skinner	22	"	"	——	"	" "
Thos Bemison	32	Painter	"	——	"	" "
Francis How	30	Labourer	"	——	"	" "
John Roberts	22	Painter	"	——	"	" "
Thos Gillard	21	Labourer	"	——	"	" "
John Pope	21	Labourer	"	——	"	" "
Michael Kenneday	33	"	"	——	"	" "
Wm Proom	21	"	"	——	"	" "
John Holding	26	Brickmake	"	——	"	" "
John Sanders	21	Sawyer	"	——	"	" "
John Garsford	22	Carpenter	"	——	"	" "
John Came	21	"	"	——	"	" "
Thomas Bryant	22	Blacksmith	"	——	"	" "
Thos Neill	22	"	"	——	"	" "
Hewill Lucas	23	Labourer	"	——	"	" "
John Williams	25	Sawyer	"	——	"	" "
John Fullerm	29	Taylor	"	——	"	" "
Francis Wilson	21	Baker	"	——	"	" "
Willm Hall	21	Labourer	"	——	"	" "

Name	*Age*	*Occupation*	*From*	*Ship*	*To*	*As a*
John Wills	30	Labourer	Willington	——	Maryland	Indented Servant
Roger Gayton	26	"	Trowbridge	——	"	" "
Robt Crawford	22	Rope Maker	Bristol	——	"	" "
Benjm Gutling	32	Baker	"	——	"	" "
John Mark	22	"	"	——	"	" "
John Griffiths	22	Labourer	Milford	——	"	" "
Duncan ONeil	24	"	Cork	——	"	" "
Willm Paintin	17	"	Bristol	——	"	" "
Robert Ellenas	25	Maltmaker	Plymouth	——	"	" "
Philip Sullevan	19	Labourer	Cork	——	"	" "
Thos Whittington	16	"	Bristol	——	"	" "
Thos Bourn	18	Baker	Bath	——	"	" "
John Pressett	20	Coachman	"	——	"	" "
Thos Dunkarn	20	Clothier	Salisbury	——	Philadelphia	" "
Willm Blackmore	16	Labourer	"	——	"	" "
John Edwards	20	"	Caumarthen	——	"	" "
Samuel Newman	24	Servant	Bath	——	"	" "
Jacob Cock	20	Labourer	Eaton	——	"	" "
Samuel Taton	15	"	Bridgewater	——	"	" "
Richd Stone	16	"	"	——	"	" "
Levi Deutch	15	"	Bristol	——	"	" "
Thos Kite	15	"	Bath	——	"	" "
Samuel Pearse	12	"	Gloucester	——	"	" "
Owen Robins	18	Wire Drawer	Wells	——	"	" "
John Williams	19	Labourer	Berkeley	——	"	" "
John McGill	29	Servant	Oxford	——	"	" "
John Felting	26	Carpenter	Barnstable	——	"	" "
Henry Stedell	26	Labourer	Wells	——	"	" "
Willm Witherley	27	"	Gloster	——	"	" "

PORT OF FALMOUTH, 30 TO 7 FEB. 1774.

Robt Bogle	50	——	London	Ann Teresa	Grenado	on his business
Robt Henston	—	——	St Vincents	Packet	"	on his return home from a Visit to his friends in England

EMIGRANTS FROM ENGLAND

Transcribed by Gerald Fothergill, Esq., of New Wandsworth, London, England, and communicated by the Committee on English Research

Port of London, 7 to 13 Feb. 1774.

Name	*Age*	*Occupation*	*From*	*Ship*	*To*	*As a*
George James	14	from School	Jamaica	Montague James	Jamaica	going home
Charles James	12	" "	"	" "	"	" "
Willm McNeader	17	Clerk	Scotland	Agnes	Cadiz	As a Clerk
Francis Simpson	22	Glass Blower	Surry	Planter	Virginia	Indenter^d Servant
John Broomfield	36	Stocking Weaver	Hereford	"	"	" "
George Wild	21	Groom	York	"	"	" "
Benj^m Badger	22	Husbandman	"	"	"	" "
Willm Payne	21	Clerk & Bookkeeper	London	"	"	" "
James Sutherland	18	Cordwainer	"	"	"	" "
Edwd Fitzpatrick	31	Surgeon	"	"	"	" "
George Adams	25	Husbandman	Derby	"	"	" "
Willm Coventry	27	Ropemaker	Southwark	"	"	" "
John Connery	40	Perukemaker	"	"	"	" "
Alex^r Burnett	25	Clerk & Bookkeeper	Westminster	"	"	" "
John Tran	20	Carpenter & Joiner	Southwark	"	"	" "
James Packer	20	Founder	London	"	"	" "
Edwd Dougharty	20	Gardner	"	"	"	" "
George Boorer	24	Clerk & Bookkeeper	"	"	"	" "
Fred^k Pampe	22	Watch & Clock Maker	"	"	"	" "
Mark Mitchell	19	Perukemaker	"	"	"	" "
James Owen	21	Bricklayer	"	"	"	" "
Robt Cowdell	17	Stocking Weaver	Leicester	"	"	" "
Law Bagnall	28	Bucklemaker	Birmingham	"	"	" "
John Turner	27	Cordwainer	London	"	"	" "
John Kennelly	21	Bricklayer	"	"	"	" "
Willm Dunn	36	"	Durham	"	"	" "
Roger Nichols	40	Breeches maker	Wilts	"	"	" "
Joseph Ormond	24	Hat Maker	Middlesex	"	"	" "

Thomas Rand	22	Butcher	Ireland	“	“	“	“
William Sibery	17	Weaver	London	“	“	“	“
Peter Cooley	38	“	“	“	“	“	“
Peter Cooley Jur	18	“	“	“	“	“	“
John Cooley	16	“	“	“	“	“	“
Joseph Cooley	12	“	“	“	“	“	“
Robert Innis	23	Groom	Bristol	“	“	“	“
Benjamin Ogle	23	Pipe Maker	Newcastle	“	“	“	“
James Freeman	20	Blacksmith	Northampton	“	“	“	“
Benjm Thompson	27	Clock & Watch maker	London	“	“	“	“
Richd Harris	29	Husbandman	Worcester	“	“	“	“
Daniel Lakeman	22	Cabinet Maker	London	“	“	“	“
Willm Wood	29	Husbandman	Northampton	“	“	“	“
John Harrower	40	Clerk & Bookkeeper	Shetland	“	“	“	“
Thos Ford	32	Carver & Gilder	London	“	“	“	“
John Williams	27	Husbandman	“	“	“	“	“
Joseph Clark	21	Cordwainer	“	“	“	“	“
Charles Avery	38	White Smith	“	“	“	“	“
Thomas Richards	22	Perukemaker	“	“	“	“	“
Edward Lawrance	41	Gardner	Middlesex	“	“	“	“
Thomas Low	17	Cabinet Maker	Chester	“	“	“	“
Mathew Fright	33	Husbandman	Kent	“	“	“	“
Peter Collins	40	Cordwainer	London	“	“	“	“
Alexr Kennedy	38	Cooper	Southwark	“	“	“	“
John Burton	22	Bricklayer	Ireland	“	“	“	“
Henry Newland	22	Silk Weaver	London	“	“	“	“
Thos Rackstrow	38	Taylor	“	“	“	“	“
James Nowland	38	Bricklayer	“	“	“	“	“
Alexr Steward	21	Footman	“	“	“	“	“
Charles Leslie	37	Taylor	“	“	“	“	“
Willm Bradley	34	Tile Maker & Turner	“	“	“	“	“
Peter Woillidge	24	Painter & Glazier	Suffolk	“	“	“	“
Willm Phillips	41	Baker	London	“	“	“	“
John Sanders	15	Husbandman	Essex	“	“	“	“
Jeremiah Stacey	19	Linen Weaver	London	“	“	“	“
Richard Green	35	Farmer	Lincoln	“	“	“	“
Daniel Turner	22	Groom	London	“	“	“	“
John Bateman	23	Clerk & Bookkeeper	Westmoreland	“	“	“	“

Name	*Age*	*Occupation*	*From*	*Ship*	*To*	*As a*
John Goldin	25	Weaver	Wilts	Planter	Virginia	Indenter[d] Servant
Roger Wren	17	Cooper	London	"	"	" "
James Downes	29	Husbandman	"	"	"	" "
John Mitchel	23	Smith & Farrier	Bristol	"	"	" "
Thomas Davis	40	Husbandman	London	"	"	" "
Henry Featson	22	Bricklayer	Southwark	"	"	" "
John Powell	36	Boat Builder	"	"	"	" "
William Hudson	20	Linen Weaver	London	"	"	" "
Samuel Mitchel	24	Cooper	York	"	"	" "
Thomas Progers	23	Cordwainer	London	"	"	" "
Will[m] Salton	42	Gardner	Middlesex	"	"	" "
Harman Heston	44	"	London	"	"	" "
Owen Roberts	18	Labourer	"	Letitia	Maryland	" "
Will[m] Laird	17	"	Middlesex	"	"	" "
James Betts	15	Husbandman	Essex	"	"	" "
Will[m] Rock	15	Labourer	London	"	"	" "
John Hubbard	20	Potter	Norfolk	"	"	" "
Solomon Baker	21	Bricklayer	Salop	"	"	" "
Hugh Walworth	45	Cook & Baker	London	"	"	" "
Lawrance Brook	21	Husbandman	Lancaster	"	"	" "
Robert Williams	22	Slater	Surry	"	"	" "
Henry Kent	25	Cordwainer	Essex	"	"	" "
John Bailey	23	Perukemaker	London	"	"	" "
Rich[d] Browing	21	Sawyer	Southwark	"	"	" "
John Hughes	45	Millwright	London	"	"	" "
John Bale	25	Husbandman	"	"	"	" "
Rob[t] Temple	33	Taylor	"	"	"	" "
Rob[t] Hazlewood	25	Hatter	"	"	"	" "
Alex[r] Ritchie	21	Miller	York	"	"	" "
Edw[d] Harvey	32	Footman	London	"	"	" "
Edw[d] Pound	32	Cordwainer	"	"	"	" "
James Lynch	24	Weaver	"	"	"	" "
Charles Lester	21	File Cutter	"	"	"	" "
Thos Shipton	21	" "	"	"	"	" "
James Needs	21	Brickmaker	Middlesex	"	"	" "

Parker Baker	29	Weaver	Middlesex	"	"	"	"
Thomas Nichols	25	Plaisterer	Herts	"	"	"	"
Richard Brown	27	Footman	London	"	"	"	"
Thomas Crouch	25	Coach Joiner	"	"	"	"	"
William Kerton	21	Hair dresser	Worcester	"	"	"	"
John Hackett	41	Husbandman	Leicester	"	"	"	"
Thomas Howard	28	Dyer	Southwark	"	"	"	"
William Paterson	21	Rope Maker	Northumberland	"	"	"	"
Thomas Arnold	27	Gardner	Herts	"	"	"	"
Samuel Cooper	22	White smith	Middlesex	"	"	"	"
Thomas Fletcher	29	Hair Dresser	"	"	"	"	"
Sarah Crosley	21	Mantua Maker & Milliner	London	"	"	"	"
Mary Williams	23	Spinster	Surry	"	"	"	"
Bridget Nash	25	Mantua Maker	London	"	"	"	"
John Jones	31	Husbandman	Surry	"	"	"	"
Samuel Pheasant	22	Taylor	London	"	"	"	"
William Child	23	Hemp and Flax dresser	"	"	"	"	"
George Long	22	Groom	"	"	"	"	"
James Muttery	23	Coachman	"	"	"	"	"
John Savatier	21	Labourer	"	"	"	"	"
Lewis Cameron	28	Hair Dresser	"	"	"	"	"
Henry Brown	35	Gardner	Kent	"	"	"	"
John Lasey	27	Butcher	London	"	"	"	"
Thomas Aldridge	24	Carpenter	Middlesex	"	"	"	"
William Dancer	21	Cordwainer	London	"	"	"	"
Abraham Vandosme	21	Weaver	"	"	"	"	"
Mary Cooper	29	Girt Maker	"	"	"	"	"
Jane Williams	26	Ladys Maid	"	"	"	"	"
Isabella Haslop	21	Spinster	"	"	"	"	"
James Davis	21	Groom	"	"	"	"	"
David Henderson	21	Husbandman	Lancaster	"	"	"	"
Mathew Ling	21	Groom	London	"	"	"	"
William Tappey	26	Cabinet Maker	Hampshire	"	"	"	"
Henry Ward	36	Cooper	London	"	"	"	"
John Deacon	15	Labourer	Coventry	Mary	Georgia	"	"
Michael Herring	37	Husbandman	London	"	"	"	"
Samuel Roberts	15	Groom	Surry	"	"	"	"
John Norton	21	Watch Engraver	London	"	"	"	"

Name	*Age*	*Occupation*	*From*	*Ship*	*To*	*As a*
John Harkett	32	Carpenter	Surry	Mary	Georgia	Indentered Servants
Richard Owen	40	Taylor	Salop	"	"	" "
John Barrow	33	Husbandman	Chester	"	"	" "
Daniel Dodd	18	"	Suffolk	"	"	" "
Edward Grenville	29	Peruke maker	London	"	"	" "
John Grant	37	Labourer	Scotland	"	"	" "
Richd Argors	16	Weaver	Coventry	"	"	" "
Sarah Finis	22	Spinster	London	"	"	" "
Mary Brooks	21	Mantua Maker	Southwark	"	"	" "
Flora Anderson	25	Singlewoman	Scotland	"	"	" "
Edward Newman	19	Labourer	London	"	"	" "
Stephen Fenn	22	Cabinet Maker	"	"	"	" "
John Humphries	21	Husbandman	"	"	"	" "
John Carver	26	Carpenter	Kent	"	"	" "
Robert Ellis	29	Cabinet Maker	London	"	"	" "
William Wilshire	28	Cooper	"	"	"	" "
John Box	26	Sawyer	Hampshire	"	"	" "
Adam Bennett	30	Husbandman	London	"	"	" "
Robert Cock	25	Turner	"	"	"	" "
James Elmes	18	Husbandman	"	"	"	" "
Alex^{r} Robinson	25	"	Northumberland	"	"	" "
Thos Hughes	21	Lath Render	Southwark	"	"	" "
Thos Driver	26	Cabinet Maker	Middlesex	"	"	" "
Joseph Walter	17	Labourer	Kent	"	"	" "
Donald Steward	18	Husbandman	Scotland	"	"	" "
Robert Lefsley	17	"	"	"	"	" "
Jane Pudeford	21	Spinster	London	"	"	" "
Lydia Wise	21	"	"	"	"	" "
Chesheave Barber	24	Perukemaker	"	"	"	" "
John Sayer	27	Husbandman	Westminster	"	"	" "
James Tawney	37	Labourer	London	"	"	" "

Port of London, 13 to 20 Feb. 1774.

Mark Brady	25	Mariner	London	Rosamond	New York	on Business
Robert Sterling	27	Gentleman	"	Lovely Betsey	Dominica	on Pleasure

Port of London, 20 to 27 Feb. 1774

Roman Schomberg	21	Seaman	London	London	Boston	for better Employment
Thomas Cuckerson	17	Gentleman	"	"	"	for pleasure
Deaphilas Hangmeyer	26	Merchant	"	"	"	going home
William Burgets	40	Gentleman	"	"	"	on Business
Elizabeth Ferguson	17	Spinster	"	Royal Charlotte	Jamaica	going to her friends
Elizabeth Carmicart	19	"	"	" "	"	" " " "
Euphemier Ferguson	16	"	"	" "	"	" " " "
Willm Bentley	15	Gentleman	Surry	" "	"	For Improvement
Willm Willis	17	"	"	" "	"	" "
Richd Nugent	20	"	"	" "	"	" "
John Henderson	25	"	"	" "	"	" "
Willm Wood	60	"	"	" "	"	going home
Mary Ann Morgan	9	Spinster	"	" "	"	" "
Harman Gades	25	Sugar Baker	London	" "	"	going to settle
Mathw Williamson	22	Carpenter	"	" "	"	" " "
Samuel Crowden	22	Grocer	Surry	" "	"	" " "
George Trupe	19	Carpenter	London	" "	"	" " "
George William	40	Perukemaker	"	" "	"	" " "
Alexr Fife	24	Husbandman	Scotland	" "	"	" " "
Willm Forsyth	17	"	Surry	" "	"	for Employment
Willm Scott	21	Malster	Scotland	Margaret & Mary	North Carolina	" "
Margaret Scott	16	Spinster	"	" "	" "	" "
Willm Sim	24	Husbandman	"	" "	" "	" "
Jane Sim	24	Wife of Willm Sim	"	" "	" "	" "
David Marshal	24	Clerk	"	" "	" "	As a Clerk
James Blakswik	21	"	"	" "	" "	" "
Ann Pake	40	———	London	Charlotte	Rhode Island	going to her husband
William Brown	22	Tanner	"	Mary & Elizabeth	Philadelphia	to follow his business
Willm Cropley	33	Husbandman	Norfolk	" "	"	" " "
John Cropley	6	Son to the above	"	" "	"	" " "

Name	*Age*	*Occupation*	*From*	*Ship*	*To*	*As a*
Thomas Bowen	27	Cabinet Maker	London	Mary & Elizabeth	Philadelphia	to follow his business
Penelope Bowen	26	Wife to the above	"	" "	"	with her husband
George Bowen	5	Child to do	"	" "	"	with their parents
William Bowen	1	" " "	"	" "	"	" " "
John Low	24	Ironmonger	Warwick			to follow his business
John Glover	28	Merchant	Yorkshire	Earl Dunmore	New York	to settle
Charles McCloud	19	Gentleman	America	" "	" "	" "
Captn McCeun	30	Mariner	Scotland	" "	" "	" "
James Thompson	25	Gentleman	"	" "	" "	" "
Mr Nichols	33	Clergyman	America	" "	" "	" "
Andrew Sutton	21	Gentleman	Scotland	" "	" "	" "
Charles Anderson	22	"	"	" "	" "	" "
Thomas Wilkins	43	Gentleman	Northampton	Mary Ann	Boston	to settle
Temperance Wilkins	46	Wife to the above	"	" "	"	" "
Ann "	17		"	" "	"	" "
Mary "	15		"	" "	"	" "
Frances "	12	Children to above	"	" "	"	" "
John "	7		"	" "	"	" "
Temperance "	9		"	" "	"	" "
William "	6		"	" "	"	" "
Richard Blencowe	25	Husbandman	London	" "	"	for Employment
Charles Sewell	29	Gentleman	Maryland	Industry	Maryland	" "
Austin Jenkins	27	"	"	"	"	going home
David Wilson	38	Merchant	London	Union	Carolina	on Business
John Machlin	24	Gentleman	Oxford	"	"	to settle
Mary Machlin	23	Wife to above	"	"	"	" "
Lewis Ogier	47	Weaver	London	"	"	" "
Catherine Ogier	40	Wife to the Above	"	"	"	" "
Thomas "	20	Silk Weaver	"	"	"	" "
Lewis "	19	" "	"	"	"	" "
Catherine "	16	Spinster	"	"	"	" "
Lucy "	13	"	"	"	"	" "
Charlotte "	9	"	"	"	"	" "
John "	8	Schoolboy	"	"	"	" "
Mary "	6	Spinster	"	"	"	" "

Peter Ogier	5	Schoolboy	"	"	"	" "
Philip Adams	30	Husbandman	"	Richd Penn	Philadelphia	for better Employment
—— Adams	26	Wife to Above	"	" "	"	" " "
George Phillips	22	Cooper	"	" "	"	" " "
Charles Richardson	23	Gentleman	"	" "	"	to settle
Thomas Richardson	30	Mariner	"	" "	"	for better Employment
Susanna Brown	20	Spinster	"	" "	"	going to service
Paul Brown	24	Servant	"	" "	"	" " "
Richard Fowler	25	Merchant	Jamaica	James Daukins	Jamaica	going home
Mrs Fowler	23	Wife to Above	"	" "	"	" "
John Serogie	28	Planter	"	" "	"	going to his plantation
Dr Chisolm	29	Docter	"	" "	"	going home
Mr Hobkirk	25	Merchant	"	" "	"	" "
Mr Croger Jur	27	Farier	London	" "		" "
Mr Croger	30	Planter	Jamaica	" "	"	" "
Mr White	36	Planter	"	" "	"	" "

PORT OF WHITEHAVEN, 20 TO 27 FEB. 1774.

Willm Bell	40	No Occupation	Westmoreland	Venus	Virginia	to look after Effects
Colquit Haywood	16	Apprentice	Cumberland	"	"	As a Factor

PORT OF PORTSMOUTH, 20 TO 27 FEBRUARY 1774.

Alexander Gordon	44	Planter	St Kitts	Pemberton	St Kitts	Came from St Kitts to settle their affairs and are now returning home again
James Farrell	42	"	"	"	" "	
Mr Burton	38	Gentleman	"	"	" "	
Francis Martin	40	"	"	"	" "	
Honble Edwd Gordon Esqre	46	"	London	Britiannia	Barbadoes	going out one of the councels at Barbadoes
Miss Mandevile	25	Lady to accompany him	"	"	"	

PORT OF LONDON, 28 FEB. TO 7 MAR. 1774.

Jane Taylor	45	Seamstress	London	Geddis	Maryland	going to her husband
David Barnes	46	Mariner	America	"	"	going home

Name	*Age*	*Occupation*	*From*	*Ship*	*To*	*As a*
Elizabeth Barnes	15		America	Geddis	Maryland	Going home
Robert "	12	Children	"	"	"	" "
Margaret "	9		"	"	"	" "
Catharine Cause	36	Seemstress	Yorkshire	Friendship	Musquiteshore	to settle there
John Cause	36	Shoemaker	"	"	"	" " "
John Stokell	26	Mariner	America	Nicholas	New England	to Settle
Charles Thomas	23	Clerk	Westminster	Tobago Planter	Tobago	On Business
Joseph Robley	25	Planter	Tabogo	" "	"	on his plantations
Lewis Cazaley	28	Surgeon	London	Hero	Grenades	to settle there
Peter White	31	Sugar Baker	"	Princess Royal	Frieseland	for Employment
Samuel Samuel	22	Cloaths Man	"	" "	"	" "
Johseph Solomon	19	" "	"	" "	"	" "
William Bowser	22	Merchant	"	Sucess	Boston	to settle
John Foster	40	Farmer	Durham	"	"	" "
David Russel	25	Cooper	Scotland	"	"	" "
John Brown	22	Merchant	London	Randolph	Virginia	" "
William Gattens	26	Carpenter	"	Speedwell	Maryland	for Employment
Jos Browning	36	Taylor	"	"	"	" "
John Brown	22	Cordwainer	"	Geddis	"	Indented servant
William Easun	37	Carpenter & Joiner	"	"	"	" "
Timothy Shean	31	Bricklayer	"	"	"	" "
John Young	18	Farmer	"	"	"	" "
John Gadsby	19	Baker	Lincolnshire	Speedwell	"	" "
Daniel Breplur	19	Bricklayer	Ireland	"	"	" "
John Moore	32	Painter	Surry	"	"	" "
John Edgerler	24	Smith	London	"	"	" "
Joseph Wright	19	Carpenter	"	"	"	" "
William Laws	22	Cordwainer	"	"	"	" "
Robert Shopshire	26	Goldsmith	"	"	"	" "
John Gurney.	25	Miller	Bedfordshire	"	"	" "
Francis Milliner	31	Glaizier	Shropshire	"	"	" "
John Smith	21	Ropemaker	London	"	"	" "
Jacob Lipdry	30	Baker	"	"	"	" "
Jacob Reybolt	45	Husbandman	Surry	"	"	" "
John Busonworth	39	Gardner	Middlesex	"	"	" "

Joseph Bolts	38	Husbandman	"	"	"	"	"
John Low	19	Turner	London	"	"	"	"
Frederick Oyle	22	Calico Printer	Essex	"	"	"	"
William Mondindale	20	Flax dresser	Lincolnshire	"	"	"	"
Samuel Green	26	" "	Denbeighshire	"	"	"	"
Robert Long	21	Jeweller	Southwark	"	"	"	"
Duncan McDonald	28	Carpenter	Hampshire	"	"	"	"
Francis Appleton	22	Ship Carpenter	Middlesex	"	"	"	"
Thomas Collins	32	Cooper	London	"	"	"	"
Richard Mathews	21	Husbandman	Kent	"	"	"	"
William Adams	45	Baker	"	"	"	"	"
Joseph Lewis	24	Clerk	South Wales	"	"	"	"
Thomas Gavin	24	Cooper	London	"	"	"	"
Richard Richardson	18	Clerk	"	"	"	"	"
Robert Lusby	21	"	"	"	"	"	"
Henry Lusby	23	"	"	"	"	"	"
John Snow	46	Gardner	"	"	"	"	"
Henry Hill	38	Carpenter	Westminster	"	"	"	"
John Barnard	24	Founder	Southwark	"	"	"	"
Marsh Sowerbutts	36	Sawyer	Lambeth	"	"	"	"
John Williamson	45	Linen Weaver	Westminster	"	"	"	"
Richard Sweenan	28	Husbandman	Essex	"	"	"	"
Thomas Bovey	27	White smith	Worcester	"	"	"	"
Benjamin Ewans	28	Weaver	London	"	"	"	"
Thomas Collins	28	Carver	"	"	"	"	"
Joseph Hall	23	Copper smith	Southwark	"	"	"	"
John Cahill	33	Black smith	Kent	"	"	"	"
John Pincock	27	Clerk	London	"	"	"	"
Thomas Gordon	23	Bleacher	Edingbourg	"	"	"	"
Thomas Lawrance	33	Gem smith	Essex	"	"	"	"
John Hamilton	21	Flax Dresser	Newcastle	"	"	"	"
Samuel Jacob	20	Taylor	Westminster	"	"	"	"
William Jacque	25	Smith	Scotland	"	"	"	"
Thomas Garthan	19	Cordwainer	Southwark	"	"	"	"
William Freeman	20	Bricklayer	York	"	"	"	"
Joseph Simmons	22	Cordwainer	London	"	"	"	"
Benjamin Fogg	19	Bricklayer	Surry	"	"	"	"
John Casey	21	Baker	London	"	"	"	"

Name	Age	Occupation	From	Ship	To	As a
James Moore	29	Baker	London	Speedwell	Maryland	Indented Servant
Drew Ridley	22	Tallow Chandler		"	"	" "
William Morgan	21	Perukemaker	Surry	"	"	" "
William Bigg	20	Groom & Farrier	London	"	"	" "
Patrick Farrel	38	Schoolmaster	"	"	"	" "
Floyd Evans	45	Sawyer	"	"	"	" "
Henry Crown	43	Watch Case Maker	"	"	"	" "
Robert Johnson	41	Husbandman	"	"	"	" "
George Willis	24	Schoolmaster	"	"	"	" "
William Oakes	23	Glass Maker	"	"	"	" "
Joseph Brittle	28	Glass Maker	"	"	"	" "
James Bird	24	Weaver	"	"	"	" "
John Gaddis	36	Farmer	Surry	"	"	" "
Thomas Dermot	25	Carpenter	"	"	"	" "
John Buck	24	Husbandman	"	"	"	" "
Stephen Winter	21	Lapidary	London	"	"	" "
Thomas Murphy	27	Plaisterer	Ireland	"	"	" "
David Calaghan	24	Hatter	"	"	"	" "
Joseph West	21	Perukemaker	London	"	"	" "
Edward Atmer	25	Tallow Chandler	"	"	"	" "
Austin Cole	20	Bricklayer	Somerset	Mermaid	"	" "
William Tyler	19	Bookkeeper	London	"	"	" "
Joseph Pinte	15	Hair Dresser	"	"	"	" "
William Holkirk	19	Taylor	Northumbland	"	"	" "
James Garton	16	Husbandman	Lancaster	"	"	" "
John Davis	21	Plaisterer & Painter	London	"	"	" "
Joseph Townsend	23	Bookkeeper	"	"	"	" "
Henry Smith	30	Miller	Norfolk	"	"	" "
Luke Sanson	26	Husbandman	Somerset	"	"	" "
George Davison	28	Shoemaker	Southwark	"	"	" "
Robert Hogg	28	Biscuit Baker	London	"	"	" "
John Sewell	29	Grocer	Norwich	"	"	" "
John Landers	28	Silk Weaver	London	"	"	" "
Robert Hooper	22	Sawyer	"	"	"	" "
Joseph Bulgin	28	"	Middlesex	"	"	" "

Joseph Hart	21	Woolcomber	Herts	"	"	"	"
John Wilson	23	Hatter	Southwark	"	"	"	"
James Creighton	33	Smith	London	"	"	"	"
Thomas Watts Osborne	35	Clerk & Bookkeeper	Devon	"	"	"	"
James Wier	23	Blacksmith & Farrier	London	"	"	"	"
John Scott	22	Tinplate Worker	"	"	"	"	"
Andrew Moir	21	Baker	Westminster	"	"	"	"
James Moir	22	Carpenter & Joiner	"	"	"	"	"
John Amsley	46	Sail Cloth Weaver	Scotland	"	"	"	"
Thomas Flice	23	Cordwainer	Southwark	"	"	"	"
George Moore	16	Labourer	Yorkshire	Patient	Virginia	"	"
Stephen Hurst	15	"	Northumbland	"	"	"	"
James Stockier	25	Husbandman	Staffordshire	"	"	"	"
William Payne	33	Husbandman	Norfolk	Betsey	"	"	"
Francis Haywood	24	Baker	Hampshire	"	"	"	"
William French	25	Gardner	London	"	"	"	"
Charles Blechynden	20	Labourer	Essex	"	"	"	"
James Rowlatt	23	Cordwainer	London	"	"	"	"
William Smith	25	Calico Printer	"	"	"	"	"
William Wilson	23	Baker & Confectioner	"	"	"	"	"
Joseph Low	23	Baker	"	"	"	"	"
Robert Everett	21	Taylor	"	"	"	"	"
Jane Withers	21	Spinster	"	"	"	"	"
Henry Morris	27	Husbandman	"	"	"	"	"
John Savage	36	Smith & Farrier	"	"	"	"	"
John Jones	27	Plaisterer	"	"	"	"	"
Stephen Chalk	32	Sawyer	"	"	"	"	"
Richard Yeoman	22	Cordwainer	Southwark	"	"	"	"
John Colman	22	Engraver	London	"	"	"	"
Colin Campbell	42	Labourer	Kent	"	"	"	"
George Binks	22	Painter	London	"	"	"	"
John Chivers	23	Smith & Farrier	Rotherhithe	"	"	"	"
Hugh Wilson	25	Smith	London	"	"	"	"
John Hay	23	Baker	"	"	"	"	"
George Mellers	21	Cordwainer	Middlesex	"	"	"	"
William Smith	20	Baker	London	"	"	"	"
Elizabeth Wilkinson	26	Spinster	"	"	"	"	"

Name	*Age*	*Occupation*	*From*	*Ship*	*To*	*As a*
James Tute	19	Breeches Maker	Ireland	Betsey	Virginia	Indented Servant
Banks Broughton	25	Clerk & Bookkeeper	London	"	"	" "
John Gardner	30	Cordwainer	"	"	"	" "
Francis Mara	23	Breeches Maker	"	"	"	" "
William Symes	21	Sadler	Scotland	"	"	" "

Port of Hull, 28 Feb. to 7 March 1774.

John Smith	29	Farmer	Yorkshire	Two Friends	Nova Scotia	Their Rents being raised so high
Mary "	25	His Wife	"	" "	" "	they cannot live
John "	4		"	" "	" "	Indentered Servant
George "	2		"	" "	" "	" "
William "	1	Children to John Smith	"	" "	" "	" "
Robert Fawceit	30	Sail Cloth Maker	"	" "	" "	going on business as agent
Samuel Pickering	23	Farmer	"	" "	" "	going to seek a better Livelihood
James Leach	27	"	"	" "	" "	" " "
Francis Layton	29	Blacksmith	"	" "	" "	" " "
Elizabeth "	26	His Wife &	"	" "	" "	" " "
Francis "		18 Months Child	"	" "	" "	" " "
John Busfield	30	Farmer	"	" "	" "	" " "
George Hayton	32	"	"	" "	" "	" " "
Anthony Hill	57	"	"	" "	" "	on acc't of his rent being raised
						by Jno Mathews his Landlord
John Willison	36	Carpenter	"	" "	" "	going to seek a better livelihood
John Layton	22	Husbandman	"	" "	" "	" " "
Richard Peck	46	Farmer	"	" "	" "	" " "
William Hodgson	22	Husbandman	"	" "	" "	" " "
John Wilson	46	Farmer	"	" "	" "	" " "
William Ward	24	"	"	" "	" "	" " "
Elizabeth "	22	His Wife &	"	" "	" "	" " "
Moses "		18 Months Child	"	" "	" "	" " "
Robert Appleby	21	Husbandman	"	" "	" "	" " "
William Brown	22	Carpenter	"	" "	" "	" " "

Jane Brown	21	His Wife &	“	“	“	“	“	“ “ “
Jane “	1	Child	“	“	“	“	“	“ “ “
James “	17	Husbandman	“	“	“	“	“	“ “ “
Mary Brown	26	Servant	“	“	“	“	“	“ “ “
John Webster	25	Taylor	“	“	“	“	“	“ “ “
Elizabeth Wrightson	20	Servant	“	“	“	“	“	“ “ “
Tomas Yate	22	Mason	“	“	“	“	“	“ “ “
Thomas Brigs	28	Blacksmith	“	“	“	“	“	“ “ “
John Sedgewick	39	Farmer	“	“	“	“	“	on acc't of his rent being raised
John Routh	22	Husbandman	“	“	“	“	“	going to seek a better livelihood
Thomas Harwood	34	Farmer	“	“	“	“	“	going to seek a better livelihood
George Firth	30	“	“	“	“	“	“	on ac't of their rents being raised
William Parker	31	“	“	“	“	“	“	“ “ “
Mary “	38	His Wife	“	“	“	“	“	“ “ “
John “	3	& Children	“	“	“	“	“	“ “ “
		18 Months	“	“	“	“	“	“ “ “
Jane Harrison	20	Maid servant	“	“	“	“	“	“ “ “
Mary Parker	74	Widow	“	“	“	“	“	going to accompany her Children
John Lumley	23	Husbandman	“	“	“	“	“	to seek a better livelihood
Arnistead Fielding	42	Farmer	“	“	“	“	“	Provision, Rents and every
Elizabeth “	40	His Wife	“	“	“	“	“	necessary of life, being so
John “	15		“	“	“	“	“	very high they cannot sup-
William “	14		“	“	“	“	“	port their family
Nicholas “	12	&	“	“	“	“	“	
Hannah “	8		“	“	“	“	“	
Esther “	5		“	“	“	“	“	
Joseph “	2	Children	“	“	“	“	“	
Richard Bare	26	Butcher	“	“	“	“	“	To seek a better livelihood
William Blinkhorn	33	Farmer	“	“	“	“	“	On account of their rents being
Ann “	29	His Wife	“	“	“	“	“	raised
William “	7		“	“	“	“	“	
John “	4	&	“	“	“	“	“	
Ann “	3		“	“	“	“	“	
Eleanor “	1	Children	“	“	“	“	“	
Abraham Mason	43	Husbandman	“	“	“	“	“	To seek a better livelihood

Name	*Age*	*Occupation*	*From*	*Ship*	*To*	*As a*
Elizabeth Abba	20	Servant	Yorkshire	Two Friends	Nova Scotia	To seek a better livelihood
John Watersworth	43	Farmer	"	" "	" "	on acc't of his rent being raised
Richard Thompson	30	Husbandman	"	" "	" "	To seek a better livelihood
John Bulmer	45	Farmer	"	" "	" "	On account of their rents being
Grace Bulmer	46	His Wife	"	" "	" "	raised by Beilly Thompson
James "	20	Children	"	" "	" "	Esqre their Landlord
George "	14	to	"	" "	" "	
Joseph "	10	John Bulmer	"	" "	" "	
Ann Bowser	60	Shopkeeper	"	" "	" "	To seek a better livelihood
Richard "	29	Farmer	"	" "	" "	On account of their rents being
Ann "	26	Servant	"	" "	" "	raised by William Weddell
Hannah Sterriker	12	"	"	" "	" "	Esqre their landlord
William Routlidge	30	Blacksmith	"	" "	" "	In hopes of a better livelihood
Sarah "	27	His Wife	"	" "	" "	
Diana "	2	&	"	" "	" "	
Joseph "		18 Months. Children	"	" "	" "	
Richard Stavely	30	Husbandman	"	" "	" "	On account of their rents being
Robert "	26	"	"	" "	" "	raised by Willm Weddell
John Linton	28	Butcher	"	" "	" "	Esqre their landlord
Robert Fenby	26	Husbandman	"	" "	" "	"
Andrew Crawford	28	"	"	" "	" "	"
Christopher Harper	40	Farmer	"	" "	" "	"
Thomas Harrison	28	Husbandman	"	" "	" "	"
William Thursby	28	"	"	" "	" "	"
John Wry	23	Weaver	"	" "	" "	"
Pickering Snowden	22	"	"	" "	" "	going to seek a better livelihood
Mary Suggett	40	Widow	"	" "	" "	" " "
Ann "	14		"	" "	" "	" " "
Mary "	12	Her	"	" "	" "	" " "
Christopher "	10		"	" "	" "	" " "
John "	8	Children	"	" "	" "	" " "
William Suggett	18	Husband	"	" "	" "	" " "
Joseph Parker	33	Rope Maker	"	" "	" "	" " "
Elizabeth "	33	His Wife &	"	" "	" "	" " "
William "	2	Child	"	" "	" "	" " "

John Fawceit	29	Farmer	"	" "	" "	On acc't of their rent being raised
Jane Fawceit	23	His Wife	"	" "	" "	" " "
Mary "	4	& Child,	"	" "	" "	" " "
Thomas Andrews	37	Husband	"	" "	" "	In hopes of a better support for himself & family every necessary of life being so dear
Lilley "	37	His Wife	"	" "	" "	
Mary "	7		"	" "	" "	
John "	5	&	"	" "	" "	
Mary "	3		"	" "	" "	
Hannah "	1	Children	"	" "	" "	

Port of Liverpool, Feb. 28 to March 7 1774.

Mary Spencer	19	Ladys Maid	Chester	Sam	Philadelphia	going to settle there & seek for Employment
Mary Bourn	25	Cook	Dublin	"	"	
Sarah Pennington	23	"	Lancaster	"	"	"
Ann Simpson	24	Dairy Maid	Upton	"	"	"
Mary Robinson	20	"	Lancaster	"	"	"
Eleanor Brow	24	Housemaid	Liverpool	"	"	"
Elizabeth Gill	20	"	Liverpool	"	"	"
George Pearson	27	A Miner	Derbyshire	"	"	"
William Carter	25	Farmer	Ulverston	"	"	"
Thomas Jones	29	Smith	Gloucesteshire	"	"	"
George Seddon	25	Barber	Ormskirk	"	"	"
Richard Taylor	25	Merchant	Derbyshire	"	"	"
William Branson	26	Weaver	Yorkshire	"	"	"
Thomas Williams	22	Farmer	"	"	"	"
James Murphy	25	"	"	"	"	"
John Turnley	24	Barber	Lancaster	"	"	"
Henry Taylor	24	Taylor	Yorkshire	"	"	"

EMIGRANTS FROM ENGLAND

Transcribed by GERALD FOTHERGILL, Esq., of New Wandsworth, London, England, and communicated by the Committee on English Research

Name	Age	Occupation	From	Ship	To	As a
PORT OF WHITEHAVEN, FEB. 28 TO 7 MARCH 1774.						
A Melatto Woman	23	a Convict	Cumberland	Cæsar	Virginia	
Charles Turner	53	Mason	Wigtoun	John & Thomas	North America	to follow their business
Charles " Jur	22	"	"	" "	" "	" " "
John Turner	17	"	"	" "	" "	" " "
PORT OF LONDON, 7 TO 14 MARCH 1774.						
William White	40	Merchant	Scotland	Jamaica Planter	Jamaica	on Business
Adam Brander	25	Carpenter	"	" "	"	to follow his business
Adam Sproule	45	Merchant	London	Minerva	Boston	to settle
William Falless	23	Mariner	Boston,England	"	"	going home
James Mellers	28	Whitesmith	London	Kitty & Nelly	Maryland	Indentured servant
John Vaughan	23	Wheelright	"	" "	"	" "
John Alexander Mackay	18	School master	Westminster	" "	"	" "
William Hiorne	26	Tallow Chandler	Surry	" "	"	" "
Joseph Weeden	39	Gardner	Kent	" "	"	" "
Peter Webb	39	Husbandman	Wilts	" "	"	" "
William Beard	24	Cordwainer	Middlesex	" "	"	" "
Edward Fame	21	Husbandman	Surry	" "	"	" "
Thomas Chilcot	25	Cabinet Maker	London	" "	"	" "
Alexander Steel	26	Taylor	"	" "	"	" "
John Flatman	35	Weaver	Suffolk	" "	"	" "
James Conolly	22	Labourer	Surry	" "	"	" "
John Scott	22	Groom	Somerset	" "	"	" "
Mark Malone	27	Cooper	London	" "	"	" "
John Fenning	28	Brick maker	Surry	" "	"	" "
John Wood	18	Husbandman	Northampton	" "	"	" "

Port of Hull, 7 to 14 March 1774.

William Harland	23	Farmer	Yorkshire	Albion	Fort Cumber-	to seek better livelihood
John Coulson	20	"	"	"	land North	" " "
Mary "	20	His Wife	"	"	America	" " "
Jonathan Patison	19	Husbandman	"	"	"	" " "
Nathaniel Smith	52	Farmer	"	"	"	their rents being raised by his
Elizabeth "	52	His Wife	"	"	"	landlord Mr Chapman they
Nathaniel "	22		"	"	"	have made a purchase of some
John "	18	&	"	"	"	land in North America
Robert "	9		"	"	"	
Elizabeth "	7	Children	"	"	"	
Rachael Smith	22	Children to	"	"	"	with their parents
Rachael "	22	Nathaniel Smith	"	"	"	
Mary Veckel	20	Maid Servant	"	"	"	To seek for better Employ^{mt}
Hannah Veckel	20	"	"	"	"	" " "
Charles Simpson	22	Husbandman	"	"	"	" " "
Thomas Scurr	34	Farmer	"	"	"	The advance of his rents by
Elizabeth "	39	His Wife	"	"	"	Fran^{s} Smith Jur Esqre his
Thomas "	9		"	"	"	landlord, he is going to pur-
William "	7	&	"	"	"	chase land abroad
Charles "	5		"	"	"	
Elizabeth "	3		"	"	"	
Alice "	1	Children	"	"	"	
Bryan Kay	28	Farmer	"	"	"	To seek for better livelihood
Dorothy "	42	His Wife	"	"	"	" " "
Robert "	42	His brother	Husbandman	"	"	" " "
Elizabeth "	16		"	"	"	" " "
Hannah "	14		"	"	"	" " "
Sarah "	12	His	"	"	"	" " "
Ann "	9		"	"	"	" " "
Jane "	7	Children	"	"	"	" " "
Anthony Thompson	20	Husbandman	"	"	"	" " "
Ann Atkinson	19	Servant	"	"	"	" " "
Ann Skelton	18	"	"	"	"	" " "
William Kay	20	Sailor	"	"	"	" " "
Joseph Palister	25	Labourer	"	"	"	" " "

Name	*Age*	*Occupation*	*From*	*Ship*	*To*	*As a*
John Atkinson	45	Labourer	Yorkshire	Albion	Fort Cumberland North America	To seek for better livelihood
Frances "	30	His Wife	"	"		" " "
Charles "	6		"	"		" " "
Martha "	4	&	"	"	"	" " "
Michael "	3		"	"	"	" " "
John "	1	Children	"	"	"	" " "
John Reed	26	Husbandman	"	"	"	" " "
George Reed	33	Farmer	"	"	"	on account of his rent being raised by his landlord Thomas Walker
Hannah "	33	His Wife	"	"	"	
Ann "	9		"	"	"	
John "	6	&	"	"	"	" " "
Isabella "	4		"	"	"	" " "
George "	1	Children	"	"	"	" " "
Mary Simpson	25	Servant	"	"	"	to seek a better livelihood
Edward Peckett	11	Husbandman	"	"	"	" " "
Lancelot Chapman	49	Farmer	"	"	"	On account of their rents being raised by the Duke of Rutland so that they could not live
Frances "	42	His Wife	"	"	"	
Thomas "	18		"	"	"	
Rachael "	14		"	"	"	
Frances "	12		"	"	"	" " "
Martin "	10	&	"	"	"	" " "
Ann "	8		"	"	"	" " "
Lancelot "	6		"	"	"	" " "
Hannah "	4	Children	"	"	"	" " "
Mary Harrison	17	Maid servant	"	"	"	To seek for better livelihood
Paul Cornforth	70	Farmer	"	"	"	" " "
Phillis "	68	His Wife	"	"	"	" " "
William Cornforth	34	Farmer	"	"	"	" " "
Mary "	26	His Wife	"	"	"	" " "
Elizabeth "	4	&	"	"	"	" " "
Mary "	1	Children	"	"	"	" " "
Michael Taylor	45	Husbandman	"	"	"	" " "
Ann "	26	His Wife	"	"	"	" " "
Robert Charlton	17	Husbandman	"	"	"	" " "
John Slee	22	"	"	"	"	" " "

Thomas Harrison	24	Taylor	"	"	"	" " "
George Taylor	25	Farmer	"	"	"	" " "
Michael Taylor	23	"	"	"	"	" " "
Giles Pickett	41	Blacksmith	"	"	"	" " "
Mary "	38	His Wife	"	"	"	" " "
James Pickett	16	Children	"	"	"	going with their
John "	7		"	"	"	
Margaret "	5	of	"	"	"	
William "	1	Giles Pickett	"	"	"	Parents
John Savage	40	Labourer	"	"	"	going to seek a better livelihood
Elizabeth "	55	His Wife	"	"	"	" " "
Anthony "	9	Son	"	"	"	" " "
John Dunning	24	Farmer	"	"	"	" " "
John Hill	25	"	"	"	"	" " "
Jane "	28	His Wife	"	"	"	" " "
Thomas "	2	&	"	"	"	" " "
Elizabeth "	2		"	"	"	" " "
Mary "	1	Children	"	"	"	" " "
James Handwick	34	Malster	"	"	"	On account of his rent being
Elizabeth "	24	His Wife	"	"	"	advanced
Edward Fenwick	28	Labourer	"	"	"	going to seek a better livelihood
Robert Appleton	24	Husbandman	"	"	"	" " "
Joseph Stockdale	24	"	"	"	"	" " "
Thomas Lumley	45	Farmer	"	"	"	On account of his rent being
Ruth "	44	His Wife	"	"	"	raised by Mr Knowsley his
Diana "	14	&	"	"	"	Landlord
John "	6	Children	"	"	"	
Thomas Shipley	31	Butcher	"	"	"	To seek a better livelihood
Elizabeth "	25	His Wife	"	"	"	
Sarah "	3	&	"	"	"	
Thomas "	1	Children	"	"	"	
Brian Kay	20	Husbandman	"	"	"	" " "
William Truman	52	Miller	"	"	"	On account of their rent being
Ann "	58	His Wife	"	"	"	raised by Durcan Esqre their
William "	22	Grocer a Son	"	"	"	landlord
John Beys	24	Husbandman	"	"	"	
Sarah Barr	21	Servant	"	"	"	A relation being dead they are
Richard Dobson	72	Gentleman	"	"	"	going to settle their affairs

Name	*Age*	*Occupation*	*From*	*Ship*	*To*	*As a*
William Pipes	49	Farmer	Yorkshire	Albion	Fort Cumber-	On account of their rent being
William "	22	Husbandman	"	"	land North	advanced
Jonathan "	20	"	"	"	America	" " "
John Smith	28	"	"	"	"	" " "
Mary Smith	26	Servant	"	"	"	" " "
George Hunter	40	Farmer	"	"	"	In hopes of making a purchase
John Watson	33	"	"	"	"	" " "
Richard Lowerson	32	Husbandman	"	"	"	" " "
John Johnson	27	Tanner	"	"	"	To seek a better livelihood
Martha "	23	His Wife &	"	"	"	" " "
William "	1	Child	"	"	"	" " "
Henry Scott	27	Husbandman	"	"	"	" " "
Mary "	29	His Wife	"	"	"	" " "
Henry "	3	&	"	"	"	" " "
Catharine "	1	Children	"	"	"	" " "
Charles Blinkey	33	Farmer	"	"	"	On account of his rent being
Sarah Blinkey	33	His Wife	"	"	"	raised by his landlord Jno
Jane "	6	&	"	"	"	Wilkinson
Mary "	1	Children	"	"	"	" " "
William Atkinson	16	Tanner	"	"	"	to seek a better livelihood
William Chapman	44	Farmer	"	"	"	On account of his rent being
Mary "	42	His Wife				raised by his landlord Lord
William "	19					Cavendish & all necessaries
Thomas "	17					of life being so dear
Jane "	15					
John "	13					
Mary "	9	&				
Henry "	7					
Jonathan "	5					
Sarah "	3					
Ann "	1	Children				
Israel Marshall	28	Husbandman				Rents being so high he goes in
						hope to make a Purchase

Henry Hammond	31	Farmer	"	"	"	" " "
Margaret "	27	his Wife	"	"	"	
Henry "	5	&	"	"	"	
Jane "	3		"	"	"	
Margaret "	1	Children	"	"	"	
Tristram Walker	27	Husbandman	"	"	"	To seek a better livelihood
William Robertson	15	"	"	"	"	" " "
Alice Dimond	24	Servant	"	"	"	" " "
Thomas Wilson	50	Joiner	"	"	"	" " "
James Wilson	19	"	"	"	"	" " "
David Bennett	30	Farmer	"	"	"	On account of his rent beingraised by Mr Bulmer his landlord
Mary Bennett	30	Wife of David Bennet	"	"	"	
Henry Charmick	31	Chandler	"	"	"	To seek a better livelihood
John Thompson	32	Farmer	"	"	"	On account of the grate advance of rents & in hopes of Purching
Joseph Thompson	26	"	"	"	"	
Joshua Gildart	48	Husbandman	"	"	"	
Robert Leming	51	"	"	"	"	" " "
Robert " Jur	17	"	"	"	"	" " "
John Gildart	19	"	"	"	"	To seek a better livelihood
Eleanor Harrison	48	Widow	"	"	"	" " "
Miles Ainson	42	Blacksmith	"	"	"	" " "
Mary "	30	His Wife	"	"	"	" " "
Miles "	6	&	"	"	"	" " "
Thomas "	3		"	"	"	" " "
Mary "	1	Children	"	"	"	" " "
Charles Clarkson	19	Husbandman	"	"	"	" " "
Richard Thompson	25	Farmer	"	"	"	Lord Bruce having raised his rent
William Sinton	21	Miller	"	"	"	To seek a better livelihood
Joseph Jacques	28	Farmer	"	"	"	On account of their rent being raised
Elenor Jacques	28	His Wife	"	"	"	
Richard Carter	27	Farmer	"	"	"	" " "
Robert Atkinson	28	"	"	"	"	" " "
Ann "	21	His Wife	"	"	"	" " "
Diana Tatum	25	Servant	"	"	"	To seek a better livelihood
Ralph Sidell	29	Cartwright	"	"	"	" " "

Name	*Age*	*Occupation*	*From*	*Ship*	*To*	*As a*
Ann Weldon	38	———	Yorkshire	Albion	Fort Cumberland North America	going to her husband who is settled abroard
Andrew "	12		"	"		
Elizabeth "	8	&	"	"		
Thomas "	4		"	"	"	
Ann "	1	Children	"	"	"	
Jacob Blackburn	27	Servant	"	"	"	
George Gibson	36	Miller	"	"	"	
Thomas Little	27	Tanner	"	"	"	To seek a better livelihood
Ann "	24	His Wife	"	"	"	" " "
William Winn	27	Farmer	"	"	"	" " "
David Winn	17	"	"	"	"	" " "
Mathew Fenwick	16	Servant	"	"	"	" " "
Mary Lowthier	21	"	"	"	"	" " "

PILL A PORT OF BRISTOL, 7th TO 14th MARCH 1774.

John Perring	22	Weaver	Worcestershire	No account of the names of Ships	Philadelphia	for want of Employment
Thomas Yearsley	33	Silk Dyer	New York		"	To return home
Willm Pearse	33	Farmer	Gloucestershire		"	for want of Employment
Wife & 2 Children	—	———	"		"	" " "
William Eycott & Wife	30	Mason	"		Jamaica	" " "
Alexander Tolme	33	Mariner	Cork		New York	" " "
Benjamine Burrows	26	Shoemaker	New York		" "	" " "
Daniel Williams & Wife	50	Cooper	Wales		" "	" " "
John Carter	30	Servant	Wiltshire		" "	" " "
Thomas Bennett	24	Linen Draper	Worcester		" "	" " "
James Carpenter	18	Carver	Bristol		" "	" " "
James Thompson	32	Cooper Smith	"		" "	" " "
Wife & 4 Children					" "	
George Stacks	23	Clerk	London		Nevis	On Business
Henry Forrest	33	Mariner	Bristol		"	" "
Thomas Rowden	17	Cutler	Birmingham		Philadelphia	Indended Servant
George Butler	17	Brick Maker	London		"	" "
John Crocker	18	Carpenter	Bristol		"	" "

Thomas Fellett	22	Carpenter	Bristol	No account of Ships	"	" "
Philip Mark	21	Servant	Dorchester		"	" "
John Taylor	15	"	Bristol		"	" "
John Burgh	20	Labourer	Exeter		"	" "
Thomas Cartwright	16	"	Worcester		"	" "
Thomas Jones	13	"	Bath		"	" "
Richard Davis	12	"	Bristol		"	" "
Thomas Seaton	16	"	Birmingham		"	" "
William Single	14	"	Bath		"	" "
Mathew McCunn	15	"	Wells		"	" "
Jos Spencer	16	"	London		"	" "
Thomas Marshall	15	"	Bristol		"	" "
John Lutton	17	"	"		"	" "
Richard Snell	13	"	Eaton		"	" "
John Dean	13	"	Oxford		"	" "
John Bartlett	12	"	Wells		"	" "
James Hatchwell	18	"	"		"	" "
William Fry	14	"	"		"	" "
Thomas Jones	18	"	"		"	" "
Thomas Thomas	17	"	Wales		"	" "
Samuel Shepherd	16	"	Worcester		"	" "
William Haile	22	Carpenter	Bath		"	" "
Andrew Taven	32	Labourer	Cornwall		"	" "
William Damead	21	"	Kent		"	" "
James Melvil	29	Taylor	Cork		"	" "
Five Women					"	" "

Port of Liverpool, 7th to 14th March 1774.

William Shakespear	40	Merchant	Yorkshire	Lydia	Philadelphia	To Trade
John Warden	21	"	Manchester	"	"	" "
James Clarke	23	"	Lincoln	"	"	" "
James Fell	34	"	Middlesex	"	"	" "
James Greenough	30	Sugar Baker	London	John	Virginia	" "
John Dunn	30	Farmer	Westmoreland	"	"	" "
Isabella Jackson	25	Servant	"	"	"	" "

Port of Whiteheaven, 7th to 14th March 1774.

Name	*Age*	*Occupation*	*From*	*Ship*	*To*	*As a*
Joseph Bowman	13	No Occupation	Maryland	Betty	Virginia	going to his Friends

Port of Bideford, 7th to 14 March 1774.

Name	*Age*	*Occupation*	*From*	*Ship*	*To*	*As a*
William Sanders	—	Merchant	——	David	Newfoundland to touch at Waterford	No account
Elizabeth Salmon	16	——				
Martin Morris	60	Banker				
William Black	—	Master of a Sloop at Cadiz		——	"	——

Port of London, 14th to 21st March 1774.

Name	*Age*	*Occupation*	*From*	*Ship*	*To*	*As a*
James Walker	50	Blacksmith	Scotland	Bellar	Philadelphia	to settle there
Ann "	50	His Wife	"	"	"	" "
Joseph "	30	Blacksmith	"	"	"	" "
Mary "	28	His Wife	"	"	"	" "
John Lewis	25	Druggist	London	"	"	On Business
John Williams	50	Cooper	"	"	"	" "
Mary Williams	10	His daughter	"	"	"	" "
Samuel Dawes	26	Merchant	"	"	"	To settle there
Richard Hotham	40	"	"	"	"	" "
Elizabeth Morris	22	Servant	"	"	"	" "
John Mayot (or Mayor)	25	Gentleman	Essex	"	"	" "
Charles Constable	13	Gentleman	Middlesex	"	"	" "
Laurance Furlong	40	Sea Captain	London	"	"	" "
Mrs Jones		Captn Jones' Lady	"	"	"	" "
William McPherson	22	Cabinet Maker	"	"	"	" "
Christopher Partridge	34	Mate to Captn Furlong	America	"	"	On his Employ
David Jones	25	Gardner	London	Brilliant	Virginia	Indented servant
John Moore	21	Weaver	London	"	"	" "
William Jones	18	Labourer	Salop	"	"	" "
Jos Usherwood	21	Perukemaker	Northampton	"	"	" "

Martin New	38	Weaver	London	"	"	"	"
William Pedder	24	Baker	"	"	"	"	"
William Barter	41	Painter	"	"	"	"	"
Richard Sewthwait	32	Blacksmith	Essex	"	"	"	"
Peter Purvis	32	Carpenter	London	"	"	"	"
John Augusts Kindon	21	Husbandman	"	"	"	"	"
Thos Hackly	29	Perukemaker	"	"	"	"	"
Thomas Hudson	22	Dyer	"	"	"	"	"
Thomas Evans	36	Joyner	"	"	"	"	"
John Congrave	23	"	"	"	"	"	"
John Dash	36	"	"	"	"	"	"
Charles Matee	26	Silk Weaver	"	"	"	"	"
Thomas Smith	22	Joyner	"	"	"	"	"
James Grant	22	White Smith	"	"	"	"	"
James Purser	21	Weaver	"	"	"	"	"
William Bartholomew	21	Husbandman	"	"	"	"	"
Robert Newson	19	Blacksmith	"	"	"	"	"
Samuel Lewis	18	Taylor	Wilts	"	"	"	"
Thomas Sanders	18	"	"	"	"	"	"
Thomas Forest	24	Schoolmaster	London	"	"	"	"
David Smith	23	Silver Smith	"	"	"	"	"
Isaac Tickner	24	Wheelright	Surry	"	"	"	"
John Knight	25	Whitster	Lancaster	"	"	"	"
Benjamin Fleet	21	Cooper	Surry	"	"	"	"
John Bryant	21	Taylor	Ireland	"	"	"	"
John Cross	19	Baker	Hertfordshire	"	"	"	"
John Merryfield	19	Husbandman	Surry	"	"	"	"
William Flower	21	Baker	Somerset	"	"	"	"
John Grinley	22	Chandler	Salop	"	"	"	"
James Wright	38	Braizier	London	"	"	"	"
Briar Brampton	31	Husbandman	"	"	"	"	"
Samuel Smith	26	Pipe Maker	"	"	"	"	"
Henry Smith	24	Husbandman	Wilts	"	"	"	"
James Lumsden	22	Baker	Scotland	"	"	"	"
Ralph Chillingworth	35	Plaisterer	Oxford	"	"	"	"
Joseph Hutchinson	27	"	London	"	"	"	"
Henry Long	23	Husbandman	Middlesex	"	"	"	"
Thomas Potter	21	Carpenter	Yorkshire	"	"	"	"

Name	*Age*	*Occupation*	*From*	*Ship*	*To*	*As a*
William Grant	24	Groom	Scotland	Brilliant	Virginia	Indented Servant
John Milsteed	22	Butcher	Middlesex	"	"	" "
Charles Giddings	32	Sawyer	Wilts	"	"	" "
Francis Haw	24	Cordwainer	Yorkshire	"	"	" "
Edward Dalton	31	Husbandman	Middlesex	"	"	" "

PILL A CREEK PORT OF BRISTOL, 14th TO 21st MARCH 1774.

Hugh Syle	45	Malster	Bristol	No Account	Maryland	On Business
David Paris	50	Merchant	"	" "	Barbadoes	" "
John James	36	"	Wales	" "	"	" "
John Brisley	28	Farmer	Somerset	" "	Maryland	Indented Servant
John Murtis	18	Shoemaker	London	" "	"	" "
Thomas Simmons	29	Labourer	Gloucester	" "	"	" "
John Sly	18	Barber	London	" "	"	" "
Thomas Lynn	17	Labourer	Shipton	" "	"	" "
James Barrett	25	Shoemaker	Portsmouth	" "	"	" "
Lawrance Caswell	15	Weaver	"	" "	"	" "
Thomas Lawrance	17	Soap Boiler	Bristol	" "	"	" "
Thomas Cooper	21	Weaver	"	" "	"	" "
Richard Samms	22	Clothier	Somersetshire	" "	"	" "
James George	29	"	"	" "	"	" "
James Sealy	22	Brazier	Frcome	" "	"	" "
William Henderson	28	Chandler	"	" "	"	" "
Guy Cole	27	Gardner	Bristol	" "	"	" "
John Witherington	27	Labourer	London	" "	"	" "
Peter Graham	18	"	Warwick	" "	"	" "
One Woman	17		"	" "	"	" "

PORT OF LIVERPOOL, 14 TO 21st MARCH 1774.

Samuel Hawbridge	40	Mercer	Yorkshire	York Packet	New York	To Trade
Jane "	39	His Wife	"	" "	" "	going with her husband

John Hutchinson	30	Farmer	"	" "	" "	To Trade
Margaret "	30	His Wife	"	" "	" "	going with her husband to trade
Francis "	10		"	" "	" "	going with their Parents
Major "	9	&	"	" "	" "	" " "
Margaret "	8		"	" "	" "	" " "
Ralph "	7		"	" "	" "	" " "
Ann "	2	Children	"	" "	" "	" " "
Richard Rowlandson	40	Farmer	"	" "	" "	going to settle there
William Appleby	18	Weaver	"	" "	" "	" "
Ralph Snowden	19	Tanner	"	" "	" "	" "
Richard Gill	40	Flax Dresser	"	" "	" "	" "
Sarah "	41	His Wife	"	" "	" "	" "
Ann "	10	Daughter	"	" "	" "	" "
Richard "	6	Son	"	" "	" "	" "
Ann "	46	Sister	"	" "	" "	" "
Elizabeth Shepherd	36	Mantua Maker	"	" "	" "	" "
Molly "	4	Daughter	"	" "	" "	" "
John "	2	Son	"	" "	" "	" "
Elizabeth Snell	24	Mantua Maker	"	" "	" "	" "
Major "	36	Flax dresser	"	" "	" "	" "
Elizabeth "	1	Child	"	" "	" "	" "
Abraham Copley	22	Blacksmith	"	" "	" "	" "
Sarah Pickler	36	Farmer	"	" "	" "	" "
Nancy "	11		"	" "	" "	" "
Mary "	9		"	" "	" "	" "
Sarah "	6		"	" "	" "	" "
Grace "	1	Children	"	" "	" "	" "
Fanny "	36	Farmer	"	" "	" "	" "
Richard Halliwell	25	Draper	"	" "	" "	" "
Richard Hiton	22	Butcher	"	" "	" "	" "
Thomas Deighton	20	Sadler	Westmoreland	" "	" "	" "
Mathew Hunter	20	Shoemaker	"	" "	" "	going to settle
John Kirkby	29	Flax Dresser	Yorkshire	" "	" "	" "
Ann "	24	His Wife	"	" "	" "	" "
Ann "	4	&	"	" "	" "	" "
John "	2	Children	"	" "	" "	" "

Name	*Age*	*Occupation*	*From*	*Ship*	*To*	*As a*
Benjamin Ambler	45	Farmer	Yorkshire	York Packet	New York	going to settle
Mary "	40	His Wife	"	" "	" "	" "
Ann "	18	&	"	" "	" "	" "
John "	14	Children	"	" "	" "	" "
Sarah Simmer	22	Servant	Ireland	" "	" "	" "
John Hannam	30	Farmer	Yorkshire	" "	" "	" "
James Hannam	45	"	"	" "	" "	" "
Thomas Authwaite	22	"	"	" "	" "	" "
William Daviner	16	"	"	" "	" "	" "
Richard Haste	30	"	"	" "	" "	" "
John Watkinson	18	"	"	" "	" "	" "
William Metcalf	16	"	"	" "	" "	" "
Robert Wilson	16	Flax Dresser	"	" "	" "	" "
James Christ	36	Taylor	London	" "	" "	" "
Richard Wilson	16	Silver Smith	Yorkshire	" "	" "	" "
John Eaton	16	Weaver	Lancashire	" "	" "	" "
William Hunt	22	"	Yorkshire	" "	" "	" "
Charles Stobbs	19	No Trade	"	" "	" "	" "
Thomas Thomson	38	Shoemaker	Westmoreland	" "	" "	" "
Joshua Robinson	12	Butcher	Yorkshire	" "	" "	To settle there
John Cunliffe	27	"	"	" "	" "	" "
John Moon	40	Carpenter	"	" "	" "	" "
James Moon	9	"	"	" "	" "	" "
Thomas Johnson	23	Merchts Clerk	"	" "	" "	" "
Jamas Watfield	22	Shoemaker	Derbyshire	" "	" "	" "
John Wright	41	Farmer	Yorkshire	" "	" "	" "
James Brown	22	Weaver	"	" "	" "	" "
Mary Brown	25	His Wife	"	" "	" "	" "
Jane Coppel	45	Nurse	Manchester	" "	" "	" "
Thomas Giude	23	Jeweller	Staffordshire	" "	" "	" "

EMIGRANTS FROM ENGLAND

Transcribed by GERALD FOTHERGILL, Esq., of New Wandsworth, London, England, and communicated by the Committee on English Research

PORT OF PORTSMOUTH, 14 TO 21st MARCH 1774.

Name	*Age*	*Occupation*	*From*	*Ship*	*To*	*As a*
John Stanley Esqre	34	Sollicitor Genl at St Kitts	London	Loyal Briton	St Kitts	to execute his office at St Kitts

PORT OF LONDON, 21st TO 28th MARCH 1774.

Name	*Age*	*Occupation*	*From*	*Ship*	*To*	*As a*
John Randall	40	Carpenter & Joiner	Gloucestershire	Sibella	Maryland	to settle there
Ann "	30	His Wife	"	"	"	" "
John Gale	25	Gentleman	"	"	"	" "
Robert Bruce	34	Carpenter	Scotland	Amherst	New England	" "
Peter Guesout	25	Merchant	Quebec	Solid Carlton	Quebec	For Pleasure
—— Le Moine	35	"	"	" "	"	" "
Mrs Brown	30	Lady	London	Boston Packett	Boston	to settle there
Mrs Copinsher	30	"	"	" "	"	for her health
Jane Chance	35	Planter	Jamaica	Rochard	Grenada	to settle there
James Rowlands	29	Taylor	London	Venus	New England	" "
Robert Scott	25	Baker	"	"	" "	" "
Edward Dalton	28	Taylor	"	"	" "	" "
Richard Whittle	24	"	"	"	" "	" "
Henry Cole	24	Gardener	Surry	Love & Unity	Maryland	Indended Servant
John Goldsborough	24	"	"	" "	"	" "
John Nichols	26	Clerk & Bookkeeper	London	Molly	"	" "
Jonathan Prinoch	21	Bricklayer	"	Sibella	"	" "
William Martin	36	Cordwainer	"	"	"	" "
Dennis Cormelly	23	Husbandman	"	"	"	" "
James Jacks	19	Baker	"	"	"	" "
William Lewis	33	Husbandman	Westminster	"	"	" "
John Old	16	"	London	"	"	" "
William Chappell	32	Millwright	"	"	"	" "

Thomas Simmons	21	Breeches Maker	"	"	"	" "
James Lawrie	28	Carpenter and Joiner	"	"	"	" "
Edward Bicknall	40	Husbandman	Surry	"	"	" "
Joseph Snook	26	"	"	"	"	" "
Edward Bailey	21	Silver Smith	London	"	"	" "
Benjamin McColley	33	Husbandman	"	"	"	" "
James Wallis	23	Taylor	"	"	"	" "
William Wallis	19	"	"	"	"	" "
Edward Pound	19	Servant	"	"	"	" "
Robert Boyle	21	Husbandman	Kent	"	"	" "
John Pleden	29	"	Gloucester	"	"	" "
William Gover	22	Smith	Surry	"	"	" "
Edward Grant	32	"	Essex	"	"	" "
Andrew Carmichael	26	Gardener	London	"	"	" "
William Gilbert	17	Clerk & Bookkeeper	Norwich	Good Intent	"	" "
James Wiggin	26	Perukemaker	London	" "	"	" "
Abraham Clack	23	Gunsmith	Cambridge	" "	"	" "
William Newcome	18	Blacksmith	Essex	" "	"	" "
Jacob Knight	21	Linen Weaver	London	" "	"	" "
James Day	24	Perukemaker	"	" "	"	" "
Thomas Evans	29	Pastry Cook	"	" "	"	" "
Robert Williams	19	Brick Maker	"	" "	"	" "
Edward Cousins	19	Husbandman	"	" "	"	" "
Andrew Law	27	Clerk & Bookkeeper	"	" "	"	" "
Richard Hill	37	Baker	"	" "	"	" "
William Cashine	33	Servant	"	" "	"	" "
Thomas Gordon	25	Sawyer	"	" "	"	" "
George Webber	21	Husbandman	"	" "	"	" "
Richard Little	21	"	"	" "	"	" "
David Smith	21	Hair Dresser	"	" "	"	" "
Thomas Gibbins	21	Cooper	Northampton	" "	"	" "
James Breverton	29	Locksmith	London	" "	"	" "
James Gwynn	26	Husbandman	"	" "	"	" "
John Thompson	32	Mathematical Inst Maker	Surry	" "	"	" "
Edward Taylor	19	Miller	Lincoln	" "	"	" "
Henry Heitland	20	Clerk	Westminster	" "	"	" "
Hugh Jopp	22	Taylor	London	" "	"	" "

Port of Liverpool, 21st to 28 March 1774.

Name	*Age*	*Occupation*	*From*	*Ship*	*To*	*As a*
John Edward	26	Farmer	Cheshire	Polly	South Carolina	To Farm
Jane "	27	His Wife	"	"	" "	going with her husband
William Simpson	23	Cooper	Lincolnshire	"	" "	To Trade
James Wilson	18	Sadler	Bedfordshire	"	" "	" "
James Clark	42	Butcher	Middlesex	"	" "	" "
William Walker	37	Merchant	Yorkshire	"	" "	" "
Captn Rainford		"	Liverpool	Mary	Jamaica	" "
Wife & 3 Children			"	"	"	
William Williams	22	"	"	"	"	" "
John Thompson	33	"	"	"	"	" "

Pill a Creek a Port of Bristol, 21st to 28th March 1774.

Name	*Age*	*Occupation*	*From*	*Ship*	*To*	*As a*
Richard Wallington	35	Gentleman	Gloster	No account	Philadelphia	On Business
Captn Hughes	40	Late of the 17 Regiment	"	———	"	to return home
John Crew	22	Tanner	"	———	"	On Business
Edward Scandred	21	Butcher	Wales	———	"	" "
Thomas Russell	34	Gentleman	Gloster	———	"	" "
William Andrews	23	Clothier	"	———	"	" "
William Heverd	20	Farmer	"	———	"	" "
William Jones	28	Carpenter	Bristol	———	"	" "
James Butland	35	Weaver	"	———	"	" "

Port of Plymouth, 21st to 28 March 1774.

Name	*Age*	*Occupation*	*From*	*Ship*	*To*	*As a*
John Reading	40	Surgeon	London	Lovely Betsey	Dominica	To reside there
Charles Court	18	Planter	"	" "	"	" "
Alexander Kukan	35	Merchant	"	" "	"	" "
Benjamin Fisher	25	Engineer	"	" "	"	" "
Edward Revely	31	Mariner	"	" "	"	To his ship

Port of Whitehaven, 21st to 28th March 1774.

John Warwick	29	Husbandman	Yorkshire	Ann	Virginia	to seek Employment
Robert Smith	20	"	Scotland	"	"	" "
John Telford	16	"	"	"	"	" "
Alexander Week	16	"	"	"	"	" "
James Boxborough	16	"	"	"	"	" "

Port of Portsmouth, 21st to 28th March 1774.

John Rime	—	Supercago	London	Am	St Kitts	To dispose of the cargo
Mr Richardson	—	Gentleman	Kent	"	"	To Settle there
Mr Rogerson	—	Planter at St Kitts	London	"	"	To his accounts at St Kitts

Port of London, 28th March to 5 April 1774.

William Markham	20	Attorney at Law	London	Mathew	St Kitts	to Act as Attorney
Simon Fraser	17	Clerk	"	"	"	" " Clerk
Thomas Gardner	44	Shoemaker	"	Harmony	Boston	to settle there
Margaret "	43	His Wife	"	"	"	" "
Simon "	16	&	"	"	"	" "
Rebecca "	7		"	"	"	" "
Thomas "	20	Children	"	"	"	" "
James Minns	60	Farmer	"	"	"	" "
James Minns Jur	30	Shoemaker	"	"	"	" "
Andrew Seaton	22	Clerk	Scotland	Industry	Grenades	" "
John Wilden	24	"	London	"	"	" "
John Ambler	35	Yeoman	"	London	Virginia	" "
Sarah "	30	His Wife	"	"	"	" "
John Petty	25	Distiller	"	Friendship	Grenades	" "
Charles Viall	19	Carpenter	Norwich	"	"	" "
William Shermer	71	Yeoman	Wilshire	Arnold	Virginia	to see his Brother
Mary Webster	30	with 3 Children	"	Baltimore	Maryland	going to her husband
Thomas Chipchase	40	Farmer	Durham	"	"	to settle there
Ann "	35	His Wife	"	"	"	" "
Thomas Wriey	21	Carpenter & Joiner	Surry	"	"	Indented Servant
Robert Cockerton	22	Clerk & Bookkeeper	London	"	"	" "

Name	*Age*	*Occupation*	*From*	*Ship*	*To*	*As a*
Thomas Gascoyne	22	Cordwainer	London	Baltimore	Maryland	Indented Servant
Thomas Boot	21	Stone Mason	Nottingham	Diana	"	" "
William Spence	23	Baker	Scotland	"	"	" "
Joseph Deborox	22	Locksmith	Stafford	"	"	" "
David Wood	37	Cordwainer	Scotland	"	"	" "
Timothy Phalon	21	Carpenter & Joiner	Ireland	"	"	" "
John Somerskill	26	Groom	London	"	"	" "
Susanna Lewis	30	Spinster	"	"	"	" "
Esther Mills	23	"	"	"	"	" "
John Sowden	23	Miller	"	"	"	" "
John Miller	26	Footman	Southwark	"	"	" "
Nathl Millington	23	Blacksmith	London	"	"	" "
George Lind	20	Carver & Gilder	"	"	"	" "
John Smith	21	Hair dresser	"	"	"	" "
Eleanor Patrick	21	Servant	Scotland	"	"	" "
Francis Crisp	25	Ship Carpenter	Norfolk	"	"	" "
William Hearnden	22	Stone Mason	Surry	"	"	" "
James Bowen	21	Perukemaker	London	"	"	" "
Thomas Hill	22	White Smith	"	"	"	" "
Edward Johnson	20	Watchmaker	"	"	"	" "
Morris Kaugho	25	Sugar Baker	"	"	"	" "
Sarah Ann Lawrance	22	Mantua Maker	"	"	"	" "
Mary Lawler	20	Servant	Ireland	"	"	" "
Elizabeth Whitsen	19	Mantua Maker	London	"	"	" "
Mary Bowen	21	Wife of James Bowen above	"	"	"	" "
Elizabeth Mansfield	20	Servant	Kent	"	"	" "
Elizabeth Skinner	20	"	London	"	"	" "
Elizabeth Morris	16	"	"	"	"	" "
Francis Suter	20	"	Rutland	"	"	" "
Jane Davis	29	"	London	"	"	" "
Charles Lake	46	Wheelright	Middlesex	"	"	" "
James Hasle	26	Watch & Clock Maker	Derby	"	"	" "
Charles Fincher	30	Sawyer	London	"	"	Indented servants for four five
Peter Ferey	25	Weaver	"	"	"	or six Years
Mary Beveridge	17	Servant	"	"	"	"

Elizabeth Burk	18	"	"	"	"	"
Thomas Salisbury	36	Grocer	"	"	"	"
George Ponay	27	Husbandman	Salop	Baltimore	"	"
John Podvin	21	Cordwainer	Kent	"	"	"
Matthew Fox	21	Butcher	Northampton	"	"	"
Edward Turner	30	Linen Weaver	Ireland	"	"	"
Thomas Bennett	19	" "	London	"	"	"
Joshua Rogers	17	Perukemaker	"	Diamond	"	"
William Biles	18	Husbandman	"	"	"	"
George Brown	18	Footman	Surry	"	"	"
John Goulby	24	Coach Harness Maker	Middlesex	"	"	"
Hugh McCullock	25	Gardener	Surry	"	"	"
William Hart	27	Carpenter & Joiner	Bedford	"	"	"
Robert Baisley	39	Cooper	London	"	"	"
James Weckman	25	Carpenter & Joiner	Surry	"	"	"
Thomas Waller	26	Husbandman	London	Diana	"	"
John Harrison	23	"	Bristol	"	"	"
Emannuel Gonsals	18	Brass founder	London	"	"	"
Samuel Davis	28	Stone Mason	Plymouth	"	"	"
George Reed	16	Tin Man	London	"	"	"
Robert Shaw	21	Baker	Scotland	"	"	"
Joseph Hack	21	Brushmaker	Surry	"	"	"
Thomas Smith	22	Cooper	"	"	"	"
Sarah Clayton	17	Servant	Berks	"	"	"
Esther Smith	16	"	London	"	"	"
Mary Murry	24	"	Kent	"	"	"
Lydia Burn	19	"	Norwich	"	"	"
Samuel Lee	32	Bricklayer	Berks	"	"	"

PORT OF BRISTOL, 28 OF MARCH TO 5th APRIL 1774.

John Donaugho	34	Planter	London	Diana	Dominica	To reside there
Elizabeth "	22		"	"	"	" "
Frederk Eligmear	24	Physician	"	"	"	" "
Campbell Voaux	30	Surgeon	"	"	"	" "

PORT OF NEWCASTLE, 28 MARCH TO 5th APRIL 1774.

Name	*Age*	*Occupation*	*From*	*Ship*	*To*	*As a*
William Elliott	33	Weaver	Sunderland	Molly	New York	for want of Employm^t
Jane Elliott	32	His Wife	"	"	" "	going with her husband

PORT OF LONDON, 5th TO 12 APRIL 1774.

Name	*Age*	*Occupation*	*From*	*Ship*	*To*	*As a*
Edward Salisbury	14	No Trade	London	St Domings	Bilboa	to serve a Gentleman
John Riley	21	Taven Waiter	"	Grate Marlow	Jamaica	to settle there
Thomas Kair	25	Clerk	Ireland	" "	"	" "
Alexander Gowie	23	Carpenter	London	" "	"	" "
Edward Davis	17	Gentleman	"	" "	"	" "
R. Ergesaged	19	Clerk	"	" "	"	" "
William Fryers	30	"	"	" "	"	" "
Jasper Wilson	36	Planter	"	Woodley	St Kitts	going to his plantation
Mary "	25	His Wife	"	"	"	going with her husband
John Winter	28	Carpenter & Joiner	London	Lousia	Maryland	Indented Servants for four & five Years
Edward Barker	24	Locksmith	"	"	"	"
Isaac Hind	32	Husbandman	"	"	"	"
Thomas Liggins	34	Butcher	"	"	"	"
Thomas Mackenzy	29	Husbandman	Ireland	"	"	"
John Teasdale	20	Cooper	London	"	"	"
Thomas Latham	20	Bookkeeper	"	"	"	"
Abraham Baker	17	Footman	"	"	"	"
Richard Patmore	17	Husbandman	Herts	"	"	"
James Molan	17	Taylor	London	"	"	"
Daniel Bloys	18	Footman	"	"	"	"
Edward Gardner	18	Labourer	Kent	"	"	"
Henry Crane	18	"	"	"	"	"
Joseph Carsley	19	Husbandman	Hants	"	"	"
Henry Crunedge	18	Footman	London	"	"	"
Thomas Aldridge	21	Groom	Essex	"	"	"
William Keymer	32	Cook	London	"	"	"
Robert Ringer	27	Carpenter & Joiner	"	"	"	"

John Fry	50	Cordwainer	Bristol	Patuxent	“	“
James Flint	15	Baker	London	“	“	“
William Cock	15	Labourer	“	“	“	“
John Brown	33	Taylor	“	“	“	“
Benjamin Looker	24	Labourer	Surry	“	“	“
James Brown	23	Gardener	London	“	“	“
John Robinson	30	Cordwainer	“	“	“	“
Ann James	21	Servant	“	“	“	“
Lydia Adams	21	“	“	“	“	“
Reuben Styles	40	Weaver	“	“	“	“
Jos Hippesley	16	Gardener	“	“	“	“
William Smith	15	Labourer	“	“	“	“
David Banks	15	“	“	“	“	“
Benjamin Ritchie	23	Clock Maker	“	“	“	“
John Newland	21	Groom	“	“	“	“
John King	21	Husbandman	Berks	“	“	“
Diana Hughes	26	Servant	London	“	“	“
John Rhodes	22	Carpenter	“	“	“	“
Edward Thompson	31	Husbandman	“	“	“	“
Thomas Daniel	21	Coach Maker	“	Stephen	“	“
John Nesbitt	21	Brass Founder	“	“	“	“
Thos Price	40	Stone Mason	“	“	“	“
William Sandlant	21	Groom	Stafford	“	“	“
Benjamin Chamberland	26	Taylor	London	“	“	“

PORT OF SCARBOROUGH, 5th TO 12th APRIL 1774.

Robert Jackson	48	Blacksmith, Wife & 3 Children	Yorkshire	No account of Ships	Nova Scotia	they could not support their families on account of the high Price of Provisions
William Ellis	24	Farmer, His Wife & 1 Child	“	“	“ “	
Thomas Blackburn	28	Farmer, Wife & 2 Children	“	“	“ “	“
John Robinson	40	Farmer	“	“	“ “	Farm being over rented could not support theirselves
John Robinson	41	Farmer, Wife & 6 Children	“	“	“ “	

Name	Age	Occupation	From	Ship	To	As a
Robert Jackson	39	Ploughwright Wife & 3 Children	Yorkshire "	No account of Ships	Nova Scotia " "	To seek for better Employment all nescessarys of life being so dear
Thomas Wilkinson	23	Blacksmith, Wife & Child	"	"	" "	
Francis Blashell	29	Farmer	"	"	" "	"
William Johnson	22	Wheelwright & Cª	"	"	" "	going with a view to better themselves
William Habishaw	18	Farmer	"	"	" "	
John Milton (or Millon)	22	Farmer	"	"	" "	"
John Johnson	20	Taylor	"	"	" "	Obliged to quit his farm being so high rented
Henry Huttson	21	"	"	"	" "	To seek for better Employ[t]
Thomas Skelton	35	Tallow Chandler	"	"	" "	" " "
Moses Andrew	34	Cooper	"	"	" "	" " "
James Dewthwaite	34	Farmer	"	"	" "	" " "
John Clark	55	"	"	"	" "	" " "
David Jukes	23	"	"	"	" "	" " "
Richard Clark	50	"	"	"	" "	" " "
Thomas Mooring	23	House Carpenter	"	"	" "	" " "
William Webster	33	" "	"	"	" "	" " "
John Lamb	21	Farmer	"	"	" "	" " "
Mary White	20	Servant	"	"	" "	" " "
Thomas Wilson	26	Farmer	"	"	" "	" " "
John Duke	25	"	"	"	" "	" " "
Robert Wilson	49	Farmer, Wife & 7 Children	"	"	" "	His rent raised so high obliged him to quit
William Webster	33	Joiner	"	"	" "	To seek for a better Employ[t]
John Witty	32	"	"	"	" "	" " "
Mathew Walker	24	Farmer	"	"	" "	All the small farms taken into large ones in his Parish, could not get Bread
John Steel	46	Farmer & Son	"	"	" "	To seek for better Employm[t]
John Jaques	26	Wife & 3 Children	"	"	" "	Provision high could not support their family
George Sharrow	26	Farmer	"	"	" "	To seek for better Employ[t]
William Wilson	23	"	"	"	" "	" " "

John Hopper	23	"	"	"	"	"	" " "
Sam Brainbridge	24	"	"	"	"	"	" " "
Adam Hawkworth	34	Joiner, his Wife & 4 Children	"	"	"	"	" " "
Richard Garbutt	34	Joiner, Wife & 6 Children	"	"	"	"	" " "
Thomas Gray	31	Blacksmith	"	"	"	"	goes as a Hired Servant
John Robinson	28	Butcher	"	"	"	"	" " "
William Jarratt	40	Farmer	"	"	"	"	going to see the country & if he likes it to settle there
George Cass	19	Gardener	"	"	"	"	goes as a hired servant
Andrew Thompson	40	Farmer	"	"	"	"	To seek Employment Provision being so dear in England
Mary "	32	His Wife	"	"	"	"	
William Jones	9	Son of Ditto	"	"	"	"	"
Michael Pickny	42	Farmer	"	"	"	"	Turned off his farm it being taken into a large one
Jonathan Barlow	24	"	"	"	"	"	To seek for better Employment
William Hardy	25	"	"	"	"	"	" " "
William Gilliat	34	Farmer	"	"	"	"	His Farm being over rented could not live upon it
Rebecca "	30	His Wife	"	"	"	"	
William "	3	&	"	"	"	"	
Elizabeth "	4		"	"	"	"	
Mary "	1	Children	"	"	"	"	
Thomas Hodgson	38	Taylor	"	"	"	"	To seek for better Employmt
William Sherwood	21	Linen Weaver	"	"	"	"	" " "
Clifford Swan	21	Joiner & Cabinet Maker	"	"	"	"	" " "
Benjamin Jackson	50	Mason) Wife & 3 Sons	"	"	"	"	" " "
William Moon	25	Weaver	"	"	"	"	" " "
Francis Boast	47	Farmer) Wife & 5 Children	"	"	"	"	" " "
Richard Topham	29	Farmer) Wife & Child	"	"	"	"	Distressed by his Landlord
William Shires	29	Farmer	"	"	"	"	To seek for better Employment
Joseph Tranner	32	Farmer) His Wife & Child	"	"	"	"	" " "
Francis Mason	33	Butcher	"	"	"	"	" " "
John Harrison	54	Farmer) Wife & 9 Children	"	"	"	"	Forced to leave the Kingdom being over rented in his farm
Robert Mennard	27	Taylor	"	"	"	"	On account of the high price of Provision and to seek better Employment
George Mennard	21	Wife & Child	"	"	"	"	
William Thomson	42	Farmer) Wife & 6 Children	"	"	"	"	
Ralph Stibbins	40	Merchant & 3 Children	"	"	"	"	"

Name	*Age*	*Occupation*	*From*	*Ship*	*To*	*As a*
William Reed	30	Farmer	Yorkshire	No account of Ships	Nova Scotia	On account of the high price of Provision and to seek better Employment
Elizabeth Reed	28	Sister to Ditto	"		" "	
Christopher Pearson	20	Farmer	"	"	" "	
William Pearson	28	Gardener	"	"	" "	"
William Hemsel	31	Farmer) Wife & 3 Children	"	"	" "	"
Robert Taylor	28	Farmer	"	"	" "	"
John Richardson	28	Smith	"	"	" "	"
John Holliday	40	Shoemaker	"	"	" "	"
Robert Dean	28	Labourer	"	"	" "	going to seek better Employt
—— Stapleton	30	Physician	"	"	" "	gave no reason
Thomas Eison	25	Joiner	"	"	" "	Being Heir to an Estate there
Richard Walker	33	Farmer	"	"	" "	going to seek for better Employt
Robert Jefferson	24	"	"	"	" "	" " "
Thomas Gibbin	31	Mason	"	"	" "	" " "
Mathw Webster	33	Taylor) his Wife & 3 Children	"	"	" "	" " "
John Orkird	30	Farmer	"	"	" "	" " "
John Holiday	46	Farmer) his Wife & 5 Children	"	"	" "	" " "
John Richardson	28	Smith	"	"	" "	" " "
Robt Jefferson	24	Farmer	"	"	" "	" " "
Michael Noddin	—	"	"	"	" "	" " "
John Cole	—	"	"	"	" "	" " "
Jonathan Milner	26	"	"	"	" "	" " "
Elizabeth Milner	50	"	"	"	" "	" " "
John Skelton	25	"	"	"	" "	" " "
Richard Oliver	19	"	"	"	" "	" " "
Elizabeth Milner	30	Servant	"	"	" "	" " "
Hugh Peebles	36	Weaver	"	"	" "	" " "

EMIGRANTS FROM ENGLAND

Transcribed by GERALD FOTHERGILL, Esq., of New Wandsworth, London, England, and communicated by the Committee on English Research

PORT OF NEWCASTLE, 5th TO 12th APRIL 1774.

Name	*Age*	*Occupation*	*From*	*Ship*	*To*	*As a*
Charles Rutherford	22	Butcher	New Castle	Willm & Elizabeth	Boston	to seek for better Employt
English Atkinson	28	Joiner	"	" "	"	" " "
John Gamsby	33	Millwright	"	" "	"	" " "
Margaret "	30	His Wife	"	" "	"	" " "
Dorothy "	10		"	" "	"	" " "
Ann "	8		"	" "	"	" " "
John "	7	&	"	" "	"	" " "
George "	6		"	" "	"	" " "
Peter "	1	Children	"	" "	"	" " "

PORT OF PORTSMOUTH, 5 TO 12 APRIL 1774.

Mr Mill	—	Planter	Grenades	Friendship	Grenades	To Superintend their plantations
Mr Carrew	—	"	"	"	"	
Mr Melville	—	"	"	"	"	"

PORT OF LONDON, 19th TO 26th APRIL.

Thomas Yates	23	Linen Draper	London	Adventurer	Maryland	going on Business
Elizabeth Barwell	21	Spinster	"	"	"	" "
Baltimore in Ireland		40 Emigrants	"			
Edward Fox	21	Clerk & Bookkeeper	"	"	"	going to settle there
William Miller	24	Surgeon	"	"	"	" "
Josha Testill	27	Clerk & Bookkeeper	"	"	"	" "
John Borwell (or Bozwell)	27	" "	"	"	"	" "

James Logan	27	Gentleman's Servant	“	“	“	“ “
Joseph Ralph	27	“ “	“	Neptune	Boston	going to his Master
John Brooks	29	Merchant	Herford	Elizabeth	Quebec	going on Business
John Johnson	25	Clerk & Bookkeeper	London	“	“	going to settle there
David Carns	21	Attorney at Law	Scotland	Amitys Desire	“	“ “
Edward Bennett	40	Merchant	Quebec	“ “	“	going home
Jane Carns	18	Spinster	Scotland	“ “	“	going with her Brother
Moses Polembo	20	Clerk	London	Britannia	Mahone	going as a Clerk
Janet Belton	20	Spinster	“	Magna Charta	Carolina	going to her friends
Tobiah Blackett	25	“	“	“ “	“	“ “
James Marshall Esqre	24	Merchant	“	Marshall	Barbadoes	going to reside there
Mrs Marshall	22	Wife of Mr Marshall	“	“	“	going with her Husband
William White	16	Gentleman	“	“	“	going to reside there
William Richardson	20	“	“	“	“	“ “
Miss Dunn	20	Spinster	“	“	“	“ “
William Singleton	15	Labourer	Hackney	Adventure	Maryland	Indented Servant
James Curry	15	“	London	“	“	“ “
Richard Marilley	15	“	Essex	“	“	“ “
Charles Blundell	21	Ropemaker	London	“	“	“ “
John Thompson	22	Husbandman	Northumberland	“	“	“ “
Thomas Spriggs	23	Weaver	London	“	“	“ “
Robert Parker	21	Baker	“	“	“	“ “
John Copland	40	Husbandman	Birmingham	“	“	“ “
Evan Davis	24	Cordwainer	London	“	“	“ “
James Holmes	21	Rope Maker	Manchester	“	“	“ “
John Rhodes	36	Cordwainer	London	“	“	“ “
Mary Philips	22	Spinster	“	“	“	“ “
Leonard Bonnet	27	Turner	“	“	“	“ “
Polin Ricard	21	Perukemaker	“	“	“	“ “
Francis Sacquetin	21	“	“	“	“	“ “
Jean Francois	28	Plasterer	“	“	“	“ “
Elizabeth Butchart	30	Pencil Maker	Essex	“	“	“ “
Henry Rees	29	Groom	London	“	“	“ “
Henry Nash	30	Stocking Weaver	Norwich	“	“	“ “
Thomas Hooker	15	Labourer	Southwark	“	“	“ “
William Johnson	16	Shag Weaver	Coventry	“	“	“ “
George Pearce	17	Labourer	London	“	“	“ “
Thomas Hughes	21	Perukemaker	Middlesex	“	“	“ “

Name	*Age*	*Occupation*	*From*	*Ship*	*To*	*As a*
Moses Banks	21	Blacksmith	London	Adventure	Maryland	Indended Servant
John Baylis	21	Husbandman	Warwickshire	"	"	" "
John Peter Obeley	25	Smith & Farrier	London	"	"	" "
James Joy	23	Husbandman	Wiltshire	"	"	" "
Charles Bush	31	Coach Harness Maker	Dorsetshire	"	"	" "
Hephribah Bush	31	Wife to the Above	"	"	"	" "
Woolaston Morris	21	Watchmaker	London	"	"	" "
William Tankard	21	Husbandman	"	"	"	" "
Sarah Witts	26	Spinster	"	"	"	" "
William Hardgrave	36	Sawyer	Yorkshire	Liberty	"	" "
Robert Masslin	28	"	Hampshire	"	"	" "
Joseph Hammond	21	Husbandman	London	"	"	" "
George Payne	21	Sawyer	Dover	"	"	" "
Francis Fowen	15	Brushmaker	Westminster	Dolphin	Philadelphia	" "
Thomas Pullen	21	Husbandman	Yorkshire	"	"	" "
Hugh Huntlong	27	Tallow Chandler	London	"	"	" "
James Wheeler	46	Flax Dresser	"	"	"	" "
Susanna Hudson	22	Spinster	"	"	"	" "
Mary Manlufmore	15	"	Middlesex	"	"	" "
Mary Fowler	22	"	London	"	"	" "
Mary Leach	21	"	"	"	"	" "
Ann Hurst	21	"	Middlesex	"	"	" "
Ann Hill	21	"	London	"	"	" "
Eliza Dawson	21	"	"	"	"	" "
Eliza Mather	25	"	"	"	"	" "
Mary Mathews	26	"	Durham	"	"	" "
Sarah Stacey	24	"	London	"	"	" "
John Parsley	23	Distiller	Ireland	"	"	" "
Daniel Furlong	22	Cordwainer	London	"	"	" "
Thomas Bennett	15	Labourer	"	"	"	" "
Samuel Canterbury	16	Husbandman	Durham	"	"	" "
Cornelius Dax	26	Turner	London	"	"	" "
William Miles	16	Labourer	Middlesex	"	"	" "
Isaac Perry	17	Weaver	London	"	"	" "
Thomas Young	19	Tallow Chandler	Surry	"	"	" "

Robert Hancock	15	Labourer	Southwark	"	"	" "
Samuel Wilson	21	Cordwainer	Middlesex	"	"	" "
Lyon Moses	24	Lapidary	London	"	"	" "
Thomas Davis	26	Groom	Hereford	"	"	" "
William Butcher	29	Felt Maker	Wiltshire	"	"	" "
Daniel Wheeland	20	Groom	Ireland	"	"	" "
Thomas Mathews	25	"	Gloucester	"	"	" "
William Whaley	28	Husbandman	Lancaster	"	"	" "
Robert Jefferson	38	Schoolmaster	London	"	"	" "
Martha Robinson	23	Spinster	"	"	"	" "
Richard Lomes	21	Husbandman	Lancaster	"	"	" "
Sarah Hinch	21	Spinster	London	"	"	" "
Elizabeth Mollet	21	"	"	"	"	" "
Eliza Gamble	21	"	Leicester	"	"	" "
Roxana Sanders	20	"	London	"	"	" "
Mary Hayfield	20	"	"	"	"	" "
Elizabeth Winter	19	"	"	"	"	" "
Rosetta Pellett	20	"	"	"	"	" "
Elizabeth Thomas	21	"	"	"	"	" "
James Winter	21	Husbandman	Huntington	"	"	" "
Edward King	24	"	London	"	"	" "
Thomas Frewin	21	Clock Maker	Hereford	"	"	" "
William Turner	17	Cordwainer	London	"	"	" "
Thomas Miles	17	Labourer	"	"	"	" "

Port of Stockton, 19th to 26th April 1774.

William Robinson	32	Tallow Chandler & Soap Boiler	Durham	Mary	Halifax	To seek for better Employt
Mary "	35	His Wife	"	"	"	going with her husband
Mary Bentley	65	Widow	"	"	"	To seek for better Employt
Nicholas Pearson	40	Shoemaker	"	"	"	" " "
Esther "	36	His Wife & 3 Children, 10, 6. 1. Years	"	"	"	" " "
John Greenwood	40	Farmer	"	"	"	" " "
Elizabeth "	36	His Wife & 4 Children, 10, 8. 6. 4. Years	"	"	"	" " "

Name	Age	Occupation	From	Ship	To	As a
John Teckle	42	Stay Maker	Durham	Mary	Halifax	To seek for better Employ[1]
Elizabeth "	40	His Wife	"	"	"	" " "
Thomas Lancaster	23	Late Linen Drapers Ápprentice	"	"	"	going with goods to dispose of
Thomas Elstob	40	Late a Farmer	"	"	"	Ditto & intends to return
Joshua Laking	41	Farmer	"	"	"	Better Employment
Ann "	39	His Wife & 1 Child age 11 Years	"	"	"	" "
John Old	30	Taylor	"	"	"	To seek for better Employment
William Pashley	70	Gardener	"	"	"	" " "
John Latham	32	Brewer	"	"	"	" " "
Jno Hutchinson	22	Butcher	"	"	"	" " "
Robt Robertson	23	"	"	"	"	" " "
William Hall	40	Labourer	"	"	"	" " "
Jane Miller	25	Spinster	"	"	"	" " "
John Harland	30	Shop keeper	"	"	"	" " "
William Paterson	34	"	"	"	"	" " "
Robert Stavely	26	Farmer	"	"	"	" " "
Joseph Pierson	34	Ship Carpenter	"	"	"	" " "
Thomas Miller	26	Shop Keeper	"	"	"	going with goods to sell & return
James Ward	28	Ship Carpenter	"	"	"	To seek for better Employment

Port of Portsmouth, 19 to 26 April 1774.

Mr Paul Bedford	—	Gentleman	Barbadoes	Favourite Betsey	Barbadoes	On his return home to settle
Mr Estick	—	"	"	" "	"	" " "

Port of London, 10th to 17th May.

James Fitter	16	———	London	Angticana	Leghorn	going to be qualified for the sea service
John Jerard	17	———	"	"	"	
Thomas Mills	18	Taylor	"	Union	Maryland	Indented Servant
Daniel Wells	20	Gardener	Suffolk	"	"	" "
John Richer	22	Sadler	Norwich	"	"	" "

William Weatherton	21	Baker	Scotland	"	"	" "
William Stockwell	23	Husbandman	Somersetshire	"	"	" "
Clement Cheeseman	26	Cordwainer	Kent	"	"	" "
Leonora Marshall	21	Spinster	"	"	"	" "
Forbes Kyll	19	Coach Wheeler	Scotland	"	"	" "
John Thompson	21	Linen Weaver	London	"	"	" "
John Harrison	24	Wool Comber	Somersetshire	"	"	" "
James Hinton	23	Back Gammon Table Maker	London	"	"	" "
George Colmer	44	Husbandman	Berkshire	"	"	" "
Mary Bird	26	Spinster	London	"	"	" "
Nathaniel Worker	25	Gentleman	"	Briton	Carolina	On Pleasure
John Grafton	25	Drawing Master	"	"	"	On Business

PORT OF WHITEHEAVEN, 10th TO 17 MAY 1774.

William Etburn	20	School Master	Scotland	Molly	Virginia	to settle in America
George Hamilton	23	Carver & Gilder	"	"	"	" "

PILL A CREEK A PORT OF BRISTOL.

Thirty two Convicts	—	from different Goales of the Kingdom			Virginia	

PORT OF LONDON, 17th TO 24th MAY 1774.

Charles Davis	25	White Smith	London	Brothers	Maryland	Indented Servant
Joseph Smith	31	Husbandman	"	"	"	" "
Richard Stewart	20	Baker	Edingbourg	"	"	" "
Charles Jones	20	White Smith	Bristol	"	"	" "
John Lish	21	Baker	London	"	"	" "
John Gilbert	20	Husbandman	"	"	"	" "
Lewis Leneveu	26	"	"	"	"	" "
John Wills	19	Groom	"	"	"	" "
Arthur Couch	45	Joiner	"	"	"	" "
Thomas Platt	20	Post Boy	"	"	"	" "
Thomas Smee	31	Boot Maker	"	"	"	" "
Mark Newson	25	Woolen Weaver	"	"	"	Indented servant for four Years
George Dent	32	Taylor	"	"	"	" " "

Name	*Age*	*Occupation*	*From*	*Ship*	*To*	*As a*
Basil Denn	18	Coach Wheeler	London	Brothers	Maryland	Indented servant for four Years
Thomas Lawrance	20	Carpenter	Berkshire	"	"	" " "
Joseph Martin	30	Stone Mason	London	"	"	" " "
John West	35	Cordwainer	Southwark	"	"	" " "
John Davis	21	Labourer	London	"	"	" " "
William Clark	19	Wheelwright	Hertfordshire	"	"	" " "
John Tice	24	Cordwainer	Southwark	"	"	" " "
Rich[d] Evans	17	Rule Maker	Birmingham	"	"	" " "
George Mercey	28	Husbandman	Somersetshire	"	"	" " "
Mathias Gainsford	28	"	"	Minerva	Maryland	" " "
John Roll	22	Gardener	Aberdeen	"	"	" " "
William Roney	21	Labourer	London	"	"	" " "
James Garriott	24	Joiner	York	"	"	" " "
Francis Daniel	27	Spinner	London	"	"	" " "
John Franler	38	Labourer	"	"	"	" " "
Owen Dunn	32	"	"	"	"	" " "
John Virgin	21	Husbandman	"	"	"	" " "
John Wood	15	Labourer	Essex	"	"	Indented Servant
John Lancaster	16	"	"	"	"	" "
Thomas Collier	21	Labourer	"	"	"	" "
William Francis	33	White Smith	Stafford	"	"	" "
Jacob Clark	23	Husbandman	London	"	"	" "
William Cornwell	27	Farrier	Ireland	"	"	" "
James Wood	22	Weaver	London	"	"	" "
Edward Coll	21	Husbandman	Ireland	"	"	" "
James Fuller	36	Tanner	London	"	"	" "
Alexander Bain	26	Groom	"	"	"	" "
Michael Howard	17	Labourer	"	"	"	" "
Patrick Denison	17	"	"	"	"	" "
Charles Johnson	21	Skinner	"	"	"	" "
James Denison	23	Cooper	"	"	"	" "
William Smith	31	Gardener	Yorkshire	Joseph & Mary	Maryland	" "
John Miller	21	Joiner	London	" "	"	" "
Robert Freemount	23	Farrier	"	" "	"	" "
William Pringley	32	Sword Cutler	Kent	" "	"	" "

Samuel Soul	23	Cloth Worker & Dyer	Gloucester	" "	"	" "
Dennis Sheeham	39	Cooper	London	" "	"	" "
Henry Bell	27	Biscuit Baker	"	" "	"	" "
Mary Bands	35	Widow	Herts	" "	"	" "
Mary Kenneday	21	Spinster	Scotland	" "	"	" "
John Brown	21	Bock keeper	Birmingham	" "	"	" "
George Taverner	21	Groom	Southwark	Friendship	North Carolina	" "
Edward Gilks	22	Leather Dresser	Coventry	"	" "	" "
John Forster	24	Printer	London	"	" "	" "
Thomas Winship	26	Clockmaker	Reading	"	" "	" "
John Darby	40	Baker	London	"	" "	" "
William Andrews	31	Carpenter	Surry	"	" "	" "

Port of Liverpool, 17th to 21st May 1774.

John Hewitt	29	Cabinet Maker	Yorkshire	Boston Packett	Philadelphia	to seek Employment
Martha "	24	His Wife	"	" "	"	going with her husband
Two Children	5	———	"	" "	"	going with their Parents
Catharine Fisher	34	Housekeeper	Chester	" "	"	To see her Brother
Elizabeth Smith	18	Ladys Maid	Yorkshire	" "	"	To see her sister
William Aperskin	45	Weaver	"	" "	"	To seek Employment
Mary "	26	His Wife	"	" "	"	going with her husband
John "	2	their Son	"	" "	"	going with his Parents
Joseph Barn	68	Potter	Staffordshire	" "	"	To take possession of an Estate
John Atkins	60	Bricklayer	Worcestershire	" "	"	" " "
Ann Atkins	39	His Wife	"	" "	"	going with her husband
John Ambler	25	Farmer	Yorkshire	" "	"	going to Trade
Thomas Scott	23	Cabinet Maker	Cumberland	" "	"	" "
Thomas Wood	24	Farmer	Stockport	" "	"	" "
John Hage	22	Weaver	Derbyshire	" "	"	" "
Thomas Thornley	42	"	Yorkshire	" "	"	" "
William Brewer	27	Shoe Maker	"	" "	"	" "
John Barnstow	42	Weaver	"	" "	"	To seek Employment
Thomas Roberts	30	Jeweller	Liverpool	" "	"	" "
Daniel Harvey	30	Gardener	Scotland	" "	"	" "
Mary "	26	His Wife	"	" "	"	" "
one Child	2	———	"	" "	"	" "
John Sutton	19	Weaver	Yorkshire	" "	"	" "
John Earle	25	Grocer	Kent	" "	"	" "

Port of Whitehaven, 17th to 24th May 1774.

Name	Age	Occupation	From	Ship	To	As a
Peter Simpson	30	Waggoner	Hensingham	Norfolk	Virginia	Transported
Mary Bragg	50		"	"	"	"
Ann Bragg	20		"	"	"	To settle there
Betty Tennant	16		Whitehaven	"	"	

Port of London, 24th to 31st May 1774.

Name	Age	Occupation	From	Ship	To	As a
Sarah Davison	34		Shropshire	Georgia Planter	Georgia	going to her husband
Thomas "	9	Her	"	" "	"	
Richard "	8		"	" "	"	
Henry "	4	Children	"	" "	"	going with their Mother
Miss Tong	16	Spinster	London	Pallas	Carolina	going on Pleasure
Mr Ginnings	25	Clerk	"	"	"	as Clerk to a Merchant
Mrs Molley	30	———	"	"	"	going to her husband
William Wild	19	Nailer	Worcester	Sally	Philadelphia	Indented servants for four five & six Years
John Hickenbottom	17	Labourer	London	"	"	
Philip Brooks	15	"	"	"	"	"
James UpJohn	15	Carpenter	"	"	"	"
Charles Edwards	15	Cordwainer	Wilts	"	"	"
John Good	17	Labourer	Leicester	"	"	"
J. F. Haller	19	"	London	"	"	Indented Servant
James Harling	17	"	Southwark	"	"	" "
Richard Hill	24	"	London	"	"	" "
John Webber	21	Ribbon Weaver	"	"	"	" "
Samuel Pendleton	22	Whitesmith	"	"	"	" "
George Garth	24	Butcher	"	"	"	" "
David Underwood	21	Cabinet Maker	"	"	"	" "
Thomas Morrison	27	Bricklayer	"	"	"	" "
Thomas Negus	21	Labourer	Middlesex	"	"	" "
Daniel McGuire	22	"	Ireland	"	"	" "
Francis Payne	25	Husbandman	Somerset	"	"	" "
David Hillier	30	"	Southampton	"	"	" "
Thomas Gest	25	"	Doncester	"	"	" "

James Cookshank	22	Taylor	London	"	"	"	"
John Lamb	39	Cordwainer	"	"	"	"	"
William Bogue	27	Gardener	Middlesex	"	"	"	"
John Randall	23	Husbandman	Salisbury	"	"	"	"
George Derry	25	Footman	London	"	"	"	"
William Burton	50	School Master	"	"	"	"	"
William Lambert	21	Watch Gilder	"	"	"	"	"
John Hogden	49	Sail Cloth Weaver	"	"	"	"	"
Ellis Jones	23	Grocer	"	"	"	"	"
Thomas Trimley	27	Husbandman	Middlesex	"	"	"	"
William Elliott	38	Glass Blower	Northumberland	"	"	"	"
John Mead	39	Carpenter & Joiner	London	"	"	"	"
Thomas Jackson	48	Gardener	Essex	"	"	"	"
George Ashling	35	Coachman	Middlesex	"	"	"	"
John Mann	30	Groom	York	"	"	"	"
Alexander Mathason	27	Husbandman	Scotland	"	"	"	"
Charles Fuller	21	"	Cambridge	"	"	"	"
John Hinam	22	Surgeon	London	"	"	"	"
Richard Fuller	15	Labourer	Portsmouth	"	"	"	"
John Salmon	17	Clerk & Bookkeeper	Oxford	"	"	"	"
George Steward	25	Miller	Salop	"	"	"	"
Robert Whielock	25	Coachman	London	"	"	"	"
Francis Weller	26	Watch Maker	"	"	"	"	"
Richard Miller	26	Husbandman	Berks	"	"	"	"
Abraham King	25	Labourer	London	"	"	"	"
John Bruce	15	"	"	"	"	"	"
James Jeffery	21	Hair Dresser	Suffolk	"	"	"	"
William Dove	24	Groom	London	"	"	"	"
John Wharton	28	Tanner	"	"	"	"	"
William Ross	40	Painter	Edingbourg	"	"	"	"
John Rish	38	Gardener	Glasgow	"	"	"	"
John Jackson	32	Surgeon	London	"	"	"	"
Michael Wall	24	Dyer	Southwark	"	"	"	"
John Norman	22	Husbandman	Cambridge	"	"	"	"
John Wills	17	Labourer	Berkshire	"	"	"	"
John Langley	27	Husbandman	London	"	"	"	"
Josiah "	25	"	"	"	"	"	"
Timothy Langley	22	"	"	"	"	"	"

Name	*Age*	*Occupation*	*From*	*Ship*	*To*	*As a*
Joseph Reade	25	Taylor	London	Sally	Philadelphia	Indented Servant
William Brooks	15	Cloth Worker	"	"	"	" "
Joseph Smith	16	Labourer	"	"	"	" "
George West	26	Husbandman	Warwick	"	"	" "
John Callaghan	22	Linen Weaver	Westminster	"	"	" "
William Cooper	27	Carpenter	London	"	"	" "
John Acton	24	Groom	Leicester	"	"	" "
John Mackay	25	Glass Polisher	London	"	"	" "
Benjamin Phaup	38	Cordwainer	Southwalk	"	"	" "
John Woodcock	33	Malster	Northampton	"	"	" "
Thomas Mack	21	Husbandman	Herts	"	"	" "
Daniel McGhie	15	Labourer	London	"	"	" "
James Harris	15	"	Gloucester	"	"	" "
John Randall	27	Sawyer	Kent	"	"	" "
John Tomkins	32	"	London	"	"	" "
John Langester	29	Watch maker	"	"	"	" "
Thomas Gerrard	28	Copper Smith & Brazier	"	"	"	" "
Ann "	33	His Wife	"	"	"	" "
John Tow	28	Husbandman	Nottingham	"	"	" "
Joseph Rich	18	Copper plate Printer	London	"	"	" "
Robert Woolett	16	Labourer	Essex	"	"	" "
Richard Thompson	15	"	London	"	"	" "
Francis Brooks	17	"	Dublin	"	"	" "
Edward UpJohn	17	Stone Mason	Dorset	"	"	" "
John Summers	20	Breeches Maker	Nottingham	"	"	" "
John Randall	19	Labourer	Salisbury	"	"	" "
Henry Bachus	19	Cordwainer	Bristol	"	"	" "
William Smith	16	Weaver	Coventry	"	"	" "
John Betteridge	56	Husbandman	Wilts	"	"	" "
Thomas Perris	21	White Smith	London	"	"	" "
Hugh Smith	28	Clerk & Bookkeeper	"	"	"	" "
George Hastings	18	" "	"	"	"	" "
William Bowser	20	" "	"	"	"	" "
Robert Stephens	22	Bricklayer	"	"	"	" "
Richard Catt	37	Shipwright	Deptford	"	"	" "

Walter Hunt	25	Husbandman	Oxford	"	"	" "
John Platt	21	"	Norwich	"	"	" "
John Forbes	30	"	London	"	"	" "
Richard Mills	23	Groom	"	"	"	" "
Robert Young	24	Plaisterer	"	"	"	" "
Edward May	35	Sail Cloth Weaver	"	"	"	" "
Thomas Shark	30	Glazier	"	"	"	" "
Philip Ticker	42	Silk Weaver	"	"	"	" "
William Edwards	40	Cordwainer	Wilts	"	"	" "
Joseph Wilson	15	Labourer	London	"	"	" "
Stewart McHean	30	Ship Wright & Caulker	Chatham	"	"	" "
Maria McHean	23	His Wife	"	"	"	" "

PORT OF LIVERPOOL, 24 TO 31st MAY 1774.

Thomas Brent	29	Farmer	Yorkshire	Cato	New York	To Trade
Richard Brooks	56	"	"	"	" "	" "
John Brooks	30	"	"	"	" "	" "
Ann Brooks	32	Dairy Maid	"	"	" "	Her Inclination
John Catchett	26	Farmer	"	"	" "	To Trade
John Fenton	21	Weaver	"	"	" "	" "
Robert Dickinson	26	Watchmaker	Lancashire	"	" "	To see his Brother
Stephen Moorhouse	28	Flax Dresser	Nottingham	"	" "	His Inclination
Christopher Hamlet	42	Farmer	Cheshire	"	" "	" "
Richard Hornsell	25	Merchant	Yorkshire	"	" "	To Trade
John Melling	32	Blacksmith	"	"	" "	" "
James Shaw (or Straw)	46	Carpenter	Derbyshire	"	" "	To see his Friends
John Ward	27	Taylor	Flintshire	"	" "	To follow his Trade
Thomas Little	22	Weaver	Yorkshire	"	" "	To see his Brother
Robert Smith	32	Merchant	"	"	" "	To Trade
Grace Smith	30	Lady's Maid	"	"	" "	To her Sister
William Smith	13	No Trade	"	"	" "	To see his Brother
George Higson	23	" "	"	"	" "	His Inclination
John Higson	43	Merchant	"	"	" "	To Trade
Charles Carr	29	Weaver	Nottingham	"	" "	To follow his business
William Downes	22	Taylor	Cheshire	"	" "	" "
John Fetter	31	Mason	Yorkshire	"	" "	" "
Henry Trotter	26	Weaver	"	"	" "	" "

Name	*Age*	*Occupation*	*From*	*Ship*	*To*	*As a*
Ellis Featter	29	Taylor	Yorkshire	Cato	New York	To Trade
Henry Swanton	36	Merchant	"	"	" "	" "
William Haywood	29	"	"	"	" "	" "
John Haywood	27	"	"	"	" "	" "

Port of London, 31st May to 7 June 1774.

Charles Skinner	28	Husbandman	Scotland	Industry	Maryland	Indented Servant
David Brennand	22	Sawyer	Ireland	"	"	" "
William Uzzell	22	Stone mason & Bricklayer	Middlesex	"	"	" "
Daniel Slade	36	Sawyer	Norfolk	"	"	" "
Michael Conlon	24	Husbandman	Ireland	"	"	" "

Port of Whitehaven, 31st May to 7th June 1774.

Thomas Mark	45	Husbandman	Cumberland	Golden Rule	New York	To settle in America
Sarah "	46		"	" "	" "	" "
Mary "	18		"	" "	" "	" "
Isaac "	16		"	" "	" "	" "
Sarah "	14		"	" "	" "	" "
Elizabeth "	9		"	" "	" "	" "
Deborah "	5		"	" "	" "	" "
George Beamont	21	Husbandman	"	" "	" "	" "
Mathew Gash	21	"	"	" "	" "	" "
John Hastwell	46	"	Westmoreland	" "	" "	" "
Mary "	34		"	" "	" "	" "
John "	23		"	" "	" "	" "
Joseph "	21		"	" "	" "	" "
Robert "	19		"	" "	" "	" "
Arthur "	17		"	" "	" "	" "
Betty "	15		"	" "	" "	" "
Mary "	12		"	" "	" "	" "

Thomas Hastwell	9		"	" "	" "	" "
Richard "	7		"	" "	" "	" "
Margarett "	5		"	" "	" "	" "
Isabella "	4		"	" "	" "	" "
Edward "	1		"	" "	" "	" "
James Aikin	41	Millwright	Scotland or Westmoreland	" "	" "	" "
William Reed	36	Plaisterer	"	" "	" "	" "
Margaret "	25		"	" "	" "	" "
William "	14		"	" "	" "	" "
Margaret "	1		"	" "	" "	" "
Mary Johnson	20		"	" "	" "	" "
Robert Shannon	26	Smith	"	" "	" "	" "
Francis Mountair	25	Merchant	Ireland	" "	" "	" "
Dorothy Mountair	26		"	" "	" "	" "
Arthur Bland	26	Husbandman	"	" "	" "	" "
Abraham Raney	28	"	"	" "	" "	" "
Richard Gildart	30	Dyer	Scotland	" "	" "	" "
John Murdock	21	Travelling Merchant	"	Lonsdale	Virginia	To settle
Samuel "	19	" "	"	"	"	" "
Thomas "	17	" "	"	"	"	" "
William Stoddart	22	Husbandman	"	"	"	" "

PORT OF LONDON, 7th TO 14th JUNE 1774.

Joseph Netherwood	19	Clerk	London	Princess Caroline	Jamaica	To settle
Robert Spence	23	Stay maker	"	" "	"	On Business
Richard Cross	38	Distiller	Paddington	" "	"	To settle
John Moody	21	Millwright	"	" "	"	On Business
Herbert Cole	18	Gentleman	"	" "	"	" "
Moses Levi	25	Poulterer	"	" "	"	" "
Hester Levi	18	His Wife	"	" "	"	" "
Ann Brook	57	Spinster	Westminster	" "	"	" "

EMIGRANTS FROM ENGLAND

Transcribed by Gerald Fothergill of New Wandsworth, London, England, and communicated by the Committee on English Research

Port of Plymouth, 7th to 14th June 1774.

Name	Age	Occupation	From	Ship	To	As a
John Smith	40	Planter	London	Grenada Galley	Grenades	To reside there
Philip Charitie	25	Merchant	"	" "	"	" "
James Thomas	16	Writer	"	" "	"	" "

Port of London, 14th to 21st June 1774.

Name	Age	Occupation	From	Ship	To	As a
Thomas Hodgson	39	Gentleman	London	Free Mason	Philadelphia	To settle
Catherine "	40	Wife to Ditto & one Child	"	" "	"	" "
John Hodgson	30	Gentleman	"	" "	"	" "
Samuel Burner	22	"	"	" "	"	" "
Ann Sumerfield	30	& one Child	"	" "	"	" "
Jno Walters	45	Gentleman	"	" "	"	" "
Maria Walters	41		"	" "	"	" "
Thomas Walters	23	Gentleman	"	" "	"	" "
Mary Young	50		"	" "	"	" "
Philip Clampton	26	Husbandman	"	" "	"	For Employment
Thomas Clampton	21	"	"	" "	"	" "
Margaret Howard	21		"	" "	"	To Settle
George Thomas	26	Husbandman	Surry	" "	"	For Employment
Mary "	32	His Wife & Child	"	" "	"	" "
Charles Wilstack	35	Sail Cloth Weaver	London	" "	"	" "
John Adkinks	41	Sawyer	"	" "	"	" "
Thomas Danny	21	Gentleman	"	" "	"	To Settle
Sarah Danny	36	& one Child	"	" "	"	" "
Samuel Danny	18	Gentleman	"	" "	"	" "
Sarah "	15	———	"	" "	"	" "

Samuel Harrison	41	Clothier	Yorkshire	" "	"	" "
Elizabeth "	32	His Wife & 4 Children	"	" "	"	" "
Samuel Hodges	35	Shoemaker	Hertford	" "	"	" "
Caleb Strang	30	Husbandman	London	" "	"	For Employment
Maria Strang	28	His Wife	"	" "	"	" "
James Thompson	38	Carpenter	"	" "	"	" "
Owen Shaw	21	Cutler	Sheffield	" "	"	" "
Thomas Jackson	26	Carpenter	London	" "	"	" "
Joseph Lafar	21	Gentleman	"	" "	"	To Settle

PORT OF LIVERPOOL, 14 TO 21st JUNE 1774.

John Lewis	16	Farmer	Ireland	Dickinson	Philadelphia	Indented Servant
Charles "	17	"	"	"	"	" "
Joshua "	19	"	"	"	"	" "
Edward Rimer	25	Blacksmith	Liverpool	"	"	" "

PORT OF LONDON, 3d TO 10th JULY 1774.

Rebecca Whitaker	35	Musical Instrument Maker	London	America	Barbadoes	Going to settle
John Short	21	Watch Maker	"	Elizabeth	Maryland	Indented Servant
James George	22	Wire drawer	Bath	"	"	" "
John Smith	24	Weaver	Kent	"	"	" "
John Pringle	30	Copper Smith & Brazier	London	"	"	" "
Richard Lewis	33	Schoolmaster	"	"	"	" "
James Wolfe	21	Groom	Westminster	"	"	" "
Robert Martin	21	Clerk & Bookkeeper	Salisbury	"	"	" "
William Smith	25	Hair Dresser	London	"	"	" "
Peter Mathew	22	Architect	Middlesex	"	"	" "
Joseph Taft	21	Footman	London	"	"	" "
George Brougham	23	Watchmaker	"	"	"	" "
Samuel Smith	21	Stay Maker	Hereford	"	"	" "
John Wallis	17	Labourer	London	"	"	" "
James Paliett	19	"	"	"	"	" "
Jacob Johnson	18	Glass Cutter	"	"	"	" "
Joseph Collins	20	Currier	Dublin	"	"	" "
William Smith	21	Taylor	Newcastle	"	"	" "
William Peate	20	Labourer	Westminster	"	"	" "

Name	*Age*	*Occupation*	*From*	*Ship*	*To*	*As a*
William Ward	19	Labourer	Reading	Elizabeth	Maryland	Indented Servant
Joseph Austin	18	Gardener	Herts	"	"	" "
Thomas Canter	18	"	Wilts	"	"	" "
John Norman	18	"	Herts	"	"	" "
David Davis	20	Taylor	London	"	"	" "
Michael Delaney	18	Labourer	"	"	"	" "
Samuel Dobbs	21	Perukemaker	Rotherhithe	"	"	" "
Isaac Hart	23	Taylor	Plymouth	"	"	" "
Thomas Ackley	24	Husbandman	Norwich	"	"	" "
John Hitchin	21	Tanner	London	"	"	" "
Simon Innis	40	Carpenter & Joiner	"	"	"	" "
Charles Hackett	22	Watchmaker	Sheerness	"	"	" "
William Proud	22	Cordwainer	Harwich	"	"	" "
William Watts	23	Miller	Essex	"	"	" "
Anthony Thorndale	25	Cabinet Maker	London	"	"	" "
Thomas Abney	48	Leather Dresser	Surry	"	"	" "
Darby Hagan	22	Husbandman	Ireland	"	"	" "
Edward Kelly	21	"	London	"	"	" "
Richard Baynham	22	Footman	Wilts	"	"	" "
Robert Beard	21	Watch & Clock Maker	London	"	"	" "
William Langford	32	Clerk & Bookkeeper	"	"	"	" "
John Parker	24	Watch Movemant Maker	"	"	"	" "
Thomas Deane	27	Groom	Southwark	"	"	" "
James Stewart	29	Husbandman	Sussex	"	"	" "
Thomas Robinson	22	Labourer	London	"	"	" "
John Finney	32	"	"	"	"	" "
Thomas Nash	28	Baker	Oxford	"	"	" "
Robert Clark	25	"	Sheerness	"	"	" "
William Jones	22	Husbandman	London	"	"	" "
Henry Horne	22	Clerk & Bookkeeper	"	"	"	" "
Stephen Phillips	23	Coach Harness Maker	Middlesex	"	"	" "
Charles Couch	22	Cordwainer	London	"	"	" "
Samuel Severn	36	Perukemaker	Westminster	"	"	" "
William Cutcliff	28	Carpenter	"	"	"	" "
Thomas Fisher	19	Sawyer	London	"	"	" "

Thomas Davis	19	Labourer	“	“	“	“ “
John Fox	16	Groom	“	“	“	“ “
William Ward	18	Cutler	Sheffield	“	“	“ “
Thomas Ward	19	Labourer	London	“	“	“ “
John Carpenter	19	Cordwainer	“	“	“	“ “
Thomas Smith	17	Sword Chain Maker	“	“	“	“ “
James Harrison	19	Cooper	Bath	“	“	“ “
Thomas Gillen	17	Cordwainer	London	“	“	“ “
John Boyden	17	Harness Maker	“	“	“	“ “
Thomas Brarenton	21	Husbandman	Gloster	“	“	“ “
Richard Reeves	21	“	Kent	“	“	“ “
John Blackwell	39	Miner	Derby	“	“	“ “
James Hillier	26	Wheelwright	Hants	“	“	“ “
Christopher Kirby	21	Taylor	London	“	“	“ “
Robert Cowley	27	Printer	“	“	“	“ “
John Robinson	23	Carpenter	Westminster	“	“	“ “
Timothy Crosby	28	Husbandman	“	“	“	“ “
John Hind	21	“	York	“	“	“ “
William Ingram	22	Lath & Stave Render	London	“	“	“ “
Robert Cruse	35	Blacksmith	Essex	“	“	“ “
Edward Johnson	22	Wheelwright	London	“	“	“ “
Thomas Bawdler	21	Brass Founder	Birmingham	“	“	“ “
John Fayne	21	Painter	Lincoln	“	“	“ “
James Powell	22	Leather Dresser	Bristol	“	“	“ “
George Mann	21	Clerk & Bookkeeper	Westminster	“	“	“ “
John Williams	30	Gardener	London	“	“	“ “
William Smith	21	Cabinet Maker	“	“	“	“ “
John Print	21	Husbandman	Deptford	“	“	“ “
Alexander Hynes	23	Perukemaker	London	“	“	“ “
John Alderton	22	“	“	“	“	“ “
William Richardson	22	Printer	Edingbourg	“	“	“ “

Port of London, 10th to 17th July 1774.

Sarah White	56	———	London	Carolina	Carolina	Going on Business
John Detlaf [? s]	30	Taylor	“	“	“	Going to settle
Sarah Detlaf [? s]	25	His Wife	“	“	“	“ “

Name	*Age*	*Occupation*	*From*	*Ship*	*To*	*As a*
William Brinkwell	22	Coach maker	Surry	Russ^{a} Merchant	Maryland	Indented Servant
Christophier Hutton	24	Bricklayer	Yorkshire	" "	"	" "
Luke Horsfield	36	Cutler	"	" "	"	" "
William Harrison	39	Bricklayer	Liverpool	" "	"	" "
Samuel Long	28	Wheelwright	London	" "	"	" "
Martin Shield	22	Plaisterer	Ireland	" "	"	" "
Robert Mills	22	Gardener	Deptford	" "	"	" "
William Wright	18	Husbandman	Hertford	" "	"	" "
Edward Higman	18	Cordwainer	London	" "	"	" "
Richard Hall	19	Waiter	"	" "	"	Indented Servants for 4, 5, & 6 Years
William Kedton	19	Miller	Yarmouth	" "	"	
Stephen Ellis	21	Taylor	Salop	" "	"	"
Patrick Tavlin	23	Husbandman	Ireland	" "	"	"
Edward Wright	23	Baker	Lincoln	" "	"	"
John Hall	25	Clerk & Bookkeeper	Chatham	" "	"	"
Mathew Moor	22	Farmer	Ireland	" "	"	"
James Bell	40	Miner	York	" "	"	"
Richard Turner	21	Brass Founder	Bristol	" "	"	"
John Yeates	24	Husbandman	Reading	" "	"	"
John Thomas	42	Clock & Watchmaker	London	" "	"	"
William Nolbrow	28	Taylor	Yarmouth	" "	"	"
John Keymester	39	Gem Maker	London	" "	"	"
Joseph Blind	25	Ship Carpenter	Kent	" "	"	"
William Turner	22	Husbandman	"	" "	"	"
John Turner.	21	"	"	" "	"	"
John Care	26	Carpenter & Joiner	London	" "	"	"
Richard Perriman	33	Collar Maker	Middlesex	" "	"	"
Joseph Horsfield	24	Smith	Sheffield	" "	"	"
Henry Snead	21	Cabinet Maker	Hereford	" "	"	"
William Wheeler	21	Carpenter	Bucks	" "	"	"
Benjamin Prior	22	Blacksmith	London	" "	"	"
William Morrison	26	Carpenter & Joiner	"	" "	"	"
Edward-Preston	38	Baker	"	" "	"	"
Jonathan Whitby	16	Husbandman	Norfolk	" "	"	"
Edward Driver	19	Glazier & Painter	London	" "	"	"

George Gardner	19	Labourer	“	“ “	“	“
Joshua Peck	18	Hairdresser	“	“ “	“	“
Thomas Judson	19	Cordwainer	Bristol	“ “	“	“
John Cook	21	Groom	Lincoln	“ “	“	“
William Monk	19	Ironmonger	Surry	“ “	“	“
Robert Randal	21	Printer and Bookbinder	Edingbourg	“ “	“	“
Thomas Field	30	Labourer	London	“ “	“	“
Edward Burrows	21	Husbandman	Suffolk	“ “	“	Indended Servant
William Lee	26	Smith	Durham	“ “	“	“ “
William Hampton	33	“	Stafford	“ “	“	“ “
Jno Solomon Balissa	31	Footman	London	“ “	“	“ “
John Connell	39	Cordwainer	Ireland	“ “	“	“ “

PORT OF HULL, 10th TO 17 JULY 1774.

Robert Medway	35	Farmer	Yorkshire	Kingston Packet	Norfolk, in Virginia	The rent of their farm raised so high they cannot live
Lydia “	33	His Wife	“	“ “	“	“
Susanna “	10		“	“ “	“	“
Elizabeth “	8	&	“	“ “	“	“
Lydia “	5		“	“ “	“	“
Robert “	2	Children	“	“ “	“	“
William Morfett	44	Farmer	“	“ “	“	To seek for better Employt
Mary “	48	His Wife	“	“ “	“	“ “ “
Hannah “	14	&	“	“ “	“	“ “ “
William “	12		“	“ “	“	“ “ “
Mary “	9	Children	“	“ “	“	“ “ “
David Wheelhouse	49	Farmer	“	“ “	“	Their rent raised so high they cannot live
Margt “	36	His Wife	“	“ “	“	
Hannah “	12	&	“	“ “	“	“
Diana “	10		“	“ “	“	“
David “	9	Children	“	“ “	“	“
Thomas Waters	24	Gardener	“	“ “	“	To seek a better Livelihood
John Brown	26	Wheelwright	“	“ “	“	“ “ “
William Mitchinson	30	Farmer	“	“ “	“	“ “ “
Thomas Wetheral	30	“	“	“ “	Virginia	To Purchase or Return
James Webster	22	Soap & Tallow Chandler	“	“ “	“	going as a Clerk
Mathew Hick	25	Schoolmaster	“	“ “	“	To seek a better livelihood
Joseph Elam	50	Gentleman	“	“ “	“	To Purchase or Return

Name	*Age*	*Occupation*	*From*	*Ship*	*To*	*As a*
William Nelson	37	Cloth Manufacturer	Yorkshire	Kingston Packet	Virginia	To transact business for two merchants
Sarah Threadgold	20	Maid Servant	"	" "	"	To seek a better livelihood
Bartho Barker	29	Farmer	"	Adventure	New York	To Purchase or return
Sarah Barker	30	His Wife	"	"	" "	" " "
James Walker	11	Servant	"	"	" "	To seek a better livelihood
Rachael Todd	19	Maid Servant	"	"	" "	" " "
Sarah Lightfoot	18	" "	"	"	" "	" " "
Thomas Corry	44	Husbandman	"	"	" "	" " "
John Packer	19	Mercer	"	"	" "	" " "
David Lessley	24	Joiner	Scotland	"	" "	" " "
Richard Henderson	34	Joiner	Hull	"	" "	Has a brother settled there who desires him to come over
Susanna "	30	His Wife	"	"	" "	"
David "	9		"	"	" "	"
Robert "	6	&	"	"	" "	"
Susanna "	4		"	"	" "	"
Ann "	1	Children	"	"	" "	"
William Sowersby	26	Farmer	Yorkshire	"	" "	To Purchase or return

PORT OF PLYMOUTH, 10th TO 17th JULY 1774.

William Smith Esqre	36	Gentlemen	London	Le Soy Planter	Dominica	To Reside
Mr Mellegan	40	"	"	" "	"	" "
Mr Burgess	26	"	"	" "	"	" "
Mr Brown	36	"	"	" "	"	" "
Mr Clark	38	"	"	" "	"	" "
Mr Roberts	20	"	"	" "	"	" "
John Edmonds	12	Servants	"	" "	"	" "
—— Violets	30		"	" "	"	" "

PORT OF LONDON, 17th TO 24 JULY 1774.

William Thomas	20	Merchant	London	St George	Philadelphia	To Settle
William Bell	29	Perukemaker	"	Rosamond	New York	" "
Robert Etherington	25	Mariner	"	"	" "	On Business

Lawrance Jones	20	Gentleman	"	"	" "	On Pleasure
Andrew Hisme	30	Physician	"	Nancy	Jamaica	To Settle
Edw[d] Earlsman	30	Bookkeeper	"	"	"	" "
William Lomas	33	Cordwainer	Northampton	"	"	" "
Will[m] Cartwright	23	"	London	"	"	" "
Joseph Johnson	14	"	"	"	"	To live with a gentleman
John Lynch	37	Farmer	Ireland	"	"	On Business
John Vaughan	59	Grocer	Shewsbury	"	"	" "
Margaret Wood	18	Spinster	London	"	"	" "
Elizabeth Ryde	18	"	Deptford	"	"	" "
Joseph Seabright	25	Millwright	Southwark	Hope	Maryland	Indented Servant
Charles Field	21	Groom	York	"	"	" "
Seth Bailey	21	Coach maker	London	"	"	" "
Edward Williams	30	" "	"	"	"	" "
William Right	31	Sawyer	"	"	"	" "
William Firmins	23	Glazier	Wolverhampton	"	"	" "
Robert Moore	37	Silversmith	London	"	"	Indented servant for four Years
Charles Kaye	30	Stone Mason	"	"	"	" " "
Thomas Hopper	32	Cooper	York	"	"	" " "
Edward Gregory	38	Painter	London	"	"	" " "
Ralph Holden	24	Chaise Driver	"	"	"	" " "
James Bankerhie	21	Husbandman	"	"	"	" " "
John Reed	30	Plate Printer	"	"	"	" " "
George Hichman	23	Glass Pollisher	"	"	"	" " "
Charles Rowland	21	House Carpenter	"	"	"	" " "
Frederick Dawson	39	Painter	"	"	"	" " "
Sam[l] Richardson	22	Book Keeper	"	"	"	" " "
Joseph Dyer	21	Groom	"	"	"	" " "

PORT OF PORTSMOUTH, 17th TO 24th JULY 1774.

Walter Robinson Esq[re]	—	Lord Chief Justice of Tobago	Tobago	Unity	Tobago "	To Execute his Office
M[r] Peter Maxwell	35	Planter	Grenada	"	"	To Superintend his plantation
M[r] Henderson	25	Gentleman	York	"	"	To settle at Tobago

EMIGRANTS FROM ENGLAND

Transcribed by GERALD FOTHERGILL of New Wandsworth, London, England, and communicated by the Committee on English Research

PORT OF HULL, 17th TO 20th JULY 1774.

Name	*Age*	*Occupation*	*From*	*Ship*	*To*	*As a*
Thomas Webster	50	Husbandman	Yorkshire	Amelia	Philadelphia	Going to seek a better livelihood
Robert Mitner	20	Grocer & Tallow Chandler	"	"	"	" " "

PORT OF LONDON, 24th TO 31st JULY 1774.

James Swallow	24	Cleat Maker	York	Charming Molly	Philadelphia	To seek Employment
Benjamin Littlewood	21	"	"	" "	"	" "
Mrs Wilcox & 3 Children		"	"	" "	"	" "
Captn Gills	—	Wife & Children	"	" "	"	" "
John Berningham	20	Gentleman	Ireland	" "	"	On his Travels
Elizabeth Stead	26	Servant	London	Earl of Dunmow	New York	Going to Service
William Hughes	34	Tallow Chandler	Deptford	Peggy Stewart	Maryland	Indented Servant
William Lilly	30	Block Maker	London	" "	"	" "
Robert Wilson	38	Footman	Northumberland	" "	"	" "
Thomas Jones	21	Joiner	London	" "	"	" "
John Bryan	30	Labourer	"	" "	"	" "
James Gunner	23	Perukemaker	"	" "	"	" "
Joseph Legard	21	Cordwainer	"	" "	"	" "
Thomas Turner	22	Gunsmith	Birmingham	" "	"	" "
William Hickison	26	Brick maker	"	" "	"	" "
Samuel Smith	24	Stay maker	Woolwich	" "	"	" "
Wm Hayes	21	Weaver	London	" "	"	" "
Simon Retallack	22	Blacksmith	Lambeth	" "	"	" "
Thomas Jacobs	25	Perukemaker	London	" "	"	" "

Ric Gardner	21	Painter	Sussex	"	"	"	" "
John Hall	21	Groom	"	"	"	"	" "
William Moland	21	Tin Plate Worker	London	"	"	"	Indented Servant for four Years
William Martin	21	Sack Weaver	Nants	"	"	"	
Richard Clayton	21	Cordwainer	London	"	"	"	"
Thomas Ireland	17	Shoemaker	Liverpool	"	"	"	"
John Slade	33	Taylor	London	"	"	"	"
Charles Roach	26	Tallow Chandler	"	"	"	"	"
Jos Godfrey	21	Groom	"	"	"	"	"
Philip Shobrooke	32	Husbandman	"	"	"	"	"
Jos Martin	16	Labourer	Somerset	"	"	"	"
William Ward	18	Footman	London	"	"	"	"
Joseph Nutting	17	Groom	"	"	"	"	"
Mark Lachman	26	Baker	"	"	"	"	"
John Munn	21	Book caser	"	"	"	"	"
Richard Jones	23	Draper	"	"	"	"	"
John Daniel	21	Perukemaker	Truro	"	"	"	"
Grifin Knight	26	Turner	London	"	"	"	"
James Johns	21	Plaisterer	Lambeth	"	"	"	"
Thomas Boyfield	20	Husbandman	Essex	"	"	"	"
Oliver Bock	21	Husbandman	London	"	"	"	"
Thomas Price	22	Groom	Monmouth	"	"	"	"
John McDonald	22	Husbandman	Scotland	"	"	"	"
Thomas Cowen	21	"	York	"	"	"	"
Daniel Hurley	21	"	London	"	"	"	"
John Phelps	24	Miner	"	"	"	"	"
James Withers	21	Jeweller	"	"	"	"	"
John Remnant	23	Joyner	"	"	"	"	"
Henry Hall	26	Cooper	Hampshire	"	"	"	"
Richard Gee	21	Weaver	London	"	"	"	"
Thomas Clark	39	Carpenter	"	"	"	"	"
James Thomas	22	Wheelwright	"	"	"	"	"
George Bradley	24	Stone Mason	Lancashire	"	"	"	"
James Powell	21	Weaver	London	"	"	"	"
John Brigham	24	Glass Frame Maker	"	"	"	"	"
Robert Ross	15	Labourer	"	"	"	"	"
John Sargood	21	Plate Worker	"	"	"	"	"
Alexr South	16	Labourer	Essex	"	"	"	"

PORT OF LIVERPOOL, 24th TO 31st JULY 1774.

Name	Age	Occupation	From	Ship	To	As a
Ralph Falkner	50	Carpenter	Staffordshire	Elizabeth	Philadelphia	To seek better Employment
Dorothy "	45	His Wife	"	"	"	" " "
Ralph "	30	Potter	"	"	"	" " "
Mary "	30	His Wife	"	"	"	" " "
Mary Harris	25	House Maid	"	"	"	" " "

PORT OF LONDON, 31st JULY TO 7th AUGUST 1774.

Name	Age	Occupation	From	Ship	To	As a
John Butler	25	Gentleman	London	Carolina Packet	Carolina	Going to settle
Ann "	25	His Wife	"	" "	"	" "
Thomas Andrews	35	Potter	"	" "	"	" "
Willm Templeman	28	Jeweller	"	" "	"	" "
John Smith	22	Cabinet Maker	"	" "	"	" "
Thomas Bailey	17	Cordwainer	Lambeth	Generous Friends	Maryland	" "
William Wall	23	Hop presser	London	" "	"	" "
Joseph Cook	24	Baker	Norwich	Beith	Virginia	Indented Servant
Thomas Atkins	24	Cordwainer	Southwark	"	"	" "
James Palmer	27	Wheelwright	Middlesex	"	"	" "
William Thompson	30	Schoolmaster	Scotland	"	"	" "
Joseph Smith	20	Baker	Surry	"	"	" "
William Lewis	20	Perukemaker	"	"	"	" "
Thomas Clark	18	Bucklemaker	Worcester	"	"	" "
John Hoskins	21	Brick Maker	Surry	"	"	" "
John Smithson	30	Blacksmith	Lincoln	"	"	" "
Jacob Seedon	24	Shipwright	Yarmouth	"	"	" "
Samuel Wilson	26	Gentleman's Servant	London	"	"	" "
Andrew McGill	25	Blacksmith	Edingbourg	"	"	" "
John Stanton	22	Wheelwright	London	"	"	" "
John Guilsbury	17	Smith	"	"	"	" "
William Bruce	15	Painter	"	"	"	" "
James Chamberlin	23	Baker	"	"	"	" "
George Bollard	21	Taylor	Ireland	Elizabeth	"	" "

John Aspley	21	Blacksmith	Birmingham	"	"	" "
William Warden	21	Schoolmaster	Middlesex	"	"	" "
John Board	36	Sawyer	Devon	"	"	" "
Thomas Brown	29	Cordwainer	York	"	"	" "
Catharine Roper	32	Spinner	London	"	"	" "
Daniel Hutchinson	21	Cordwainer	Dublin	"	"	" "
William Castake	21	Sawyer	London	"	"	" "
Charles Wise	21	Rope Maker	"	"	"	" "
Thomas Rudkin	28	Currier	"	"	"	" "

PORT OF WHITBY, 31st JULY TO 7th AUG. 1774.

Robert Harrison	38	Innholder & Shopkeeper	Yorkshire	Marlborough	Savanna in America	Going to seek for better Employt to stay there or return
David Black	19	Book binder	Scotland	"	"	" " "
Richard Fenton	26	Canvas Weaver, Wife & Children	"	"	"	" " "
Ralph Cock	37	Linen Weaver & Wife	"	"	"	" " "
John Tate	25	Carpenter, Wife & 4 Children	"	"	"	" " "
Thomas Oliver	29	Blacksmith, Wife & 2 Children	"	"	"	" " "
Jane Wilson	22	Spinster	"	"	"	" " "
James Elliot	35	Husbandman & his Wife	"	"	"	" " "
James Berry	31	Linen Weaver with 1 Child	Lancashire	"	"	" " "
Adam Dryden	28	Gardener	Scotland	"	"	Going to seek better Employment to stay there or return
William Alexander	32	Labourer, Wife & 3 Children	Yorkshire	"	"	

PILL A CREEK A PORT OF BRISTOL, 31st JULY TO 7th AUG. 1774.

Samuel Hughes	19	Labourer	Bristol	Restoration	Maryland	Indented Servant
John Wilkins	18	"	"	"	"	" "
John Perry	16	"	Bath	"	"	" "
Thomas Russel	17	Servant	Bristol	"	"	" "
One Woman	—	———	———	"	"	" "
William Keater	29	Smith	Bristol	"	"	A Convict

Port of London, 7th to 14th Aug. 1774.

Name	*Age*	*Occupation*	*From*	*Ship*	*To*	*As a*
Mary Fraser	30	Weaver	London	Cæsar	Philadelphia	Going to settle
William Fraser	40	Weaver & 3 Children	"	"	"	" "
Charles Webster	36	Husbandman	Scotland	Mercury	Quebec	" "
Jenna "	33	His Wife & 3 Children	"	"	"	" "
Margaret Weshelt	28	Spinster	"	"	"	" "
George Grant	22	Joiner	London	Ross	Virginia	Going to settle
James Scotland	21	Cabinet Maker	"	"	"	" "
Alex^r Ploughton	27	Clerk	"	"	"	" "
M. A. Hunter	28	"	"	"	"	On Business
Elizabeth Spence	16	Spinster	"	"	"	" "
Judith Worthson	70	———	"	"	"	" "
James Hunter	27	Merchant	"	"	"	" "
Ann Bell	21	Spinster	"	Success's Increase	Pensocla	To Settle
Murray McLinzey	28	Cartwright	Scotland	" "	"	" "
William Stephens	23	Carpenter	"	" "	"	" "
Gerard Byrne	22	Carpenter & Joiner	Kent	" "	"	" "

Port of Hull, 7th to 14th Aug. 1774.

John Willman	43	Clothier	Yorkshire	America	New York	To seek a better Livelihood
Stephen Fisher	30	Joiner	"	"	" "	" " "
Georg Waterworth	45	Cloth Dresser	"	"	" "	" " "

Port of Liverpool, 7th to 14 Aug. 1774.

Thomas Fisher	27	Carpenter	Lancashire	Betsey	Virginia	To seek for better Employ^t
Henry "	25	Weaver	"	"	"	" " "
John Betty	29	Farmer	Westmoreland	"	"	" " "
James Bread	30	Smith	Liverpool	"	"	" " "
Robert Ferry	44	Farmer	Yorkshire	"	"	" " "
James "	19	"	"	"	"	" " "
Joseph "	17	"	"	"	"	" " "

Port of London, 14th to 21st Aug. 1774.

David Adkins	22	Cooper	Lincoln	William	Carolina	Indented Servant
James Nichols	24	Silver Caster	London	"	"	" "
Thomas Winter	21	Husbandman	Leicester	"	"	" "
John Rixon	22	Brazier & Copper Smith	Birmingham	"	"	" "
Benjamin Evans	22	Sail Cloth Weaver	Cornwall	"	"	" "
John Anthony	21	Baker	Middlesex	"	"	" "
James Smith	21	Painter & Glazier	Nottingham	"	"	" "
Michael Delancy	21	Husbandman	Ireland	"	"	" "
John Gear	17	Blacksmith	London	Patience	Virginia	" "
Henry Edwards	17	Perukemaker	"	"	"	" "
David Rees	22	Carpenter	Middlesex	"	"	" "
Thomas Ball	33	Bricklayer	London	"	"	" "
George Pratt	22	Cordwainer	"	"	"	" "
George Blackburn	22	Clerk & Bookkeeper	"	"	"	" "
William Seymour	27	House Carpenter	Hereford	"	"	" "
John Tatham	32	Taylor	Middlesex	"	"	" "
Daniel Graham	25	Clock Maker	Gloucester	"	"	" "
Elizabeth Davis	21	Spinster	Westminster	"	"	" "
Elizabeth "	21	"	"	"	"	" "

Pill a Creek a Port of Bristol, 14th to 21st Aug. 1774.

Edward Ryan	21	Labourer	Bristol	Charming Nancy	Philadelphia	Indented Servant
Timothy Connelly	22	"	"	" "	"	" "
George James	18	Hooper	Hereford	" "	"	" "
James Lynn	20	Brickmaker	Bristol	" "	"	" "
John Weeks	22	Weaver	"	" "	"	" "
John Kenneday	26	Labourer	Ross	" "	"	" "
William Power	18	"	"	" "	"	" "
John Carrel	25	Shoemaker	Bristol	" "	"	" "
B. Kelly	26	Labourer	"	" "	"	" "
John Flemming	21	"	"	" "	"	" "
Henry Havell	25	Cooper	Cork	" "	"	" "
R. Seaton	22	Shoemaker	"	" "	"	" "

Name	*Age*	*Occupation*	*From*	*Ship*	*To*	*As a*
P. Butler	23	Seaman	Cork	Charming Nancy	Philadelphia	Indented Servant
Jno Cass	18	Book binder	Wells	" "	"	" "
James Faulkner	20	Cork Cutter	Bristol	" "	"	" "
One Woman	—	——	——	" "	"	returning Home

Port of London, 21st to 28th Aug. 1774.

George Messenberg	19	Gentleman	London	Royal Exchange	Virginia	On Business
James Jones	43	Fell Monger	"	Lovely Lass	Philadelphia	" "
James Forrester	20	Hat Maker	"	" "	"	to settle
Robert Cory	16	Draper	Norfolk	" "	"	" "
John Simmons	52	Merchant	London	" "	"	On Business
William Stockwell	19	Draper	Norfolk	" "	"	to settle
Leonora Gilman	30	& 3 Children	——	——	——	——
Anthony "	40	Merchant	London	Benjamin & Mary	Campvere	On Business

Pill a Creek a Port of Bristol, 21st to 28th Aug. 1774.

John Simpson	27	Labourer	Bristol	Glorious Memory	Philadelphia	Indented Servant
Thomas Fletcher	26	"	"	" "	"	" "
Daniel Shiels	21	"	"	" "	"	" "
Robert Hurst	30	Soap Maker	Kent	" "	"	" "
Twelve Women	—	——	——	——	——	" "

Port of London, 28th Aug. to 4 Sept. 1774.

James Keen	22	Cook	London	Rebecca	Maryland	Indented Servant
William Nainby	16	Clerk & Bookkeeper	Southwark	"	"	" "
Robert Moore	37	Silversmith	London	"	"	" "
Seth Bailey	21	Carpenter & Joiner	Westminster	"	"	" "
Charles Stuteville	22	Husbandman	Greenwich	"	"	" "
William Collins	24	Butcher	Westminster	"	"	" "
John Johns	24	Carpenter & Joiner	Kent	"	"	" "
James Barker	23	Cloth Dresser	Manchester	"	"	" "
William Wright	33	Sawyer	London	"	"	" "

Elizabeth Haynes	22	Spinster	Westminster	“	“	“ “
Ann Tucker	21	“	Southwark	“	“	“ “
Mary Cormick	24	“	London	“	“	“ “
Andrew Bagge	23	Baker	“	“	“	“ “
Henry Hughes	18	Silversmith	“	“	“	“ “
William Stoakes	16	Husbandman	Nottingham	“	“	“ “
Henry Desterberg	16	Weaver	London	“	“	“ “
John Lynch	16	Taylor	Bucks	“	“	“ “
John Gates	17	Labourer	Newcastle	“	“	“ “
William Lewis	16	“	London	“	“	“ “
Sarah Flaker	16	Spinster	“	“	“	“ “
Ann Baker	16	“	“	“	“	“ “
Arthur Honeywood	22	Cock Founder	Sussex	“	“	“ “
Thomas Pearson	23	Husbandman	London	“	“	“ “
Archibald Laikie	24	Engraver	“	“	“	“ “
Abraham Bass	25	Buckle Maker	“	“	“	“ “
William Archer	23	Surgeon	Newcastle	“	“	“ “
Frederick Dawson	39	Painter	London	“	“	“ “
Thomas Hopper	32	Cooper	York	“	“	“ “
Matthew Branan	21	Smith	London	“	“	“ “
James Keith	24	Clerk & Bookkeeper	Northumberland	“	“	“ “
William Pitman	24	Carpenter & Joiner	Worcester	“	“	“ “
John Benefold	29	Labourer	London	“	“	“ “
William Cooley	21	Founder	Dublin	“	“	“ “
Isaac Kilburn	21	Butcher	York	“	“	“ “
William Linton	21	Skinner & Glover	Northumberland	“	“	“ “
Lawrance Hackett	32	Weaver	Westminster	“	“	“ “
Charles Wightman	26	Surgeon	London	“	“	“ “
Elizabeth Derbyshire	21	Milliner	Surry	“	“	“ “
William Rouse	17	Cloth Weaver	York	“	“	“ “
William Holmes	17	Labourer	Essex	“	“	“ “
Isaac Bury	17	Weaver	London	“	“	“ “

PORT OF LONDON, 5th TO 12 SEPT. 1774.

Martin Crew	29	Taylor	London	Neptune	Maryland	Indented Servant
Mary “	28	His Wife	“	“	“	“ “

Name	*Age*	*Occupation*	*From*	*Ship*	*To*	*As a*
John Heard	21	Schoolmaster	London	Neptune	Maryland	Indented Servant
Samuel Landers	25	Broker	"	"	"	" "
Carl Thale	19	Footman	"	"	"	" "
Richard Nicholas	22	Husbandman	Devon	"	"	" "
Edward Dunn	21	Hatter	Stafford	"	"	" "
Richard Assick	20	Gentleman's Servant	London	"	"	" "
William Clifford	22	Gardener	Bristol	"	"	" "
Thomas Durant	20	Blacksmith	London	"	"	" "
Cornelius Thompson	25	Perukemaker	Milton	"	"	" "
William Ohlson	29	Cabinet Maker	London	"	"	" "
John Uppord	21	Carpenter	"	"	"	" "
Thomas Burn	22	Brickmaker	Surry	"	"	" "
John Byam	18	Groom	Dublin	"	"	" "
John Taylor	33	Cheese Monger	York	"	"	" "
Hersford Johnson	21	Carpenter	Norfolk	"	"	" "
Charles Williams	23	Dyer	Somerset	"	"	" "
James Perkle	22	Printer	Edingbourg	"	"	" "
William George	24	Scrivener	Wilts	"	"	" "
Patrick Hopkins	25	Gentleman's Servant	London	"	"	" "
Jos Butterworth	37	Bookkeeper	"	"	"	" "
John Strong	25	Silversmith	"	"	"	" "
John Rose	22	Schoolmaster	"	"	"	" "
William Lazinby	21	Butcher	"	"	"	" "
Joseph Mead	37	Brickmaker	Wells	"	"	" "
Thomas Jackson	21	Butcher	London	"	"	" "
Benjamin Loftman	16	Gentleman's Servant	York	"	"	" "
John Carroll	22	Husbandman	Dublin	"	"	" "
William Kidder	20	Leather Dresser	London	"	"	" "
James Worker	23	Blacksmith	"	"	"	" "
John George	37	Gentleman's Servant	"	"	"	" "
John Williams	40	Hair Dresser	"	"	"	" "
Margdin Mullunly	25	Groom	"	"	"	" "
Thomas Archdale	40	Stone Mason	"	"	"	" "
George Wood	25	Groom	"	"	"	" "
John Reilly	26	Brass founder	London	"	"	" "

Frederick Mathey	21	Coach Maker	“	“	“	“ “
Jos West	44	Shipwright	Greenwich	“	“	“ “
Abraham Tucker	25	Blacksmith	Surry	“	“	“ “
Charity Armstead	21	Milliner	London	“	“	“ “
Sarah Timmins	21	Servant	“	“	“	“ “
William Pearse	23	Surgeon	“	“	“	“ “
John Butler	23	Linen Weaver	“	“	“	“ “
Thomas Paterson	23	Taylor	“	“	“	“ “
Charles David	26	Schoolmaster	Wales	“	“	“ “
Francis Lester	18	Hair Dresser	Edingbourg	“	“	“ “
Thomas Loyd	28	Footman	London	“	“	“ “
Thoma Warren	31	Trunk Maker	“	“	“	“ “
John Cale	42	Taylor	“	“	“	“ “
Robert Peacock	24	Joiner	“	“	“	“ “
John Braithwait	24	Sawyer	“	“	“	“ “
William Jenner	50	Cloth Weaver	“	“	“	“ “
Martin Pandel	21	Baker	“	“	“	“ “
John Long	23	Tinman	“	“	“	“ “

Port of Lo[illegible]dom, 12th to 19th Sept. 1[illegible]74.

James Underwood	27	Schoolmaster	Salop	Nancy	Maryland	Indented Servant
Elias Making	30	Taylor	London	“	“	“ “
William Miller	29	Plaisterer	Dorset	“	“	“ “
Samuel Moor	38	Gardener	Surry	“	“	“ “
Thomas Tamer	21	Brickmaker	London	“	“	“ “
Samuel Griffiths	19	Gardener	Islington	“	“	“ “
John Rutherford	21	Turner	Westminster	“	“	“ “

Pill a Creek a Poet of Bristol, 12th to 19th Sept. 1774.

Wm Gussick	17	Labourer	Wells	Concord	Philadelphia	Indented Servant
James Haskins	13	“	“	“	“	“ “

EMIGRANTS FROM ENGLAND

Transcribed by GERALD FOTHERGILL of New Wandsworth, London, England, and communicated by the Committee on English Research

PORT OF LIVERPOOL, 12th TO 19th SEPT. 1774.

Name	Age	Occupation	From	Ship	To	As a
John Jones	27	Watchmaker	Staffordshire	Liverpool	Philadelphia	To work at his Trade
Wm Whiteside	25	Merchant	London	"	"	To Trade

PORT OF LONDON, 12 TO 19st SEPT. 1774.

Thomas Brown	22	Blacksmith	Westminster	Nancy	Maryland	Indented Servant
Peter Credy	25	Taylor	London	"	"	" "
Charles Cook	23	Box and Trunk Maker	"	"	"	" "
Williams Elkins	25	Sawyer	"	"	"	" "
Joseph Law	21	Husbandman	Middlesex	"	"	" "
George Hamilton	19	"	Worcester	"	"	" "
Henry Halworth	23	Weaver	Lincoln	"	"	" "
John Gordon	28	Husbandman	Westminster	"	"	" "
George Ward	22	Carpenter	Surry	"	"	" "
Robert Watson	28	Shipwright	Greenwich	"	"	" "
John Lucas	23	Cordwainer	Middlesex	"	"	" "
Thomas Rubidge	37	Leather Dresser	Surry	"	"	" "
William Lyon	30	Surgeon & Apothecary	Liverpool	"	"	" "
Edward Davis	25	Cooper	London	"	"	" "
Thomas Edwards	19	Cordwainer	Westminster	"	"	" "
John Neave	25	Farmer	Lincoln	"	"	" "
John Paterlange	21	Clerk & Bookkeeper	London	"	"	" "
Thomas Charnock	26	Brickmaker	"	Neptune	Philadelphia	" "
Samuel Wherrett	25	Watch Movement Maker	"	"	"	" "
Edward Jones	21	Labourer	"	"	"	" "
John Christian Haffner	28	Taylor	"	"	"	" "
Ephraim Christian Mickell	34	Butcher	"	"	"	" "

Port of Hull, 19th to 26th Sept. 1774.

Thomas Layton	32	Horse Jockey	Malton	Jamaica Packet	Jamaica	To seek a better livelihood
John Fletcher	15	Native of the Country	Hull	" "	"	Going to his Friends
Daniel Bridges	25	Merchant	"	" "	"	To settle in business

Port of Plymouth, 26th Sept. to 3rd Oct. 1774.

Cousin Richard Esqre	29	Gentleman	London	Proudfoot	Grenada	Going to reside
Clozier Esqre	21	Planter	"	"	"	" "
Duval Esqre	16	"	"	"	"	" "
Deglapion Esqre	23	"	"	"	"	" "
Mr Niel	18	Merchant	"	"	"	" "
Monbrun	26	Servant	"	"	"	" "
Antoine	25	"	"	"	"	" "
Francois	15	"	"	"	"	" "
Rosette	25	"	"	"	"	" "
John Henry	30	Clerk	"	"	"	Going to Settle
Peter Bossile	21	"	"	"	"	" "
Stephen Clerk	26	"	"	"	"	" "

Port of London, 3rd to 10th Oct. 1774.

Rachel L'Fabeure	40	Lady	London	London	Carolina	Going for Pleasure
Jane Bignell	47	Severt of Do	"	"	"	Going with Mrs L' Fabeure
Ann Bowie	36	" "	"	"	"	" " "
Eliza Batty	16	A Native of Carolina	"	"	"	Going home
Ann Weston	30	Lady	"	"	"	Going for Pleasure
John West	28	Gentleman	"	"	"	" "
John Auldjo	15	"	"	"	"	" "
Alexr Auldjo	16	"	"	"	"	" "
Robert Dee	33	"	"	"	"	" "
Henry Houseman	35	"	"	"	"	" "
Hezekiah Johnson	22	Land Surveyor	"	Standlinch	Jamaica	Going for Encouragement
William Finch	11	A Youth	"	"	"	Going under the care of Mr Johnson

Name	*Age*	*Occupation*	*From*	*Ship*	*To*	*As a*
John Forbes	25	Blacksmith	Scotland	Standlinch	Jamaica	Indented Servant
William Middleton	23	Carpenter	"	"	"	" "
John Lindsey	23	Mercer	"	"	"	" "
George Allerdyer	22	Carpenter	"	"	"	" "
William Brown	21	Blacksmith	"	"	"	" "
Thom^s Craig	22	Mason	"	"	"	" "
James Flanagan	21	Husbandman	"	"	"	" "
William Lamb	21	"	"	"	"	" "
Hugh Price	15	Labourer	London	London Packet	Philadelphia	" "
John Sollicoffre	17	Cabinet Maker	"	" "	"	" "
Charles Foggett	17	Labourer	"	" "	"	" "
Charles Wallis	22	Baker	"	" "	"	" "
William Sparrow	22	Worsted Weaver	Northampton	" "	"	" "
William Chester	24	Gardener	London	" "	"	" "
Abraham Bryant	22	Buckle Maker	"	" "	"	" "
Daniel Briarly	45	Plaisterer	Lancaster	"	"	" "
Joseph Savage	22	Bookkeeper	London	" "	"	" "
John Mason	21	Baker	"	" "	"	" "
George Jones	21	Ironfounder	"	" "	"	" "
Willm Hayman	22	Carpenter	"	" "	"	" "
John Clare	22	Servant	Colchester	" "	"	" "
John Williams	22	Sawyer	London	" "	"	" "
William Good	21	Perukemaker	"	" "	"	" "
Richard Briggs	25	Shipwright	"	" "	"	" "
Richard Jones	21	Labourer	"	" "	"	" "
William Jones	38	Printer	"	" "	"	" "
James Poyton	40	Woolcomber	Somerset	" "	"	" "
John Stallard	32	Cook	London	" "	"	" "
Thomas Williamson	23	Taylor	"	" "	"	" "
Robert Colbrook	28	Miller	Kent	" "	"	" "
Aaron Bowler	21	Labourer	London	" "	"	" "
Jos Wyatt	27	Woolcomber	Essex	" "	"	" "
Richd Mitchell	15	Labourer	London	" "	"	" "
William Davenport	15	"	"	" "	"	" "
John Wetherel	15	"		" "	"	" "

Joseph Palmer	16	"	"	"	"	"	"	"
Henry Carwebe	15	"	"	"	"	"	"	"
Charles Pemberton	16	"	"	"	"	"	"	"
John Meech	17	"	Lincoln	"	"	"	"	"
George Dowson	16	"	Northampton	"	"	"	"	"
Edward Arnold	16	"	London	"	"	"	"	"
William Brymer	18	"	York	"	"	"	"	"
John Watts	22	Brass Founder	London	"	"	"	"	"
John Bryant	21	Husbandman	"	"	"	"	"	"
David Brown	35	Gardener	"	"	"	"	"	"
James Hay	29	"	"	"	"	"	"	"
William Noll	27	Stone Mason	Kent	"	"	"	"	"
Charles Hallett	21	Musician	London	"	"	"	"	"
John Gelling	23	Pavior	"	"	"	"	"	"
Richard Roily	28	Breeches Maker	"	"	"	"	"	"
James Lee	26	Tobacconist	Surry	"	"	"	"	"
John Dunilton	21	Baker	Dublin	"	"	"	"	"
Jonas Turner	25	Dyer	London	"	"	"	"	"
Thomas Taylor	21	Brickmaker	"	"	"	"	"	"
John Clark	18	Joiner	"	"	"	"	"	"
Alexander Gray	36	Taylor	"	"	"	"	"	"
William Manning	16	Labourer	Kent	"	"	"	"	"
Samuel Meekham	15	Letter Founder	London	"	"	"	"	"
John White	22	Labourer	Suffolk	"	"	"	"	"
John Brown	17	Clerk & Bookkeeper	Northumberland	"	"	"	"	"
John Topping	23	Boat Builder	Newcastle	"	"	"	"	"
Jos Dayman	21	Blacksmith	London	"	"	"	"	"
Richard Francis	26	Stocking Weaver	"	"	"	"	"	"
Jos Doyle	24	Cabinet Maker	Warwick	"	"	"	"	"
Lakey Kelly	25	Husbandman	London	"	"	"	"	"
James Feull	24	"	"	"	"	"	"	"
Joseph Rudsdell	15	Labourer	Norwich	"	"	"	"	"
Luke Wilmott	15	Blacksmith	London	"	"	"	"	"
John Rolph	15	Labourer	"	"	"	"	"	"
John Alsop	15	"	"	"	"	"	"	"
William Chisham	19	Net Maker	"	"	"	"	"	"
Thomas Fenton	15	Labourer	"	"	"	"	"	"
John Bailey	15	Thread Maker	Birmingham	"	"	"	"	"

Name	*Age*	*Occupation*	*From*	*Ship*	*To*	*As a*
William Leonard	15	Pavior	London	London Packet	Philadelphia	Indented Servant
Joseph Wright	16	Labourer	"	" "	"	" "
Robert Merryfield	15	"	"	" "	"	" "
Andrew Flogden	16	"	Norfolk	" "	"	" "
Thomas Bissell	17	"	Lincoln	" "	"	" "
James Mooring	17	Brick maker	Suffolk	" "	"	" "
John Lee	16	Rope Maker	Durham	" "	"	" "
Owen Williams	18	Husbandman	Durham	" "	"	" "
Bobert Jones	22	House Painter	London	" "	"	" "
Alexander Abrahams	23	Clerk	"	" "	"	" "
Thomas Rolph	21	Cordwainer	"	" "	"	" "
John Alexander	23	Hatter	"	" "	"	" "
George Smith	21	Baker	Liverpool	" "	"	" "
James Elliott	32	Cordwainer	London	" "	"	" "
William Johnston	26	Gardener	Herts	" "	"	" "
Benjamin Palmer	25	Footman	London	" "	"	" "
Thomas Dailey	24	Baker	"	" "	"	" "
Joseph Watley	22	Cloth Weaver	Wilts	" "	"	" "
John Frost	25	Woolcomber	London	" "	"	" "
Patrick Boylan	24	Cordwainer	Dublin	" "	"	" "
Dean Taylor	28	Surgeon	London	" "	"	" "
John Baldry	22	Gardener	"	" "	"	" "
Thomas Salver	30	"	Nottingham	" "	"	" "
William Lye	18	"	"	" "	"	" "
John Heap	15	Labourer	London	" "	"	" "
John Forster	17	Gardener	"	" "	"	" "
Thomas Walter	19	Labourer	"	" "	"	" "
William Hodson	15	"	Bristol	" "	"	" "
John Ford	17	Taylor	"	" "	"	" "
William Dodd	17	Watch Gilder	London	" "	"	" "
William Dawson	17	Husbandman	"	" "	"	" "
William Chapman	18	"	Essex	" "	"	" "
John Tyre	16	"	"	" "	"	" "
Jo^{s} Medget	16	"	Norwich	" "	"	" "
James Hooper	22	Printer	Dorset	" "	"	" "

Joel Simmel	21	Hair dresser	London	" "	"	" "
John Allen	21	Groom	"	" "	"	" "
Francis May	21	Cabinet Maker	"	" "	"	" "
Samuel Hook	38	Printer	London	" "	"	" "
William Oldaker	22	Sawyer	"	" "	"	" "
John Mingay	44	Cooper	"	" "	"	" "
Robert Cobham	39	Joiner & Carpenter	"	" "	"	" "
Lawrence Kamey	23	Husbandman	Ireland	" "	"	" "
Laughlin Birn	21	Farmer	Ireland	" "	"	" "
Lewin Coey	21	Butcher	London	" "	"	" "
Dederick Griskin	30	Carpenter	"	" "	"	" "

Pill a Member of the Port of Bristol, 3rd to 10th Oct. 1774.

One hundred & Six Convicts from the different Jails in the Kingdom	William	Maryland	To be transported

Port of Newcastle, 3rd to 10th Oct. 1774.

Thomas Stead	17	Butcher	Hull	Rockingham	Cape Fear	Going to his Father who lives there

Port of London, 10th to 17th Oct. 1774.

James Reed	27	Taylor	London	Lady Tuliana	Jamaica	Going to settle
Thomas Chisham	15	Clerk	"	" "	"	Going as a Clerk
William Hall	16	"	"	" "	"	" "
James Pottinger	15	Labourer	"	Two Friends	Philadelphia	Indented Servant
John Graves	25	Stocking Weaver	Nottingham	" "	"	" "
Thomas Payne	22	Carpenter & Joiner	Southampton	" "	"	" "
Jonathan Allan	19	Glass Grinder	London	" "	"	" "
James Stewart	22	Clerk & Bookkeeper	Edingbourgh	" "	"	" "
Alary Collin	22	Spinster	Kent	" "	"	" "
Moses Burt	15	Husbandman	Somerset	Mary	"	" "
John Lander	19	"	Edingbourgh	"	"	" "
George Sadler	26	"		"	"	" "
Elizabeth Savigny	21	Spinster	London	"	"	" "
Jonathan Grover	17	Groom	Surry	"	"	" "

Name	*Age*	*Occupation*	*From*	*Ship*	*To*	*As a*
William Stone	18	Husbandman	Oxford	Mary	Philadelphia	Indented Servant
Joseph Harris	15	Labourer	Warwick	"	"	" "
Michael McDonald	21	Plaisterer	London	"	"	" "
Jane Tiberson	21	Spinster	"	"	"	" "
Wm Burt	18	Husbandman	Somerset	Two Friends	"	" "

PORT OF LONDON, 17th TO 24th OCT. 1774.

Name	*Age*	*Occupation*	*From*	*Ship*	*To*	*As a*
Rebecca Wildie	22	Spinster	London	Britannia	Barbadoes	Going to Settle
Thomas Evans	26	Servant	"	"	"	Going to his Master
Wiloughby Day	14	Lad	"	"	"	Going to his Friends
Stephen Eglin	25	Draper	"	Newmarket	Carolina	Going to Settle
Jasper Scouler	30	Carpenter	"	"	"	" "
Thomas Wilcox	25	Currier	"	Suekey	Salem	Going on business
James Berry	15	Servant	"	"	"	Going to his Master
Andrew Wright	22	Millwright	Jamaica	George Booth	Jamaica	Going home
Mary "	22	His Wife	"	" "	"	" "
James Brookson	18	Gentleman	Surry	" "	"	Going to Settle
Robert Maxwell	18	Clerk	Scotland	James	Carolina	Going to Settle
Willson Dabrall	25	Jeweller	"	"	"	" "
Berobeer Forsyth	22	Gentleman	"	"	"	" "
Sarah Eastwood	16	Spinster	London	Lowther	St Carolina	Indented Servant
Joseph Dyer	21	Waiter	"	"	" "	" "
William Kennedy	25	Perukemaker	"	"	" "	" "
Ralph Richardson	35	Gardener	Surry	"	" "	" "
John Ayliffe	17	Husbandman	Suffolk	Sims	Maryland	" "
Elizabeth Magguire	17	Spinster	Westminster	"	"	" "
Ann Tapp	16	"	London	"	"	" "
James Read	20	Bricklayer	Middlesex	"	"	" "
James Yeo	21	Carpenter & Joiner	"	"	"	" "
Francis Sedly	21	" "	Ireland	"	"	" "
Jos Gibbs	26	Surgeon	London	"	"	" "
Thomas Wood	22	Glazier & Painter	Middlesex	"	"	" "
Jas Scarborough	25	Perukemaker	London	"	"	" "
Thomas Morgan	27	Skinner	"	"	"	" "

William McColl	37	Gardener	Kent	"	"	"	"
Jesse Scudder	21	Husbandman	"	"	"	"	"
William Williams	16	Gardener	Bristol	"	"	"	"
Mary Le Fount	19	Spinster	London	"	"	"	"
John Salmon	15	Taylor	"	"	"	"	"
Charles Savin	24	Painter & Glazier	Westminster	"	"	"	"
John Hipsley Standen	29	Brewer & Clerk	"	"	"	"	"
John Freeman	23	Butcher	Oxford	"	"	"	"
Charles Ferrier	31	Taylor	London	"	"	"	"
Penelope Anderson	23	Book Binder	"	"	"	"	"
Jane Smart	23	Spinster	"	"	"	"	"

PORT OF LONDON, 24th TO 31st OCT. 1774.

John Somersal	22	Clock Maker	London	Sophia	Maryland	Indented	Servant
George Finlayson	21	Taylor	Southampton	"	"	"	"
Edward Burchal	21	Labourer	London	"	"	"	"
Ralph Hague	24	Painter	Edingburgh	"	"	"	"
Anthony Paine	23	Groom	Worcester	"	"	"	"
Thomas Butcher	22	Gardener	"	"	"	"	"
Joseph Lawton	30	Dyer	Somerset	"	"	"	"
James Masterson	36	Gardener	London	"	"	"	"
John Barnard	24	Weaver	"	"	"	"	"
William Dunster	40	Taylor	"	"	"	"	"
Elizabeth Dunster	21	His Wife	"	"	"	"	"
John Peacock	39	Husbandman	Kent	"	"	"	"
Elizabeth Peacock	34	His Wife	"	"	"	"	"
Mary Alford	21	Spinster	London	"	"	"	"
Mary Thompson	26	"	"	"	"	"	"
John Parkinson	34	Joiner	"	"	"	"	"
Thomas Titcomb	25	Stone Mason	Bristol	"	"	"	"
William Wintent	22	Groom	London	"	"	"	"
John Remonda	30	Hair dresser	"	"	"	"	"
Robert Ambrose	22	Surgeon	"	"	"	"	"
Thomas Anderson	22	Husbandman	Bristol	"	"	"	"
George Graham	17	"	Cumberland	"	"	"	"
John Oliver	17	"	"	"	"	"	"

Name	*Age*	*Occupation*	*From*	*Ship*	*To*	*As a*
Saml Davidson	15	Watch Maker	London	Sophia	Maryland	Indented Servant
John Davidson	22	Surgeon	"	"	"	" "
John Wilson	39	Perukemaker	"	"	"	" "
John Chandler	19	Clock Maker	Suffolk	"	"	" "
C. Spingen	21	Linen Weaver	London	"	"	" "
John Turner	22	" "	"	"	"	" "
William Cook	24	Paper Hanger	"	"	"	" "
Christopher Roan	22	Weaver	"	"	"	" "
William Banks	24	"	"	"	"	" "
William Sisson	21	Cordwainer	"	"	"	" "
William Alford	26	Printer	"	"	"	" "
Nathaniel Norton	26	Taylor	"	"	"	" "
John Wright	30	Book Keeper	"	"	"	" "
Samuel Mashman	36	Clock Maker	Wiltshire	"	"	" "
Daniel Smith	38	Wire Drawer	London	"	"	" "
Amos Blackwell	43	Weaver	"	"	"	" "
Henry Perriman	22	Husbandman	"	"	"	" "
James Bencroft	27	Carpenter	"	"	"	" "
Mathias Bonner	28	Taylor	"	"	"	" "
Hannah Butler	27	Cook & Dairy Maid	"	"	"	" "
Mathew Simpson	48	Joiner	"	"	"	" "
James Gosling	34	Whitesmith	"	"	"	" "
Thomas Gilchrist	27	Carpenter	"	"	"	" "
John Furger	19	Book Keeper	"	"	"	" "
Jonathan Ridge	22	Joiner	"	"	"	" "
William Willoughby	22	Cordwainer	"	"	"	" "
John Reynolds	22	Weaver	"	"	"	" "
John Cooper	29	Schoolmaster	"	"	"	" "
Samuel Freeman	27	Book Keeper	"	"	"	" "
Edward Steed	25	Husbandman	Essex	"	"	" "
Charles Field	21	Engraver	Ireland	"	"	" "
William Cook	21	Husbandman	Plymouth	"	"	" "
Peter Deacon	25	Breeches Maker	London	"	"	" "
Charles Stone	21	Husbandman	"	"	"	" "
Walter Prior	32	Carpenter	"	"	"	" "

Elizabeth Hilint	21	Spinster	"	"	"	" "
Andrew Russel	24	Gardener	Kent	"	"	" "
Robert Henry	36	Cooper	"	"	"	" "
John Griffiths	26	Groom	"	"	"	" "
Samuel Vincent ✓	23	Plaisterer	London	"	"	" "

PORT OF PORTSMOUTH, 24th TO 31st OCT. 1774.

John Robinson	50	Planter at Dominica	Gosport	Aurora	Dominica	To Superentend his plantation

PILL A CREEK A PORT OF BRISTOL, 31st OCT. TO 7 NOV. 1774.

James Nash	18	Labourer	Westbury	Sampson	Maryland	Indented Servant
John Philips	15	"	Hereford	"	"	" "
William Pope	18	"	Bath	"	"	" "
N. Murray	30	Weaver	Cork	"	"	" "
John Foster	26	Shoemaker	Newport	"	"	" "
John Knight	19	"	"	"	"	" "
James Straham	18	Labourer	Scotland	"	"	" "
William Whitehead	27	"	Bristol	"	"	" "
John Lane	17	"	"	"	"	" "
William Lane	19	"	"	"	"	" "
Robert Aston	18	"	Salop	"	"	" "
B. Murphy	26	"	Dublin	"	"	" "
James Grace	19	"	Leicester	"	"	" "
Robert Ward	17	Barber	Wiltshire	"	"	" "
James Butler	29	Labourer	Falmouth	"	"	" "
Edward Bennett	27	"	"	"	"	" "
John Williams	18	Shoemaker	Bristol	"	"	" "
Thomas Reece	19	Labourer	Wales	"	"	" "
Robert Evans	15	"	"	"	"	" "
John Stallard	19	"	Bath	"	"	" "
William Read	15	"	"	"	"	" "
John Felley	17	"	London	"	"	" "
Samuel Trotman	16	"	"	"	"	" "

PORT OF WHITEHAVEN, 31st OCT. TO 7th NOV. 1774.

William Birbeck	16	Merchants Clerk	Cumberland	Prince George	Jamaica	To keep a Store

Port of London, 7th to 14 Nov. 1774.

Name	Age	Occupation	From	Ship	To	As a
William Ripley	22	Farmer	York	Mary & Hannah	Carolina	Going to Settle
John Sanderson	45	"	"	" "	"	" "
John Blyth	32	Gentleman	London	" "	"	On Pleasure
James Downing	20	Surgeon	"	Turnbull	Tortola	to Settle
Nicholas Purcel	23	Planter	"	"	"	" "
John Burke	16	"	"	"	"	" "
John Belinder	45	Merchant	"	Good Intent	Antigua	On Business
Jane Ross	21	———	"	Harlequin	Nevis	To see her Friends
John Arthurton	22	Merchant	Nevis	"	"	Going home
James Flatt	25	Taylor	London	Mary & Hannah	Carolina	Indented Servant for two Years
James Trenham	22	Butcher	York	" "	"	" " "

Port of Portsmouth, 7th to 14th [Nov.] 1774.

Mr Beckford & his family			London	New Duckinfield	Jamaica	To settle on his Estate at Jamaica

Pill a Member of the Port of Bristol, 7th to 14th Nov. 1774.

William Hensley	40	Gentleman	Jamaica	Chorlotte Pegr	Jamaica	to return Home
John Saunders	36	Gentleman	"	" "	"	" "

Port of London, 14th to 21st Nov. 1774.

John Sanbatch	13	———	London	Marquis of Rockingham	Grenades	Going to his friends
Jos Nappier	15	A Native of the	Grenades		"	Going home
Mary Powell	33	———	London	Dawes	Jamaica	Going to her husband
David Smith	21	Clerk	Scotland	"	"	To Settle
Thomas Banister	19	"	London	"	"	" "
James Pringle	16	Gentleman	"	"	"	On Pleasure
James Afflick	35	Carpenter	"	"	"	To Settle
James Meldram	42	Docter	America	Catharine	America	Going home
Charles Constable	19	Gentleman	London	"	"	To Settle

Robert Martin	23	“	“	William & Elizabeth	Antigua	“ “
Thomas Powell	15	Youth	Jamaica	Catharine	Jamaica	Going to their Friends
George Forster	11	“	Bedford	“	“	“ “ “
Henry Forster	12	“	“	“	“	“ “ “
John Thompson	17	Clerk	London	“	“	As a Clerk
Richard Clark	30	Cooper	“	Mars	“	To Settle
William Kettle	30	Blacksmith	“	“	“	“ “
William Barker	30	“	“	“	“	“ “
James Giddons	25	Millwright	“	“	“	“ “
George Hearton	27	Gentleman	“	Crook	St. Vincent	On Business
Robert Carson	20	Surgeon	“	Simond	Grenades	To Settle
George Nicholson	27	Merchant	“	“	“	“ “
William Francey	30	Woolcomber	“	Elizabeth	Virginia	Indented Servant
Marten Mills	22	Husbandman	Hampshire	“	“	“ “
Thomas Hamerston	22	Dyer	London	“	“	“ “
Daniel Sabouren	21	Weaver	“	“	“	“ “
Robert Simpson	31	Taylor	“	“	“	“ “
Charles May	22	Poulterer	“	“	“	“ “
Alexander Watson	44	Baker	Suffolk	“	“	“ “
John Tucker	39	Cloth Weaver	Devon	“	“	“ “
Charles Humphry	25	Coachman	London	“	“	“ “
John Bates	21	Baker	Norwich	“	“	“ “
Edward Coombs	21	Skinner	Bristol	“	“	“ “
John Bailey	21	“	“	“	“	“ “
Richard Green	18	Husbandman	Canterbury	“	“	“ “
Samuel Brown	19	Labourer	Middlesex	“	“	“ “
Robert Pearce	15	“	“	“	“	“ “
Ann Wright	20	Spinster	London	“	“	“ “
Elizabeth Wright	20	“	“	“	“	“ “
Mary Hooper	18	“	“	“	“	“ “
Charles Bush	18	Labourer	“	“	“	“ “
Thomas Thomson	18	Clerk & Bookkeeper	Norfolk	“	“	“ “
William Gray	17	Labourer	London	“	“	“ “
Robert Salter	21	Groom	“	“	“	“ “
John Flower	21	“	“	“	“	“ “
William Williamson	21	Baker	“	“	“	“ “
John Williamson	21	“	“	“	“	“ “

Name	Age	Occupation	From	Ship	To	As a
William Hillyer	21	Baker	Portsmouth	Elizabeth	Virginia	Indented Servant
John Tolson	30	Taylor	London	“	“	“ “
James Fromny	32	Weaver	“	“	“	“ “
Samuel Poulter	39	Gardener	“	“	“	“ “
John Pele	21	“	“	“	“	“ “
Thomas Dore	23	Groom	“	“	“	“ “
Jos March	21	Labourer	Gloucester	“	“	“ “
Alexr McDaniel	26	Rope Maker	Liverpool	“	“	“ “
Benjamin March	29	Husbandman	Portsmouth	“	“	“ “
George Gibbs	21	Labourer	London	“	“	“ “
Patrick Thomas	27	Sawyer	Berks	“	“	“ “
Joseph Smith	24	·Painter	Herts	“	“	“ “
William Lee	25	Cooper	London	“	“	“ “
John Clark	28	Groom	Kent	“	“	“ “
Jos Bromley	22	Husbandman	Bucks	“	“	“ “
John Shine	31	Perukemaker	London	“	“	“ “
Amos Beck	28	Husbandman	Norfolk	“	“	“ “
John Wood	27	Bricklayer	London	“	“	“ “
Henry Stone	21	Surgeon	“	“	“	“ “
Francis Turner	33	Cordwainer	Somerset	“	“	“ “
William Brazier	19	Labourer	London	“	“	“ “
William Brock	23	“	“	“	“	“ “
John Bowen	34	Husbandman	“	“	“	“ “
William Ramsey	22	Baker	“	“	“	“ “
Hugh Reed	23	Woolcomber	Scotland	“	“	“ “
Charles King	21	Groom	Herts	“	“	“ “
John Newton	21	Clerk & Bookkeeper	“	“	“	“ “
William Smith	26	“ “	Waterford	“	“	“ “
Owen Keefe	27	Husbandman	London	“	“	“ “
Henry Honsdon	21	Cordwainer	“	“	“	“ “
John Proudfoot	24	Hairdresser	Scotland	“	“	“ “
Robt Wentherhead	26	Weaver	London	“	“	“ “
Thomas Parsons	25	Carpenter	Kent	“	“	“ “
John Morres	30	Husbandman	Berks	“	“	“ “
John Curtis	27	“	“	“	“	“ “

William Stephens	22	Gardener	“	“	“	“ “
Dorothy Stephens	22	His Wife	“	“	“	“ “
John Colgrove	23	Labourer	Ireland	“	“	“ “
Thomas Doyle	22	“	London	“	“	“ “
Charles Stevens	22	“	“	“	“	“ “
Wm Molling	19	“	“	“	“	“ “
John Leach	17	Cordwainer	Surry	“	“	“ “
Thomas Himler	34	Sawyer	Durham	“	“	“ “
George Darling	35	Hair dresser	London	“	“	“ “
John Brown	23	Husbandman	Huntingdon	“	“	“ “
John Head	17	“	London	“	“	“ “
Mary Read	16	Spinster	“	“	“	“ “
Ann Refane	22	Glove Maker	“	“	“	“ “
Jane Paterson	22	Spinster	“	“	“	“ “
Ann Leverston	22	Glove Maker	“	“	“	“ “
Ann Philips	22	Spinster	“	“	“	“ “
Mary Jones	22	“	Birmingham	“	“	“ “
James Wright	22	Baker	London	“	“	“ “
James Philips	23	Groom	“	“	“	“ “
John Parlow	30	Hatter	“	“	“	“ “
Alexander Andrews	29	Bricklayer	“	“	“	“ “
George Thomas	22	Butcher	“	“	“	“ “
George Davidson	38	Husbandman	“	“	“	“ “
Samuel Penn	24	Baker	Deptford	Catharine	Philadelphia	Indented Servant
John Pye	24	Clock Maker	London	“	“	“ “
John Peyerden	32	Sugar Baker	“	“	“	“ “
Thomas Hayler	35	Perukemaker	“	“	“	“ “
Patrick Clarke	21	Husbandman	Essex	“	“	“ “
David Payne	38	Dyer	“	“	“	“ “
Robert Samuel	22	Printer	“	“	“	“ “
Lawden Halliburton	25	Hairdresser	London	“	“	“ “
Thomas Phipps	21	Husbandman	Middlesex	“	“	“ “
Philip Clarke	21	“	Essex	“	“	“ “
John Bell	36	Ship Carpenter	Cumberland	“	“	“ “
John Thornton	30	Pewterer	London	“	“	“ “
James Povey	29	Tallow Chandler	“	“	“	“ “
Justice Walker	40	Seaman	“	“	“	“ “
Mrs Walker	30	His Wife	“	“	“	“ “

EMIGRANTS FROM ENGLAND

Transcribed by Gerald Fothergill of New Wandsworth, London, England, and communicated by the Committee on English Research

Port of London, 21st to 28th Nov. 1774.

Name	*Age*	*Occupation*	*From*	*Ship*	*To*	*As a*
Robert Anderson	16	Clerk	Edingbourgh	Warnees	Antigua	Going to his Uncle
Joseph Wesley	15	Cabinet Maker	Norfolk	Britannia	Philadelphia	Going to settle
Mary Wesley	22	Spinster	"	"	"	" "
Ann Wesley	48	Mother to the Above	"	"	"	" "
Elizabeth Wesley	13	Spinster	"	"	"	" "
Charles Wesley	25	Husbandman	"	"	"	" "
Thomas Foulger	42	"	"	"	"	" "
Mary "	40	His Wife	"	"	"	" "
Rebecca "	18		"	"	"	" "
Thomas "	16	&	"	"	"	" "
Benjamin "	14	Children	"	"	"	" "
John Rant	40	Woolen draper	London	"	"	" "
John Graven	40	Gentleman	"	Catharine	St Kitts	Going on pleasure
Thomas Bradshaw	35	"	"	"	" "	" "
Robert Guld	21	Clerk	"	"	" "	As a Clerk
John Young	24	Merchant	"	"	" "	On Business
John Robinson	15	Youth	"	Westerhall	Grenades	As a Clerk
Thomas Boyse	15	"	"	"	"	" "
Thomas Wood	25	Groom	Middlesex	Active	Virginia	Indented Servant
George Morris	23	Carpenter & Joiner	London	"	"	" "
Catharine Simpson	23	Milliner and Mantua Maker	"	"	"	" "
William Tilley	21	Tinker	Kent	"	"	" "
Andrew Haines	16	Labourer	Middlesex	"	"	" "
Robert Perry	20	"	Southwark	"	"	" "
Archibald Miller	27	Gardener	Kent	"	"	" "
Patrick Rinney	22	Husbandman	London	"	"	" "

James Gogin	22	"	Essex	"	"	"	"
Joseph Cooper	26	Schoolmaster	London	"	"	"	"
John Baptist	26	Husbandman	"	"	"	"	"
James Johnson	42	Silk Weaver	"	"	"	"	"
Charles Bruing	23	Groom	"	"	"	"	"
Stephen Rust	28	Gardener	Middlesex	"	"	"	"
Reuben Longust	35	Tallow Chandler	London	"	"	"	"
Joseph Cobudge	22	Husbandman	Essex	"	"	"	"
Thomas Felton		"	Middlesex	"	"	"	"
J Burges	21	"	London	"	"	"	"
Susanna Staples	22	Spinster	"	"	"	"	"
Jane Budgman	29	Widow	Kent	"	"	"	"
Sarah Lowe	29	Spinster	London	"	"	"	"
Elizabeth Everett	21	"	Kent	"	"	"	"
James Elgian	23	Clerk & Bookkeeper	Scotland	"	"	"	"
George Coles	15	Labourer	Oxford	"	"	"	"
John Hadley	25	Cabinet Maker	Gloucester	"	"	"	"
Robert Allen	16	Footman	London	"	"	"	"
Thomas Newman	16	Stocking Weaver	Leicester	"	"	"	"
Thomas Cooper	16	Groom	Durham	"	"	"	"
Jeremiah Murphy	23	Gardener	London	"	"	"	"
Michael Nugent	22	Paviour	Essex	"	"	"	"
John Calaghan	23	Husbandman	Southwark	"	"	"	"
William Melson	24	"	Kent	"	"	"	"
John Willison	16	Labourer	Surry	"	"	"	"
George Gretton	19	Gun Stock Maker	Warrick	"	"	"	"
Alexander Ford	26	Cooper	Surry	"	"	"	"
Edward Hewkes	36	Butcher	Suffolk	"	"	"	"
Thomas Bradshaw	32	Blacksmith	Middlesex	"	"	"	"
Thomas Young	29	Carpenter	Somerset	"	"	"	"
Joseph Mathershaw	21	Cutler	York	"	"	"	"
George King	35	Husbandman	London	"	"	"	"
John Catheral	38	Gardener	"	"	"	"	"
Joseph Bennett	22	Carpenter	Bristol	"	"	"	"
Samuel Fox	22	Bricklayer	Surry	"	"	"	"
William Cooke	30	Cordwainer	London	"	"	"	"
Solomon Taylor	25	Smith	"	"	"	"	"
Ann Taylor	27	His Wife	"	"	"	"	"

Name	*Age*	*Occupation*	*From*	*Ship*	*To*	*As a*
William Peters	15	Labourer	London	Active	Virginia	Indented Servant
Hannah Burdon	27	His Wife [*sic*]	"	"	"	" "
Elizabeth Poplett	28	Cook Maid	"	"	"	" "
Edward Walker	20	Stocking Weaver	"	"	"	" "
Jonathan Forster	20	Husbandman	"	"	"	" "
Luke Brady	23	Labourer	Westminster	"	"	" "
Thomas Etridge	26	Husbandman	"	"	"	" "
Stephen Williamson	31	Perukemaker	"	"	"	" "

Port of Portsmouth, 21st to 28 Nov. 1774.

Bazil Cooper Esqre	36	Merchant	Georgia	John	Georgia	Going to Settle
William Thompson Esqre	20	Gentleman	London	"	"	To Settle his private Affairs

Port of London, 28th Nov. to 6th Dec. 1774.

Nicholas Herbert	34	A Wine Merchant	Surry	Beaufort	Georgia	Going to Settle
Nicholas "	9	His Son	"	"	"	Going with his father
Thomas Forestreet	24	Clerk	London	New Shoreham	Jamaica	Going to settle
John Wellery	20	Gentleman	Jamaica	" "	"	Going Home
D Tavans	14	"	"	" "	"	" "
W. Clarke	18	"	"	" "	"	" "
Thomas Sabin	15	A Youth	Oxford	Generous Friend	Antigua	Going as a Merchants Clerk
Thomas Secker	14	" "	London	" "	"	" " "
Philip Spence	14	" "	Kent	" "	"	" " "
Francis Colle	25	Carpenter	Hertfordshire	Richmond	Barbadoes	Going as a Surveyor
Peter Martin	35	Linen Weaver	Scotland	William	Virginia	Indented Servant
Silvanus Ball	22	Clerk & Bookkeeper	Salop	"	"	" "
William Wigley	23	Miller		"	"	" "
William Jackson	30	Bricklayer	Yorkshire	"	"	" "
James Spree	31	Husbandman	Kent	"	"	" "
Richard Hodges	22	Perukemaker	London	"	"	" "
William Terry	22	Gardener	Essex	"	"	" "

William Pelham	34	Sawyer	Kent	"	"	" "
Mary Pelham	31	His Wife	"	"	"	" "
John Widdows	31	Groom	Warwick	"	"	" "
William Thompson	21	Labourer	Kent	"	"	" "
Thomas Ormond	40	Cabinet Maker	Dorset	"	"	" "
Thomas Batt	25	Baker	London	"	"	" "
Thomas Carter	26	Shipwright	Warwick	"	"	" "
Joseph Croxford	23	Husband	Bedford	"	"	" "
Dennis Dowlin	27	"	Cork	"	"	" "
John Rowley	29	"	Stafford	"	"	" "
John Weedham	16	Cutler	York	"	"	" "
Samuel Fletcher	16	Husband	Stafford	"	"	" "
William Alleman	15	Labourer	Liverpool	"	"	" "
William Dytche	20	"	Stafford	"	"	" "
Benjamin Agar	27	Breeches Maker	Northampton	"	"	" "
Cornelius Fogarty	30	Husbandman	Surry	"	"	" "
James Haiste	34	Linen Weaver	Middlesex	"	"	" "
Jeremiah Bowley	23	Groom	"	"	"	" "
John Cookson	26	Sail Maker	Kent	"	"	" "
Edward Ellis	27	Turner	London	"	"	" "
James Fogerty	27	Husband	Surry	"	"	" "
James Smith	30	Gentleman	Natives of Ja-	William & Mary	Jamaica	Going home
Samuel Cunningham	19	"	maica	" "	"	" "
Thomas Yatman	18	"	"	" "	"	" "
Willm Sangster	19	Clerk & Bookkeeper	London	Friendship	Monserat	Going to Settle
John Mackenzie	16	Clerk & Bookkeeper	Scotland	Briton	Carolina	" "
Alexander Douglas	22	Husbandman	"	"	"	" "
Christopher Smith	49	"	Switzerland	"	"	" "
Esther Smith	35	His Wife	"	"	"	" "
Andrew Milborn	7		"	"	"	" "
Christopher Milborn	2	Children	"	"	"	" "
Richard Hall	16	Labourer	London	William	Virginia	Indented Servant
Elizabeth Bly	21	Spinster	"	"	"	" "
Sarah Parker	19	"	"	"	"	" "
Elizabeth Lone	21	"	"	"	"	" "
William Wilson	22	Breeches Maker	Southwark	"	"	" "
John Smith	22	Husbandman	Berks	"	"	" "
Mary Smith	22	His Wife	"	"	"	" "

Name	Age	Occupation	From	Ship	To	As a
Marmaduke Mason	22	Gentleman's Servant	York	William	Virginia	Indented Servant
George Orrage	29	Husbandman	Essex	"	"	" "
John Woodhouse	36	Shipwright	Portsmouth	"	"	" "
John Turtle	23	Sawyer	Essex	"	"	" "
Thomas Allen	22	Breeches Maker	London	"	"	" "
Samuel Taylor	28	Brass Founder	Warwick	"	"	" "
John Latham	16	Labourer	London	"	"	" "
John Hunt	19	"	"	"	"	" "
James Lyon	18	"	"	"	"	" "

Port of Bristol, 28 Nov. to 6th Dec. 1774.

William Hamilton	26	Merchant	Bristol	Campbell	Grenada	Going on Business

Port of London, 5th to 12th Dec. 1774.

Francis Smith	34	Clergyman	Jamaica	Fanny	Jamaica	Going home
Susanna Dawson	16	Seemstress	London	"	"	Going to Settle
Mark Gorden	28	Carpenter	"	Mary	New York	" "
Alexander Anderson	26	Gardener	"	Beulah	" "	" "
Daniel McFasson	38	Taylor	New York	"	" "	" "
Ralph Sadler	25	Groom	Jamaica	Amity Hall	Jamaica	" "

Port of London, 12th to 19th Dec. 1774.

Thomas Warge	27	Planter	Berwick on Tweed	Jamaica	Jamaica	Going to Settle
James House	17	"		"	"	" "
Thomas Austin	20	Attorney	Dorsetshire	Northampton	"	" "
Martha "	18	His Sister	"	"	"	" "
Ann "	17	" "	"	"	"	" "
Thomas Wise	19	Surgeon	Jamaica	"	"	" "
Charles Schaw	17	Planter	"	"	"	Going Home
Robert Avis	45	Gentleman	London	Woodley	"	Going on Business
George McKenzie	22	"	Scotland	"	"	" "

Stephen Palmer	26	Husbandman	Berks	Carolina	Virginia	Indented Servant
William Stockley	26	Sawyer	Kent	"	"	" "
John Mead	17	Husbandman	London	"	"	" "
William Duncan	21	Clerk & Bookkeeper	Scotland	"	"	" "
William Bird	29	Dyer	London	"	"	" "
Robert Snape	38	Husbandman	Lancaster	"	"	" "
John Cooke	21	Groom	Lincoln	"	"	" "
Edward Farr	18	Weaver	London	"	"	" "
John Gilbert	16	Husbandman	Norfolk	"	"	" "
John Godfrey	22	Musical Inst Maker	London	"	"	" "
James Tomling	25	Copper Plate Printer	"	"	"	" "
William Jones	22	Clerk & Bookkeeper	"	"	"	" "
Nathaniel Adams	35	Labourer	"	"	"	" "
Timothy Kennedy	21	Schoolmaster	Westminster	"	"	" "
Robert Lee	22	Husbandman	Kent	"	"	" "
William Goldie	38	"	Scotland	"	"	" "
James Wright	28	Printer	London	"	"	" "
John Smith	27	Husbandman	Worcester	"	"	" "
Robert Edwards	22	Grocer	Chester	"	"	" "
John Little	30	Husbandman	Scotland	"	"	" "
John Saul	37	Forgeman	Surry	"	"	" "
Mary "	21	His Wife	"	"	"	" "
S L. "	17	Forgeman His Son	"	"	"	" "
Jno "	13	" " "	"	"	"	" "
Jno Taylor	21	Coach Wheelwright	London	"	"	" "
T P Parent	25	Silk Weaver	"	"	"	" "
Esther Parent	24	His Wife	"	"	"	" "
Willm Beman	39	Whitesmith	"	"	"	" "
Alexander Lee	21	Taylor	"	"	"	" "
John Harwood	21	Perukemaker	"	"	"	" "
John Gray	21	"	"	"	"	" "
James Kelly	25	Husbandman	"	"	"	" "
William Bladen	16	Labourer	"	"	"	" "
James Marr	17	"	Surry	"	"	" "
John Holt	26	Smith	London	"	"	" "
John Darry	22	Gardener	Middlesex	"	"	" "
Thomas Wright	22	Breeches Maker	London	"	"	" "
John Green	25	Perukemaker	"	"	"	" "

Name	*Age*	*Occupation*	*From*	*Ship*	*To*	*As a*
Martin Doyle	22	Labourer	London	Carolina	Virginia	Indented Servant
Oliver Stevens	18	Groom	Oxford	"	"	" "
Edward Mahon	23	Taylor	Ireland	"	"	" "
Jos Mahony	23	Groom	"	"	"	" "
Dennis Craigen	37	Husbandman	London	"	"	" "
James Lilley	23	Schoolmaster	"	"	"	" "
Francis Pankhurst	20	Bricklayer	"	"	"	" "
George Smith	18	Labourer	Surry	"	"	" "
James Lilley	37	Husbandman	Essex	"	"	" "
Moses Puckridge	29	Watch Case Maker	London	"	"	" "
James Doyle	28	Husbandman	"	"	"	" "
Robert Brinder	32	Stone Mason	"	"	"	" "
Mathew Oliver	32	Bricklayer	"	"	"	" "
James Woosencroft	23	Cabinet Maker	Manchester	"	"	" "
John Atheridge	37	Carpenter	Sussex	"	"	" "
John May	37	Wool comber	Devon	"	"	" "
David Stewart	21	Cabinet Maker	London	"	"	" "
Elizabeth Allenten	21	Housemaid	"	"	"	" "
Richard Clean	34	House Carpenter	"	"	"	" "
Elizabeth Speirs	22	Governess	"	"	"	" "
William Pase	29	Bricklayer	"	"	"	" "
Joseph Reed	23	"	"	"	"	" "
Cornelius Crow	48	Turner	"	"	"	" "
Morris Maney	23	Bricklayer	"	"	"	" "
Thomas Aubony	22	Footman	"	"	"	" "
Henry Gibbard	35	Husbandman	Middlesex	"	"	" "
Joseph Daniel	29	"	"	"	"	" "
Joseph Moore	27	"	Leicester	"	"	" "
John Mitson	21	Footman	Middlesex	"	"	" "
Martin Mealey	25	Painter Glazier	"	"	"	" "
John Jones	26	Clerk & Bookkeeper	London	"	"	" "
Joseph Thompson	30	Bricklayer	Exeter	"	"	" "
Wm Whiting	24	Sawyer	London	"	"	" "
John Hammond	37	Bricklayer	Bucks	"	"	" "
Wm Gill	30	Husbandman	Essex	"	"	" "

George Gordon	39	Labourer	"	"	"	"	"
Willm Robinson	25	Sawyer	Northumberland	"	"	"	"
Charles Rowland	23	Carpenter	London	"	"	"	"
John Blackwell	33	Sawyer	Bucks	"	"	"	"
Willm Colton	22	Joiner	Oxford	"	"	"	"
James Doves	28	Malster	Kent	"	"	"	"
Valentine Strong	39	Tallow Chandler	Middlesex	"	"	"	"
M. A. Vaines	26	Lady's Maid		"	"	"	"
Jno Hamilton	32	Cabinet Maker	Northumberland	"	"	"	"
Hugh Vaughan	28	Groom	London	"	"	"	"
George Sarratt	27	Husbandman	York	"	"	"	"
Benjamin Hambury	15	Labourer	London	"	"	"	"
Edward Pink	32	Husbandman	Kent	"	"	"	"
Willm Barnard	20	Groom	London	"	"	"	"
Thos Cradick	16	Labourer	Somerset	"	"	"	"
John Journ	16	Labourer	Dorset	"	"	"	"
Wm Doulan	24	Perukemaker	Dublin	"	"	"	"
Wm Phillips	21	Buckle Maker	Somerset	"	"	"	"
Jno Follard	20	Husbandman	London	"	"	"	"
Jas Keep	19	Bricklayer	Bedford	"	"	"	"

Pill a Creek a Port of Bristol, 19th to 26th Dec. 1774.

Thomas Adding	40	Labourer	London	Sally	Maryland	Indented	Servant
William Keene	34	Joiner	Wilts	"	"	"	"
Nathaniel Stacey	36	Labourer	Somersetshire	"	"	"	"
William Nangle	20	Carpenter	"	"	"	"	"
John Redding	21	Taylor	"	"	"	"	"
Michael Casan	23	Labourer	"	"	"	"	"
Thomas Grant	25	"	"	"	"	"	"
Thomas Johnson	16	"	"	"	"	"	"
John Stafford	15	"	"	"	"	"	"
Thomas Sullivan	17	"	"	"	"	"	"
William Barry	25	Butcher	"	"	"	"	"
James Nash	18	Labourer	"	"	"	"	"
Thomas Philps	16	"	"	"	"	"	"
John Pope	14	"	"	"	"	"	"

Name	Age	Occupation	From	Ship	To	As a
Thomas Forster	18	Labourer	Somersetshire	Sally	Maryland	Indented Servant
John Knight	16	"	"	"	"	" "
Job Whitehead	27	Carpenter	"	"	"	" "
John Lane	17	Labourer	"	"	"	" "
Richard Aston	24	"	"	"	"	" "
James Groree	15	"	"	"	"	" "
John Ward	27	Mason	"	"	"	" "
Samuel Butler	15	Labourer	Cornwall	"	"	" "
Richard Bond	17	"	"	"	"	" "

PORT OF PORTSMOUTH, 19th TO 26th DEC. 1774.

Sherland Swanston	44	Merchant	London	London Packet	Nevis	To settle his private affairs
Richard Pinney	35	Planter	Nevis	"	"	To superentend their Plantations
William Tucket	37	"	"	"	"	

PORT OF PLYMOUTH, 26th DEC. 1774 TO 3rd JAN. 1775.

Jean Degarne Esqre	30	Planter	London	Reward	Grenada	Going to reside
Madam "	27	———	"	"	"	" "
John Peschier	31	Planter	"	"	"	" "
Madam "	25	———	"	"	"	" "
Mr Deschamps	40	Planter	"	"	"	" "
Mr Nolonier	40	Eclesiastick	"	"	"	" "
Mr Grant	40	Planter	"	Laurent	"	" "
Mrs "	36	———	"	"	"	" "
Three Servants belonging to Mrs Grant			"	"	"	" "
Mr Lithgow	34	Planter	"	"	"	" "
Mr Bull	40	Gentleman	"	"	"	" "
James Clifton	50	"	"	Generous Planter	St Kitts	Going to reside
Richard Riddie	25	"	"	" "	" "	" "
Mary Tayton	18	Spinster	"	" "	" "	" "

PORT OF LONDON, 3rd TO 10 JAN. 1775.

Paul Simons	18	Carpenter & Joiner	London	York	New York	Indented Servant
Thomas Pitkin	15	Labourer	Herts	"	" "	" "
James Barton	18	"	London	"	" "	" "
William Creamer	35	Husbandman	Northampton	"	" "	" "
James Gingell	32	Gardener	Middlesex	"	" "	" "
Robt Holliday	30	Sawyer	"	"	" "	" "
Samuel Lockweer	17	Gentleman's Servant	Yorkshire	"	" "	" "
George Suffrin	18	Labourer	Kent	"	" "	" "
John Reiley	19	Groom	London	"	" "	" "
James Ould	15	Mathematical Inst Maker	Bristol	"	" "	" "
Thomas Lawrence	18	Labourer	Hertford	"	" "	" "
John Newberry	19	Husbandman	Devon	"	" "	" "
Anthony Blank	17	Labourer	London	"	" "	" "
John Jones	15	"	Berks	"	" "	" "
Henry Geo Ohlen	16	Footman	London	"	" "	" "
William Bingley	18	Stocking Weaver	Nottingham	"	" "	" "
Michael Tobin	18	Labourer	Ireland	"	" "	" "
Oliver Tate	21	Husbandman	"	"	" "	" "
William Tear	31	"	"	"	" "	" "
James Butler	24	Sawyer	"	"	" "	" "
Thomas Holmes	31	Clerk & Bookkeeper	London	"	" "	" "
Randal Ilsley	17	Groom	Middlesex	"	" "	" "
William Wyer	18	Brass Founder	London	"	" "	" "
Joseph Dyer	17	Buckle Maker	"	"	" "	" "
Joseph Boothey	19	Labourer	"	"	" "	" "
Jacob Byer	17	"	Northampton	"	" "	" "
John Leathergough	19	Buckel Maker	Worcester	"	" "	" "
Adam Heindrick	15	Labourer	London	"	" "	" "
Richd Bennett	15	"	"	"	" "	" "
John Lyons	29	Clerk & Bookkeeper	Dublin	Adventurer	Virginia	Indented Servant
Jane Berners	29	Cook Maid	London	"	"	" "
Sarah Farley	20	Spinster	"	"	"	" "
Catharine Lithman	18	"	"	"	"	" "
Sarah Holiday	22	House Maid	"	"	"	" "

Name	*Age*	*Occupation*	*From*	*Ship*	*To*	*As a*
Ann Merritt	20	Spinster	London	Adventurer	Virginia	Indented Servant
Edward Walker	32	Brickmaker	Rutland	"	"	" "
Thomas Cooper	22	Baker	Essex	"	"	" "
Joseph Simpson	28	Clerk & Bookkeeper	Salop	"	"	" "
Thomas White	42	Husbandman	Bedford	"	"	" "
Thomas Smith	19	Footman	Essex	"	"	" "
John Collins	25	Carpenter & Joiner	London	"	"	" "
William Benson	23	Taylor	Warwick	"	"	" "
William Chapman	27	Tavern Waiter	Somersetshire	"	"	" "
Thomas Woodward	21	Gardener	"	"	"	" "
William Ashton	26	Carpenter & Joiner	London	"	"	" "
Abraham Osborn	16	Labourer	Somersetshire	"	"	" "
Richard Buck	29	Carpenter	Suffolk	"	"	" "
Joseph Moss	21	"	Essex	"	"	" "
Thomas Hodges	24	Husbandman	Kent	"	"	" "
Thomas Fowler	28	Baker	Somersetshire	"	"	" "
Daniel Finana	36	Clerk & bookkeeper	Ireland	"	"	" "
William Herring	27	" "	Berks	"	"	" "
Robert Warner	27	Groom	Westminster	"	"	" "
James Nelson	21	Painter	"	"	"	" "
Henry Wetheral	40	Clerk & Bookkeeper	"	"	"	" "
John Jameson	23	Tin Plate Worker	"	"	"	" "
Willm Evans	19	Gardener	London	"	"	" "
John Davis	26	Weaver	"	"	"	" "
Robert Dawson	28	Plaisterer	"	"	"	" "
James Howard	25	Engraver	"	"	"	" "
Edward Mackrell	25	Husbandman	Berks	"	"	" "
Jno Arnett	20	Flax dresser	Kent	"	"	" "
J W. Cunliffe	22	Schoolmaster	Westminster	"	"	" "
Jas Mackrell	21	Husbandman	Berks	"	"	" "
Robt Mason	17	Gunsmith	London	"	"	" "
Stephen Grange	38	Blacksmith	"	"	"	" "
John Connor	19	Clerk	"	"	"	" "
Joseph Shute	20	Waiter	"	"	"	" "
Josiah Bailey	22	Glover	"	"	"	" "

John Moore	23	Coach Maker	“	“	“	“ “
Philip Folkard	29	Clerk & Bookeeeper	“	“	“	“ “

PORT OF LONDON, 10th TO 17 JAN. 1775.

Thomas Hodges	25	Shipwright	Bedford	Price Frigate	Jamaica	Going to Settle
Roderick McCloud	17	Clerk	Scotland	Nautilus	Tobago	Going as a Clerk
William Dunkley	18	Husbandman	Bedford	Baltimore	Maryland	Indented Servant
James Bourman	21	Surgeon	Scotland	“	“	“ “
William Hudson	25	Butcher	York	“	“	“ “
Simon Taylor	21	Silk Weaver	Middlesex	“	“	“ “
James Eaton	32	Linen Dyer	London	“	“	“ “
Thomas Furlong	26	Coach Maker	“	“	“	“ “
Edward Burford	21	Groom	Harts	“	“	“ “
Charles Murphy	27	Clerk & Bookkeeper	Ireland	“	“	“ “
John Stevens	21	Bricklayer	Gloucester	“	“	“ “
Lydia Davis	32	Cook Maid	Kent	“	“	“ “
William Jenkins	34	Carpenter & Joiner	London	“	“	“ “
Josiah Hattersley	21	Schoolmaster	“	“	“	“ “
Willm Tucker	23	Perukemaker	“	“	“	“ “
Joseph Carter	26	Cordwainer	Westminster	“	“	“ “

PORT OF LONDON, 17th TO 24th JAN. 1775.

Matthew Skinner	40	Weaver	Norfolk	Wren	Maryland	Indented Servant
John Johnson	22	“	Northampton	“	“	“ “
John Chamberlain	22	Cordwainer	London	“	“	“ “
John Pricker	22	Sawyer	Wilts	“	“	“ “
Thomas Beard	39	Husbandman	Stafford	“	“	“ “
Edward Luck	22	Gardener	London	“	“	“ “
Daniel Har	30	Husbandman	“	“	“	“ “
John Harvey	35	“	“	“	“	“ “
Christopher Beck	21	“	“	“	“	“ “
John Welling	21	“	“	“	“	“ “
Timothy Donovan	23	“	“	“	“	“ “
John Hamilton	22	Clerk & Bookkeeper	Norfolk	“	“	“ “
Nathaniel Palmer	22	Weaver	Northampton	“	“	“ “

Name	*Age*	*Occupation*	*From*	*Ship*	*To*	*As a*
Thomas Dutton	23	Joiner	Norfolk	Wren	Maryland	Indented Servant
John Hullatt	22	Weaver	Northampton	“	“	“ “
Jonas Chamberlain	22	Cutler	Bristol	“	“	“ “
John Sheston	23	Cordwainer	London	“	“	“ “
Daniel James	22	Blacksmith	“	“	“	“ “
Philip Chamberlain	22	Cutler	“	“	“	“ “
William Braithwaite	22	Footman	“	“	“	“ “
John Tool	22	Bucklemaker	“	“	“	“ “
Michael Calam	27	Coachman	“	“	“	“ “
Andrew Conaly	23	Footman	Dublin	“	“	“ “
John Sutherland	28	Clerk & Bookkeeper	London	“	“	“ “
George King	21	Cooper	“	“	“	“ “
William Allendar	39	White Smith	“	“	“	“ “
Samuel Squiar	21	Baker	“	“	“	“ “
James Still	21	Perukemaker	“	“	“	“ “
William Sugars	21	Clerk & Bookkeeper	“	“	“	“ “
John Smith	21	Taylor	“	“	“	“ “
William Westlake	28	Baker	Kent	“	“	“ “
Patrick Collins	25	Weaver	Ireland	“	“	“ “

PORT OF WHITEHAVEN, 17th TO 24 JAN. 1775.

George Stevens	40	Virginia Planter	Virginia	Mary & Ann	Virginia	Returning Home
George Craike	28	Schoolmaster	Whitehaven	“ “	“	Going to follow his Occupaton
Sarah Cherry	22	Indented Servant	“	“ “	“	Indented
Edwd Strickland	14	A Convict	Carlisle	Hero	“	Transported there
Mary Graham	34	“ “	“	“	“	“ “
John Wallace	22	Shoemaker	Cumberland	Ann	“	To follow their trade
William Wallace	24	Currier	“	“	“	“ “ “

EMIGRANTS FROM ENGLAND

Transcribed by Gerald Fothergill of New Wandsworth, London, England, and communicated by the Committee on English Research

Pill a Creek a Port of Bristol, 17th to 24th Jan. 1775.

Name	*Age*	*Occupation*	*From*	*Ship*	*To*	*As a*
Daniel McGilchrist	53	Gentleman	Jamaica	Hector	Jamaica	Going on Business
William Jordan	36	"	"	"	"	" "
John Griffiths	27	"	Bath	"	"	" "
William Shuring	19	"	Bristol	"	"	" "
William Walters	18	"	Andover	"	"	" "
Aaron Gover	16	Labourer	Somerset	Chalkley	Philadelphia	Indented Servant
Thomas Draysey	15	"	"	"	"	" "
William Dormant	25	"	"	"	"	" "
John Holbrook	12	"	"	"	"	" "
Charles Stewart	20	"	"	"	"	" "
Samuel Jones	18	"	"	"	"	" "
Benjamin Taylor	15	"	"	"	"	" "
William Adam	16	"	"	"	"	" "
Roger Roe	23	"	"	"	"	" "
John Williams	20	"	Wales	"	"	" "
Samuel Kemgs	14	"	"	"	"	" "
John Page	20	"	Somersetshire	"	"	" "
Alexander Biggs	15	"	"	"	"	" "
John Chestmore	14	"	"	"	"	" "
Jos Wilkins	14	"	"	"	"	" "
William Hall	17	"	"	"	"	" "
Samuel Jordan	15	"	"	"	"	" "
William Collins	14	"	"	"	"	" "
Jos Padmore	20	"	"	"	"	" "
Edward Barnes	27	"	"	"	"	" "
Richard Baker	11	"	Exeter	"	"	" "
Richard Gough	15	"	"	"	"	" "

William Smith	16	"	"	"	"	" "
William Vaughan	22	Shoemaker	Hereford	"	"	" "
Francis Horrell	14	Labourer	Somersetshire	"	"	" "
William Fair	22	"	"	"	"	" "
William Snead	18	Joiner	"	"	"	" "
William Harman	25	Labourer	"	"	"	" "

PORT OF LONDON, 24th TO 30 JAN. 1775.

John Slowcuna	16	A Clerk	Kent	Elenor	Antigua	To follow their Calling
Samuel Alsebrook	17	" "	Nottingham	"	"	" " "
John Alsebrook	15	" "	"	"	"	" " "
John Gibson	22	Groom	Norfolk	Diana	Maryland	Indented Servant
Thomas Howard	29	Labourer	Surry	"	"	" "
Peter Godona	17	"	London	"	"	" "
Jasper Mahony	16	"	"	"	"	" "
James Chantley	21	Husbandman	Northington	"	"	" "
Thomas Kidman	27	Carpenter	Kent	"	"	" "
James Doyley	26	Clerk & Bookkeeper	Ireland	"	"	" "
William Primrose	43	Sail Maker	London	"	"	" "
John Beble	26	Pavior	Hereford	"	"	" "
David Conolly	21	Bricklayer	Ireland	"	"	" "
Lewis Fountain	28	Cordwainer	London	"	"	" "
Mary Thompson	24	Spinster	York	"	"	" "
Elizabeth Crompton	25	"	Surry	"	"	" "
Penelope Powell	23	"	Kent	"	"	" "
Jane Stewart	35	Widow	London	"	"	" "
Eliza Stewart	11	Daughter of Above	"	"	"	" "
Thomas Barefoot	25	Weaver	"	"	"	" "
William Smith	20	Labourer	Southwark	"	"	" "
Middleton Merriott	20	Groom	Windsor	"	"	" "
Elizabeth Jarrott	16	Spinster	London	"	"	" "
Mary Sievens	17	"	"	"	"	" "
Mary Hetchcock	15	"	Southwark	"	"	" "
Charlotte Palmer	18	"	Warwick	"	"	" "
James Mann	31	Shipwright	Suffolk	"	"	" "
John Archer	23	Sawyer	Oxford	"	"	" "

Name	*Age*	*Occupation*	*From*	*Ship*	*To*	*As a*
John Harding	22	Joiner	London	Diana	Maryland	Indented Servant
Joseph Wale	30	Weaver	Norfolk	"	"	" "
Anthony Lambert	36	Brazier	Middlesex	"	"	" "
John Field	28	Paviour	London	"	"	" "
William Hotchkiss	31	Watchmaker	"	"	"	" "
George Johnson	24	Sawyer	"	"	"	" "
Camlin Purellio	18	Mariner	"	"	"	" "
Samuel Galland	39	Husbandman	Norfolk	"	"	" "
William Pitts	32	Cordwainer	Southwark	"	"	" "
John Chapman	22	Husbandman	London	"	"	" "
Ambrose Lumpey	26	Mariner	"	"	"	" "
Edward Wright	28	"	York	"	"	" "
William Burton	22	Husbandman	Surry	"	"	" "
Nicholas Chily	30	Hair dresser	London	"	"	" "
John Lepo	30	Weaver	"	"	"	" "
Elzabeth Strange	30	Widow	"	"	"	" "
Elzabeth Haywood	25	Spinster	"	"	"	" "
Susanna Houchen	30	"	"	"	"	" "
Sarah Houchen	26	"	"	"	"	" "
Walter Clemenshaw	24	Cordwainer	Southwark	"	"	" "
Elizabeth Gibson	19	Spinster	"	"	"	" "
Martha Smith	15	"	"	"	"	" "
Susanna Scotney	19	"	Middlesex	"	"	" "
William Nash	26	Carpenter	Kent	"	"	" "
Scriven Jones	22	Clerk & Bookkeeper	"	"	"	" "
John Crook	33	Shipwright	"	"	"	" "
William Anderson	34	Husbandman	Scotland	"	"	" "
Adam Garrett	22	Waiter	London	Jane	"	N.B. All these People that have
James Williams	21	Servant	Somerset	"	"	shipped themselves on Board
Charles Hare	22	Cabinet Maker	York	"	"	the Jane, are going to settle
David Rose	21	Carpenter	London	"	"	abroad & by an agreement
William Patterson	24	Seaman	"	"	"	with the Captn are to pay him
Francis Miles	21	Waiter	"	"	"	so much for their passage to
John Ferndon	22	Weaver	"	"	"	Maryland, on their arrival, but
George Booth	31	Servant	"	"	"	if they cannot then the Captn

Thomas Jones	22	Blacksmith	“	“	“	is to dispose of them for a number of years to defray the expences of their passage
James Connor	24	Grocer	Norfolk	“	“	
Samuel Tyler	35	Printer	London	“	“	
John Tanch	35	Farmer	Bedfordshire	“	“	“
William Hudson	32	Seaman	London	“	“	“
Henry Dismore	21	Farmer	“	“	“	“
Samuel Chandler	22	“	“	“	“	“
James Simpson	34	Seaman	“	“	“	“
William Caton	22	Blacksmith	“	“	“	“
Lewis Morgan	15	Gentleman's Servant	Surry	“	“	“
Charles Penny	15	“ “	Hertford	“	“	“
Peter White	18	“ “	London	“	“	“
John Bullen	18	“ “	Devonshire	“	“	“
Rednd Roach	18	“ “	Pembroke	“	“	“
Edward Sutton	16	“ “	Ireland	“	“	“
William Broughton	18	“ “	Norwich	“	“	“
James Dutch	16	“ “	London	“	“	“
Robert Wilmot	17	“ “	Hampshire	“	“	“
Robert Gray	15	“ “	Somerset	“	“	“
Cornelius Dutch	27	Weaver	London	“	“	“
Thomas Dutch	21	“	“	“	“	“
Hugh Stephens	22	Painter	Bristol	“	“	“
James Robinson	36	Groom	London	“	“	“
John Crut	36	Joiner	“	“	“	“
Charles Dowling	30	Shoemaker	“	“	“	“
James Wade	25	Brewer	Rotherhithe	“	“	“
Stephen Tester	22	Sawyer	Essex	“	“	“
Jane Tester	22	His Wife	“	“	“	“
Thomas Alliton	35	Farmer	Surry	“	“	“
Lydia “	29	His Wife	“	“	“	“
Dennis Carter	22	Weaver	London	“	“	“
John Benjamin	40	Miner	Flintshire	“	“	“
C. F. Newman	24	Surgeon	London	“	“	“
Evan James	22	Watch Gilder	“	“	“	“
Evans Tames [? *dup.*]	22	Watch Gilder	“	“	“	“
Thomas Bean	45	Shoemaker	“	“	“	“
J. P. Fevete	22	Clerk	“	“	“	“
Jn° Cornish	38	Weaver	“	“	“	“

Name	*Age*	*Occupation*	*From*	*Ship*	*To*	*As a*
William Snuvre	22	Groom	Essex	Jane	Maryland	N. B. All the People that have
Charles Warner	21	Turner	London	"	"	shipped themselves on Board
Peter Bowles	21	Waiter	"	"	"	the Jane, are going to settle
John Dutch	23	Weaver	"	"	"	abroad & by an agreement
Mary "	23	His Wife	"	"	"	with the Captn are to pay him
Gilbert Samuel	21	Servant	"	"	"	so much for their passage to
Thomas Newland	32	Hair dresser	"	"	"	Maryland, on their arrival, but
Thomas Wilinore	32	Bricklayer	"	"	"	if they cannot, then he is to
Letitia "	35	His Wife	"	"	"	dispose of them for a number
William Ryder	25	Bricklayer	"	"	"	of years to defray the ex-
Ralph Gadsby	21	Farmer	Derby	"	"	pences of their passage
Thomas Sammonds	24	Weaver	Norwich	"	"	"
Stephen Morris	36	Carpenter	Middlesex	"	"	N.B. All these People are going
George Gilbert	33	Butcher	Essex	"	"	to settle abroad, and by an
Richard Kitcher	36	Mason	London	"	"	agreement with the Captn are
James Mead	27	Farmer	"	"	"	to pay him so much for their
William Perches	32	Blacksmith	Dorset	"	"	passage to Maryland on their
Mathew Hart	24	Carpenter	London	"	"	arrival, but if they cannot,
J. B. Carier	45	Schoolmaster	Westminster	"	"	then the Captn is to dispose
William Fenton	23	Miller & Baker	"	"	"	of them for a number of years
Benjamin Miles	21	Shuttle Make[r]	Surry	"	"	to defray the Expences of their
Charles Brewer	21	Carpenter	Middlesex	"	"	passage
William Smith	26	Farmer	Oxford	"	"	"
William Wilson	29	Anchor Smith	Surry	"	"	"
Josiah Bendal	35	Sawyer	"	"	"	"
John Howard	22	Painter	Sussex	"	"	"
Thomas Slade	22	Wool Comber	"	"	"	"
John Cotton	40	Biscuit Baker	Kent	"	"	"
John Mansfield	23	Carpenter	Salisbury	"	"	"
John Flimaning	31	Clerk	London	"	"	"
Francis Reynolds	22	Barber	"	"	"	"
Edward Dillon	22	Clerk	Kent	"	"	"
Michael Gray	25	Farmer	London	"	"	"
Leonard Miller	22	"	"	"	"	"
Farrol Lister	23	"	Kent	"	"	"

John Farmer	22	Clerk	London	"	"	"
William Boyde	36	Cotton Factor	"	"	"	"
Leonora "	27	His Wife	"	"	"	"

PORT OF PLYMOUTH, 24 TO 30 JAN. 1775.

William Forbes	30	Planter	London	London	Tobago	Going to reside there
John Petrie	30	"	"	"	"	
Thomas Bigby	28	"	"	"	"	
James Wallern	21	"	"	"	"	
Thomas Campbell	30	"	"	Albion	St. Vincents	Going to reside at St. Vincent
William Walker	26	"	"	"	" "	" " "
Evan Bailie	28	Merchant	"	"	" "	" " "
Martin Jolly	22	Planter	"	"	" "	" " "
Thomas Sharp	30	"	"	"	" "	" " "
Patrick Connor	35	"	"	"	" "	" " "

PORT OF WHITEHAVEN, 24th TO 30 JAN. 1775.

John Lewthwaite	21	Sadler	Whitehaven	Saint Bees	Virginia	Going to follow his trade

PORT OF LONDON, 30 JAN. TO 6th FEB. 1775.

Thomas Winderbank	15	Breeches Maker	Surry	Nancy	Maryland	Indented Servant for 7 Years
Francis Frazer	15	Labourer	London	"	"	" " "
Joseph Peper	21	Husbandman	"	"	"	Indented Servant for 4 Years
John Harrin	40	Groom	"	"	"	" " "
John Crook	34	Shipwright	Kent	"	"	" " "
John Bebb	26	Paviour	London	"	"	" " "
James Rowland	22	Weaver	"	"	"	" " "
John Ridpeth	30	Cordwainer	"	"	"	" " "
John Strickland	22	Gardener	"	"	"	" " "
William Denton	23	Woolcomber	Berks	"	"	" " "
Thomas Jackson	23	Stone Mason	Kent	"	"	" " "
William Compton	25	Husbandman	London	"	"	" " "

Name	Age	Occupation	From	Ship	To	As a
William Love	24	Groom	Suffolk	Nancy	Maryland	Indented Servant for 4 Years
William Deane	36	Taylor	Middlesex	"	"	" " "
John Brande	23	Husbandman	Kent	"	"	" " "
William Walker	24	Lathrender	Norfolk	"	"	" " "
Abraham Wood	26	Cook	Bath	"	"	" " "

PORT OF LONDON, 6th TO 13 FEB. 1775.

Name	Age	Occupation	From	Ship	To	As a
Henry Lisper	38	Print Cutter	London	Britannia	Philadelphia	Indented Servant for 4 Years
James Wright	26	Bricklayer	Suffolk	Mary	Virginia	" " "
John Lewis	30	Husbandman	Glamorgan	"	"	" " "
William Dashall	24	"	Ireland	"	"	" " "
William Metcalf	25	"	Yorkshire	"	"	" " "
John Litchfield	21	"	Bedfordshire	"	"	" " "
John Barbet	21	"	London	"	"	" " "
Richard Collins	37	Smith	Warwick	"	"	" " "
Elizabeth Young	21	Spinster	London	Maryl Planter	Maryland	" " "
Mary Hall	26	Widow	"	" "	"	" " "
Samuel Richards	16	Weaver	"	" "	"	" " "
John Palmer	16	Taylor	Herts	" "	"	" " "
Thomas Berry	16	Cordwainer	Southwark	" "	"	" " "
William Welch	17	"	"	" "	"	" " "
Samuel Brasington	19	Husbandman	Gloster	" "	"	" " "
Jane Tucker	20	Spinster	Southwark	" "	"	" " "
Elizabeth Tate	20	"	London	" "	"	" " "
Ann Booker	19	"	"	" "	"	" " "
George Castell	40	Husbandman	"	" "	"	" " "
George Wood	35	Dyer	"	" "	"	" " "
Isaac Bailey	30	Clerk & Bookkeeper	"	" "	"	" " "
Edward Edwards	22	Stone Mason	Surry	" "	"	" " "
Ambrose Lops	26	Mariner	London	" "	"	" " "
John Chapman	22	Labourer	"	" "	"	" " "
James Roberts	22	Cordwainer	Ireland	" "	"	" " "
John Harding	22	Joiner	London	" "	"	" " "

George Jennings	22	Weaver	"	"	"	"	"	"	"
George Squires	22	"	"	"	"	"	"	"	"
James Jolly	40	Wire Worker	"	"	"	"	"	"	"
James Walker	23	Sawyer	"	"	"	"	"	"	"
James Barr	32	Water Gilder	"	"	"	"	"	"	"
Henry Taylor	22	Sawyer	Somerset	"	"	"	"	"	"
William Primrose	39	Sail Maker	London	"	"	"	"	"	"
William Holloway	21	Butcher	"	"	"	"	"	"	"
Samuel Newth	23	Dyer	"	"	"	"	"	"	"
John Slater	27	Butcher	"	"	"	"	"	"	"
John Catt	28	"	"	"	"	"	"	"	"
Christopher Aldridge	24	Labourer	"	"	"	"	"	"	"
John Cook	29	Brick Maker	"	"	"	"	"	"	"
Newman Betts	24	Husbandman	"	"	"	"	"	"	"
Edward Wright	28	Caulker	Yorkshire	"	"	"	"	"	"
William Anderson	34	Distiller	London	"	"	"	"	"	"
James Makar	25	Husbandman	Ireland	"	"	"	"	"	"
Anthony Byrne	16	Labourer	London	"	"	"	"	"	"
Mary Staines	27	Widow	"	"	"	"	"	"	"
Ann Roe	35	Cook Maid	"	"	"	"	"	"	"
Robert Moss	40	Weaver	Lancaster	"	"	"	"	"	"
Robert Scotland	27	Plaisterer	London	"	"	"	"	"	"
Isaac Martin	22	Silk Weaver	"	"	"	"	"	"	"
John Griffin	20	Labourer	"	"	"	"	"	"	"
Thos Kedman	28	Joiner	Kent	"	"	"	"	"	"
Wm Sawyer	35	Gardener	London	"	"	"	"	"	"
Joseph Henson	35	Bookkeeper	Northampton	"	"	"	"	"	"
Edward McFading	24	Husbandman	London	"	"	"	"	"	"
Thomas Kinslow	25	"	"	"	"	"	"	"	"
Wm Tidd	21	Blacksmith	"	"	"	"	"	"	"
Thos Wilkins	21	Husbandman	Herts	"	"	"	"	"	"
Mercy Beedle	21	Spinster	London	"	"	"	"	"	"
Elizabeth Somerville	21	"	"	"	"	"	"	"	"
James Harris	23	"	"	"	"	"	"	"	"
Jane Managan	15	Labourer	"	"	"	"	"	"	"
Francis Knet	15	"	Wilts	"	"	"	"	"	"
Wm Morris	17	Cabinet Maker	London	"	"	"	"	"	"
Mary Heeds	19	Spinster	Kent	"	"	"	"	"	"

Name	Age	Occupation	From	Ship	To	As a
Mary Hoons	18	Spinster	London	Maryl Planter	Maryland	Indented Servant for 4 Years
Barbara Kermet	21	"	Isle of Man	" "	"	" " "
Richard Mason	15	Cordwainer	Surry	" "	"	" " "
Thomas Butcher	15	Tallow Chandler	London	" "	"	" " "
John Bowling	18	Footman	"	" "	"	" " "
Wm Staples	17	Labourer	"	" "	"	" " "
Peter Equidoney	15	Mariner	"	" "	"	" " "
Johanna Eremeath	15	"	"	" "	"	" " "
William Clark	29	Husbandman	"	" "	"	" " "
John Gordon	27	Shipwright	Southampton	" "	"	" " "
William Nash	26	Carpenter & Joiner	London	" "	"	" " "
Daniel Gorrie	29	Perukemaker	"	" "	"	" " "
William Cole	21	Weaver	"	" "	"	" " "
George Taylor	29	Husbandman	"	" "	"	" " "
Anthony Lambert	36	Brazier	"	" "	"	" " "
Daniel Sanders	27	Brickmaker	"	" "	"	" " "
John Wilson	39	Gardener	Surry	" "	"	" " "
Joseph Sale	30	Worsted Weaver	Norfolk	" "	"	" " "
Hannah Fotts	22	Spinster	London	" "	"	" " "
Elizabeth Hewlett	26	"	Lincoln	" "	"	" " "
William Rands	33	Husbandman	London	" "	"	" " "
John Fowler	36	Taylor	"	" "	"	" " "
Daniel Linch	22	Cordwainer	"	" "	"	" " "
Michael Jackson	39	Clerk	"	" "	"	" " "
William Dean	19	Brazier	Southwark	" "	"	" " "
Elizabeth Beedler	22	Spinster	Middlesex	" "	"	" " "
George Green	15	Husbandman	Essex	" "	"	" " "
George Mercer	22	"	Northumberland	" "	"	" " "
Lucy Graystock	21	Spinster	Hants	" "	"	" " "

PORT OF YARMOUTH, 6th TO 13 FEB. 1775.

Samuel King	24	Husbandman	Suffolk	Norfolk	Jamaica	These four Persons, lived at or near Somerlyton in Suffolk &
William Gilbert	25	"	"	"	"	

Robert Newstead	28	"	"	"	"	followed the Employment of Husbandry and now go to Jamaica under Patronage of Wm Beckford Esqre to follow the same business in that Island
Samuel Smith	13	"	"	"	"	

Port of London, 13 to 20 Feb. 1775.

Arthur Morris	36	Mariner	Ireland	Baltimore Packet	Maryland	Indented Servant for 4 Years
John Hall	22	Painter	London	" "	"	" " "
John Atkins	23	Carpenter	Berks	" "	"	" " "
Fanny "	29	His Wife	"	" "	"	" " "
James Morris	21	Jeweller	Westminster	" "	"	" " "
Roger Brickstock	21	Weaver	Northampton	" "	"	" " "
Joseph Lamb	21	Steel Worker	Surry	" "	"	" " "
Henry Prescott	39	Clerk	Kent	" "	"	" " "
Charles Singleton	30	Labourer	Cambridge	" "	"	" " "
John Langdon	18	"	Leicester	" "	"	" " "
John Jones	36	Iron Founder	Wales	" "	"	" " "
John Richard	22	Weaver	Southwark	" "	"	" " "
Abraham Holden	37	Husbandman	Sussex	" "	"	" " "
Richard Wood	26	"	London	" "	"	" " "
Charles Smith	24	Weaver	"	" "	"	" " "
Jane Mason	25	Spinster	"	" "	"	" " "
Wm Brickstock	22	Weaver	Northumberland	" "	"	" " "
George Pinder	21	"	"	" "	"	" " "
Daniel Longest	40	Farrier	Surry	" "	"	" " "
Thomas Wilkinson	21	Labourer	"	" "	"	" " "
Thomas Smith	26	Bricklayer	"	" "	"	" " "
George Smith	23	Coach Maker	Wilts	" "	"	" " "
William Blake	19	Tavern Waiter	Oxford	" "	"	" " "
William Court	18	Carpenter & Joiner	Gloucester	" "	"	" " "
William Fillwood	17	Husbandman	Middlesex	" "	"	" " "
John Hoare	22	Weaver	London	" "	"	" " "
John Bradford	30	"	"	" "	"	" " "
William Clarke	18	Perukemaker	"	Hopewell	"	" " "

Name	*Age*	*Occupation*	*From*	*Ship*	*To*	*As a*
Thomas Elsworthy	21	Butcher	Bristol	Hopewell	Maryland	Indented Servant for 4 Years
Henry Keeble	27	Painter	London	"	"	" " "
John Stephenson	27	Butcher	"	"	"	" " "
William Poyntell	21	Clerk	"	"	"	" " "
Thomas Ryley	22	Gardener	Stafford	"	"	" " "
Thomas Smith	24	Dyer	Southwark	"	"	" " "
Stephen Pitt	15	Gentlemans Servant	Westminster	Adventure	"	" " "
William Bond	16	Groom	Gloster	"	"	" " "
Richard Calder	21	Husbandman	Salop	"	"	" " "
Thomas Merrick	22	Clerk	London	"	"	" " "
Jno Scarf	34	Husbandman	Hertford	"	"	" " "
Willm Jones	23	Gardener	Surry	"	"	" " "
George Boyd	25	Currier & Tanner	London	"	"	" " "
Richard Atkins	22	Butcher	"	"	"	" " "

PORT OF LONDON, 27th FEB. TO 6th MARCH 1775.

Susanna Stapleton	35	Widow	Middlesex	Fanny	Virginia	Indented Servant for 4 Years
Thomas Hall	28	Stay Maker	London	Liberty	Maryland	" " "
Thomas Wager	19	Weaver	Gloucester	"	"	" " "
Edward McEnnis	15	Labourer	London	"	"	" " "
John Moore	15	"	"	"	"	" " "
Joseph Lilley	16	"	"	"	"	" " "
Samuel Minphey	15	"	"	"	"	" " "
Stephen Walker	27	Weaver	"	"	"	" " "
Thomas Humphry	22	Carpenter	"	"	"	" " "
Mary Phepol	21	Spinster	"	"	"	" " "
Joseph Butler	17	Tavern Waiter	"	"	"	" " "
Henry Townley	18	Labourer	"	"	"	" " "
James Deacon	15	Cordwainer	"	"	"	" " "
William Turner	16	Labourer	"	"	"	" " "
Henry Gardner	21	Baker	"	"	"	" " "
William Adams	22	Groom	"	"	"	" " "
George Chambers	30	Cordwainer	"	"	"	" " "

Thos Bedford	35	Bricklayer	"	"	"	" " "
Charles Sealy	35	"	"	"	"	" " "
William Collins	24	Butcher	"	"	"	" " "
Thomas Rowland	37	Buckle Maker	"	"	"	" " "
Francis Day	30	Clerk & Bookkeeper	"	"	"	" " "
Thomas Swanick	32	Carpenter	"	"	"	" " "
Robert Butler	29	Footman	"	"	"	" " "
John Groves	44	Glover	"	"	"	" " "
Willm Adams	23	Cooper	"	"	"	" " "
Martin Robinson	27	Husbandman	Lincoln	"	"	" " "
Philip Jones	27	"	"	"	"	" " "
Thomas Holden	27	Coach Harness Maker	"	"	"	" " "
John Word	26	Cordwainer	"	"	"	" " "
Mathew Lampen	23	"	"	"	"	" " "
Thomas Gilbert	26	Groom	"	"	"	" " "
Francis Burton	21	Husbandman	Derby	"	"	" " "
Henry Goodwin	30	Groom	Oxford	"	"	" " "
Edward Richards	22	Joiner	Kent	"	"	" " "
Jane "	22	His Wife	"	"	"	" " "

PORT OF HULL, 27 FEB. TO 6th MAR. 1774.

Mary Smith	25	Spinster	Hull	Shipwright	Maryland	From the Charity Hall Hull going as Indented Servants for 4 Years
Mary Hemingway	27	"	"	"	"	
Mary Williamson	17	"	"	"	"	
Elizabeth Fitzgerald	16	"	"	"	"	"
Ann Butler	16	"	"	"	"	"
Maria Harrison	16	"	"	"	"	"
George Williams	19	Baker	Scotland	"	"	Indented Servant for 4 Years
Robert King	23	Cordwainer	Norfolk	"	"	" " "
William Dannot	17	Labourer	Lincoln	"	"	" " "

PORT OF BRISTOL, 27th FEB. TO 6th MAR. 1775.

John Thomas	30	Seaman	Bristol	Ann	Philadelphia	Indented Servant
Amos Rudd	25	Clothier	Wilts	"	"	" "
Thomas Bishop	19	Labourer	"	"	"	" "

Name	*Age*	*Occupation*	*From*	*Ship*	*To*	*As a*
George Thomas	30	Sadler	Wilts	Ann	Philadelphia	Indented Servant
Nicholas Linch	26	Brazier	Bridgewater	"	"	" "
John Berry	26	Weaver	"	"	"	" "
John Sutton	22	Labourer	Minehead	"	"	" "
Edward Walton	37	"	"	"	"	" "
John Sacker	39	Carpenter	London	"	"	" "
John Radcliffe	24	"	"	"	"	" "
William Manley	31	Labourer	Bristol	"	"	" "
William George	29	"	"	"	"	" "
Edward Cole	17	"	"	"	"	" "
Richard Reynolds	19	"	"	"	"	" "
Samuel Bird	20	"	"	"	"	" "
Henry Gower	23	"	"	"	"	" "
Richard Edwards	23	"	Bath	"	"	" "
William Carroll	29	"	"	"	"	" "
William Mays	22	"	"	"	"	" "
Peter Franklyn	24	Labourer	"	"	"	" "
Thomas Bryon	22	Coach Maker	"	"	"	" "
Charles Morgan	31	Labourer	"	"	"	" "
John Abbot	20	Tyler	Bristol	"	"	" "
William Spring	24	Labourer	Exeter	"	"	" "
Richard Jenkins	34	"	"	"	"	" "
Daniel Hollis	24	"	"	"	"	" "
S. Williams	22	"	"	"	"	" "
S. Allom	23	"	"	"	"	" "
S. Bond	27	Blacksmith	Wells	"	"	" "
Ja[s] Jones	24	"	"	"	"	" "
Rob[t] Knight	25	Labourer	"	"	"	" "
Jn[o] Mathews	26	Weaver	"	"	"	" "
James Pitt	23	Labourer	"	"	"	" "
Fourteen Women	—	———	"	"	"	" "
William Williams	17	Labourer	Bath	Sally	"	" "
Henry Emmett	32	"	"	"	"	" "
John Pembroke	24	"	"	"	"	" "
John Burne	20	Shoemaker	Bristol	"	"	" "

William Keaton	25	Shoemaker	"	"	"	" "
William Child	21	———	"	"	"	" "
Three Women	—	———	———	"	"	" "
Samuel Edwards	15	Labourer	Bath	Olive Branch	Maryland	" "
James Griffiths	16	"	Bristol	" "	"	" "
Thomas Benson	29	"	"	" "	"	" "
John Burridge	20	"	"	" "	"	" "
John Hurd	14	"	"	" "	"	" "
Mich[l] Cockran	22	"	"	" "	"	" "
John Goman	20	Taylor	Wells	" "	"	" "
John Griffiths	19	"	"	" "	"	" "
John Thomas	29	Barber	Salisbury	" "	"	" "
Richard Mayer	35	Labourer	"	" "	"	" "
John Young	19	"	"	" "	"	" "
Four Women	—	———	———	" "	"	" "
David Grumble	21	Labourer	Bristol	William	"	" "
Samuel Short	28	"	"	"	"	" "

Port of London, 6th to 13th Mar. 1775.

James Spencer	34	Carpenter	London	Marg[t] & Rebecca	Antigua	Going to settle
Nicholas Stear	47	Carpenter & Joiner	Devon	Nelly Frigate	Maryland	Indented Servant for 4 Years
Thomas Lloyd	27	Schoolmaster	London	" "	"	" " "
Thomas Harrison	21	Blacksmith	Warwick	" "	"	" " "
Duncan M[c]Clean	21	Perukemaker	Edingburgh	" "	"	" " "
Ann Falles	21	Spinster	Wilts	" "	"	" " "
Joseph Martin	24	Husbandman	Cheshire	" "	"	" " "
William Cooper	40	Cordwainer	Sussex	" "	"	" " "
William Harrison	21	Gardener	Warwick	" "	"	" " "
Thomas Smith	21	Gentleman's Servant	London	" "	"	" " "
William Bruff	33	Husbandman	Stafford	" "	"	" " "
Elizabeth Davidson	21	Spinster	Surry	" "	"	" " "
Mathew Keeling	25	Husbandman	Cheshire	" "	"	" " "
Thomas Law	26	Schoolmaster	London	" "	"	" " "
Richard Wiseman	24	Shoemaker	Middlesex	Fanny & Janny	"	These People are called Redem-
William Greedy	28	Millwright	Somerset	" "	"	tioners, they give Notes on
Henry Fisher	30	Labourer	Wilts	" "	"	Bond to pay for their pas-

Name	*Age*	*Occupation*	*From*	*Ship*	*To*	*As a*
James Davison	22	Carpenter	London	Fanny & Janny	Maryland	sage after arrival, if not the
Alexander Wright	27	Silversmith	"	" "	"	Capt^{tn} is to dispose of them
Edward Haydon	30	Carpenter	Hertford	" "	"	for a number of Years per
John Eyre	22	Baker	London	" "	"	agreement
Joseph Reeves	31	Farmer	Suffolk	" "	"	"
John Jackson	29	Miller	London	" "	"	"
Thomas Arthurs	35	Woolcomber	"	" "	"	"
Mary Arthurs	36	Servant	"	" "	"	"
Sarah Jackson	28	"	"	" "	"	"
Mary Harris	26	"	Surry	" "	"	"
Mary Fowler	22	"	London	" "	"	"
Elizabeth Long	22	"	"	" "	"	"
Rebecca Howell	21	"	"	" "	"	"
Ann Kendal	21	"	Derby	" "	"	"
Sarah Howell	21	"	London	" "	"	"
Elizabeth Limford	21	"	Middlesex	" "	"	"
Catharine Rigdel	22	"	Kent	" "	"	"
Mary Cooper	30	"	London	" "	"	"
Rose Mason	23	"	Warwick	" "	"	"
Elizabeth Brown	30	Schoolmistress	London	" "	"	"
William Mathews	25	Painter & Glazier	Westminster	" "	"	"
Ralph Ford	22	Cock Founder	Surry	" "	"	"
George Okell	24	Gold Beater	London	" "	"	"
James Luckman	37	Silk Weaver	"	" "	"	"
John Johnson	23	Carpenter	"	" "	"	"
Wm Cook	21	Buckel Maker	Stafford	" "	"	"
Jno Thomas	42	Glass Grinder	London	" "	"	"
H^{y} Poole	21	Jeweller	"	" "	"	"
George Anson	21	Servant	"	" "	"	"
Wm Lee	21	Labourer	"	" "	"	"
Jno Mitchell	21	Cooper	"	" "	"	"
Thos Mills	22	Clockmaker	"	" "	"	"
Thos Warner	21	Shoemaker	Hertford	" "	"	"
Ja^{s} Dale	22	Labourer	"	" "	"	"
Evan Edmonds	46	"	Monmouth	" "	"	"

Danl Aldham	27	"	Lincoln	"	"	"	"
Jno Roberts	23	"	Kent	"	"	"	"
Thos Dennison	30	Baker	Southwark	"	"	"	"
William Huggin	30	Labourer	London	"	"	"	"
Thos Bear	21	"	"	"	"	"	"
Thos Jones	21	Shoemaker	"	"	"	"	"
Wm Birch	27	Woolcomber	"	"	"	"	"
Jas Cato	28	Sawyer	"	"	"	"	"
Jno Ashton	27	Labourer	"	"	"	"	"
Wm Pagram	30	"	"	"	"	"	"
Peter Watson	42	Taylor	"	"	"	"	"
Henry Lawson	32	Painter	"	"	"	"	"
Jno Malone	30	Labourer	"	"	"	"	"
Jno Chapman	21	"	Hertford	"	"	"	"
Jno Briggs	29	Taylor	Essex	"	"	"	"
Thos Barnett	22	Farmer	Berks	"	"	"	"
Peter Swan	40	Stocking Weaver	Nottingham	"	"	"	"
Daniel Crumpler	26	Labourer	London	"	"	"	"
Adam Bale	24	"	Norfolk	"	"	"	"

PORT OF LIVERPOOL, 6th TO 13th MARCH 1775.

George Tunniby	40	Mercer	Staffordshire	Lydia	Philadelphia	Going to trade
John Tunniby	21	Sadler	"	"	"	to follow his trade
John Bohannan	30	Merchant	Ireland	"	"	To Trade
Ann Taylor	40	Lady	Staffordshire	"	"	On Business
Ann Naylor	21	"	Cheshire	"	"	" "
Elizabeth "	12	Her Sister	"	"	"	" "
Sarah Freeborn	24	Spinster	London	"	"	" "
A Gwin, his Lady & six Servants			Lancashire	John	Jamaica	" "

EMIGRANTS FROM ENGLAND

Transcribed by Gerald Fothergill of New Wandsworth, London, England, and communicated by the Committee on English Research

Port of London, 13th to 20th Mar. 1775.

Name	Age	Occupation	From	Ship	To	As a
Mary Anderson	54	———	London	Betsey	Virginia	Going to her Husband
George "	12		"	"	"	
Robert Jno "	11	Her	"	"	"	
Ann "	5		"	"	"	
Letitia "	3	Children	"	"	"	Going with their Mother
Wm Paine	24	Gentleman	"	Minerva	Boston	Going to settle
R. Chandler	25	"	"	"	"	" "
John Sprague	23	Surgeon	"	"	"	" "
Susanna Jackson	11	———	Essex	Angnes	Quebec	Going to her Aunts by her Friends Consent
Jas Robinson	17	White Smith	Scotland	Betsey	Virginia	Indented Servant for four Years
Jos Naterlow	16	Weaver	London	"	"	" " "
Henry Adge	73	Miller	Stafford	Montreal	Montreal	Going to Settle
Mary Adge	44		Warwick	"	"	Going to her husband
Samuel "	16	Children	"	"	"	Going with their Mother
Mary "	14		"	"	"	" " "
Wm "	9	of	"	"	"	" " "
Margaret "	5	Mary Adge	"	"	"	" " "
Nicholas Watson	15	A Youth	Lancaster	"	"	Going to be a Clerk
Benjamin Boswell	15	Baker	Warwick	Pensilvania	Philadelphia	Indented Servant for 7 Years
George Warren	14	Labourer	London	Packet	"	" " "
Condery Bolton	16	"	"	Culvert	Maryland	" " "
Henry "	15	"	"	"	"	" " "
Edward Beaton	20	Cordwainer	Somerset	Pensilvania	Philadelphia	Indented Servants for 4, 5 & 7
Thomas Watkins	21	House Painter	London	Packet	"	Years
John Thomas	26	Smith	"	"	"	"
Thomas Martin	23	Taylor	"	"	"	"

Richard Noxon	25	Perukemaker	Worcester	"	"	"
Moses Hiams	24	Jeweller	London	"	"	"
Moses Jacobs	22	"	"	"	"	"
Wm Edwards	36	Painter	"	"	"	"
William Chase	23	Cordwainer	"	"	"	"
John Haynes	22	Hair dresser	"	"	"	"
John Forster	30	Clerk & Bookkeeper	"	"	"	"
Robert Hayward	22	Carpenter	Essex	"	"	"
William Longwood	23	Groom	"	"	"	"
William Mitchell	21	Stone Mason	Westmoreland	"	"	"
William Harrison	23	Husbandman	Surry	"	"	"
John Humble	21	Footman	Northumberland	"	"	"
George Woodford	21	"	Salisbury	"	"	"
John Wallis	21	Baker	Essex	"	"	"
John Row	21	"	Berks	"	"	"
William Dickerson	25	Butcher	London	"	"	"
Daniel Teffoe	24	Clock & Watch Maker	Middlesex	"	"	"
William Avey	21	Taylor	London	"	"	"
Paul Courtney	23	Plaisterer	"	"	"	"
John McCunn	22	Cabinet Maker	Ireland	"	"	"
James Russel	24	Stone Mason	Westmoreland	"	"	"
Samuel Lecount	24	Printer	London	"	"	"
John Crab	22	Groom	Surry	"	"	"
William Baslay	23	Clerk	Ireland	"	"	"
John Amos	27	Hatter	London	"	"	"
John Graves	36	Perukemaker	"	"	"	"
William Gray	21	Woolcomber	Suffolk	"	"	"
James Vaulotte	17	Watch Finisher	London	"	"	"
John Logan	19	Husbandman	Kent	"	"	"
Theophilus Dunning	15	Labourer	London	"	"	"
Thomas Thompson	15	"	Kent	"	"	"
James Lover	15	"	Harts	"	"	"
William Hayes	15	Hair dresser	Warwick	"	"	"
William Brown	15	Labourer	Kent	"	"	"
Richard Peplow	18	"	London	"	"	"
Valentine Kirby	16	Groom	"	"	"	"
Francis Phain	16	"	Worcester	Calvert	Maryland	Indented Servant for 4 to 7 Years
John Smith	16	Labourer	London	"	"	" " "

Name	Age	Occupation	From	Ship	To	As a
George Hollingworth	21	Tavern Waiter	London	Calvert	Maryland	Indented Servant for 4 to 7 Years
Willm Vincent	25	Throwster	Kent	"	"	" " "
Thomas Manders	33	Milwright	Southwark	"	"	" " "
Thomas Landon	24	Breeches Maker	"	"	"	" " "
Peter Bradshaw	22	Painter	"	"	"	" " "
John Furrance	21	Husbandman	Surry	"	"	" " "
Samuel Price	25	Cordwainer	London	"	"	" " "
Patrick Sheen	21	Gardener	Essex	"	"	" " "
Henry White	30	Sawyer	Kent	"	"	" " "
John Burch	30	Cooper	Somerset	"	"	" " "
Willm Power	24	Gardener	Essex	"	"	" " "
James Cave	46	Millwright	Winchester	"	"	" " "
John Blount	28	Surgeon	Hereford	"	"	" " "
John Barlow	21	Perukemaker	Salisbury	"	"	" " "
James Handley	21	Groom & Coachman	Newcastle	"	"	" " "
Dennis Sullivan	26	Husbandman	London	"	"	" " "
William Rumford	22	"	Bedford	"	"	" " "
William Pomfrey	38	Cooper	Gloster	"	"	" " "
Richd Tomlinson	34	Cabinet Maker	London	"	"	" " "
F. B. McDonald	33	Upholsterer	"	"	"	" " "
John Tapley	44	Harness Maker	"	"	"	" " "
John Lishman	35	Blacksmith	"	"	"	" " "
John Johnson	45	Joiner	Yorkshire	"	"	" " "
John Allington	21	Skinner	Southwark	"	"	" " "
John Halliday	26	Cloth Dresser	London	"	"	" " "
Jos Dennis	21	Husbandman	"	"	"	" " "
Paul Hurley	48	Baker	"	"	"	" " "

PORT OF LONDON, 20th TO 27 MAR. 1775.

Adam Irvine	38	Ship Joiner	London	Canadian	Quebec	Going to Settle
Elizabeth "	36	His Wife & 3 Small Children	"	"	"	" "
John Roberts	30	Merchant	Scotland	Georgia Diana	Georgia	" "
Margaret "	23	His Wife	"	" "	"	" "

Sarah Brooke	21	Spinster	Somerset	Patuxant	Maryland	Indented Servant for 4 Years
James Dawson	25	Woolcomber	London	"	"	" " "
Margaret Dennison	35	Widow	Durham	"	"	" " "

PORT OF PORTSMOUTH, 20th TO 27 MAR. 1775.

Mr Holdman	—	Gentleman	———	Ipswich	Jamaica	To be store keeper in His Majestys Yard Jamaica
Mr Taylor	22	"	———	"	"	N. B. the Particulars (from this
Mr Johnson	22	"	———	"	"	Port) that are not inserted
Mr Frankland	58	"	———	Pensilvania Packet	Philadelphia	cannot be ascertd

PORT OF LONDON, 27th MAR. TO 3d APRIL 1775.

Charles Connor	24	Merchant	London	Noble	Dominica	Going on Business
William Barrett	28	Baker	Southwark	Royal Charlotte	Maryland	Indented Servant for 4 Years
Thomas McVael	19	Labourer	London	" "	"	" " "
George Ryan	15	"	"	" "	"	" " "
James Lipcombe	35	Butcher	Isle of Wight	" "	"	" " "
John Williams	22	Footman	Middlesex	" "	"	" " "
Thomas Jones	17	Groom	Essex	" "	"	" " "
James Ward	21	Farrier	London	Neptune	"	These People, on their arrival
Benjamin Bateman	35	Last Maker	"	"	"	at Maryland, are to be dis-
Anthony Hopper	19	Painter	Ireland	"	"	posed of for a number of years
Daniel Whilton	29	Weaver	Norfolk	"	"	Provided they are not found
Rachel Sampson	23	"	London	"	"	capaple to pay the Captn for
Thomas Savage	33	Bricklayer	Surry	"	"	their passage, as Per agreemt
Mark Moses	23	Schoolmaster	London	"	"	"
Lawrance Crane	23	Clerk	"	"	"	"
John Connor	21	Hair dresser	"	"	"	"
James Cranston	25	Stationer	"	"	"	"
Rice Price	30	Farmer	Southwark	"	"	"
Mary Dealy	22	Servant	Middlesex	"	"	"
Charles Connor	24	Merchant	London	Noble	Dominica	On Business
Nicholas Miller	34	Labourer	"	Neptune	Maryland	These People, on their arrival
Michael Griffin	21	"	"	"	"	at Maryland, are to be dis-

Name	*Age*	*Occupation*	*From*	*Ship*	*To*	*As a*
Jane Wood	22	Servant	London	Neptune	Maryland	posed of for a number of years,
Mary "	24	"	"	"	"	Provided they are not found
Thomas Branson	21	Gardener	Leicester	"	"	capable to pay the Captⁿ for
C. I. Selby	27	Butcher	Nottingham	"	"	their Passage as Per agree-
Low Paine	21	Chair Maker	London	"	"	ment
Elizabeth Paine	21	Servant	"	"	"	"
Thomas Jones	27	Gun Smith	"	"	"	"
C. D. Fitzgerald	30	Labourer	Suffolk	"	"	"
George Linton	21	"	London	"	"	"
John Dealy	31	Joiner	Buckingham	"	"	"
Charles Harding	21	Weaver	London	"	"	"
Susanna Wing	17	Servant	"	"	"	"
Hannah Thompson	19	"	"	"	"	"
Rebecca Hosser	16	"	Middlesex	"	"	"
Margᵗ Goodson	18	"	London	"	"	"
Elizabeth Barnes	18	"	"	"	"	"
Alice Harvey	18	"	"	"	"	"
Sarah Neale	17	"	"	"	"	"
Thomas Barclay	16	Labourer	"	"	"	"
Benjamin Wise	18	Weaver	Norwich	"	"	"
George Wassel	17	Cordwainer	Cheshire	Bland	Virginia	Indented Servant for 4 Years
William Figg	19	Hair dresser	Hertford	"	"	" " "
John Madden	17	Weaver	London	"	"	" " "
James Sampell	32	Husbandman	"	"	"	" " "
Barnabas Clarke	21	Clerk & Bookkeeper	"	"	"	" " "
Stephen Rose	26	" "	Kent	"	"	" " "
John Shephard	23	Apothecary	Westminster	"	"	" " "
James Paulson	43	Do & Chymist	London	"	"	" " "
George Edie	28	Husbandman	Essex	"	"	" " "
Thomas Bareford	26	Silk Weaver	London	"	"	" " "
Thomas Barr	22	Baker	Warwick	"	"	" " "
Samuel Waples	21	Butcher	London	"	"	" " "
Michael Wickers	35	Woolcomber	York	"	"	" " "
John Flemming	27	Clerk	London	"	"	" " "
John Clough	40	Schoolmaster	Essex	"	"	" " "

Thomas Holland	20	Ironmonger	London	"	"	" " "
Thomas Atkins	19	Twine Spinner	Middlesex	"	"	" " "
William Francis	15	Fisherman	Essex	"	"	" " "
Benjamin Stickland	15	Labourer	Southwark	"	"	" " "
James Little	16	Husbandman	Wexford	"	"	" " "
Arthur Hughes	17	Brass Founder	Worcester	"	"	" " "
George Jarvis	21	Groom	Derby	"	"	" " "
John Brown	21	"	Surry	"	"	" " "
Samuel Sherry	22	Husbandman	Westminster	"	"	" " "
John Richardson	24	Cooper	London	"	"	" " "
James Bowtell	24	Plaisterer	"	"	"	" " "
George Woodhouse	22	Husbandman	"	"	"	" " "
William Fox	26	Bricklayer	"	"	"	" " "
Luke Field	22	Linen Weaver	"	"	"	" " "
William Clarke	21	Carpenter	Southwark	"	"	" " "
John Gibbs	27	Breeches Maker	Kent	"	"	" " "
Henry Cook	32	Sash Maker	London	"	"	" " "
James Spence	41	Ship Wright	Kent	"	"	" " "
Barnabas McVicar	22	Watch Maker	London	"	"	" " "
Barnat Marry	32	Husbandman	Lincoln	"	"	" " "
Charles Hall	16	Labourer	London	"	"	" " "

Port of London, 3d to 10th April. 1775.

Elizabeth Cheine	24	Spinster	Surry	George	Montreal	Servants to Gentlemen
Hannah Pool	24	"	London	"	"	" "
Mary Stainer	30	"	"	"	"	" "
Sarah North	27	Cook Maid	Essex	Nancy	Maryland	Indented Servant for four Years
Charles Blundell	29	Footman	Surry	"	"	" " "
Mary Blundell	29	His Wife	"	"	"	" " "
John Taylor	21	Husbandman	Stafford	"	"	" " "
William Skelly	29	Gentleman's Servant	Middlesex	"	"	" " "
Charles Drabwell	29	Taylor	London	"	"	" " "
Thomas Forsyth	47	Husbandman	Kent	"	"	" " "
John Robertson	21	School Master	Scotland	"	"	" " "
James Hanlan	29	Husbandman	London	"	"	" " "
Kenrick Anwyl	27	Silversmith	"	Fleetwood	"	" " "

Name	Age	Occupation	From	Ship	To	As a
George Scarr	21	Engraver	London	Fleetwood	Maryland	Indented Servant for four Years
Thomas Davis	22	Cutler	"	"	"	" " "
John Clark	23	Cabinet Maker	Southwark	"	"	" " "
Richard Biggs	21	Groom	Middlesex	"	"	" " "
William Dean	35	Gardener	Surry	"	"	" " "
Theodore Jennings	40	Pewterer	Middlesex	"	"	" " "
Thomas Brogden	21	Cabinet Maker	Norwich	"	"	" " "
Job Hain	32	Malster	Somerset	"	"	" " "
Wiloughby Harvey	38	Perukemaker	London	"	"	" " "
Sarah Powell	21	Beaver Puller	"	"	"	" " "
Roger Shephard	27	Cordwainer	Surry	"	"	" " "
William Baldwin	24	Joiner	London	"	"	" " "
William Smith	27	Upholsterer	Oxford	"	"	" " "
William Sadler	21	Leather dresser	Southwark	"	"	" " "
John Strattard	27	Tin Plate Worker	London	"	"	" " "
William Sanders	22	Hat Maker	Worcester	"	"	" " "
Benjamin Burdock	23	Brazier	London	"	"	" " "
Charles Cumming	26	Gardener	Middlesex	"	"	" " "
Thomas Thompson	23	Waiter	London	"	"	" " "
William Spencer	25	Husbandman	Harford	"	"	" " "
Mathew Simpson	35	Hatter	Southwark	"	"	" " "
James Bradshaw	22	Smith	London	"	"	" " "
Christiana Town	32	Housemaid	York	"	"	" " "
Elizabeth Brown	22	"	Coventry	"	"	" " "
Jane Harley	22	Seamstress	Kent	"	"	" " "
William Clements	20	Rope Maker	London	"	"	" " "
Mary Newton	21	Lady's Maid	"	"	"	" " "
Susanna Southwell	26	House Keeper	"	"	"	" " "
Mary Simmonds	16	Milliner	"	"	"	" " "

Port of Portsmouth, 3d to 10th Mar. 1775.

Robert Rawlings Esqre & Family, Gentleman			London	Dorsetshire	St. Christophers	Going to settle at St. Christophers
Mr John Stanley	—	Planter	"	"	" "	
Mr Willm Maynard	—	Gentleman	Nevis	"	" "	Going to settle at Nevis

Port of Hull, 3^d to 10th April 1775.

William Black	43	Linen Draper	Yorkshire	Jenny	Fort Cumber-	Having made a purchase is going
Elizabeth "	36	His Wife	"	"	land	with his family to reside there
William "	14		"	"	"	"
Richard "	11	&	"	"	"	"
John "	15		"	"	"	"
Thomas "	9		"	"	"	"
Sarah "	7	Children	"	"	"	"
Mathew Lodge	20	Servant & House Carpenter	"	"	"	Going to seek a better Liveli-
Elizabeth Redfield	25	Servant	"	"	"	hood
Jane Hurdy	16	"	"	"	"	"
Elizabeth Beaver	30	Housekeeper to the Goverer	"	"	"	"
Bridget Sedel	38	———	"	"	"	Going with her Children to her
Mary "	7		"	"	"	husband
Francis "	6	Her	"	"	"	
Sarah "	1	Children	"	"	"	
Christopher Horsman	27	Farmer	"	"	"	Going to seek a better Liveli-
Robert Colpits	28	"	"	"	"	hood
Christopher Harper	45	"	"	"	"	Having made a purchase is go-
Elizabeth "	40	His Wife	"	"	"	ing to reside there
Hannah "	15		"	"	"	"
Elizabeth "	14		"	"	"	"
John "	13		"	"	"	"
Thomas "	12	&	"	"	Fort Cumber-	Going with their parents
Catharine "	7		"	"	land in Nova	" " "
Charlotte "	6		"	"	Scotia	" " "
William "	4	Children	"	"	"	" " "
Thomas King	21	Blacksmith	"	"	"	Going to purchase or return
William Johnson	28	Gentleman	"	"	"	" " "
Mary Lowry	27	———	"	"	"	Going over to her husband
Mary Lowerson	27	———	"	"	"	" " "
Thomas Wheatley	53	Farmer	"	"	"	Going to purchase or Return
William Clark	42	Farmer	"	"	Anapolis in	" " "
Mary "	13		"	"	Nova Scotia	" " "
William "	10	His	"	"	"	" " "
Richard "	9		"	"	"	" " "
Rachael "	3	Children	"	"	"	" " "

Name	Age	Occupation	From	Ship	To	As a
John Skelton	38	Servant	Yorkshire	Jenny	Annapolis in Nova Scotia	Going to seek a better Livelihood
Jane Skelton	36	——	“	“		
Francis Watson	18	Taylor	“	“	“	“
John Bath	23	Servant	“	“	“	“
William Johnson	49	Farmer	“	“	Halifax in Nova Scotia	Having purchased An Estate is going over with his Family & Servants to reside
Margaret “	48	——	“	“		
George “	26	Servant & Carpenter to Wm Johnson	“	“	“	
William Johnson	23	Son of Wm Johnson	“	“	“	“
Emanuel “	16	“ “ “	“	“	“	“
Joseph “	14	“ “ “	“	“	“	“
James Hutton	15	Apprentice to Wm Johnson	“	“	“	“
Elizabeth Anderson	36	——	“	“	“	Going over with her Children to her husband who is Cooper to William Johnson
Mary “	9		“	“	“	
Jane “	7		“	“	“	
Moses “	5	Her	“	“	“	“
William “	4		“	“	“	“
John “	1	Children	“	“	“	“
Thomas Walton	24	Husbandman	“	“	“	Going to seek a better Livelihood
William Robinson	42	——	“	“	“	Having Purchased, is going over with his family
Elizabeth “	30	——	“	“	“	
Elizabeth “	9	Children	“	“	“	Going with their Parents
Jonathan “	5	of	“	“	“	“
Francis “	3		“	“	“	“
William “	2	William Robinson	“	“	“	“
Thomas Kalin	24	Servant to Wm Robinson	“	“	“	Going with William Robinson
Patience Fallydown	22	“ “ “	“	“	“	“ “ “
John Robinson	47	Husbandman	“	“	“	To make a purchase or return
Ann “	15	His Daughter	“	“	“	Going with their father
Jenny “	9	“ “	“	“	“	“ “ “
Mary Parker	40	——	“	“	“	Going over to her husband he having a Farm there
Elizabeth “	9	Her	“	“	“	
James “	2	Children	“	“	“	“

Richard Peck	47	Husbandman	"	"	"	Having made a purchase is going with his family to reside
Jane "	42	His Wife	"	"	"	
Mary "	20		"	"	"	Going with their parents
Jane "	17		"	"	"	" " "
Helen "	15		"	"	"	" " "
Isaac "	13		"	"	"	" " "
Robert "	10		"	"	"	" " "
Rose "	7		"	"	"	" " "
Richard "	5		"	"	"	" " "
Joseph "	2	Children of R^d Peck	"	"	"	" " "
Sarah Fenton	15	———	"	"	"	Going over to their Father
Mary "	9	———	"	"	"	" " "

PORT OF LONDON, 10th TO 17th APRIL 1775.

Charles Steward	22	Labourer	London	Adventure	Maryland	Passengers & Redemptioners
John Chandler	22	Watch Maker	"	"	"	" "
Samuel Griffiths	22	Silk Weaver	"	"	"	" "
William Turner	45	Gun Barrel Maker	"	"	"	" "
John Desertembbo	25	Hatter	"	"	"	" "
William Whitewith	22	Farmer	"	"	"	" "
Benjamin Kelsey	16	Labourer	"	"	"	" "
Benjamin Corby	15	"	"	"	"	" "
Thomas McBone	26	Farmer	"	"	"	" "
Thomas Cleaver	22	Labourer	"	"	"	" "
Jeremiah Regan	23	Taylor	"	"	"	" "
James Warner	31	"	"	"	"	" "
James French	25	Hair dresser	"	"	"	" "
Richard Mondy	22	Glazier	"	"	"	" "
William Townsend	16	Brewer	"	"	"	" "
James Jackson	19	Silversmith	"	"	"	" "
John Hopkins	19	Woolen Weaver	"	"	"	" "
Thomas Morgan	16	Tin Man	"	"	"	" "
William Tune	17	Labourer	"	"	"	" "
Henry Emerton	21	Shoemaker	"	"	"	" "
Joseph "	21	Bookbinder	"	"	"	" "
Richard Lord	15	Bricklayer	"	"	"	" "

Name	Age	Occupation	From	Ship	To	As a
Edward Dobbis	21	Carpenter	London	Adventure	Maryland	Passengers & Redemptioners
Mary Dobbis	29	Milliner	"	"	"	" "
Samuel Nash	40	Shoemaker	"	"	"	" "
Samuel English	23	Waiter	"	"	"	" "
William Higgins	22	"	"	"	"	" "
Francis Broome	42	Servant	"	"	"	" "
Sarah "	27	"	"	"	"	" "
George Hunt	15	Labourer	"	"	"	" "
Robert Byrne	22	Smith	"	"	"	" "
Thomas Smith	23	Gardener	"	"	"	" "
William Jones	24	Cooper	"	"	"	" "
Edward Hynes	22	Farmer	"	"	"	" "
George Wilkinson	18	Labourer	"	"	"	" "
William Dennison	16	Painter	"	"	"	" "
William Wood	21	Farmer	"	"	"	" "
Sarah Harper	21	Trimming Maker	"	"	"	" "
Samuel Penny	19	Watch Maker	"	"	"	" "
William Cull	21	Labourer	"	"	"	" "
Esther Cunliffe	28	Servant	"	"	"	" "
Thomas Woodford	30	"	Essex	"	"	" "
Mary Roberts	35	"	"	"	"	" "
Elizabeth Woodford	30	"	"	"	"	" "
Richard Boniface	16	Postillion	"	"	"	" "
John Nage	29	Cabinet Maker	Kent	"	"	" "
William Flint	26	Labourer	"	"	"	" "
Mary Robinson	26	Servant	"	"	"	" "
Elizabeth Hood	30	"	"	"	"	" "
Ashton Lever	21	Carpenter	Sussex	"	"	" "
John Shove	29	Schoolmaster	"	"	"	" "
John Salmon	16	Founder	Birmingham	"	"	" "
John Harris	29	Baker	Somersetshire	"	"	These People on their arrival at
Isaac Taplan	16	Labourer	"	"	"	Maryland are to be disposed
William Howard	15	"	"	"	"	of for a number of Years pro-
Mary Hughes	15	Servant	Glasgow	"	"	viding they are not found
Daniel McPhee	21	Joiner	"	"	"	capable to pay the Captn for

William Welsh	30	Farmer	Birmingham	“	“	their passage as per Agreement
Gilbert Carty	21	“	Ireland	“	“	
Sarah Bateman	21	Servant	Hertfordshire	“	“	“
Thomas Kersey	22	Clerk	Norfolk	“	“	“
Thomas Crampton	15	Labourer	Nottingham	“	“	“
Philip Kingsford	23	Turner	Cornwall	“	“	“
James Roads	15	Labourer	Northampton	“	“	“
Edward Horrabin	22	Farmer	Staffordshire	“	“	“
Robert Bray	16	Labourer	Norfolk	“	“	“
Francis Goodbern	25	Painter	Shropshire	“	“	“
Edward Williams	45	Wool comber	Devonshire	“	“	“
Thomas Barne	25	Sawyer	Liverpool	“	“	“
John Morrison	36	“	Cheshire	“	“	“
John Price	22	Labourer	Berkshire	“	“	“
Jane Monkhouse	42	Servant	Cumberland	“	“	“
Stephen Jackson		These People did not choose to Answer the required questions				
Joseph Eastman		“ “ “ “				
Thomas Wright		“ “ “ “				
Charles Dean		“ “ “ “				
Jane Beamont		“ “ “ “				

PORT OF EXETER, 10th TO 17 APRIL 1775.

Sir John Colliton His Wife & three Children & three Women Servants	40	——	Exeter	A New York Ship	Charles Town S. Carolina	Going to look after an Extensive Estate belonging to him
		——	“	“ “		
		——	“	“ “	“	
		——	“	“ “	“	

PORT OF NEWCASTLE, 17th TO 24 APRIL 1775.

Mathew Newton	30	Yoeman	Durham	Providence	Halifax	In expatation of better Employ

PORT OF LONDON, 24th APRIL TO 1st MAY 1775.

Mary Dyal	23	Servant	London	St. James	Jamaica	Going to settle at Jamaica
Mary Rolfe	20	“	“	“ “	“	“ “ “
Catharine Welmore	29	“	“	“ “	“	“ “ “
Thomas Motral	26	“	Norwich	“ “	“	“ “ “
Charles Robinson	22	Gardener	Middlesex	Elizabeth	Virginia	Indented for 4 Years

Port of Portsmouth, 24th April to 1st May 1775.

Name	Age	Occupation	From	Ship	To	As a
Mr David Young	—	Planter	London	Unity	Tobago	Going to superintend his Plantation
Mr Deponthe	—	"	"	"	"	
Mr Pearson	—	Merchant	"	"	"	Going to settle at Tobago
Mr Carrick	—	"	"	"	"	" " "

Pill a Creek a Port of Bristol, 24th April to 1st May 1775.

Name	Age	Occupation	From	Ship	To	As a
One Hundred & Six Convicts from different Jails of this Kingdom				Elizabeth	Maryland	N. B. Could not take their names, or any other Particulars, as the ship came down & Sailed immediately

Port of Exeter, 1st to 8th May 1775.

Name	Age	Occupation	From	Ship	To	As a
Jane Bell	25	Spinster	Exeter	Starr & Garter	Maryland	Going to seek a better Livelihood
Ann Williams	23	"	"	" "	"	
Mary Gilliford	24	"	"	" "	"	"
Mary Ridgway	29	Wife of one of the Convicts, who was Transported in the said Vessel				

Port of London, 8th to 15th May 1775.

Name	Age	Occupation	From	Ship	To	As a
Thomas Rice	17	Husbandman	Worcester	Elkridge	Maryland	Indented Servant for 4 Years
William Ayre	24	"	Lincolnshire	"	"	" " "
Edward Toothacre	22	Cordwainer	London	"	"	" " "
Robert Sharman	22	Carpenter	Wales	"	"	" " "
Charles Evans	32	Butcher	London	"	"	" " "
William Reading	24	Husbandman	"	"	"	" " "
John King	24	Carpenter	Birmingham	"	"	" " "
Joseph Fellows	39	Flax Dresser	Sheffield	"	"	" " "
William Davison	29	Cutler	London	"	"	" " "
Elizabeth Harris	19	Spinster	"	"	"	" " "

Rebecca Hilditch	27	Cook	“	“	“	“	“	“
John Lusher	23	Taylor	Surry	“	“	“	“	“
Edward Harris	37	Comb Maker	London	“	“	“	“	“
Catharine Hany	33	Cook	“	“	“	“	“	“
John Wiltshire	21	Husbandman	Suffolk	“	“	“	“	“
Benjamin Gray	24	Butcher	London	“	“	“	“	“
William Rogers	21	White Smith	“	“	“	“	“	“
William Jones	15	Labourer	Southwark	“	“	“	“	“
Luke Linley	21	Smith	Wiltshire	“	“	“	“	“
Francis Gray	21	Plaisterer	Surry	“	“	“	“	“
John Robinson	17	Labourer	Portsmouth	“	“	“	“	“
Thomas Harvey	23	Clerk	Huntingdon-shire	“	“	“	“	“
George Markham	24	“	London	“	“	“	“	“
John Gough	33	Sawyer	Salop	“	“	“	“	“
Robert Manning	31	Gardener	Southwark	“	“	“	“	“
Thomas Brooks	30	Cooper	Middlesex	Ashton Hall	“	“	“	“
Edward Dennis	21	Butcher	London	“ “	“	“	“	“
Thomas Hancock	29	White Smith	Staffordshire	“ “	“	“	“	“
Henry Crocket	21	Horse Farrier	London	“ “	“	“	“	“
Thomas Brotherton	21	Cordwainer	“	“ “	“	“	“	“
Joseph Miller	29	Mercer	“	“ “	“	“	“	“
Bennettetto Fallevolte	40	Surgeon	“	“ “	“	“	“	“
William Wheatley	30	Butcher	Nottingham	“ “	“	“	“	“
John Percival	25	Labourer	London	“ “	“	“	“	“
Andrew Dove	15	“	“	“ “	“	“	“	“
William Hull	15	“	“	“ “	“	“	“	“
Eleanor Ludley	35	———	Durham	“ “	“	“	“	“
Thomas Jordan	17	Labourer	London	“ “	“	“	“	“
Susanna Staples	22	Spinster	“	“ “	“	“	“	“
Sarah Bennett	22	“	Nottingham	“ “	“	“	“	“
Mary Pledge	21	“	Sussex	“ “	“	“	“	“
Mary Abercrombie	27	“	Southwark	“ “	“	“	“	“
Elizabeth Brown	19	“	London	“ “	“	“	“	“
Ann Smith	21	“	Warwick	“ “	“	“	“	“
James King	22	Clerk	London	“ “	“	“	“	“
J. P. Pettyt	30	Vinter	“	Camden	“	“	“	“
Charles Flynn	24	Carpenter	“					

PORT OF WHITEHAVEN, 15th TO 22nd MAY 1775.

Name	*Age*	*Occupation*	*From*	*Ship*	*To*	*As a*
Richard Todd	21	Block Maker	Whitehaven	Woodcock	South Carolina	To follow his trade
William Brace	20	Musician	Dumfries	Tyger	Jamaica	" "

PORT OF PORTSMOUTH, 15th TO 22nd MAY 1775.

Miss Rawlins	25	Lady	St. Christophier	Weatheral	St. Christophers	To return Home
Miss Ama Rawlins	18	"	" "	"	" "	" "

PORT OF LONDON, 22nd TO 29th MAY 1775.

William Dobberhow	23	Cooper	London	Mermaid	Maryland	Indented Servant for 4 Years
John Pringle	27	Taylor	"	"	"	" " "
William Jones	25	Smith	"	"	"	" " "
William Jackson	24	Groom	"	"	"	" " "
William Hatton	21	Clerk & Bookkeeper	"	"	"	" " "
William Browning	21	Surgeon	"	"	"	" " "
William Chambers	28	Cook	"	"	"	" " "
Harriet Colebrooke	21	Lady's Maid	"	"	"	" " "
Joanna Lander	28	" "	"	"	"	" " "
Mary Banse	25	" "	"	"	"	" " "
Mary Brown	21	" "	"	"	"	" " "
John Coleby	21	Painter	"	"	"	" " "
John Gray	28	Joiner	"	"	"	" " "
Thomas Carter	22	Smith	"	"	"	" " "
William Bury	22	"	"	"	"	" " "
William Walton	20	Groom	"	"	"	" " "
Brill Dancer	18	Pou[l]terer	"	"	"	" " "
Joseph Floyd	16	Plaisterer	"	"	"	" " "
Henrietta James	18	Servant	"	"	"	" " "
Susanna Sweatman	22	Housemaid	"	"	"	" " "
William Young	16	Labourer	"	"	"	" " "

James Edwd Smith	31	Pewterer	"	"	"	"	"	"
Henry Wright	21	Cabinet Maker	"	"	"	"	"	"
John Maxwell	25	Gardener	"	"	"	"	"	"
William Jones	21	Apothecary	"	"	"	"	"	"
Robert Boyle	21	Gentlemans Servant	"	"	"	"	"	"
James Tarmdy	21	Flax dresser	"	"	"	"	"	"
Mary Jones	21	Muff Maker	"	"	"	"	"	"
William Brown	21	Plumber	"	"	"	"	"	"
William Woard	32	Husbandman	"	"	"	"	"	"
George Ummell	32	Smith	"	"	"	"	"	"
Elizabeth Ummell	21	Wife of Do	"	"	"	"	"	"
John Woods	16	Weaver	"	"	"	"	"	"
George Harding	21	Groom	Southwark	"	"	"	"	"
Sarah Wilson	22	Housemaid	"	"	"	"	"	"
Margaret Evans	23	"	"	"	"	"	"	"
Ann Bishop	21	"	"	"	"	"	"	"
Susanna Valnant	22	"	"	"	"	"	"	"
Mary Farrod	28	"	"	"	"	"	"	"
William Knox	37	Husbandman	Surry	"	"	"	"	"
John Russell	21	Taylor	"	"	"	"	"	"
Francis Eales	21	Butcher	Kent	"	"	"	"	"
Patrick Stephens	24	Joiner	Essex	"	"	"	"	"
William Shaw	21	Clerk & Bookkeeper	Yorkshire	"	"	"	"	"
James Favell	26	Husbandman	"	"	"	"	"	"
Richard Halford	21	"	Leicester	"	"	"	"	"
Thomas Waters	16	"	Dorset	"	"	"	"	"
Edward Walter	15	Labourer	"	"	"	"	"	"
William Sayer	27	Wheelwright	Tunbridge	"	"	"	"	"
William Hawksford	21	Plater	Birmingham	"	"	"	"	"
James Ham	21	Cordwainer	Salisbury	"	"	"	"	"
William Munton	21	Grocer	Lincoln	"	"	"	"	"
David Johnson	48	Cooper	Middlesex	"	"	"	"	"
John Roberts	15	Labourer	Northampton	"	"	"	"	"
George Turdy	23	Bricklayer	Norfolk	"	"	"	"	"
William Wright	27	Clerk & Bookkeeper	Liverpool	"	"	"	"	"
King English	35	Land Surveyor	Bristol	"	"	"	"	"
Robert Daile	21	Labourer	Deptford	"	"	"	"	"
John Smith	42	Cooper	Norfolk	"	"	"	"	"

Name	*Age*	*Occupation*	*From*	*Ship*	*To*	*As a*
Thomas Smith	25	Shop man	Hertford	Mermaid	Maryland	Indented Servant for 4 Years
Charles Girdler	17	White Smith	Berkshire	“	“	“ “ “
James Oliver	18	Shoemaker	Herefordshire	“	“	“ “ “
Elizabeth Jenkins	24	Housemaid	“	“	“	“ “ “
Samuel Hanson	15	Labourer	London	Patowmack	“	“ “ “
James Thompson	30	House Carpenter	“	“	“	“ “ “
Catharine Lewis	36	Cookmaid	“	“	“	“ “ “
Robert Robertson	25	Carpenter	“	“	“	“ “ “
Elizabeth Brind	20	Housemaid	“	“	“	“ “ “
John Carswell	44	Weaver	“	“	“	“ “ “
Brian O. Brian	24	Carpenter	“	“	“	“ “ “
Michael Carry	23	“	“	“	“	“ “ “
Henry Turner	24	Upholsterer	“	“	“	“ “ “
John Atkinson	26	Cabinet Maker	“	“	“	“ “ “
John Redpeth	30	Cordwainer	“	“	“	“ “ “
Mary “	31	His Wife	“	“	“	“ “ “
William Ranson	35	Shoemaker	“	“	“	“ “ “
Alexander Burleigh	16	Comb Maker	Worcester	“	“	“ “ “
Isaac Reynsbottom	16	Labourer	Norwich	“	“	“ “ “
Margaret Love	22	Housemaid	Newcastle	“	“	“ “ “
Thomas Hobec	20	Husbandman	Bedford	“	“	“ “ “
George Collin	30	Brewer	Sussex	“	“	“ “ “
Thomas Jones	22	Sawyer	Southwark	“	“	“ “ “
John Taylor	21	Husbandman	Bucks	“	“	“ “ “
James Halton	16	Labourer	Nottingham	“	“	“ “ “
Edward Hanks	16	Miller	Shewsbury [*sic*]	“	“	“ “ “
John Woodstock	25	Carpenter	Birmingham	“	“	“ “ “
George Watson	29	Gardener	York	“	“	“ “ “
Edward Church	23	Clerk & Bookkeeper	Cornwall	“	“	“ “ “
Mary Atkinson	21	Wife of John Atkinson	London	“	“	“ “ “

EMIGRANTS FROM ENGLAND

Transcribed by Gerald Fothergill of New Wandsworth, London, England, and communicated by the Committee on English Research

Port of Poole, 22nd to 29th May 1775.

Name	*Age*	*Occupation*	*From*	*Ship*	*To*	*As a*
John Phillips	50	Baker	Poole	——	Quebec	Going to settle at Quebec being sent for by his father is a brick-layer & working for his majesty on the garrison there
Sarah "	45	His Wife	"	——	"	

Port of Plymouth, 22nd to 29th May 1775.

Thomas Pearson	27	Planter	London	Chaming Nancy	Tobago	Going to reside

Pill a Creek a Port of Bristol, 22nd to 29th May 1775.

Thomas Rosse	35	Carpenter	Wells	Isabella	Maryland	Indented Servant
Charles Jones	25	Labourer	"	"	"	" "
Seventy five Convicts from Bristol Jail			——	"	"	——

Port of Whitehaven, 29th May to 5th June 1775.

James Blair	24	Factor	Virginia	Union	Virginia	Going to Trade
Edward Fisher	28	Farmer, Wife & 2 Children	Yorkshire	Favourite	New York	Going to follow their respective trades & callings
Christopher Hetherington	45	" " & 7 Children	"	"	" "	
John Waite	50	" " & 6 Children	"	"	" "	"
Joseph Pescod	48	" " & 5 Children	"	"	" "	"
William Parker	45	Shoemaker, Wife & 5 Children	"	"	" "	"
James Hendry	40	Farmer, Wife & 3 Children	"	"	" "	"

Margaret Moore	21	———	"	"	" "	"
David Carson	40	Farmer, Wife & 4 Children	"	"	" "	"
Robert Hamilton	42	" " " 3 "	"	"	" "	"
John Sutton	43	Shoemaker	"	"	" "	"
William Bond	21	Mason	"	"	" "	"
William Scott	23	Farmer & Wife	"	"	" "	"
John Moor	24	Farmer, Wife & 1 Child	"	"	" "	"
Richard Nixon	25	" & Wife	"	"	" "	"
Bridget Pattison	40	——— & Child	"	"	" "	"
Nicholas McIntosh	35	Taylor	"	"	" "	"
John Armstrong	25	Smith & Wife	"	"	" "	"
James Scott	40	Farmer, Wife & 3 Children	"	"	" "	"
Alexander Connell	24	Farmer, & Wife	"	"	" "	"
John Brown	30	Shoemaker	"	"	" "	"
Thomas Patterson	27	Farmer, Wife & 1 Child	"	"	" "	"
John Patterson	30	" " " 3 Children	"	"	" "	"
Margaretta Varley	35	— & 2 Children	"	"	" "	"
John Peel	30	Farmer	"	"	" "	"
John Carrick	31	"	"	"	" "	"
David Edger	40	Farmer, Wife & 2 Children	"	"	" "	"
William Armstrong	30	Smith	"	"	" "	"
Robert Boyde	28	Farmer, Wife & Child	"	"	" "	"
James Hutchinson	40	" " " 4 Children	"	"	" "	"

PORT OF LONDON, 5th TO 12th JUNE 1775.

Samuel Phillips	24	Linen Weaver	London	Baltimore	Baltimore	Redemptioners, these people on their arrival at Maryland are to be disposed of for a number of years providing they are not capable to pay the Captn for their passage as per Agreement
Agnes Carswel	17	Servant	"	"	"	
Jane Giss	17	"	"	"	"	
Christopher Morris	22	Farmer	Dublin	"	"	
Mary Durham	21	Housekeeper	Scotland	"	"	
Cornelius Hagarty	19	Gardener	Ireland	"	"	
Ann Norris	17	Servant	Bedford	"	"	
Mary Barker	31	"	Portsmouth	"	"	"
William Combes	15	"	Devonshire	"	"	"
John Burley	28	Coulor Maker	Nottingham	"	"	"
Ann Hopkins	29	Ladys Maid	Shrewsbury	"	"	"

Name	*Age*	*Occupation*	*From*	*Ship*	*To*	*As a*
John Button	21	Miller	Essex	Baltimore	Baltimore	Redemptioners, these People on their arrival at Maryland, are to be disposed of for a number of years provided they are not found capable to pay the Captn for their passage as per agreement
Thomas Gatley	17	Servant	Somerset	"	"	
William Forbey	15	"	Norfolk	"	"	
John Constable	24	Pastry Cook	Surry	"	"	
William Griffin	24	School Master	Ireland	"	"	
John Moore	16	Servant	Warwick	"	"	
Dennis Mahany	27	Sailor	Ireland	"	"	
Turns White	24	Farmer	Dublin	"	"	"
James Brooks	22	Linen Weaver	Cork	"	"	"
Edward Pulley	30	Gardener	Worcestershire	"	"	"
John Pennington	35	Farmer	Staffordshire	"	"	"
William Mead	15	Servant	Warwickshire	"	"	"
James Stile	22	Brass Founder	"	"	"	"
Robert Smith	24	Carpenter	Southwark	"	"	"
Ann Money	24	Servant	"	"	"	"
Sarah Austin	25	"	"	"	"	"
Elizabeth Grindal	32	Housekeeper	Bucks	"	"	"
William Crane	26	Farmer	Cambridge	"	"	"
Samuel Dennis	21	"	Essex	"	"	"
Joseph Gibbs	25	Brass Founder	Southwark	"	"	"
William Cole	22	Gardener	Surry	"	"	"
James Silk	21	Baker	London	"	"	"
Joseph Moobat	40	White Smith	Warwick	"	"	"
Henry Couley	21	Black Smith	York	"	"	"
Peter Green	25	Gardener	Hampshire	"	"	"
Charleton Smith	36	Surgeon	Cumberland	"	"	"
Robert Elcock	22	Book Keeper	London	"	"	"
John Moore	25	Butcher	"	"	"	"
Thomas Milton	28	Gardener	Middlesex	"	"	"
William Poynton	21	Bookkeeper	London	"	"	"
George Milton	22	Gardener	Middlesex	"	"	"
Hannah Scholar	25	Servant	"	"	"	"
Ann Watson	20	"	"	"	"	"
James Dimpsey	23	Cooper	"	"	"	"
William Chamberlin	28	Wheeler	London	"	"	"

John Restley	21	Servant	Middlesex	"	"	"
William Smith	44	Perukemaker	"	"	"	"
Catharine Wyborne	37	Housekeeper	"	"	"	"

PORT OF LONDON, 12th TO 19 JUNE 1775.

John Twedy	28	Rope Maker	Yorkshire	Nancy	Baltimore	Redemptioners, these People on their arrival at Maryland, are to be disposed of for a number of years provided they are not found capable to pay the Captn for their passage as per agreement
Edward Keen	23	Butcher	Somersetshire	"	"	
Thomas Palmer	21	Shoemaker	London	"	"	
John Toomy	27	Weaver	Essex	"	"	
Thomas Edwards	21	Farrier	"	"	"	
Thomas Courtman	28	Blacking Ball Make[r]	"	"	"	
Thomas Clarke	21	Labourer	Bedfordshire	"	"	
Henry Cooper	22	Weaver	London	"	"	"
Patrick McKernelly	25	Labourer	"	"	"	"
William Moreran	21	Servant	Surry	"	"	"
John Reeby	24	Miller	Berkshire	"	"	"
William Yerrow	36	Tin Plate Worker	London	"	"	"
Edward Green	42	Coal Breaker	"	"	"	"
William Dunster	22	Bookkeeper	"	"	"	"
Edward Kent	21	Servant	"	"	"	"
John Onchard	31	Taylor	Warwickshire	"	"	"
Thomas Spencer	30	Carpenter	"	"	"	"
William Johnson	30	Cooper	Berwick	"	"	"
Duncan Keith	30	Carpenter	Scotland	"	"	"
Joseph Yiffard	30	Schoolmaster	Kent	"	"	"
Bryan Lamb	21	Carpenter	London	"	"	"
James Wilson	23	Brazier	"	"	"	"
John Fraiser	28	Carpenter	Surry	"	"	"
Beavis Shirey	25	Gun Maker	Bristol	"	"	"
Samuel Piveyer	22	Brick Maker	Northampton-shire	"	"	"
James Chapman	23	Tin Plate Worker	London	"	"	"
William Elmes	30	Weaver	Hants	"	"	"
William Barnard	22	Shoemaker	London	"	"	"
Lawrance Kelly	39	Mason	"	"	"	"
John Turner	21	White Smith	Newcastle	"	"	"

Name	*Age*	*Occupation*	*From*	*Ship*	*To*	*As a*
Samuel Budden	22	Cordwainer	Dorsetshire	Nancy	Baltimore	Redemptioners, these People on
Thomas Turbelt	21	White Smith	London	"	"	their arrival at Maryland are
John Symonds	21	Farmer	Kent	"	"	to be disposed of for a number
Henry Strudwick	33	Gardener	Surry	"	"	of years provided they are not
Isaac Founier	24	Weaver	London	"	"	found capable to pay the Captn
Edward Palmer	44	Woolcomber	Hants	"	"	for their passage as per agree-
George Johnson	25	Sawyer	London	"	"	ment
Robert Delbridge	21	Smith	"	"	"	"
Thomas Parrott	21	Rope Maker	"	"	"	"
John Hoy	21	Accountant	Scotland	"	"	"
Morris Morrison	25	Bricklayer	London	"	"	"
Christopher King	21	Farmer	Coventry	"	"	"
Thomas Watton	22	"	Warwickshire	"	"	"
Charles Pillar	25	Hair dresser	Scotland	"	"	"
John Pearson	40	Cordwainer	London	"	"	"
John Lewisger	26	Farmer	Herts	"	"	"
John Roworth	21	Servant	London	"	"	"
William Javes	41	Cooper	"	"	"	"
William Mee	24	Servant	Yorkshire	"	"	"
John Williams	29	Blacksmith	Monmouth	"	"	"
Thomas Morgan	25	Hair dresser	Westminster	"	"	"
John Dufton	27	Corn Chandler	London	"	"	"
Samuel Isaacs	21	Servant	"	"	"	"
John Lewce	24	"	"	"	"	"
John Simpson	22	Blacksmith	Northampton	"	"	"
Thomas Merrick	21	Servant	London	"	"	"
James Herdie	30	Surgeon	"	"	"	"
John Shaw	22	Servant	Kent	"	"	"
Nathaniel Parr	45	Taylor	Nottingham	"	"	"
Thomas Mullender	26	Hat Maker	London	"	"	"
John Grove	23	Servant	"	"	"	"
Benjamin Kidder	15	"	"	"	"	"
James Hudson	16	"	Leicester	"	"	"
Robert Abbert	15	"	"	"	"	"
Joseph Haydon	18	Baker	"	"	"	"

William Thomas	15	Servant	Somersetshire	"	"	"
George Brooks	15	"	Berks	"	"	"
James Miller	15	"	Chester	"	"	"
Thomas Green	15	"	Poole	"	"	"
Joseph Lyon	16	"	London	"	"	"
John Lack	21	Weaver	Reading	"	"	"
William Wybot	15	Servant	Ware	"	"	"
John Stepney	16	Weaver	London	"	"	"
Samuel Gray	16	Cordwainer	"	"	"	"
Mary Cure	19	Housemaid	"	"	"	"
Sarah Dobson	17	Servant	Glostershire	"	"	"
Ann Slack	19	Housemaid	London	"	"	"
Martha McBride	16	Servant	"	"	"	"
Elizabeth Forrest	26	"	"	"	"	"
Mary Hudson	22	"	Somersetshire	"	"	"
Margaret Crouch	27	Milliner	London	"	"	"
Sarah Smith	21	Servant	Leicester	"	"	"
Grace Smith	27	"	Devon	"	"	"
Martha Newman	23	"	Rotherhithe	"	"	"
Elizabeth Draper	26	"	London	"	"	"
Ann Cabell	27	"	"	"	"	"
Ann Powell	21	Milliner	Glostershire	"	"	"
Mary Wilson	22	"	Hants	"	"	"
Elizabeth Willis	22	"	London	"	"	"
Margaret Goodson	18	Servant	Kent	"	"	"
Elizabeth Morgan	22	"	London	"	"	"
John Yeats	26	Farmer	Wilts	"	"	"
William Patrick	22	Bookkeeper	London	"	"	"
Henry Jones	23	Hat Presser	"	"	"	"
Richard Younger	23	Clerk	"	"	"	"
Margaret Clark	26	Servant	"	"	"	"
Elizabeth Brittlebank	21	"	"	"	"	"
Thomas Eldridge	26	Carpenter	Kent	"	"	"

PILL A CREEK A PORT OF BRISTOL, 12th TO 19th JUNE 1775.

James Clarke	21	Blacksmith	Birmingham	Elizabeth	Philadelphia	Indented Servant
William West	25	Clothier	Plymouth	"	"	" "

Name	*Age*	*Occupation*	*From*	*Ship*	*To*	*As a*
Edward Jackson	22	Labourer	Plymouth	Elizabeth	Philadelphia	Indented Servant
William Tingle	15	"	Bristol	"	"	" "
Seven Women	—	———	———	"	"	" "

PILL A CREEK A PORT OF BRISTOL, 26th JUNE TO 3rd JULY 1775.

Anthony Dewyer	20	Taylor	Cork	Mary	Maryland	Indented Servant
Samuel Lewis	28	Labourer	Westbury	"	"	" "
John Williams	30	Smith	Wales	"	"	" "
James Williams	31	Labourer	"	"	"	" "
John Evans	24	"	Gloster	"	"	" "
Andrew Mooring	29	"	"	"	"	" "
John Page	26	"	"	"	"	" "
Humphry Carpenter	25	Carpenter	Bristol	"	"	" "
John Parset	16	Labourer	"	"	"	" "
William Williams	21	"	"	"	"	" "
James Newport	19	"	Bideford	"	"	" "
John Templar	17	"	"	"	"	" "
Forteen Women	—	———	———	"	"	" "

PILL A CREEK A PORT OF BRISTOL, 10th TO 17 JULY 1775.

Joseph Priest	19	Clock Maker	London	Fortune	Maryland	Indented Servant for four Years
Thomas Huddleston	18	Bricklayer	Norwich	"	"	" " "
Thomas Adamson	21	Tanner	Scotland	"	"	" " "
Elizabeth Hardcastle	27	Wife of Samuel	Leeds	"	"	" " "
Samuel Hardcastle	28	Cordwainer	"	"	"	" " "
Thomas Flaxman	44	Hemp Dresser	Maidstone	"	"	" " "
William Pocock	21	Weaver	London	"	"	" " "
Robert Child	21	Baker	Essex	"	"	" " "
William Reed	21	Weaver	London	"	"	" " "
Hugh Norris	17	Labourer	Essex	"	"	" " "
Robert Hamilton	24	Tin Plate Worker	London	"	"	" " "
Thomas Williamson	21	" " "	Sunderland	"	"	" " "

Peter Macquire	17	Labourer	Ireland	"	"	" " "
Richard Harris	16	Frame Work Knitter	Oxford	"	"	" " "
William Glover	16	Labourer	London	"	"	" " "
John Bolney	15	Sawyer	"	"	"	" " "
John Spray	15	Husbandman	Nottingham	"	"	" " "
Thomas Burch	16	Frame Work Knitter	"	"	"	" " "
Edward Gardener	18	Husbandman	Oxford	"	"	" " "
Joseph Gray	19	Weaver	London	"	"	" " "
William Atkinson	18	Labourer	Kent	"	"	" " "
Mary Stanley	17	Nursery Maid	London	"	"	" " "
John Merrill	36	White Smith	York	"	"	" " "
Roger Parke	21	Clerk	Dublin	"	"	" " "
Thomas Glover	24	Cabinet Maker	London	"	"	" " "

PORT OF LONDON, 10th TO 17 JULY 1775.

John Smith	28	Gentleman's Servant	London	Fortune	Maryland	Indented Servant for four Years
William Hening	25	Cordwainer	Surry	"	"	" " "
Jordan Castallo	31	Clerk	Dublin	"	"	" " "
Francis Crago	30	Carpenter	London	"	"	" " "
George Field	29	Butcher	Portsmouth	"	"	" " "
Christopher Seymour	23	Woolcomber	Essex	"	"	" " "
Nicholas Morrough	21	Dyer & Lace Weaver	Cork	"	"	" " "
Thomas Adams	32	Shipwright	Plymouth	"	"	" " "
Thomas Palmer	28	Cordwainer	London	"	"	" " "
William Latewood	21	Silk Weaver	"	"	"	" " "
William Middleton	21	Coach Tyre Smith	"	"	"	" " "
William Bolton	34	Cooper	Plymouth	"	"	" " "
Roger Regan	21	Cook	Dublin	"	"	" " "
Joseph Hill	21	Labourer	London	"	"	" " "
John Oliver	33	Tanner	"	"	"	" " "
Thomas Simpson	36	Clerk	Greenwich	"	"	" " "
Edward Davis	25	Gentleman's Servant	Westminster	"	"	" " "
Michael Cotton	30	Lock Smith	Dublin	"	"	" " "
John Gover	15	Labourer	Bath	"	"	" " "
Andrew Power	15	"	London	"	"	" " "
James Taylor	15	"	Wilts	"	"	" " "

Name	*Age*	*Occupation*	*From*	*Ship*	*To*	*As a*
Thomas Penifold	16	Labourer	Hertford	Fortune	Maryland	Indented Servant for four Years
Willm Browing	16	"	London	"	"	" " "
Thomas Satchwell	17	Smith	"	"	"	" " "
William Anderton	18	Groom	"	"	"	" " "
John Tait	18	Labourer	Liverpool	"	"	" " "
Thomas Pinder	16	"	London	"	"	" " "
John Bean	16	Cordwainer	Canterbury	"	"	" " "
John Jones	19	Labourer	London	"	"	" " "
Stephen Turner	24	Carpenter	"	"	"	" " "
James Dodsworth	25	Clerk	Southwark	"	"	" " "
John Hodgson	26	Cloth Worker	York	"	"	" " "
John Speakman	20	Bricklayer	Middlesex	"	"	" " "
William Brant	26	Painter	London	"	"	" " "
John Sunmary	21	Joiner	Exeter	"	"	" " "
Thomas Gould	21	Groom	London	"	"	" " "
Ralph Core	22	Clerk	Southwark	"	"	" " "
James Couling	21	Taylor	London	"	"	" " "
George "	31	Upholsterer	"	"	"	" " "
Michael Murphy	22	Clerk	Cork	"	"	" " "
John Bend	21	Gentlemans Servant	Coventry	"	"	" " "
Richd Wildman	23	Butcher	Southwark	"	"	" " "
Joseph Triggs	33	Weaver	Newbury	"	"	" " "
Charles Barker	21	Cutler	London	"	"	" " "
Christopher Mitcham	25	Perukemaker	Deptford	"	"	" " "
Robert Harpham	31	Labourer	Lambeth	"	"	" " "
Samuel Hutchinson	24	Clerk	Middlesex	"	"	" " "
John Plumber	33	Labourer	Herts	"	"	" " "
William Northey	37	Serge Weaver	Plymouth	"	"	" " "
Anthony Hale	17	Cordwainer	London	"	"	" " "
Stephen Hancock	16	Labourer	"	"	"	" " "

PORT OF LONDON, 7th TO 14th AUG. 1775.

Francis Wright	24	Gentleman	London	Black Prince	Philadelphia	On Business
Elizabeth Ward	14	Servant	"	Lively	St John's Island	To live there

Charlotte Burton	13	"	"	"	" "	" "
John Hawkins	15	"	"	"	" "	" "
Ann Cleaveland	14	"	"	"	" "	" "
William Graham	14	"	"	"	" "	" "

PORT OF LONDON, 14th TO 21st AUG. 1775.

James Townsend	41	Farmer	Berkshire	Elizabeth	St John's Island	Going to Settle
Elizabeth "	47	His Wife	"	"	" "	" "
John "	19		"	"	" "	Going with their parents
James "	10		"	"	" "	" " "
Lucy "	18	&	"	"	" "	" " "
Richard "	13		"	"	" "	" " "
Mary "	5	Children	"	"	" "	" " "
Thomas Edmonds	19	Their Servant	"	"	" "	" " "
Marshall Hall	22	Carpenter	London	Hawk	Philadelphia	Indented Servant for four Years
Bryan Burn	22	Husbandman	Ireland	"	"	" " "
George Wright	32	Butcher	Yorkshire	"	"	" " "
James Colealough	24	Groom	London	"	"	" " "
Thomas Ward	39	Gardener	Portsmouth	"	"	" " "
Richard Hogg	15	Labourer	London	"	"	" " "
John Collins	42	Stationer	"	"	"	" " "
Thomas Reed	40	Clothier	"	"	"	" " "
Edward Bird	26	Husbandman	Bristol	"	"	" " "
William Hawkins	21	Plaisterer	Plymouth	"	"	" " "
Edward Evander	23	Groom	London	"	"	" " "
William Reych	21	Brass Founder	Birmingham	"	"	" " "
Isaac Hanks	25	Parchment Maker	Bristol	"	"	" " "
Thomas Sims	21	Taylor	London	"	"	" " "
Jeremiah Dowsing	30	Cordwainer	"	"	"	" " "
Thomas Wood	30	Stocking Frame Maker	"	"	"	" " "
John Selley	34	Currier	"	"	"	" " "
John Badger	22	Groom	"	"	"	" " "
Richard Selden	31	Taylor	Essex	"	"	" " "
John Bates	27	Hatter	Bristol	"	"	" " "
Susanna Jordan	21	Housemaid	London	"	"	" " "
James Bull	15	Cordwainer	"	"	"	" " "

Name	*Age*	*Occupation*	*From*	*Ship*	*To*	*As a*
Ann Kentish	17	Housemaid	London	Hawk	Philadelphia	Indented Servant for four Years
William Newman	25	Husbandman	"	"	"	" " "
George Nonis	23	Silversmith	"	"	"	" " "
Robert Southam	23	Husbandman	"	"	"	" " "
Richard Thompson	34	Tavern Waiter	"	"	"	" " "
John Biddle	25	Mercer	"	"	"	" " "
Aaron Colling	25	Labourer	"	"	"	" " "
William Allen	22	Taylor	"	"	"	" " "
John Wainwright	25	Late bookkeeper to William Cartwright Esqr	Nottingham	Marlborough	Savanna in Georgia	Going to seek better Employment
Ralph Bland	18	Butcher	Durham	"	"	"
Joseph Armistead	17	Brush Maker	"	"	"	"
Mark Morton	42	Wheelwright, Wife & 3 Children	Hull	"	"	"
Robert Buttle	35	& Ann his Wife & 5 Children	Yorkshire	"	"	"
William Charles	24	Labourer	Preston	"	"	"
George Bennington	32	"	Yorkshire	"	"	"
Isaac Herbert	23	Agent & Att to Jonas Brown	"	"	"	"

Port of Poole, 21st to 28th Aug. 1775.

Sr John Nesbitt	30	Merchant	Philadelphia	Sampson	Philadelphia	To secure their Effects at Philadelphia
Mr Hyam	42	"	"	"	"	
2 Servants belonging to the above Gentlemen			"	"	"	Going with their Masters
A Lady & Three Children		———	———	"	"	———

Port of London, 4th to 11th Sept. 1775.

Robert Dee	33	Gentleman	London	Beaufort	Georgia	Going to settle
George Surr	19	"	"	"	"	" "
Francis Finmore	50	"	"	"	"	" "
John Butler	25	"	Carolina	"	"	" "

John Air	23	"	Georgia	"	"	Going home
John Lord	34	Carver	"	"	"	" "
James Harris	20	Surgeon	London	Betsey	St Kitts	Going to settle
Francis Brown	20	Gentleman	"	"	" "	" "
Rev John Bucannon	28	——	——	Rachael	Virginia	Going to reside
James Fry	35	Merchant	Maryland	"	Maryland	Going to settle
William Barton	35	Butcher	Lincolnshire	"	"	" "
Justina Zoci	—	——	——	"	"	These people are all going to settle at Maryland, but being Germans could not sufficiently understand them to get further information of their Ages and other Particulars
Joannes Frentein	—	——	——	"	"	
Felix Masserback	—	——	——	"	"	
Martin Vieland	—	——	——	"	"	
Martin Kumlert	—	——	——	"	"	
Geo Adam Clein	—	——	——	"	"	
Gabriel Clein	—	——	——	"	"	"
Johan Geo Mohr	—	——	——	"	"	"
Joseph Seegar	—	——	——	"	"	"
Zeonhard Wieland	—	——	——	"	"	"
Jonas Clean Ceanfas	—	——	——	"	"	"
Samuel Billus	—	——	——	"	"	"
Fridering Cekrer	—	——	——	"	"	"
Jacob Cubler	—	——	——	"	"	"
Geo Meinrich Friedering	—	——	——	"	"	"
David Sausseleer	—	——	——	"	"	"
Johan Michale Sautteer	—	——	——	"	"	"
Martin Veisz Bachs	—	——	——	"	"	"
Ottelia Veisz Bachs	—	——	——	"	"	"
Justina Buzin	—	——	——	"	"	"
Jacobina Santerin	—	——	——	"	"	"
Frederick Frentle	—	——	——	"	"	"
Peter Frentle	—	——	——	"	"	"

PORT OF NEWCASTLE, 4th TO 11th SEPT. 1775.

Francis Wallace	18	Keelman	Newcastle	Georgia Packet	Georgia	Going to seek better Employt
Edward Jackson	15	Ribbon Weaver	Coventry	" "	"	" " "

Name	*Age*	*Occupation*	*From*	*Ship*	*To*	*As a*
John Dean	19	Shoemaker	Shields	Georgia Packet	Georgia	Going to seek better Employ[t]
Thomas Purdy	17	Keelman	Sunderland	“ “	“	“ “ “
James Fairface	20	Barber	Newcastle	“ “	“	“ “ “
William Linnon	19	Taylor	Scotland	“ “	“	“ “ “
John Dick	46	Upholsterer	Newcastle	“ “	“	“ “ “
Mary “	33	His Wife	“	“ “	“	“ “ “
Jane “	13	&	“	“ “	“	“ “ “
Grizel “	4	Children	“	“ “	“	“ “ “
Samuel Briggs	28	Dyer	Scotland	“ “	“	“ “ “
John Douglas	20	Gardener	“	“ “	“	“ “ “
John Wark	30	Millwright	“	“ “	“	“ “ “
Simon Porteus	49	Mason	“	“ “	“	“ “ “
William Stewart	24	“	“	“ “	“	“ “ “
Hugh Gordon	22	Yeoman	“	“ “	“	“ “ “
Robert Robson	28	Yeoman	“	“ “	“	“ “ “
Jane “	28	His Wife	“	“ “	“	“ “ “
Eleanor “	6		“	“ “	“	“ “ “
James “	4	&	“	“ “	“	“ “ “
Mary “	1	Children	“	“ “	“	“ “ “
James Oliphant	34	Yeoman	“	“ “	“	“ “ “
David Maxwell	19	Barber	Newcastle	“ “	“	“ “ “
Robert Martin	26	Yeoman	Scotland	“ “	“	“ “ “
John Scott	30	Yeoman	“	“ “	“	“ “ “
Margaret “	35	His Wife	“	“ “	“	“ “ “
William “	13		“	“ “	“	“ “ “
John “	10		“	“ “	“	“ “ “
Mary “	8	&	“	“ “	“	“ “ “
Agnes “	4		“	“ “	“	“ “ “
Margaret “	2	Children	“	“ “	“	“ “ “
Robert Crawford	16	Yeoman	“	“ “	“	“ “ “
George Liddle	15	“	“	“ “	“	“ “ “
David Murry	23	Shoemaker	Newcastle	“ “	“	“ “ “
David Arnott	20	Smith	Scotland	“ “	“	“ “ “
George Watson	36	Shoemaker	Newcastle	“ “	“	“ “ “
Mary “	33	His Wife	“	“ “	“	“ “ “

Thomas “	12		“	“	“	“	“	“	“
Isabella “	10	&	“	“	“	“	“	“	“
Mary “	5		“	“	“	“	“	“	“
Douglas “	2	Children	“	“	“	“	“	“	“
William McCullock	24	Barber	Scotland	“	“	“	“	“	“
Barbara “	24	His Wife	“	“	“	“	“	“	“
Charles Brokey	25	Gardener	“	“	“	“	“	“	“
James Scott	25	Carpenter	“	“	“	“	“	“	“
George Bulman	46	“	“	“	“	“	“	“	“
Elizabeth “	36	His Wife	“	“	“	“	“	“	“
George “	5	&	“	“	“	“	“	“	“
Diana “	4	Children	“	“	“	“	“	“	“
Andrew Lithcow	37	Breeches Maker	Sunderland	“	“	“	“	“	“
Elizabeth “	35	His Wife	“	“	“	“	“	“	“
Andrew “	11		“	“	“	“	“	“	“
Robert “	4	&	“	“	“	“	“	“	“
Elizabeth “	2		“	“	“	“	“	“	“
Jane Lithcow	1	Children	“	“	“	“	“	“	“
John Hume	28	Farmer	Scotland	“	“	“	“	“	“
John McIntosh	32	Rope Maker	“	“	“	“	“	“	“
William Budge	22	Joiner	“	“	“	“	“	“	“
John Cobb	31	Butcher	“	“	“	“	“	“	“
Alexander Bean	23	Shoemaker	“	“	“	“	“	“	“
Christianna Bean	18	His Wife	“	“	“	“	“	“	“
Whitaker Shadforth	21	Watchmaker	“	“	“	“	“	“	“
Charles Salisbury	30	Yeoman	“	“	“	“	“	“	“
Robert “	11	His	“	“	“	“	“	“	“
Thomas “	10	Sons	“	“	“	“	“	“	“
William Macwell	33	Yeoman	“	“	“	“	“	“	“
John Dick	14	Labourer	“	“	“	“	“	“	“
Henry Graham	26	Yeoman	“	“	“	“	“	“	“
William Jackson	16	“	London	“	“	“	“	“	“
Thomas Tulip	36	Taylor	Newcastle	“	“	“	“	“	“
Jane “	40	His Wife	“	“	“	“	“	“	“
Alexr McAndrew	18	Yeoman	Scotland	“	“	“	“	“	“
David Weatherspoon	23	Weaver	“	“	“	“	“	“	“
Andrew Watson	21	Smith	“	“	“	“	“	“	“
Andrew “	45	Joiner	London	“	“	“	“	“	“

Name	Age	Occupation	From	Ship	To	As a
Thomas Manson	16	Yeoman	Scotland	Georgia Packet	Georgia	Going to seek better Employ[t]
Barbara "	23	Spinster	"	" "	"	" " "
Thomas Taylor	22	Surgeon	Sunderland	" "	"	" " "
William Hewison	20	"	Newcastle	" "	"	" " "
Thomas Thompson	29	Labourer	Scotland	" "	"	" " "
John Eives	31	Soapboiler	Shields	" "	"	" " "
Elizabeth "	24	His Wife	"	" "	"	" " "
William "	7	& Son	"	" "	"	" " "
Margaret Brown	19	Spinster	Whitby	" "	"	" " "
Elizabeth Milburn	20	"	Scotland	" "	"	" " "
Jane Blackett	20	"	Newcastle	" "	"	" " "
Jane Dunn	20	Mantua Maker	Blythe	" "	"	" " "
Mary Foster	18	Spinster	Newcastle	" "	"	" " "
Jane Mibross	30	"	"	" "	"	" " "
Mary Wullins	20	"	Sunderland	" "	"	" " "
Jane Taylor	23	"	Newcastle	" "	"	" " "
Eleanor Peakstone	26	"	Stockton	" "	"	" " "
Eleanor Foreman	20	"	Newcastle	" "	"	" " "
Jane Garthwaitt	22	"	"	" "	"	" " "
Ann Pearson	19	"	Rudwith	" "	"	" " "
Elizabeth Wall	19	"	South Shields	" "	"	" " "
Margaret Manson	25	"	Scotland	" "	"	" " "
Elizabeth "	26	"	"	" "	"	" " "
Elizabeth "	9	"	"	" "	"	" " "
John Derry	45	Joiner	London	" "	"	" " "

Port of Portsmouth, 4th to 11th Sept. 1775.

William Stewart	—	Gentleman	——	Richmond	Jamaica	Going to settle there
Ralph Skelton	—	"	——	"	"	" "
Duncan Monroe	—	"	——	"	"	" "
Alexander Peterkin	—	"	——	"	"	" "
Thimothy Walker	—	"	——	"	"	" "
John Palmer	—	"	——	"	"	" "
Mr How	—	"	——	"	"	" "
Three Miss Myries	—	Ladies	——	"	"	" "

PORT OF LONDON, 25th SEPT. TO 2nd OCT. 1775.

Richard Spate	27	Druggist	New York	Robert	New York	Going home
John Whetham	40	Gentleman	London	"	" "	Going to settle
John Head	43	Merchant	Boston	William	Nantucket	" "
Nathaniel Black	41	Hatter	"	"	"	" "

PILL A CREEK A PORT OF BRISTOL, 2nd TO 9th OCT. 1775.

John Brewer	24	Merchant	———	Ann	Jamaica	Going on Business

PORT OF NEWCASTLE, 9th TO 16th OCTOBER 1775.

John Thomas	45	Gentleman	———	Experiment	Jamaica	To inspect into his affairs on the Island

PORT OF LONDON, 23rd TO 30th OCT. 1775.

Joseph Hodge	37	Gentleman	London	Fortune	Carolina	Going to settle
Robert Ford	40	Clergyman	"	"	"	" "
Ann Hill	24	———	"	"	"	Going to her husband
Jane Martin	30	———	"	"	"	" " "
Elizabeth Barker	19	Spinster	"	"	"	Going to her Friends

PILL A CREEK A PORT OF BRISTOL, 23rd TO 30 OCT. 1775.

William Smith	27	Accountant	Bristol	Egale	Jamaica	On Business
John Powell	25	"	"	"	"	" "

PORT OF PORTSMOUTH, 23rd TO 30th OCT. 1775.

Messr Thos Richardson	36	Gentleman	London	Darlington	Dominica	Going to Excute some private business there
" Edmond Disabie	45	"	Dominica	"	"	Going to return home to their plantations at Dominica
" Arear	50	"	"	"	"	

Pill a Creek a Port of Bristol, 30th Oct. to 6th Nov. 1775.

Name	Age	Occupation	From	Ship	To	As a
Mr David Paris	50	Merchant	Bristol	Barbads Packet	Barbadoes	Going on Business

Port of Poole, 30th Oct. to 6th Nov. 1775.

Name	Age	Occupation	From	Ship	To	As a
Abraham Osgood	43	Merchant	Casct Bay	Squrriel	Nova Scotia	Going to traffic and Intends to return
Thomas Palmer	49	Mariner	New Hampshire	"	" "	All Masters of Ships on their return Home having left their ships in England for Sale
Josiah Shackford	47	"	" "	"	" "	
Stephen Meads	25	"	" "	"	" "	
John Hart	25	"	" "	"	" "	"
Gideon Crawford	39	"	Rhode Island	"	" "	"

Port of Yarmouth, 20th to 27 Nov. 1775.

Name	Age	Occupation	From	Ship	To	As a
George Riches	24	Clerk	Yarmouth	Effingham	St Christopher	Going to Mr Beekfords
Thos Manning	30	Ostler	"	"	Jamaica	To look after horses at Jamaica
John Hounsby	30	Weaver	Suffolk	"	"	To seek Employment

Port of Yarmouth, 4th to 11th Dec. 1775.

Name	Age	Occupation	From	Ship	To	As a
John Riches	23	Clerk	Yarmouth	Antonetta	St Christopher	To carry on Merchandize or Factory at St Kitts

Port of Portsmouth, 11th to 18 Dec. 1775.

Name	Age	Occupation	From	Ship	To	As a
William Young	27	Gentn Planter	London	Dawes	Jamaica	To superentend an Estate there
David Kerr	30	" Surgeon	"	"	"	To practice Surgery
Walter Murry	36	"	Jamaica	"	"	To return home
Mrs Scott	36	Lady	"	"	"	" "

Pill a Creek a Port of Bristol, 11th to 18th Dec. 1775.

Mr Jas Peckett	50	Gentleman	Bath	Eleanor	Barbadoes	Going on Business
" Jas Hanstey	19	"	"	"	"	" "
" Jas Tite	17	"	"	"	"	" "

Port of Portsmouth, 24 to 31st Dec. 1775.

Lieut Man	—	Gentn Engineer	London	Grenville Bay	Grenada	To execute their Office their with a recommendation
Mr Flowers Officer of his Majestys Ordnance			"	" "	"	
Mr Winfield	—	Gentleman	"	" "	"	"
Mrs Finley	—	Lady	"	" "	"	"

Port of Newcastle, 31st Dec. 1775 to 7 Jan. 1776.

William Watson	26	Gentleman	London	Proudfoot	Grenada	In Expatation of better Business
Joseph Hyam	17	"	"	"	"	
Thomas Smith	22	Blacksmith	Durham	"	"	"

Port of Portsmouth, 31st Dec. to 7th Jan. 1776.

Mr Samuel Scott	—	Merchant	London	Gibbons	Barbadoes	To Collect his property at Barbadoes
" John Willson	—	"	"	"	"	To take possession of an Estate there
" Martin Williams	—	Planter	Jamaica	St James Planter	Jamaica	To superintend his plantations at Jamaica

Pill a Creek a Port of Bristol, 7th to 14th Jan. 1776.

James Peckett	56	Gentleman	Bath	Eleanor	Barbadoes	To re[illegible] Home
James Hanstey	19	"	"	"	"	Going on [illegible]siness
James Tite	17	"	"	"	"	" "

Port of Portsmouth, 28th Jan. to 4th Feb. 1776.

Name	Age	Occupation	From	Ship	To	As a
Robert Sewell Esqr	25	Gentleman	London	Judith & Hilaria	Jamaica	To Practice in the Island of Jamaica as a Barrister
Mrs "	20	His Wife	"	" "	"	
Mary Lewis	18	Young Lady	"	" "	"	Returning to Jamaica having been in England for Education
Maria "	15	" "	"	" "	"	
Catharine "	13	" "	"	" "	"	
Mrs Elliston	50	Lady	"	" "	"	Going with the above Family

Port of London, 11th to 18 Feb. 1776.

Name	Age	Occupation	From	Ship	To	As a
David Mitchell	38	Merchant	London	Lady's Adventure	Jamaica	Going on Business
Thomas Goldwin	30	"	"	" "	"	" "
Thomas Waller	22	"	"	" "	"	" "
Paul Parker	19	"	"	" "	"	" "
William Brown	25	Gentleman	"	" "	"	" "

Port of Portsmouth, 3rd to 10th March 1776.

Name	Age	Occupation	From	Ship	To	As a
Mr William Lester	—	Planter	Musquito Shore	Hope	Musquito Shore	To return to his Plantation at Musquito Shore
Rev Mr Stanfold	—	Clergyman	London	"	" "	To Excute his Function
John Jenison	—	Planter	Musquito Shore	"	" "	To return home
Mr Willm Whitlock	—	"	Jamaica	Thetis	Jamaica	To return to his Plantations
John Crief	—	Sadler	London	"	"	To carry on a business of a Saddler at Jamaica
Mr Hamilton	—	Planter	Tobago	Picairi	Barbadoes	To return to his Plantations
Mr George Craig	—	"	London	"	"	To superintend Plantation at Tobago

Their ages cannot be ascertained

Port of Portsmouth, 10th to 17 March 1776.

Mr Rowe Jones	—	Planter	Barbadoes	Three Brothers	Barbadoes	On their return to Barbadoes to their respective Plantations
— Colton	—	"	"	" "	"	
— Hasler	—	"	"	" "	"	"
— Whitaker	—	"	"	" "	"	"

Port of Portsmouth, 17th to 24th Mar. 1776.

Mr Charington & Family			Barbadoes	Polly & Charlotte	Barbadoes	To return to his Estate at Barbadoes

Pill a Creek a Port of Bristol, 17th to 24th March 1776.

William Brown	47	Merchant	London	Aurora	Tortola	Going on Business

Port of Plymouth, 24th to 31st March 1776.

Sr George Macartney Esqr	34	Govenor	London	Earl of Erroll	Grenades	Going to reside there
John Peter Ricker	30	Gentleman	"	" "	"	" " "
James Bartlett	30	"	"	" "	"	" " "
Alexandr Houstown	22	"	"	" "	"	" " "
William Grant	28		"	" "	"	" " "
Thomas Urquhart	25		"	" "	"	" " "
William Isaac	22		"	" "	"	" " "
Lady Macartney	—	Lady	"	" "	"	" " "
Elizabeth Ricker	25	"	"	" "	"	" " "
Mrs Bartlet	30	"	"	" "	"	" " "

Port of Brighthelmstone, 31st March to 7 April 1776.

John Amory	50	Merchant	London	Eagle	Boston	To Reside
Mrs Catherine	44	Wife of do	"	"	"	" "
Samson Blowers	19	Attorney	"	"	"	" "

PASSENGER ARRIVALS AT SALEM AND BEVERLY, MASS., 1798-1800

Contributed by MRS. GEORGIE A. HILL, of Bernardsville, N. J.
With an Introduction by MEREDITH B. COLKET, JR., of Washington, D. C.

So great an interest has been manifested in early lists of passengers to America that genealogists have published most of the extant lists of the pre-Federal period. One of the most valuable transcripts of passenger lists was prepared by John Camden Hotten under the title "Lists of Persons of Quality, Emigrants. . . ". It concerns seventeenth century arrivals. More recently Strassburger and Hinke in their three-volume "Pennsylvania German Pioneers", published transcripts of lists of most of the continental European immigrants to Pennsylvania, 1727-1808. Publications dealing generally with the arrivals to America were listed by A. Harold Lancour in his modest but thorough bibliography: "Passenger Lists of Ships Coming to North America, 1607-1825". This was reprinted from the May 1937 issue of the *Bulletin of the New York Public Library* but is now out of print.

Very few records of passenger arrivals for the early Federal period have been preserved. Some records were kept by the country from which the passengers emigrated, as shown by the transcripts of lists of passengers from British ports prepared by Gerald Fothergill for volumes 60, 61, 62, and 66 of THE NEW ENGLAND HISTORICAL AND GENEALOGICAL REGISTER. Some records were kept by certain States to which emigrants migrated, as illustrated by transcripts covering Pennsylvania in the work of Strassburger and Hinke just cited. Finally, some records were kept by the Federal Government. Since little or nothing has been written about the earliest Federal records listing passenger arrivals, it seems appropriate to describe the legislation under which these records were created.

The Federal Government at the close of the eighteenth century enacted two laws, one in 1798 and the other in 1799, which resulted in some few records of arrivals. The act approved 25 June 1798, one of the Alien and Sedition Laws, required that for a period of two years all aliens coming into the country should be recorded by the customs officials and a report of their arrivals should be made periodically to the Department of State. This act reads in part:

> That every master or commander of any ship or vessel which shall come into any port of the United States after the first day of July next, shall immediately on his arrival make report in writing to the collector or other chief officer of the customs of such port, of all aliens, if any, on board his vessel, specifying their names, age, the place of nativity, the country from which they shall have come, the nation to which they belong and owe allegiance, their occupation and a description of their persons . . . and on failure every such master and commander shall forfeit and pay three hundred dol-

ars. . . . And shall be the duty of such collector or other officer of the customs, forthwith to transmit to the office of the department of state true copies of all such returns.

Unfortunately, most of these records have been lost or destroyed. Examination of Department of State records for this period has failed to reveal the whereabouts of these transcripts required by law. Nine original lists for Salem and Beverly turned up among the customs records now deposited in the National Archives (Records of the Bureau of Customs, Record Group 36). Transcripts prepared by Mrs. Georgie Hill are the basis of this article.

An act approved 2 March 1799, regulating the collection of duties on imports and tonnage, required the listing of the names of those passengers, whether aliens or natives, who brought in baggage. Section 23 of this act reads in part:

That no goods shall be brought into the United States . . . in any . . . vessel unless the master of such . . . vessel shall have a manifest . . . in writing . . . containing the name or names of the several passengers on board the vessel, distinguishing whether cabin or steerage passengers, or both, with their baggage, specifying the number and description of packages belonging to each respectively. . . .

Unfortunately, past generations often did not regard such records as of sufficient value to be preserved, and it is believed that the records were destroyed for most ports. In cases where they do exist they are not separately filed as baggage lists, but appear on or with manifests, which contain much unrelated data. So small a percentage has been preserved and so difficult of access are those that are preserved that efforts to obtain information about a given arrival under these acts are not at the present time worthwhile. But it is hoped that all such lists will be published as they are found.

Records of the port of Philadelphia for this period are among the best, if not the best, now preserved. They include not only records of baggage owners, but also more detailed records of aliens, 1798–1800. One baggage list is of more than usual interest because it appears to give the names of all individuals in a family and not merely the names of heads of families directly responsible for baggage. This list, part of a document affixed to the ship's manifest, was signed by the master on 29 Oct. 1799, shortly after the arrival of the vessel at Philadelphia. Entitled "Report of Passengers, Baggage, and Stores on Board Ship *Pacific*, Perkins Salter, master, from Hull to Philadelphia", it contains the following names of passengers: Thomas Webster, James Havvister [*sic*], Elizabeth Havister, Maud Havister, Elizabeth Havister, James Havister, Rebe(c)kah Havister, Valentine Shaw, Ann Shaw, Rebeckah Shaw, David Shaw, Maud Shaw, and William Bu(s)hnell. Thomas Webster was a cabin passenger but the others listed went steerage. The report also contains rather detailed information about the contents of each piece of baggage.

Not until 2 March 1819 was there enacted a Federal law requiring masters to submit to customs authorities lists of passengers, with the occupation, sex, and age of each. Most of these extant passenger lists for the nineteenth century are in the National Archives, but no lists for the western ports have been accessioned. For the most part these lists are not indexed; and they are so voluminous that they cannot be consulted readily unless very specific information is furnished.

Upon request the National Archives will consult a partial index to the names of passengers arriving in Philadelphia if the inquirer can supply the name of the passenger and the approximate year of arrival. It will consult some other nineteenth century indexes, which are especially useful for the period 1820–1846; but most of these indexes are so incomplete that the following specific information in addition to the name of the passenger is usually necessary for a successful search: the port of entry, the name of the vessel, and the approximate date of arrival, or the port of embarkation and the exact date of arrival. If such information cannot be supplied, the National Archives will furnish the names of private persons willing to search the records for a fee.

1798

List of the names of Passengers arived in

Ship Fanny — Joseph Lindsay from Martinico

Mrs. Hurd	5 feet 10 inch High	dark Complexion
Mr. Hurd		Light do
Son Mr. Hurd		do do
Daughter		do do
Mr. Simon	5 feet 8 Inch High	dark complexion
John Charles	5 feet 6 Inch High	Negro
Prince	5 feet 8 Inch High	Negro
Elus	5 feet High	Negro

H,sman

Accot. of Alien Passengers
on board Scho Eliza
Elisha Payson Master,
Sept. 19. 1798

Report of Alien Passengers on board the Schooner Eliza of which Elisha Payson is master, arrived at the Port of Salem in the State of Massachusetts on the eighteenth day of September 1798.

Names	Ages	Places of Nativity	Country from which they have come	To what nation they belong and owe allegiance	Their occupation	Description of their persons
Ebenezer Porter	Sixty	Beverly, Massachusetts	Grand Passage Nova Scotia	Great Britain	Yeoman	Light eyes & hair, five feet six inches high
Sarah Porter (wife to said Ebenezer)	fifty eight	———	ditto	———	———	light eyes & hair
Sereno U. Jones	twenty seven	Massachusetts	ditto	Great Britain	yeoman	dark hair & eyes five feet six inches high
Reuben Tucker	forty	ditto	ditto	ditto	ditto	Sandy hair, light eyes, five feet eleven inches high

Salem 19 Sept 1798
(Signed) Elisha Payson

Brig Six Brothers
Newham

	Age	Heighth	born	comp.
John W. Dongal	15	4′ 7½	London	dark
Vonreman ———	10	4′ 5	Curacoa	black

Came in Brig Six Brothers Jno Newham
Master from Curacoa ———

Ship Barbara-Clarke

Report of Alien Passengers on board the Ship Barbara of which Henry Clarke is master arrived at the port of Salem in the State of Massachusetts on the thirtieth day of December 1798.

Names	Ages	Places of Nativity	Country from whence they have come	To what nation they belong and owe allegiance	Their occupation	Description of their persons
Johan D. Kreiger	twenty six	frankford	Hamburg	Prusian	Baker	light complexion, five feet two inches high
Johan Martin	twenty nine	frankford	Hamburg	Prusian	Baker	dark complexion, five feet four inches high
Johan S. Cairever	thirty	Rushland	Hamburg	Prusia	Baker	light complexion five feet six inches high
Johan Ruio	twenty five	Rushland	Hamburg	Prusia	Saddler	dark complexion five feet two inches high
Francis G. Nioss	twenty one	Hamburg	Hamburg	Hamburgers	Baker	dark complexion, five feet two inches high
Johan Poerscheke	twenty seven	inselburg	Hamburg	Prussian	Baker	dark complexion-five feet three inches high

Salem 31 December 1798

Ship John, Putnam

John Wyers 44 years Copenhagen Denmark
Military officer Light complexion,
five feet three inches high

Ship John, Levi Putnam Master arrived Jan 17. 1799 —

Ship Belisarius, Crowninshield.

Ship Belisarius, Benjamin Crowninshield from Copenhagen — 16 January 1799 —

Names		Born	From	
Thomas Gunning Bashford	24 years	Belfast in Ireland	Denmark	Great Britain

merchant — 24 years — light complexion 6 feet

Scho. Sally Snow
Schooner Sally, James Snow master, arrived at Salem March 30, 1799 —

Fuslam More	28	Ireland	Newbown Sarmrordy	Gr Britain	Yeoman	6 feet	dark
John Gunning	26	Do	Belly Mony	do	merchant	6 feet	light
Daniel M Colmuck	29	Do	Belly Castle	do	check manufacturer	5.9 inches	light

Note The above persons were received on board the Ship Andromache, Capt. Cutler from back for New York

Salem 1 Ap 1799

J. S.

[On outside of document]

Return of Alien Passengers on board
Brig Rajah, Carnes, from Sumatra

[Inside document]

Report of alien passengers on board the brig Rajah of which Jonathan Carnes is master arrived at the port of Salem in the State of Massachusetts on the 14th day October A. D. 1799.

Names	Ages	Places of Nativity	Country from whence they came	To what nation they belong & owe allegiance	Their occupation	Description of their persons
Jacob Benson	Fourteen	Padang	Sumatra in the East Indies	English	Come for education	About five feet high and very dark complexion

Jon Carnes

Z. Woodberry's Report of Passengers

Come passengers in the Schooner Britton

Capt. Stephen Smith of Nova Scotia
Aged twenty five years five feet nine
Inches high Light complection

Nathan Harris c/o Aged twenty one years five feet
five Inches high Light Complection

Beverly July 21 1800

PASSENGER LISTS TO AMERICA.

Communicated by GERALD FOTHERGILL, Esq., of New Wandsworth, London, England.

IT was formerly the duty of an official to keep a strict account of all persons leaving the shores of England or Ireland, and this was no doubt at all times carried out in a more or less perfect way.

As regards England, these were all burnt by a fire at the Custom House, London. In some few cases, however, duplicates had been made for various official reasons, and these were printed, so far as then discovered, by Hotten.*

In making researches among the British Archives, I have discovered others. One series of these has been printed and is called a "List of Emigrant Ministers to America." Others I hope to print from time to time in the pages of the REGISTER.

The following are lists of passengers who left Ireland between the years 1805–1806, and contained in a British Museum Manuscript numbered Add. 35032.

The following is an example of a list, affidavit and certificate, showing that some trouble was taken in making the records:

Thomas Ryan	Patrick Ryan
John Cronnan	Mich[l] Enright
John Daly	Pat Hennesy

Edward Kellerman maketh oath that the above is a true list and description of the passengers engaged to go in the Ship *Numa* to America, and that not any of them is or are atrificers, artisans, manufacturers, seamen or seafaring men, and that he will not take any other passengers but those expressed in the above list, and that this list is a duplicate of the original one transmitted to the Lord Lieutenant and Council save and except six of the passengers mentioned therein who are not to proceed.

Sworn before the Custom House, Limerick, 2 Ap[l]., 1803. } EDW[d] KELLERAN.

I certify that I have personally examined the Men in the above List and that to the best of my knowledge I do believe they are of the occupation above discribed. Limerick, 3 Ap[l]., 1803.

WM. PAYNE, Brig[r] Gen[l].

* "The Original Lists" of Emigrants to America, 1600–1700, edited by John Camden Hotten. New York, 1874.

A List of Passengers who have sailed on board the *Mars* for America from Dublin, 29 March, 1803.

Wm Ford	gent	Robert Gibson	American merchant
John Morris	servant	——— Teeling	clerk
Wm Sherlock	merchant	James Murphy	labourer
Hugh Jackson	"	John Hobleton	"

A List of Passengers on the Ship *Portland* for Charlestown, 29 Mch., 1803.

Charles Adams	age 48	farmer of	Limerick
Marg^t^ Adams his wife	" 39		"
Ric O'Carroll	" 22	"	Bolinbroke
Danl O'Carroll	" 20	"	"
Thos Egan	" 29	writing clerk	Limerick
Martin Corry	" 58	labourer	"
John Connery	" 29	"	"
Mary Egan	" 60		"
Eliza Corry	" 33		"
Mary Connory	" 24		"
Mary Egan jun^r^	" 27		"
Betty Fitzpatrick	" 26		"
Mich^l^ Quillan	" 48	gent	"
Mary Quinlan	" 46		"
Mary Quinlan jun^r^	" 13		"
Thos O'Duyer	" 22	gent	"
Mich^l^ O'Donnovan	" 26	"	"
John Mullins	" 26	labourer	"
James Meehan	" 26	"	Clare
Pat^k^ Kernan	" 24	"	"
Terence Murray	" 18	"	"
Patrick Magrath	" 21	"	"
Andrew Lee	" 26	"	Caperas
Ric Ennery	" 19	writing clerk	Limerick
Hugh Morgan	" 22	labourer	"
James Kerly	" 37	farmer	Ballyhoben
John Walsh	" 27	labourer	Limerick
Ann Considen	" 22		"
John Cummins	" 21	"	Claraline co. Tipp^y^
W^m^ O'Brien	" 26	"	Thomas Town
Margaret Fehilly	" 24	"	Limerick
Marg^t^ Hayes	" 18		"
Mary Callaghan	" 14		"
Joseph Fihilly	7		"
Mich^l^ Fihilly	5		"
John Fihilly	3		"
Mary Fihilly	2		"

A List of Passengers on the Ship *Eagle* for New York, 29 Mch., 1803.

Alex Radcliffe	age 23	farmer	Ballyroney
John Menter	" 28	labourer	Belfast
Wm Calvert	" 33	"	Killeagh
Ann Calvert	" 24	spinster	"
James Bryson	" 27	farmer	Kilrock
Peter Leonard	" 28	"	Hillsboro

Wm Logan	age 36	labourer	Dromore
Thos Bain	" 18	farmer	Dounpatrick
Joseph Webb	" 25	labourer	Cockslem
Wm Wilson	" 22	"	Derrylea
Margt Wilson	" 20	spinster	"
Wm Kineard	" 52	farmer	"
Robt Kineard	" 18	labourer	"
Wm Hancock	" 19	"	"
Thos Wilson	" 23	"	Armagh
James Diennen	" 19	"	Dovehill
John English	" 40	"	Tynan
Isabella English	" 32		"
Wm Kerr	" 18	"	"
James Lister	" 20	"	"
George Lister	" 25	"	"
John Graham	" 24	"	"
Thos Spratt	" 50	farmer	Clough
John Browne	" 24	"	Saintfield
Saml Campbell	" 18	labourer	Banbridge
Charles Martin	" 20	farmer	Ballymoney
Robert Halridge	" 16	clerk	"
Robt Eakin	" 38	farmer	Coleraine
Wm Rafield	" 23	"	Ballymena
Wm Woods	" 27	labourer	Sea Patrick
Neha Kidd	" 20	"	Keady
John Shields	" 20	farmer	"
John Cully	" 24	"	"
David Clement	" 22	"	"
Andrew Clement	" 20	"	"
Wm McAlister	" 20	"	Ballycastle

A List of Passengers on the Ship *Susan* for New York from Dublin, 5 Apl., 1803.

John Dornan	age 43	bookseller	Dublin
Mrs Mary Dornan	" 40	spinster	"
Three small children			
Mrs Frances Russel	age 40	grocer	Dublin
Mrs Annie Russel	" 38	spinster	Louth
Three small children			
John Midleton	age 29	merchant	Louth
James Erwin	" 28	physician	"
Wm Erwin	" 26	"	"
Chas Rivington	" 25	merchant	New York
Robert Noble	" 60	"	"
Mrs Nelly Welch	" 31	spinster	Wexford
Miss MaryAnn Finly	" 21	"	Meath
James Truer	" 22	farmer	County Meath
Thomas Fitzgerald	" 23	"	County Wexford
James Byrne	" 19	"	County Meath
John Byrne	" 21	"	" "
Wm Finly	" 18	"	County Wexford
James Kelly	" 24	"	" "
John Riley	" 31	"	" "
James Kelly	" 25	"	" "

A List of Passengers to go on board the American Brig *Neptune*, Seth Stevens Master, for Newcastle and Philadelphia, burthen per admeasurement 117 tons, at Warren Point, Newry, 29 Mch., 1803.

John Grimes	labourer	aged 28
Agnes "	his wife	" 26
James Crummy	farmer	" 45
Agnes "	his wife	" 30
Mary "	their daughter	" 15
Sarah "	ditto	" 12
James "	their son	" 6
David	ditto	" 4
Susan Dene	spinster	aged 18
David Gallon	farmer	" 40
John Henry	ditto	" 40
Hanna "	his wife	" 30
Nancy "	their daughter	" 13
James "	their son	" 11
William Countes	labourer	" 26
Mary Countes	his wife	" 21

List of Passengers to proceed by the American Ship *Rachel*, Benjamin Hale, Master, to New York from Sligo, 15 Apl., 1803.

Robert Ormsby	clerk
James Gillan	farmer
John Read	clerk
James Henderson	clerk
Peter McGowan	schoolmaster
Chas Armstrong	clerk
Lauce Christian	labourer
Patt "	"
James Donald	"
Wm Corry	"
Danl McGowan	"
Owen McGowan	labourer
Fredk Corry	"
Pat Gilmartin	"
Pat Gilan	"
Pat Foley	"
Pat Feeny	
Michl Horan	
John Farrel	
John Commins	
Danl Gilmartin	

List of Passengers on board the Ship *Margaret*, Thomas Marsh, Master, bound for New York, from Newry, 18 Apl., 1803.

Eliz Brothers		aged 44	
Mary "		" 19	
Saml "	labourer	" 12	
James "		" 10	
William "		" 7	
M Ann Anderson		" 30	
Matu Doubly		" 12	
James Farrell		" 3	
James Harkness	labourer	" 40	
Jane "		aged 36	his family
Thos "		" 12	his family
Margt "		" 10	his family
Sarah "		" 10	his family
Abigal "		" 8	his family
Robt "		" 6	his family
James "		" 4	his family
Eliz Story		aged 47	
Ben Story	farmer	" 18	
Ann Story		" 16	
Hugh Alexander	labourer	aged 29	
Jane "		aged 22	his family
Jane "		" 3	his family
Sarah "		" 2	his family
Robert Goocy	farmer	aged 20	
Samuel Douglas	"	" 18	
Thomas Haxten	labourer	" 19	
John Rolston	"	" 27	
Ann Beard		" 24	
Ann Beard		" 2	
James McClean	farmer	" 60	
Eliz McClean		" 60	
David McClean	labourer	" 24	
John "	"	" 22	
George "	"	" 28	
William Riddle	"	" 19	
Samuel Magil	"	" 21	
Samuel Magil	"	" 39	
Biddy Enery	"	" 35	

List of passengers intending to go from Belfast to Philadelphia in the Ship *Edward*, from Belfast, 19 Apl., 1803.

James Greg	farmer	age 46
Thomas Greg	"	" 18
James Fox	labourer	aged 40
Ja. Mooney	"	" 16

John Greg	farmer	age	19	James Towel	labourer	aged	22
Thomas Fleming	labourer	"	19	James Burns	"	"	20
Hugh Porter	"	"	24	Rob[t] Labody	gent	"	32
John Martin	"	"	21	Hers M[c]Cullough	farmer	"	27
Alex[r] M[c]Meekin	"	"	21	W[m] Scott	"	"	22
Ad[m] Dunn	farmer	"	30	James Kirkman	"	"	40
Thomas Monks	farmer	"	60	W[m] Bingham	"	"	40
Robert Monks	"	"	22	James Bingham	"	"	14
Joseph Monks	"	"	20	John Norris	labourer	"	16
Thomas Monks	"	"	17	Hugh Murphy	"	"	18
John Smith	labourer	"	20	Edw[d] Wilson	gent	"	18
Hu M[c]Bride	"	"	26	Ardsal Hanlay	laborer	"	22
W "	"	"	25	James Read	"	"	23
W Dawson	"	"	28	Jos Haddock	"	"	27
Jno Craven	"	"	25				

A List of Passengers who intend going to Newcastle, Wilmington and Philadelphia in the Ship *Pennsylvania*, Elhana Bray, Master, from Londonderry, 16 Apl., 1803.

Patrick Lealer	aged	50	of Shabane	labourer
Robert Donaldson	"	46	"	"
Bell Donaldson	"	36	"	spinster
Mary "	"	24	"	"
Jane "	"	25	"	"
Mary "	"	20	Clanely	"
Nancy Maxwell	"	30	"	"
Robert "	"	10	"	labourer
Nash Donald	"	26	"	"
Patrick Donal	"	50	"	"
Margaret Steel	"	26	"	spinster
Peter Derin	"	56	"	labourer
James M[c]Gonagal	"	26	Tulerman	"
Charles Canney	"	28	"	"
Richard Dougherty	"	36	"	"
Margaret Heaton	"	28	"	spinster
Patrick M[c]Callon	"	33	"	labourer
Hugh Breeson	"	40	"	"
Mary O'Donnell	"	25	Strabane	spinster
Samuel Gilmour	"	20	Sr Johnston	*spinster*
Ann Gilmour	"	15	"	"
Jas Elgin	"	10	"	labourer
James Boyd	"	26	"	"
William Oliver	"	26	Sr Johnstown	"
Thomas Wilson	"	25	"	"
Nancy Wilson	"	26	"	spinster
Nancy Wilson jun[r]	"	24	"	"
Ja[s] Wilson	"	20	Muff	labourer
John Wilson	"	56	"	"
Sam[l] "	"	45	"	"
Eleanor "	"	36	Newton Limavady	spinster
John Moore	"	22	" "	farmer
Bridget Dever	"	55	" "	spinster

John Lewis	aged 33	Newton Limavada		labourer
Fanny Lewis	" 70	"	"	spinster
Fanny Lewis junr	" 15	"	"	"
And^{w} Lewis	" 20	"	"	labourer
Susan "	" 36	"	"	spinster
George "	" 33	"	"	labourer
James Stewart	" 25	Dungiven		"
Ja^{s} King	" 45	"		"
Willm McBride	" 50	"		"
Will Parker	" 61	"		"
Alex^{r} Houston	" 45	"		"
Francis "	" 20	"		"
John Brigham	" 26	"		farmer
Jane "	" 25	Ballyshannon		spinster
Eliz Brigham	" 26	"		"
Ezek^{l} Brigham	" 25	"		labourer
David Brigham	" 22	"		"
Wm White	" 18	"		"
Ja^{s} Mitchell	" 22	Derry		"
Fra^{s} Dormet	" 20	"		"
Wm Montgomery	" 22	"		"
May "	" 41	"		spinster
Saml "	" 12	"		labourer
Rebecca Montgomery	10	Ballendreat		spinster
Robert Little	" 26	"		labourer
John Little	" 24	"		"
Math^{w} Armstrong	" 23	"		"
Ja^{s} Todd	" 20	"		"

PASSENGER LISTS TO AMERICA.

Communicated by GERALD FOTHERGILL, Esq., of New Wandsworth, London, England.

A List of Passengers who intend going to New York in the Ship *Cornelia* of Portland, sworn at Londonderry, 15 Apl., 1803.

Andrew Little	age	35	labourer	James Tracy	age	30	farmer
Jane "	"	26	spinster	Rose Tracy	"	32	spinster
John "	"	12	labourer	Margaret Tracy	"	2	a child
Margaret "	"	9	spinster	James M^c^Carron	"	29	farmer
William "	"	6	a child	Jane M^c^Carron	"	29	spinster
Eliza "	"	4	"	John M^c^Carron	"	5	labourer
Jane "	"	2	"	Fanny "	"	3	a child
Hugh McAvery	"	24	farmer	John M^c^Quoid	"	20	labourer
Jane McAvery	"	30	spinster	Robert Leonard	"	22	"
Jane McAvery	"	1	a child	Jane "	"	20	spinster
Simon Neilson	"	25	labourer	John Kelly	"	21	labourer
Mary "	"	25	spinster	Eliz Bruce	"	26	spinster
Archibald Armstrong	"	18	farmer	Robert Harper	"	30	farmer
James Neilson	"	3	a child	Jane Harper	"	24	spinster
Catherine Rodgers	"	30	spinster	Charles Harper	"	35	farmer
Wm Brown	"	20	labourer	John Forster	"	24	labourer
James McCann	"	25	"	Jane Little	"	21	spinster
David Henderson	"	20	"	James Harper	"	7	labourer
Con^s^ Dougherty	"	20	"	Anthony O Donnell	"	19	"
Thos McDonogh	"	50	farmer	Manus Brown	"	19	"
Catherine "	"	50	spinster	Edwd Brown	"	20	"
" "	"	50	"	Patrick Collin	"	22	"
James "	"	15	farmer	John Gallougher	"	22	"
Hugh McDonogh	"	13	"	Chas Dougherty	"	23	"
Richard "	"	11	"	Rebecca Beatty	"	21	spinster
Thomas "	"	2	a child	James Muldoon	"	24	labourer
Hugh Donnelly	"	32	labourer	James King	"	25	farmer
Mary "	"	28	spinster	John Lenox	"	30	"
Hugh Kennen	"	51	labourer	William Coldhoune	"	30	labourer
Catherine Donnelly	"	4	a child	Patrick Caldwell	"	25	"
Hugh Kennen	"	3	"	Jane "	"	20	spinster

Thomas McKennen	age 3	a child	Mary McIver	age 17	spinster
John Beatty	" 28	farmer	Judith "	" 19	"
Isabella Beatty	" 22	spinster	Shane "	" 25	farmer
Stephen "	" 2	a child			

A List of Passengers who intend going to New York on the Ship *American*, 340 Tons burthen, Alexander Thompson Master, sworn at Londonderry, 9 Apl., 1803.

David Kerr	aged 28	of Donegal	farmer
Hannah Kerr	" 25	"	spinster
Robert Virtue	" 22	"	farmer
Ann Virtue	" 25	"	spinster
Alexander Thompson	" 21	Fermanagh	farmer
L Jenkin	"	"	labourer
Andw Brander	"	"	"
L Miller	"	"	"
James McCafferty	"	"	"
John Ward	"	"	"
Robert Fitzpatrick	"	"	"
Robert Stinson	"	"	"
William Taylor	"	Sligo	"
Elinor "	"	"	spinster
Mary "	"	"	"
John Longhead	"	Donegal	labourer
R Longhead	"	"	spinster
Robt Longhead	"	"	labourer
John Longhead	"	"	"
John Whiteside	"	"	"
Ann "	"	"	spinster
Arthur Johnston	"	"	farmer
Mary "	"	"	spinster
Thomas Longhead	"	"	labourer
Thomas "	" 28	"	"
James McCrea	" 20	Ballantra	"
John "	" 25	"	"
Barbara Spence	" 24	"	spinster
Catherine "	" 23	"	"
John Coulter	" 23	Petigo	labourer
Dennis Carr	" 22	"	"
Catherine Carr	" 21	"	spinster
James Tremble	" 26	Donegal	farmer
Patk McGeragh	" 22	"	"
Alex McKee	" 27	"	"
Fanny McKee	" 26	"	spinster
Patrick McMullen	" 29	"	labourer
Hugh Devarney	" 26	Monaghan	"
Bryan Devine	" 28	"	"
Ann "	" 25	"	spinster
Mary McGinn	" 22	Cavan	"
Thos McGinn	" 27	"	labourer
James Murphy	" 27	"	"
Thomas Murphy	" 23	"	"

Thomas M^c^Surgan	aged 26	Cavan	labourer
Mary "	" 23	"	spinster
Mark O'Neill	" 25	Drunguin	labourer
Jane "	" 23	"	spinster
Henry "	" 17	"	labourer

A List of Persons who intend going to Philadelphia in the Ship *Mohawk* of and for Philadelphia, burthen 500 tons, John Barry Master, sworn at Londonderry, 23 Apl., 1803.

Neal Callaghan	aged 19	Ardmalin	labourer
Darby Dougherty	" 25	"	"
John Thompson	" 35	"	"
Charles Hethrington	" 40	Dungannon	"
Christ^y^ Hethrington	" 36	"	"
Sus^na^ "	" 40	"	
Jos^h^ "	" 14	"	
Eliza "	" 16	"	
George "	" 10	"	
James Walker	" 32	Enniskillen	house servant
Ann Walker	" 30	"	
Ralph "	" 36	"	labourer
Anne "	" 32	"	
Alex^r^ Wood	" 26	Lisnaska	"
Mary "	" 20	"	
Wm Alexander	" 32	Donagheady	"
Jane "	" 30	"	
James "	" 11	"	
Martha "	" 10	"	
William Bacon	" 28	Taughbone	"
Elizabeth "	" 27	"	
William "	" 12	"	
John M^c^Grenan	" 18	"	house servant
Pat M^c^Gafferty	" 19	"	labourer
Tho Donan	" 23	"	"
Anne Martin	" 20	Enneskillen	
Thomas Drum	" 36	"	"
Nathl Drum	" 34	"	"
Francis Smyth	" 29	"	
William Drum	" 20	"	"
Mary Drum	" 16	"	
Pat Lunny	" 20	"	
John Bates	" 21	Donamanagh	"
James Murray	" 20	"	"
Richd Jones	" 24	Strabane	house servant
Barry M^c^Ana	" 24	"	labourer
William Glin	" 25	Letterkenny	"
Owen M^c^Dade	" 28	Carne	"
Robert Hopkins	" 21	Bolea	"
Robert Graham	" 20	"	"
Abraham Philips	" 35	Urney	"
Robert M^c^Crea	" 30	Strabane	house servant
Pat Diven	" 28	"	"

Henry Forrester	aged	24	Clonis	labourer
Saml Faggart	"	30	"	"
Margt "	"	28	"	
Elizth Niely	"	21	Newton	stewart
John McCoy	"	20	Clougher	labourer
John Hastings	"	21	Stewartstown	"
John Simpson	"	25	"	"
George Walker	"	20	"	"
Samuel Thompson	"	28	Dungannon	"
Anna "	"	30	"	
Andw "	"	25	"	"
James	"	6	"	
Sarah	"	22	"	
James Campbell	"	28	"	"
Mary "	"	20		
Patk Brodley	"	19	Londonderry	house servant
Alexr "	"	28	Newtonstewart	labourer
Archd Anderson	"	19	Armagh	"
James Tait	"	36	"	"
James McGonegall	"	25	Buncrana	"
Ferrol McAward	"	21	"	"
Patk McDonnell	"	20	"	"
Denis Lynchakin	"	20	"	"
Neal Dougherty	"	20	"	"
William Kelly	"	23	"	"
John Carton	"	35	Claggen	"
David McConaghy	"	10	Ballyarton	"
Robert McQuistin	"	26	Dungiven	"

List of Persons who have engaged their Passage on board the ship *Ardent*, Burthen 350 tons, Richard Williams Master, bound for Baltimore, sworn at Londonderry, 23 Apl., 1803.

Thomas Ramsey	aged	28	Nr Muff	co. Donegal	farmer
Hugh Elliott	"	40	Rancel	"	"
Mrs "	"	54	"	"	
James "	"	20	"	"	"
Hugh "	"	14	"	"	
Jean Elliott	"	18	"	"	
James Richey	"	58	Donan	"	"
Mrs "	"	52	"	"	
Wm "	"	18	"	"	"
Cath "	"	16	"	"	
Ann "	"	14	"	"	
John "	"	20	"	"	"
Andw "	"	12	"	"	
Ellen "	"	10	"	"	
Andw McKee	"	38	"	"	"
Mrs "	"	34	"	"	
Eliza Richey	"	9	"	"	
Nancy McKee	"	16	"	"	
Pat "	"	14	"		
Eliz Finlay	"	57	"		

John Finlay	aged 22	Donan	Donegal	farmer
James "	" 17	"	"	"
Pat Cunigan	" 60	Killaughter		drover
James Manilus	" 26	Kilcar		"
Hugh Clark	" 30	Donan	"	farmer
Mrs Clark, Senr	" 28	"	"	
James "	" 17	"	"	"
Wm "	" 26	"	"	"
Mrs " Junr	" 22	"	"	
Alexr	" 8	"	"	
Mrs Richey	" 38	"	"	
George Richey	" 9	"	"	
Charles "	" 44	"	"	"
Andw McCullough	" 40	"	"	"
Mrs Mc "	" 34	"	"	
Andw "	" 16	"	"	
Jean "	" 14	"	"	
George "	" 12	"	"	
Alexr "	" 10	"	"	
John Montgomery	" 24	Killybegs	"	gentleman
John Jones	" 20	"	"	"
Wm Graham	" 22	Tyrough	"	farmer
Francis "	" 22	"	"	"
James Cunningham	" 17	Glenery		
John Crawford	" 28	Ballybofey		"
John Erwin	" 56	"	"	"
George Crawford	" 32	Doren	"	"
Ann Boyle	" 14	Mt Charles	"	
David Graham	" 48	Dergbridge co. Tyrone		"
Sarah "	" 41	"	"	

PASSENGER LISTS TO AMERICA.

Communicated by Gerald Fothergill, Esq., of New Wandsworth, London, England.

List of Passengers who intend to proceed on board the American Ship *Jefferson* to New York from Sligo, James Adams, Master, sworn at Sligo, 16 Apl., 1803.

Peter Gonagle	Labourer	Pat Nelis	Labourer
James Clenten	"	Edmd Gilfeader	"
Edm^{d} Leyonard	"	Thomas Reily	"
Pat. Waterson	"	James McKey	"
John McGan	"	James Curry	"
Thos Wymbs	Dealer	Danl Gilmartin	"
Mich^{l} Wymbs	"	Thos Farrel	"
Pat Hangdon	Labourer	John Higgins	
John Harken	"	William Kalens	
Fran^{s} Kelly	"		

The following duplicate of the foregoing, sworn 28 Apl., 1803, by James Adams, the Master, gives fuller information.

Peter Nangle	aged 40	of Sligo		Labourer
James Clenton	26	Clurbagh	Sligo	"
Edm^{d} Leynerk	20	"	"	"
Pat Waterson	55	"	"	"
John McGan	32	Carns	Sligo	"
Thos Wymbs	36	"	"	Dealer
Mich^{l} "	30	"	"	"
Pat Haregdon	41	Moneygold	"	Labourer
John Harken	26	Grange	"	"
Fra^{s} Kelly	29	Bunduff	"	"
Pat Nelis	27	Creery	"	"
Edm^{d} Gilfeader	23	Mt Temple	"	"
Thos Reilly	29	" "	"	"
Ja^{s} McKey	36	Sligo		"
Ja^{s} Curry	28	"		"
Danl Gilmartin	29	"		"
Thos Farrell	23	Clurbagh	Sligo	"
Jno Higgins	37	"	"	"
Wm Kalens	42	"	"	"

A List of Passengers who intend going to Baltimore in the Ship *Serpent* of Baltimore, Arch^{d} McCockell, Master, sworn at Londonderry, 30 Apl., 1803.

Joseph	Neilson	26	Farmer	Strabane
Margt	"	24	———	"
Jane	"	14	spinster	"
Elizabeth	"	12	"	"
John	"	10	———	"
James	"	10	———	"

Saml McCarthy		25	Labourer	Omagh
Dav^{d} Falls		25	"	"
Saml Turner		30	"	Strabane
Jno Neilson		27	"	"
Pat Mounigle		28	"	Rosquill
Neal McPeak		30	"	"
Mich^{l} McCann		40	Farmer	"
Phelix McCann		35	"	"
Pat^{k}	"	28	"	"
Peter	"	18	"	"
Nelly	"	37	———	"
Susan	"	40	———	"
Hannah	"	16	spinster	"
Mary	"	14	"	"
James McBride		25	Farmer	"
Catherine	"	24	———	"
Peter Corbitt		25	Farmer	Rathmullen
Isabella	"	23	———	"
John Mundell		40	Farmer	Gortgarn
Margaret Mundell		39	———	"
Samuel	"	46	Farmer	"
W^{m} Jno	"	25	"	"
Isabella	"	37	———	"
Isabella	"	20	spinster	"
Jane	"	16	"	"
Mary	"	14	"	"
Eliz^{h}	"	12	"	"
Margt Craig		36	———	"
Geo Laird		25	Farmer	"
Saml	"	22	"	"
Mary	"	24	———	"
Rach^{l}	"	25	spinster	"
Peter Kenedy		27	Farmer	"
Margaret	"	25	———	"
Emelia	"	6	———	"
James Reed		40	Farmer	Maghera
Agnes Reed		37	———	"
Sally	"	15	spinster	"
Mary McCool		45	———	"
James McCool		24	Farmer	"
Jn	"	20	"	"
Nelly Ross		35	———	"
James Rolls		18	Labourer	"

Passengers List of the Ship *Strafford* for Philadelphia, sworn at Londonderry, 14 May, 1803.

John	McGan	aged 34	Farmer of	Coagh
Elizabeth	"	30	Spinster	"
Sarah	"	2	———	"
Elinor	"	infant	———	"
W^{m}	Walker	30	Farmer	"
Mary Anne	"	20	Spinster	"
Eliz	"	18	"	"

Wm Mitchel	20	Farmer	Cumber
Thos Coningham	18	"	Ballymony
Alexr Stewart	20	Labourer	Ketreights
John Moore	19	"	Loughgin
James Hamilton	23	"	"
Wm Smily	23	"	Ketreights
Edw Clarke	40	Farmer	Enniskillen
John Milley	45	"	"
Wm Loughridge	30	"	Cookstown
Mg "	24	———	"
Jane "	7	———	"
James "	5	———	"
Eliza "	2	———	"
Nancy Harkin	30	Seamstress	Birdstown
Nelly "	4	———	"
Wm "	6	———	"
John Chamber	20	Farmer	County Tyrone
Wm Gray	24	"	" "
James Ralston	45	"	" "
Mary Ralston	40	———	" "
James Ralston	15	———	" "
Mary "	12	———	" "
Davd "	9	———	" "
Josh "	5	———	" "
Anne "	2	———	" "
Anne "	34	Seamstress	" "
Robt "	19	Labourer	" "
Davd "	15	"	" "
John "	11	———	" "
Jane "	8	———	" "
Anne "	5	———	" "
Josh "	2	———	" "
John "	40	Farmer	" "
Sarah "	40	Seamstress	" "
Davd "	9	———	" "
Andw "	7	———	" "
Wm "	3	———	" "
James "	5	———	" "
Elinor Shean	60	———	County Down
Mary Anderson	24	———	" "
Mary "	2	———	" "
John Wilson	22	Farmer	———
Wm Carr	20	"	———
James Moore	19		Ballykelly

A List of Passengers to go on board the Ship *Patty*, sworn at Newry, 5 May, 1803.

Wm Griffis	34	Labourer	Down
Andrew Hurs	30	"	"
John Kenedy	41	"	"
Saml McBride	28	"	Tyrone
John Gibson	50	Farmer	"

Pat[k] Lynch	27	Laborer	Tyrone
David Hunter	28	"	"
Edward "	34	"	"
George "	14	"	"
Alex[r] Armstrong	29	"	Armargh
Mary Harvey	45	Spinster	"
Eliza "	23	"	"
Rob[t] "	48	Farmer	"
Biddy Brown	38	Spinster	Down
Henry Williams	28	Gentleman	Armagh
Sam[l] Patton	32	Laborer	Down
Joseph "	36	"	"
George Tilforde	28	"	"
John Blair	29	"	"
John M[c]Dale	36	"	"
Walter Potts	25	"	"
William Roncy	19	"	"
James Eakin	46	Farmer	"
Samuel "	50	"	"
James Fitspatrick	37	"	"
Mary "	32	Spinster	"
Edward Maugher	26	Laborer	Queens County
John Fleming	24	"	" "
Thomas Dick	32	Farmer	Down
James Nelson	28	"	"
John Armstrong	29	"	"

PASSENGER LISTS TO AMERICA.

Communicated by GERALD FOTHERGILL, Esq., of New Wandsworth, London, England.

A Report of Passengers on board the American Ship *Active*, whereof Robert McKown is Master, burthen 138 tons, bound for Philadelphia, sworn at Newry, 6 May, 1803.

James Moore	aged 21	Clerk		Martha Parnell	aged 18	———
James Rendles	" 40	Labourer		Robert Mills	" 40	Labourer
John Rendles	" 38	"		Eliza Barnett	" 16	———
Eliza "	" 16	———		Jane "	" 12	———
Thomas "	" 12	Labourer		William Stewart	" 50	Labourer
John Barnett	" 38	"		Margaret "	" 38	
Margaret "	" 34	———		Ann "	" 24	

Eliza Laverty	"	20	———	Agness Stewart	aged	20		
Andrew Barnett	"	24	Labourer	Susannah "	"	18		This one is crossed out
Annabella "	"	20	———					

A Report of Passengers on board the American Ship *Diana* of New Bedford, Burthen 223 Tons, whereof Henry Hurter is Master, bound for New York, sworn at Newry, 18 May, 1803.

Isabella Allen	aged	32		of Market-hill
John Collins	"	36	Labourer	" "
Pat[k] Crowley	"	39	"	" "
Mary "	"	39	———	" "
Rich[d] Burden	"	28	Labourer	Fentona
James Farrel	"	40	"	Stewartstown
Patrick Philips	"	24	"	Stralane
Thomas Rooney	"	40	"	Banbridge
Mary Martin	"	20		"
Charlotte Brothers	"	26		"
Isaac Collins	"	30	Labourer	Monaghan
John Martin	"	36	"	"
John Brothers	"	30	"	"
Thomas Lewis	"	30	"	"
John Michael	"	30	"	Dundalk
William Sleith	"	23	"	"
Henry Ells	"	30	"	Newry
Tho[s] Fure	"	39	"	"
Tho[s] Smith	"	37	"	Bathfriland
Rebecca Brothers	"	45	———	Newry
Benjamin Philips	"	30	Labourer	Dundalk
Hanna Mytrood	"	25	———	Newry
James Downs	"	30	Labourer	Coatehill
Samuel Crawley	"	35	"	"
John Burden	"	32	"	Ballybery
Sarah Barder	"	31	———	"
Rebecca Deblois	"	24	———	Ballyconnell
Eliza Whithom	"	23		Killyshandon
Mary Cahoone	"	22		Cavan
Mary Overing	"	25		"

A List of Passengers intended to go from this Port by the Ship *Hopewell* of and for New York, burthen 125 tons, sworn at Newry, 6 June, 1803.

Peter Downey	aged	22	Labourer	Joseph Humphies	aged	26	Labourer
William Thornbury	"	40	"	Robert Humphries	"	40	"
W[m] Daly	"	30	"	Moses "	"	17	"
Geo Ferrigan	"	32	"	James Couser	"	18	"
W[m] Martin	"	36	"	Robert Humphies	"	19	"
Sam Smyley	"	35	"	James Reed	"	20	"
John M[c]Ceaverell	"	35	"	Tho[s] M[c]leherry	"	21	"
Pat Cullager	"	20	"	John Anderson	"	25	"
David Humphies	"	52	"				

A List of Passengers intending to go from Belfast to New York in the Ship *Wilmington*, Thomas Woodward, Master, 360 Tons, sworn 9 July, 1803.

John Houston	aged	30	Farmer	John Curry	aged	9	———
Mrs Houston	"	27		Robt Warwick	"	30	gen^t
Houston	"	7	Children	Hen Garrett	"	33	Farmer
"	"	5	"	S Ann "	"	27	———
"	"	2	"	Mary Maucally	"	23	———
Robert Stewart	"	27	Farmer	John Browne	"	45	gen^t
M^rs "	"	24		Robt Jackson	"	30	"
——— "	"	2	Child	John Murphy	"	28	"
James Galway	"	18	Farmer	John Thompson	"	26	"
Thomas Allen	"	25	"	Thos McCrellos	"	34	Farmer
Willm Erskin	"	32	"	Thos McConaghy	"	27	"
Isabella Dick	"	16	———	John Cameron	"	39	"
John Cross	"	35	Farmer	Lavinia "	"	20	———
Wm Crozier	"	26	"	Agnus "	"	17	———
Henry McHenry	"	40	gent^n	Martha "	"	14	———
Hen Read	"	30	"	Elinor "	"	9	———
Jane Curry	"	36	———	Saml Chestnut	"	30	gen^t
Mary "	"	14	———	Mary Cameron	"	36	———
Eliza "	"	12	———				

List of Passengers engaged to sail on board the American Ship *Margaret*, Wm. M. Boyd, Master, for Wiscasset in the United States, sworn (indorsed from Dublin) 12 July, 1803.

Edwd Irwin	aged	50	Labourer	Wexford
Geo Phillips	"	30	"	"
Thos Maguire	"	32	"	"
Patrick Irwin	"	31	"	"
Jo^s Cavaneagh	"	34	"	"
Tho Bent	"	22	"	"
Mary Irwin	"	40	———	"
Ann Irwin	"	9	———	"

A List of Passengers intending to go in the Brig *Sally*, Tim^y Clifton, Master, for New York, burthen 147 Tons, now lying in the Harbour of Dublin, sworn 5 Aug., 1803.

Alice Flood	aged	22	spinster	Dublin
Margaret Kelly	"	45	"	"
Elizabeth Flood	"	24	"	"
Alicia Purfield	"	18	"	"
Ann Eagle	"	10	"	"
George Eagle	"	9	———	"
Mary Bennett	"	30	spinster	"
Nich Campbell	"	24	Labourer	"
Nancy Fallis	"	20	spinster	"
James Grant	"	17	Scotch Labourer	———
Hugh Kelly	"	24	Labourer	Dublin
Bernard Fitzpatrick	"	38	Farmer	Tullamore
Ellen "	"	28	his wife	"
Mary "			a child	"
John Lyons	"	30	Farmer	"
& an infant				

A List of Passengers engaged to sail on board the Brig *George* of New Bedford, burden 172 tons, Jacob Taber, Master, for New York, sworn 16 Aug., 1803.

John OBrien	aged 28	Clerk	Dublin
Michael Brannon	" 23	Farmer	Mayo
John Lyons	" 30	Farmer	Tullamore
Mark Evans	" 30	"	Queens Co.
Mary Evans		his wife	
James Henney	" 25	Farmer	Dublin County
Pat^k Doyle	" 20	"	Mayo
Bern^d Fitzpatrick	" 36	"	Tullamore
his wife & child			
Henry OHara	" 23	"	Clare

A List of persons who have engaged their passage in the Ship *Eagle*, Andrew Riker, Master, of and for New York, sworn 27 Aug., 1803.

Robert Small	aged 27	height 5– 5	Labourer	Ballymony
Wm Conoy	40	5–10	Farmer	Pensilvania
Alex^r McKeown	18	5– 5	Labourer	Belfast
Wm Williamson	25	6– 1	"	Killinchy
Owen Miskelly	25	5–10	"	"
Kitty "			spinster	"
Wm Magill	23	5–11	Labourer	"
Roger Welsh	24	6– 1	"	"
James Reid	22	5– 7	"	Saintfield
Thomas Armstrong	31	5– 9	Farmer	Clonfeakle
Mary ———			spinster	
John Treanor	25	5– 9	Farmer	Killinchy
John Murphy	24	5– 9	Labourer	"
Alex^r Orr	21	5– 9	gentleman	Ballymoney
Jas Boyd	30	5– 9	merchant	N^r Ballameane
Saml B Wiley	30	5–10	clergyman	Philadelphia
John Moorhead	24	5– 7½	merchant	Antrim
Marcus Heyland	22	5– 3	"	Coleraine
Wm Freeland	20	5– 8	farmer	co Armargh
Wm Deyrman	25	5–10	labourer	Drumbo
Ja^s Mild	25	5–10	farmer	Aughaloo
Jo^s Caldwell	22	5– 8	merchant	Ballymony
Mrs Orr				Tobermore
John Breene	15	5– 7	farmer	Killenely
Saml McNeill	20	5– 8	grocer	Ballymeana
Jas Campbell	30	5– 5	labourer	Carmoney
Saml Miniss	21	5– 7	"	Saintfield
James Mcauley	22	5–11	"	"
Wm Dixin	22	5– 7	"	"
Saml Moore	18	6–	gentleman	Portglenone
Alexr Graham	34	5– 8	M.D.	last residence Glasgow
Thos Neilson	24	5– 5	merchant	Ballinderry
Saml "	11	5– 8	none	"
Robt "	28	5– 7	merchant	"
James Grant	28	5– 7	"	Armahilt

PASSENGER LISTS TO AMERICA.

Communicated by Gerald Fothergill, Esq., of New Wandsworth, London, England.

Passengers on the Brig *George* of New Bedford, bound for New York, in addition to the list before laid before the Privy Council, sworn at Dublin, 29 Aug., 1803, Jacob Taber, Master.

Peter Roe	aged	30	Ross	Merchant
Stephen French	"	45	Carrick on Suir	"
Hugh Madden	"	30	Dublin	Clerk
Mat^{s} Joyce	"	18	"	"

Passengers engaged to sail on board the Brig *George* of New Bedford, Jacob Taber, Master, for New York, sworn at Dublin, 29 Aug., 1803.

John O'Brien	aged	28	Dublin	clerk
Mich^{l} Bannon	"	23	Mayo.	farmer
John Lyons	"	30	Tullamore	"
Mark Evans	"	30	Queens county	"
Ann Evans	"	—	his wife	
James Hennesy	"	25	Dublin	labourer
Patrick Doyle	"	20	May	farmer
Bernard Fitzpatrick	"	36	Tullamore	"
His wife & child				
Hen^{y} OHara	"	23	Clare	"
Peter Roe	"	30	Ross	merchant

Shepherd French	aged 45	Carrick on Suir	merchant
Mat[s] Joyce	" 18	Dublin	clerk

Passengers of the American Ship *Susan*, John O'Connor, Master, from Dublin to New York, sworn 6 Sept., 1803.

Abraham Bell	aged 28	New York	merchant	cabben
Robert Bleakly	" 26	Armagh	linen merchant	"
Dav[d] "	" 24	"	" "	"
M[rs] Mathews	" 45	Londonderry		"
Simon Felix Gallagher	" 45		Catholick pastor	"
John Carbery	" 36	Danish Island	merchant	"
John Watters	" 27	Navan	clerk	steerage
James Hornidge	" 25	New York	surveyor	"
John Curtis	" 28	Dublin	super cargo	"
Thomas Roberts	" 25	England	farmer	"
John North	" 36	America	gentleman	"
Laurence Toole	" 22	Dublin	labourer	"
Walter Fleming	" 21	New York	clerk	"
Hugh Maddin	" 23	Dublin	clerk	"
Roger Morris	" 28	"	"	"
William Sedgwick	" 36	"	"	"
Arthur Fulham	" 12	Edinderry	———	"
Jane Hughes	" 22	Down	———	"
Mary Kelly	" 40	Dublin	———	"
Mary Mathews	" 12	"	———	"
Mary OBrien	" 9	"	———	"
Ann "	" 8	"	———	"
Eliza Langley	" 22	Kilkenny	———	"
Margaret Nowlan	" 22	"	———	"
Biddy OConnor	" 14	Wexford	———	"
Mary Larkin	" 16	"	———	"
Mary Ann Reilly	" 22	Dublin		"

List of passengers on the *Fortitude* of New York, Hezekia Pinkham, Master, bound for New York, sworn at Cork, 1 Sept., 1803.

John Sullivan Scully	aged 35	Cork	merchant
Mary " "	" 28	"	wife to same
James Ryan	" 34	Bantry	farmer
Mary "	" 30	"	wife to same
James Long	" 22	"	shop keeper
Denis Sullivan	" 21	"	" "
Corn "	" 17	"	farmer
John Barry	" 25	"	"
Mary Harte	" 40	Cove	sailors wife
Mary Harte	" 10	"	child to same
John Harte	" 5	"	" "
Tho[s] Johnson	" 30	Cork	clerk
Mary Stewart	" 55	"	gentlewoman
W[m] Devayne	" 60	Exter Devon	now in Cork gentleman
Harriott "	" 24	"	daughter to same
Charlotte "	" 22	"	" "
James Hughes	" 30	Richmond, America, now in Cork, gent	
Mary "	" 28	" "	wife to same

A List of Passengers of the ship *American* of New York, from Londonderry to New York, sworn at Londonderry, 10 Sept., 1803.

John Patton	aged	34	New York	merchant
Robert Boreland	"	20	Strabane	farmer
Mary "	"	19	"	spinster
Hannah McGhee	"	45	"	"
Edward McGowan	"	25	Tamlaght, Derry	labourer
William Dunn	"	25	Gellygordon	farmer
Thomas Buchannon	"	22	"	"
John Donahy	"	21	N T Lamavady	labourer
John Patterson	"	30	Moneymore	farmer
Mathew "	"	27	"	"
George "	"	26	"	"
Eliza "	"	20	"	
James Dougherty	"	23	Ramullen	labourer
James Cormick	"	28	Strabane	clerk
Rebecca "	"	20	"	spinster
Alexander McKinley	"	23	"	farmer
John Torbet	"	18	Tyrone	labourer
Thomas Miller	"	28	Coagh	farmer
David "	"	24	"	"
Marth "	"	50	"	
Eliz^h "	"	23	"	spinster
Robert Foster	"	22	"	farmer
Martha Foster	"	22	"	spinster
William Browne	"	34	"	farmer
Margaret Browne	"	26	"	spinster
Philip McGowan	"	34	Glock Tamlaght	farmer
Grace "	"	27	"	spinster
Philip " jun^r	"	12	"	
John McKenney	"	38	New York	merchant
David Birket	"	30	Castlefin	farmer
William Beatty	"	25	New York	trader
George Lindsey	"	32	Pettijoe	farmer
William Cook	"	26	"	"
Isaac Cockran	"	27	New York	merchant
James McFarland	"	24	Tyrone	farmer
Alex McIntire	"	29	Waterside, Londonderry	"
Edward McClary	"	21	Tamlaght, Derry	"
Mary McGhee	"	38	Cookstown	spinster

Additional list of Passengers intending to proceed to New York on board the American Ship *Susan*, from Dublin, sworn 13 Sept., 1803.

John Price	aged	35	New York	Surgeon	Cabbin
Thomas Dawdal	"	25	Dublin	Labourer	Steerage
John Gavan	"	30	Dublin	Attorney	"
Thos Flood	"	20	Dublin	Clerk	"
Andrew Flinn	"	23	Dublin	Clerk	"
Patrick Sennott	"	25	Wexford	Farmer	"
Francis Murphy	"	50	America	Farmer	"
Owen "	"	25	Monaghan	"	"
Andrew Connor	"	45	Dublin	Merchant	"

Names of persons who wish to go to Philadelphia in the Snow *George* of Philadelphia, indorsed from Belfast, sworn 22 Sept., 1803.

Ephraim Lee	aged 26	Kilishandon	co.	Cavan	Farmer
Edw[d] Lee	" 23	"		"	"
Hugh Gably	" 18	Killinchy	co.	Down	Labourer
Rob[t] Walsh	" 22	Downpatrick		"	Dealer
Alex[r] Fulton	" 34	Loughsill		"	Farmer
Tho[s] Kelly	" 36	Grange		"	"
Edw[d] Donelly	" 27	Lessan		Tyrone	"
Will Lowry	" 29	Killinchy		Down	Labourer
Tho[s] Service	" 18	Brochan		Antrim	"
Sarah Dawson	" 17	Connor		"	———
Marcus Toole	" 39	Belfast	co.	"	Servant
Jane Toole	" 28	"		"	
John Dodds	" 30	Dromal		"	Farmer
Henry Wilson	" 24	Belfast		"	Schoolmaster
John Thompson	" 28	Ballymony		"	Dealer
Patrick Mullan	" 21	Tynan		Armagh	"
James Strachan	" 20	Connor		Antrim	Farmer
John Johnson	" 19	"		"	"
Nath[l] Byst	" 30	Gencany		"	Dealer
Jane Develin	" 32	Ballymow		Armagh	
Roger "	" 35	"		"	Farmer
Patrick M[c]Key	" 38	Drumgoland		Down	"
Alex[r] Stewart	" 21	Tullylisk		"	"
James Ganet	" 30	Annalult		"	Dealer
Mathew Timoly	" 28	Ballymasaw		"	Labourer
Tho[s] Armstrong	" 31	Clonfeech		Armagh	Farmer
Mary Armstrong	" 27	"		"	———
Tho[s] Mathews	" 27	Belfast		Antrim	Dealer
Eliza "	" 25	"		"	———
Joseph Wilson	" 22	"	co.	"	Dealer
John Pumphy	" 29	"		"	Farmer

A List of Passengers on board the *Betsy* for New York, sworn at Newry, 22 Sept., 1803.

James Kilheath	aged 25	Kilkeel	Farmer
Jane "	" 26	"	
Pat Murray	" 28	Hillsborough	Labourer
Sarah "	" 26	"	
Robert Smith	" 28	Clough	Farmer
Jenny "	" 26	"	
James Conwell	" 28	Armagh	Farmer
Catherine "	" 27	"	
Anthony "	" 26	"	"
Bernard "	" 25	"	"
Jeremiah "	" 24	"	"
Mick Burns	" 25	"	Labourer
George Tedford	" 28	Down	"
Eliza "	" 28	"	"
Rachael Weston	" 20	Charlestown, America	Lady
Pat M[c]Cullough	" 26	Armagh	Farmer

Sally M^c^ullough	aged 27	Armagh		
Pat Cassidy	" 17	"	Farmer	
John Humphry	" 32	Richmond, America.	At present in Lisburn, Ireland. Merchant	
Owen M^c^Uraney	" 22	Carrickadrummond	Labourer	
James Moore	" 45	Cranfield	"	
Nelly Small	" 30	Down		
Saml Patterson	" 21	Grange	"	

A List of Passengers who have engaged to go in the Brig *Lady Washington*, John Luscombe, Master, from Belfast to Charleston, sworn 22 Sept., 1803.

Jane M^c^Cance of Blackumigo, So. Carolina		age	54
William Craig of Mageradroll, Co. Down	Farmer	"	54
Agnes Craigh his Wife, child & servant boy, of Magerdroll			
Hugh M^c^Cance of Magerdroll	Farmer	"	55
Elizabeth " his Wife "		"	57
Hugh " his Son "		"	19
Samu^l^ " " "		"	22
Jane " his Daughter "		"	19
John Blackwood of Clough	Farmer	"	15
David Bell of Belfast, Co. Antrim	Merchant	"	26
Saml Carson " " "	"	"	36
Arthur ONeill of Drumarra, Co. Down	Farmer	"	24
Saml Leslie of Kilmore "	"	"	22
Willm Leslie " " "	"	"	20
John Wilson & Wife of Ballycam "	"	"	{ 43 / 35 }
William Hooy of Ballykill, Co. Antrim	"	"	18
John Young of Glenary, Co. Antrim	Labourer	"	22
John Sherlock " " "	Labourer	"	23
Saml Rabb of Ballinahurch "	Farmer	"	29
Thomas Caldwell of Broad Island	Labourer	"	20
William Caldwell " " "	"	"	18
Widow Lamont " Charleston, S^o^ Carolina			
John Lowry of Garvagh, Co. Down	Farmer	"	35

A List of Passengers of the ship *Independance* who have contracted to take their Passage to New York in the said ship being of the burthen of 300 Tons and upwards, Mathias Fleming, Master, sworn at Londonderry, 31 Oct., 1803.

Edward M^c^Kelvy	aged 35	Farmer	L Kenny
M^rs^ M^c^Kelvy	" 35	House Wife	"
Three Children to the above			"
Luke Creyon	aged 20	Labourer	Sligo
Roger Creyon	" 18	"	"
John C Steward	" 24	Farmer	"
Francis Wood	" 26	Labourer	L Kenny
Isabella Wood with her infant Child			"
Thomas Leary	aged 28	Farmer	Raphoe
Michael Leary	" 20	"	"

Rose Caffry	aged 18	Spinster	Raphoe
Thomas Laughlin	" 18	Farmer	"
Thomas Caffry	" 20	Labourer	"
John Hopkins	" 24	"	L Kenny
John Fisher	" 26	"	"
Wm Latemore	" 30	"	"
Mary Latemore	" 29		"
James Ward	" 25	"	"
Henry Tory	" 28	"	"
Jaseph Robinson	" 20	"	"
Marg^t^ Miller	" 20	Spinster	Derry
Mathew M^c^Dole	" 36	Labourer	Carrikfergus
T. M^c^Dole	" 20	Spinster	"

List of Passengers intending to go to Norfolk in America with the Ship *Venus*, Resolve Waldron, Master, Burthen 246 Tons, sworn at Dublin, 14 Nov., 1803.

John Sherman	aged 18	Merchant	Dublin, No 13 Little Britten st
Edward Rooney	" 30	"	Smithfield, No. 45
George M^c^Entire		Physician	17 Crampton Court
M^rs^ M^c^Entire	" 22		" " "
Edward Dempsy	" 22	Farmer	Klimbullock, Kings Co
Thos Dempsy	" 18	"	" "
Mary "	" 50		" "
Esther "	" 20		" "
Judy "	" 19		" "
Catherine "	" 16		" "
Thos Best	" 17	Gent^n^	Smithfield

List of Passengers on board the *Fortitude* bound to New York, sworn at Cork, 18 Feb., 1804.

Margaret Mahony	aged 30	gentlewoman	Dunmanaway
Anne "	" 9	her daughter	"
Goody Burke	" 30	gentlewoman	Kilkenny
Ellen "	" 12	her daughter	"
Edward "	" 9	her son	"
Biddy "	" 7	her daughter	"
Denis "	" 5	her son	"
John Buen	" 55	farmer	County Waterford
Pierce Corbett	" 22	farmer	" "
Saml Grace	" 19	"	" Cork
Thos Mackay	" 30	"	" "
Ellen "	" 25	his wife	" "
Ellen "	" 2	her daughter	" "
Thos Brien	" 23	farmer	" "
Thos Brook	" 36	gentleman	" "
Denis Flanigan	" 28	farmer	" Limerick

List of Passengers going to New York on the *George* of New Bedford, sworn at Belfast, 25 Feb., 1804.

Andrew Smith	aged 24	farmer	Downe
James Sprowl	" 30	"	"

Alexr Cochran	aged 36	farmer	Downe	
Agnes "	" 28	spinster & four children from 1 to 8 years old		
Elenor Martin	" 70	spinster	Downe	
Margt Fleming	" 20	"	"	
Wm Hinger	" 20	gentleman	Drumara	
Peter OHamill	" 27	labourer	Antrim	
Thomas Duncan	" 18	"	"	
John Johnston	" 50	farmer	"	
John Crothers	" 44	"	"	
Wm Crothers	" 34	"	"	
Rt "	" 30	spinster & four children from 1–8 years old		
Thos Gray	" 30	farmer	Antrim	
Jane Gray	" 27	spinster	"	
Hans Wilson	" 24	farmer	Bangor	
Edw Templeton	" 20	"	Coleraine	
Jane Templeton	" 18	spinster	"	
John Dawson	" 18	farmer	Antrim	
David Rea	" 24	farmer	Downe	

PASSENGER LISTS TO AMERICA.

Communicated by GERALD FOTHERGILL, Esq., of New Wandsworth, London, England.

List of Passengers on board the *Prudence*, of Philadelphia, Sworn at Dublin, 9 March, 1804.

Thos Maitland	aged 22	One family from Baltinglass, Wicklow
Ann "	56	
and child	7	
Mary Ann Maitland	19	
James Barry	25	Apothecary, Dublin
John McDermott	26	Clerk "
James McCarty	26	" "
John Gitten	30	" "
and child	8	"
Jane Hines	22	Glasnevin "

Additional List of Passengers taken on board since the above was sworn to:

John Nixon	26	Farmer, Manor Hamilton, Leitrim
John Trevin	27	" " " "
James Gore	24	Clerk, Dublin

List of Passengers in the *Eagle*, for New York, sworn at Belfast, 10 March, 1804.

Josiah Kerr	age 28	height 5– 8	Clerk, Loughbickyard. Thin faced and pretty fair
Joseph "	21	5–10	Farmer, Hillsborough. Smooth and fair faced
Hamilton "	17	5– 0	Farmer, Hillsborough. Smooth and fair faced
John McMurdy	30	5– 7	Farmer, Banbridge. Pitted with the small-pox

James McMullen	age 28	height 5– 6	Farmer, Loughbrickland. Red haired, smooth faced, and lame of a knee
Robert Cavart	36	5– 2	Labourer, Rathfyland. Smooth and fair faced
Jas Fulton	22	5– 8	Labourer, Maghrolin. Smooth and fair faced
Arthur Walker	27	5– 9	Labourer, Drumore. Yellow and smooth faced
Thos Gordon	28	5– 5	Labourer, Drumore. Yellow and pitted with small-pox
Robert Whany	28	5– 7	Farmer, Drumore. Ruddy, a little pitted
Robt Smith	21	5– 6	Labourer, Hillsborough. Sallow thin and smooth faced
Hu Hanison	13	5–11	Farmer, Drumore. Ruddy Complexion and black eyed.
Paul Rogan	30	5– 8	Labourer, Loughbuckland. Spare faced
Wm McKee	26	5–10	Labourer, Mt Stewart. Thin faced & ruddy
Archd Williams	21	5– 8	Farmer, Castle Dawson. Smooth faced, fair haired
John Benson	19	5– 3	Labourer, Near Drumore. Little pitted, black hair
Robert Patterson	24	5–11	Farmer, Ballindeny. Black hair and ruddy
Adam Patterson	20	5– 6	Farmer, Ballindeny. Fair haired, a little pitted
John Dickson	33	5– 7	Farmer, Banbridge. Smooth face, black hair
James Black	34	5–11	Linnen draper, Banbridge. Smooth faced, black hair
James Moones	21	5– 7	Farmer, Ballendeny. Little pitted, fair hair
Anthy McMordy	44	6– 0	Farmer, Banbridge. Ruddy complexion.
Eliz Kerr	49	5– 4	Spinster, Loughbickland. Brown complexion
Eliz Kerr	30	5– 6	Spinster, Hillsborough. Brown and smooth faced
Sarah Kerr	49	5– 4	Spinster, Hillsborough. A little pitted with the small-pox
Marg Cavart	28	5– 0	Spinster, Rathpiland. Fair and smooth faced
Eliza Walker	24	5– 3	Spinster, Dromon. Fair, a little pitted
Margaret Gordon	21	5– 4	Spinster, Dromon. Fair and smooth faced
Margaret Walker	25	6– 0	Spinster, Hillsboro'. Yellow and a little pitted
Jane Whany	35	4– 0	Dromon. Tender eyed and fair
Nancy Williams	23	5– 6	Spinster, Castle Dawson. Black haired, a little pitted

Jane Dickson	age 21	height 5– 3	Spinster, Bambridge. Smooth and fair faced.
Hamilton Brown	35	5– 4	Farmer, Killnechy. Pale faced and pitted
Jane "	35	5– 3	Spinster, Killnechy. Pale faced and pitted
Wm Whaly a child	7		

List of Passengers to go on board the American Ship *Maria*, of Wilmington, bound for Philadelphia, sworn at Londonderry, 10 March, 1804.

Nancy McKeever	aged 45	Spinster
Robert Fulton	43	Labourer
John Rice	38	"
Mary Ann Hammond	27	Spinster
Nancy Fulton	31	"
Robert Millar	26	Labourer
Arthur Murphy	49	"
James Dougherty	33	"
Jas McKinley	23	"
Sarah Murphy	21	Spinster
Mary McGomery	17	"
Margt Pearson	52	"
Frans Scott	47	Labourer
James Dogherty	51	"
Saml McKinley	33	"
Patt Karlin	42	"
John McConway	29	"
Mary McConway	26	Spinster
Hugh Smith	44	Labourer
Humphry Graham	50	"
Thos Graham	36	"
Barny McCanna	43	"
Robert Leonard	21	"
Henry Rankin	17	"
Wm Anderson	58	"
Wm Edmond	41	"
John Anderson	28	"
Heny Anderson	46	"
Wm Harkin	25	"
Jos Arskine	56	"
Jas Waker	40	"
Saml Bellman	33	"
John Bellman	35	"
Saml Anderson	46	"
Margt Anderson	36	Spinster
Ann Walker	24	"

List of Passengers to New York on the *Charles and Harriott*, sworn at Sligo, 29 March, 1804.

Martin Carney	of Mogherow	Labourer
Peter Carroll	"	"
Wm Curry	Conought	"

Fras McGowan	of Mogherow	Clerk
Roger Gill	Co. Fermanagh	Labourer
Bryan McManus	" "	"
Philip Rogers	Sligo	"
Robert Muns	Drumclief	"
Alexr Rutledge	Tyrecagh	"
Hugh Murray	Sligo	Clerk
Wm Moreton	Co. Fermanagh	Labourer
Thos McIntire	Sligo	Clerk
Bryan Collen	Brenduff	Labourer
John Flynn	Drumcliff	"
Michael Golden	"	"
John Elliott	Mulloghmore	"
Michl Dunn	"	"
Peter McGarry	Colooney	"
Michl OHara	Co Sligo	"
James "	" "	"
Edwd "	" "	"
Payton Farrell	Boyle	"
Patt Fox	"	"
Mark McGowan	Carney	"
Thos "	"	"
Con. Hart	Co Fermanagh	"
James McMorrow	Sligo	"
Alexr Martin	Sligo	"
Wm Chambers	Leitrim	"
Edwd Chambers	"	"

A List of passengers from Londonderry to New York, on the ship *American*, sworn at Londonderry, 31 March, 1804.

Patk McKay	aged 40	of Moghera	Farmer
Alexr "	21	"	"
Nancy "	40	"	———
Thomas Bradley	20	"	"
John Dougherty	20	Ballyarlin	"
James Parks	28	Rushbank	Gentleman
Thomas McGomeray	19	Londonderry	Clerk
Captain Sterling	25	New York	Mariner
James Bond	18	Londonderry	Clerke
John Clyde	13	Rushbank	Servant
Geo Crawford	19	Coningham	Farmer
Robert Johnston	20	Nn Cumber	"
Thos Ramsey	21	Ballyauret	"
Gerard Twine	23	Nn Stewart	"
Owen McGlenhy	34	Cumber	Labourer
Mary McGlenhy	32	"	———
John Donaghy	41	Ennishowin	Labourer
James Dougherty	39	Nn Limavady	"
Elenor Dougherty	38	Nn Limavaddy	
James Patterson	25	Desartmarten	Farmer
Alexr McDonald	19	Moneymore	Labourer
Hugh Ramsay	29	"	"
Alexr "	23	"	"

James Dougherty aged	29	Moneymore	Tanner?
William Donaghy	48	"	Farmer
John "	19	"	"
Alex "	24	"	"
Sarah "	39	"	
William McLaughlin	50	Cain	Farmer
John McLoughlin	28	"	"
Alexr "	25	"	"
Mary "	48	"	"
James Buchannon	35	"	Labourer
William Miller	28	Nn Clinavady	Servant
Alex Dougherty	35	Magilligan	Labourer

A List of Passengers intending to go by the British Brig *Alexis*, of Greenock, to Wilmington, North Carolina, sworn 29 March, 1804.

Hu. McNight	40	Near Belfast	Farmer
Jas "	54	" "	"
Batty "	36	" "	"
Margt "	age uncertain	" "	
John "	child	" "	
Batty " junr	"	" "	
Eliza "	"	" "	
James Flanagan	uncertain	Dundalk	Labourer
James Gordon	"	"	Farmer
Hu Wilson	"	"	"
Thos Gormen	"	Creggans	Labourer
Wm Greyson		"	"
Oliver Plunket	"	"	"
Michael Mackay	"	Cullaville	"
Terence Murphy	"	Carricknacross	"
Willm Vance	"	"	"
Patrick Fenor	"	"	"

Indorsed from Newry.

A List of Passengers from Sligo to New York, sworn 29 March, 1804.

Wm Jeffers	Loghadill	Farmer
Alex Griffith	"	"
John Hodman	"	"
Geo Taylor	"	Labourer
Robt Griffith	"	"
Jno Low	Moghean	"
Robt Elliott	"	"
Archd "	"	"
David Ellis	Tilton	Farmer
Thos Armstrong	"	"
Andw Taylor	"	Labourer
Geo Young	"	"
Michl Farrill	"	"
Jno McMorrow	Cloghfin	"
Peter Brady	"	"
Jno Carty	Ardnaston	"
Patt McDonogh	Ardnastran	"

And^{w} McNossen	Ardnastran	Clerk
Mc Donogher	"	Labourer
James "	"	"
" McDonogher jun	"	"
Robt Cracy	Loghfin	"
Edwd Crawford	"	"
Ben Caffry	"	"
Jas Caffuny	"	"
Wm Vaugh	"	Clerk
Henry Dowler	Barton	"
Jno Duffy	"	Labourer
Hugh Crawford	"	"
Thos Pattinson	"	"
Hugh Davis	"	"

List of Passengers of the Ship *Susan*, of and for New York, sworn at Dublin, 28 March, 1804.

Patrick Glenning aged	22	Fair, Monasterever, Kildare, Labourer
Mary "	24	" " " Spinster
Michael Cawlin	23	Dark, Nober, Meath, Labourer
Mary Kenny	36	" Dublin, Married
Edward Donagan	21	Fair, Connotwood, Queens Co^{y}, Labourer
Michael Branghill	30	Sallow, Bala Braughin, Kings County, Labourer
Eliza Fullard	26	Fair, Edenderry, Kings Co^{y}., Spinster
Frances Fullard	11	" " " " "
Jane Fullard	10	" " " " "
Nicholas Caffrey	21	Light, Monastereven, Kildare, Farmer
Patrick Wogan	20	Fair, Dublin, Gentleman
Good Rhind	23	Light, " "
Keeron Carrill	23	" " Servant
Thomas Durm	28	Dark, Bala Braughen, Kings Co^{y}., Labourer
Michael Taylor	38	Sandy, Dublin, Labourer
Thomas Matland	21	Light, Dunlavan, Wicklow, Labourer
Anne Matland	56	Dark, " " Married
Mary Ann Matland	20	Fair " " Spinster
James Barry	23	Fair, Dublin, Gentleman
Edward McDermott	30	Dark, " "
Robert Dyas	19	Light, Kings Court, Cavan, Gentleman
James Gore	26	Sandy, Dublin, Gentleman
James Yates	34	" Newry "
Joseph Dempsey	18	Fair, Upper Wood, Queens Co^{y}., Servant
Judith Campbell	25	Brown, Knockmack, Meath, Married
Jane Hyres	30	" Drogheda, Married
Mark Kelly	30	" Monastereven, Kildare, Farmer
Mary Kelly	30	" " " Married
John Foran	35	Sandy " " Labourer
Simon Donnolly	22	Dark, Naas " "
Luke Toole	28	Fair, Donnybrook, Dublin, Clerk
William Christian	25	Fair, Dublin, Labourer
Nicholas Hobart	30	Dark, Mullingar, Meath, Labourer
Michael Murthe	25	Lurganlyseen, South, Labourer

PASSENGER LISTS TO AMERICA.

Communicated by GERALD FOTHERGILL, Esq., of New Wandsworth, London, England.

A List of Passengers to Philadelphia on board the *Brothers* of Philadelphia, sworn at Londonderry, 14 April, 1804.

Margaret Osburn	aged 27	Spinster,	Omagh, Tyrone
Thom Thompson	23	Farmer,	Castlefin, Donegal
Ann Hearney	35	Spinster,	Dungiven, Derry
Pat[k] "	12	Child	" "
John "	9	"	" "
Biddy "	7	"	" "
Nanny "	4	"	" "
Noble Young	22	Farmer,	Pethgow, Fermanagh
Ja[s] "	21	Labourer	" "
Sarah "	50	Spinster	" "
J Hibran	30	Labourer,	Castlefin, Donegal
Jo[s] "	22	"	" "
Jane Himton*	35	Spinster	" "
Ja[s] Boyd	26	Farmer,	Pettigo, Fermanagh
Marg[t] Wishart	21	Spinster	" "
Jas "	51	Labourer,	Dungannon, Tyrone
Chas Kelly	21	"	Drunmore, "
Hugh "	22	"	Dunmore "
Marg[t] Osburne	27	Spinster,	Omagh, "
Jane "	6	Child	" "
Ja[s] "	4	"	" "
Cha[s] Flanigan	34	Labourer,	Ballyshannon, Donegal
Mary Flanigan	28	Spinster	" "
Jn[o] "	6	Child	" "
Hu Kelly	30	Labourer	" "
Jn[o] Kane	24	"	" "
Ja[s] Boyle	40	"	" "
W[m] Robinson	32	"	Coloraine, Derry
Ann "	22	Spinster,	Innishannon, Donegal
John Doherty	30	Labourer	" "
Mary "	26	Spinster	" "
Pat M[c]Loughlin	32	Labourer	" "
R M[c]Loughlin	24	"	" "
W[m] Doherty	23	"	" "
Ja[s] "	28	Farmer,	Beet, "
Ja[s] Dunn	24	Farmer,	Beet, "
Mary Dunn	19	Spinster	" "
Ja[s] Porter	35	Farmer	" "

List of Persons who wish to go to Baltimore, sworn 14 April, 1804.

Robert Gibson	aged 28	Farmer,	Dromon, Down
Sarah "	27	———	" "

* This may be intended for Hibran, it is in the same brackets.

Mary Gibson	aged 60	———	Hillsborough, Down
John “	30	Farmer	“ “
David “	28	“	“ “
Ann “	20	———	“ “
Elizabeth “	18	———	“ “
Jane Taggart	40	———	Dromon, “
Ann “	14	———	“ “
Jane “	12	———	“ “
Wm Cotter	28	Labourer,	Ballymona, Antrim
Ann Cotter	26		“ “
Felix Divine	38	Dealer,	Philadelphia, America
Robert Nesbit	40	“	Killinchy, Down
James McCausland	30	Farmer,	Cookstown, Tyrone
Susanna “	28	———	“ “
Alexander Richardson	28	Dealer,	Baltimore, America
Mary Ann “	26	———	“ “
William Greer	25	Dealer	“ “
James Cleland	24	“	Ballymillon, Down
George “	21	Farmer	“ “
William Lindley	20	“	“ “
Robert Lowry	55	Dealer,	Killinchwood, “
Mary Lowry	55	“	“ “
Robert “	26	Farmer	“ “
James “	24	Labourer	“ “
W^{m} “	20	“	“ “
Jane “	18	———	“ “
George Hutton	21	Farmer	“ “
Francis Delap	50	“	Comber “
Alexander “	22	“	“ “
Jane “	50	———	“ “
Jane “	20	———	“ “
Christian “	18	———	“ “
Andrew Morrow	40	Labourer,	Ballyargin “
Jane “	30	———	“ “
Mary Boyd	31	———	Dromon “
Daniel Boyd	34	Farmer	“ “

A List of Passengers who intend going to New York in the American Ship *William and Jane* from Belfast, sworn at Belfast, 14 April, 1804.

John Eaton	aged 30	Farmer,	Tanlagh, Derry
Ja^{s} “	28	“	“ “
Saml “	29	“	“ “
Mary “	25	Spinster	
Mat^{w} Maxwell	25	Gentleman,	Ballooly, Rathfryland, Down
Robt Loughran	23	Labourer,	Near Cookstown, Tyrone
Brizb^{r} “	25	Spinster	“ “
Wm Henderson	21	Farmer,	Raloe near Larne, Antrim
John Lundy	34	“	Near Tandragee, Armagh
Phil^{p} McKevy	25	“	Raloe near Larne, Antrim
Alex^{r} Robb	24	Labourer,	Broadisland “
Wm Alexander	20	“	“ “
Widow Brown	60	Spinster,	Kelleleagh, Down

Marg^t Brown aged	25	Spinster	Kelleleagh, Down
Barbara Brown	18	Spinster,	Killilegh "
John McCulloh	21	Labourer,	Drumbo "
Marg^t Withers	25	Spinster	" "
John Robinson	28	Labourer,	Near Porlavo Archin, Down
John Steen	13	"	Near Coan, Antrim
John Burns	30	"	Drumgolan near R^t Fayland, Down
Denis Doyle	34	"	Drumgolden n^r R^t Fayland, Down
Margt "	34	Spinster	" " "
Mich^l "	27	Labourer	" " "
Eliza "	27	Spinster	" " "
Arthur ONeal	23	Farmer,	Near Castlereagh, Down
Saml Morrison	27	"	Killinchy "
Mary "	25	Spinster	" "
James Rusk	23	Farmer,	Derriaghy near Lisburne
George McCray	20	"	Donerisk n^r Cookstown, Tyrone

A List of Passengers in the American Ship *Jane* of New Bedford for New York, sworn at Dublin, 17 April, 1804.

James Normidge	26	Dark,	Surgeon, Britan Street, Cabin
Mary Normidge his wife aged	19	"	Britan Street, Cabin
George Nalleran	34	"	Clerk, Britan Street, Cabin
Jane Nalleran his wife	26	"	Britan Street, Cabin
Edward Dartnell	27	Fair,	Clerk, Britan Street, Single, Cabin
Catherine Corish	32		James Street, Married, Cabin
Miss Corish	8		" " Cabin
Michael Smith	24	Dark,	Farmer, Clighen, Cavan, Single, Steerage
John Mullahy	22	"	Farmer, Callan, Kilkenny, Single, Steerage
John Shilly	35	"	Farmer, Callan, Kilkenny, Single, Steerage
Denis Finning	25	Fair,	Steerage
Thomas Mahir	21	Dark,	Farmer, Callan, Kilkenny, Married, Steerage
Mary Mahir his wife	22		Callan, Kilkenny, Married, Steerage
infant child			
Patrick Cormack	17	"	Farmer, Callan, Kilkenny, Single, Steerage
William Carty	17	"	Farmer, Barton, A. N., Married, Steerage
Alice White	50		Callan, Kilkenny, Single, Steerage
May White	20		" " " "
Catherine White	22		" " " "
Eleanor White	18		" " " "
Margaret Cormick	20		" " " "
John Rossiter	22	Dark,	Farmer, Wexford, " "
James Rossiter	24	Dark	" " " "
Thomas Bahan	26	Dark,	Clerk, Bride Street, " "

List of Passengers of the American Ship *Mary* of New Bedford to Philadelphia, sworn at Dublin, 17 April, 1804.

Richard Fell	aged 50	Dark,	Merchant, Philadelphia, Married, Cabin
Patrick Kenney	39	"	Clergyman, Lusk, Dublin, Single, Cabin
James R Bainbridge	20	Fair,	Clerk, Bride Street, Single, Cabin
Lawrence Cafsidy	25	Dark,	Clerk, Coombe, Single, Cabin
Oliver W Stone	22	Fair	" Largan, Armagh, Single, Cabin
Elizabeth Hudson	22		Grafton St., Single, Cabin
Ann Mullhollan	17		Ballycumber, Kings Co., Single, Cabin
Miss Gordon	17		Philadelphia, Single, Cabin
William Coogan	40	Dark,	Farmer, Pensylvania, Married, Steerage
James Fagan	30	"	Farmer, M^{t}rath [?], Queens Co., Single, Steerage
James McCarty	25	"	Farmer, Wexford, Single, Steerage
Henry Byrne	30	"	" " " "
Owen Garter	26	"	" M^{c}rath " "
William Power	28	"	" Fitthind, Tippe^{y}, Single, Steerage
Mathew Daily	25	"	Farmer, Kilkullen, Kildare, Single, Steerage
Thomas Daily	23	"	Farmer, Kilkullen, Kildare, Single, Steerage
Edward Gumen	35	"	Farmer, Ruihale, Queens Co., Single, Steerage
Mathew Boyn	30	"	Labourer, Kildare, Single, Steerage
Catherine Daily	22		Kilkullen, Single, Steerage
William Gathan	10	child	Dublin, Single, Steerage
Mary Fagan	25		M^{c}rath, Married, Steerage
Robert Dickinson	30	Dark,	Farmer, Wickton, Married, Steerage
Rose Dickinson his wife	25		"
Patrick Kogan	30	Dark	" Barris in Opary, Single, Steerage
Anthony Hagdon	25	"	Barris in Opary, Single, Steerage
Ann Field Porter	20	"	" " " " "

A List of Passengers on the American Ship *President* of New Bedford from Newry for New Castle in America, sworn 21 April, 1804.

Edward Lynch	22	Armagh,	Labourer
Robt Frances	30	Cavan,	Farmer
Jane Frances	28	"	
Mary Frances	2	"	
Marg^{t} Farley	20	"	
Wm Gilmor	54	"	Labourer
Jane Gilmore	50	"	
Frances "	21	"	
James "	19	"	Labourer

Rose Gilmore	17	Cavan,	
Jourdan "	16	"	
Bartley Hart	17	"	
Andw McQuillan	40	"	Farmer
Margt McMullen	41	Cavan	
John McMullen	20	"	Farmer
Saml "	13	"	
Wm Wright	40	"	Labourer
David Ferguson	54	Armagh	"
Robt "	25	Down,	Farmer
Wm "	21	"	"
Hugh "	19	"	"
Jas "	16	"	"
Eliza "	14	"	
Jas McBride	aged 37	Down,	Farmer
Wm McBride	22	"	"
Sarah "	10	"	
Jas Lard	30	Armagh	"
Margt "	31	"	
Jane "	8	"	
Sarah "	2	"	
Jas Murphy	36	"	"
Mary "	30	"	
James "	5	"	

A List of the Passengers for Philadelphia on the American Ship *Commerce,* sworn 28 April, 1804.

Hugh Jelly	35	Labourer,	Loughinisland, Down
Hugh Thomson	36	"	Kilmore "
Joseph Lindsey	33	"	Sea Patrick "
James Beck	30	Farmer,	Ashegarg "
John Beck	25	"	" "
Margt Bock	24	Spinster	" "
Thomas Kilpatrick	37	Farmer,	Kellead, Antrim
Patt Cunningham	30	"	Loughinisland, Down
Sarah Mitchell	25	Spinster	" "
Wm McGowan	35	Farmer,	Dunmurray, Antrim
John Gordon	36	"	Keddy, Armagh
Willm Dinwiddie	40	"	Dunaghy, Antrim
Geo Logan	30	Labourer,	Killinchy, Down
Geo Logan jr	25	"	" "
Robt McCaughty	25	Farmer,	Cammoney, Antrim
Jane "	20	Spinster	" "
Isaac Dickey	20	Farmer,	Magheragill, Down
Anne Stewart	18	Spinster,	Belfast, Antrim
Thos Stevenson	21	Farmer,	Dunaghy, Antrim
John Douglass	38	"	Seaford, Down
Mary Douglass	38	Spinster	" "
Agniss McAfee	20	"	Belfast, Antrim
Geo Martin	35	Farmer,	Blaris, Down
John Shery	34	"	" "
Patrick McCarroll	26	"	Augher, Tyrone

John Duross	21	Farmer,	Dublin
Francis ONeill aged	27	Labourer	"
Emelia ONeill	22	Spinster	"
Rich[d] Courtney	25	Farmer,	Clough, Dublin
Margt Courtney	24	Spinster	" "
Mathew Bailie	48	Farmer	" "
Eliza "	46	Spinster	" "
Stewart "	20	Farmer	" "
Matty "	18	Spinster	" "
William Ferris	25	Farmer,	Ballymina, Antrim
Ann " his wife	32	Spinster	" "

A list of Passengers in the American Ship *Diligence* of New Bedford for New York, sworn at Dublin, 30 April, 1804.

Richard Despard aged	25	Married, Fair, New York, an American, Cabin, Merchant
Mary his wife	28	Married, Fair, Cabin
James M[c]Annally	47	" " Old Merion, Dublin, Cabin, Merchant
Thomas Taylor	25	Single, Light, Bellywater, Wexford, Steerage, Farmer
William Berford	19	Single, Dark, Bellywater, Wexford, Steerage, Farmer
Thomas Price	24	Married, Fair, Dublin, Steerage, Labourer
Hanoia his wife	17	" Yellow " "
Mary Doland	26	Single, Dark, Mountrath, Servant to M[rs] Despard
Geo Reynolds	50	Married, Fair, St. Margaret, Dublin, Steerage, Farmer
Mary his wife	40	Dark, St. Margaret, Dublin, Steerage
Jonathan son	9	Single, Fair, St. Margaret, Dublin, Steerage
Thomas son	7	" " " " "
Eliza their daughter	5	" " " " "
William Davison	28	Married, Sandy, Laiterbeag, Cavan, Steerage, Farmer
Mary his wife	28	Married, Brown, Laiterbeag, Cavan, Steerage
William their son	5	Single, Fair " " "
Edward "	4	" " " " "
Easter Brown	20	" " Servant to M[r] Davison
Betsy M[c]Mullin	60	Widow, Dark, Caverhalman, Cavan, Steerage
Jane her daughter	28	Single, Dark " " "
Fany M[c] M[c]Mullin	18	Single, Fair " " "
(Query if these last three are also servants to M[r] Davison)		
Henry Sheilds	30	Married, Dark, Kings Court, Cavan, Steerage, Farmer
Ann his wife	29	Married, Dark, Kings Court, Cavan, Steerage
James Higgins	27	Single, Dark, Caverhalman, Steerage, Farmer
John Brady	27	" " " " "
John M[c]Mullin	50	Married, Fair, Pattle, Cavan, Steerage, Farmer
Mary his wife	50	" " " " "
Jonathan their son	20	Single " " " "
William " "	18	" " " " "

Thomas their son	16	Single, Fair,	Pattle,	Cavan,	Steerage		
Andrew " "	13	"	"	"	"	"	
Easter their daughter	9	"	"	"	"	"	
Alexandrew M^c^Mullin	22	Married "	"	"	"	"	Farmer
Barbara his wife	22	"					
Patrick Redmond	47	"	Dark,	Baley,	Wexford,	Farmer	
Bridget his wife	35	"	"	"	"		
Jonathan their son	12	Single, Fair		"	"		
Nicholas "	10	"	"	"	"		
Eliz daughter	7	"	"	"	"		
Bridget "	5	"	"	"	"		

PASSENGER LISTS TO AMERICA.

Communicated by GERALD FOTHERGILL, Esq., of New Wandsworth, London, England.

A List of Passengers who have contracted to take their passage to Baltimore on board the Ship *Serpent* of Baltimore, burthen 280 tons, Arch[d] McCorkell, master, sworn at the Custom House, Londonderry, 5 May, 1804.

Charles Cochran aged	24	Farmer,	Fermanagh
Elizabeth "	24	Spinster	"
Henry "	3	Child	"
John Irvin	21	Farmer,	Drunhing
Charlotte Irvin	45	Spinster	"
Andrew McGee	21	Farmer,	Killygordon
William Brandon	21	Labourer,	Crumlin
Henry "	20	"	"
Gerard "	18	"	"
James "	16	Farmer	"
John "	14	Labourer	"
Mary "	18	Spinster	"
Edward "	15	Labourer	"
Isabella "	10	Spinster	"
Christopher "	8	Child	"
Mary "	40	Spinster	"
Thomas "	4	Children,	"
Jane "	6		
Oliver McCausland	22	Farmer,	Omagh
Thomas Harvey	22	"	"
James Davis	26	"	Dungannon
Margaret Davis	25	Spinster	"
Samuel Scott	60	Farmer,	Cosquin
Ann Scott	69	Spinster	"
Rebecca Scott	30	"	"
Francis Scott	22	"	"
Ann Scott	20	"	"
Samuel Scott	28	Farmer	"
Jane Carter	30	Spinster	"
John Carter	35	Farmer	"
John Johnston	22	"	Ardshaw
James McColley	19	Labourer,	Linamore
Stephen Johnston	21	"	Adderny
John Ball	36	Farmer,	Higham
Prudence Ball	30	Spinster	"
Edward Ball	14	Labourer	"
John Ball	12	"	"
John Doherty	21	Farmer,	Clonmany
George Doherty	21	"	"

A muster roll of Passengers to go on board the Brigantine *Sally*, Timothy Clifton, Master, for New York, Burthen 156 tons, Port of Newry, sworn 9 May, 1804.

Wm McBerney	35	Diamary,	Down,	Farmer
Alice McBerney	32	"	"	
Three children under	5	"	"	
David Kelly	36	"	"	"
Mary "		"	"	
Six children under	10	"	"	
Eliza Martin	30	Killevey,	Armagh	
James McCrum	30	Tynan	"	
Sarah "	30	"	"	
Two children under	4	"	"	

Richard Stewart			Tynan,	Armagh,	Labourer
John Famister	aged	30	Armagh,	Farmer	
Ann	"	22	"		
Jane	"	25			
Robt Kinmar		25	Keady,	Armagh,	Labourer

Roll of Passengers by the Brig *Jefferson* of Newberry Port in the U. S. A., Burthen 138 tons, bound from Ballyshannon to New Castle and Philadelphia, Daniel Kmight, Master, sworn 10 May, 1804.

Francis Maquire	aged	38	Barony of Lurg,	Fermanagh,		Sandy,	Labourer
Bridget		36	"	"	"	Dark	
Edward Thompson		34	"	"	"	Fair	"
John "		24	"	"	"	Dark	"
Mary "		22	"	"	"	Fair	
Edward "	junr	8	"	"	"	"	"
Patt Conolly		33	Resinuer,	Leitrim,		Dark	"
Rose "		31	"	"		"	
Charles Stephenson		29	Firehugh,	Donegal,	Farmer		
John Stephenson		27	"	"	"		
Margaret Stephenson		22	Firehugh,	Donegal,	Fair		
Thomas Diver		25	"	"	Fair,	Chapman,	Cabin
Mary Diver		26	"	"	"		"
Robert Johnson		15	Donegal		"	Clerk	"
William Stephenson		20	"		"	Farmer	
John Connor		20	Drumcliffe,	Sligo,	Dark,	Labourer	
Francis Cullin		16	Resinner,	Leitrim,	Sallow	"	
Hugh McPartlan		23	Ballyshannon,		Dark	"	
Mary "		22	"		Fair		
Daniel Tiffany		24	Resinuer,	Leitrim	Fair	"	

List of Passengers in the *William and Mary* of New York, burthen 420 tons, to sail from Londonderry to New York, sworn at Londonderry, 18 May, 1804.

James Crawford	aged	45	Farmer,	Kinnaty
John Robinson		40	"	Omagh
Jane "		36	"	"
Robt "		20	"	"
Joseph "		18	Labourer	"
James "		11	"	"
John Robinson		16	Farmer,	"
Mary "		7	Spinster	"
Barber "		5	"	"
Ann "		3	"	"
Henry Mills		35	Farmer,	Ballogrey
James Fulton		30	Farmer,	Umagh
Patrick McNamee		25	Labourer,	Augher
Joseph Gray		40	Farmer	"
Hugh Doherty, senr		38	Labourer	"
Hugh " junr		16	"	"
John "		14	"	"
Unity "		32	Spinster	"

Elinor Doherty	19	Spinster,	Augher
John Caldwell	30	Farmer	"
Elizabeth "	29	Spinster	"
James "	·9	Farmer	"
Elizabeth "	7	Spinster	"
Jane "	17	"	"
Thomas "	30	Farmer	"
John Crawford	28	"	"
Elizabeth Caldwell	29	Spinster	"
Isabella "	13	Spinster	"
Joseph "	11	Farmer	"
Joseph "	9	"	"
Isabella "	7	Spinster	"
Alex[r] "	10	Farmer	"
Jane "	7	Spinster	"
Joseph Watt	30	Farmer	"
Patrick M[c]Canne	24	Labourer	"
Joseph Lowther	24	"	"
Thomas Quin	25	"	Hollyhill
Edw[d] Divin	24	"	"
James Hargan	25	"	"
John Mulheron	26	"	"
Sarah Gray	30	Spinster,	Shabane
Boshale Gray	28	Labourer,	N. Town Stewart
Neal Crosby	24	"	"
John Rodgers	21	"	"
Robert Rodgers	23	"	"
James M[c]Divitt	24	"	"
William Trevine	27	"	"
Sam[l] M[c]Mellan	24	"	"
Robert Willson	24	Labourer	"
Robert M[c]Cay	24	"	"
John Read	25	"	Bollindret
Alex[r] Hunter	21	"	"
Robt "	19	"	"
John Ross	26	"	New York
John King	32	"	"
Susanna Armstrong	38	Spinster,	Carns
Mary Armstrong	23	"	"
John "	18	Labourer	"
James M[c]Guire	30	"	"
John Getty	50	"	Loughinwale
Abigail "	45	Spinster	"
James "	26	Labourer	"
Robert Adems	45	"	"
Elizabeth "	45	Spinster	"
John Adems	15	Labourer	"
Archebald Adems	12	"	"
Mary "	10	Spinster	"
Elizabeth "	8	"	"
Martha "	6	"	"

PASSENGER LISTS TO AMERICA.

Communicated by GERALD FOTHERGILL, Esq., of New Wandsworth, London, England.

List of Passengers on Board the American Ship *Mechanic* of Baltimore, Peter Thorn, Master, from Dublin to Baltimore, Navigated with ten men, 203 tons burden, sworn 28 May, 1804.

Benjamin Clegg	22, Single,	Fair, Stradbally, Queens Co., Cabin, gent
George Clegg	26, Single,	Dark, Stradbally, Queens Co., Cabin, gent

Rev Matthew Ryan	60,	Single,	Fair, Dublin, Steerage, Clergyman
James Carney	56,	Married,	Dark, Athy, Kildare Co., Steerage, Farmer
Mary Carney	50,	Married,	Fair, Athy, Kildare, Steerage, Farmer
Thomas Carney	30,	Single,	“ “ “ “ “
John Carney	20	“	“ “ “ “ “
Nicholas Carney	19	“	“ “ “ “ “
Martin Carney	11	“	“ “ “ “ “
Elinor Carney	16	“	“ “ “ “ “
Ellen Dobbyn	20	“	Fair, Stradbally, Queens Co., Steerage, Farmer
William Rogers	30	“	Brown, St. Margarets, Dublin, Steerage, gent
John Hay	23	“	Fair, Newry, Down, Steerage, gent
George Reynolds	42,	Married,	Brown, St. Margarets, Dublin, Steerage, gent
Mary Reynolds	—	Married,	Fair, St. Margarets, Dublin, Steerage
Matthew Christian	22,	Single,	Brown, Borris, Queens Co., Steerage, Labourer.

List of Passengers who have contracted to take their passage on board the Ship *Duncan* of Whitehaven, Burthen 238 tons, Abraham Sebson, Master, for New York, sworn at Londonderry, 26 May, 1804.

George Cuthbert	35,	Labourer,	Coleraine
James Alcorn	40	“	Glenvenogh, co. Donegal
Michael “	16	“	“ “ “
John “	17	“	“ “ “
Mary Gallagher	35,	Spinster	“ “ “
Ann Cuthbert	13	“	“ “ “
Fanny Cuthbert	12	“	“ “ “
John Coyle	20,	Farmer	“ “ “
James McCaran	20	“	“ “ “
Edward McCaran	22	“	“ “ “
James Todd	19,	Labourer,	Largilly
John Gibson	19	“	Ballycloy
Thomas Paul	20	“	County Down
George Elliot	24,	Farmer	“ “
James Gamble	25	“	Donaghady, co. Tyrone
Samuel Patterson	26,	Labourer,	“ “ “
George Watson	29	“	“ “ “
William Sanderson	35	“	Langfield “ “
Margaret “	18,	Spinster	“ “ “
Sidney “	28	farmer	“ “ “
James Davitt	24,	Farmer,	Astraw “ “
Patrick McGawly	26,	Labourer,	Urney “ “
John Ginn	28	“	Drumceeran “ “
Margaret “	26,	Spinster	“ “ “
Jane “	20	“	“ “ “
Ann “	50	“	“ “ “
Matthew Gibson	38	Farmer	“ “ “
Eliza “	28	Spinster	“ “ “
Fanny Gibson	18	Spinster	“ “ “

Charles Johnston	38,	Labourer,	Co. Fermanagh
Ann Johnston	26,	Spinster,	" "
Thomas Keys	24,	Farmer,	Magheramny
Eliza Keys	20,	Spinster	"
Francis Crow	22,	Labourer	"
Richard Guthrie	34,	Labourer	"
James Crozier	22	"	Dromash
James Brisland	26,	Farmer,	County Tyrone
Margaret Woods	28,	Spinster,	Lissenderry

A List of Passengers intending to go by the American Brig *Ceres* of New York, Herbert Forrester, Master, from Newry for New York, sworn 31 May, 1804.

Robert Tronson	17,	Newtown, Hamilton,	gent
Thomas Hanlon	26,	Armagh	Farmer
Judith "	26	"	
Joseph Love	23	"	Labourer
Rose Love	18	"	
John Peebbes	43	Hamiltonsbawn,	gent
Ann "	37		
Marg^t^ "	14		
Sarah "	9		
Annebella "	5		
Mary Jane "	Infant		
Ann Murry	26,	Fivemiletown	
Betsy "	23		
Mary Patterson	34,	Lisdromore	
Patt M^c^Conell	24,	Moy,	Labourer
Ketty "	22		

A List of Passengers intended to be taken on board the Ship *Live Oak* of Scarboro, Christopher Dyer, Master, burthen 400 tons, bound to New York in America, sworn at Londonderry, 23 June, 1804.

Henry Wilson	24,	Farmer,	Dungannon
Jane "	20,	his Wife	"
Mary "	2 mo^s^,	Child	"
Mark M^c^Quillan	21,	Farmer,	Nughnacloy
William Pedin	22,	Labourer,	Nughadown, Derry
William Davidson	20	"	Nughnacloy
Susan Greer	40,	Married,	Cookstown
Sarah "	20,	Spinster	"
Susan "	15	"	"
Mary "	14	"	"
Hannah "	12	"	"
Anna "	7	"	"
Joseph "	4,	Child	"
Sarah Dougal	20,	Servant Girl	"
John Webb	50,	Farmer	"
John Webb	19	"	"
Susan "	16,	Spinster	"
Janet "	44,	Married	"

Thomas Webb	15,	Farmer	Cookstown
Maria "	10,	Spinster,	"
Jane "	5	"	"
Alas "	8	"	"
William Hannah	22,	Labourer,	Armagh
John Hannah	20	"	Newtown Stewart
William Patrick	19	Farmer	" "
Samuel Steel	16	"	" "
Jane Patrick	18,	Spinster	" "
Nancy "	4 mo^{s},	Child	" "
Alex^{r} McKeever	21,	Labourer,	Gortin, N. Stewart
David Anderson	20	"	" "
Alex Irvine	21	"	" "
James Russell	22	"	Dunnamany
Elizabeth Russell	22,	Married	"
Isabella "	5 mo^{s},	Child	"
James Sands	26,	Labourer,	Cranah, Moneymore
Mary "	26,	Married	" "
Robert "	7,	Child	" "
John "	5	"	" "
Ellen "	1	"	" "
Mary "	22,	Spinster	" "
Jo Hunter	45,	Farmer	Gortmurry, Moneymore
William McKeon	23	"	Lisabany, Moneymore
Ann "	24,	Spinster	" "
William Blair	20,	Farmer,	N. Lemevady
John Murdock	20	"	Glass Lough, Monaghan
Patrick Gallagher	21,	Labourer,	Furmeny, Omagh
John "	22	"	" "
John McQuin	15	"	Cookstown
Ann "	17,	Spinster	"
Ostin Allen	19,	Farmer	"
James Crooks	60	"	"
Jane Crooks	50,	Married	"
Mary Crook	20,	Spinster	"
Margaret Crooks	18	"	"
Saml "	17,	Farmer	"
John Crooks	16	"	"
Sarah Crooks	14,	Spinster	"
James Crooks	12,	Farmer	"
Benjam Crooks	11	"	"
James Crooks	6,	Child	"
Alex^{r} McKeon	20,	Labourer,	Lisabany, Moneymore
John McCue	20	"	Ternamenter, Tyrone
James Walker	54	"	Dromagalagh
Wm Dick	30	"	Kilane Ceepeyt, near Ballymena
Samuel Gault	30	"	Kilane, etc.
Samuel Reed	30,	Farmer,	Castledaunt, n^{r} N. Stewart
Alex "	28	"	" " "
William "	23	"	" " "

PASSENGER LISTS TO AMERICA

Communicated by Gerald Fothergill of New Wandsworth, London, England

Roll of Passengers to be received on Board the Ship *Catherine* of Dublin, 170 Tons Burthen as per Register, George Thomas, Master, now in the Port of Killybegs and bound for New Castle & Philadelphia. Sworn at Ballyshannon 9 June 1804

John Conyngham of Monargin in Killybegs, Donegal Dark age 55 Farmer Hold
Isabella Conyngham of Monargin in Killybegs, Donegal Dark age 49 Hold
William Conyngham of Monargin in Killybegs, Donegal Fair age 26 Labourer Hold
Isabella Conyngham of Monargin in Killybegs, Donegal Dark age 23 Hold
Alexr Conyngham of Monargin in Killybegs, Donegal Fair age 21 Labourer Hold
Jas Conyngham of Monargin in Killybegs, Donegal Fair age 18 Labourer Hold
John Conyngham of Monargin in Killybegs, Donegal Fair age 15 Labourer Hold
Catherine Conyngham of Monargin in Killybegs, Donegal Fair age 12 Hold
George Conyngham of Monargin in Killybegs, Donegal Dark age 40 Schoolmaster Hold
Andrew Conyngham of Lochris in Mishue, Donegal Dark age 34 Farmer
Elitia Conyngham of Lochris in Mishue, Donegal Fair age 34 Hold
John Conyngham of Lochris in Mishue, Donegal Fair age 12 Hold
Andrew Conyngham of Lochris in Mishue, Donegal Fair age 6 Hold
Robt Johnston of Donegal Fair age 15 Cabin
Robt Henderson of Lochris in Mishue, Donegal Dark age 45 Farmer Hold
Elenor Henderson of Lochris in Mishue, Donegal Dark age 44 Hold
Elenor Henderson of Lochris in Mishue, Donegal Dark age 18 Hold
Jane Henderson of Lochris in Mishue, Donegal Dark age 15
Prudence Henderson of Lochris in Mishue, Donegal Dark age 13 Hold
George Henderson of Lochris in Mishue, Donegal Dark age 11 Hold

Ann Henderson of Lochris in Mishue, Donegal Dark age 8 Hold
Alexr Henderson of Lochris in Mishue, Donegal Fair age 6 Hold
Arthur Fawcet of Lochris in Mishue, Donegal Fair age 19 Labourer Hold
John Porter of Lochris in Mishue, Donegal Dark age 43 Farmer Hold
Elitia Porter of Lochris in Mishue, Donegal Dark age 44 Hold
Catherine Porter of Lochris in Mishue, Donegal Dark age 22 Hold
William Porter of Lochris in Mishue, Donegal Fair age 20 Labourer Hold
Alexr Porter of Lochris in Mishue, Donegal Fair age 18 Hold
William Harran of Carrick East, Drumhome, Donegal Black age 37 Farmer Hold
Elizabeth Harran of Carrick East, Drumhome, Donegal Dark age 37 Hold
Ann Harran of Carrick East in Drumhome, Donegal Dark age 15 Hold
Jane Harran of Carrick East in Drumhome, Donegal Dark age 13 Hold
John Harran of Carrick East in Drumhome, Donegal Dark age 10 Hold
Alexr Harran of Carrick East in Drumhome, Donegal Fair age 7 Farmer(?) Hold
Matthew Brown of Carrick East in Drumhome, Donegal Dark age 18 Labourer Hold
William Harran of Carrick Breeny in Drumhome, Donegal Dark age 37 Farmer Hold
Jane Harran of Carrick Breeny in Drumhome, Donegal Fair age 32 Hold
Barbara Harran of Carrick Breeny in Drumhome, Donegal Fair age 11 Hold
Jane Harran of Carrick Breeny in Drumhome, Donegal Fair age 8 Hold
Thos Grier of Big Park in Drumhome, Donegal Dark age 30 Hold
Jane Grier of Big Park in Drumhome, Donegal Fair age 23 Hold
John McCrea of Lignanornan in Drumhome, Donegal Black age 24 Labourer Hold
Cath Fawcett of Mt Charles Inver in Drumhome, Donegal Dark age 21 Hold
Elinor Devenny of Benro in Killartie, Donegal Fair age 27 Hold
Archd Scott of Tullymore in Misheel, Donegal Black 26 Farmer Hold
Elenor Scott of Tullymore in Misheel, Donegal Dark age 29 Hold
Wm Scott of Ardara in Killybegs, Donegal Dark 20 Labourer Hold
Jas McDade of Killarhel in Misheel, Donegal Fair age 22 Labourer Hold
Andw Lamon of Ardegat in Misheel, Donegal Black 18 Labourer Hold
Patt Kennedy of Meenhallu in Killymard, Donegal Dark age 52 Farmer Hold
Susan Kennedy of Meenhallu in Killymard, Donegal Dark age 52 Hold
Edward Kennedy of Meenhallu in Killymard, Donegal Dark age 24 Hold
John Kennedy of Meenhallu in Killymard, Donegal Dark age 19 Labourer Hold
Patrick Kennedy of Meenhallu in Killymard, Donegal age 16 Labourer Hold
James Kennedy of Meenhallu in Killymard, Donegal Fair age 13 Labourer Hold

Charles Kennedy of Meenhallu in Killymard, Donegal Fair age 11 Hold
Biddy McCafferty of Meenhallu in Killymard, Donegal Dark age 20 Hold
Danl Sheerin of Ardara in Killybegs, Donegal Dark age 24 Hold
Michl Carlain of Killybegs, Donegal Dark age 26 Hold
Geo Maxwell of Raferty in Killartie, Donegal Dark age 24 Hold
Jas Syms of Bractcla in Killartie, Donegal Dark age 45 Farmer Hold
Mary Syms of Bractcla in Killartie, Donegal Fair age 40 Hold
Samuel Syms of Bractcla in Killartie, Donegal Fair age 6 Hold
Elizabeth Syms of Bractcla in Killartie, Donegal Fair age 4 Hold
Tera Allis of Drimahy in Done, Donegal Fair age 30 Hold
James Allis of Drimahy in Done, Donegal Fair age 14 Labourer Hold
Owen McGloghlin of Glen, Donegal Dark age 29 Farmer Hold
Nelly McGloghlin of Glen, Donegal Dark age 30 Hold
——— McGloughlin of Glen, Donegal Dark age 5 Hold
Patt Gillespy of Glen, Donegal Fair age 35 Hold
Pegy Gillespy of Glen, Donegal Fair age 24 Hold
John McClosky of Drimreny in Inver, Donegal Fair age 25 Labourer Hold
Rose McClosky of Drimreny in Inver, Donegal Fair age 19 Hold
John Syms of Glen, Donegal Fair age 30 Hold
Catherine Syms of Glen in Donegal Fair age 21 Hold

PASSENGER LISTS TO AMERICA

Communicated by GERALD FOTHERGILL of New Wandsworth, London, England

PASSENGERS Engaged to Sail on Board the American Brig *Atlantic*, Robert Askins, Master, burden 196 tons, for Boston. Sworn at Dublin 19 June 1804.

Sydenham Davis of Summerhill, Kilkenny, age 20, height 5–2, dark, farmer.
Ralph Morgan of Raheen, Kilkenny, aged 20, height 5–11, sallow, labourer.
Mich[l] Ryan of Thomastown, Kilkenny, age 22, height 5–7, fair, labourer.
John O'Hara of Kilmurray, Kilkenny, age 31, height 5–3, dark, labourer.
Hugh Hefferman of Clonsart, Kings Co., age 22, height 5–6, dark, labourer.
Walter Madigan of Thomastown, Kilkenny, age 35, height 6, fair, labourer.
Catherine Madigan of Thomastown, Kilkenny, age 28, his wife.
And[w] Shortell of Thomastown, Kilkenny, age 21, height 5, dark, labourer.
Danl Nowlan of Tullow, Carlow, age 21, height 5–10, dark, clerk.
John Boulger of Dublin, age 36, height 5–5, dark, labourer.
Catherine Boulger of Dublin, age 36, his wife.
Saml Duke of Thomastown, Kilkenny, age 21, height 5–5, dark, labourer.
Martin Switzer of Navan, Meath, age 28, height 5–10, fair, labourer.
James Maxwell of Dublin, age 20, height 5–8, dark, labourer.
William Gorman of Dublin, age 32, height 5–10, dark, clerk.

Additional Passengers engaged to Sail on Board the Brig *Atlantic*, Robert Askins, Master, for Boston. Sworn 26 June 1804.

Wm O'Brien of Dublin, age 20, height 5–6, dark, clerk.
Michael Kane of Dublin, age 25, height 5–6, fair, clerk.
Michael Mallon of Dungannon, Tyrone, age 33, height 5–6, dark, brewer.
*Henry Bowerman, age 40, height 5–8, fair, Lieut. Novascotia Inf'y.
Anthony Kearns of Dunleer, Louth, age 23, height 5–7, dark, labourer.
Andrew Melvin of Bray, Wicklow, age 25, height 5–9, dark, clerk.
Thomas Reynolds of Klena, Longford, age 22, height 5–6, fair, clerk.

List of Passengers for New York on the Ship *Eagle*, Charles Thompson, Master, sworn at Belfast 4 Aug. 1804.

Wm Biggem, farmer, Bushmills. His name was sent in by the High Sheriff, who does not know his age.
Alex Beggs, age 30, height 5–9, farmer, Ballyroban, pale faced.
Margt Beggs, age 30, height 5–9, spinstress, Ballyroban, fair faced, his wife.
Thos Clyde, age 21, height 5–9, farmer, Ballyroban, fair faced.
Wm McQueen, age 39, height 5–8, farmer, Bangor, pockpitted.
Jane McQueen, age 36, height 5–2, spinstress, Bangor, dark colored, his wife.
Jane Robinson, age 26, height 5–5, spinstress, Belfast, fair faced.
John Searight, age 30, height 5–9, farmer, Banbridge, fair faced.
Jane Searight, age 30, height 5–5, spinstres, Banbridge, fair faced.
John Henry, age 18, height 5–6, farmer, Banbridge, fair faced.
Jas Anderson, age 28, height 5–6, farmer, Banbridge, fair faced.
Tho. Norris, age 56, height 5–10, farmer, Belfast, sallow.
Jas. Warden, age 21, height 5–9, labourer, Randalstown, brown.
Robt McCroy, age 30, height 5–7, labourer, Randalstown, fair.
Hu Liddy, age 20, height 5–6, labourer, Randalstown, brown.
David Bell, age 47, height 5–7, farmer, Banbridge, brown.
Patience Bell, age 45, height 5–5, spinstress, Banbridge, brown, his wife, & their child
George Bell, age 16, height 5–3, Banbridge, brown } their sons
Thos. Bell, age 14, height 5–0, Banbridge, brown }
Alex^r Ellis, age 36, height 5–8, farmer, Ballymena, pitted
Margt. Ellis, age 30, height 5–6, spinstress, Ballymena, fair faced, his wife
Jno. Crothers, age 44, height 5–8, farmer, Randalstown, brown
Laifanny Crothers, aged 32, height 5–4, spinstres, Randalstown, fair, his wife
Jenny Crothers, age 68, Randalstown.
Nanny Acheson, age 21, height 5–4, spinstress, Randalstown, fair
Jane Wilson, age 30, height 5–5, spinstress, Randalstown, brown, servant to Lafanny Carrothers
Joseph Warden, age 26, height 5–8, farmer, Randalstown, pitted
James Warden, age 22, height 5–8, farmer, Randalstown, brown.
Robt. Carrothers, age 35, height 5–8, farmer, Randalstown, brown, brother to John Carrothers
William Carrothers, age 29, height 5–7, farmer, Randalstown, brown, brother of John Carrothers
Eliza Carrol, age 22, height 5–4, spinstress, Randalstown, brown, servant to Jenny Carrothers.

* This line has been crossed out in the MS.

Isaiah Young, age 28, height 5–6, farmer, Monaghan, fair.

Henry Hose, age 25, height 5–7, Merchant, a Citizen of the United States of America.

PASSENGER LIST, LIVERPOOL, 1830

PASSENGER LIST, LIVERPOOL, ENGLAND, 1830.—The following list contains the names of passengers who sailed from Liverpool, England, in 1830, on the *Mexico*, 273 tons burden, Actor P. Patterson of Kennebunkport, Maine, captain. The *Mexico* was rebuilt in Liverpool in May and June 1830 in order to carry passengers. The original list is in the possession of the contributor, a granddaughter of Captain Patterson.

The items are in order, name of passenger, age, place of nativity, country from which passenger came, name of nation to which passenger belonged, occupation, description of passenger, and height. In many cases some of these items are omitted in the original copy.

Thomas Reeves, 40, Horn Castle, British, Schoolmaster, Dark, 5 ft. 7½ in.
Mary Reeves, 31, Horn Castle, Engl[and], 5 ft. 3 in.
William Reeves, 13, Horn Castle, Engl[and], British, 4 ft. 7½ in.
John Reeves, 10, Horn Castle, Engl[and], 4 ft. ½ in.
Thomas Reeves, 9, Horn Castle, 4 ft.
Joseph Reeves, 7, Horn Castle, Engl[and], 3 ft. 5 in.
Henery Reeves, 5, Horn Castle, Engl[and], 3 ft. 2 in.
Frederick Reeves, 3, Horn Castle, Engl[and], 2 ft. 7½ in.
Luke Malloy, 24, Nergen [?], Ireland, British, Labourer, Light, 5 ft. 6 in.
John O Connor, 13, Limirick, Ireland, British, Gentelman, 4 ft. 11¼ in.
Thomas Quinn, 11, Limirick, Ireland, British, 4 ft. 8¾ in.
John Quail, 23, Isle Man, England, British, Labourer, Dark, 5 ft. 6¾ in.
Ann Quail, 25, Isle Man, England, British, Light, 5 ft. 8¾ in.
Patrick Quail, 10, Isle Man, England, British, 4 ft. 4 in.
John Quail, 1, Isle Man, England, British, Infant
Ellen Shimmin, 40, Isle Man, England, British, Light, 5 ft. 2 in.
Mary Shimmin, 13, Isle Man, England, British, Light, 5 ft. ¾ in.
Catharine Shimmin, 12, Isle Man, England, British, Light, 5 ft. ¾ in.
William Shimmin, 9, Isle Man, England, British, Light, 4 ft. 5¾ in.
Ellen Shimmin Jr, 6, Isle Man, England, British, Light, 3 ft. 10¾ in.
Ann Shimmin, 4, Isle Man, England, British, Light, 3 ft. 4 in.
John James Shimmin, 2, Isle Man, England, British, Light, 2 ft. 11 in.
Thomas Murphy, 23, Dongennon[?], Ireland, British, Labourer, Light, 5 ft. 6 in.
Jacob Locke, 29, Wilberstone, England, British, Weaver, Light, 5 ft. 8¾ in.
Ann Locke, 37, Wilberstone, England, British, Dark, 4 ft. 9½ in.
Esther Locke, 8, Wilberstone, England, British, Light, 3 ft. 8 in.
Lydia Locke, 7, Wilberstone, Light, 3 ft. 4 in.
Elizabeth Staine, 12, Coventry, Dark, 4 ft. 4½ in.
Mary Ann Staine, 9, Coventry, Dark, 3 ft. 10 in.
Robert Lane, 48, Norwich, Engl[an]d, British, Cabinet Maker, Light, 5 ft. 7 in.
Judith Lane, 51, Norwich, Engl[an]d, British, Dress Maker, Light, 5 ft. 2½ in.
Judith Lane Jr, 26, Norwich, Engl[an]d, British, Dress Maker, Light, 5 ft. 4¼ in.
Charlotte Lane, 20, Norwich, Engl[an]d, British, Dress Maker, Light, 5 ft. 4¼ in.
Robert Lane Jur, 18, Norwich, Engl[an]d, British, Printer, Light, 5 ft. 4 in.
Henery Lane, 16, Norwich, 5 ft. 2½ in.
Walter Lane, 13, Norwich, 4 ft. 11½ in.
Mary Ann Lane, 10, Norwich, 4 ft. 1 in.
Alfred Lane, 8, Norwich, 3 ft. 11 in.
Ann Hill, 28, St Foiths, Engl[an]d, British, School Mistress, Light, 5 ft. 3¼ in.
James Sparrow, 37, Croxtown, Engl[and], British, Weaver, Light, 5 ft. 7½ in.
Ann Sparrow, 46, Dodington, Engl[and], British, Light, 5 ft. 4¾ in.
William Sparrow, 14, N Thorpe, Engl[and], British, Weaver, Light, 5 ft. 1¼ in.
James Bond, 30, Yarmouth, Engl[and], Brit[ish], Hatter, Light, 5 ft. 3½ in.
Matilda Bond, 31, Bungay, Engl[and], Brit[ish], Light, 5 ft. 2¼ in.
George Page, 19, Yarmouth, Engl[and], Brit[ish], Tailor, Light, 5 ft. 9½ in.
Robert Anderson, 34, Derham, England, British, Shoemaker, Dark, 5 ft. 8 in.
Samuel Allen, 46, Norwich, England, British, Wool comer, Dark, 5 ft. 5½ in.
Thomas M. Warrant, 23, Yarmouth, England, British, Braizer, Dark, 5 ft. 8¼ in.
Elizabeth Hoggatt, 36, Loddon, Engl[and], British, Dress maker, Dark, 5 ft. 6 in.
Elizabeth Hoggatt Jr, 13, Loddon, Engl[and], British, Dress maker, Light, 4 ft. 11 in.
William Hoggatt, 13, Loddon, Engl[and], British, Dark, 4 ft. 7½ in.
Samuel Hoggatt, 9, Loddon, Dark, 4 ft. 3 in.
Edward Hoggatt, 2, Loddon, Engl[and], British, Infant
Samuel Ward, 42, Bungay, Engl[and], British, Weaver, Dark, 5 ft. 7 in.
Mary Ward, 44, Norwich, Engl[and], British, Weaver, Light, 5 ft. 1 in.
Mary Bryan, 40, Wexford, Ireland, British, Light, 5 ft. 5¾ in.
Mary Bryan Jr, 9, Wexford, Ireland, British, Light, 4 ft. 2½ in.
Ann Bryan, 7, Wexford, Ireland, British, Light, 4 ft. 1 in.
William Dickins, 20, Sanbrook [?], Engl[and], British, Carpenter, Light, 5 ft. 5¼ in.
John Poole, 20, Soldrop, Engl[and], British, Farmer, Dark, 5 ft. 6¾ in.

George Jarvis, 16, Buckinghamshire, Engl[and], British, Blacksmith, Dark, 5 ft. 5¼ in.
Thomas Nonn, 25, Thornbay, Engl[and], British, Farmer, Light, 5 ft. 10½ in.
Elizabeth Nonn, 23, Litterworth, Engl[and], British, Dark, 5 ft. 5 in.
Patrick Dolan, 25, McGuire Bridge, Ireland, British, Labourer, Light, 5 ft. 9¾ in.
Watkins Jones, 23, Marionethshire, Wales, British, Farmer, Light, 5 ft. 9½ in.
Henery Parry, 23, Clondethshoth[?], Wales, British, Farmer, Dark, 5 ft. 7¾ in.
John Davis, 19, Llanderfel, Wales, British, Carpenter, Dark complective, 5 ft. 8¼ in.
Hugh Jones, 40, Marionshire, Wales, British, Farmer, Dark, 5 ft. 8¼ in.
Jane Jones, 37, Marionshire, Wales, British, Light, 5 ft. 1¾ in.
Susan Jones, 13, Marionshire, Wales, British, Light, 4 ft. 9¼ in.
Hugh Jones Jr., 10, Marionshire, Wales, British, 4 ft. 4 in.
Sarah Parry, 45, Marionshire, Wales, British, 5 ft. 2¼ in.
David Parry, 14, Marionshire, Wales, British, Farmer, 4 ft. 9¼ in.
Edward Parry, 14, Marionshire, Wales, British, Farmer, 4 ft. 10½ in.
Robert Parry, 9, Marionshire, Wales, British, 4 ft. 5 in.
Hugh Perry, 6, Marionshire, Wales, British, 4 ft. 2 in.
Howland Perry, 4, Marionshire, Wales, British, 3 ft. 4 in.
Catherine Henry, 28, Carvan, Ireland, British, Dark, 5 ft. ½ in.
Eleanor Timmins, 21, Carrigan, Ireland, British, Dark, 5 ft. 2 in.
Edward Hawkins, 23, Donnegall, Ireland, British, Labourer, Dark, 5 ft. 4½ in.
Richard Stevens, 33, Cornwall, Engl[and], British, Miner, Dark, 5 ft. 9½ in.
William Owens, 26, Newtown, Engl[and], British, Farmer, Dark, 5 ft. 6 in.
James Cooper, 31, Brighton, Engl[and], British, Farmer, Dark, 5 ft. 8 in.
James Booth, 33, Rochdeal, England, British, Weaver, Light, 5 ft. 7¼ in.
Richard Hamer, 34, Rochdeal, England, British, Weaver, Dark, 5 ft. 6¾ in.
Hannah Hamer, 23, Rochdeal, England, British, Weaver, Light, 5 ft. 5½ in.
Mary Hamer, 2, Rochdeal, England, British, Infant
Joseph Crossley, 34, Rochdeal, England, British, Weaver, Dark, 5 ft. 6¼ in.
John Brown, 48, Paisley, Scotland, British, Weaver, Dark, 5 ft. 4¼ in.
Lawrence Crawford, 43, Paisley, Scotland, British, Weaver, Light, 5 ft. 7¾ in.
Thomas Lomax, 24, Rochdeal, Eng[land], British, Fuller, Light, 5 ft. 7½ in.
Charles Baker, 29, Nottingham, Eng[land], British, Merchant, Dark, 5 ft. 7¼ in.
Margaret Muldown, 30, Longfird, Ireland, British, Dark, 5 ft. 1¾ in.
James Hickey, 25, Longford, Ireland, British, Labourer, Dark, 5 ft. 8½ in.
Michell McColley, 21, Longfird, Ireland, British, Labourer, Dark, 5 ft. 5 in.
Samuel Ross, 33, Barnsley, Eng[land], Brit[ish], Farmer, Light, 6 ft. 1½ in.
Margaret Ross, 30, London, Eng[land], Brit[ish], Dark, 5 ft. 2½ in.
Joseph Wilkinson, 34, Huddersfield, Eng[land], Brit[ish], Cloth Dresser, Dark, 5 ft. 8¾ in.
Craven Cookson, 50, Barnsley, England, British, Weaver, Dark, 5 ft. 7½ in.
Andrew Allen, 47, Alman, Ireland, British, Weaver, Dark, 5 ft. 5¼ in.
John Garibold, 58, Nice, Itally, Farmer, Dark, 5 ft. 2¾ in.
John Garibold Jr, 39, Nice, Itally, organ maker, Dark, 5 ft. 6 in.
Angelino Garibold, 35, Nice, Itally, Cordwainer, Dark, 5 ft. 1½ in.
Dominick Garibold, 27, Nice, Ittally, Farmer, Dark, 5 ft. 8 in.
Augustine Garibold, 43, Nice, Ittally, Musician, Dark, 5 ft. 8¼ in.
John Bogon, 38, Nice, Ittally, Musician, Dark, 5 ft. 4½ in.
Augustine Rook, 31, Genoa, Itally, Farmer, Dark, 5 ft. 5¼ in.
Robert Llewellyn, 28, Bermingham, Engl[and], British, Brass Terner, Dark, 5 ft. 3 in.
Antoni Sinia, 33, Genoa, Itally, Farmer, Dark, 5 ft. 4½ in.

Kennebunkport, Maine. MISS MARY P. LORD.

MISCELLANEOUS LISTS

The following persons embarked for New England in the "Susan and Ellen," April, 1635

Men:	*Women:*	*Women:*
Jo: Atherson, 24.	Grace Bewlie, 30.	Precilla Jarman, 10.
Edmond Gordon, 18.	Ann Blason, 27.	Margaret Leach, 25.
John Jones, 20.	Joan Broomer, 13.	Elizabeth Nicholls, 25.
Wm. Lambart, 26.	Tomazin Carpenter, 35.	Marie Riddlesden, 17.
Thos. Sydlie, 22.	Marie Clifford, 25.	Hanna Smith, 30.
Walter Thornton, 36.	Jane Coe, 30.	Marie Smith, 21.
George Wilby, 16.	Barbara Ford, 16.	Alice Street, 28.
	Ann Fowle, 25.	Elizabeth Swayne, 16.
	Ann Gilson, 34.	

MISS A. H. THWING.

"A LYST OF THE PASINGERS ABORD THE SPEEDWELL OF LONDON, ROBERT LOCK MASTER, BOUND FOR NEW ENGLAND.

Richard Stratton,	aged		Shudrack Hopgood,	aged	14
John Mulfoot,	"		Thomas Goodynough,	"	20
Richard Smith,	"	43	Nathaniel Goodinough,	"	16
Francis Brinsley,	"	22	John Fay,	"	8
Thomas Noyce,	"	32	William Tayler,	"	11
Mathew Edwards,	"		Richard Smith,	"	28
Joseph Boules,	"	47	Muhuhulett Munnings,	"	24
William Brand, (Q) *	"	40	Margarett Mott,	"	12
John Copeland, (Q)	"	28	Henry Reeue,	"	8
Christopher Holder, (Q)	"	25	Henery Seker,	"	8
Thomas Thurston, (Q)	"	34	John Morse,	"	40
Mary Prince, (Q)	"	21	Nickolus Dauison,	"	45
Sarah Gibbons, (Q)	"	21	John Baldwin,	"	21
Mary Weatherhead, (Q)	"	26	Mary Baldwin,	"	20
Dorothy Waugh, (Q)	"	20	Rebeca Worster,	"	18
Lester Smith,	"	24	John Wigins,	"	15
Christopher Clarke,	"	38	John Miller,	"	24
Edward Lane,	"	36	Thomas Home,	"	11
Tho: Richardson,	"	19	John Crane,	"	11
John Earle,	"	17	Charels Baalam,	"	18
Thomas Barnes,	"	20			

"The persons aboue named past from hence [in] the shipp aboue mentioned, and are, according to order, registred heare. Dated, Searchers office, Grauesend, 30th May, 1656.

EDWARD PELLING, }
JOHN PHILPOTT. } *Searchers.*

"Theese were Landed at Boston in N. E. the 27th of the moneth, 1656.

J. E."

PASSENGERS TO NEW-ENGLAND IN 1670.—[I find the following in the court files of county Essex.—H. F. WATERS.]

"June ye: 21th: 1670,—Rec: off Mr Stephen heskotte the summe off fortenne pounds in silver and A Bill from Mr petter Lidgett drawen on mr nathamell pryer in piscatequoy for Accõ of sd Stephen heskotte Being in full for ye pasage off Thomazin the wife off Rob Bray and Robert and margette ther sonne and daughter in ye shipe hapy Returne off plymo Geo Orchard mr from plymo in old england to Boston in new england pr me GEORGE ORCHARD."

"and is in full off all other debts and Accos due to me."

PASSENGERS FOR NEW ENGLAND.

1671. A List of the Names of the Passengers on board the Ship Arabella Richard Sprague Master for New England, May ye 27th, 1671.

William Shoars,
William Hadwell,
William Syton,
George Ash,
George Bearbeik,
Robert Collins,
William Bently,
Josiah Hobbs,
John Clarke,
Robert Halworthy,
Eliza Coleman,
Andrew Rodgers,
Joseph Read,
Thomas Webb,
John Parker,
Stephen Bustells,
Joseph Bortes,
Samuel Borthamer,
Robert Gibbert,
Henry Mumford,
Henry Tarlton,
William Twide,
Cooleman.

Grauesend May 27th: 1671. The Passengers aboue mentioned were all willing to goe to New England as are Regestered according to order.

William Burnney
Clarke of ye Passage

This is a True Coppie as attests Free Grace Bendall
Cleric.

APPENDIX*

FIRST SETTLERS OF NEW HAMPSHIRE.

Perhaps we cannot do better than to preface the important documents now for the first time printed, with some historical matters from the *Rev. Mr. Hubbard's* History of New England. We say the following documents are "now for the first time printed," which is believed to be the fact, although *Mr. Adams* has, in his "*Annals of Portsmouth*," given the names of the early planters sent out by *Captain Mason*, but, as is seen, with several evident and important mistakes, taking it for granted that our copy (which is a very old one) is correct. Whether *Mr. Adams* used originals or copies, we have no means of knowing. *Dr. Belknap* does not appear to have known of the existence of these papers, and *Mr. Farmer*, his excellent editor, knew them only from the Annals of Portsmouth.

We have no certain knowledge of the exact time of the arrival of the people, a list of whose names we give, but there can be little doubt that many of them were among the first who commenced the settlements at the mouth of the Pascataqua. We will now hear what *Mr. Hubbard* says, in his quaint and pleasing style, upon the early beginnings at Pascataqua:

"Some merchants and other gentlemen in the West of England, belonging to the cities of Exeter, Bristol, Shrewsbury, and towns of Plymouth, Dorchester, &c., incited no doubt by the fame of the plantation begun at New Plymouth in the year 1620, having obtained patents for several parts of the country of New England, from the grand council established at Plymouth, (into whose hands that whole country was committed,) made some attempt of beginning a plantation in some place about Pascataqua river, about the year 1623. For being encouraged by the report of divers mariners that came to make fishing voyages upon that coast, as well as by the aforementioned occasion, they sent over that year one *Mr. David Thompson*, with *Mr. Edward Hilton*, and his brother, *Mr. William Hilton*, who had been fishmongers in London, with some others, that came along with them, furnished with necessaries for carrying

*By any construction of the term the lists in this section cannot be considered ship passenger lists; however, since they are cited in Lancour's *Bibliography of Ship Passenger Lists, 1538-1825*, it is well to include them here, if for no other reason but to reveal the full extent of Lancour's citations to *NEHGR*.

on a plantation there. Possibly others might be sent after them in the years following, 1624 and 1625; some of whom first in probability, seized on a place called the Little Harbour, on the west side of Pascataqua river, toward, or at the mouth thereof; the Hiltons in the mean while setting up their stages higher up the river, toward the northwest, at or about a place since called Dover. But at that place called the Little Harbour, it is supposed was the first house set up, that ever was built in those parts; the chimney, and some part of the stone wall are standing at this day, and certainly was it, which was called then, or soon after, Mason Hall, because to it was annexed three or four thousand acres of land, with intention to erect a manor, or lordship there, according to the custom of England; for by consent of the rest of the undertakers, in some after division, that parcel of land fell to his share; and it is mentioned as his propriety, in his last will and testament, by the name of Mason Hall. Sir Ferdinando Gorges and Capt. John Mason might have a principal hand in carrying on that design, but were not the sole proprietors therein; there being several other gentlemen that were concerned therein, and till after the year 1631, there seems to have been not many other buildings considerable erected in any other place about Pascataqua river, all which is evident by an indenture yet extant [1680?] in the hands of some gentlemen now living at Portsmouth, a town seated down near the mouth of the said river."

The "indenture" above referred to, bears date 8 Nov., 1631, from which it is evident that many persons had some time before settled at Pascataqua; for in naming the property sold, "an house" is mentioned, "wherein Capt. Neal and the colony with him do or lately did reside." Notwithstanding this statement, *Mr. Adams* has introduced his list of settlers under 1631, as though they all had arrived in that year, which gives a wrong impression.

The contracting parties were "the President and Council of New England on the one part, and Sir Ferdinando Georges, Capt. John Mason, John Cotton, Henry Gardner, George Griffith, Edwin Guy, Thomas Wannerton, Thomas Eyre, and Eleazer Eyre, on the other part." Then follows, "as the forementioned have by their agents there, taken great pains, and spent much time in the discovery of the country, all which hath cost them, (as we are credibly informed,) £3000, and upwards, which hithertunto they are wholly out of purse for, upon hope of doing good for time to come, to the public, and for other sufficient causes," have sold, &c.

We must draw a few sentences more from *Mr. Hubbard*, who, it will be remembered, was living and wrote while many of the first settlers were alive, and who evidently communicated with them upon their beginnings at Pascataqua. He writes, "and whereas there is mention in this indenture of *Capt. Neal*, and the colony with him, there residing in the said house, it must be understood, that the agents of *Sir Ferdinando Gorges* and *Capt. Mason*, with the rest, had by their order built an house, and done something about saltworks, sometime before the year 1630; in which year *Capt. Neal*, with three other gentlemen, came over to Pascataqua, in the bark Warwick. He was said to be sent as governor for *Sir Ferdinando Gorges* and the rest; and to superintend their affairs there. Another occasion of their sending over, was said to be searching, or making a more full discovery of an imaginary province, supposed to be up higher into the country, called Laconia. But after three years spent in labor and travel for that end, or other fruitless endeavors, and expense of too much estate, they returned back to England with a *non est inventa provincia.* Nor is there anything memorable recorded as done by him, or his company, during the time of his three years stay, unless it were a contest between him and *Capt. Wiggans*, employed in like manner to begin a plantation higher up the river, for some of Shrewsbury, who being forbidden by him the said *Neal*, to come upon a point of land, that lieth in the midway betwixt Dover and Exeter, *Capt. Wiggans* intended to have defended his right by the sword; but it seems both the litigants had so much wit in their anger, as to wave the battle, each accounting himself to have done very manfully in what was threatened; so as in respect, not of what did, but what might have fallen out. The place to this day retains the formidable name of Bloody Point." The following are the documents:

The Names of Stewards and Servants sent by John Mason, Esq., *into this Province of New Hampshire.*

Walter Neal, *Steward,*
Ambrose Gibbins, *Steward,*
Thomas Comock,*
William Raymond,
Francis Williams,
George Vaughan,
Thomas Wonerton,† *Steward,*
Hinry Jocelyn, *St.*,
Francis Norton, *Steward,*
Sampson Lane, *Steward,*
Reginald Furnald,‡ *Chirurgeon,*
Ralph Gee, §
Henry Gee, §
William Cooper,
William Chadborn,
ffrancis Matthews,
Humphrey Chadborn,
William Chadborn, Junr,
ffrancis Rand,
James Johnson,
Ant. Ellins,
Henry Baldwin,
Thomas Spencer,
Thomas Furral,
Thomas Herd,
Thomas Chatherton,
John Crowther,
John Williams,
Roger Knight,
Henry Sherburn, ||
John Goddard,
Thomas Furnold,
Thomas Withers,
Thomas Canney,
John Symonds,
John Peverly,
William Seavy,
Henry Langstaff,
William Berry,
Jeremy Wolford, ¶
James Wall,
William Brookin, **
Thomas Walford,
Thomas Moor,
Joseph Beal,
Hugh James,
Alexander Jones,
John Anlt, ††
William Bracket,
James Newt,
Eight Danes,
Twenty Two Women.

* *Carnocks* in Adams.
† *Warnerton*, ib.
‡ *Renald Fernald*, ib.
§ This name is perfectly plain in our MS., but in *Adams's Annals of Portsmouth*, it is *Goe*. Which is right remains to be discovered. We feel quite sure of the present spelling.
|| *Sherborn*, ib.
¶ *Jeremiah Walford*, ib.
** Also perfectly plain on our copy, but in Adams's Annals it is rendered *Brakin*. The name of John Brookin occurs in the early conveyances, in Suffolk Deeds, Boston, where he owned a house and land, 1672. One error causes many more. Farmer was misled by this.
†† *John Ault*, ib.

TIME OF THE ARRIVAL IN NEW ENGLAND OF THE FOLLOWING MINISTERS.

1630.

Rev. John Maverick.
Rev. John Warham.
Rev. John Wilson.
Rev. George Phillips.

1631.

Rev. John Eliot.

1632.

Rev. Thomas Weld.
Rev. Thomas James.
Rev. Stephen Bachiler.

1633.

Rev. John Cotton.
Rev. Thomas Hooker.
Rev. Samuel Stone.
Rev. William Leveredge?

1634.

Rev. John Lathrop.
Rev. John Miller?
Rev. James Noyes.
Rev. Thomas Parker.
Rev. Zechariah Symmes.
Rev. Nathaniel Ward.

1635.

Rev. Peter Bulkley.
Rev. John Avery.
Rev. George Burdet?
Rev. Henry Flint.
Rev. Peter Hobart.
Rev. John Reyner?
Rev. Richard Mather.
Rev. Hugh Peters.
Rev. John Norton.
Rev. Thomas Shepard.
Rev. William Walton.
Rev. John Jones.

1636.

Rev. Ralph Partridge.
Rev. Samuel Whiting.
Rev. Nathaniel Rogers.
Rev. John Wheelwright.
Rev. Thomas Jenner.
Rev. Samuel Newman.

1637.

Rev. John Allin.
Rev. Edmund Brown.
Rev. Thomas Cobbet.
Rev. Timothy Dalton?
Rev. John Davenport.
Rev. John Fiske.
Rev. John Harvard.
Rev. George Moxon.
Rev. William Thompson.
Rev. John Prudden.
Rev. Samuel Eaton.

1638.

Rev. Ezekiel Rogers.
Rev. Robert Peck.
Rev. Edward Norris.
Rev. Charles Chauncy.
Rev. Thomas Allen.
Rev. Henry Phillips?
Rev. Marmaduke Matthews.

1639.

Rev. John Knowles.
Rev. Henry Whitfield.
Rev. Richard Denton?
Rev. Jonathan Burr.
Rev. Ephraim Hewett.
Rev. Henry Smith.
Rev. John Ward.
Rev. William Worcester.
Rev. Abraham Pierson?

1640.

Rev. Henry Dunster.

1641.

Rev. Richard Blinman?

A LIST OF NAMES FOUND AMONG THE FIRST SETTLERS OF NEW ENGLAND.

[Those names which are starred are not contained in Farmer's Genealogical Register, and concerning those which are not starred, additional facts are related. The article is prepared entirely from unpublished manuscripts, by Mr. S. G. Drake.]

ADAMS, SAMUEL, Chelmsford, authorized to solemnize marriages there, 1664.

ALLEN, BOZOUN, Boston, constable, 1680.

ALLIN, ONESIPHORUS,* Ipswich, 1679.

ALLYNE, THOMAS,* Barnstable, 1644, a witness to a sale of land by the Indian *Seacunk.*

ANDREWS, THOMAS,* and THOMAS JR.,* Dorchester, 1664.

ANGIER, ANDREW, first inhabitant at Dunston, Me.—ARTHUR, born about 1625.

ANNABLE, ANTHONY, Barnstable, 1644.

ARCHARD, SAMUEL,* church member, Salem, 1640.

ARDELL, RICHARD,* Boston, merchant, 1686.

ATWOOD, JOHN,* ensign, Boston, juror, 1686.

AVERY, WILLIAM* and JONATHAN,* members of the church, Dedham, 1677.

BAXTER, DANIEL, Salem, 1638. Carried the charter of R. Island from Boston to Newport, 1663. [*Farmer's MS.*]

BENTLEY, WILLIAM,* came to New England in the ship Arabella, Richard Sprague master; sailed from Gravesend, May 27, 1671.

BEZBEANE, JOHN,* Woburn, 1677.

BERRY, RICHARD,* Medford, 1636.

BLAKE, FRANCIS,* Dorchester, 1664.—WILLIAM,*—JAMES, a. 24 in 1677.

BLOWERS, JOHN, a. 36 in 1663, a lessee of an island in Boston harbor for seven years.

BOTT, ISAAC,* Boston, 1675.

BRADLEY, WILLIAM,* Dorchester, 1664.

BROUGHTON, THOMAS, Boston, 1655, petitions general court against imposing duties on importations.

BULL, WILLIAM, Charlestown, 1638, heard Squaw Sachem say then, that she had given all her lands to Mr. Gibbons; was 43 years of age in 1662.

CAPEN, BARNARD, witnesses the Indian deed of Dorchester, 1671; SAMUEL,* also a witness to the same.

CARPENTER, WILLIAM, Hingham, 1641, witnessed, and seems to have drawn the deed of a tract of land there from the Indians "to John Tower the elder." His autograph, and the instrument to which it is attached, are a most elegant specimen of the chirography of that age.

CHEEVER, EZEKIEL, married the widow of Capt. Lothrop, who was killed in Sudbury fight, before May 19, 1680.

CHILD, RICHARD,* Watertown, juror, 1680.

CHURCH, GARRETT, Watertown, 1636, aged 51 in 1662.—RICHARD, Plymouth, 1631; went there from Wessaguscussett.

CLARKE, JONAS, constable of Cambridge, 1680.—THEODORE,* York, 1663.

CLAY, NATHANIEL,* Dorchester, 1664.

COBB, HENRY, Barnstable, 1644.

COOK, GEORGE, Colonel, &c., Cambridge, Ms., in which place and vicinity he had large possessions; returned to England in or about the beginning of the Civil War, in which he took a part, went into Ireland, where he was killed in 1652. He was twice married, and left by one of his wives, two daughters: 1. MARY, m. to "her mother's younger brother," Mr. Samuel Annesley, 1681. In 1669 she resided at Martins in the Fields, London; in 1691 she resided with her husband in the city of Westminster. 2. ELIZABETH, m. 1st, Rev. John Quick, of St. Giles, Cripple Gate, London, and perhaps, 2ndly, Joseph Cawthorne.

CRISPE, BENJAMIN, "Misticke als Meadforde," 1636.

CURWIN, GEORGE, Salem, 1682, aged 70; went there near 44 years before.

CUSHIN, JEREMIAH,* Boston, juror, 1680.

DAVIS, LAWRENCE,* York, 1663.

DINSDALE, WILLIAM, aged 47 in 1663. Hired an island of John Leverett, in Boston harbor, for seven years.

DOGGETT, JOHN, Hingham, 1662, where he witnessed an Indian deed.

DURGIE, WILLIAM,* came to Ipswich, Nov. 9, 1663, and was then 33 years old. Had been in the W. Indies, and came here from thence. Wife, Martha. Perhaps this name is that since written *Durgin.*

EDGECOMBE, MILES,* a. 25, 1676. Was at "Black Point the day and tyme when nine of Winterharbor men were fighting with the Indians upon the sands opposite to the said place."

EEDY, JOHN,* Plymouth, left there to reside in Massachusetts, before Feb., 1632.

EUERS, MATHIAS,* Dorchester, 1664.

EVERETT, JOHN, Chelmsford, 1664, where he is authorized to unite people in marriage.

FOOTE, PASCO, Salem church, 1640.

FOSTER, JAMES,* Dorchester, constable, 1680.

FOX, THOMAS, Ms., about 52 in 1659, wife, Elinor.

FOXWELL, RICHARD, Dunston, Me., 1654.

Franklin, Benjamin, Boston, before 1678, wife, Katherine.

Friend, John, Salem, church memb., 1640.

Goddard, Giles,* Boston, 1679, had wife and servants.

Gray, John,* buys Nantasket of the Indians, 1622.

Greenleafe, Enoch,* Boston, saddler, 1693.

Greenough, Robert,* Rowley, 1701.

Green, John, Cambridge, juror, 1680. Nathaniel, 1675.

Harrod, Thomas,* Boston, juror, 1680.

Hews, Jeremiah,* Dorchester, 1664.—Eleazer,* Dorchester.

Hauxworth, Thomas,* Salisbury. Had a daughter married to Onesiphorus Page. His widow was living there, 1667.

Hayden, Samuel,* Dorchester or vicinity, 1666.

Hills, Joseph, Medford, a. 60 in 1662. Capt. James,* [Hill] grand juror, Boston, 1686

Hoar, William,* Boston, baker, 1670.

Hodman, John, Dorchester, 1679, born 1659.

Hood, Jeremiah,* Massachusetts, 1676.

Hopin, Steven,* born 1626, Dorchester, in Capt. Roger Clapp's employ, 1642. Witness to Indian deed of Dorchester, (8: 4: 1649.)

Houghton, Ralph, Lancaster, 1670, where he was constable, collector of taxes, treasurer, &c. There were at the same place in 1703, Henry, Jonas, Robert, John, Sen., John, Jr., Joseph and Jacob.

Howard, Jacob,* Dorchester, 1664.

Hudson, William, lived at "Wading River" in 1670, "where King Philip and Squamaug (brother of Josias deceased) met to settle the bounds between them, which had for some time been in dispute.

Johnson, Edward, a. 60 in 1660, at which time he gives evidence about land in Charlestown. Francis, Marblehead, 1660, nephew of Mr. Christopher Coulson, a merchant adventurer of London.

Joyliffe, John, Boston, will dated 1699-1700. Had a brother, Dr. George Joyliffe, in England; sisters, Dorothy Cane, in England, Martha Cook, in England, Rebecca Wolcott, Margaret Drake, and Mary Biss, "sometime wife of James Biss of Shepton Mallet, in the county of Somerset," Eng.

Key, Joshua,* probably married a daughter of Capt. Thomas Lothrop, who was killed by the Indians in 1675, as his children received a legacy out of Lothrop's estate.

King, Thomas, was an inhabitant of Exeter, 1675.

Knight, Walter, aged 66 in 1653, at which time he was at Boston. The same person was at Nantasket in 1622. John, Charlestown, juror in the witch trials, 1680.

Latham, Cary, was born in 1612; Boston, 1663.

Lawrence, Thomas, Hingham, 1661.

Loephelin, Peter,* Frenchman, Boston, 1679.

Leach, Richard, Salem, a. 60 in 1678, leased a farm of Gov. Endecott, 1657.

Long, Robert, Marblehead, a. 70 in 1660.

Lothrop, Capt. Thomas; his widow married Joseph Grafton, before May 19, 1680. After her decease, the property left her by Lothrop was ordered by court to the wife of Ezekiel Chever, and her issue, heirs of Capt. Lothrop. It is also ordered Mrs. Grafton to pay to the children of Joshua Key, £20.

Lyon, Peter, Dorchester, 1664.

Marriner, Andrew,* Boston, 1693, leather dresser.

Mather, Timothy, Dorchester, 1667.

Mayhew, Thomas, hired a farm in Medford, 1636.

Mellen, John,* Charlestown, where he died before 1695.

Middlecott, Mr. [Richard?] Boston, juror at trials for witchcraft, 1680.

Mokall, James,* b. 1660, Massachusetts, 1680.

Morse, William, Newbury; wife, Elizabeth, accused of practising witchcraft, finally acquitted at Boston, 1680.

Mose, John, Watertown, 1680, constable.

Mott, Nathaniel, a. 10, or thereabouts, in 1681.

Naramore, Thomas,* Dorchester, 1664. Persons of this name are in N. Hampshire at this time.

Neighbor, James,* Massachusetts, 1662.

Odiorne, John and Phill., Portsmouth, N. H., 1657, subscribed toward the support of public worship.

Page, Onesiphorus,* Salisbury, 1667, married daughter of Thomas Hauxworth [Hawksworth].

Parsons, Mark,* Sagadahock, 1665.

Pateshall, Robert,* Boston, 1655, petitions General Court against duties on importations.

Peaslee, Joseph, went to Haverhill before 1653.

Philips, John,* Massachusetts, 1630, styled servant, went to Plymouth, 1631.

Pole, William,* Dorchester, 1649. The name is since written *Pool.*

Pray, Ephraim,* born 1661, Dorchester, 1680.

Rainsford, Samuel,* Boston, killed with Capt. Turner, at Pawtucket, in Philip's war, leaving no relative in the country.

Rice, Henry, Charlestown, juror, 1662.

Richard, Gyles,* Sen., Massachusetts, 1666.

ROBBINS, RICHARD, juror at trials for witchcraft, 1680.

ROOT, THOMAS, Lynn, 1674, where he attempted to gather a church.

RYALL, JOSEPH,* Charlestown, constable, 1680.

SAUNDERS, MARTIN,* born 1630, Boston, 1679.

SEALE, EPHRAIM,* Lieutenant, Boston, juror, 1686.

SEARES, JOHN,* Boston, Lieutenant, 1652.

SEWALL, HENRY; was residing at Manchester, Lancaster co., Eng, in 1623, only son of HENRY SEWALL, who came to N. England with his family, and settled in Newbury.

SHERBURNE, GEORGE, b. 1602, Portsmouth, 1650, m. Rebecca, dau. Ambrose Gibbins, and had children, SAMUEL, ELIZABETH, m. Tobias Lear, MARY, HENRY, JOHN, AMBROSE, SARAH, and REBECCA. [*Farmer's MS.*]

SIBLY, JOHN, church member, Salem, 1640.

SMITH, JOHN,* Barnstable, 1644.

SPRAGUE, SAMUEL,* Charlestown, 1695.

STILEMAN, ELIAS, Boston, constable, 1673.

STONE, JOHN,* Watertown, juror, 1680.

STUDSON, ROBERT,* one of the commissioners for settling the bounds between Plymouth and Massachusetts, 1664.

SUMNER, WILLIAM,* Dorchester, 1670.

SWAIN, JOHN,* Salisbury, b. 1633, Nantucket, 1703. A Lieutenant SWAIN had been under Major Appleton against the Indians at Narraganset, in 1675. He was afterwards a captain.

TAYLER, JOHN,* Shipcot, [Sheepscot,] 1665.

THAYER, RICHARD, Massachusetts, went to England, and returned in 1679.

TINKHAM, EPHRAIM, Massachusetts, 1666, at which time he was a witness to the sale of lands to Richard Thayer of Braintree, by the Indian chief *Josias*. He attests to it in 1678.

TOWER, JOHN, Hingham, buys a large tract of land of several Indians in that place; deed dated June 17, 1641. In an endorsement on said deed, (made by Ri: Bellingham, 19: 1: 1662-3,) JOHN TOWER is called senior. But in the TOWER GENEALOGICAL TREE there are assigned as the children of JOHN TOWER of Hingham, (1637) only AMBROSE, BENJAMIN, JONATHAN, HANNAH, and JEREMIAH.

TRAVIS, DANIEL,* "chiefe gunner in ye town of Boston, to salute shipps and look after ye artillery," at £5 per annum, 1680.

WAIT, JOHN, Charlestown, juror, 1662, [spelt *Wayte*,] Boston, juror at the trials for witchcraft, 1680. RICHARD, Boston, a. 82 in 1678. He was marshal. RICHARD, Springfield, 1680, wounded by Indians, Oct. 5, 1675.

WALES, JOHN,* and JOHN, JR.,* Dorchester, 1677.

WALKER, ROBERT, Boston, aged 72 in 1679. He came from Manchester, Eng., where he was living in 1623.

WAY, RICHARD, Lieutenant, Boston, juror, 1680. HENRY, Dorchester, 1664.

WEBB, THOMAS, came to N. England in 1671, in the ship Arabella, Capt. Richard Sprague, which sailed from Gravesend May 27.

WHITTINGHAM, RICHARD,* Charlestown, 1693; had been in England in 1691.

WILLEY, EDWARD,* Boston, juror, 1686.

WILLIAMS, WILLIAM,* Boston, 1675, wife, Johanna; was pressed to go against the Indians in Philip's war, and was killed at Medfield, leaving "four small children."

WILLIS, LAWRENCE,* Barnstable, 1644.

WINSOR, JOSHUA,* Boston, constable, 1686.

WISWALL, JOHN, Dorchester, witnesses a new deed of the town, (8: 4: 1649,) made "because ye old deed was something decayed with ill keeping."

FIRST SETTLERS OF RHODE ISLAND.

BY THE LATE JOHN FARMER, ESQ.

Roger Williams,
John Thockmorton,
William Arnold,
William Harris,
Stukeley Westcot,
Thomas Olney, Sen.
Thomas Olney, Jun.
John Greene,
Richard Waterman,
Thomas James,
Robert Cole,
William Carpenter,
Francis Weston,
Ezekiel Holleman,
Robert Williams,
John Smith,
Hugh Bewitt,
William Wickenden,
John Field,
Thomas Hopkins,
William Hawkins,
William Hutchinson,
Edward Hutchinson, Jun.
John Coggeshall,
William Aspinwall,
Samuel Wildbore,
John Porter,
John Sandford,
Edward Hutchinson,
Thomas Savage,
William Dyre,
William Freeborn,
Philip Sherman,
John Walker,
Richard Carder,
William Baulston,
Henry Bull,
William Coddington,
John Clark,
Edward Cope,
Chad. Brown,
Daniel Brown,
Henry Brown,
John Brown,
Samuel Bennett,
Hugh Bewett,
Adam Goodwin,
Henry Fowler,
Arthur Fenner,
Henry Reddock,
Thomas Sucklin,
Christopher Smith,
Richard Pray,
Nicholas Power,
Stephen Northup,
Edward Hart,
Benjamin Herenden,
Edward Inman,
John Jones,
James Matthewson,
Henry Neale,
William Man,
——— Jinckes,
Roger Mawry,
Edward Manton,
Shadrach Manton,
George Shepard,
Edward Smith,
Benjamin Smith,
John Smith, (the Mason,)
John Smith, (Sen.)
John Smith, (Jun.)
John Smith, (Jamaica,)
Epenetus Olney,
Lawrence Wilkinson,
Daniel Williams,
Christopher Onthank,
Joshua Verin,
John Sayles,
Richard Scott,
Joan Tyler,
Joshua Winsor,
Valentine Whitman,
George Way,
William White,
Thomas Walling,
John Warren,
John Whipple,
Matthew Waller,
Robert Williams,
Joseph Williams,
William Wickenden,
Robert R. West,
Pardon Tillighast.

TRANSPORTATION FROM HERTFORDSHIRE, ENGLAND TO AMERICA, 1646-1775

By Anthony J. Camp, of Walkern, Herts, England

The following list of persons transported from Hertfordshire, England, to America has been extracted from the ten volumes of printed *Hertfordshire Quarter Sessions Records* (Hertford, 1905-57) and includes all those prior to 1775 and the commencement of the war. These cover the Sessions Rolls for 1581-1850 and the Sessions Books for 1619-1843. Over 500 other transportations are recorded between 1776 and 1843, but these were presumably all to Australia.

The information here given should be treated as an index only as the printed volumes are fuller and give exact references to the original volumes now deposited in the Hertford County Record Office. The volume number only is given as the person may be mentioned several times on different pages. In many cases, as will be noted, no exact parish of origin or period of transportation is given.

The references to volume 4 are to the *Sessions Records of the Liberty of St. Alban Division* which rarely give the place of origin. The jurisdiction of this Liberty may be roughly defined as the south-westerly part of the county, stretching from Rickmansworth to East Barnet on the south and on the west a line from Rickmansworth, Abbots Langley and Leverstock Green to Redbourn. The north-eastern boundary of the area came down from Sandridge, North Mimms and Northaw to Chipping Barnet.

The following abbreviations have been used:

- * destination definitely stated to be America
- † destination definitely stated to be Virginia or Maryland
- ‡ destination definitely stated to be Barbadoes
- § destination definitely stated to be Jamaica

These are followed by the number of years (if stated) and the printed volume number.

The reason for transportation, which often appears in the printed volumes, is not here given. It was usually straightforward theft, although there is a group of five in 1664 for "attending unlawful meetings."

AYLOTT or AYLETT, William	Watton-at-Stone	Labourer	1774	*	7	2 & 8
BALDWIN, Samuel			1774			4
BASTEN, John			1737	†		2
BATES, John	Coleshill	Labourer	1767	*	7	8
BIBBY, William	Bishops Hatfield	Tripeman	1768		7	8

BOSWELL, Bush			1740			7
BOSWELL, Charles (senior)			1740			7
BOSWELL, Charles (junior)			1740			7
BOSWELL, Hannah			1740			7
BOSWELL, Letitia			1740			7
BOTSFORD, John	Essendon		1753	*		8
BRANDON, William			1774			4
BRIDGES, John			1740			7
BRITT, William			1740			7
BROOKS, Edward			1740			7
BROWN, William	Berkhamsted St. Peter	Labourer	1766	*	7	8
BURDEN, John			1740			7
BURGESS, Thomas			1772			4
CASTLE, William	Berkhamsted St. Peter	Labourer	1767	*	7	8
CHANDLER, John			1758	*	7	4
CHAPPEL, William	Meesden	Labourer	1764		7	8
COCKS, James	Bishops Hatfield	Labourer	1772	*	7	8
CONNOR, Mary			1775	*	7	1
CRAMPHORN, William	Bishop Stortford	Labourer	1775	*	7	2 & 8
DENNISS, Mary			1697			1
DOCKRELL, James			1740			7
EDGECOMBE, George			1774			4
EDMONDS, Joseph	St. Albans [?]		1776	*	7	4
FAIRMAN, William	Hertford	Brewer	1664	‡		1
FEATHERSTONE, Mary	Foxon, Cambs.,	servant at Ware	1790		7	7
FEILD, Roland			1740			7
FLIXON, William			1697			1
FORSTER, John			1771			4
FULLER, George			1740			7
GIBBARD, Thomas			1770	*	7	4
GILL, Thomas	Much Hadham	Labourer	1768	*	7	8
GREENHAM, Richard	Bishops Hatfield	Sawyer	1768		7	8
HAMPTON, Esther	Wife of John Hampton, yeoman of Sawbridgeworth and Great Hadham		1733			7
HARRIS, Thomas			1740			7
HAWLEY, Joseph	Great Gaddesden	Chimney-sweeper	1765	*	7	8
HOW, Benjamin			1774			4
HOWARD, Eignon			1758	*	7	4
HUMPHREYS, Thomas	Watford [?]		1763	*	7	4
HUNT, William			1740			7
INGRAM, Jacob	Berkhamsted St Peter	Labourer	1766	*	7	8
JARVIS, Benjamin			1646			7
JENNINGS, Edward			1646			7
KNIGHT, William	Hemelhempstead	Paper-maker	1768	*	7	8
LEE, John	Graveley	Labourer	1770	*	7	8
LEVINGS, Edward			1759	*	7	4
LEWIS *alias* TRAHERNE, Samuel	Tewin	Yeoman	1664	§		1 & 4
LONG, Mary			1744			2 & 7
MARSHALL, Henry			1664			1
MCKEAN, James	Hertford St Andrew	Labourer	1767	*	7	8

MONTGOMERY, John	Aston	Labourer	1766	*	7	8
MORDRUM, Henry			1770		7	4
MORE, Thomas			1775	*	14	4
NOAR, William			1740			7
PALLET *alias* AYLOTT, William	Watton-at-Stone	Labourer	1774	*	7	2 & 8
PARKIN, Edward	Hertford	Tailor	1664	‡		1
PENNINGTON, John	Graveley	Labourer	1774	*	7	2 & 8
PIGGOTT, Ralph			1774			2 & 7
PITTMANN, James			1646			7
PREIST, James *alias* Joseph SUTTON			1744			2 & 7
PRESTAGE, John			1740			7
REID, Andrew			1744			7
RIXON, Jacob			1744/6			2 & 7
ROLFE, John	Berkhamsted St Peter	Labourer	1767	*	7	8
RUSSELL, William			1771			4
SCOTCHER, Ann			1646			7
SHERSTON, John			1744			2 & 7
SHIPROLL, Richard			1740			7
SMITH, John	Hertford St John	Labourer	1765	*	7	8
SMITH, Martha			1646			7
STAINES, Thomas			1737	†		2
STRICKETT, Arthur			1744			2 & 7
STROUD, Richard			1770	*	7	4
STURGEON, John			1740			7
SULTON or SUTTON, James *alias* Joseph PREIST			1744			2 & 7
TATTON, Joseph			1646			7
TAYLOR, William			1744/6			2 & 7
TAYLOR, William			1771			4
TILL, John	Rickmansworth	Labourer	1763	*	7	4
TITMUS, William	Stevenage	Butcher	1765	*	7	8
TRAHERNE, *alias* LEWIS, Samuel	Tewin	Yeoman	1664	§		1 & 4
TRIPP, John			1740			7
UNCLE, Benjamin (junior)	Albury	Labourer	1765		7	8
UNDERWOOD, Jacob			1646			7
Fosbrooke			1646			7
WALBY, Elizabeth			1646			7
WATTS, John			1770			4
WATTS, Thomas			1770	*	7	4
WHITE, William	St Albans [?]		1776	*	7	4
WHITENAIL, Thomas	Hertford St Andrew	Cordwainer	1763	*	7	8
WHITING, Thomas			1740			7
WHITTENBURY, Mary	Cottered & Bengeo	Spinster	1664	‡		1
WILLIAMS, John			1646			7
WILSON, Robert			1772		7	4
WOOD, John	Berkhamsted St Peter	Labourer	1768	*	7	8
WOODARD, William			1697			1
WOODWARD, Thomas	Hertford St Andrew	Labourer	1764		7	8
WRIGHT, Lucretia	Broxbourn, wife of John		1764		7	8
YOUNG, James			1770			4

EMIGRANT MINISTERS—ADDITIONS

EMIGRANT MINISTERS.—Since the publication of "A List of Emigrant Ministers to America" (see *ante*, vol. 58, page 408), the following additions have been found, and it has been thought better to publish the information in the REGISTER than to wait for a second edition.

In Bodley's Library, Oxford, England, is Rawlinson MS., A 306, it being a Receipt book of secret service money from 20 April, 1689, to June, 1691, with autographs of receivers. The signatures may prove of some value as a means of identification.

Baron, Humberton, Jamaica, 24 Aug., 1689, Rawl. A 306: 41.
Bosseam, James, clk, Virginia, 11 Nov., 1689, Rawl. A 306: 65.
Clarke, Josias, clk, Jamaica, 8 Nov., 1689, Rawl. A 306: 64. Son of Sabothi Clarke of Tavin, Chester, matric. 1611 (Foster).
Cox, Samuel, clk, Leeward Islands, 12 Nov., 1689, Rawl. A 306: 66.
Gellbrand, Andrew, New York, 9 June, 1690, Rawl. A 306: 142.
Gray, Samuel, clk, Virginia, 1 Dec., 1689, Rawl. A 306: 73.
Gregory, Thomas, Virginia, 15 May, 1691, Rawl. A 306: 264.
Hanmer, Joseph, D.D., New York, 9 June. 1690, Rawl. A 306: 143. Another grant to Dr. Joseph Hanmer, 16 Sept., 1690, Rawl. A 306: 183.
Lidford, Mathew, clk, Virginia, 20 Oct., 1690, Rawl. A 306: 197. Son of James Lidford of Sandwich Purbeck, Dorset, B. A. 1686 (Foster).
Lightfoote, William, clk, Jamaica, 22 Oct., 1689, Rawl. A 306: 60.
Lillingstone, John, clk, Maryland, 29 Oct., 1689, Rawl. A 306: 62. Son of George Lillingstone of Kingsey, Bucks, B. A. 1676 (Foster).
Mitton, Roger, clk, Virginia, 15 Nov., 1689, Rawl. A 306: 69.
Philips, James, schoolmaster, at New York, 8 May, 1691, Rawl. A 306: 263.
Scaife, Thomas, clk, Virginia, 3 Jan., 1689-90, Rawl. A 306: 92.
Smith, Peter, clk, Newfoundland, 2 Aug., 1689, Rawl. A 306: 32.
Stuart, Robert, schoolmaster, to Jamaica, 3 Jan., 1689-90, Rawl. A 306: 93.
Ware, Jacob, clk, Virginia, 11 Nov., 1689, Rawl. A 306: 65.

The following three documents are to be found in the same Library:

Testimonial in favour of Mathew Blewett, M. A., signed by Wicks, D. D., and Samuel Harris, Rector of St. Ethelburga, London, 13 Apr., 1692, Rawl. MS. 983: 66.

Bond in £40 from John Span of Queen's College, Oxford, that he will within three months proceed to Virginia as a Chaplain; signed by John Span and Sir Robert Dunckley, knt., of Tower St., London, 20 Oct., 1710, folio 179, Rawl. MS. 983: 68.

Bond in £40 from Joseph Cleator of Hestholme, Cumberland, that he will within six months proceed to Rye in the Province of New York, as schoolmaster; signed by Jos. Cleator, and Abraham Isaac, merchant, of London, 9 July, 1766, folio 180, Rawl. MS. C 983: 69.

GERALD FOTHERGILL.

77 Brussels Road, New Wandsworth, London, Eng.

EMIGRANT LIVERYMEN OF LONDON

LIST OF EMIGRANT LIVERYMEN OF LONDON.—The following list is of some value as, besides the fact of a man having emigrated, we get the name of the Livery to which he belonged, and from this the record of apprenticeship can be obtained, giving age, parentage and place of birth.

The book from which this information is taken has no title page nor is it dated, but it was made about 1801-2, Sir John Eamer, knt., being Lord Mayor.

The names in the body of the book are under wards and streets, then follows that part of London outside the city, next the near counties, then the distant counties, Wales and Scotland, and finally a list of the Liverymen whose addresses are unknown or are abroad.

Those who are stated to be in America or abroad are here printed, but some of the others may have been in America, unknown to the Clerk of the Company, so the list might repay a search for any individual in America thought to have come from England.

Bakers.
William Lovell in America.

Barbers.
James Sparks abroad.

Blacksmiths.
John Batchelor in America.
William Batchelor in America.

Brewers.
James Harvey in America.

Broderers.
John Davidson abroad.
John Greenfield in America.

Clock-makers.
James Upjohn in America.

Cooks.
John Davis in America.
Henry Pace in America.

Coopers.
Isaac Patching in America.
John Toulmon abroad.

Cordwainers.
James Gautier abroad.

Curriers.
David Compigre in America.
John Cooke Pettit in Philadelphia.

Distillers.
John Field in America.

Drapers.
Zachariah Clark abroad.

Dyers.
George Cooke abroad.
Thomas Mitchell abroad.

Felt Makers.
James Bliss in America.

Fishmongers.
Stephen Addington in America.
Thomas Horne abroad.
William Price, supposed in America.

Framework Knitters.
Arthur Lee abroad.
Robert Mason abroad.
Stephen Tayre abroad.

Girdlers.
William Carnaly abroad.

George Illman abroad.
Robert Ledlee abroad.
John Tayleure abroad.

Glass Sellers.

Samuel Anderson abroad.
James Ansell abroad
Joseph Fielder abroad

Goldsmiths.

Philip F. Fatio East Flordia.

Grocers.

John Parker Church abroad.
John Fox.

Innholders.

John Banks in America.

Joiners.

Peter Banner abroad.

Leathersellers.

James Lapins abroad.
Richard Oakes abroad.
James Spiring abroad.

Mercers.

John Chamberlain Robson abroad.
Stevens Direly Totton esq abroad.

Musicians.

Thomas Knott in America.
Thomas Wilkinson in America.

Pewterers.

Thomas Giffen Jamaica.

Stationers.

Daniel T. Eaton in America.
William Harryman New York.
John Miller America.
John Martin in America.
James Rivington in New York.
Robert Wilson in Philadelphia.
Samuel Wakeling in America.

Tinplate Workers.

William Falkner in America.

Tylers and Bricklayers.

John Bell in America
Benjamin Chamberlain in America.
John May Evans in America.
James Fullick in America.

Vintners.

Samuel Durham jun abroad.
John Rider abroad.
Richard Waller abroad.

GERALD FOTHERGILL.

11 Brussells Road, New Wandsworth, London, Eng.

FAMILIES IN FRESSINGFIELD, ENG., 1836, WISHING TO EMIGRATE TO AMERICA.

Communicated by Rev. JOHN J. RAVEN, D.D., F.S.A., Vicar of Fressingfield, Suffolk, Eng.

IN turning over some parochial records this 27th of February, 1895, I lighted on the following memoranda:—

"Fressingfield April 14th 1836.

Families wishing to emigrat to America

	John Knights	35
	Sarah Knights	37
	Benjamin	11
	John	10
	James	6
	Robert	2
7	Sarah	3 months
	Jarvis Mutimer	38
	Susan Mutimer	26
	Frederick	12
	Ann	8
5	Esau	6
1	George Smith, single.	17
1	Robert Borrett, single	16
	Richard Evans	37
	Martha Evans	36
	Mary Ann	9
	James	8
	Martha	7
	Richard	6
	John	5
	William	4
	Robert	3
	Rebecca	2
11	Elizabeth	3 months
25 total		

25		
	Charles Buggs	40
	Sophia Buggs	41
	William	20
	Mary	17
5	Charles	10
	Charles Elmer	22
2	Hannah Elmer	24
32	William Seaman	38
	Hannah Seaman	30
	Lucy	2
35		

W. R. Lepingwell, Esq.
Benj. Harris
Edwd. Clatten for M^{rs} C.
John Rope for M^{rs} R.
S. Chandler for J. C.
Ja^{s}. Ebden
David Green
Saml Death
William Moore

Proposed by E. Barkway and seconded by M^{r}. R. Read That Two Hundred pounds be borrowed to pay the expences of the above named persons, and others, to America, to be repaid in 5 years, in equal annual instalments.

carried unanimously.

25 at 4 . 10 ca.	112 . 10 . 0	Passage & Provisions
	37 . 10 . 0	on Landing
	14 . 0 . 0	M^{rs}. Churchyard & Barfield
	10 . 0 . 0	Shoemakers
	3 . 0 . 0	Tailors
	2 . 0 . 0	Bryant. Stradbrooke
	12 . 0 . 0	Conveyance to Ipswich
	191 . 0 . 0	
	3 . 0 . 0	
	194 . 0 . 0	
	43 . 8 . 0	
	237 . 8 . 0	

We the undersigned do hereby authorise the payment of the several sums set opposite the above names amounting to £37 . 10/-, for & on behalf of the Parish of Fressingfield.

E B[arkway]
Churchwarden
& Guardian

W. R. L[epingwell]
Guardian."

This record of emigration is worth note, and it is possible that some of the children in this list may be still living. My sexton, H. E. Barber, remembers the event. They started in an eclipse of the sun, and the waggon broke down after they had gone a little way. When they reached Ipswich they lay a fortnight at "Pin Mill" before the ship started. The families—Groves, Knights, Smith and Snowling went out at the same time.

INDEX OF NAMES

--- B ---

--- D ---

--- F ---

--- H ---

--- I ---

--- K ---

--- L ---

--- M ---

--- N ---

--- O ---

--- P ---

--- Q ---

--- R ---

-- S --

--- T ---

--- U ---

--- V ---

--- X ---

--- Y ---

--- Z ---

INDEX OF SHIPS